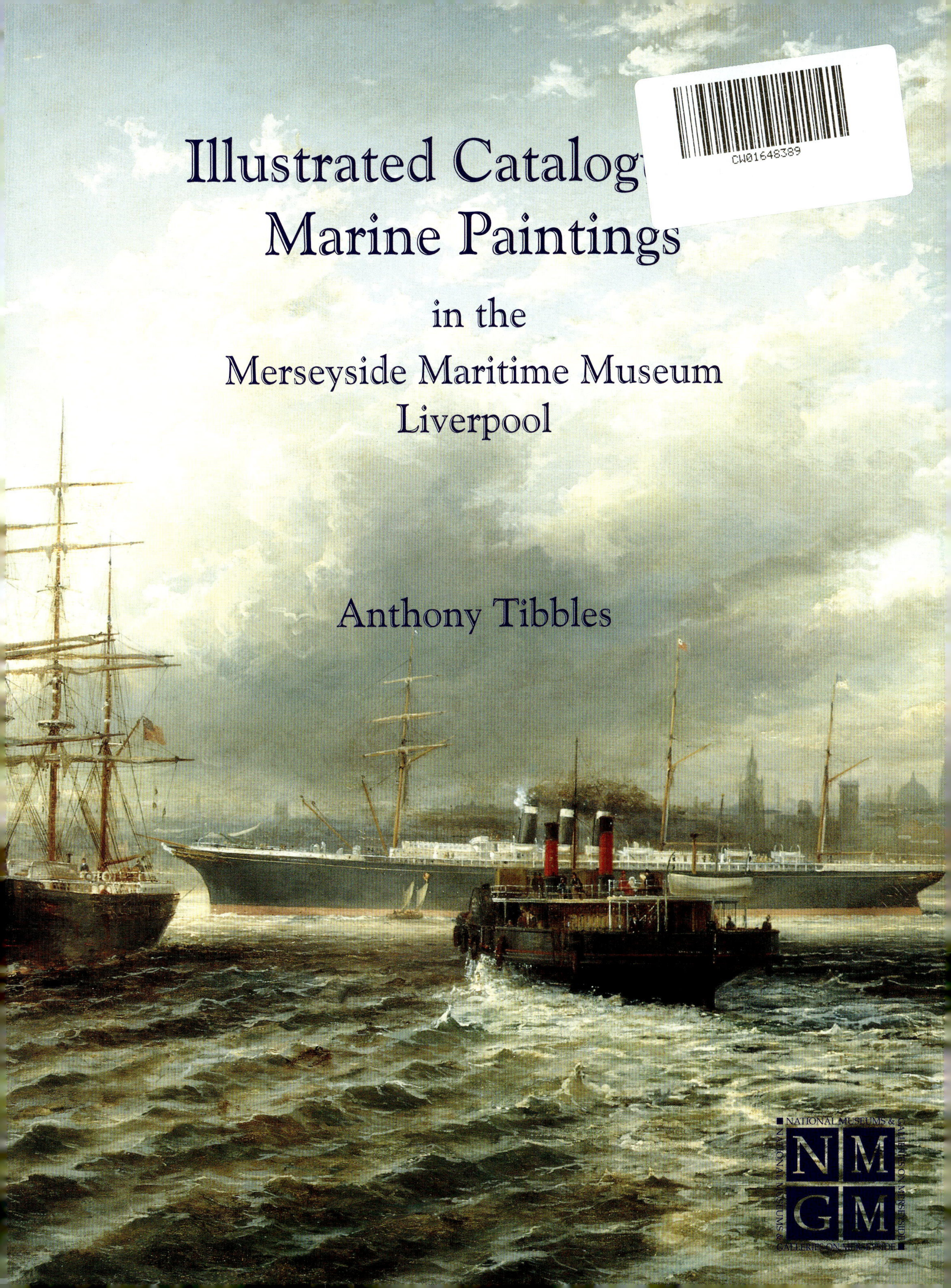

Illustrated Catalog

Marine Paintings

in the

Merseyside Maritime Museum

Liverpool

Anthony Tibbles

NATIONAL MUSEUMS & GALLERIES ON MERSEYSIDE
NMGM

This book was made possible with the financial support from
NatWest

First Published in Great Britain in 1999 by
JONES-SANDS PUBLISHING
8 Trimley Close
Upton
Wirral
L49 6PQ
England

ISBN 0-947764-57-7 hardback
ISBN 0-947764-67-4 softback

Published and Marketed by
JONES-SANDS PUBLISHING

TITLE PAGE (detail):
In The Mersey
Max Sinclair
This evocative scene off Liverpool waterfront in 1889 captures the Mersey bustling with activity. The Inman liner *City of New York* is just getting underway on her voyage across the Atlantic whilst the Woodside ferry *Lancashire* heads for the Landing Stage (*see* No. 207).

OPPOSITE (detail):
The Port and Harbour of Whitehaven, (c.1840)
Samuel Walters
In one of Walters' most accomplished canvases, the barque *Gunga* is shown off Whitehaven heading for the harbour. Although less important than it had been in the eighteenth century, Whitehaven was still an active port, as this busy scene shows (*see* No. 237).

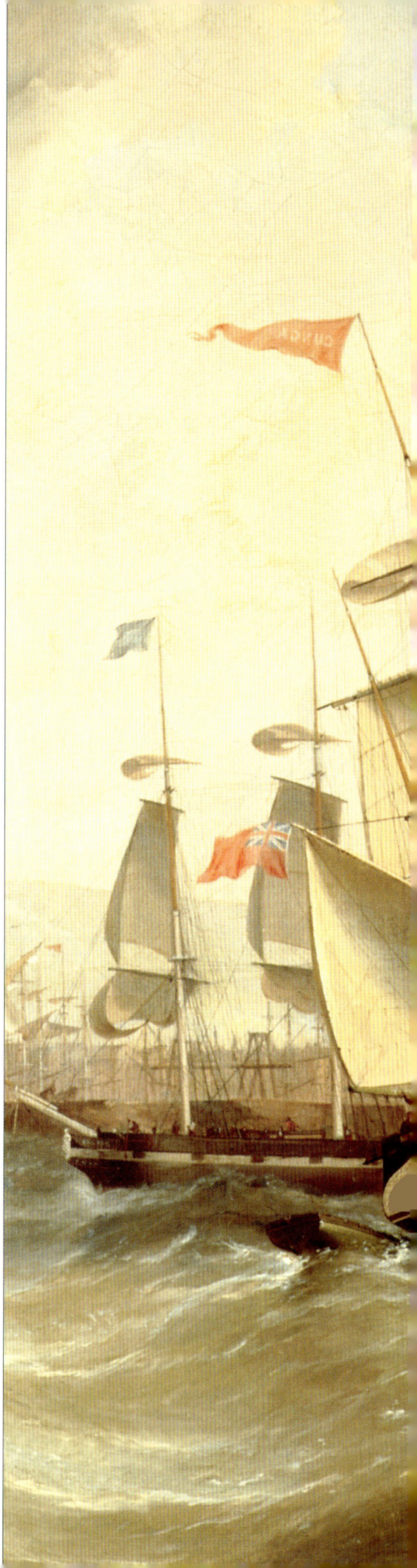

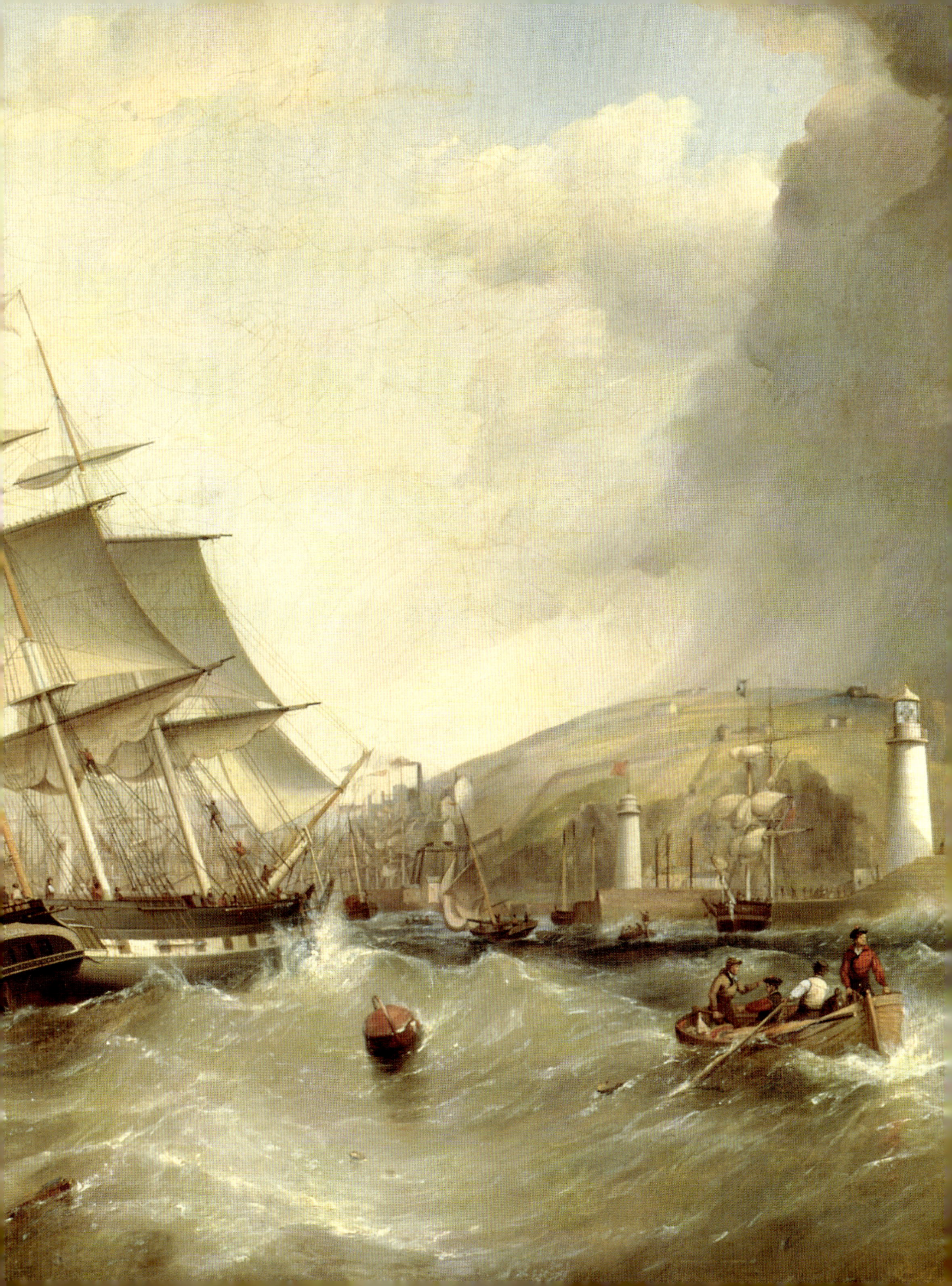

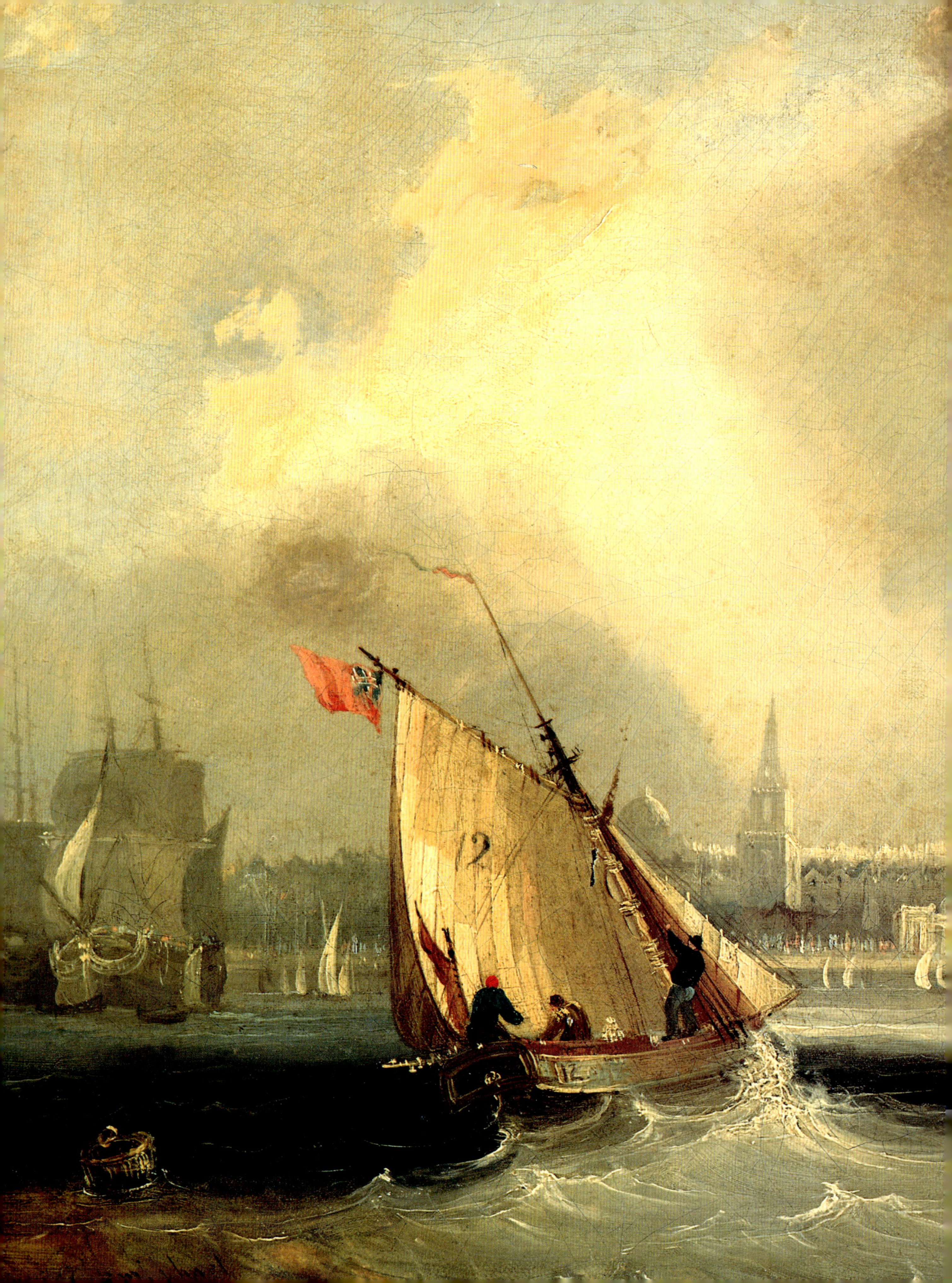
12
12

Foreword

Ever since its establishment in 1986, National Museums & Galleries on Merseyside has laid great emphasis on making its collections known to specialists and a wider public. It has sought to do this by publishing catalogues, guides and hand lists. This new catalogue of the marine paintings at the Merseyside Maritime Museum is the latest in a series of publications which documents the maritime collections, including ship models, boats and archives.

The collection of marine paintings has been built up over many years not primarily on the basis of artistic value, impressive though this often is, but as a documentary record of merchant shipping. Almost all the artists represented here were very knowledgeable about ships and many had themselves served at sea. They thus produced extremely accurate representations of the vessels they painted. Indeed, many of these paintings are the only visual record we have of some of these vessels, particularly in the era before photography was widely practised.

Although many maritime museums have published catalogues of their collections of paintings, this catalogue sets new standards by providing a critical and systematic analysis of the visual and documentary evidence. As these entries show there is much to learn from this approach.

I would like to thank NatWest for sponsoring the production of this catalogue. The bank initially supported the museum's *Art & The Sea* Gallery opened by HRH Princess Margaret in 1988. This additional support for the catalogue has enabled us to do justice to the paintings both in the quality of the production and in the extensive use of colour illustration.

Finally, I would like to thank Tony Tibbles, curator of Maritime History, whose patient study and research has produced an informed and scholarly record of an outstanding collection.

Richard Foster
Director

Shipping off George's Baths, Liverpool
J W Carmichael
This small oil sketch shows a variety of shipping off the main Liverpool waterfront in the second quarter of the nineteenth century (*see* No. 51).

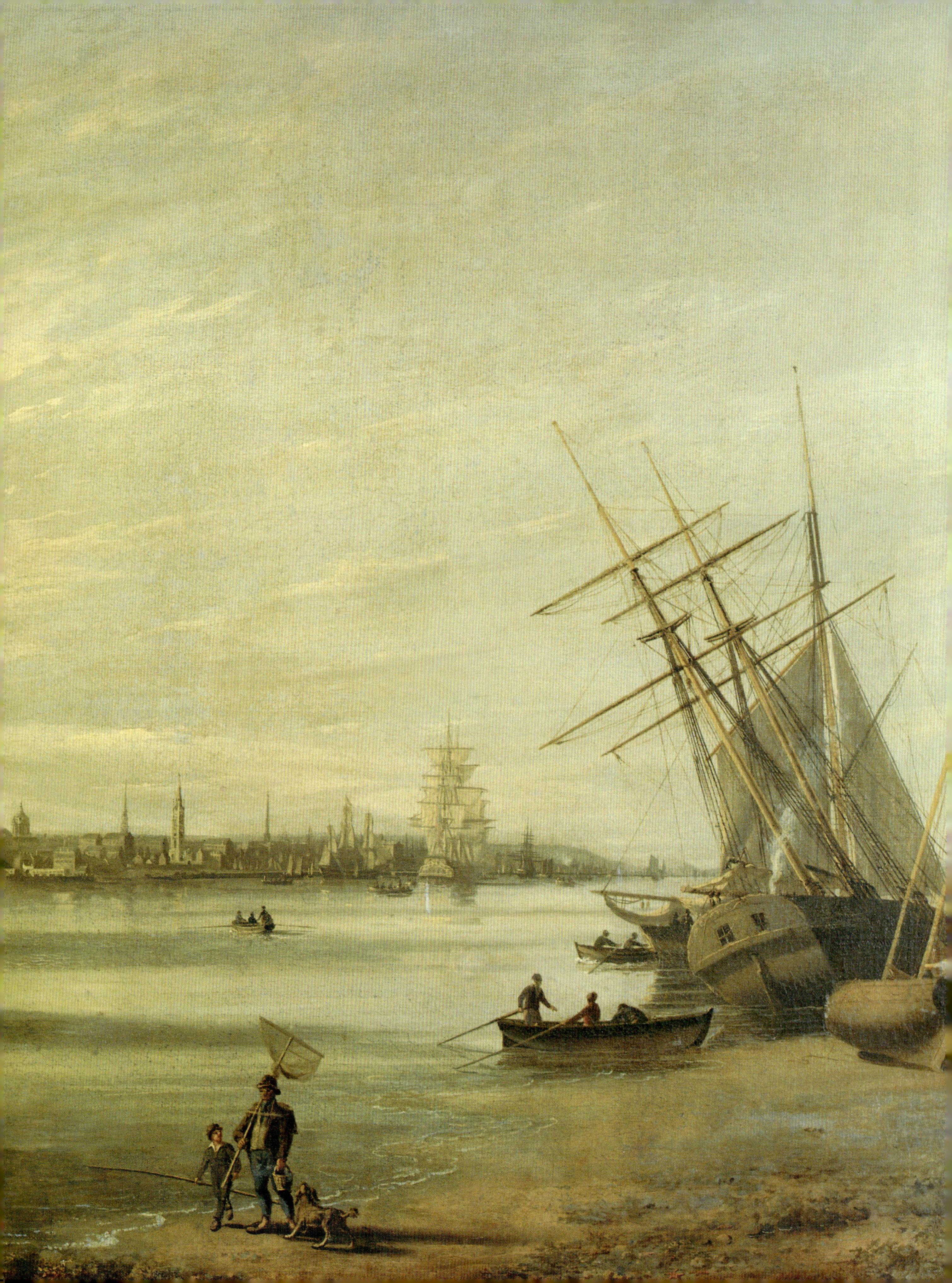

Contents

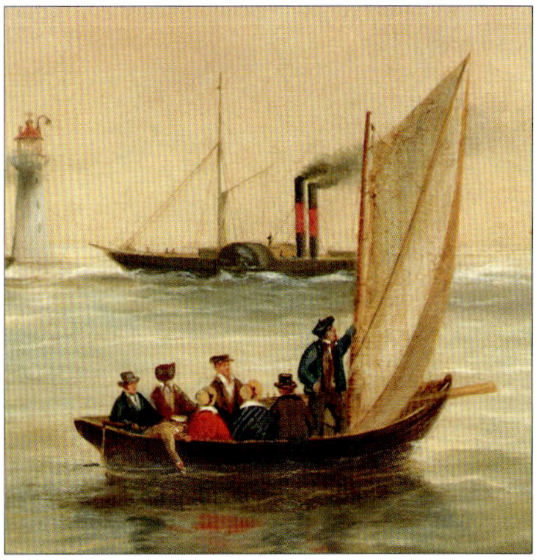

Detail from No. 156

(Left) *A view of Liverpool*
John Jenkinson
Jenkinson painted several views of Liverpool across the Mersey from the Wirral shore, including this view from the area known as The Magazines. He enlivens the scene with details of the everyday life of the river including the shrimper in the foreground (see No. 137).

Acknowledgements

I first started taking an interest in the museum's maritime paintings nearly ten years ago and I undertook to prepare this catalogue when I took curatorial responsibility for the collection in 1990. My initial enthusiasm was brought to an abrupt halt when I agreed to take charge of the development of the museum's Transatlantic Slavery Gallery in 1991. I was only able to take up my work on the paintings collection in earnest again in 1995.

Every author of a catalogue owes an immense debt of gratitude to a host of other people. Firstly, I must mention my colleagues within NMGM. In particular, my curatorial colleagues in the Merseyside Maritime Museum, both past and present, who have worked on the collections and more lately have assisted me in the care of the collections and with my research. Assistance has also been generously provided by staff of the Maritime Archives and Library, Conservation Division and the Walker Art Gallery. Michael Stammers, Keeper of the museum, has provided advice, support and the benefits of his wide knowledge of matters maritime. I am also grateful for the support and occasional cajolery of Richard Foster, Director of NMGM, who has take a personal interest in this work from its inception.

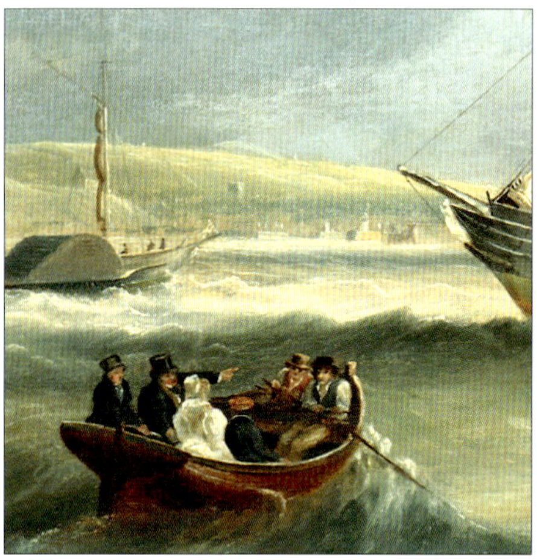

Detail from No. 150

A number of friends and colleagues have helped with my researches. These include Michael Charles, Arthur Credland, Christopher Foley, David Jenkins, Richard Kelton, Julia Korner, Brian Lavery, Charles Omell, Rina Prentice, Roger Quarm, Caroline Roberts, Colin White. I have also benefited from examining collections in the United States and am grateful in this regard for the assistance of H Crosby Forbes, Fritz Gold, Tony Lewis, Charles Sachs and Paul Winfisky.

My greatest debt, like anyone else who has taken an interest in Liverpool ship portraiture in the last twenty years, is to Sam Davidson. Sam's fascination with the marine artists of Liverpool dates back many years and has seen fruition in his two invaluable volumes, *Marine Art & Liverpool* and *Samuel Walters*. But he has also been a sterling friend to the museum supporting and helping with the many curatorial activities for more than two decades. In personal terms he has been a great mentor and friend who has freely shared his knowledge and expertise and who never fails to surprise me with his ability to spot a detail or to recall some vital clue which otherwise I would have overlooked. He has not only contributed generally to the documentation of the collection but has read, discussed and dissected every entry in this catalogue. We may not always fully agree but I have been saved from many errors and have been forced to re-think and justify many of my conclusions. I am sure that any errors that remain are mine.

Finally I would like to thank those who have made the publication of this catalogue possible. Firstly to NatWest for sponsoring the production of this book. I am also grateful to David Flower, NMGM's senior photographer, who took the majority of the photographs for this catalogue and to my colleagues Claire Birtwisle and Caroline Delahunty, who made the practical arrangements. Richard Sands has been a sympathetic and enthusiastic publisher and must take credit for the fine appearance of the book. He has also made my task as author as painless as he could and I thank him for that.

Anthony Tibbles
December 1998

Introduction

The collection of marine paintings in the Merseyside Maritime Museum is one of the key holdings of the museum. It provides a comprehensive record of merchant vessels and shipping activity, particularly related to Liverpool, from the late eighteenth century to the present day.

The majority of the paintings in the collection are portraits of merchant vessels, owned in Liverpool or associated with the port. They were produced for people who knew these vessels - their owners, builders, masters and crew. There are also views of the port of Liverpool, the Mersey and general shipping scenes set against local and other British coastal backgrounds. There are only a handful of portraits of people.

The paintings date predominantly from the nineteenth century, though there is a representative selection of twentieth century works and a small number of important works from the last years of the eighteenth century. They are mostly by artists who were based in Liverpool or worked in the town at some point in their careers. There is also a small but significant group of paintings by artists of the nineteenth century Chinese School.

History of the Collection

Although other maritime artefacts had been collected by the museum during the late nineteenth century, the first marine oil painting was only acquired in 1912. Additions to the collection were slow but increased after the opening of the Shipping Gallery in Liverpool Museum in 1931. However, by the end of the Second World War the collection numbered less than 35. A significant increase in the rate of acquisition took place over the following years and a further 130 works were added between 1950 and 1970. This was partly the result of the decision in 1957 to establish a separate department to curate the maritime collections and to engage in a positive effort to build up the museum's holdings with a view to establishing a separate maritime museum. The changes which took place in the shipping industry, and particularly the merging of many shipping companies, saw significant collections and individual items being offered to the museum for safe keeping. A greater awareness of the historical importance of paintings in private hands also brought further offers to the collection. In recent years, there have been fewer additions, partly through the adoption of more stringent collecting policies. Whilst there are still generous individual benefactors, most works are now acquired by purchase whether from dealers, private owners or at auction.

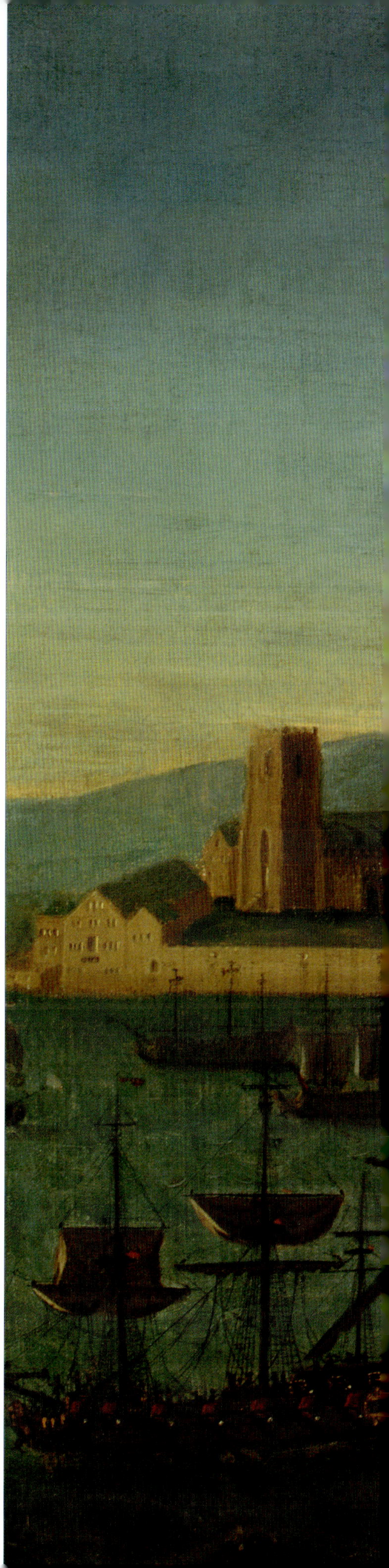

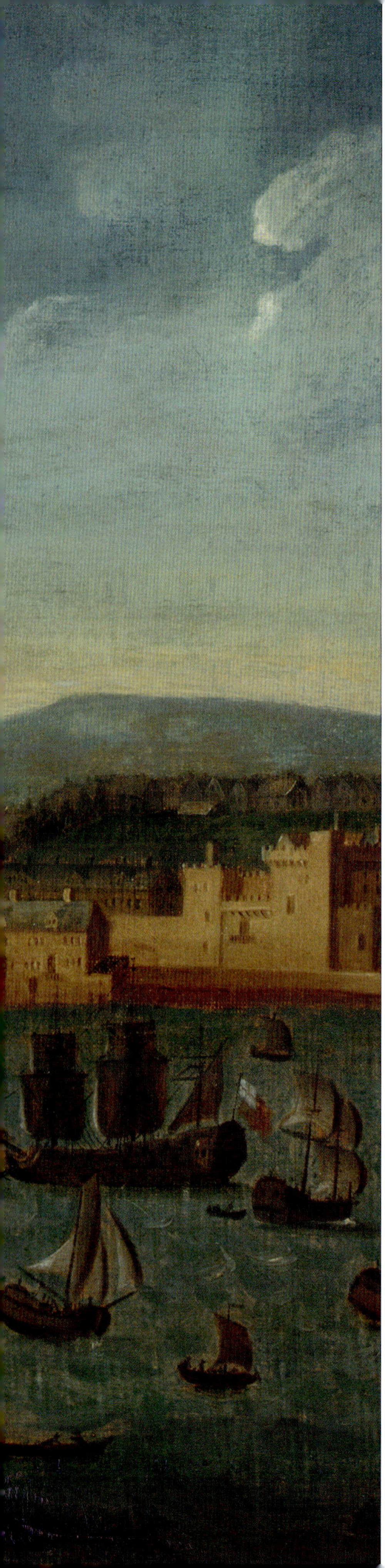

History of Marine Painting in Liverpool

There is no evidence of any significant activity or interest in marine painting in Liverpool before the late eighteenth century. The first recognised Liverpool born marine artist was Richard Wright (1723-1775), though he had moved to London by 1762 and none of his work relates specifically to the port. From this point there were two parallel but generally separate traditions of marine painting - the academic and ship portraiture.

The academic tradition of marine art, encompassing Wright, was founded by the van der Veldes in the 1670s and developed accordingly over the following centuries.[1] In nineteenth century Liverpool it is represented by artists such as W J J C Bond, Henry Dawson and Samuel Williamson.[2] These artists produced general marine and coastal scenes where the vessels are usually part of the overall composition and are normally generic not specific representations. Such works are well seen within the history of British painting and are well represented in the collection of the Walker Art Gallery.[3] Few of this type of work is found in the maritime collection.

The tradition of ship portraiture follows a different course. In fact, the first representations of named vessels appear on pottery,[4] and particularly on the ship bowls produced by the Liverpool factories from the early 1750s onwards.[5] Not surprisingly, the first recognised Liverpool ship portraitist, William Jackson, began his career as a painter of ship bowls and only later graduated to canvas painting.[6] His earliest known painting is probably the *Liverpool Slave Ship* (no. 125) which dates from about 1780.[7] The earliest dated Liverpool ship portrait is Joseph Parry's *Return of a Liverpool Privateer*, (no. 190) signed 1780. Parry left Liverpool soon afterwards but Jackson continued painting until his death in 1803 and a small number of extant works are known. A number of other artists began appearing on the scene and these include John Jenkinson, Henry Collins and Robert Salmon working in the port at various periods from the 1790s until the 1820s.

Jenkinson died in 1821, Collins in 1824 and Salmon went to the United States in 1828 just as Miles Walters and his son Samuel arrived in the town. Miles gave up painting after 1832 but for the next 50 years Samuel Walters dominated the local maritime scene. His career coincide with a period of rapid growth for Liverpool and in particular a huge increase in the number of vessels visiting the port. It is not surprisingly that there was a large and sustained demand for ship portraits not only from local people but from visiting captains and others associated with the vessels. This large market provided opportunities for local talent like John Hughes but mainly drew other young but often established artists to settle in the port. Joseph Heard came from Whitehaven, William McMinn from Workington, Duncan McFarlane from Scotland and Thomas Dove from Whitby. This was the hey-day of Liverpool's ship portraiture.

The latter years of the nineteenth century saw a gradual decline in the interest in ship portraiture. The reasons for this decline are a moot point - was it the loss of artists of the calibre of Walters and Heard, the onset of photography, the loosening of personal links between ships and their owners and crew or perhaps a combination of these factors? In general the Liverpool artists of this period - such as W H Yorke, Ogilvy, Witham and Parker Greenwood - are less creative and talented than their earlier counter-parts. Many patrons trading in the East also turned to Chinese artists when the opportunity arose.

The early and middle decades of the twentieth century saw a new generation of artist working in the port - including Samuel Brown, Odin Rosenvinge and Walter Thomas. They rarely painted in oil and worked mainly in water-colour or within the printing industry. This latter was particular important as advertising material for shipping companies proliferated, stimulated by the advances in colour printing and the increased competition between passenger liner companies. These artists produced a considerable amount of very attractive and now evocative artwork for posters and other promotional material. Since the Second World War there have been huge changes in the nature of the shipping industry. Although Liverpool is still a thriving port, there are virtually no passenger services and with the globalisation of shipping ownership, none of the major ship owning companies is based in the city. There have been few marine artists working on Merseyside in recent decades. Where previously most artists produced work of contemporary subjects, practitioners like Gordon Ellis and Keith Griffin have broadened their range to include retrospective paintings of historic vessels long since gone and have found this a popular and successful line.

The Liverpool School

So is there a Liverpool School of ship portraitists? The answer is no in the sense of a group of artists working closely together. There were undoubtedly some connections and cross influences - there was a dynamic relationship between the father and son team of Miles and Samuel Walters for a short period and Joseph Heard seems to have had at least one close associate in the artist here called "Old Ensign". Artists also presumably saw each other's work at times whether directly or through reproductions. Paintings by Walters, for instance, were regularly engraved and in later years his entrepreneurial spirit encouraged him to produce several of his paintings as small photographic prints in cartes de visite. They no doubt influenced his contemporaries.

The term is, however, useful in identifying those artists who worked in the port during the late eighteenth and nineteenth centuries. Whilst many of the artists did have distinctive personal styles, in some cases not enough signed works survive to establish clear personal attributes. However, there are often many similarities of composition and style which make an attribution to an artist working in Liverpool very likely. These are most obvious in the use of local backgrounds - whether in the Mersey or off North Wales, particularly around Anglesey - or in the use of a local flag code, but there is often a close affinity in style.

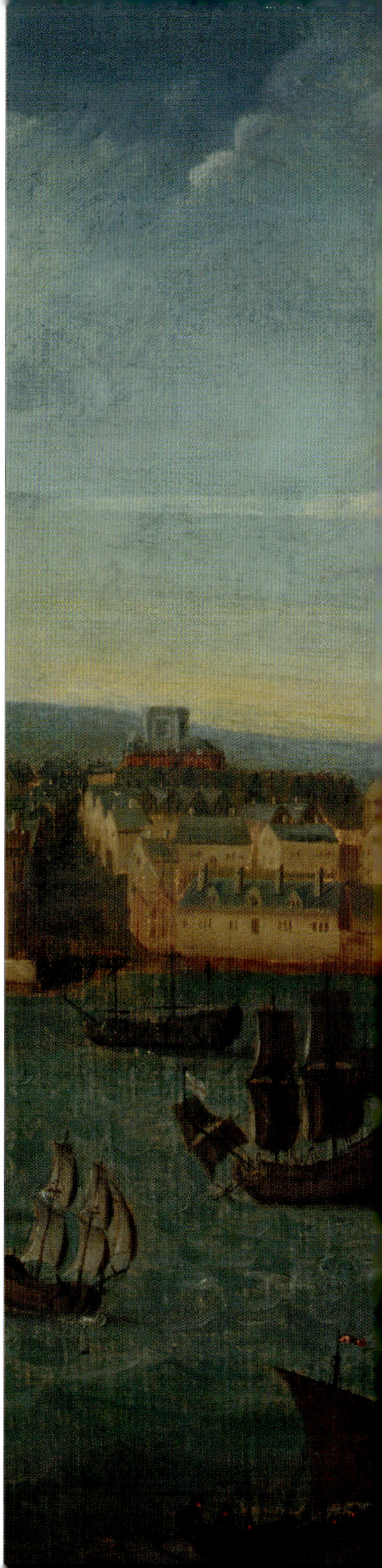

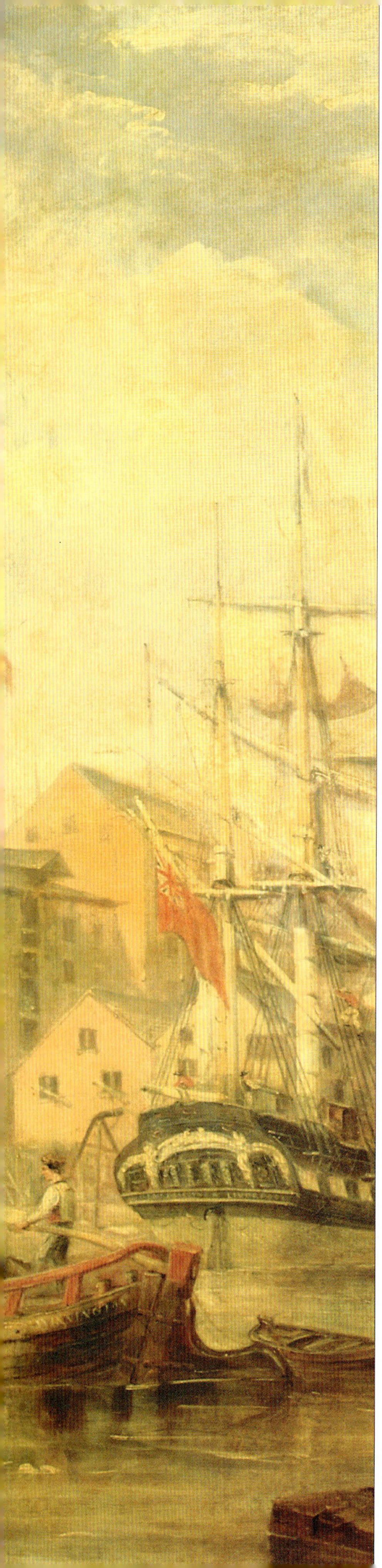

Inevitably the attribution of some unsigned works has proved problematic and some paintings have moved between different artists. For instance, works by Jenkinson have previously been attributed to Robert Salmon, his better known contemporary. Within the collection, *Amity* (no. 116) has moved from Walters to Dove and is here attributed to "Old Ensign".

The nature of ship portraiture

It is true that many ship portraits were done to a formula - a standard port or starboard profile either at sea or against a background, sometimes a generalised coastline but more often a specific location. However, these portraits frequently offer very significant information about the vessel depicted and in many cases the composition is more complex and there is a significant amount to learn from a close examination of the painting. The artist often tells a story of either a limited or more complicated nature. At its most simple it may show a vessel in two positions entering a port, changing direction, waiting for a pilot or riding out a storm. More occasionally a vessel is shown in three positions, such as Walters' *Helen* entering the Mersey. In others, an incident may be depicted, such as the Cunarder *Scotia* dropping the New York mail off Cape Race (no. 242). It can also be a very specific one off incident such as Greenwood's *Germanic rescuing the crew of Hurworth* (no. 94) or *Siam* taking a tow from the paddle steamer *Windsor* (no. 115). Both are actual well-documented occurrences. Sometimes an artist produced two related canvases such as *Knight Errant* at calm and in a storm (nos. 2 and 3) or the *Sir Henry Pottinger* pair (nos. 112 and 113) where Heard shows the vessel being dis-masted in a storm and returning to port under a jury or temporary rig. In many of these cases it is possible to find independent documentary evidence to substantiate the particular incident and the details that the artist has incorporated.

In other cases the story is more difficult to discern. There is likely to be a relationship between the vessels in the double portrait of *Rimac* and *Ariel* by Heard but this cannot be firmly established. However, on occasions the subject can be very specific: Heard's masterly *Jumna and other Brocklebank vessels* (no. 108) uniquely encapsulates the career of Captain Pinder by featuring his commands and the ship on which he served his apprenticeship in one canvas.

A painting is often the only evidence for a particular vessel other than its inclusion in standard contemporary reference works like Lloyd's Register or records of its working life such as Lloyd's Lists or the Customs Bills of Entry. Indeed, such is the accuracy of most ship portraits that in the era before photography they are often the most important surviving evidence for the actual appearance of the vessel.

The majority of ship portraitists were extremely knowledgeable about the technical detail of the vessels they depicted, indeed a number of them probably had sea-going experience. The level of detail includes everything about the vessel from such things as the shape of the hull, the figurehead, position of deck-houses to the intricacies of the rigging being accurately portrayed. Sails are shown in their correct position for the weather conditions or when a vessel is manoeuvring and with the best artists it is often possible to work out exactly what the vessel is doing and what it will do next. Relatively small details such as what other vessels are present and what they are doing are addressed. In Walters' *The Duke* (no. 244) there is a steamer in the background but it is not just a generic vessel but identifiable as a Collins liner. Specific features are included. Several of the paintings feature vessels whose topsails were fitted with patent reefing devices, including those devised by Howe, Cunningham and Colling and Pinkey around 1850. A clear example is Walters' *Domitila* (no. 228). On several occasions – *Prince Louis* (no. 6) and *Morocco* (no. 236) – artists depict a pole compass, raised on a wooden tripod to avoid the effects of the metal hull of the vessel. This is interesting detail but can also incidentally confirm identification or aid dating. The topographical detail is usually very accurate and often very detailed, allowing specific landmarks to be identified and again in some cases providing evidence for very precise dating. For instance, the inclusion of the telegraph station above Hong Kong provides an earliest date for the *Scawfell* (no. 144).

The degree of accuracy is not surprising given that most of these portraits were being painted for people who often knew the vessel intimately - their owners, builders, captains and crews. Unfortunately there is very little surviving information on the nature of patronage of these artists and contemporary references to collectors are rare. One early reference is to the ship owner James Ewing whose drawing room in 1856 "abounded in marine paintings, chiefly of his own ships."[8] There must have been others like him.

A survey of the museum's collection provides some evidence for the patterns of patronage based on inscriptions, documentation and provenance. Details are known or can be inferred for more that a third of the collection. The largest group, about 45 paintings, are associated with the owner of the vessel. A further 25-30 are associated with the master or crew and 4 with the builder. Approximately 10 have other connections or have come directly from the artist or their family.

These patterns of patronage are confirmed by looking at the lenders to the first major exhibition of marine paintings in Liverpool in 1907. Apart from the museum and collectors like Robert Gladstone, the principal lenders were major ship companies like Cunard, Lamport & Holt and Brocklebanks, other ship owners such as C W Kellock and the Beazley family and ship builders like Graysons and Quiggins. Many of these firms maintained their collections through decades of business and one or two such collections survive in company offices until the present day.

Unfortunately no documentation illustrating the commissioning arrangements has been found in connection with any of the paintings in the collection and little is known of the exact process and the arrangements between patron and artist. Occasional references to payment are known, such as the receipt for

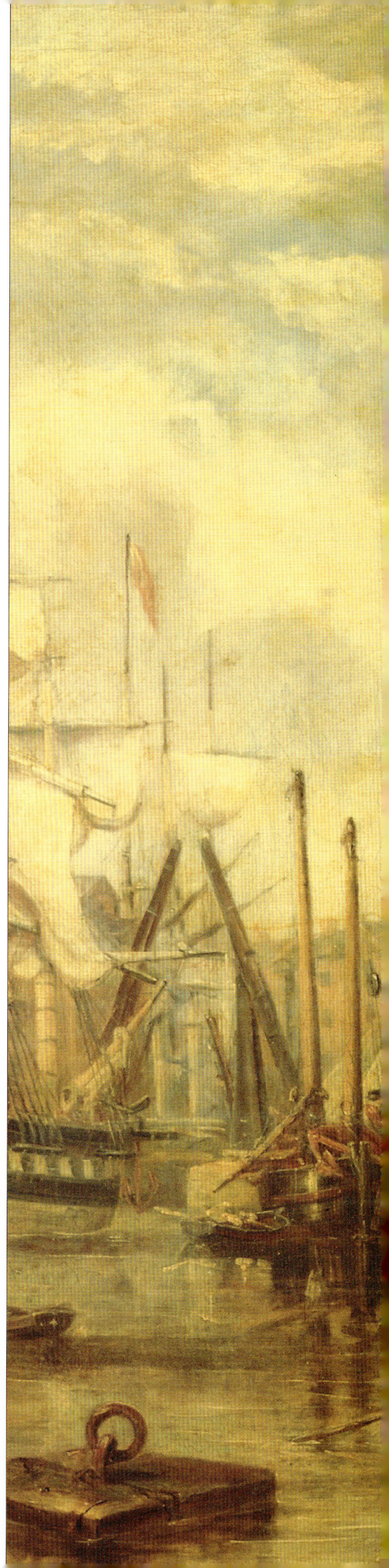

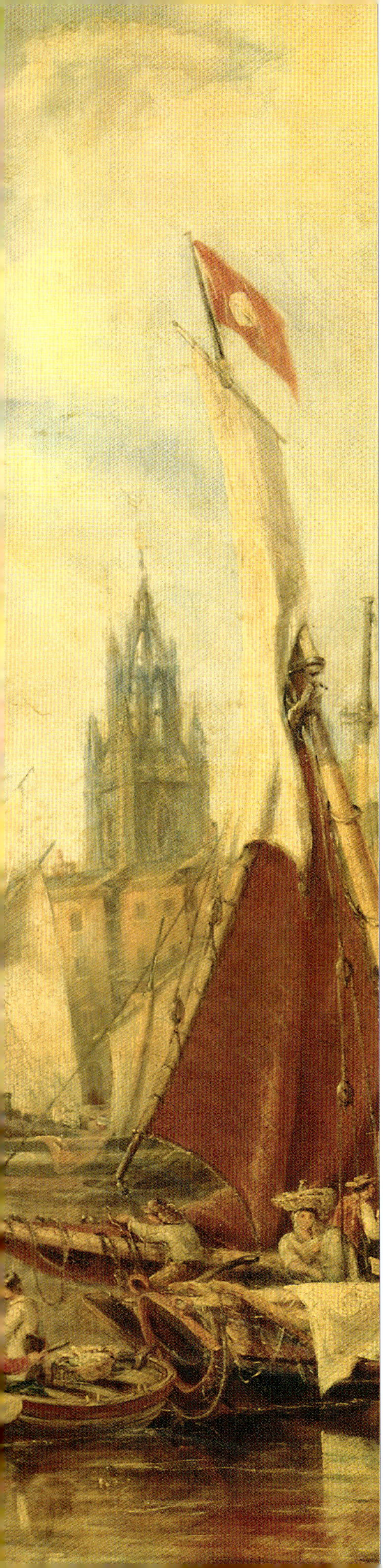

£7 for a painting by Miles Walters to Captain Hammond in 1830 "for painting the Portrait of his Ship *Morea* in three Views sailing into Liverpool with a View of the Ches[t]er Coast, with Gold frame complete."[9]

In some cases artists showed considerable commercial acumen. This is particularly true of Samuel Walters. He painted many popular occasions such as vessels leaving on their maiden voyages and had them engraved for sale. A revealing example is the painting of the paddle steamer *Liverpool* in mid-Atlantic on her maiden voyage (no. 233). In fact, the painting had been completed before the vessel left Liverpool and engravings of it were available the week she sailed. No doubt he had his eye on the hundreds of well-wishers who lined the waterfront on her departure.[10] In later years he was an early supporter of the photographic print.

Conclusion

The present catalogue seeks to provide comprehensive and detailed information about the paintings in the collection and to describe the ships and other subject matter depicted. It is hoped that this catalogue will draw attention to the collection as a major source for the history of ship portraiture and of Liverpool and its shipping, particularly in the nineteenth century.

[1] See Oliver Warner *An Introduction to British Marine Painting*, London 1948, and for a more up-to-date survey James Taylor *Marine Painting: Images of Sail, Sea and Shore*, London, 1995
[2] See H C Marillier *The Liverpool School of Painters: Liverpool Academy, 1810 - 67*, Liverpool, 1904.
[3] See Bennett, 1978.
[4] The earliest dated examples, from 1747, are in Bristol City Museums. See F Britton *English Delftware in the Bristol Collection*, London, 1982.
[5] See M K Stammers 'Liverpool Ship Bowls - the Maritime Historian's View' in L P Lipski *Dated English Delftware: Tin-glazed Earthenware 1600 - 1800*, London.
[6] For William Jackson, see pp.118-120.
[7] His *Mentor and Carnatic*, formerly in the LCL but destroyed in bombing in 1940, is probably from about the same period. Illustrated in G Chandler *Liverpool*, London, 1957, p.302.
[8] *The diary of a Maritimer, 1861 - 1901: The Life and Times of Joseph Salter*, ed. N R Ross, St John's, Newfoundland, 1996, p. 147.
[9] Davidson 1992, pp. 56-7 (ill).
[10] GGA (25 October 1838) has an account of the departure of the vessel and an announcement of the engraving in the same issue.

First boat race on the Mersey between cadets of HMS Conway and HMS Worcester, 11 June 1891. (detail)
Charles W Wyllie
This detail shows the crew of the winning boat from *Conway* celebrating their victory at the end of the race. *Conway* herself appears to the right with other Mersey-based training ships in the background (see No. 261).

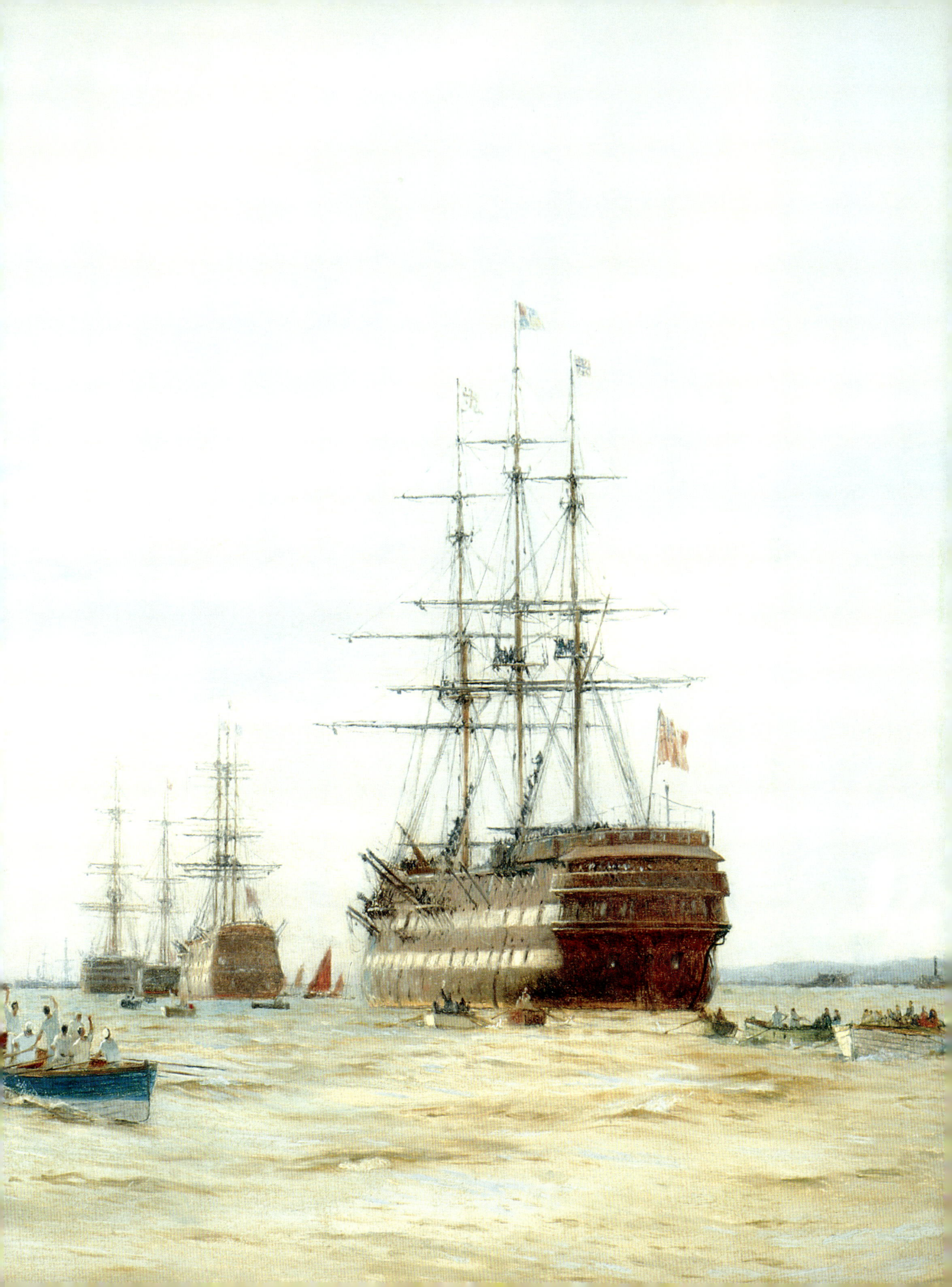

Guidance Notes

Entries are arranged alphabetically by artist's surname and then alphabetically by the title of the work but ignoring abbreviations, the definite and indefinite article, except where this forms part of the ship name (e.g. *The Highfields*). Each artist is listed with year of birth and death. "Active" indicates the dates when the artist is known to have been working. A brief biography, where known, is given.
Where a work is included under the artist's name, it is considered to be by that artist on the basis of a signature or firm art historical evidence or in some cases on the basis of tradition where there is no reason to doubt the attribution. Where a work is "attributed" it is suggested that the work is by that artist but some doubt remains as to its authorship.
The title is generally that which has been used to described the painting historically or is based on the subject matter. Where a title was given by the artist this is shown in inverted commas.

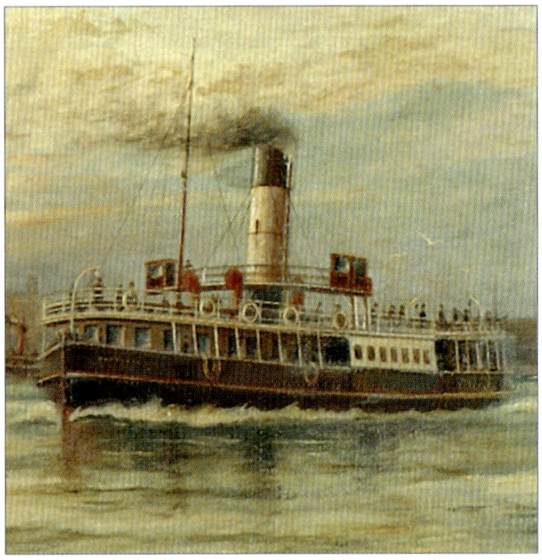
Detail from No. 73

Each catalogue entry is presented in the following format:

The main text includes a full visual description of the work and includes historical information related to the subject. In the case of ship portraits this generally includes a brief history of the vessel. Where the history of a vessel is well-known and available in published sources, only an outline is given. All important sources are annotated, except for confirmation of the identity of house flags and funnel colours (see below).

The dimensions of vessels are generally those relating to the vessel as launched and do not include subsequent changes. Exceptionally changes which are relevant to the vessel as portrayed in the painting are given in the main text. Dimensions are given according to contemporary conventions and it should be noted that the method of calculation varied at different periods.

Technical detail of each work is provided on the following basis:

All accession numbers include the date of acquisition, sometimes in abbreviated form. Since 1990 all accessions numbers adopt the format of "MMM" followed by the year of acquisition and a running number.

Medium and support.

Dimensions of the work, in centimetres, height followed by width.

Signatures, with dates and inscriptions if included, are noted as they appear on the work. The position in which the signature appears is given in brackets using the following abbreviations: bl bottom left, br bottom right, bc bottom centre.

Provenance (Prov) includes the date, method and source of acquisition together with any known details of the previous ownership of the painting.

Exhibition history (Exh) lists all occasions on which the painting has been included in a specific exhibition. Abbreviations, as given in the list of exhibitions, are used.

All known published references (Ref) to the painting are included. However, these do not include occasions where only an illustration of a painting has been included without comment. Abbreviations, as given in the bibliography, are used.

Flags

Three main signal codes are referred to in the text. Generally artists depict the flag hoist providing a number to identify the vessel.
The Marryat Code (in use from 1817 to about 1880), was devised by Captain Frederick Marryat RN, later a novelist. The code employs one of up to four distinguishing pennants (annotated as 1 d.p., 2 d.p. etc.) hoisted over the number or occasionally on another masthead. A major re-numbering took place with the seventh edition, published between 1837 and 1841.
The Watson or Liverpool Code (in use from about 1826 to about 1843) was devised by Lt. B L Watson, instigator of the Liverpool to Holyhead Telegraph. This was only used locally.
The Commercial Code (known as the International Code from about 1870) was introduced in 1857. It was published with the authority of the British Board of Trade.

Full details of these codes can be found in Davidson 1986.

The identification of house flags and funnel colours has been confirmed in one or more of the following sources:
J.L. Loughran, *A Survey of Mercantile Houseflags and Funnels*, Wolverhampton, 1979
F.J.N. Wedge, *Brown's Flags and Funnels*, Glasgow, 4th edition, 1940
Flags of Merchant Shipping issued by Liverpool Journal of Commerce, various dates from 1885
Lloyds Book of House Flags and Funnels of the Principal Steamship Lines of the World, London, 1904
John T. Jackson, *Mercantile Marine Signals*, 1889. Manuscript in Athenaeum Library, Liverpool.

Ship portraits in other NMGM Collections

A number of ship portraits and other marine paintings by artists featured in this catalogue are to be found in the Walker Art Gallery. Basic information is included in the *Concise Illustrated Catalogue of British Paintings in the Walker Art Gallery and Sudley* by Sandra Penketh, Liverpool, 1995. More detailed entries on Merseyside related paintings, including important works by Robert Salmon and Samuel Walters, can be found in *Merseyside Painters, People & Places, Catalogue of oil paintings in Walker Art Gallery*, by Mary Bennett, Liverpool, 2 vols, 1978.

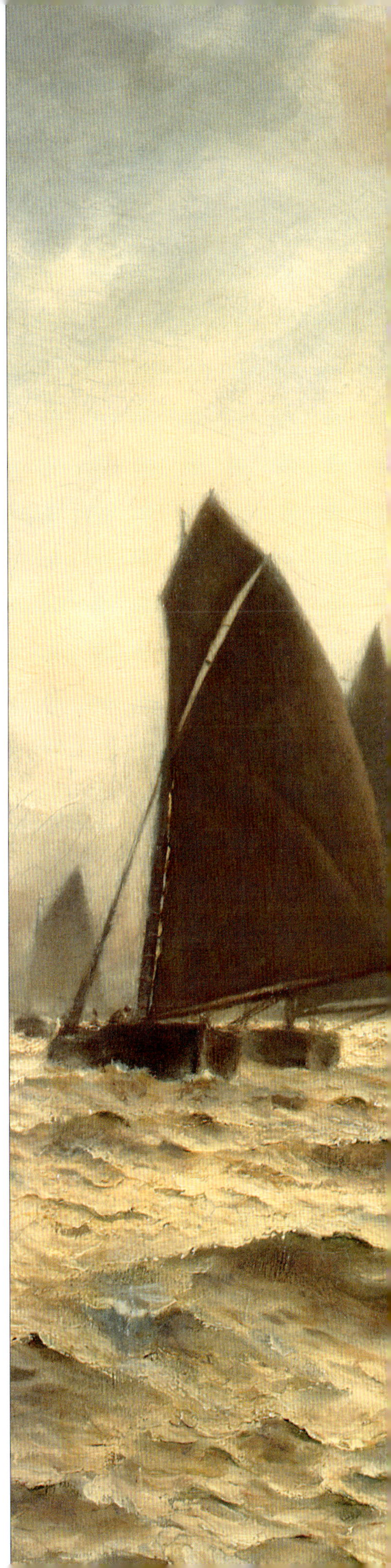

Abbreviations

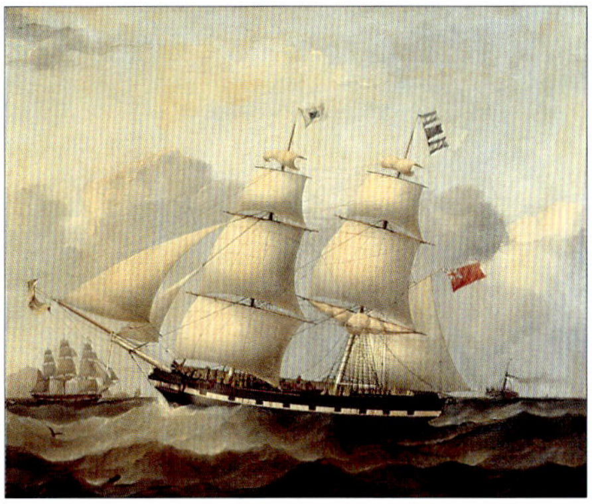

Detail from No. 240

Anderson	R Anderson *White Star*, Prescot, 1964
Annals	Annals of Liverpool in GDL
Archibald	E H H Archibald *Dictionary of Sea Painters*, Woodbridge, 1980
Ath Flags	*Mercantile Marine Signals*, compiled by J T Jackson, 1889, Robert Gladstone Bequest, Athenaeum Library, Liverpool
Beard	Captain J. Beard *Index of Sailing Ships*, mss., MAL
Baines	E. Baines *History, Directory and Gazetteer of the County Palatine of Lancaster*, Liverpool, 2 vols., 1825
Bennett	Mary Bennett *Merseyside Painters, People & Places, Catalogue of oil paintings in Walker Art Gallery*, Liverpool, 2 vols, 1978
Bonsor North	N R Bonsor *North Atlantic Seaway*, 5 vols, Newton Abbot, 1975-80
Bonsor South	N R Bonsor *South Atlantic Seaway*, Jersey, 1983
Brewington 1982	D E R Brewington *Dictionary of Marine Artists*, Mystic, 1982
Brewington KWM	M V and D Brewington *Kendall Whaling Museum Paintings*, Sharon, 1965
Brewington PM	M V and D Brewington *The Marine Paintings and Drawings in the Peabody Museum*, Salem, 1981
Brook-Hart	D Brook-Hart *British 19th Century Marine Painting*, Woodbridge, 1974
Brown	F J N Wedge *Brown's Flags and Funnels of British and Foreign Steamship Companies*, Glasgow, 1940
Celebration	*A Celebration of Marine Art: Fifty Years of the Royal Society of Marine Artists*, London, 1996
Chronology	*Civil War Chronology*, Naval History Division, Navy Department, Washington, 1971
Concise NMM	*Concise Catalogue of Oil Paintings in the National Maritime Museum*, Woodbridge, 1988
CR	Copy Register of Merchant Ships, Chief Registrar of Shipping in PRO
Credland	A G Credland *Marine Painting in Hull through Three Centuries*, Hull, 1993
Crossman	C L Crossman *TheDecorative Arts of the China Trade*, Woodbridge, 1991
Davidson, 1986	A S Davidson *Marine Art and Liverpool*, Wolverhampton, 1986
Davidson, 1992	A S Davidson *Samuel Walters, Marine Artist*, Coventry, 1992
DCF	Departmental Collection Files, Merseyside Maritime Museum
DNB	Dictionary of National Biography
Duckworth	C L D Duckworth & G E Langmuir *West Coast Steamers*, Prescot, 1956
Elliot & McNairn	R S Elliot and A D McNairn *Reflections of an era: Portraits of 19th century New Brunswick Ships*, New Brunswick, 1987
Fairburn	W A Fairburn *Merchant Sail*, 6 vols., Maine, 1955
Falkus	M Falkus *The Blue Funnel Legend. A History of the Ocean Steam Ship Company, 1865-1973*, London, 1990
Finamore	D Finamore *Across The Western Ocean: American Ships By Liverpool Artists*, Peabody Essex Museum, Salem, 1995
Finch 1975	R Finch *The Ship Painters*, Lavenham, 1975
Finch 1983	R Finch *The Pierhead Painters: Naive Ship-Portrait Painters 1750 - 1900*, London, 1983
GDL	*Gore's Directory of Liverpool*
Gibson	J F Gibson *Brocklebanks, 1770-1950*, 2 volumes, Liverpool, 1953
Griffiths	Denis Griffiths *Brunel's Great Western*, Wellingborough, 1985
GGA	*Gore's General Advertiser*, Liverpool
Hague	D B Hague & R Christie *Lighthouses : Their Architecture, History and Archaeology*, Dyfed, 1975
Handbook 1932	*Handbook and Guide to the Shipping Gallery in the Public Museums, Liverpool*, Liverpool, 1932
Handbook 1935	*Handbook and Guide to the Shipping Gallery in the Public Museums, Liverpool, Part II*, Liverpool, 1935
Haws Blue Funnel	D Haws *Merchant Fleets 6: The Blue Funnel Line*, Hereford, 1988
Haws Cunard	D Haws *Merchant Fleets 12: Cunard Line*, Burwash, 1987
Haws Ellerman	D Haws *Merchant Fleets 16: Ellerman Lines*, Hereford, 1989
Haws Harrison	D Haws *Merchant Fleets 15: T & J Harrison*, Hereford, 1988
Haws PSNC	D Haws *Merchant Fleets 8: Pacific Steam Navigation Company*, Burwash, 1986
Haws Royal Mail	D Haws *Merchant Fleets 5: Royal Mail Line*, Crowborough, 1982

Hay	D. Hay *Whitehaven: An Illustrated History*, Whitehaven, 1979
Heaton	P M Heaton *Lamport and Holt*, Newport, 1986
Hyde	F E Hyde *Blue Funnel. A History of Alfred Holt and Company of Liverpool from 1865 to 1914*, Liverpool, 1956
Iron Registry	*Underwriters' Registry for Iron Vessels*, Liverpool, 1862 -1885
JRGS	*Journal of the Royal Geographical Society*
Kennedy	J Kennedy *The History of Steam Navigation*, London, 1903
Kennedy 1933	N W Kennedy *Records of Early British Steamships*, Liverpool, 1933
Kerchove	R de Kerchove, *International Maritime Dictionary*, New York, 1948
LL	Lloyds List, 1741- date
LCR	Liverpool Statutory Register of Merchant Ships, 1786-, MAL
LCpR	Lloyd's Captains' Register, 1869
LR	Lloyd's Register, 1764 - date
LRO	Liverpool Record Office, City of Liverpool Libraries, William Brown Street, Liverpool
Loughran	J L Loughran *A Survey of Mercantile Houseflags and Funnels*, Wolverhampton, 1979
Lubbock	Basil Lubbock *The Last of the Windjammers*, 2 vols, Glasgow, reprinted 1963
MacGregor 1980	D R MacGregor *Merchant Sailing Ships, 1775-1815. Their Design and Construction*, Watford, 1980
MacGregor 1983	D R MacGregor *The Tea Clippers, their history and development 1833-1875*, London, 1983
MacGregor 1984a	D R MacGregor *Merchant Sailing Ships, 1815 - 1850*, London, 1984
MacGregor 1984b	D R MacGregor *Merchant Sailing Ships, 1850 - 1875*, London, 1984
MacGregor 1988	D R MacGregor *Fast Sailing Ships, Their Design and Construction, 1775 - 1875*, London, 1988
Maginnis	A J Maginnis *Atlantic Ferry*, London, 1900
MAL	Maritime Archives & Library, Merseyside Maritime Museum, Liverpool
Marcil	E R Marcil *The Charley-Man: A History of Wooden Shipbuilding at Quebec 1763-1893*, Kingston, 1995
McCarron	K McCarron *Fort Perch Rock and the Defence of the Mersey*, Birkenhead, 1991
Mountfield	Stuart Mountfield *Western Gateway: A History of the Mersey Docks and Harbour Board*, Liverpool, 1965
McNeill 1969	D B McNeill *Irish Passenger Steamship Services, 1, North of Ireland*, Newton Abbot, 1969
McNeill 1971	D B McNeill *Irish Passenger Steamship Services, 2, South of Ireland,* Newton Abbot, 1971
Nicholson	Susan Nicholson, ed., *The Changing Face of Liverpool, 1207-1727*, Liverpool, 1981
Nottingham	Lucie Nottingham *Rathbone Brothers 1742-1992*, Liverpool, 1992
Parker & Bowen	H Parker & F C Bowen *Mail and Passenger Steamships of the Ninenteenth Century, The Macpherson Collection*, London, 1928
Penketh	Sandra Penketh, ed., *Concise Illustrated Catalogue of British Paintings in the Walker Art Gallery and at Sudley*, Liverpool, 1995
Rees	J S Rees *The History of the Liverpool Pilot Service*, 1949
Rees Brocklebank	J S Rees *Brocklebank family notes*, file TI, B/BROC, MAL
Richie-Noakes	N Ritchie-Noakes *Liverpool's Historic Waterfront*, London, 1984
Royden	Sir E B Royden *Thomas Royden & Sons, Liverpool, 1818-1893*, Liverpool, 1953
Smith	P C F Smith *More Marine Paintings and Drawings in the Peabody Museum*, Salem, 1979
Sniffen Checklist	Harold S Sniffen *Antonio Jacobsen - The Checklist : Paintings and Sketches by Antonio N. G. Jacobsen, 1850 - 1921*, Newport News, 1984
Sniffen 1994	Harold S Sniffen *Antonio Jacobsen's Painted Ships on Painted Oceans*, Newport News, 1994
Spratt	H P Spratt *Transatlantic Paddle Steamers*, 1980
Tibbles	Anthony Tibbles *Art & the Sea*, Liverpool, 1988
THSLC	Transactions of the Historical Society of Lancashire and Cheshire
Underhill	H A Underhill *Masts and Rigging*, Glasgow, 1946
Williams	Gomer Williams *History of the Liverpool Privateers and Letters of Marque with an account of the Liverpool Slave Trade*, London & Liverpool, 1897
Wilmerding	John Wilmerding *Robert Salmon, Painter of Ship and Shore*, 1971
Wilson	Arnold Wilson *A Dictionary of British Marine Painters*, Leigh-on-Sea, 1967
Wilson Flags	T Wilson *Flags at Sea*, London, 1986

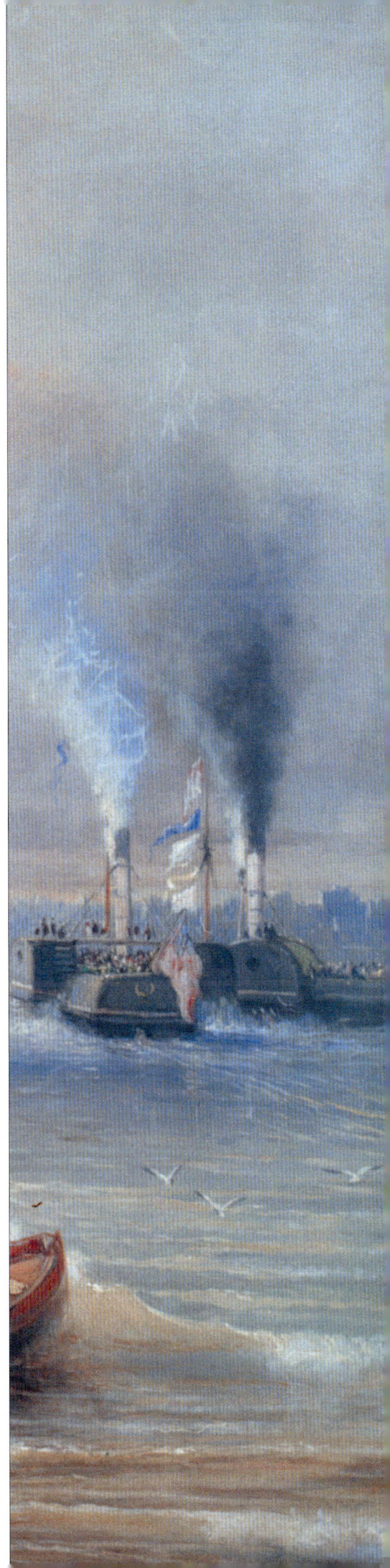

Exhibitions

Art Council, 1965	*Marine Paintings*, Art Council Touring Exhibition, Hull, Southampton, Plymouth, Cardiff, Sunderland, Kendal, 30 October 1965 - 16 April 1966
Bootle, 1959	*Samuel Walters, Marine Painter*, Bootle Art Gallery, Bootle, 6 April - 2 May 1959
Crosby, 1951	*Festival of Britain, Shipping Exhibition*, Crosby, Lancashire, August 1951
Liverpool, 1907	*Foundation of Liverpool, 700th Anniversary, Historical Exhibition of Liverpool Antiquities*, Walker Art Gallery, Liverpool, 15 July - 10 August 1907
Liverpool, 1931	*Liverpool Shipping Week Exhibition*, St Georges Hall, Liverpool, 29 August - 5 September 1931
Liverpool, 1957	*Liverpool Charter Celebrations, 1207 to 1957, Maritime Exhibition*, Littlewoods Central Clubrooms, Liverpool, 17 - 29 June 1957
Liverpool, 1974	*New Shipperies Exhibition*, Merseyside County Museums, Liverpool, 1 October 1974 - 28 September 1975
Liverpool, 1986	*Port Panorama*, Merseyside Maritime Museum, Liverpool, 17 July 1986 - 25 January 1988
Liverpool, 1987a	*Australia 1788, 'A mine of botanical novelty'*, Liverpool Museum, Liverpool, 26 September 1987 - 24 April 1988
Liverpool, 1987b	*100 years of the Alexandra Towing Company*, Merseyside Maritime Museum, Liverpool, 6 May - 31 December 1987
Liverpool, 1991	*Liverpool Liners*, Merseyside Maritime Museum, Liverpool, 24 May 1991 - 31 March 1992
Wembley, 1924	*Liverpool Civic Week at Wembley*, Wembley, 18 - 25 September 1924

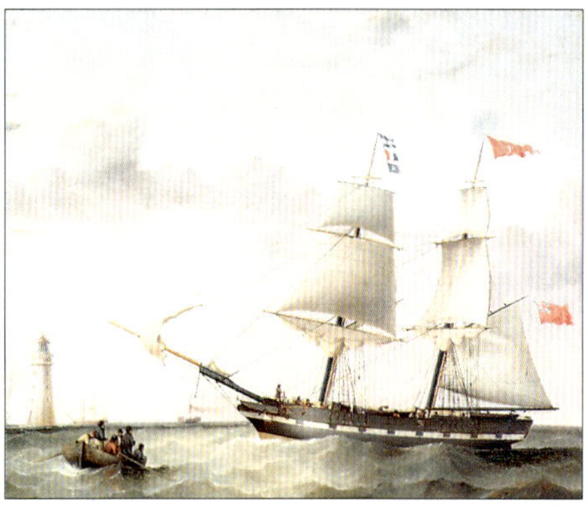

Detail from No. 245

Edouard Marie Adam (1847-1929)

Adam was born near Paris and moved to Le Havre in 1873 or 1874. His earliest painting dates from 1877.[1] His portraits tend to follow a pattern with the vessel placed in the centre with the headland and two lighthouses of Cap de la Heve on one side and a pilot cutter on the other. He often painted two birds above or near his signature. He generally signed his works "Ed. Adam" and included an anchor, the date and "Havre". His work is sometimes confused with that of his son, Edouard Victor Charles Adam (1868-1938) who painted mainly steamers and who was less skilled than his father, particularly in his depiction of the sea.[2]
The main collections of his work are in the Musée de la Marine, Paris and the Musée des Beaux Arts, Le Havre.

1 *Castine* signed and dated 1877. See Brewington, p.5, illus.
2 I have made use of the unpublished researches of H V Sulkowski of Paris in preparing these notes.

1 *Glenorchy*

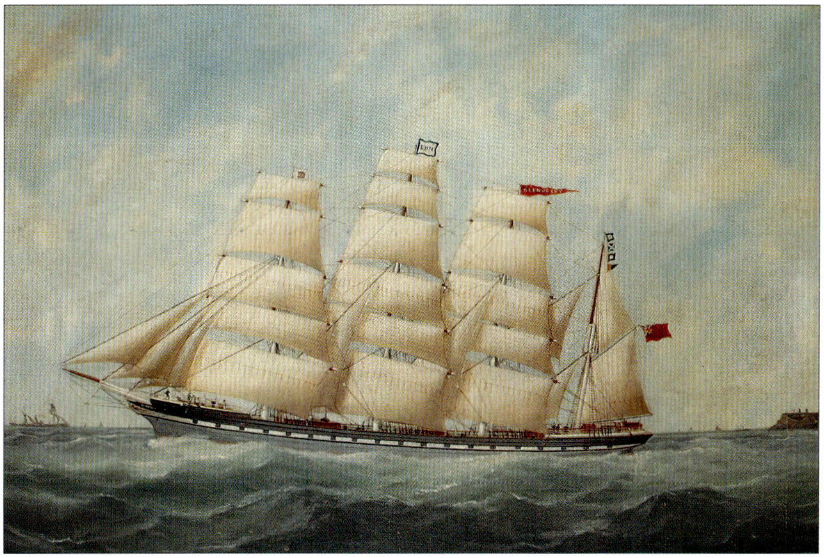

1962.260.1
Oil on canvas mounted on board
57 cm x 86.5 cm[1]
Prov: Captain H S Taylor; by descent to grandson; then to Mrs M. T. MacDonald (daughter of Captain Taylor), Nova Scotia, who presented it, 1962

Vessel: 280.7 ft (l), 42 ft (b), 24.8 ft (d); 2229 gross tons

The 4 masted iron barque *Glenorchy* is shown in port profile under full sail off Cap de la Heve, Le Havre. She is identifiable by her bow name, a name pennant at the mizzen and her commercial flag code (W M P G) from the jigger mast. The pilot jack flies at the foremast, the McIntyre house flag at the main and the red ensign at the after peak. A brigantine rigged steamer is visible under the bowsprit.
Glenorchy was built by the Sunderland Shipping Co. for L H McIntyre of Liverpool in 1882. She was the largest of the five vessels the company then owned and the fleet stayed of similar proportions during its short life. She traded mainly to Calcutta, with an occasional voyage to Australia. *Glenorchy* was sold to the Red Cross Shipping Co., managed by C T Bowring of Liverpool, in 1893 and was converted to barque rig about this time. She was sold to Italian owners in 1899 and sank following a collision off Cape de Gata, on the southern coast of Spain in 1915.[2]
The painting belonged to Captain Herbert S Taylor who was master of the vessel from March 1887 until March 1892.[3] Although the donor suggested that the artist may be R B Spencer, an attribution to Adam seems much more consistent with the location and the treatment of the sea, figures and other details. The vessel was in Le Havre undergoing repairs in January 1892 returning from San Francisco on Taylor's last voyage.[4] A very similar painting in composition and style of the 4 masted barque *Cedarbank* exists but is unattributed.[5]

1 Cut down by former owner according to donor, see DCF. The canvas was presumably mounted on board at the same time.
2 LCR, vol.94, no. 141, 25 September 1882; LR 1882; Beard
3 CR, no. 141, 25 September 1882. For Bowring and the Red Cross Line see D Keir *The Bowring Story*, London, 1962.
4 LL 30 December 1891, 6 February 1892. The vessel did not visit the port on any other occasion during Taylor's captaincy. (Index to LL, 1887-92).
5 Finch 1975, p. 118 (ill)

2 Knight Errant

1955.258.1
Oil on canvas
62.5 cm x 92 cm
Prov: Unknown, in collections, 1955

Vessel: 330 ft (l), 43.5 ft (b), 29 ft (d);
3453 gross tons

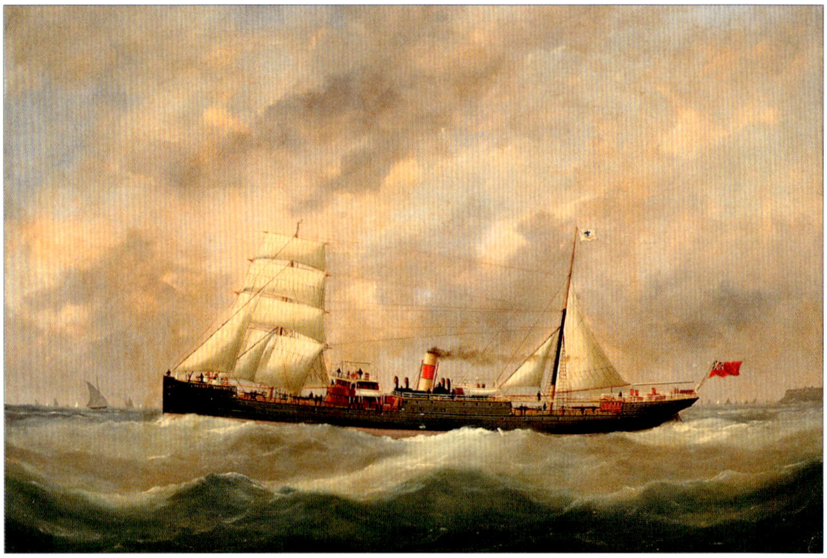

This is one of a pair, with no. 3, of the steam ship *Knight Errant* in calm waters and in a storm. Here the vessel is portrayed in port profile off Cap de la Heve, Le Havre. There are several yachts and small craft in the distance. Members of the crew are on watch or are relaxing on various parts of the decks. One man is on the catwalk between the fore and aft decks. The vessel is identifiable by her name on the bow and she also flies a house flag of a blue fleur-de-lys over a bar of alternate bands in red and blue on a white ground. The red ensign is at the stern.

Knight Errant was built by the Palmer Shipbuilding & Iron Co. Ltd of Jarrow on the Tyne in 1885 for the Knight Line of Greenshields, Cowie and Co. of Liverpool. They had established the line in 1877 largely for Far Eastern services across the Pacific. By 1885 they had six other *Knights* in service, three of them also steamers of a similar size. *Knight Errant* was sold to two Glasgow ship owners, William Raeburn and John Visel, in 1896 and renamed *Kensington*. She was broken up in 1910. Knight Line was acquired by Blue Funnel in 1917.[1]

The style of the painting and in particular the treatment of the sea and the other shipping suggests an attribution to Adam. The vessel occasionally visited Le Havre during her career.[2]

1 CR no. 129, 19 December 1885. For a history of Knight Line see David Burrell 'Fortunes of the Knight Line', *Sea Breezes*, vol. 60, 1986, pp. 337-58.
2 For example in October 1886. LL 30 October 1886.

3 Knight Errant in a storm

1955.258.2
Oil on canvas[1]
62.5 cm x 92 cm
Prov: Unknown, in collections, 1955

1 Relined, 1982; printed label on rear for Harriet Owen Hughes, Picture Restorer, Liverpool.

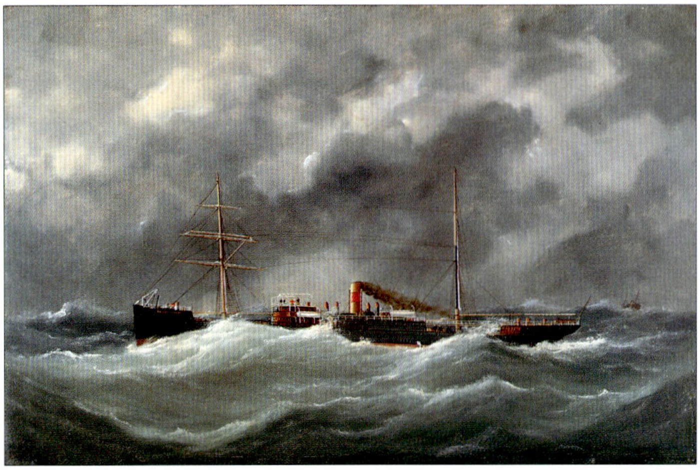

In this view, a companion to no. 2, *Knight Errant* is shown in port profile battling against a storm; waves are breaking against the hull and over the deck and all the sails have been furled. Members of the crew can be seen on the bridge ensuring the vessel keeps her head to the wind. The vessel is identifiable by the name on her bow and her funnel is painted as in no. 2. Another steamer, possibly intended to be a second view, is just visible on the horizon on the right hand side of the canvas.

This canvas is slightly more accomplished than no. 2, for instance, the crew are more realistically portrayed.

4 *Lumen*

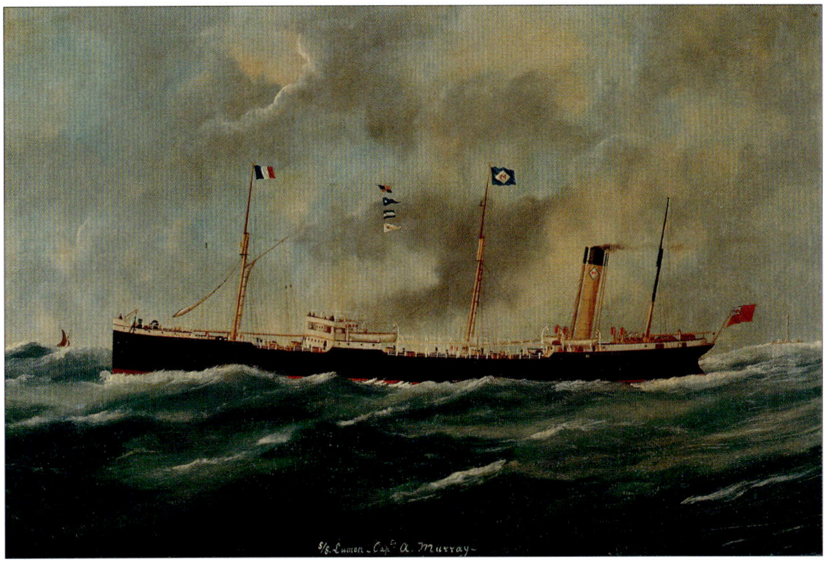

1971.14.1
Oil on canvas[1]
61 cm x 91 cm
Signed and dated (br) "Teddy. Adam 1906." Inscribed along centre bottom "S/S. Lumen - Cap^tn A. Murray"
Prov: H E Moss & Co. Tankers Ltd.; Cunard Brocklebank Ltd; Private Collection, on permanent loan.
Exh: Liverpool 1957

Vessel: 294 ft (l), 37.7 ft (b), 26.6 ft (d); 2357 gross tons

The steamer *Lumen* is shown in port profile off a lighthouse. This steel vessel was schooner rigged and is one of the earliest vessels designed specifically as a tanker. The tanker section is aft of the bridge and there is a derrick over the forward hatch which is probably for ordinary cargo. Sails are shown furled on the main and fore masts. She wears the house flag on the main mast and the house colours are repeated on her funnel. Her commercial code (L D J C) flies on a signal hoist between the fore and main masts. The red ensign is at the stern and she also flies the French flag from her foremast - indicating that she is bound for a French port, probably Rouen.
Lumen[2] was built by Armstrong, Mitchell & Co. of Low Walker, Newcastle Upon Tyne in 1889. She was registered to the Lumen Steam Ship Company, which was a wholly owned subsidiary of the Liverpool firm of H E Moss. She was used to carry petroleum and remained in their ownership until 1924 when she was sold to Harvis and Dixon of London and renamed *Ivor*.[3]
The lighthouse is probably le Gros du Raz off Cap de la Hague on the north-west corner of the Cherbourg Peninsula. *Lumen* was a regular visit to Rouen at this period bringing oil from the Black Sea port of Kustendje (now Constanta, Roumania).[4]
Captain A Murray was master of *Lumen* from 1902 until 1909 and the painting was presumably commissioned by him.
This is a well executed painting and is most likely the work of Adam senior. The main element of the signature is consistent with its use on other canvases, in particular the long descender on the letter "m".[5] The use of the diminutive "Teddy" is perhaps a concession to his English patron.[6]
There is a half-model of the vessel in the collections, accession no. L1970.244.31.

1 Relined. Label on rear stretcher for J Davey of Liverpool.
2 Lumen, a unit of light
3 LCR, vol. 96, no. 48, 9 May 1889
4 For example, see LL 2 June 1905, 18 October 1906, 21 November 1907.
5 See signature on *Sunningdale* in Brook Hart, pl. 165, p.165 and on *Victoria* in Archibald, pl.613.
6 A painting signed "Ted Adam" and dated 1912 was sold at Sotheby's, London, 1 April 1998, lot 38.

5 *Polestar*

This view of the iron barque *Polestar* shows the vessel in port profile off Cap de la Heve, leaving Le Havre. All her sails are set, except the main course and the upper main topsail gallants, as she gets under way in the open sea. Various members of crew can be seen around the decks at their duties. An unusual feature is the pole compass, a wooden tripod lifting the compass away from the effects of the metal hull of the vessel.[1] She flies a house flag at the main mast, a name pennant at the mizzen and her commercial code (N G P H) under the red ensign at the after peak. There is a raised painted star at the bow in lieu of a figurehead. In the background are many small sailing craft.

1971.137
Oil on canvas
61 cm x 91.5 cm
Signed and dated (br) "Ed. Adam (anchor on side) 1881 / Havre"
Prov: Francis Norman; Miss E Jenkins (niece of F Norman) who presented it, 1971.
Ref: E W C Beggs 'Looking Back', *Sea Breezes*, 9, 1950, p.348-9, (ill.)

Vessel: 175.7 ft (l), 28.2 ft (b), 19 ft (d); 647 gross tons

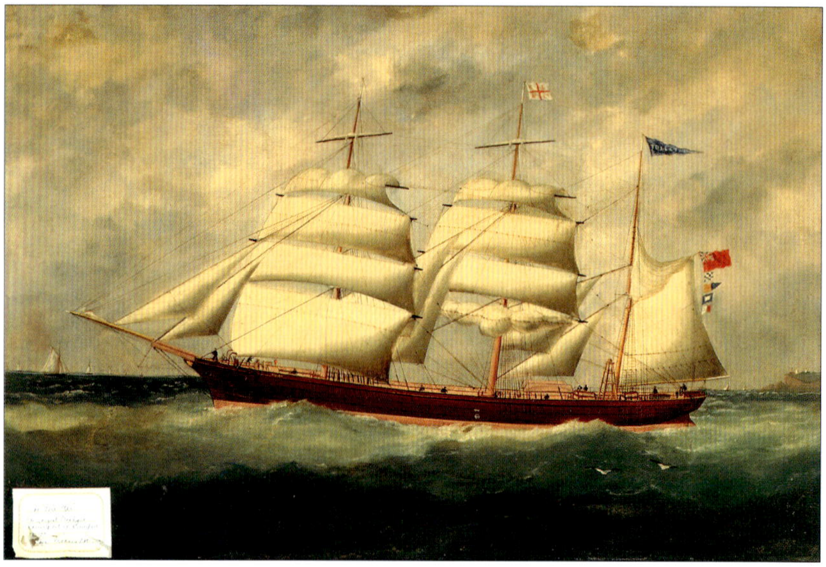

Polestar was built in 1858 by Martin Samuelson of Hull for Cotesworth, Lyne & Co. of Liverpool. She was mainly employed in the San Francisco and west coast of South America trades and was stranded on Doolach Rocks in Galway Bay in March 1891 on a voyage from Peru to Galway with a cargo of guano. After refloating she was sold to A J de Souza of Para, Brazil in 1895. She was converted to a coal hulk for Booth Line (one of the main companies working between Liverpool and Brazil) in 1900.[2]

The picture was probably painted for Frank Norman, her master from 1881 until 1887.[3] *Polestar* was in Le Havre on a voyage from Valparaiso to Liverpool in 1881 and the picture was probably painted at that time.[4]

1 See H Pasch *Illustrated Marine Encyclopaedia*, Antwerp, 1890, p.203.
2 CR, no. 154, 29 June 1858; CR, no. 146, 16 August 1870. LR 1889-90. Reminiscences of her career are in E W C Beggs 'Looking Back', *Sea Breezes*, 9, 1950, p.349.
3 There is a paper label in the left hand corner of the canvas which reads "The "Pole Star" / The largest Barque / sailing out of Liverpool / in 1884 / Captain Francis Norman" and similar labels on the rear read "This is the Pole Star / owners / Cotesworth Lyne & Co." and "Uncle Frank Norman / sailed her for / some years in the early 1880s." Exact dates for the captaincy are given in CR, 1870.
4 *Polestar* was in Le Havre from 16 September until 5 October. LL 17 September, 7 October 1881.

6 *Prince Louis*

The 3 masted ship rigged *Prince Louis* is shown in port profile under full sail off Cap de la Heve, Le Havre. The artist shows the vessel slightly tilted so that the viewer can see the deck where various members of crew are about their duties. The vessel is identifiable from her name on the bow and aft hull and she flies the red ensign at the peak. In the background are various small sailing craft.

1981.735.1
Oil on canvas
62 cm x 92.5 cm
Prov: Captain James Cope Page by descent to the Misses Pearl Leuwin and Ildefonso Page, daughters; presented by them to the International Cape Horners Association; transferred to National Maritime Museum; transferred July 1987.

Vessel: 206.3 ft (l), 38.3 ft (b), 23.5 ft (d); 1374 gross tons

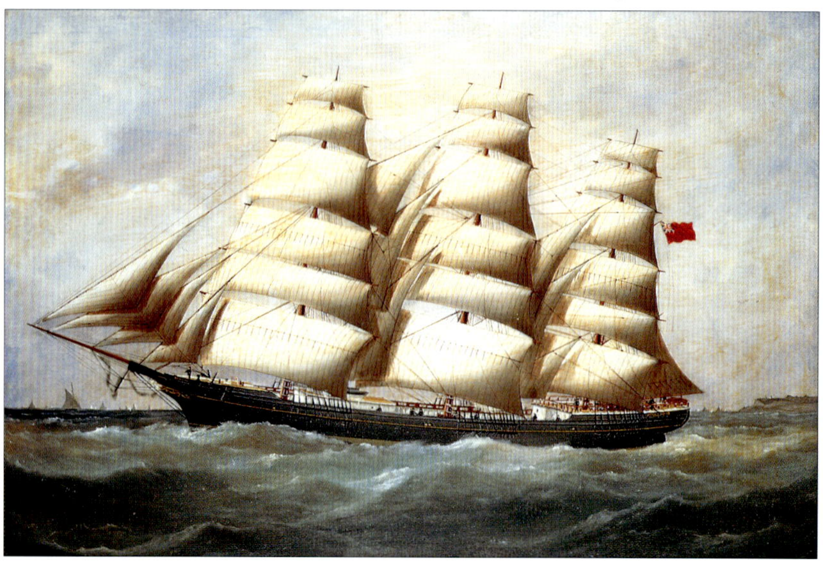

Prince Louis was built in New Brunswick in 1873 by J H Moran of St Martins. In 1882 ownership was transferred to R G Moran, trading as Moran, Galloway Ltd in Liverpool. At that time the firm owned six other *Prince* vessels varying in size from 1200 to 1600 tons. She traded between Europe, India and North and South America. She was sold to Norwegian owners in 1889 and broken up in 1903.[1]

James Cope Page, the first known owner of this painting, had a particular affection for *Prince Louis*. He was master of the vessel from March 1884 and also owned two shares between April 1885 and September 1887.[2] It was during this time, in December 1886, that she collided with a sunken vessel near the mouth of the Hoogly river on a passage from Chittagong to Boston. Despite considerable damage and at some risk, Page safely navigated *Prince Louis* to Boston, arriving on 11 April 1887. As a mark of appreciation the Liverpool Underwriters presented Page with a gold watch and a purse of 57 sovereigns. The watch and archival material relating to Captain Page's career are in the museum collections.[3]

The composition is very similar to *Polestar*, no. 5, and is stylistically attributable to Adam. In particular, the rather dumpy figures are characteristic. The picture may have been commissioned when the vessel was in Le Havre in February 1886.[4]

1 LCR vol. 95, cert. No. 183, 6 November 1882; LR, 1882
2 LCR, op. cit.; TB9, p.309
3 *Mercantile Marine Service Association Reporter*, vol. XIII, July 1888 (copy in DX302).
4 Arrived from New Orleans on 1 February and passed west of the Lizard on 19 February bound for Newport. LL 3 February, 20 February 1886.

James Aitken (active 1870-1935)

Aitken exhibited between 1870 and 1935, mainly coastal scenes and seascapes. He lived in Egremont on the Wirral and in North Wales.

7 *Entrance to the Mersey at Flood Tide*

1957.146.3
Oil on canvas[1]
66.5 cm x 97 cm
Signed (br) "J Aitken"[2]
Prov: C J W Crichton, Liverpool, who presented it, 1957.

This view of the entrance to the Mersey at flood tide shows a group of vessels with New Brighton Pier and Landing Stage in the far distance. There is an easterly wind blowing down the Mersey, as smoke from the steamers and local chimneys indicates. To left of centre is a group of Mersey flats and in the background a steamer and

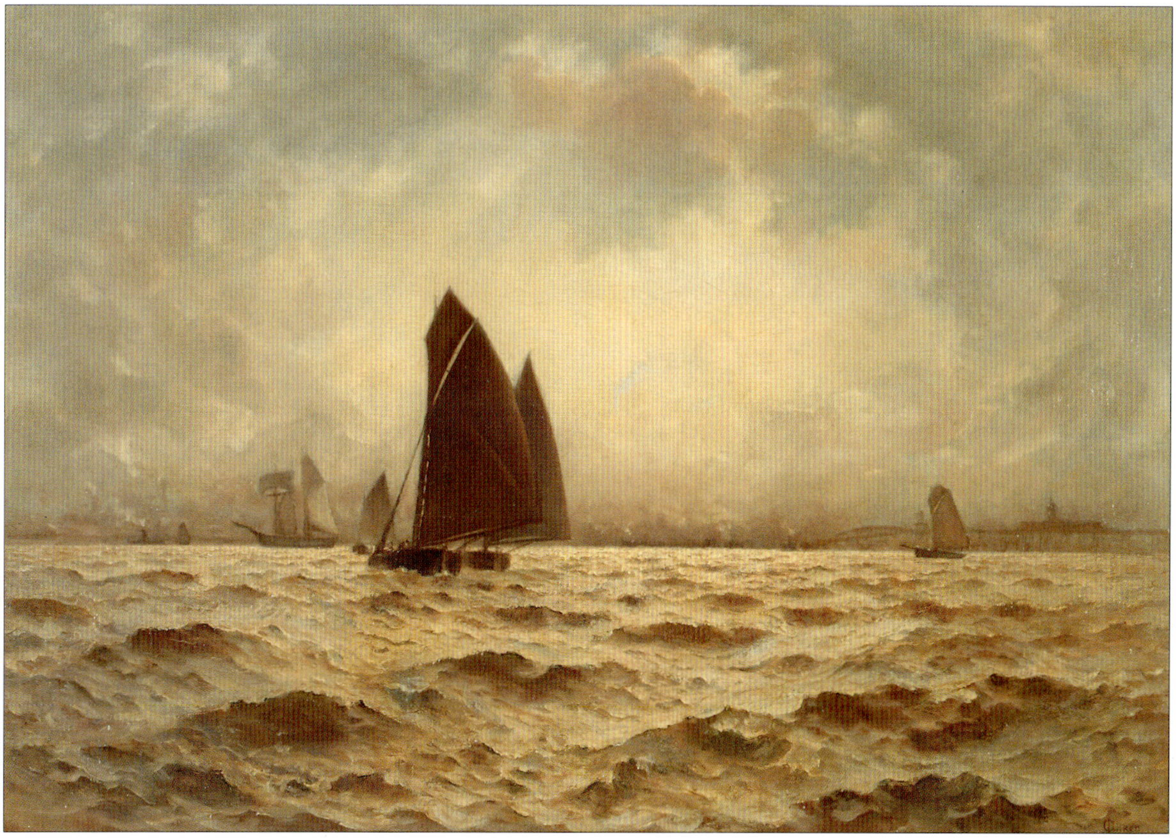

topsail schooner are also visible. The artist's main interest is in producing a seascape in which the vessels depicted are used for compositional effect and the emphasis is on the creamy sea and sky.
New Brighton Pier was opened in September 1867. The painting dates to before the erection of the New Brighton Tower (completed in 1900).

1 Printed label on rear stretcher for John H Paris / 15-17 Leece Street / Liverpool
2 J and A are interlaced

George Anthony (active 1811)

8 *Site of the Regent's Dock in Liverpool, 1811*[1]

1955.409
Oil on canvas
64 cm x 89.5 cm
Signed (bl) "George Anthony"
Inscribed (br) "Site of the Regent's Dock Liverpool in 1811"
Prov: Mr Thomas Branch, who presented it before 1951.[5]
Exh: Crosby, 1951, no. 105.

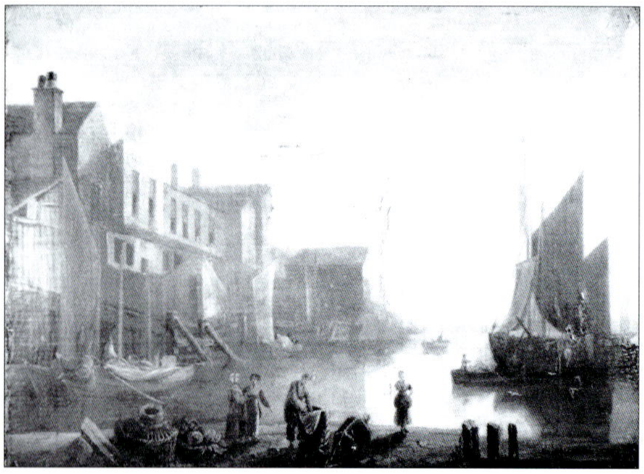

This atmospheric view shows the site of what was to become Prince's Dock, the first dock built north of St Nicholas' Church. The observer is probably looking out into the river from New Quay with a group of timber and brick warehouses and other buildings to the left.[2] The right hand side of the canvas is taken up with a couple of fishing vessels and a small rowing boat. In the foreground various figures can be seen amidst the baskets and other fishing equipment on the quay side. The sun is setting and gives a gentle light over this seemingly peaceful scene.
Work on constructing Prince's Dock began in 1811 but was initially half hearted due to a series of problems relating to shortage of money and labour and difficulties over the site compounded by mismanagement and fiddling. The name of Prince's Dock was confirmed by the Dock Committee in July 1811. It was completed and officially opened in 1821.[3]
The collections also contain two watercolours by J McGahey of this same area, dating from 1809. The first shows a view from the river of the north end with the Old Fort; the other is of the south end with St Nicholas and the dry dock, again from the river.[4]

1 This canvas is currently covered with eldoline paper for conservation reasons and a full examination has not been possible.
2 If the viewpoint was from the Fort one would expect to see the Baths which were described as "commodious and elegant" in [W Moss] Liverpool Guide 1796, p.56
3 For a detailed history of the dock see A E Jarvis *Prince's Dock: A Magnificent Monument of Mural Art*, Birkenhead, 1991.
4 Accession nos. 1970.39.1/2. The southern view is signed and dated.
5 Information from label on stretcher

Mrs A Argent (active about 1953)

9 *No.1 pilot boat Sir Thomas Brocklebank*

1982.799
Oil on canvas[1]
31 cm x 25.5 cm
Prov: Mr A Argent, who presented it, 1982

Vessel: 176 ft (l), 32 ft (b), 11 ft (d); 2 diesel electric engines, 675 gross tons.

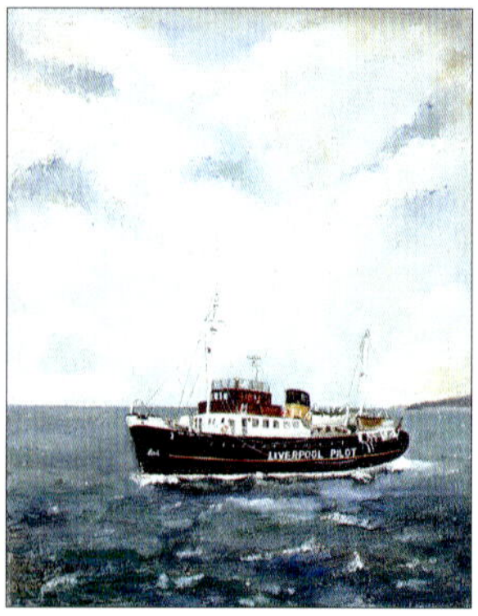

The No.1 Liverpool pilot boat *Sir Thomas Brocklebank* is shown in port quarter view off Point Lynas about 1953.
Sir Thomas Brocklebank was built in 1950 by Phillip & Sons of Dartmouth, the first of three diesel electric motor driven vessels[2]. She was withdrawn from service in 1974 and sold to Danish owners two years later. She was named after Sir Thomas Brocklebank (1899-1953), of the famous shipping family, who was the Chairman of the Pilotage Committee from 1936 to 1941.

1 canvas stamped "GRANGE COTTON CANVAS"
2 One of the other two vessels *Edmund Gardner*, built by Phillip & Son in 1953, is preserved in dry dock in the *Ships and Quaysides* area of the museum.

James Bell (active about 1890-about 1910)

James Bell is listed in the 1905 Liverpool directory as a marine artist but little else is known about him.[1] He is said to have been a sailor and served on board *S S Politician*[2] and *R M S Karina*.[3] All his surviving work follows one of two almost identical designs painted on small milk glass panels. They all appear to date from the period of the late 1890s to the early 1900s. An example, in a private collection, of *S S Gallia*, can be dated with some accuracy to 1898-9.[4] There is a further published example in the Peabody Collection of *S S Bencliff*.[5] There are several examples in the British Mercantile Marine Memorial Collection, including one in a presentation cardboard box.[6]

1 GDL, 1905. Living at 1 Lander Road, Litherland.
2 Information from donor. DCF
3 Information from potential donor whose grandfather served with him on *Karina*. DCF
4 The masthead flies the Beaver Line house flag. *Gallia* was operated by Beaver for only four months from late November 1898.
5 Smith, p.4
6 This latter was sold at Phillips, Bristol, 27 May 1996, lot 331.

10 *R M S Atlantic*

This follows the first of the standard designs with the vessel shown at sea within a lifebelt. The name of the vessel and its home port is painted on the belt which has a spray of blue flowers and a ribbon fed into the grab rope. The ribbon bears the legend "*MIZPAH*". This was a favourite Victorian tag often found on jewellery and meaning "I will watch over thee."[2] A mast head with appropriate house flag is placed diagonally behind the belt.

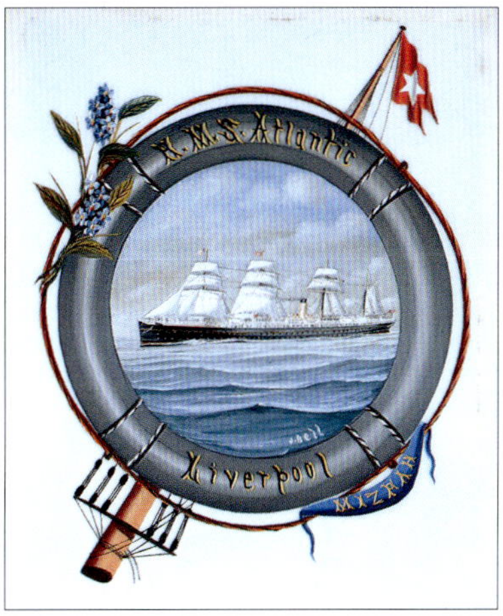

MMM.1997.107
Oil on milk glass panel[1]
33 cm x 27 cm
Signed (br) "J. Bell"
Prov: Mr Youlston by descent to grand-daughter, Mrs Heaney, Wirral, who presented it, 1997.

Vessel: 420.4 ft (l), 40.9 ft (b), 31 ft (d); 3707 gross tons

RMS Atlantic is shown in port profile at sea under full auxiliary sail. She flies the Stars and Stripes, the White Star house flag and a red ensign at the stern. The mast head flies the White Star house flag.

Atlantic was the second of the first four ships built by Harland and Wolff to establish White Star's transatlantic service in 1871. Her engines were supplied by Forrester of Liverpool. She was wrecked near Halifax, Nova Scotia, in April 1873 with the loss of more than 500 lives, the worst North Atlantic disaster to date and the subject of acrimonious debate.[3]

Although this could be a contemporary painting dating from the early 1870s, the degree of standardisation and the dating of all other known examples, suggests that it is most likely to be a retrospective work. The donor's grandfather was a member of the crew who survived the loss of the vessel and he was given this painting at an unknown date.

1 In its original red velvet frame.
2 This also appears on the Peabody version.
3 See R Anderson *White Star*, Prescot, 1964, pp.53-59.

11 *S S Boulama*

This example adopts the second standard design where a spray of flowers replaces the ribbon on the belt. *Boulama* is shown in standard port profile with a bluey-grey sea. She flies the British & African Steam Navigation Company flag, which also features on the mast head behind the lifebelt. The legend "R. M. S. Boulama / Liverpool" is included on the belt.

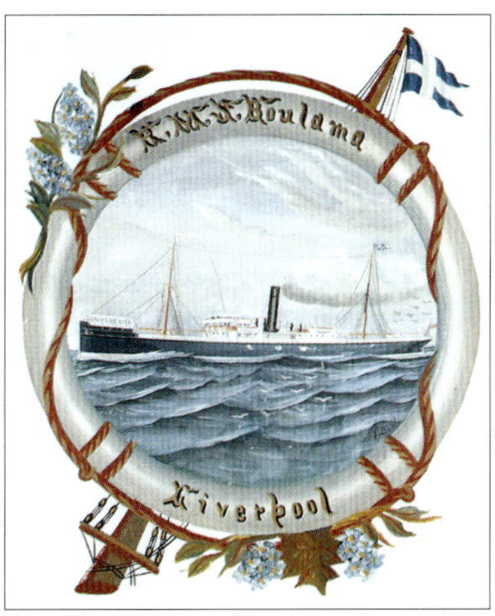

MMM.1995.96.25
Oil on milk glass panel
30.5 cm x 25.5 cm
Signed (br) "J. Bell"
Prov: Elder Dempster Co.; Ocean Group; presented by the P H Holt Trust, 1995

Vessel: 324.8 ft (l), 45 ft (b), 19.6 ft (d); 2613 gross tons

Boulama, named after a small port in Portuguese Guinea, was built by the Londonderry Shipbuilding & Engineering Co. Ltd. in 1901 for Elder Dempster of Liverpool. She was transferred to their British & African Steam Navigation Company in 1903 and was sold in January 1923.[1]

1 Cowden & Duffy, p.106.

12 *R M S Pavonia*

1980.874
Oil on milk glass panel[1]
34 cm x 27 cm
Signed "J. BEll"
Prov: Mr G H Crosbie, Preston, who presented it, 1980

Vessel: 430.6 ft (l), 46.3 ft (b), 34.9 ft (d); 5588 gross tons

R M S Pavonia is shown in port profile under steam with her auxiliary sails furled. She flies the Stars and Stripes, the Cunard house flag and the red ensign. The lifebelt carries the legend "R.M.S. *PAVONIA / LIVERPOOL*" with the *MIZPAH* ribbon. The mast head behind the lifebelt also flies the Cunard house flag.

Pavonia was built by J & G Thomson & Co. of Glasgow for Cunard in 1882. She served on the Liverpool - New York service and from 1884 to Boston. She made her last voyage for Cunard in 1899 and was broken up in 1900.[2]

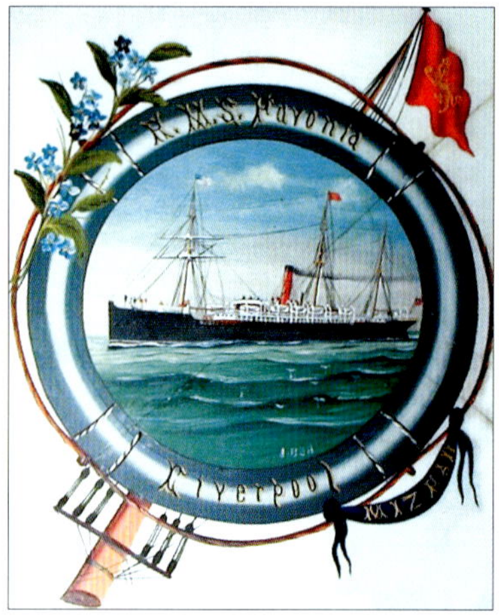

1 Panel cracked top right to bottom left and to right.
2 Bonsor North, p. 153.

13 *S S Politician*

1990.113
Oil on milk glass panel
33 cm x 27 cm
Signed (br) "J. Bell"
Prov: Mrs Evans, Wallasey, who presented it, 1990.

Vessel: 470 ft (l), 56.2 ft (b), 31.9 ft (d); 7228 gross tons

Politician is shown in port profile at sea. Her name and home port are carried on the lifebelt with the two sprays of flowers and the masthead behind flies the Harrison Line house flag.

Politician was built in 1899 for T & J Harrison of Liverpool by Swan & Hunter of Sunderland. She was sold in 1922 to Christian Salvesen for use as a whale oil processing ship and survived until 1946.[1]

The panel was painted by Bell, a seamen on *Politician*, for his ship mate Robert William Wilde, grandfather of the donor. Wilde died about 1905.[2]

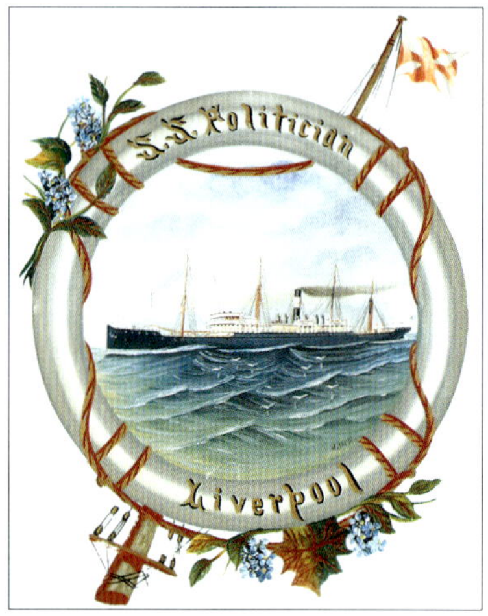

1 Haws Harrison, p. 58.
2 Information from donor, DCF

William J J C Bond (1833-1926)

Bond was a marine and landscape artist rather than a ship portraitist. He was born in Liverpool in 1833 and was apprenticed to Thomas Griffiths, a "local picture restorer and cleaner". He exhibited at the British Institution, Royal Academy, Liverpool Academy and other exhibitions. Watercolours formed a significant part of his output. There are a number of works in the Walker Art Gallery.[1]

1 Bennett, pp. 43-5.

14 *Liverpool from Wallasey Pool about 1850*[1]

This long panoramic view shows the Liverpool waterfront from across the Mersey with Wallasey Pool in the foreground. Building works have begun for the new Birkenhead docks and there are a number of men working in the right foreground. Various coastal vessels are sheltering in the pool itself, including a hulk and beached Mersey flat in the left foreground. This latter has a large winch on her mast, perhaps for lifting stone. Both steam and sailing ships can be seen in the river in the background.

The Liverpool shore is shown in considerable detail from its northern boundary, with Bootle to the left, down to Toxteth in the south, encompassing virtually all the shore-side development of the time. The principal landmarks are, from the left, the

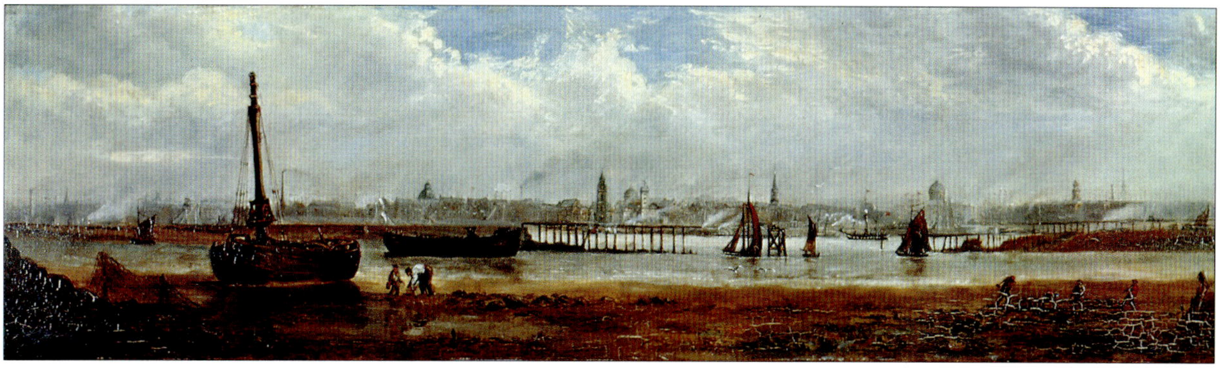

Bootle chimney and Seaforth Church, the Muspratt Chimney (by the mast of the flat), the dome of St Paul's Church, St Nicholas, the Town Hall, Tower Buildings with the semaphore station on top (in the centre), St George's Church, the Custom House, Albert Dock (including the clock turret erected in 1848[2]) and the spire of St Michael's Church. Each of the principal docks can be pinpointed by the cluster of masts breaking the skyline.

In the foreground is part of Wallasey Pool, a natural inlet between the high ground of Wallasey to the north and Bidston Hill to the south. In 1844 it was described as "silting up rapidly; it is quite dry at half-tide; at no very distant period the pool will be quite lost."[3] There were plans from the early nineteenth century to develop a system of docks and parliamentary approval was given in 1844. The project was riven with intrigue and incompetence and took more than 20 years to complete.[4]

1970.246.7.1
Oil on panel
24.5 cm x 86.5 cm
Prov: Cunard Steam Ship Company Ltd; Private Collection, on permanent loan.
Exh: Liverpool, 1974; Liverpool, 1986
Ref: Port Panorama 1986, p.3(ill.)

1 Inscribed on rear 'Mr Bond saw this picture in April 1887 and said he painted it about 1850'
2 Situated on the north-east warehouses, this was designed by the architect Philip Hardwick, see Ritchie-Noakes, p. 52.
3 T Webster *The Port and Docks of Birkenhead*, London, 1847, p.62
4 K McCarron *The Fall and Rise of Birkenhead Docks*, unpublished mss., MAL; summarised in K McCarron & D Marks, ed. P Rees, *Birkenhead's Docks and Railways*, NMGM, 1997.

J Bourne (active 1890s)

Although other paintings by the artist survive, principally in the British Mercantile Marine Memorial Collection, no biographical information is known.[1]

1 See Davidson, 1986, p. 126.

15 *The Pilot Boat Francis Henderson*

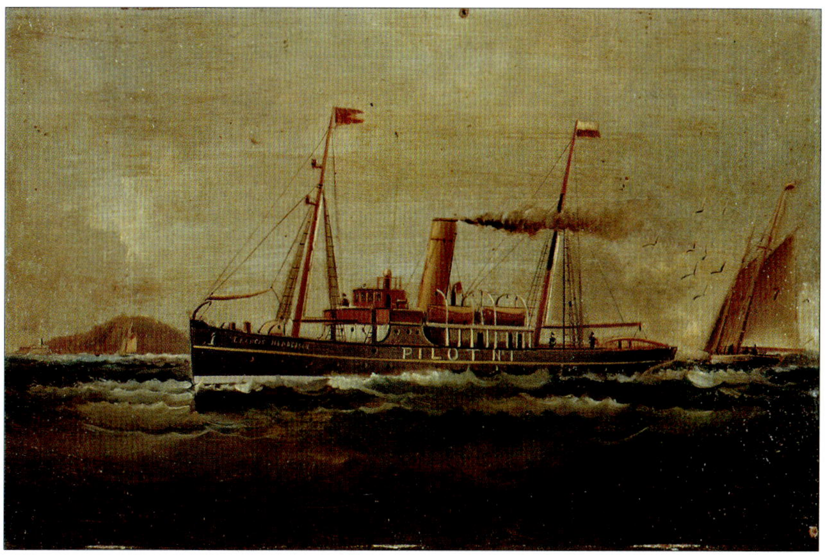

1962.26.1
Oil on panel[1]
30.5 cm x 47 cm
Signed (bl) "J. BourNE."
Prov: R Thompson, Wallasey, who presented it, 1962.
Exh: Liverpool 1986
Ref: Port Panorama, 1986, p.3

Vessel:
Francis Henderson 128.2 ft (l), 24.1 ft (b), 11.7 ft (d); 275 gross tons
Lancashire Witch 80.7 ft (l), 18 ft (b), 9.6 ft (d); 56 gross tons

This small painting of *Francis Henderson*, the first steam vessel used by the Liverpool Pilotage Service, shows her off Anglesey in the company of one of the sailing vessels she was introduced to replace. The pilots had resisted the introduction of steam vessels because they felt they were less manoeuvrable than the existing schooners. As can be seen in the painting, *Francis Henderson* was fitted with sails to assist when lying to in rough conditions. She is shown in port profile under full steam on station, probably off Point Lynas. A red swallow tail flies from the fore and the pilot flag from the main. The No. 7 boat *Lancashire Witch* is shown in port stern view astern of the steam boat. A second unidentified pilot boat can be seen in the far distance near Lynas.

Francis Henderson and her sister, the No.2 boat *Leonard Spear*, were built by Murdock and Murray of Glasgow in 1896. Named after the Chairman of the Pilotage Committee, she took up her duties at Point Lynas on 26 October of that year. Two further steam vessels were introduced in 1898 and all but one of the sailing boats were sold. *Francis Henderson* remained in service until 1917 when she was sold and became the coasting vessel *Pickavance*. She was scrapped on the Clyde in 1929.[2]

The schooner rigged *Lancashire Witch* had been built in 1863 by Michael Ratsey of West Cowes. She was withdrawn in 1896 and sold to owners in Leith in 1897.[3]

There is a model of *Francis Henderson* in the collections (1933.166)

1 Label on rear for J Davey, 5 South John Street, Liverpool
2 Rees, pp. 178-80, 205
3 ibid. p.204

W. Bradley (active 1920s)

Known only by two other paintings,[1] biographical information has not been found.

1 DCF.

16 *A Monks Coaster*

1952.2.2A
Oil on canvas[1]
34 cm x 52 cm
Signed and dated (bl) "W. BRADLEY. 1921."
Prov: C & H Crichton Ltd., Liverpool, who presented it, 1952
Exh: Liverpool 1986
Ref: Port Panorama 1986, p4 (ill)

Vessel: 142.3 ft (l), 25.2 ft (b), 11.4 ft (d); 461 gross tons.

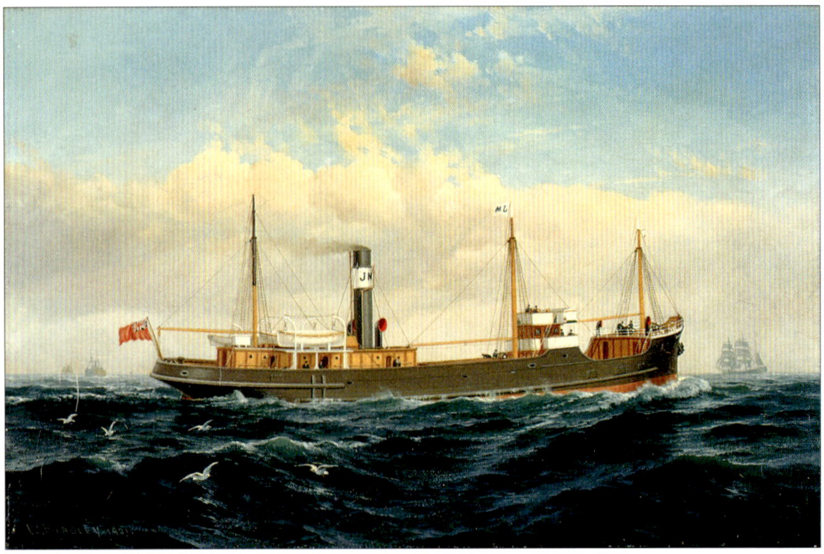

In this attractive composition, a steam coaster belonging to the Liverpool firm of J H Monks is shown in starboard profile at sea. Other shipping is shown in the background, including a 3 masted barque. She flies a house flag at the main mast and the funnel is painted in the company's livery; the red ensign is on the stern jack. The artist adopts a viewpoint which allows him to portray a considerable amount of detail including the deckhouse aft and the two storey bridge amidships. Various members of the crew can be seen on deck at work.

The vessel is probably *T P Tilling* named after a member of one of the owning families. She was built by the Lytham Shipbuilding and Engineering Company and completed by J Crichton & Co. of Saltney, Chester in 1920. She was one of three coasters built in 1920-1 for the company which usually purchased second-hand. She was broken up in 1954. Monks were one of the leading operators of small tramp steamers on the west coast.[2] There is a model of *Clara Monks,* the other coaster built for the firm in 1920, in the collections, accession no. 1963.236.1.

1 Relined 1982
2 See R S Fenton *Monk's Ferry*, World Ship Society, Monograph 3, Kendal, 1981. *T P Tilling* is illustrated on p.35, probably late in her career, less her mizzen mast.

British School

These works are probably by artists working in Britain in the nineteenth century for which a more certain attribution cannot be offered.

17 *Alcester*

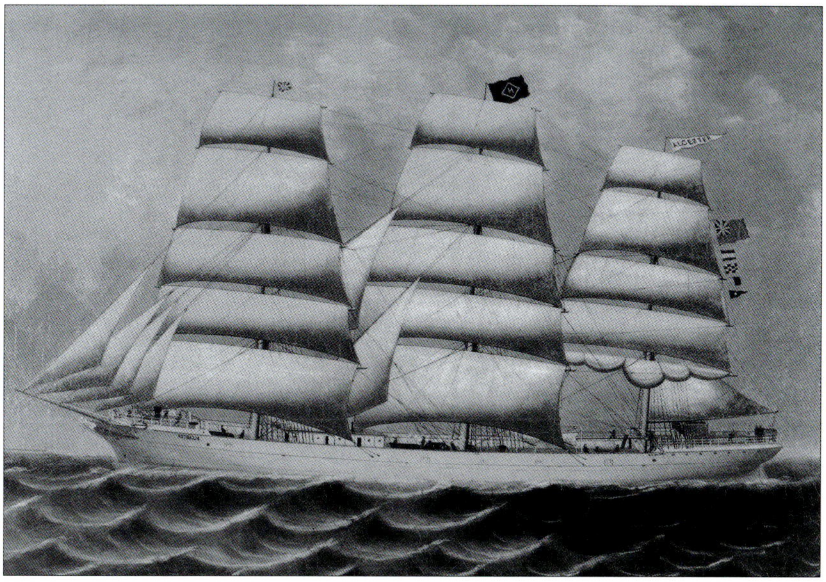

1934.29
Oil on canvas[1]
73.5 cm x 114.5 cm
Prov: by descent in Haws family, Captain G W Haws, Fife, who presented it, 1934
Ref: Handbook 1935, p.20; Finch 1975, p.69 (ill).

Vessel: 257 ft (l), 38.2 ft (b), 23.2 ft (d); 1657 gross tons

The 3-masted ship *Alcester* is shown in port profile at sea. She is under full sail, except for the mizzen course which is furled. Various members of her crew are on deck about their duties, including a group who are making the jib sails secure. The deckhouse and gear on board ship are clearly, if rather schematically, shown and there is a catwalk between the decks. She flies the pilot jack from her foremast, the house flag of her owners, Haws, on the main mast and a name pennant at the mizzen. The red ensign and her commercial flag code (J N K D) fly from the peak. At the far sides of the canvas a sailing ship and two masted steamer are shown on the horizon. The iron hulled *Alcester* was built at Greenock by Archibald Russell & Co. in 1883 for J R Haws of Liverpool.[2] She was named after Lord Alcester, the former Admiral Sir Beauchamp Seymour, who was ennobled for his part in the bombardment of Alexandria in 1882. *Alcester* was used in the deep sea trades, particularly to India, and went aground in February 1897 off Atherfield, Isle of Wight, on a passage from Calcutta to Hamburg with a cargo of jute.[3]

1 Relined; label on rear stretcher for J Davey & Son Liverpool
2 LCR 10 November 1883, vol. 95, no. 182
3 Notes compiled by Captain G Caldecott on Haws, Lawson & Co. in MAL (540.HAW/1/PM). For a graphic description of the wreck by the master, A D Haws, see K Phillips *Shipwrecks of the Isle of Wight*, Newton Abbot, 1988, pp.86-92

18 *S S America*

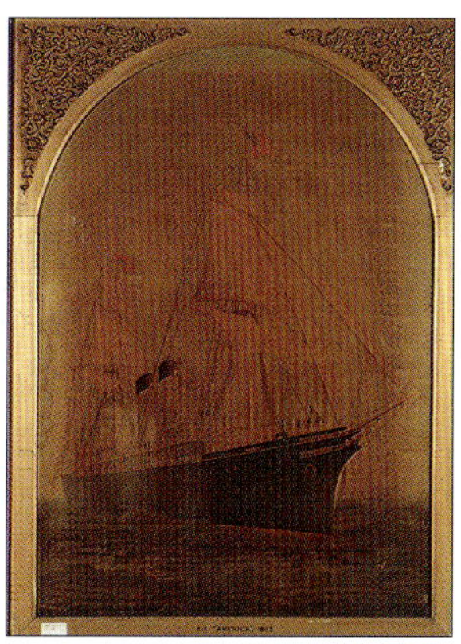

1955.227
Oil on canvas
86.5 cm x 61 cm
Prov: Unknown; in collection, 1955.

Vessel: 441.8 ft (l), 51.2 ft (b); 5528 gross tons

The unknown artist has chosen an unusual portrait format for the National Line's *America* which is portrayed at sea in a starboard bow view and provides a dramatic view of her clipper bow. She is under steam and sail and flies the Stars and Stripes at the foremast and the house flag at the main.[1]

America was built by J & G Thomson of Clydebank in 1884 for the National Steam Ship Company. She had accommodation for 300 first class passengers and 700 steerage. She made some of the fastest transatlantic crossings of her time but had a high consumption of coal which made her very expensive

1 The colours of the house flag are worn but the design is correct.
2 LCR vol. 95, no. 73, 23 May 1884; Bonsor North, pp. 607, 614
3 Illustrated in C R Vernon Gibbs *Passenger Liners of the Western Ocean*, London, 1957, frontispiece.
4 Sniffen Checklist
5 Illustrated Maginnis, p. 79

to run and she was sold to the Italian Navy in 1887. As *Trinacria* she was employed as cruiser, transport, torpedo school, royal yacht and exhibition ship. She was scrapped in 1925.[2]
This painting is almost identical to a poster of the ship and may explain the unusual composition.[3] Jacobsen painted the vessel three times[4] and John Hall also produced a port view in 1886.[5]
There is a builder's model of the vessel in the collections, accession no. 16.3.88.

19 A "Blackwall Frigate"

1964.227.1
Oil on canvas
50.5 cm x 61 cm
Prov: Manx Museum, Isle of Man; transferred 1964

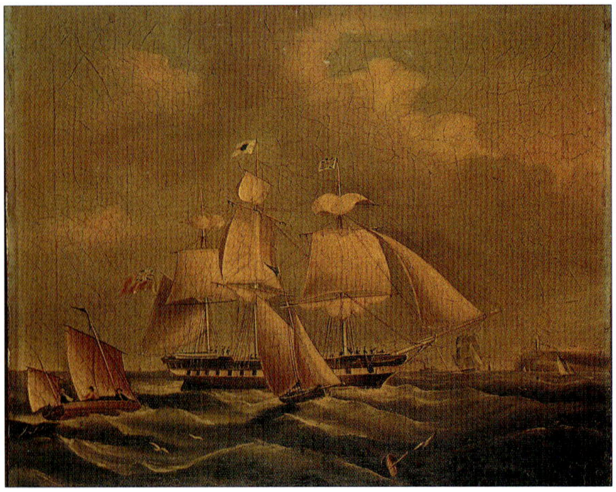

A "Blackwall Frigate" is shown hove-to in starboard view having just taken a pilot on board. The No.4 pilot boat, which can be seen in a starboard bow view in the foreground, is heading away from the frigate. She flies a diagonally divided blue and white flag. The frigate flies a red ensign at the after peak, a pilot jack at the foremast and the house flag of the Blackwall Line at the main.[1] In the left foreground is a small lugger boat with three men aboard. A marker buoy is keeling over in the centre foreground.
The scene is set off a headland with crudely drawn lighthouse or similar structure, shown to the right of the canvas, presumably on the south coast. There is other shipping including a steamer and both deep sea and coastal craft in the background.
The term "Blackwall Frigate" is a twentieth century invention to describes ships built for the East India trade, after the abolition of the East India Company's monopoly of trade to China in 1833. Contemporaries called them "frigates" and they sailed from Blackwall on the Thames. Many of them were also built at the Blackwall Yard of Green, Wigram and Green.[2]

1 The Blackwall Line (Green & Wigram) house flag had a white ground with a red St George's Cross behind a central blue square and was used by Money, Wigram after the split with Green. See Basil Lubbock *The Blackwall Frigates*, Glasgow, rep. 1962, pp. 39-40
2 MacGregor 1984a, pp.161, 173-6

20 RMS Carmania at sea

1980.327a
Oil on canvas[1]
23 cm x 31 cm
Prov: Mrs J V Joyce, Eastham, Wirral, who presented it, 1980.

Vessel: 650 ft (l), 72.2 ft (b), 40.2 ft (d); 19,524 gross tons

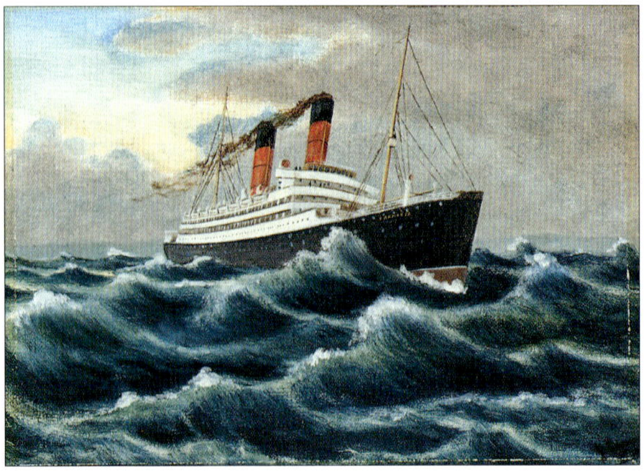

This view of *RMS Carmania* in a starboard bow profile in heavy seas is probably a piece of sailor's art and entered the collection with papers related to the Royal Naval career of C E Joyce who served 1903 - 1917.[2]
Carmania was built by John Brown & Co. of Glasgow for the Cunard Steam Ship Co. in 1905. She served on the Liverpool - New York run until the outbreak of the first world war when she was requisitioned as an armed cruiser. She sank a German armed cruiser in 1914 and resumed her duties for Cunard in 1916. She was scrapped in 1932.[3]

1 Stamped "ROWNEY / CANVAS"
2 Charles Edward Joyce. Papers in MAL, SAS/23A/6/8
3 Bonsor North, pp.156-7

21 S S Daylight

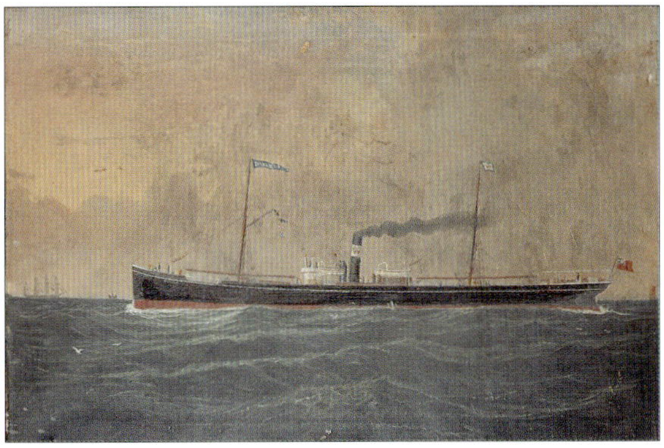

This is a conventional portrait of the iron cargo steamer *Daylight* in port profile at sea. She is identifiable by a name pennant and her flag code in the Commercial Code (L G V N) on her foremast. She flies a house flag on the main mast of a red W on a white ground bordered in dark blue and has the funnel colours (black funnel with red W on white band) of John Wood of West Hartlepool. The red ensign is at the stern. In the far distance a 4 masted ship and paddle tug are sketched.

Daylight was built by Raylton, Dixon and Co. of Middlesborough, with triple expansion engines by T Richardson & Sons, for John Wood of West Hartlepool in 1889. She was lost off Cape Vilano, Spain, on a voyage from Barry docks to Buenos Aires with a cargo of coal in February 1897.[1]

1965.128
Oil on canvas
46 cm x 67 cm
Prov: Mr G H Booth, West Kirby, who presented it, 1965

Vessel: 295.1 ft (l), 38.2 ft (b), 20.1 ft (d); 2338 gross tons

1 LR 1891-2; LL 12 February 1897

22 Duleep Singh

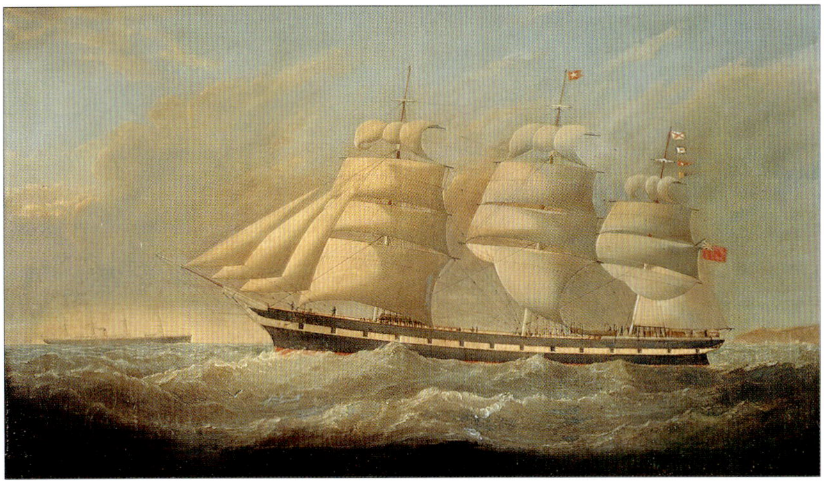

The ship rigged *Duleep Singh* is shown in port profile off an unidentified coast with all sails set, except the upper topgallants and the main and mizzen courses which are clewed up. Her name is visible on the bow and is confirmed by the flag hoist (V W F G in the Commercial Code) at the mizzen. She flies a flag of a five pointed white star on a red ground, the house flag of Imrie & Co., on her main mast. On the horizon under her bow is a starboard view of a steamer, identifiable by her funnel colours (black above yellow) of a White Star liner, probably the first *Oceanic* or one of her sisters.[2]

The iron-hulled *Duleep Singh* was built by T Vernon & Son of Liverpool in 1863 for Imrie & Co. also of Liverpool.[3] This firm formed the original owners of the White Star Line when it was a sailing ship company prior to the partnership with Thomas Ismay which launched the more famous line of that name. The vessel was named after Maharajah Sir Duleep Singh,[4] no doubt because she was intended to sail to India though later she was employed on the route to Australia. She was sold

1955.236
Oil on canvas[1]
69 cm x 117 cm
Prov: In collection, 1955.

Vessel: 210.7 ft (l), 34.6 ft (b), 22.7 ft (d); 1198 gross tons

1 Relined.
2 *Oceanic* built 1870, sisters 1871. See Bonsor North, pp. 732-6
3 LCR no. 50, vol. 86, 1864, TB4, p.439, TB6, p.74, TB10, p.265
4 Maharajah Sir Duleep Singh, (1838-1893), one of the Indian princes removed from his throne in the Punjab by the British and who 'lived extravagantly in England, alternating between chorus girls and the country.' (Mark Girouard *The Victorian Country House*, Yale UP, 1979).
5 CR, no. 50, 3 February 1864; CR no. 19, 9 February 1871. John William Jennings born Dublin, 1817, LCpR 1869.

to Walsh Bros., a small Liverpool company, in 1876 and passed through other small companies before being sold to owners in Santos in Brazil in 1917.

Although the provenance of this painting is not known, John William Jennings master of *Duleep Singh* from February 1864 to October 1871 was also captain of *Oceanic* in 1874-5.[5] Given that both vessels probably feature in the painting it is possible he was the original purchaser. The painting almost certainly dates from the 1870s.

23 *First Lancashire*

1957.47
Oil on canvas mounted on board
46 cm x 56 cm
Prov: F G Smith, Liverpool, who presented it, 1957.

Vessel: 232.6 ft (l), 36.9 ft (b), 22.6 ft (d); 1405 gross tons

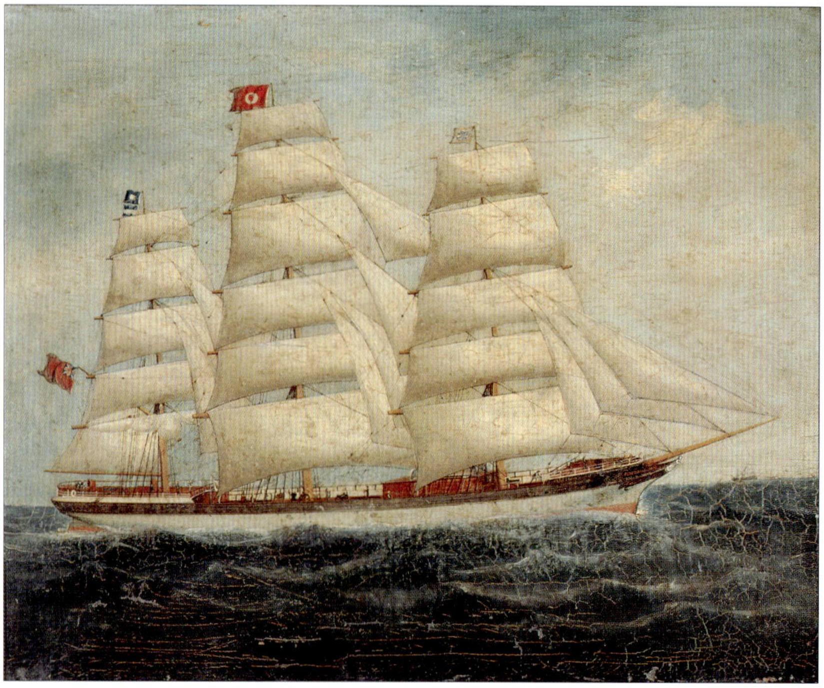

The iron ship *First Lancashire* is shown in standard starboard profile under full sail. She is identifiable by her name which appears twice at the bow. She flies the red ensign at her stern, the first two letters of her flag code (P J C F) are visible on the mizzen and an unidentified house flag of a red ground with a central white circle with a head in red on the main. The pilot jack flies at the foremast. The figures of the crew are nicely drawn in realistic poses.

First Lancashire was built by Osbourne, Graham & Co of Hylton, County Durham in 1875.[1] Her first owner was W H Owen of Anglesey but she was registered in Liverpool. She was sold to J C & G S Richardson of Swansea in 1891 for £22,000[2]. In 1896 she was sold on to Finnish owners and renamed *Endymion*. She was sunk by a German submarine off south-west Ireland in April 1917.[3]

1 She was built for Richard Clayton, a banker of Wylam on Tyne. LCR vol. 92, no. 207, 17 December 1875.
2 See Maritime Wales, I, 1976, p.69
3 Beard

24 *The Barque Glandinorwig*

The iron barque *Glandinorwig* is shown at sea in starboard profile under plain sail. She is identifiable by the inscription, by the name on her hull and her flag code (W T S R) flown from the mizzen. She flies an unidentified house flag of a white bird on a red ground and the letters 'E S C Co.' at the main and the red ensign at the after peak. The crew are on watch at various points around the deck.

Glandinorwig was built in Sunderland by W Doxford & Co. in 1876. She was owned initially by W E Jones of Caernarvon but was bought by D P Williams of

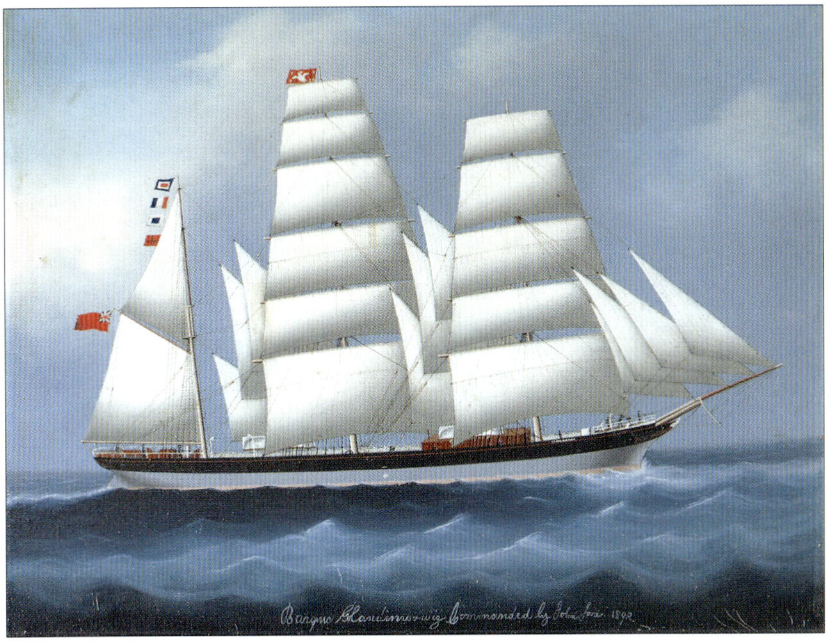

1965.206
Oil on canvas
62 cm x 79.5 cm
Inscribed (bottom) "Barque Glandinorwig Commanded by John Jones. 1890"
Prov: Mr T D Rye, Bebington, who presented it, 1965.

Vessel: 219 ft (l), 35.1 ft (b), 21.3 ft (d); 1107 gross tons

Llanberis in 1877, who traded as Williams, Jones & Co., from about 1889. John Jones was her master in the late 1880s and presumably joined Williams in ownership. Williams himself had limited shipping interests and was principally a druggist who became first Chairman of Caernarvonshire County Council. *Glandinorwig* is typical of the sailing ships owned in North Wales in the latter days of sail by seamen and small scale owners. Most of her voyages were to the ports of northern Europe. She was sold to Scandinavian owners in 1899 and renamed *Sivah*. She was broken up in Germany in 1923.[1]

1 LR 1877-1923; Beard; for a discussion of the North Welsh Shipping industry in the late nineteenth century, see Aled Eames *Ventures in Sail*, London, 1987.

25 *Hilbre Islands*

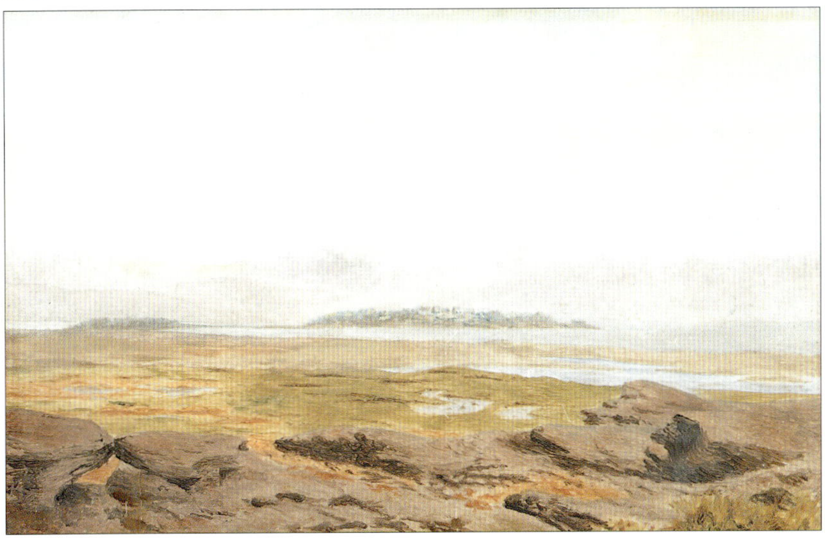

1966.301.7
Oil on canvas[1]
22.5 cm x 36 cm
Prov: Mrs E Woods, Paignton, who presented it, 1966

This is a view of Hilbre Islands in the Dee estuary off the north-west corner of the Wirral peninsula.The main island is in the centre of the canvas with Little Hilbre to the left. In the foreground are the rocks of Hilbre Point on the mainland.

1 Printed label on rear for R Jackson & Sons, Slater Street, Liverpool

26 *Hildebrand on the Amazon*

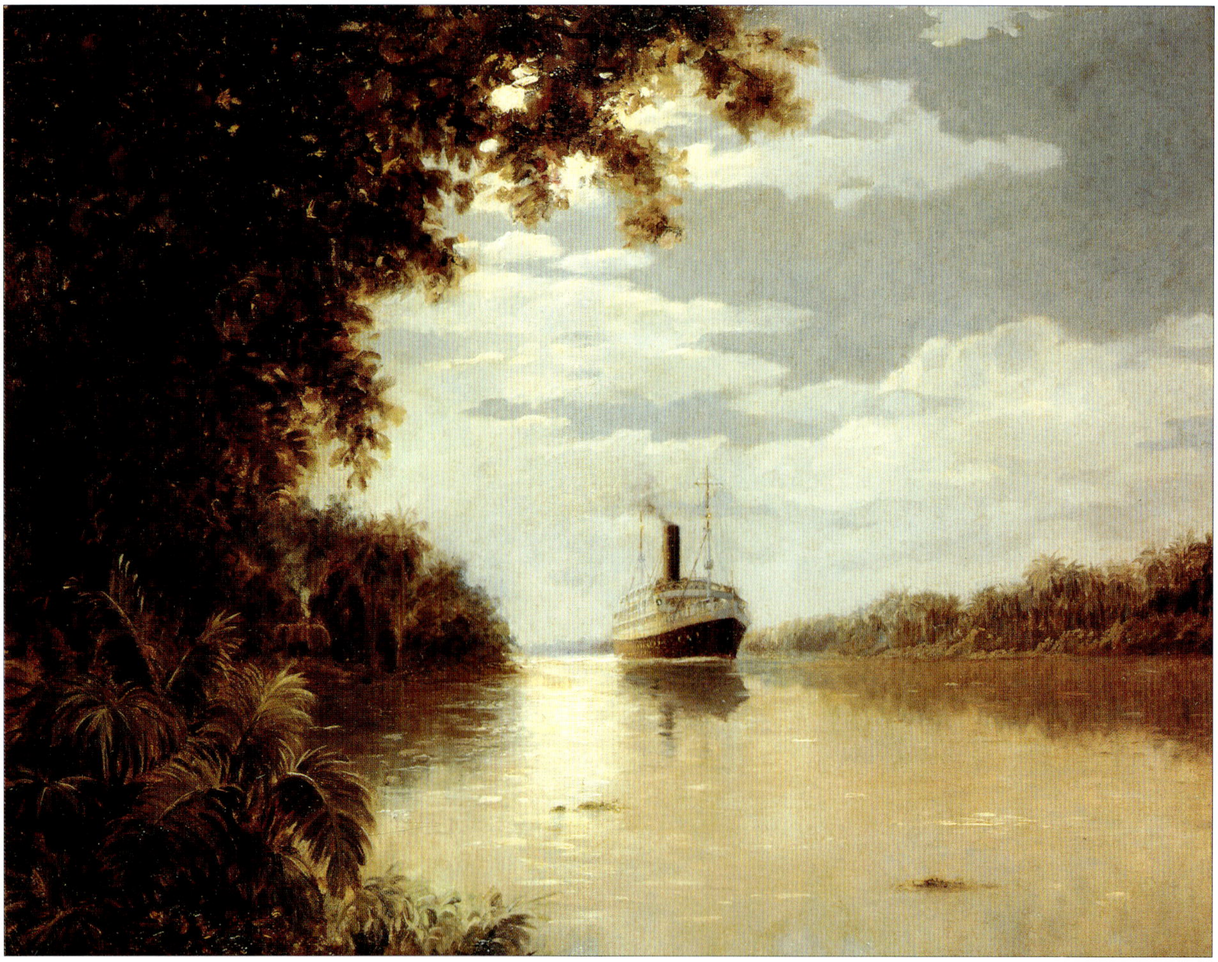

1987.307
Oil on canvas[1]
41 cm x 51 cm
Signed and dated (bl) "?S A Wright?[2] / 1925"
Prov: Mrs M Harte[5], Bournemouth, who presented it, 1987
Exh: Liverpool 1991

Vessel: 440.3 ft (l), 54.1 ft (b), 27.3 ft (d); 6995 gross tons

1 Relined
2 The signature is difficult to read. No artist of this name has been traced.
3 Gregory VII, c.1020 - 1085. Most company vessels were named after Saints and Early Christian fathers.
4 Heaton, p. 60.
5 Daughter of Charles Goode, a captain with the Booth Line.

This atmospheric view shows the Booth Line *Hildebrand* in a starboard quarter view on the Amazon. The vessel is placed in the centre of the canvas in a middle distance view framed by the trees and shrubs of the river banks.

Hildebrand was built by Scott's Shipbuilding and Engineering Company of Greenock in 1911 for the Booth Steamship Company of Liverpool. She was named after the German ecclesiastic who became Pope Gregory VII.[3] She was for many years the largest ship in the fleet and was the mainstay of the passenger service to Para and Manaos in Brazil with accommodation for 218 first class and 406 third class passengers. After serving as an armed merchant cruiser during the First World War, she was laid up in 1932 and broken up in Newport in 1934.[4]

There is a builder's model of the vessel in the collections, accession no. 34.37.

27 *Holt Hill*

The 4 masted barque *Holt Hill* is shown in standard starboard profile with all sails set making her way through a slightly choppy sea. She flies a series of flags from her masts which confirm her identity, including her commercial code (L S T K) at the jigger, a name pennant at the mizzen and the house flag of her owners, William Price, at the main mast. The pilot jack flies at the foremast and the red ensign at the peak. About a dozen of her crew can be seen at work on various parts of the deck. There is a catwalk between the fore and aft decks for when the decks are awash and a member of the crew can been seen using it.

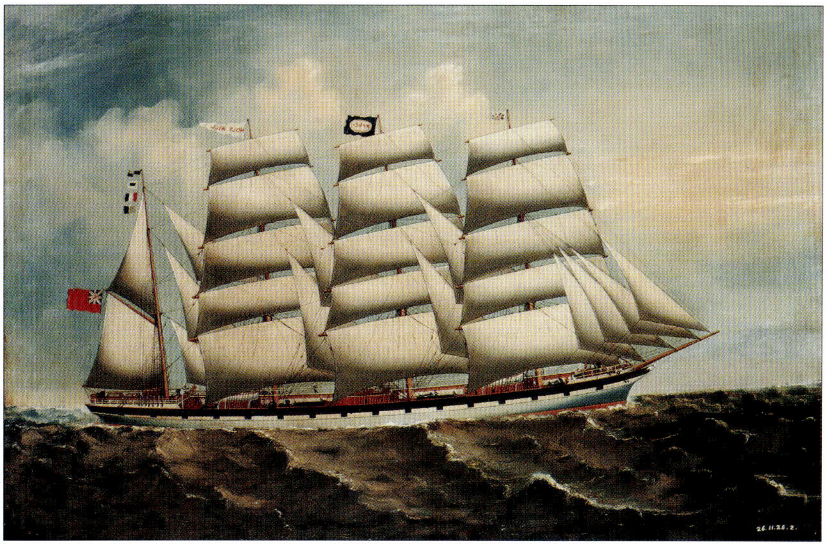

26.11.25.2[1]
Oil on canvas[2]
61 cm x 91.5 cm
Prov: William Price & Co., who presented it, 1925.
Ref: Finch 1975, p.116 (ill).

Vessel: 300 ft (l), 42.2 ft (b), 24.7 ft (d); 2449 gross tons

The iron framed *Holt Hill* was built in Liverpool by W H Potter & Sons for the locally based owner William Price and Co. in 1884. Her career was cut short when she was wrecked on the French island of St Paul in the Indian Ocean in November 1889 on her way to Calcutta from Rio de Janeiro. All her crew were rescued. [3]

1 Painted on canvas (br)
2 Relined
3 LCR, vol. 95, no. 74, 26 May 1884

28 *The Hon. F. G. Wynn*

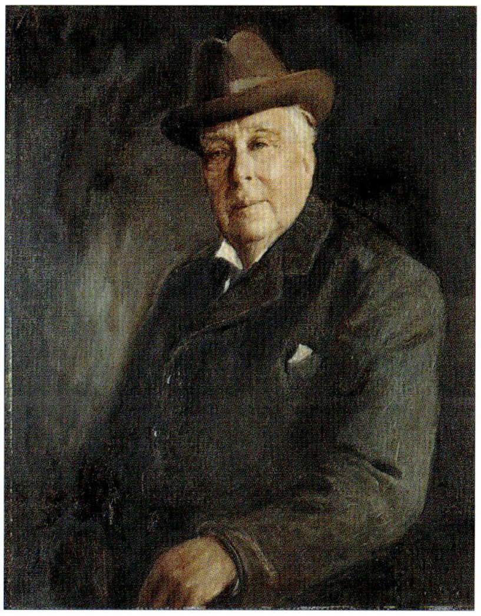

The Hon. Frederick George Wynn (1853 - 1932) of Glynllifon and Bodvean, was the fourth son of the 3rd Lord Newborough. He was a great boating enthusiast and was responsible for commissioning a number of the family boats including two large steam yachts, *Mira* (built 1891) and *Mora* (built 1904), the steamer paddle yacht *Firefly* (built 1900)[1] and the steam tender *Birdie* (built 1899).[2] He was a frequent visitor to the family's summer home, Fort Belan on the Menai Straits, and was responsible for preserving many of the historic relics at the fort.[3] The museum acquired the Wynn Collection of boats and historic artefacts in 1986. This portrait was completed in the 1920s but the artist is not known.

1986.201.182
Oil on canvas
73 cm x 60 cm
Prov: by descent in family, 7th Lord Newborough, from whom purchased, 1986
Exh: *Fort Belan*, Merseyside Maritime Museum, Liverpool, 1987-90

1 Two tenders from *Firefly* are in the collections, 1986.201.12-13. See M Tanner *The Ship and Boat Collection: Merseyside Maritime Museum*, Liverpool, 1995, pp. 72-3. The engine, paddles and paddle boxes are also in the collection, 1986.201.32
2 *Birdie* is in the collections, 1986.201.1. See Tanner, op. cit., pp. 74-5
3 R V Wynn *Short History of Belan Fort* (privately printed)

29 *Liverpool in 1682* (page 38)

This painting of Liverpool, dated 1682, shows an almost identical view to the Peters painting *Liverpool in 1680*, no. 217. However, although the layout of the town and the location, appearance and condition of the buildings is virtually the same, there are differences in detail and particularly in the vessels shown in the river.

The layout of the town corresponds very closely with the Peters painting and the overall description need not be repeated. The principal difference is that this panel shows the castle with only one tower to the right, which is surely an error on the artist's part. The number and disposition of vessels on the Mersey, however, is quite different and their rendering more problematic. The nearest vessel in the centre

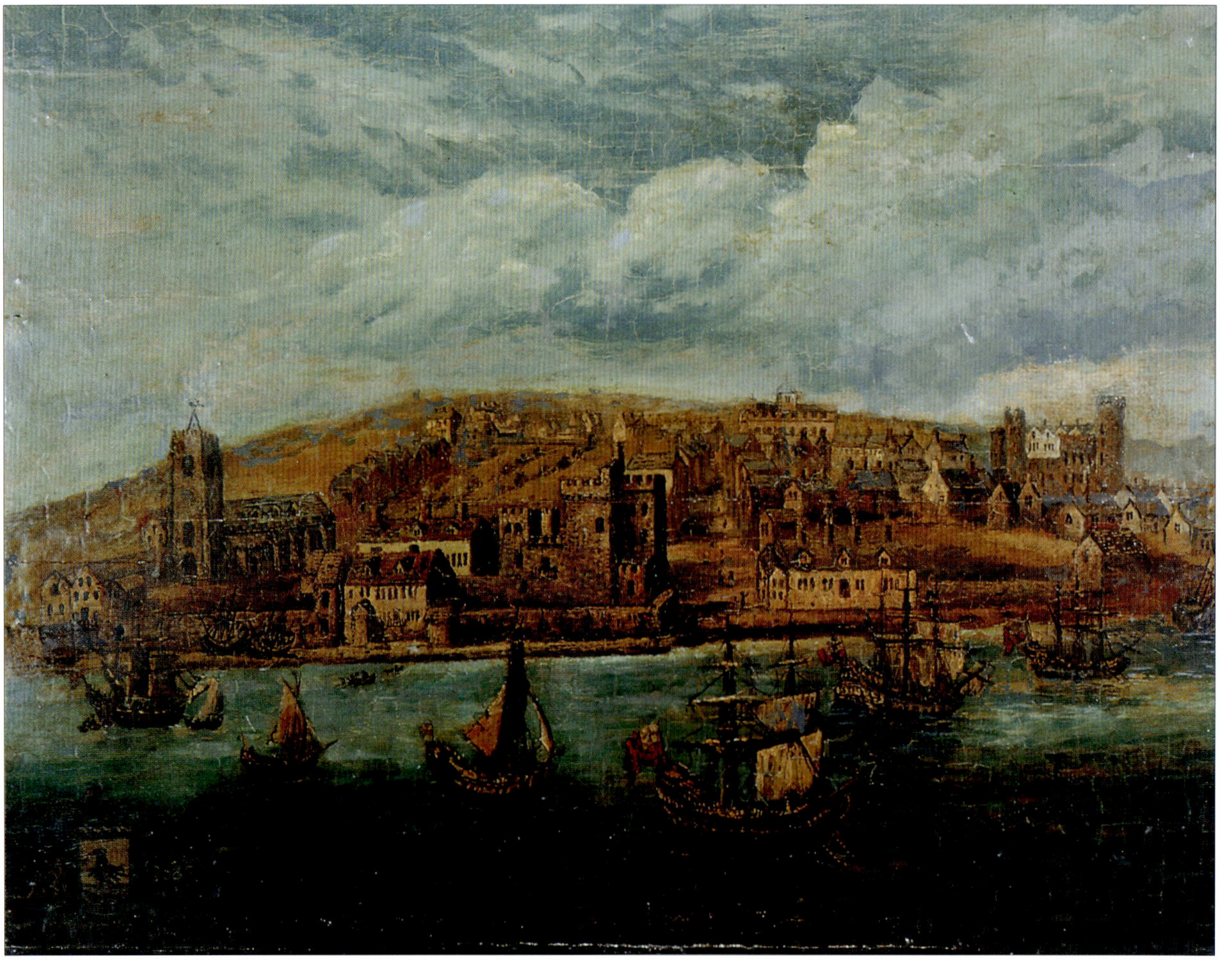

1931.211.1
Oil on wood panel[1]
42 cm x 65 cm
Prov: Skillicorn family, Liverpool (c.1860); Miss Skillicorn; purchased by Charles R Hand, Liverpool, 1907; purchased by Robert Gladstone, Liverpool, 1931, who presented it, 1931.
Exh: Liverpool, 1931, no. 435; Crosby, 1951, no. 106; Liverpool, 1986
Ref:[Underhill] History of Liverpool, c.1830, mss. quoted in R Stewart-Brown, op. cit.; Port Panorama, 1986, p.4 (ill)

foreground is a brig but the high poop looks odd for a vessel of this date and royals would not be expected. To the right are two ships. The one nearest the custom house has a broad band on the hull which is more characteristic of vessels a century or more later. In the left foreground are two single masted vessels which are perhaps inaccurate renderings of coastal craft. The overall impression is one of potential anachronism and of an artist who is not expert at depicting sailing vessels.

The tide is out and there are two beached ships below the quay wall by St Nicholas and two further vessels on the shore to the right of the Castle.

Given the similarities, it is difficult to believe that the two paintings were produced independently of each other, though this must remain a slight possibility. However, the exact relationship of the two paintings is not immediately clear. Whereas the physical condition of no. 217 is consistent with a seventeenth century date, there are significant elements about this painting which cause concern. These relate particularly to the paint layer which shows no age cracks or other physical characteristics of an aged oil film.[2] The inclusion of the arms of Richard Windall and the date of 1682, which has previously been thought to authenticate the painting[3] may be a later addition.

In stylistic terms and in some elements of detail, this painting is more closely related to the Eyes engraving of 1766[4] than no. 217. This is particularly true of the angularity of the buildings, the inclusion of trees in the Common Garden and the dome like structure on top of the Town Hall. However, the inscription on the 1766 engraving makes it clear that Eyes was copying the Peters painting (no. 217). One possible explanation would be that this panel painting was copied from the Eyes engraving, probably in the late eighteenth or early nineteenth century. Whilst it should be

1Conserved 1931, 1971, 1977. Panel is stuck to a piece of Sundela fibre board for support.
2 Report of NMGM Conservation Department, December 1995. This concludes that "the whole of the visible painted design is somewhat suspect and highly unlikely to date from 1682."
3 Letter of Robert Gladstone, 3 November 1931, DCF
4 Engraving "*The West Prospect of the Town of Liverpool, as it appeared about the year 1680. Taken from a painting in the possession of Ralph Peters Esqr.*" John Eyes, 1766.
5 R Stewart-Brown, op. cit., p.41 quoting Underhill mss. Stewart-Brown doubts the existence of a second painting, suggesting that Underhill was mistaking either the Eyes engraving or the Peters painting. It is perhaps surprising that he was unaware that no. 29 had surfaced in 1907 and could be a candidate.

noted that there is little correlation with the vessels in the Eyes engraving, the depiction of the vessels with its inaccuracies and anachronisms would perhaps support a later date.

It is possible, from documentation associated with its acquisition, to trace the history of the painting back to about 1860 with some confidence. There is reference to a second painting being in existence in about 1830 in the possession of G. Crump, who was probably George Crump an attorney of Seacombe and Liverpool.[5] This could well be the present painting.

Given all the uncertainties surrounding this painting, any attribution is clearly impossible.

30 *P S Pacific*

This schooner rigged paddle steamer is shown in port profile at sea with various sailing vessels and other small craft in the background and the hint of land on the horizon to the left. She flies the house flag of the Pacific Steam Navigation Company from her main mast and the red ensign at the stern. The deck accommodation, equipment and crew are painted in attractive detail.

The canvas bears no evidence regarding the identity of the vessel and it has previously been assumed to be one of three P S N C's sisterships built in 1851 and 1852 - *Quito*, *Lima* or *Bogota* - from a plaque on the frame. In fact the vessel depicted answers to the description of a later generation of paddle steamer and is one of four sisters – *Pacific, Santiago, Limena* and *Panama* – built by Randolph and Elder of Glasgow in 1865. They could carry cargo and nearly 200 passengers and the increased deck accommodation can be seen in the painting. Although intended for the Valparaiso - Callao service, they were transferred to inaugurate the company's Liverpool to Valparaiso service in 1868. This was provided under contract with the

1984.269.5
Oil on canvas
75 cm x 111 cm
Prov: Pacific Steam Navigation Company, on permanent loan.

Vessel: 267.5 ft (l), 40.2 ft (b); 17.5 ft (d); 1631 gross tons

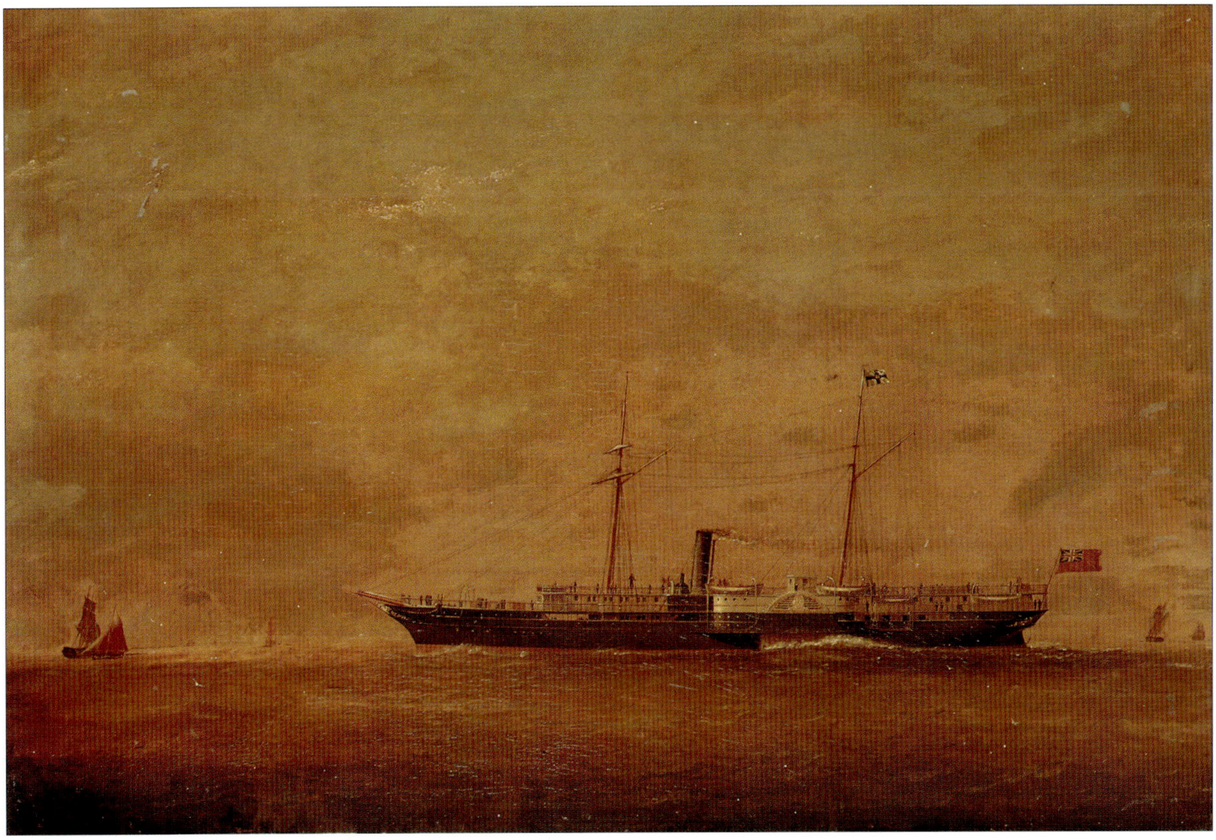

Chilean government and was a significant success. *Santiago* was lost in the Straits of Magellan in 1869, *Limena* was sold to the Peruvian government in 1877 and *Pacific* and *Panama* were hulked in 1881 when screw steamers had taken over.[1] Although no artist has been identified, this painting is well executed and details, such as the water round the paddles, are convincingly depicted. It is almost certainly by the same hand as no. 40, *P S Valparaiso*.

1 A C Wardle *Steam Conquers the Pacific*, London, 1940, J Lingwood *By Royal Charter. The Steam Conquistadors. A History of the Pacific Steam Navigation Company*, Liverpool, 1977.

31 *Parthian*

1955.237
Oil on canvas[1]
61 cm x 77 cm
Prov: Unknown, in collections, 1955.

Vessel: 291 gross tons

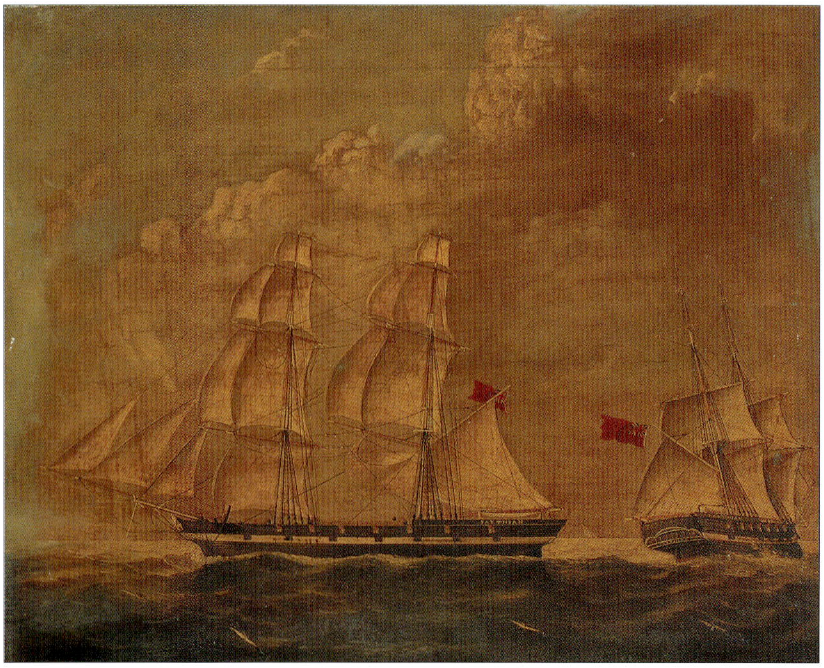

The snow *Parthian* is shown in two views at sea. In the main view she is shown in port profile under full sail with weather stunsails but with her main clewed up. Her name can be seen painted clearly on the stern boards. She flies a red ensign but no identifying flags. The secondary view placed to the right of the canvas shows the vessel departing from the scene in a starboard view with all her sails set. Again her name is visible on the side and on the stern. The combination of views is unusual in that by facing different ways the one position does not lead naturally into the other. Also unusual is the vantage point which allows the masts and rigging to be clearly shown.

Parthian[2] was built in Sunderland in 1846. She spent all her career in Sunderland ownership, initially with C Alcock then from 1859 to 1867 with M. Simpson and finally with Morgan & Company. Her principal trade was to the Mediterranean but she made occasional voyages to North America and her final voyage was to the Baltic.[3] She was abandoned in 1868.

The painting is likely to be the work of an artist working on the East coast but no attribution has been suggested to date.

1 Printed label rear stretcher for W Rosenberg & Co., Picture Framers, 46-48 Lime Street, Liverpool with a hand written note of a date of August 1913
2 Parthia was an ancient kingdom of western Asia.
3 LR 1846-1868/69

32 *Princess Charlotte*

Princess Charlotte is shown in port profile outward bound from Liverpool with the port's waterfront in the background. To her stern an unidentified ship is also outward bound and in the far left-hand foreground a small ferry boat full of passengers crosses the Mersey from the Wirral shore.

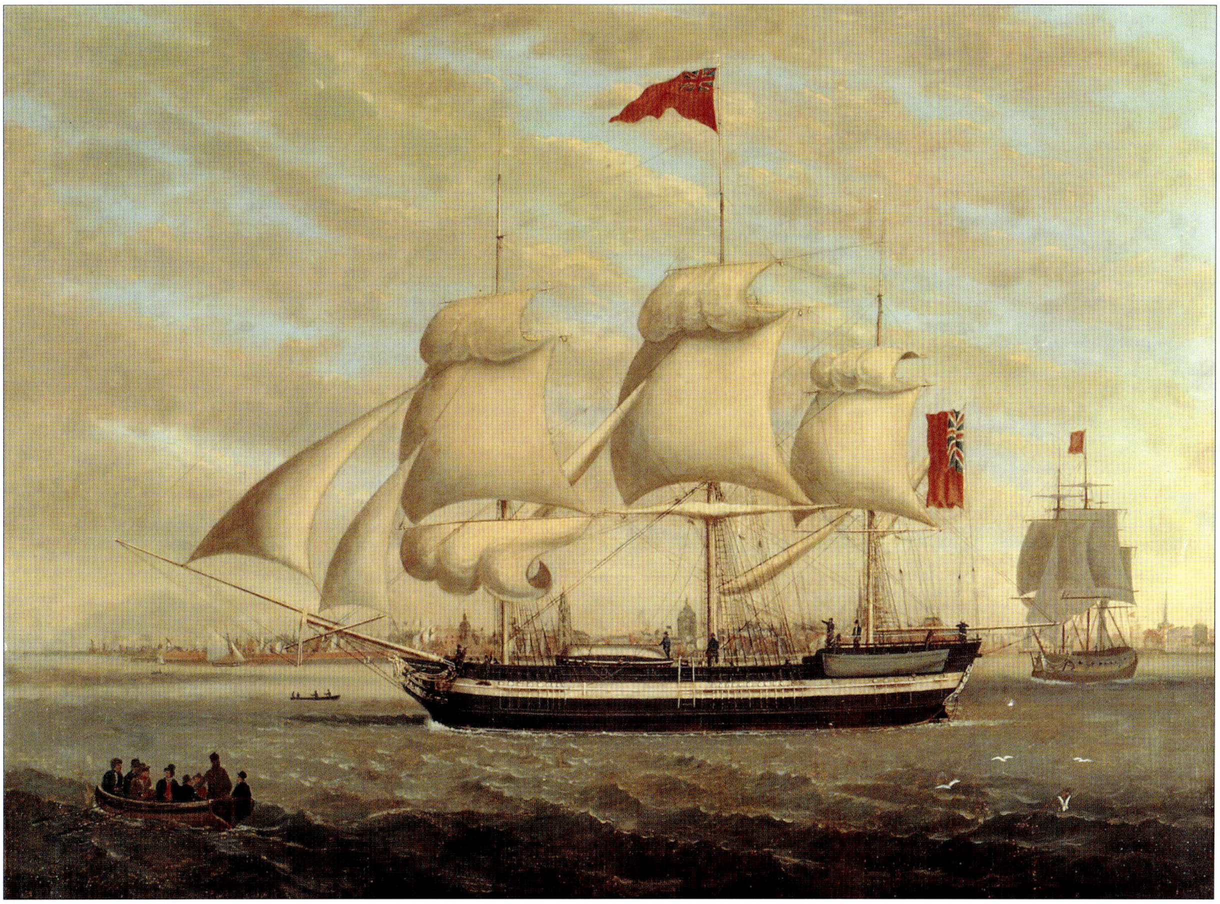

The vessel, named after the Prince Regent's daughter, can be identified from the name on her bow and the artist has depicted a very fine figurehead. She flies the red ensign at the main mast and the after peak. *Princess Charlotte* was built by Brocklebanks, then of Whitehaven, in 1815. At 514 tons she was the largest ship that the company had yet built and was described as "a vessel of uncommon strength and beauty."[1] She was armed with 22 guns. Intended to enter the Far Eastern trade, following the lifting of the East India Company's monopoly in 1813, she spent her career almost exclusively in trade to Bombay and Calcutta. She was sold to Willis & Co. of Scarborough in 1845 and abandoned at sea in 1854.[2]

Princess Charlotte made her maiden voyage to Batavia (present day Djakarta) from Whitehaven in February 1816, returning to Liverpool in March 1818.[3] Thereafter she sailed from Liverpool and she is shown making her way down the estuary under topsails and jibs with topgallants and forecourse in the process of being set. There is a long detailed view of the Liverpool shore in the background. To the extreme left under the bowsprit, Bootle Bay is visible with windmills in the distance, then forward of the foremast is the familiar landmark of St Paul's dome and between the fore and main masts the tower of St Nicholas and the dome of the Town Hall with St George just before the mizzen mast and to the far right the spire of St Thomas, Park Lane. Although traditionally attributed to Henry Collins (1782-1824), this canvas is stylistically different from other surviving works by the artist particularly in the handling of the sea and the general warm atmosphere. There is a more accomplished painting of *Princess Charlotte* which is signed and dated "H. Collins 1816" showing the vessel off Whitehaven, with which this may have been confused.[4] The vessel was also painted in a view off Anglesey by Miles Walters in 1831.[5]

1970.246.5
Oil on canvas
84 cm x 114 cm
Prov. T & J Brocklebank Ltd., Cunard Brocklebank Ltd., Private Collection, on permanent loan
Exh: Liverpool 1986
Ref: Gibson 1953, p.56, ill. opp. p.36; Port Panorama, p.10

Vessel: 119 ft 3 in (l), 31 ft 2 in (b), 18 ft 6 in (d); 514 tons

1 *Cumberland Pacquet*, 12 September 1815, quoted Rees Brocklebanks, p.52.
2 For a history of the vessel see Gibson I, especially pp. 52, 54-59, 212 and Rees Brocklebanks, pp. 52-57.
3 Although Djakarta was in the Dutch East Indies, it which was under British control between 1811 and 1818. *Princess Charlotte* was taken over by the East India Company for troop carrying when she arrived in Batavia. See Rees Brocklebanks, pp. 56-7.
4 Photograph in DCF; in Brocklebank family ownership, 1934, see Rees Brocklebank, file, p6, MAL, B/BROC.
5 See Davidson 1992, p.71 (ill).

33 *Shipping off a port*

1959.72.2
Oil on canvas
43 cm x 53.5 cm
Prov: Dr D Chapman, Liverpool, who presented it, 1959

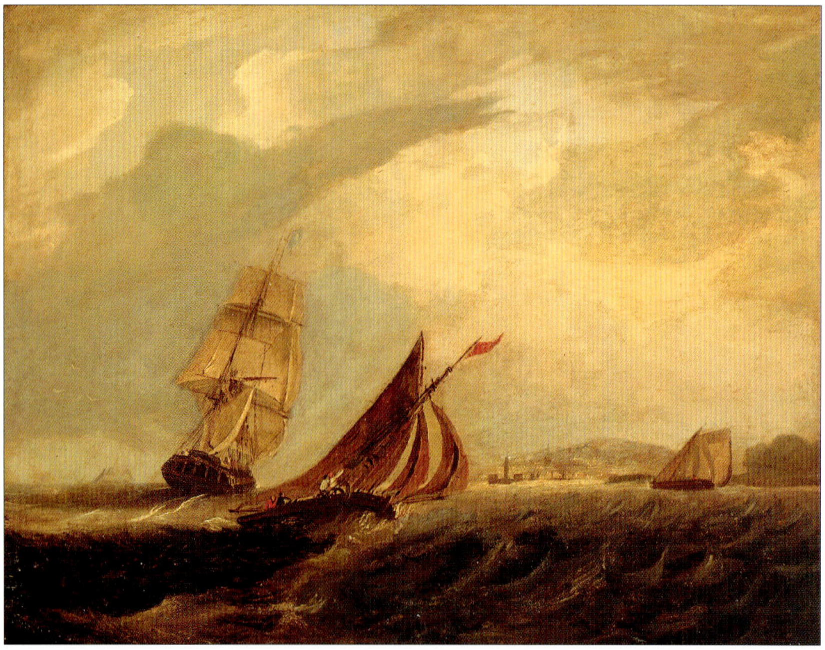

This view shows a group of unidentified vessels off an unknown port, perhaps on the East coast. In the centre a cutter is shown in starboard quarter profile fighting heavy seas and winds with a barque in starboard stern view. Other vessels are in the background.

34 *Shipping off South Shields*

1959.72.3
Oil on canvas[1]
45.5 cm x 61 cm
Prov: Dr D Chapman, Liverpool, who presented it, 1959

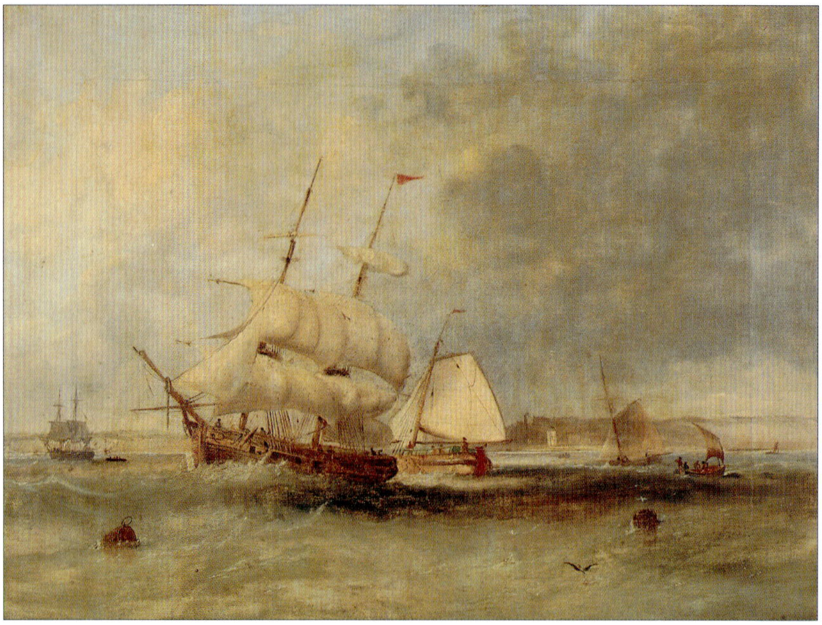

This view shows a variety of East coast shipping off the South Shields lighthouse. The main vessel depicted is a port bow view of a collier brig with full billowing sails which are in the process of being trimmed. A Dutch vessel is astern of this brig and heading for the coast. Her mainsail is triced up to allow a clear view for the helmsman. In the distance to the left is another brig, probably another Dutch coasting vessel and there are other small coasting vessels to the right. This is probably the work of an East coast artist.

1 Remains of label on rear stretcher "…….Shields"

35 *Sir Percy Bates*

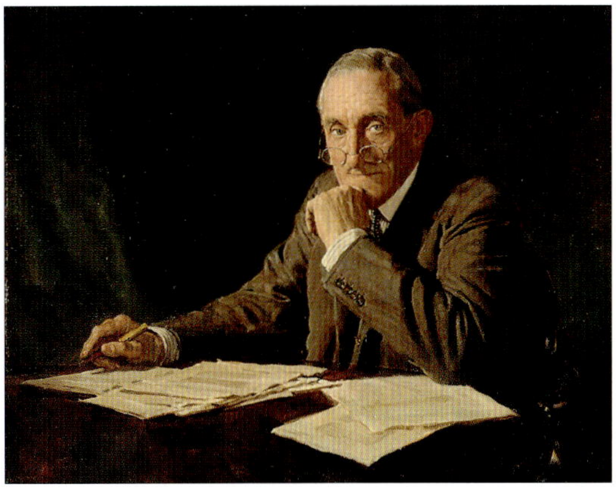

Sir Percy Bates was Chairman of Cunard from 1930 to 1946, a crucial period in the company's history. He is shown here seated at his desk on which various papers are laid out. This portrait was one of two painted from a photograph by the famous Liverpool photographer E Chambre Hardman (1898-1988). This one hung in the main boardroom of Cunard's office in Liverpool and the other one went to the New York office.[3]

Sir Percy Elly Bates was born in 1879 and initially became a partner in Edward Bates & Co., the Liverpool ship owners. He joined Cunard in 1910 and became Deputy Chairman in 1922 succeeding Lord Royden as Chairman in 1930. Bates played an important role in the merger with White Star and the financial problems involving the building of *Queen Elizabeth* and *Queen Mary*. He was a Director of the *Morning Post* 1924-37 and served on the Ministry of War Transport Advisory Council, 1939-45. He succeeded to the baronetcy in 1903, was created GBE in 1920 and died in 1946.[4] There are also portraits by A T Nowell and Sir Gerald Kelly.[5]

1972.148
Oil on canvas[1]
71.5 cm x 92 cm
Signed (br) monogram HG-
Prov: Philip E Bates[2], Hampshire, who presented it, 1987
Exh: National Maritime Museum, Greenwich, 1981-1991

1 Two printed labels on rear for Boydell Galleries, Liverpool; canvas stamped "National Canvas / No 2 / Prepared by Windsor 7 Newton / London, England"
2 Philip Bates is a nephew of Sir Percy and himself was Managing Director and Deputy Chairman of Cunard.
3 Information from Philip E Bates, 30 January 1987 (DCF)
4 *DNB, 1941-1950*, Oxford, 1959
5 ibid.

36 *P S Sirius* (page 44)

Inscribed 'STEAM - VESSEL SIRIUS', Lieutenant RICH[D]. ROBERTS; R.N. off NEW YORK. The first BRITISH Steam-Vessel that ever crossed the Atlantic: performed her Voyage from Cork in 18 days !!'

The commemorative nature of this picture is underlined by the size and comprehensiveness of the inscription, which also succinctly summarises the subject depicted.

The paddle steamer *Sirius* is shown in central port profile under steam and sail arriving off New York. The vessel flies the Stars and Stripes from her foremast and the English national flag with the red cross of St George on the main mast. The figurehead of a dog and 6-pointed star is a reminder of Sirius's more common name, the dog-star. The figures on deck are well-drawn, in particularly the group of passengers at the stern. Two schooners of the New York pilot service are depicted to the left and right of the vessel, flying a blue and white flag and the Stars and Stripes respectively. The Battery at the southern tip of Manhattan can be seen in the distance on the left hand side of the picture.

Sirius was built in 1839 by Robert Menzies and Co. of Leith, with engines by T Wingate & Co. of Whiteinch, Glasgow, for the St George's Steam Packet Company of Cork, for their service to London. She was chartered by the British and American Steam Navigation Company[2] when their own vessel *British Queen* was delayed in completion, at the height of the race to make the first westbound crossing of the Atlantic under steam. She arrived in New York only hours before her rival *Great Western*, having burned her cabin furniture and every available piece of timber to maintain steam. She made one further transatlantic crossing before returning to her intended career. She was fitted with new engines in Hull and transferred to the Cork Steam Ship Company in 1844. She was wrecked near Youghal, just north of Cork, in January 1847.[3]

1 Relined
2 The funnel is here painted in the company's colours, white with black top.
3 Bonsor North, pp. 54-5, 59; R Greenwood and F Hawks *The Saint George Steam Packet Company, 1821-1843*, Kendal, 1995, p.20; D D C Pochin Mould *Captain Roberts of the Sirius*, Cork, 1988.
4 See Maginnis, p. 13 (ill)
5 For the engraving see Kennedy, p.72 and the drawing see E K Chatterton *Steamships and their history*, London, 1910, ill. opp. p.96.
6 Parker and Bowen, 1938, pp. 270-1.

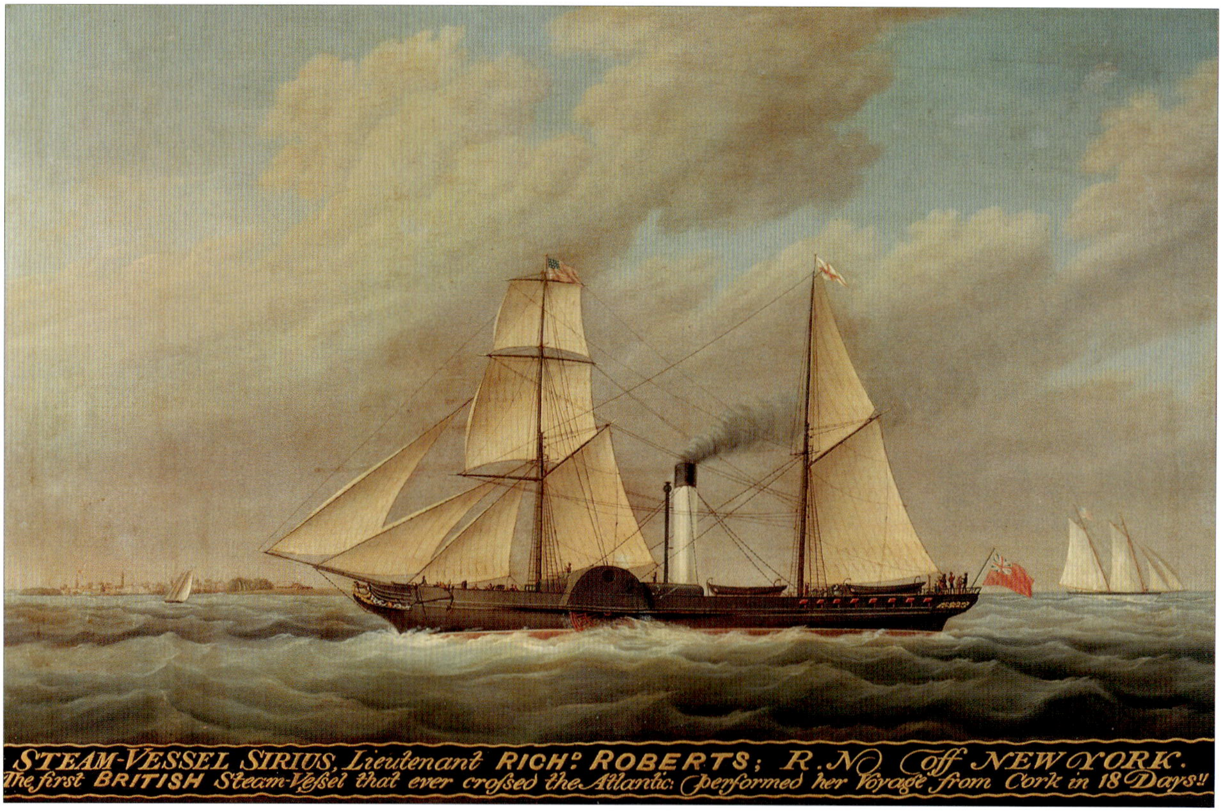

17.6.27.1
oil on canvas[1]
61 cm x 91.5 cm
Provenance: Mrs Stewart, from whom purchased 1927.
Ref: Handbook 1932, pp. 50-1, Finch 1983, p.134 (ill)

Vessel: 178 ft (l), 25 ft 6 in (b), 18 ft 3 in (d); 703 tons.

There is another unattributed painting of *Sirius* arriving in New York in the South Street Seaport Collections, New York. A third unattributed painting of the vessel nearing New York is also known.[4] An engraving shows her on arrival being greeted by a fleet of small boats and there is also a drawing of her at sea.[5] There are engravings of her off Cork by Wadmore and at sea by Atkinson.[6]
There is an exhibition model of the vessel in the collections, accession No. 37.37. The figurehead of the vessel is in Hull Maritime Museum.

37 *S S Sirius*

1958.22
Oil on canvas
59 cm x 94.5 cm
Prov: Mr T Gough, Liverpool, who presented it, 1958

Vessel: 316.2 ft (l), 34 ft (b), 21.7 ft (d); 2169 gross tons

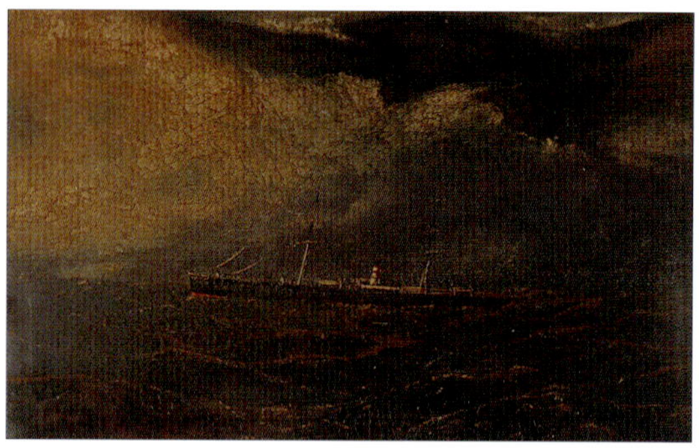

This extremely dark scene shows *S S Sirius* in port profile at sea. She has an auxiliary brig rig but all her sails are stowed. The vessel is identifiable by the name on her bow and by the funnel colours, of black, red and white bands of her owners, the Star Navigation Company.The iron steamship Sirius was built by A Leslie & Co. with a compound engine by R Stephenson in Newcastle upon Tyne in 1869 for the Star Navigation Company of Liverpool. This company had been formed in that same year by Rathbone Brothers, the well established firm with banking, mercantile and shipping interests. The Star Line was intended to run a monthly service to Calcutta and Sirius was one of four ships built between 1869 and 1875 especially for this purpose[1] . She was sold to Lamport & Holt of Liverpool in 1878[2] and was fitted with a new engine by Fawcett, Preston. In 1899 she was sold to Italian owners and broken up.[3]

1 For brief details of Star Line see Nottingham 1992, pp. 67-68.
2 The other Star steamers were sold to T & J Harrison of Liverpool in 1889. ibid.
3 LCR, vol. 90, no. 246, 6 December 1869, vol. 99, no. 43, 4 March 1899. Heaton p.114.

38 *Susannah*

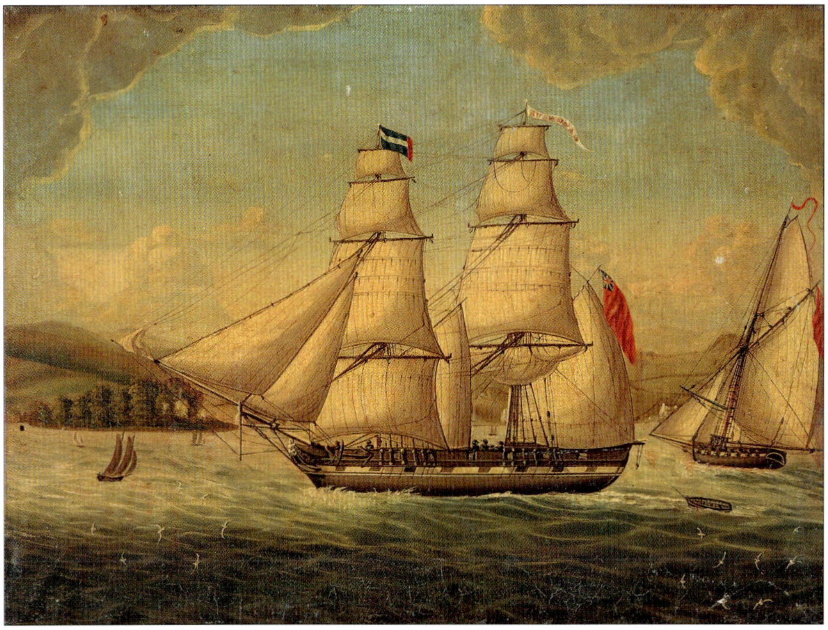

1954.5
Oil on canvas
43.5 cm x 58.5 cm
Prov: A Grierson, Cheadle Hulme, who presented it, 1954.

Although the overall style is rather naive, the vessels in this painting are accurately depicted and provide an accurate record of sail plan and rigging. The brig *Susannah* is shown in port profile off an unidentified coast. The vessel is making good progress under sail with only the main course partly furled. She is towing the ship's boat which is unoccupied. A name pennant flies from the main mast and an unidentified house or signal flag from the foremast. This consists of a white horizontal band between two blue bands, the fly having a red edge. To the right in port quarter view is an armed sloop of 14 guns. Although appearing to fly a red ensign, this may be a revenue boat or possible a mail boat. The hilly coast line, with a wooded headland or island below *Susannah*'s bowsprit, has not been identified.

Without some independent evidence, it is almost impossible to identify the vessel precisely. The name *Susannah* was a popular one in the first half of nineteenth century when this painting was most probably completed[1]. If this is a north-west vessel, the most likely candidate is the 140 tons brig built at Harrington, Cumbria, in 1824 and owned in Whitehaven.[2]

1 There are twelve brigs with the name *Susanna* or *Susannah* listed in LR 1830/1.
2 LR 1830/1, 1840.

39 *Traveller*

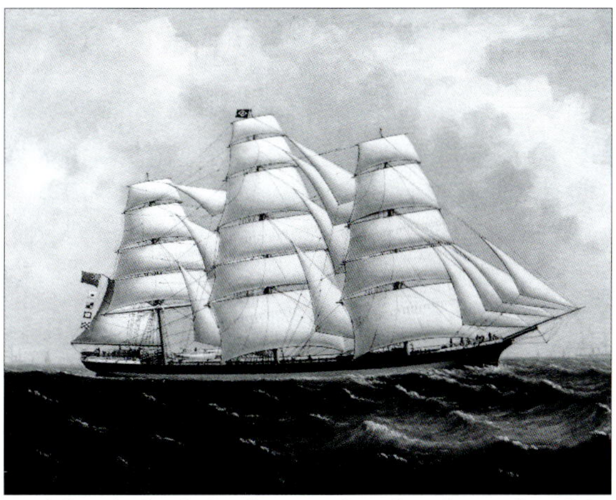

1934.30
Oil on canvas
61 cm x 91.5 cm
Prov: By descent in Haws family, Captain G W Haws, who presented it, 1934
Exh: Crosby 1951, no.97
Ref: Handbook 1935, p.20

Vessel: 228.1 ft (l), 38.1 ft (b), 23.9 ft (d); 1492 gross tons

The 3 masted iron ship *Traveller* is shown at sea in starboard profile under all plain sail. There is a variety of unidentified shipping sketched along the horizon, including coastal and deep sea vessels. Various members of crew are shown on board, including sailors making fast the anchor cable. The vessel flies the red ensign above her commercial code flag hoist (S L W N) at the after peak and the

1 Notes compiled by Captain G Caldecott on Haws, Lawson & Co. in MAL (540.HAW/1/PM). CR, no. 11, 20 February 1879.

house flag of Haws, Lawson & Co. of Liverpool at the main. *Traveller* was built by Birrell, Stenhouse & Co. of Dumbarton in 1879. She was the first iron ship owned by R C Haws who had originally been based in St John, New Brunswick. In February 1897 she was wrecked on the island of Rodriguez in the Indian Ocean with a cargo of sugar from Java to Delaware.[1]

40 *P S Valparaiso*

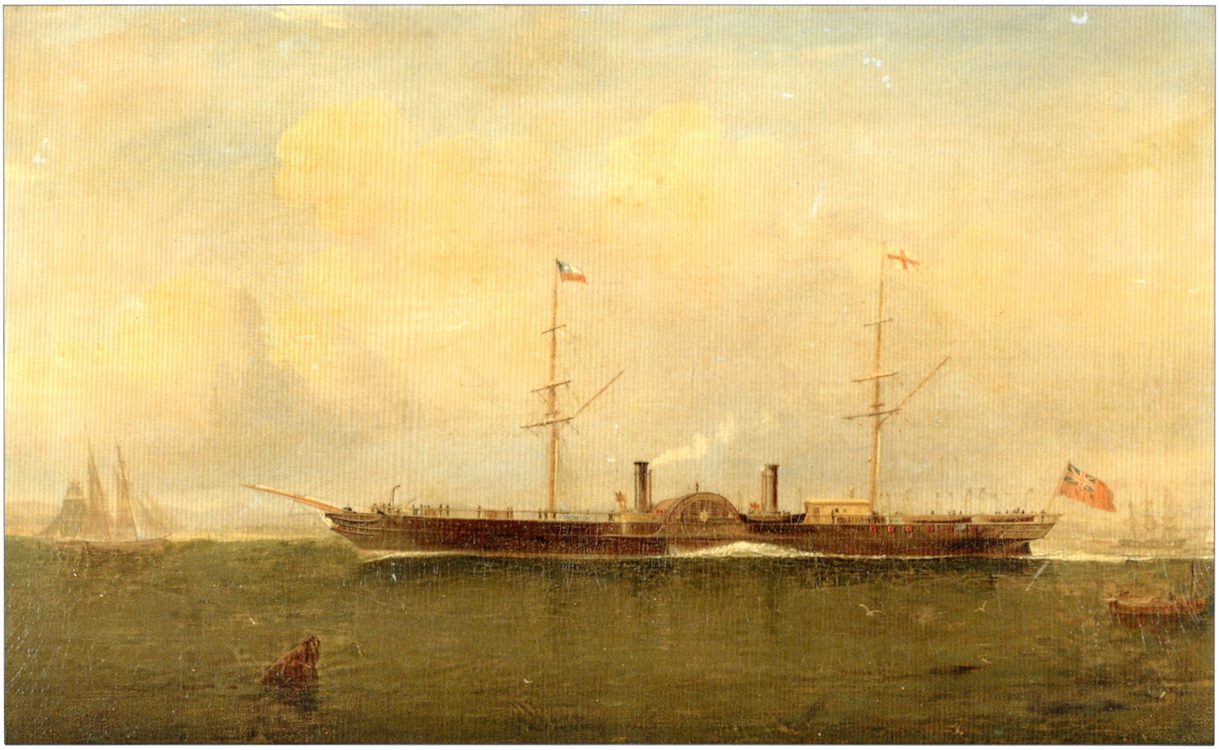

1984.269.6
Oil on canvas
68 cm x 111 cm
Prov: Pacific Steam Navigation Company, on permanent loan.
Ref: A C Wardle *Steam Conquers the Pacific*, London, 1940, p.80 (ill).

Vessel: 234.1 ft (l), 29.1 ft (b), 14.4 ft (d); 1059 gross tons

The iron paddle steamer *Valparaiso* is shown in port profile off an unidentified harbour, probably on the western coast of South America. Although she has an auxiliary brig rig, her sails are stowed. Like other paddle driven vessels of the period, she retains strong affinities with sailing ship design, in particular her lofty rig, figurehead and clipper bow. She flies the Chilean national flag at the foremast, a variation of the PSNC house flag from the main mast and the red ensign at the stern.[1] There is a small single masted boat in the right foreground and there are other vessels in the background towards the coast. There appears to be a long sandy beach in the far left distance and a group of buildings on the shore.

Valparaiso was built by John Reid of Glasgow for the Pacific Steam Navigation Company of Liverpool in 1856. She was the first major vessel to be fitted with compound engines, supplied by Randolph, Elder & Company of Glasgow after the PSNC's directors were convinced of the savings in fuel consumption by John Elder.[2] She served on the company's Valparaiso - Chiloe express steamer service calling at nine Chilean ports until wrecked off Lagartija Island in the straits of Chiloe in 1872.[3] The painting probably dates from early in the vessel's career. There are significant differences between this painting and a photograph of the vessel taken at Puerto Montt in 1870.[4] The paddle box is much smaller in the photograph which may be the result of new wheels being fitted in 1860.[5] The rig had also been simplified to a schooner rig by 1870.

Although no artist has been identified, this painting is almost certainly by the same hand as no. 30, *P S Pacific*.

1 Although of the standard PSNC flag design, this version has a red rather than the usual blue cross and letters in blue not red. The letters are also mis-arranged, reading S P N C. There is no obvious explanation and artist error must be a possibility.
2 She consumed approximately 30% less coal than other ships of her size. See A C Wardle *Steam Conquers the Pacific*, London, 1940, p. 92.
3 PSNC Minute Books, vol. 3, passim and LCR, vol. 81, no. 309, 10 November 1856
4 See drawings in Haws PSNC, p.33 based on this painting and the photograph
5 Minute of 31 July 1860 noted the vessel's improved performance due to new wheels. PSNC Minute Books, vol. 4, p.106 (MAL)

41 *Yola*

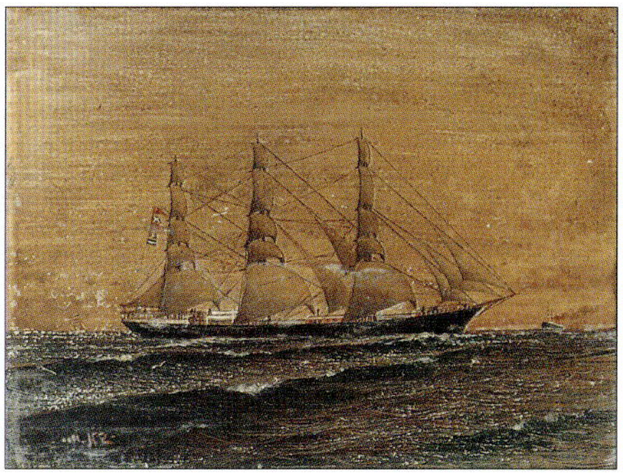

The steel ship rigged *Yola* is shown in a port profile at sea under full sail. She flies her commercial code (M R T J). There is a liner approaching from the starboard side in the far distance. *Yola*[1] was built by J Reid & Company of Whiteinch, Glasgow in 1892 for McDiarmid, Greenshields & Co. of Liverpool. She was sold to Norwegian owners in 1910.[2]

1965.223
Oil on hardboard
24.5 cm x 32 cm
Signed and dated (br) "S.H. 1900"
Prov: Mr M B Glasier, Liverpool, who presented it, 1965.

Vessel: 228 ft (l), 38.5 ft (b), 23 ft (d); 1490 gross tons

1 Yola in a town in Eastern Nigeria.
2 LCR vol. 97, no. 89, 19 August 1892

42 *Zemindar*

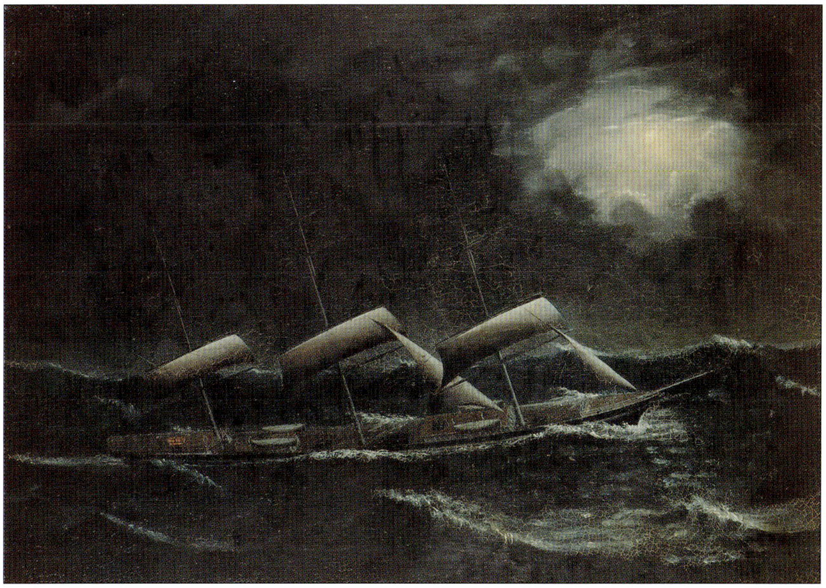

1970.246.10.1
Oil on canvas[1]
66 cm x 88.5 cm
Prov: T & J Brocklebank Ltd; Cunard Brocklebank Ltd; Private Collection on permanent loan.

Vessel: 292.5 ft (l), 39.6 ft (b), 23.4 ft (d); 2053 gross tons.

The ship rigged *Zemindar* is seen from a bird's eye view in starboard profile battling against a storm at night. A shaft of moonlight illuminates this awesome scene from a gap in the clouds. Waves are breaking over the port bulwark and the crew are sheltering below deck. She has been close reefed with just her topsails and two staysails. Although there is no identification of the vessel on the painting, this causes no concern because of the provenance.

Zemindar[2] was the first steel ship owned by Brocklebanks and was built for them by Harland and Wolff in Belfast in 1885. She voyaged mainly to Calcutta with one trip to Rangoon and made her last voyage for the company to Buenos Aires. She was sold in 1900 and renamed *Otto Gildermeister* and had a long career mainly in the Pacific under various different names and owners in the United States and Japan until converted to a barge in Vancouver in 1937.[3]

There is a companion painting of her sister ship *Talookdar* depicted in similar circumstances and almost certainly by the same artist.[4] The collections also contain a half-model of the vessel, accession no. L1970.244.32.

1 Relined
2 A zemindar was an Indian landed proprietor who paid land tax to the government.
3 Gibson I, pp. 156, 286; Beard.
4 Formerly Cunard Brocklebank Ltd, present location unknown, illustrated in Gibson I, opp. pp.148

Arthur James Wetherall Burgess (1879 - 1957)

Burgess was born in New South Wales, Australia and studied art in Sydney before settling in England in 1901. He established his reputation in oils but also worked as an illustrator for the *Graphic* and the *Illustrated London News*. He was a founder member of the Society of Marine Artists and later its vice-president.[1] There are five works by him in the National Maritime Museum.[2]

1 Celebration, p.157-8.
2 Concise NMM.

43 *Cunard "A" Class Liner*

1971.107.2
Oil on canvas
51 cm x 76 cm
Signed (bl) "ARTHUR J BURGESS"
Prov: Cunard Brocklebank Ltd, Private Collection, on permanent loan, 1971

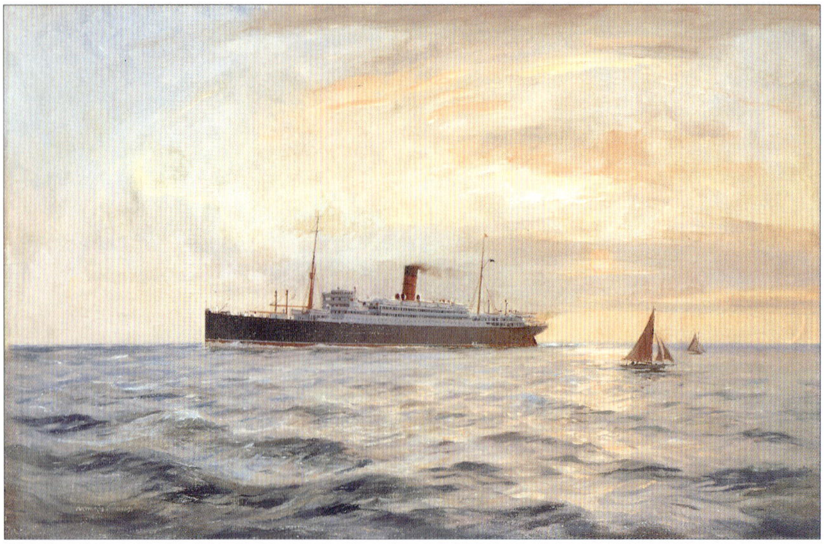

This atmospheric view shows a Cunard "A" Class Liner against a pink sky as the sun is setting. The vessel is shown in port profile in the middle distance probably having just left port. There are two small yachts to the right hand side of the canvas and a hint of land.

The liner is one of three sister ships built in 1922 to operate on the Canadian service: *Andania* built by Hawthorn, Leslie of Hebburn on the Tyne, *Antonia*, built by Vickers Armstrong of Barrow or *Ausonia* built by Armstrong, Whitworth of Newcastle. A further three vessels with slight variation of design were built in 1924/5 also for the Canadian service from Liverpool and Southampton.[1]

1 Bonsor North, pp. 113-4, 164

44 *R M S Oropesa*

1984.269.12
Oil on canvas[1]
56 cm x 92 cm
Signed (bl) "ARTHUR J BURGESS"
Prov: Pacific Steam Navigation Company, on permanent loan.

Vessel: 530 ft (l), 66.2 ft (b), 41.6 ft (d); 14118 gross tons

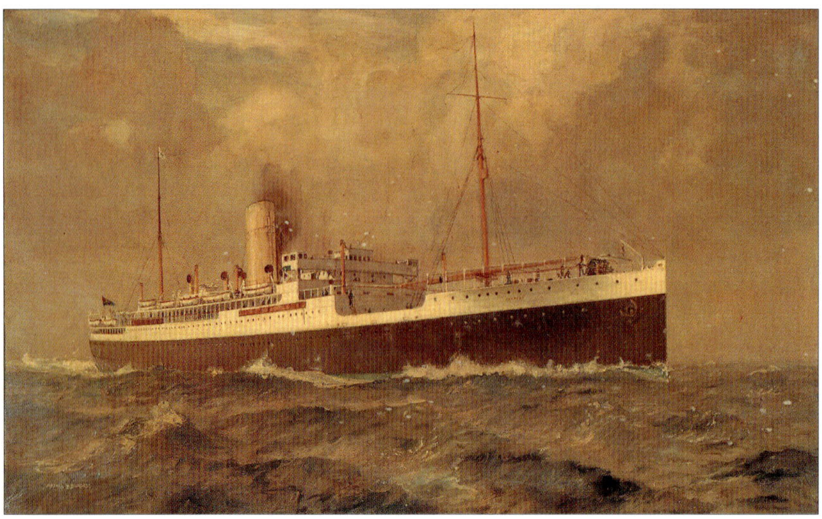

R M S Oropesa is shown in starboard bow profile under full steam at sea. She is identifiable by the name on her hull. She flies the Pacific Steam Navigation Company house flag from the main mast and the blue ensign at the stern. This latter almost certainly indicates that the vessel is shown during her period of war service.[2] *Oropesa* was built by Cammell Laird for PSNC in 1920 and was the first new ship to enter the fleet after the first world war. Named after the town in Central Spain,[3] she made her maiden voyage to Buenos Aires and thereafter sailed between Liverpool and Valparaiso. She was overhauled in 1931 to act as consort to the company's new liner *Reina Del Pacifico* but in fact spent most of the next six years laid up because of the depression. She was taken over for trooping duties in 1939 and was sunk by U-96 off Ireland in 1941 with the loss of 113 lives.[4]

1 Canvas stamped "CHAS. N. WEST / 117 FINCHLEY ROAD". Label on rear "ROBERT BUNTING / FINE ART DEALER / THE REMBRANDT GALLERY / 12 WATER STREET / LIVERPOOL 2"
2 The blue ensign could also be worn by ships commanded by a master who was also in the Royal Navy Volunteer Reserve with a minimum number of crew who were also in the RNVR.
3 From 1879, PSNC's mail passenger ships had names with the prefix "Or". This was only broken with the naming of *Reina Del Pacifico* in 1931.
4 Haws PSNC, p78

L Burke (active 1864)

45 *Boarding A Slaver*

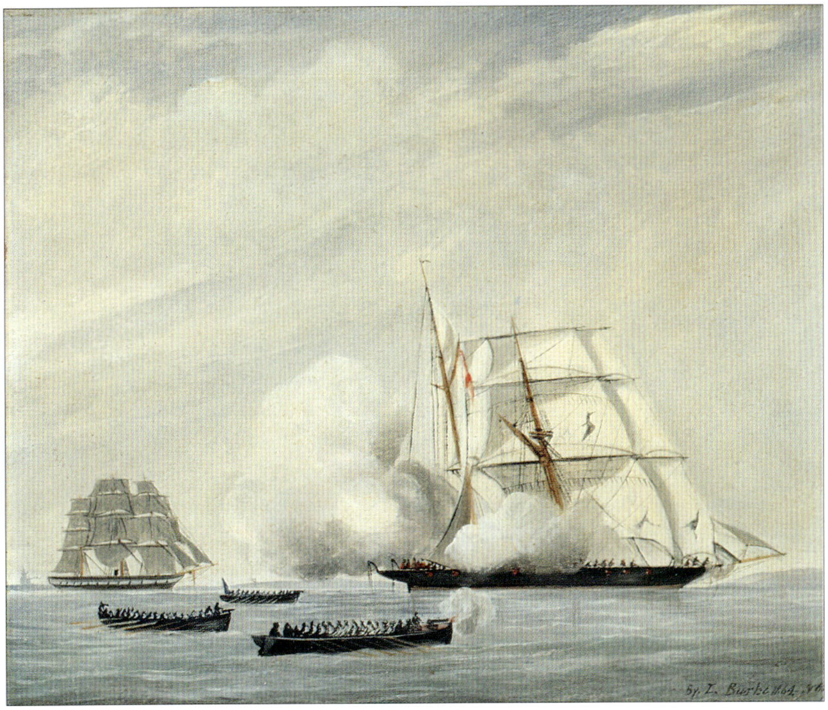

MMM.1995.164
Oil on paper covered fibre board
16 cm x 27.5 cm
Signed and dated (br) "By. L. Burke 1864. N. ???? / 15"
Prov: Auctioned by D M Nesbit & Co, Southsea, 27 June 1995, Lot 203; Michael Graham-Stewart, London; from whom purchased, 1995

Vessel: 185 ft (l), 36 ft (b), 20 ft (d); 722 gross tons

This action filled painting shows boats from *U S S Saratoga* about to board the American clipper *Nightingale* which was correctly suspected of being involved in the illegal slave trade. The slaver is shown in starboard profile with all her sails set. She is resisting the boarding and clouds of smoke from her guns are drifting over her hull and stern. *Saratoga* is also portrayed under full sail in the far distance astern of *Nightingale*. Three boats[1] from the warship carrying the boarding parties are approaching the slaver in the foreground and the nearest one is returning fire.
The artist is not a recognised marine artist and his depiction of the vessels is questionable. The position of the sails on *Nightingale* do not relate to a realistic situation and there seems an excessive number of gunports for a vessel of her size and type.
A handwritten note by the artist, attached to the back of the painting, records his comments:

"Boarding A Slaver
A Right of Search Treaty with America has been Concluded and American Cruizers may now render good service in the Capture of Slavers - President Lincoln has by this Treaty done more towards the Suppression of the horrid slave traffic than all his Predecessors. The Capture of the Nightingale With several hundred Slaves on board has Brought to light the Astonishing fact that the American Vessel actually fitted out as a Slaver in Liverpool. We hope that all the Guilty parties will speedily be visited With their Just Deserts.

Cruizer boats about to Board A Slaver

By L. Burke 1864"

Nightingale had left New York in September 1860 with a cargo of grain bound for London under the command of her owner, Captain Francis Bowen.[2] In fact she arrived in Liverpool on 6 October. She was resupplied by Holzberg & Bowen (the latter was Thomas, brother of Francis) and sailed for St Thomas on 24 November with a cargo of cotton goods, rice, beans, earthenware, muskets and gunpowder. She was in St Thomas in January 1861 but was sighted off the West African coast by *Saratoga* on 17 April behaving suspiciously. On 20 April she was caught off Kabanda, Angola, boarding enslaved Africans. It is this scene that the painting depicts.

The seized vessel was taken to Liberia to discharge the enslaved Africans but fever broke out and 160 of the 961 captives had died by the time *Nightingale* reached Monrovia on 13 May. She arrived in New York on 13 June. Although a case was brought to court, Bowen had escaped from custody on the night of the capture and continued to evade punishment.

The case caused a great deal of comment and the Liverpool connection came under close scrutiny. It was apparently common knowledge in Liverpool that the vessel was destined for slaving and questions were raised about why the authorities took no action. Bowen had previously been involving in slaving on his former ship *Sultana* and was referred to by one who knew him as "The Prince of Slavers."

Nightingale was an unusual vessel with an interesting history. She had been built by Samuel Hanscomb junior at Eliot, Maine as a "yacht-like clipper" in 1851. The original intention had been to sail her to London with a group of exclusive passengers to visit the Great Exhibition and to anchor her in the Thames as a floating hotel. The promoters were short of money and she was sold and began a commercial career trading between the east coast of the United States, London, the Far East and Australia. After her slaving involvement she was used by the Federal Government but resumed a commercial career in 1865. After a brief period exploring for cable laying she returned to the Pacific and Eastern trades. She was transferred to Norwegian ownership in 1878, reduced to barque rig in 1885 and was finally abandoned at sea in April 1893 on a voyage from Liverpool to Halifax.

There are engravings of *Nightingale* at anchor and getting under weigh off the New York Battery by Currier (published 1854), after paintings by J E Buttersworth; a view at anchor by a Chinese artist (Marine Historical Society, Mystic) and a painting with barque rig.[3]

1 According to a letter of the Captain of the *Saratoga* "At 10 P.M. we anchored and sent two boats under Lieutenant Guthrie to surprise her...." Quoted in Fairburn, V, p.3091
2 I am grateful to Marika Sherwood for sharing the fruits of her research on the *Nightingale*. Her as yet unpublished article "Who killed Cock Robin?" tells the full story and examines the wider political and moral implications of illegal slaving. The basic story is told in Fairburn, V, pp. 3088-3092 and the vessel's earlier career is covered in ibid., IV, pp. 2340-2343.
3 DCF. Copies of engravings in Peabody Essex Museum, Salem.

John Callow (1822-1878)

John Callow was the younger brother of William Callow (1812-1908) the watercolourist, with whom he studied in Paris and London. His oil paintings are mainly coastal shipping scenes and he also worked extensively in watercolour. He lived in London and also taught drawing.[1]

1 Archibald, p.78.

46 *Blowing Hard: Billy Boys off Bridlington*[1]

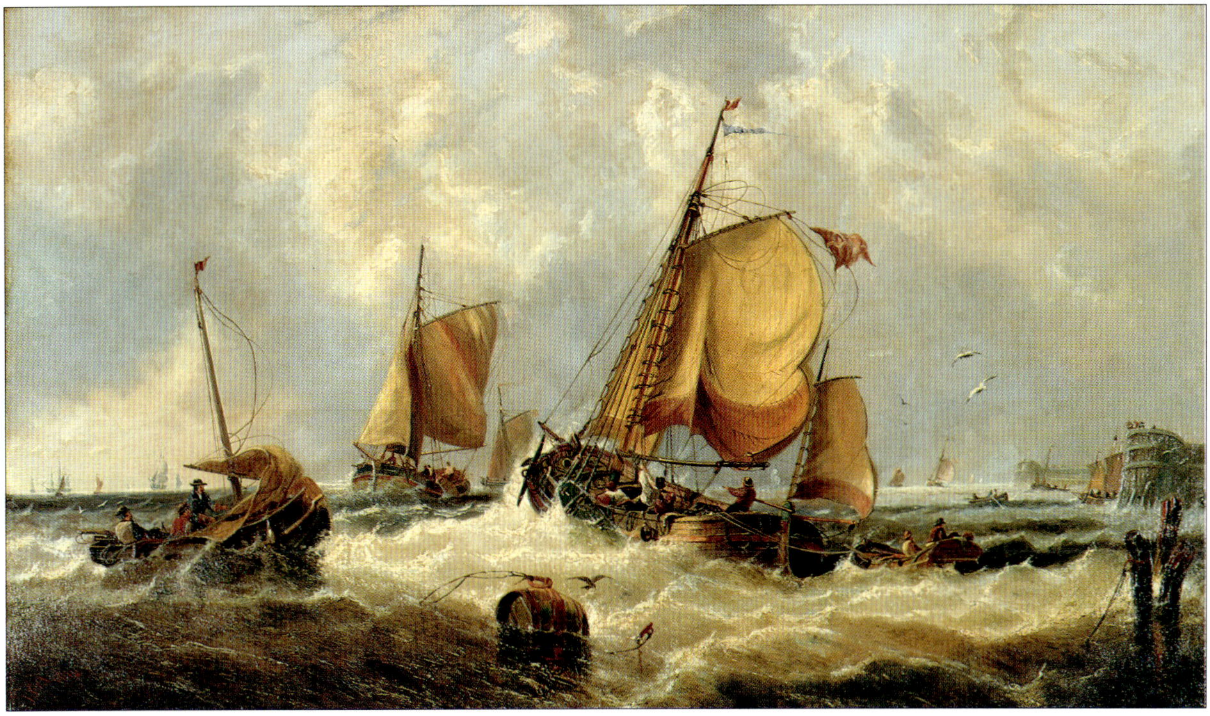

This lively scene by Callow shows a group of coastal trading vessels, known as Billy Boys, off Bridlington. The various boats are shown getting under way as they battle to raise their sails in the face of a strong wind and choppy conditions. On the vessel in the centre of canvas one man is straining to raise the main sail, whilst his companion struggles at the tiller. They are towing a small boat which is being buffetted by the waves. The piers of the entrance to Bridlington harbour are shown on the far right with further vessels emerging to sea and on the horizon on the far left there are a couple of deep sea sailing ships.

Billy Boys were clinker built flat bottomed vessels with a rounded bow. They were generally built on the river Aire and though used for general trading in the Humber and along the coast and rivers of Yorkshire, they commonly sailed to other East coast ports, the Thames and even as far as Plymouth. They remained in use until the early decades of the twentieth century. Originally they were single masted vessels with a trysail, but later they adopted a ketch rig and some of the larger ones had square topsails and topgallants.[2] Callow shows a number of vessels with different rigs including the small single masted boat in the left foreground.

The painting probably dates from the late 1860s or early 1870s.

1957.146.2
Oil on canvas
61 cm x 105.5 cm
Signed (bl) "J Callow"
Prov: C J W Crichton, Liverpool, who presented it, 1957

1 Title as given in pencil note on reverse of canvas.
2 See Roger Finch *Sailing Craft of the British Isles*, 1976, pp. 78-9

Frederick Calvert (active 1815-1844)

Born in Cork, Calvert moved to London in 1827. His marine paintings are generally coastal shipping scenes in the Dutch tradition. He was also produced topographical work and was a watercolourist and engraver.[1]

1 Archibald, p.79; Brook-Hart, pp. 36-7.

47 *View of Liverpool about 1830*

1957.80.1
Oil on canvas
25.5 cm x 35.5 cm
Signed (bl) "F. Calvert"
Prov: Miss M Baxendale, Liverpool, from whom purchased, 1957

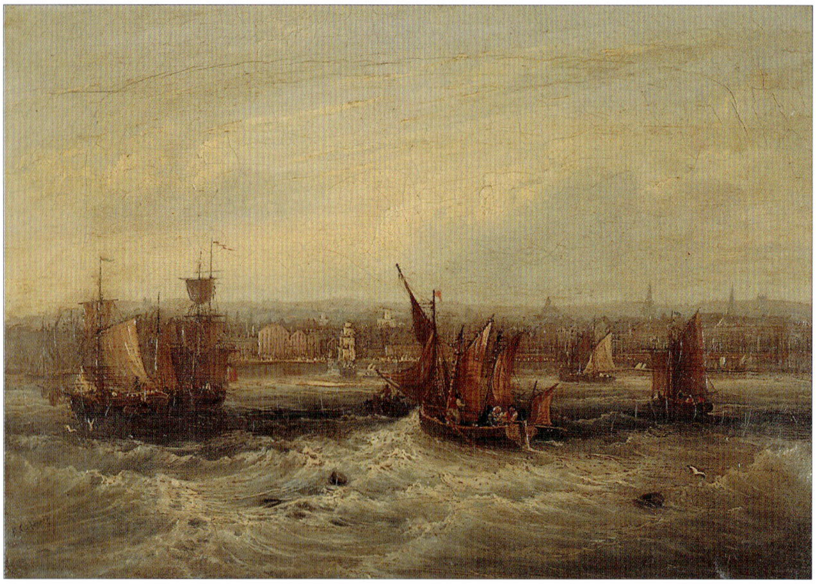

This is a pair with no. 48. They are typical Calvert canvases showing a variety of shipping in demanding conditions off a coastline. The identity of the vessels is immaterial and Calvert seeks to present a pleasing and lively picture with the small craft and their crew overcoming the forces of nature.

Here several groups of vessels are shown off the northern end of the Liverpool waterfront. The left hand group shows a brig with some coastal sloops and cutters, whilst in the centre is a two masted ferry boat. There are some Mersey flats in the right middle ground. In the far distance between the two groups a square rigged vessel is emerging from Prince's Dock Basin. To the left of this entrance are the early warehouses of Waterloo Dock and to the right the long wall of Prince's Dock itself. This may be exaggerated by the perspective. The spire and church of St George, Everton can be seen on the hillside and to the right are the dome of St Paul's church and the spires of St Nicholas' and St George's churches.

There is a similar painting by the artist in the Walker Art Gallery dated 1830. Although the vessels depicted are quite different, the background view of the town is virtually identical to the present painting. There are two further views of shipping in the Mersey in Wallasey Public Library and there is a view of Birkenhead in the Williamson Art Gallery, Birkenhead.[1]

1 WAG 1493 Shipping in the Mersey, signed and dated F Calvert 1830. See Bennett p.67

48 *View of Liverpool about 1830* (top illustration, page 53)

In this second canvas of the pair, the view is off Bootle Bay and the vessels include a brig in the left distance and a sloop and small ferry boat to the right. The sloop has temporarily scandalised the mainsail (that is dropped the peak) to pursue a squall. The main features of the background are the Bootle shore marks, two 100 foot brick columns erected in September 1829 below the high water mark. They were "intended to aid the navigation of vessels through the Rock channel" which lay opposite.[1] The rest of the shore was undeveloped at this period.

1 GGA, 3 September 1829.

George F Campbell (active 1960s)

George Campbell was a naval architect, historian and artist. He was born near Liverpool but lived in New York from the mid-1960s until about 1980, when he

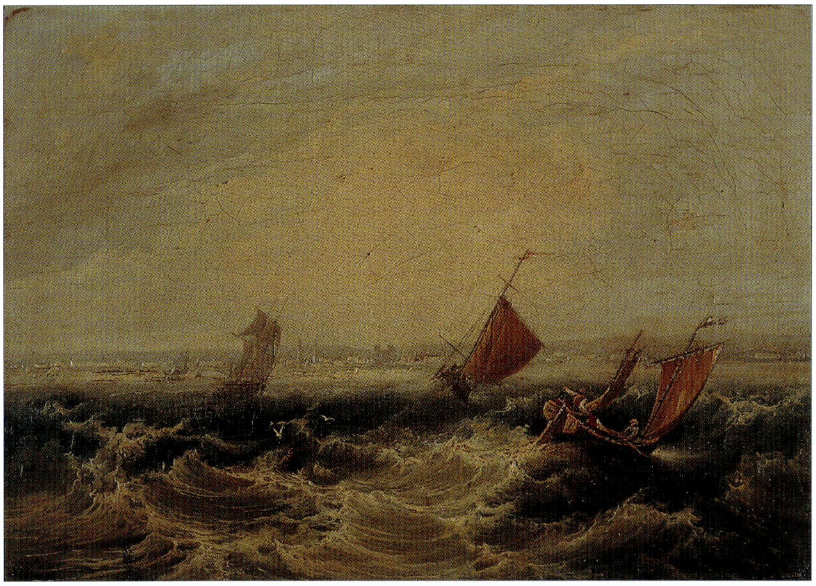

1957.80.2
Oil on canvas
25.5 cm x 35.5 cm
Signed (bl) "F. Calvert"
Prov: Miss M Baxendale, Liverpool, from whom purchased, 1957

moved to Brighton. He was involved in historic ship restoration as architect for *Cutty Sark* in Greenwich and for *Wavertree* at South Street Seaport Museum, New York.

49 *James Monroe in the Mersey*

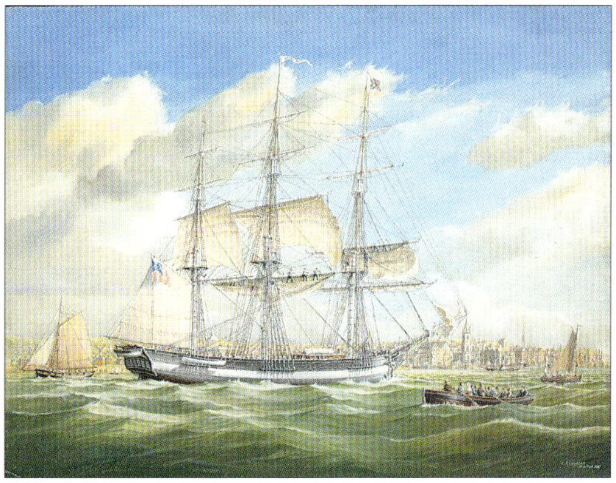

This retrospective painting is almost certainly based on an existing painting or engraving. It shows the American ship rigged *James Monroe* in starboard profile arriving off the Liverpool waterfront.

James Monroe was built by A Brown of New York in 1817 for the Black Ball Line. Named after the 5th President of the United States, she was one of four ships which established a regular packet service between New York and Liverpool. She served in this capacity until 1823 and was then a Cuban trader and a whaler for seventeen years.[1]

1967.349
Oil on canvas covered board
45.5 cm x 60.5 cm
Signed and dated "G. F. Campbell / New York 1967"
Prov: Presented by the artist, 1967.

Vessel: 118 ft (l), 28.3 ft (b), 14.1 ft (d); 424 gross tons

1 Fairburn, II, p. 1297, III p. 1626

50 *Wanderer*

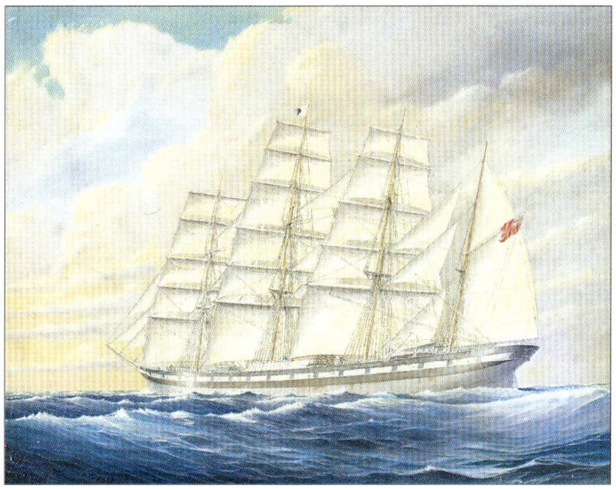

The 4 masted steel barque *Wanderer* is shown in a retrospective painting under full sail in port quarter profile at sea. The view provides a very full and accurate depiction of the sail plan and rigging, including well-placed shading.

Wanderer was built by W H Potter of Liverpool in 1891 and was operated by them as

1968.123
Oil on masonite panel
61 cm x 77 cm
Signed and dated (br) "G. F. Campbell / 66 / N.Y."
Prov: presented by the artist, 1968

Vessel: 309 ft (l), 46 ft (b), 25.8 ft (d); 2903 gross tons.

1 Lubbock, Windjammers, II, pp. 199-202; quotation p.199. A first-hand account of her maiden voyage by Harry Watson, one of her crew, is in *Sea Breezes*, vol. 29, 1960, pp. 238-244
2 John Masefield *The Wanderer of Liverpool*, New York, 1930; also contains a number of photographs of the vessel.

the Wanderer Sailing Company Ltd.. She had an unlucky career and Lubbock describes her as behaving "like a siren luring man after man to his doom". She was lost after being hit whilst lying at anchor in 1907.[1] She was the subject of John Masefield's book and poem *Wanderer*.[2]
There is an exhibition model of the vessel in the collections, L60.25.

John Wilson Carmichael (1799-1868)

1 See Diane Villar *John Wilson Carmichael, 1799-1868*, Portsmouth, 1995. A view of the Perch Rock Fort and Lighthouse by Carmichael was owned by Sir Ernest Royden and exhibited Liverpool 1957.

Carmichael was born in Newcastle and was trained as a ship's carpenter. He set up as an artist in about 1825, moved to London in 1846 and spent his final years from 1863 in Scarborough. He favoured general maritime and shipping views, including naval encounters rather than ship portraits.[1]

51 *Shipping off George's Baths, Liverpool*

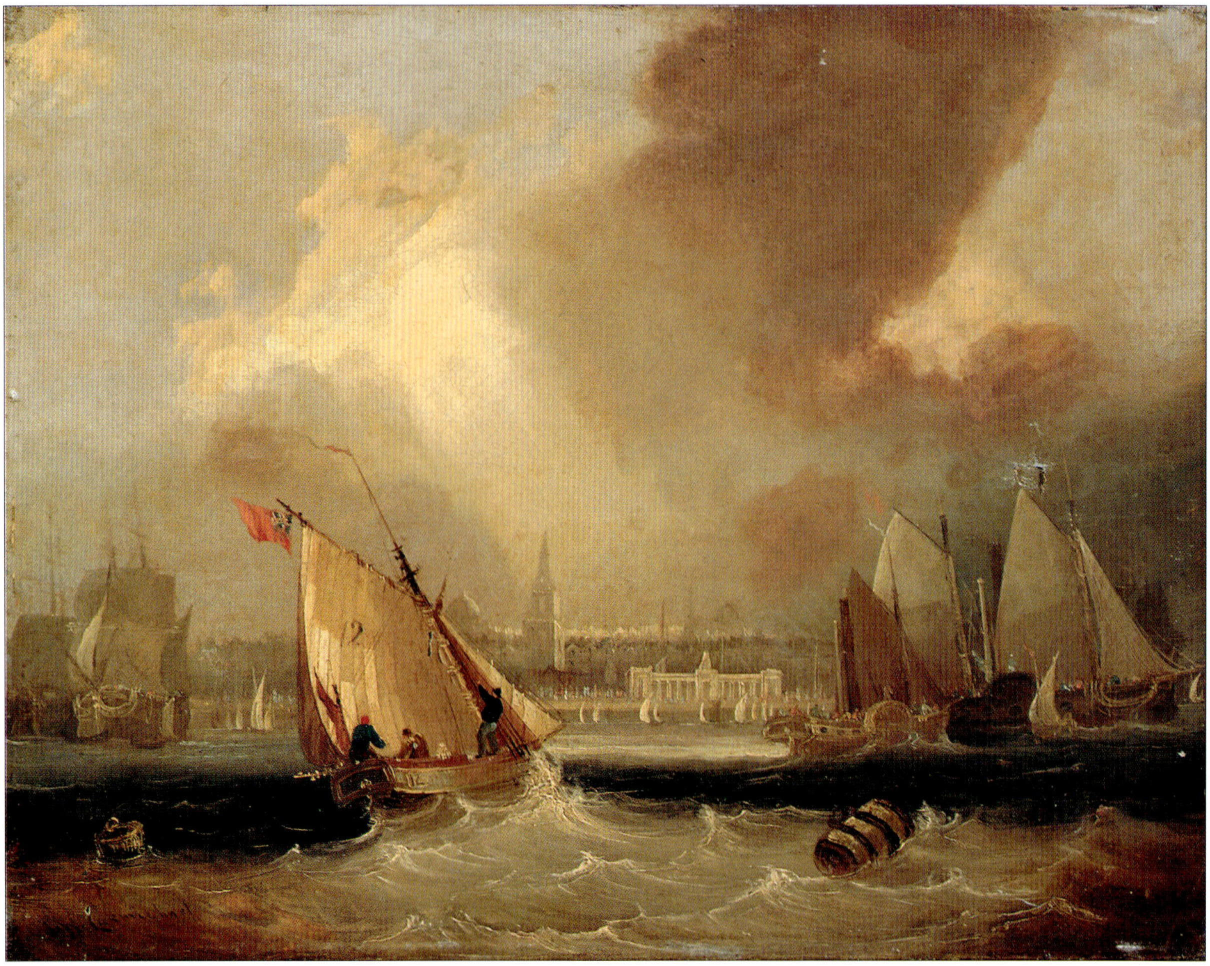

7.4.22.2
Oil on canvas[1]
30.5 cm x 40.5 cm
Signed (bl) 'J W Carmichael'
Prov: In collection, 1922.

This small oil sketch shows a variety of shipping off the main Liverpool waterfront in the second quarter of the nineteenth century. To the left of centre is a rather inaccurate depiction of the No.12 pilot cutter, (with its number on the hull and main sail), towing a small punt and heading for shore. In the middle distance to the left is a group of sailing vessels and to the right a further group of sailing vessels and a paddle steam-driven ferry. Typical additional details are the barrel and fishing pot in the sea in the foreground.

In the far distance is the waterfront with the George's Baths (completed 1829) in the centre and a mass of sailing ship masts in George's Dock in front of the tower of St Nicholas and the dome of the St Paul's to the left.
The No.12 Pilot Cutter *Perseverance* was built by Thomas Royden of Liverpool in 1842 and remained in service until 1860, when replaced by a schooner.[2]

1 There is a printed biographical label on the rear of the stretcher.
2 Rees, p. 202

Leo Cauyrigham (active about 1940)

52 *S. S. Ascanius*

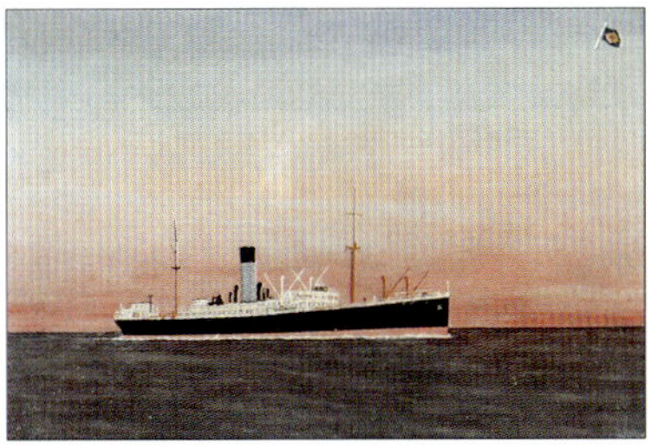

Ascanius is shown in a starboard quarter view against a nearly black sea and a pink sky in a style very reminiscent of the Chinese School. A Blue Funnel Line flag is included in the top right hand corner of the canvas.
Ascanius was built by Workman Clark of Belfast in 1910 as one of three sister ships operating to Australia for the Ocean Steam Ship Company. They could each carry 288 first class passengers but had significant cargo capacity, one sixth of which was refrigerated holds. After war service as a troopship for the Australian Expeditionary Force she was refitted in 1922. She again served as a troopship in World War II but was torpedoed in July 1944 and limped into Liverpool. After being repaired at Cammell Laird she was sold to Genoese owners in 1949 and broken up in 1952.[1] As the inscription infers, the painting was completed for W Eccles, a member of the ship's crew from 1926 to 1949.

1980.494
Oil on board
37.5 cm x 54.5 cm
Inscribed rear (br) "Ascanius Belfast 1910 / W.E. Joined Lpool 3.12.1926 / W. E. Paid off do. 24.6.1949 / Drawing by Leo. Cauyrigham / Ships Carpenter / 5.12.48 / W Eccles"
Prov: Mr L Prince, Liverpool, who presented it, 1980.

Vessel: 493 ft (l), 60 ft (b), 29 ft (d); 10048 gross tons

1 Falkus, p. 48; Haws Blue Funnel, pp. 79-80.

Chinese School

During the period from about 1850 until 1910, a number of Chinese artists working in the main ports of India and the Far East established a profitable line in producing ship portraits for Europeans. Although the following paintings exhibit the characteristics of this group, it has not been possible to attribute any of them to known artists. See also entries for Kwong Sang, Lai Fong, Lai Sung and Namcheong.

53 *Anjer Head*

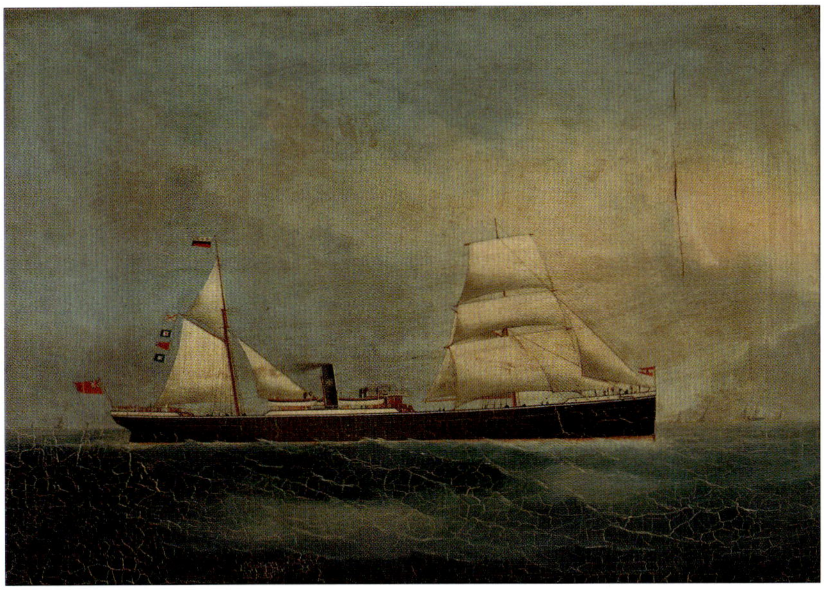

1954.72.2
Oil on canvas
66 cm x 90.5 cm
Prov: Mr E Stewart, Bebington, who presented it, 1954.

Vessel: 274.5 ft (l), 36 ft (b), 24.4 ft (d); 2015 gross tons

Anjer Head was a brigantine rigged iron steamer and is shown here in starboard profile at sea under full sail and steam. The vessel is identifiable from her flag hoist (V W B P) and the name on her hull. The Angier Bros house flag flies at the main mast and the flag on the bow jack staff is unidentified[1]. The funnel is painted in house colours and she flies the red ensign at the stern. Other shipping is sketchily shown in the background.

Anjer Head was built by R Dixon & Company of Middlesborough in 1881 for Angier Bros of London. She was the largest of their four ships at the time of building and was used in trade to the East, particularly Hong Kong. She disappears from Lloyds Register after 1895/96.[2]

1 Red ground with white central horizontal band with central emblem of blue encircling red cross on white ground.
2 LR 1882-1895/6

54 *Cyclops*

1988.122
Oil on canvas
45 cm x 59.5 cm
Prov: N R Omell Gallery; purchased 1988, with assistance from the P H Holt Trust and George Palmer Holt Esq..

Vessel: 485 ft (l), 58.3 ft (b), 31 ft (d); 8998 gross tons

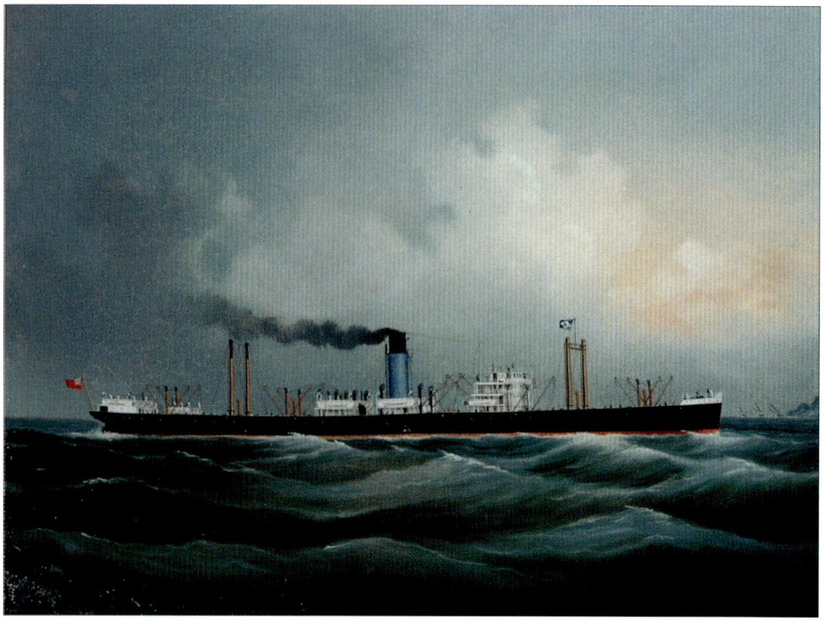

The Blue Funnel Line's *Cyclops*, with her famous 'goal post' masts, is shown in starboard profile approaching Hong Kong harbour. The mountainous coastline appears on the far right hand edge of the canvas where a group of three rigged vessels can be seen. The line's house flag, with its linked initials of Alfred Holt the founder, is flying from the bow pair of masts. The red ensign is on the stern jack.

Cyclops was one of five sister ships built in 1906. They were the largest Holt vessels to date and had a new form of deck construction to provide the minimum of obstruction and the maximum capacity in the hold. The so-called goal post masts were to allow the derricks to work at maximum outreach over the side. *Cyclops* was the second Holt vessel named after the one-eyed giant of Greek mythology. She was built by D W Henderson & Co. of Glasgow, who also provided the twin triple expansion engines. She was torpedoed off the New England coast by a German U-boat in 1942 with the loss of 87 lives.[1]

The unknown artist uses a very blue palette in both sea and sky, except for the red burst amongst the clouds over the coast. A painting of one of the sister ships, *Titan*, by the same artist is in private hands.[2]

There is a mirror-backed half-model in the collections, accession no. 1968.268.

1 For details on the construction see Hyde 1956, pp. 134-5, 179
2 Correspondence (1991) in DCF

55 *Dardanus*

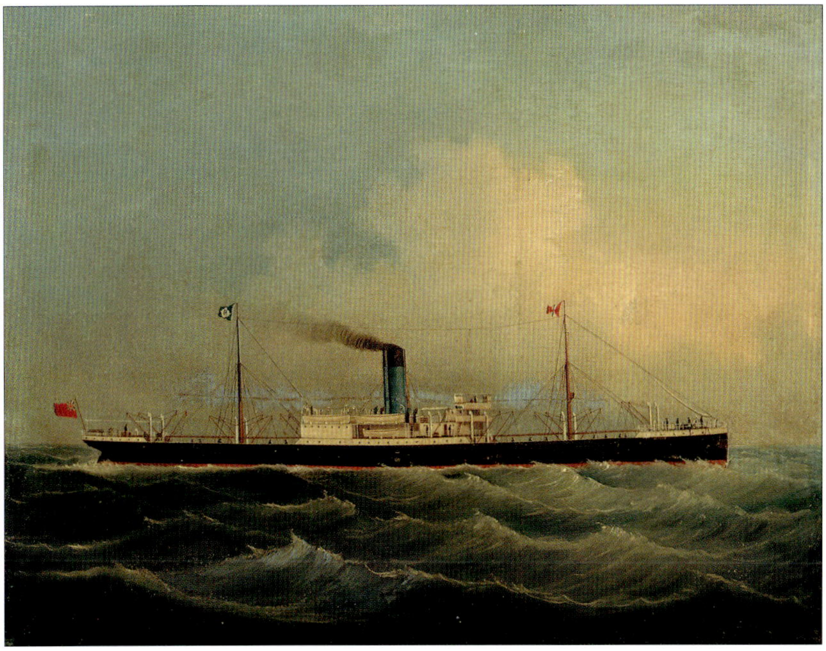

1955.245
Oil on canvas[1]
44 cm x 58.5 cm
Prov: Unknown, in collections, 1955.

Vessel: 392 ft (l), 47.1 ft (b), 26 ft (d); 4653 gross tons

This is one of a number of surviving examples of portraits of Blue Funnel ships painted by Chinese artists in the late nineteenth and early twentieth centuries. Here *Dardanus* is shown in starboard profile steaming through a lively but formalised sea. She is identifiable by her name on the starboard bow and she flies the Blue Funnel flag of Alfred Holt's entwined initials. At her foremast she also flies the flag of the China Navigation Company which was closely allied with Holts and indicating a joint service.[2] The red ensign is at the stern. A number of the crew can be seen standing on various parts of the deck - indeed, they seem to have their hands in their pockets!
Dardanus was one of six sister ships built by Workman Clark for Blue Funnel in 1894 and 1895 with powerful new cargo handling gear.[3] This can be clearly seen in the painting over the fore and aft holds. They were the first ships designed by Henry Bell Wortley[4] (with Alfred Holt's involvement) and gave Holts the ability to respond to the boom in international trade which took place from around 1896. *Dardanus* was the second vessel named after the mythical founder of Troy. She was launched in 1894 and was transferred to the Dutch subsidiary NSMO in 1911. She was sold and renamed in 1923 and broken up in 1927.[5]
The painting presumably dates to the period 1902-11, after the acquisition of China Mutual but before the transfer to NSMO.

1 Relined.
2 China Navigation had been founded by John Swire in Shanghai in 1872. The Holts had been original shareholders and Alfred advised on ship design. See Falkus 1990, pp. 63 - 70.
3 See Falkus. The other ships were *Orestes, Sarpedon, Diomed, Menelaus* and *Hector*.
4Henry Bell Wortley (1868-1919).Wortley was to make a significant contribution to the firm as Naval Architect until his early death. See Falkus 1990, pp. 151-3.
5 Haws Blue Funnel, pp. 59-60; Falkus 1990, pp. 151-3.

56 *Elizabeth Nicholson* (page 58)

Although the vessel depicted carries no means of identification, apart from the red ensign at the peak, this painting entered the collection as *Elizabeth Nicholson*. This ship rigged vessel is shown from the leeward side in starboard profile under full sail. An anchored Chinese junk is visible under the bowsprit. The artist depicts Cunningham's roller-reefing gear, patented in 1851, on all the topsails and on the main topgallant. This allowed them to be rolled from the deck.
Elizabeth Nicholson was built in 1863 by B E Nicholson of Annan, Dumfriesshire, for their own use in the tea trade. She was built of wood with Muntz metal sheathing and had two steel masts. She made one of the fastest runs from China in 1867-68 when she reached London from Foochow in 92 days. Sold to Montgomerie Workman

5.10.15.4
Oil on canvas
44 cm x 59 cm
Prov: William Honour, who presented it, 1915.
Ref: Finch 1975, p.97 (ill); MacGregor 1983, pp.143-5(ill).

Vessel: 192.5 ft (l), 32.5 ft (b), 22.2 ft (d); 904 gross tons

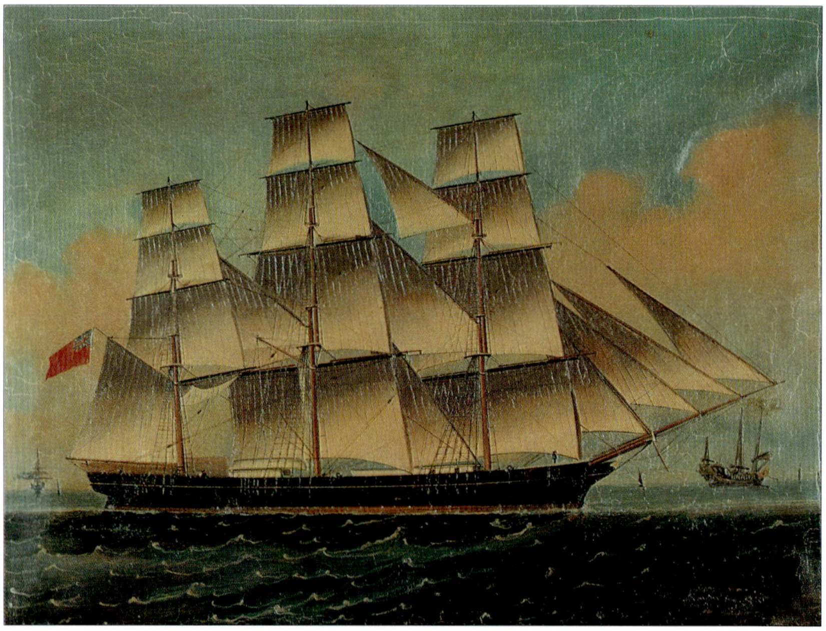

of London in 1888, she then spent time in Chile under the name *Elisa* from 1892 until 1901. She returned to her original name and British ownership in 1901 when she was acquired by S C Farnham of Shanghai. Her final days were spent as a hulk at Shanghai.[1]

1 MacGregor 1983, pp. 143-5; F Tweedie 'The Era of Shipbuilding at Annan' in *Mariner's Mirror*, 37, 1951, pp. 128-142.

57 *Empress of China*

1961.130.20
Oil on canvas
45 cm x 59.5 cm
Prov: J A Howard Watson, Liverpool, who presented it, 1961.

Vessel: 455.6 ft (l), 51.2 ft (b), 33.1 ft (d); 5905 gross tons

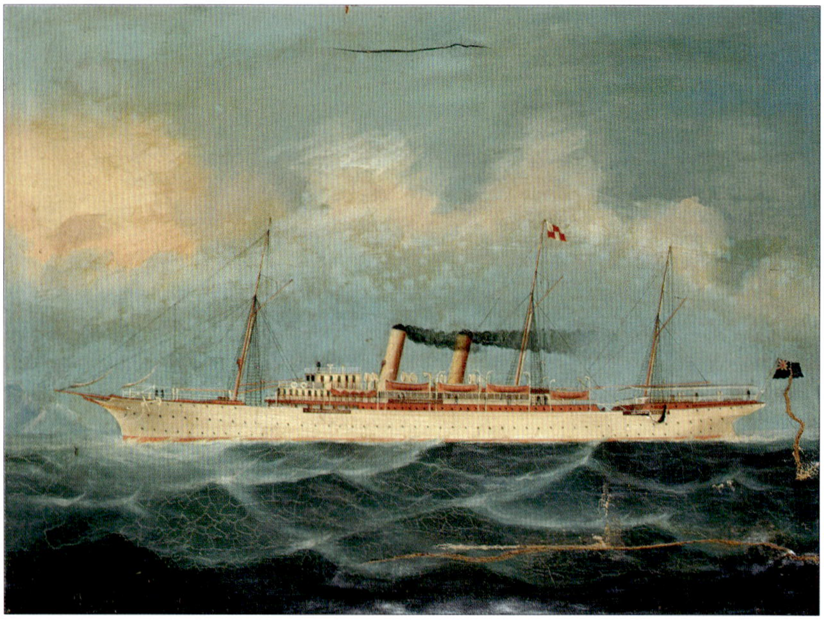

The triple screw steamer *Empress of China* is shown in port profile under full steam at sea. This is a typical Chinese School work with a characteristic pink sky. The vessel flies the Canadian Pacific house flag on her main mast and a blue ensign at the stern. This latter indicates that the master and a contingent of the crew were members of the Royal Naval Volunteer Reserve.

Empress of China was one of three steel twin-screwed sister ships which were built for the Canadian Pacific Railway Company when they won the British Mail contract for the transpacific route in 1889. They were known as the White Empresses from their splendid white hulls. *Empress of China* was built 1891 by the Naval

Construction and Armaments Company of Barrow in Furness and took passengers on the first leg of a World Tour from Liverpool via the Suez Canal in the course of taking up her station at Vancouver. After a successful career on the transpacific route she ran aground on the Mera Reef in Tokyo Bay in July 1911. Although refloated she was written off in the following year.[1]

There is another painting of the vessel by a less accomplished and anonymous hand in the collections, no. 58.

1 For a history of the vessel see George Musk *Canadian Pacific*, 1981, pp. 15, 127-30

58 *Empress of China*

1955.228
Oil on canvas[1]
32 cm x 45.5 cm
Prov: In collections, 1955.

Vessel: 455.6 ft (l), 51.2 ft (b), 33.1 ft (d); 5905 gross tons

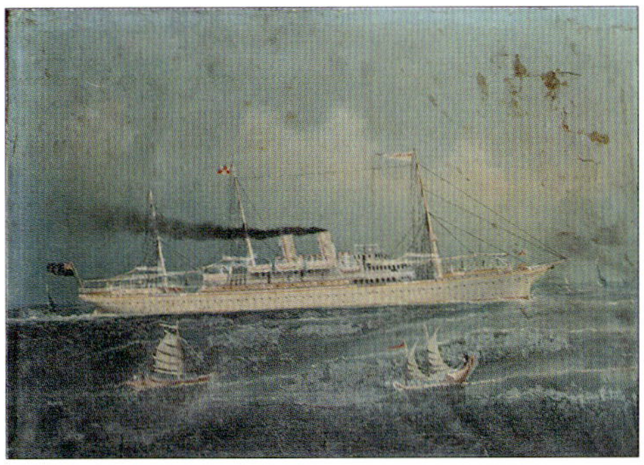

This rather naive painting shows the *Empress of China* in starboard profile at sea under full steam. She flies the house flag of the Canadian Pacific Railway on her main mast and on a jack at the bow; a white pennant with the legend *Royal Mail* in red flies on the foremast and the Canadian flag from her stern. Her name is painted on the bow and the painter has included the vessel's distinctive dragon figurehead. There are two junks in the foreground, indicating that the scene is probably intended to be in the South China Sea.

There is another painting of this vessel in the collections, no. 57, also attributed to a Chinese artist. For the history of the vessel see no. 57.

1 Relined with strips of canvas.

59 *Holkar*

1951.30
Oil on canvas
45 cm x 59.5 cm
Prov: Mrs Pennant, Liverpool, who presented it, 1951

Vessel: 329.3 ft (l), 45.2 ft (b), 26.7 ft (d); 3088 gross tons

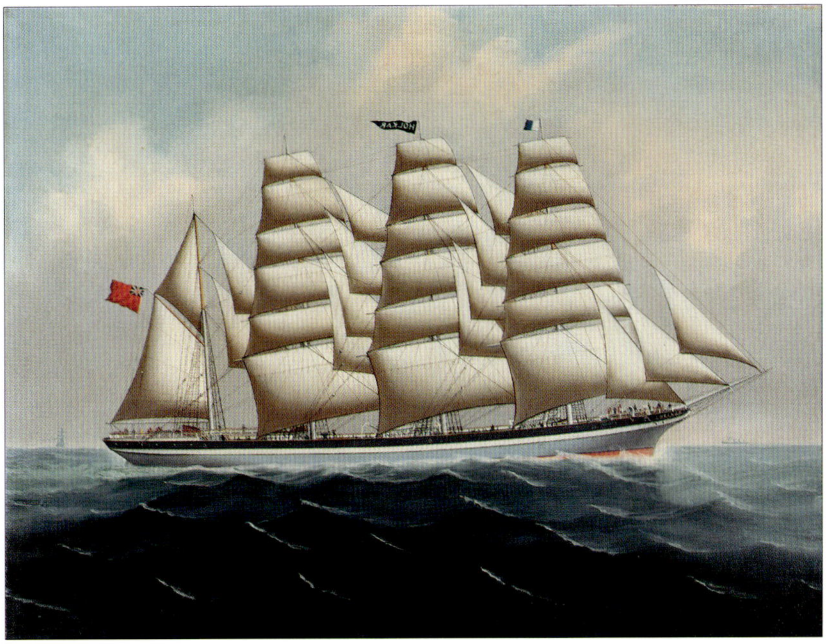

The 4 masted steel barque *Holkar* is shown in starboard profile under full sail with her crew busy on deck. Her name is on the bow and she flies a name pennant from her main mast together with the blue and white Brocklebank house flag in its traditional place on the foremast. The red ensign is at the peak.

Holkar and her sister *Sindia* were the last two sailing ships built for Brocklebank and were constructed at Belfast by Harland & Wolff in 1887 and 1888. These fine ships were the largest sailing ships of the time.[1] They both spent their Brocklebank careers voyaging to Calcutta, initially from Liverpool but later loading at Middlesborough and returning to Dundee. *Holkar* was sold in 1901 having German and Norwegian owners under a variety of names until broken up in 1925.[2]
There is an exhibition model of the vessel in the collections, accession no. L1970.246.4. A painting of her sister ship *Sindia* by R H Neville-Cummings is in a private collection.

1 There is a sail plan in Lubbock Windjammers, opp. p.58
2 Gibson I, p.165-166.

60 *Maiden Queen*

1970.244.65
Oil on canvas
44.5 cm x 59.5 cm
Prov: Cunard Brocklebank Ltd, Private Collection, on permanent loan, 1970
Ref: MacGregor 1983, p.125 (ill).

Vessel: 178 ft (l), 32.3 ft (b), 21.1 ft (d); 814 gross tons

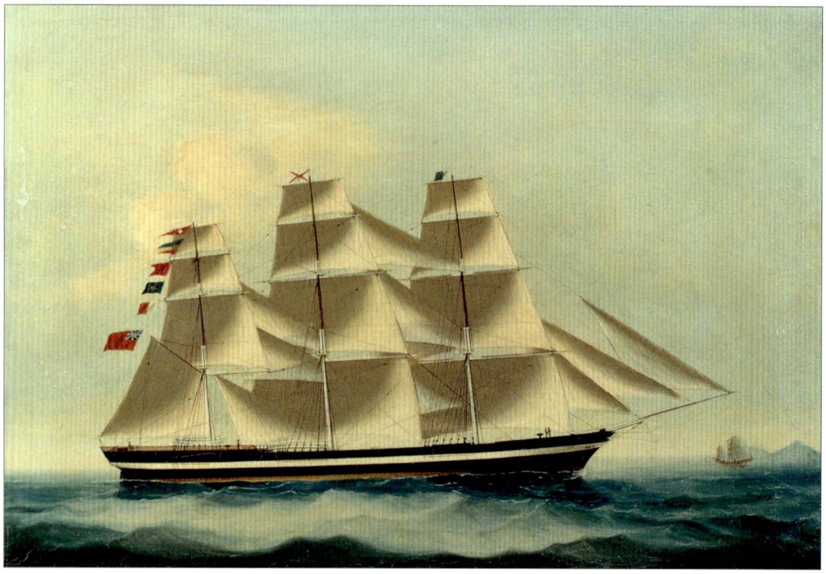

Although this is a standard Chinese School painting, it is of particular interest because it still has its original Chinese lacquered frame. The ship *Maiden Queen* is shown in leeward starboard profile off the Chinese coast. She is shown under full sail, including staysails. She exhibits the typical Brocklebank broad white hull band and flies the company's house flag from her foremast. Her Marryat number (3 d.p. 6 5 8 3) is displayed on her mizzen mast and she flies an unidentified flag of red St Andrew's Cross on a white ground[1] at the main and the red ensign at the peak. A junk and a mountainous coastline are visible in the far distance under the bowsprit. *Maiden Queen* was built by R Williamson & Son of Harrington, Cumbria, in 1860 and was owned by Brocklebanks until 1874. She was used in the tea trade and sailed principally to Hong Kong with occasional visits to Shanghai, Manila and Foo Chow. She was renamed *Betty* in 1886 and was hulked at Santos, Brazil by 1892.[2]

1 This is also V in the Commercial / International code but has no relevant meaning at this time.
2 Gibson I, p.272; MacGregor 1983, pp. 125, 222.

61 *Merioneth*

1964.306
Oil on canvas
64 cm x 92.5 cm
Prov: Mr R R Froom, Liverpool, who presented it, 1964.

Vessel: 231.4 ft (l), 38.9 ft (b), 23.6 ft (d); 1366 gross tons

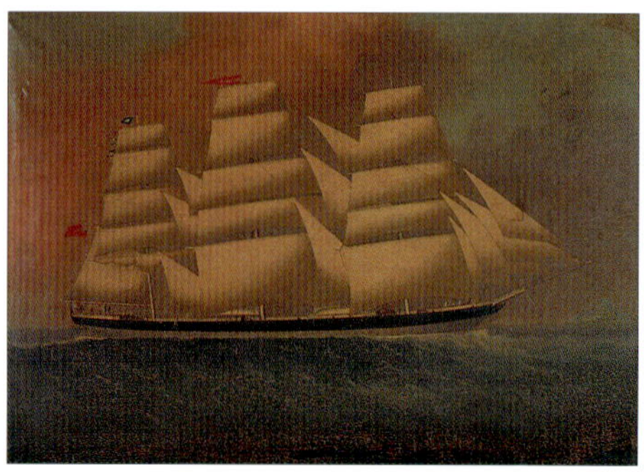

The 3 masted ship *Merioneth* is shown in starboard profile with all sails set except the mizzen course, making her way towards land. A number of men are on deck, including a small group about to take in the headsails. In the far distance a mountainous peak or island is visible with a brig rigged steamer close by. *Merioneth* is identifiable by the name

on her bow, her name pennant on the main mast and her commercial flag code (P H N J) at the mizzen. She flies the red ensign at the after peak.
Named after the former Welsh county, the iron built *Merioneth* was built in Liverpool by Thomas Royden & Sons for Hughes & Co. of Menai Bridge, Anglesey in 1875. She is remembered for a record breaking run from Cardiff to San Francisco, via Cape Horn, and back in 1887-8 when she undertook the outward run with a cargo of coal in 96 days and the homeward voyage in 95 days. In recognition of the outward voyage, the Californian sugar merchants Spreckels presented Captain Robert Thomas with a huge silk flag. The vessel was sold to Italian owners in 1902 and renamed *Santa Felice*. She was broken up in 1922.[1]

1 Lubbock, Windjammers I, pp. 203-4

62 *S S Moyune in a tropical storm*

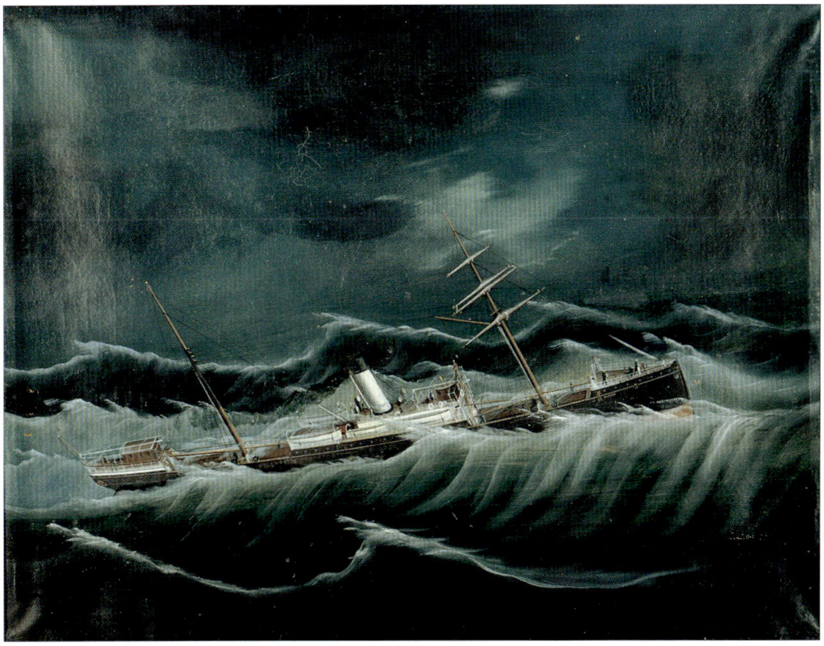

1955.249
Oil on canvas
45 cm x 59.5 cm
Prov: Unknown, in collections in 1955.

Vessel: 340 ft (l), 40.1 ft (b), 25.5 ft (d); 2690 gross tons

This unknown artist depicts the brigantine rigged screw steamer *Moyune* in a dramatic starboard profile riding out a tropical storm. Her auxiliary sails on the foremast are furled and she is using her engines to keep her head into the sea and winds. Waves are towering over the ship and pounding over the deck and members of the crew can be seen at the bow trying to make sure all is secure.
Moyune was built by J L Thompson & Sons of Sunderland in 1886 for the China Shippers' Mutual Steam Navigation Company, formed in 1882. The company was a major competitor on the Far Eastern routes to the Liverpool-based Blue Funnel Line.[1] She was sold to Japanese owners in 1894 and was later owned in Hong Kong and Turkey before being sold for scrap in 1935.

1 The Ocean Steam Ship Company (Blue Funnel) purchased China Mutual in 1902 (see Falkus 1990)

63 *Pegasus* (page 62)

This portrait of a 4 masted barque is identifiable as *Pegasus* by her Commercial flag hoist (J P D T) flying under the red ensign at the after peak and the flying horse figurehead, which was a trademark of her owner. She flies a house flag for D Corsar and Sons at the main mast. She is typically shown in starboard profile at sea under full sail with other shipping off a rather rocky and mountainous coast in the far right distance.
Pegasus was built in 1884 by W H Potter of Liverpool for W T Dixon & Co in association with W H Corsar, the well-known Liverpool canvas maker. She was managed by Dixons until 1895 when Corsars took over the management. She worked

1960.62
Oil on canvas[1]
65 cm x 89 cm
Prov: John Kennaugh, Liverpool, c.1910 [2], by descent to Mr T Kennaugh, Liverpool, who presented it, 1960.

Vessel: 314 ft (l), 42.3 ft (b), 24.9 ft (d); 2564 gross tons

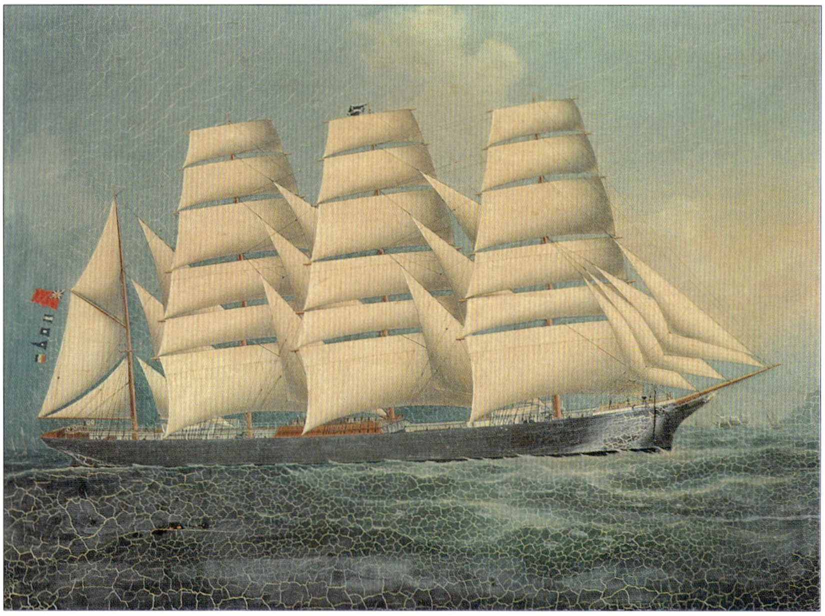

mainly on the Pacific coast of America and to Australia carrying coal and nitrates. She was sold on to C Neilsen & Co. of Larvik, Norway, in 1909. In August 1912 she was stranded on Market Island in the Gulf of Bothnia and though towed to Revel was condemned and broken up.[3] Her figurehead and anchor are now in the Swedish National Maritime Museum and her wheel is preserved in the Waddo Museum, Sweden.[4] There is a painting of her sister ship *Reliance* by Witham (no. 266) in the collections. The painting presumably dates to the period 1895 to 1909.

1 Written in pencil on stretcher "Mr Kennaugh / 2 Clarendon Terrace / ?Be[aumont Street] / B[ ]" There is a John Kennaugh, foreman sailmaker listed at this address in GDL 1910
2 see n.1 above.
3 LCR, vol. 95 no. 118, 4 Sept 1884, LCR TB9 p.15, LCR TB11, p.129; Lubbock, Windjammers I, pp. 307-8
4 Information in DCF, anchor seen August 1990.

64 *Sierra Cordova*

1957.198
Oil on canvas
45 cm x 60 cm
Prov: Miss N Vooght, Liverpool, who presented it, 1957

Vessel: 232 ft (l), 37.9 ft (b), 22.8 ft (d); 1491 gross tons

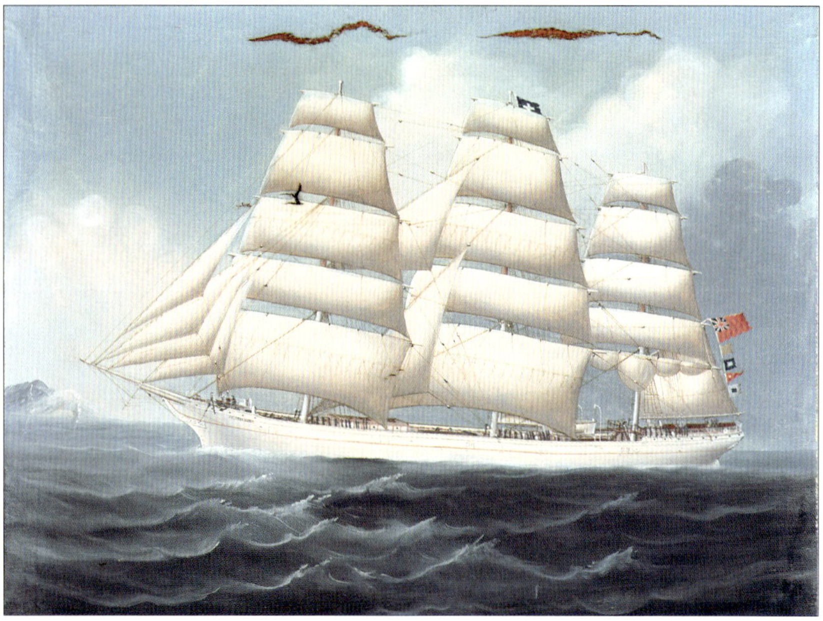

The *Sierra Cordova* is shown in port profile with all her sails set off a rocky headland. She has her name on the bow and a simple scroll instead of a figurehead. The house flag of the Sierra Line flies from the main mast and the red ensign flies above the commercial code (Q P F S) at the after peak.

The iron ship *Sierra Cordova* was built as *Lucile* by Thomas Royden & Sons of Liverpool for their own use in 1877. She was acquired by the Sierra Shipping

Company, managed by Thompson, Anderson & Co. in 1882. Like other vessels of the line she traded principally to Rangoon in Burma in the rice trade. She was sold to Leif Grendersen of Norway and renamed *Heimal* in 1903 and was broken up in 1913.[1] The general appearance of this canvas is reminiscent of the Chinese School which is supported by the fine linen canvas.

1 LCR 14 May 1877, no. 134, vol. 93, TB vol. 7, p.148, TB vol. 10, p.286. Brief details of the Sierra Line are in *Sea Breezes*, vol. 9, 1927, pp. 379-80 and Lubbock Windjammers, pp. 201-2.

65 *Tantalus at sea*

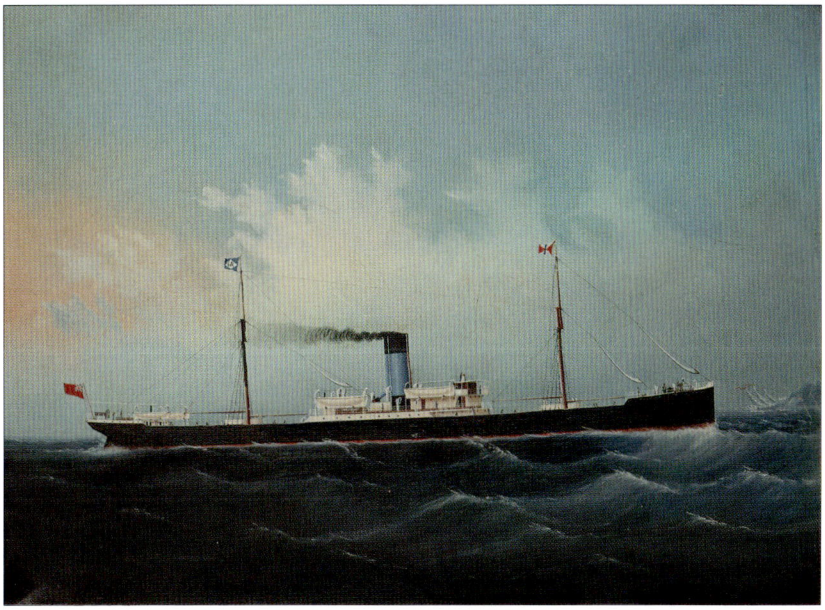

1970.173.2
Oil on canvas
44.5 cm x 59.5 cm
Prov: Miss C Spencer, Liverpool, from whom purchased, 1970

Vessel: 354.9 ft (l), 42.8 ft (b), 26.7 ft (d); 3621 gross tons.

Pairs of ship portraits, typically a vessel depicted in a calm sea and in a storm, were a frequent subject for artists. This unknown Chinese artist adopts this pairing for *Tantalus*, here and in no. 66. In this view the vessel is shown in starboard profile in calm conditions. She flies the Alfred Holt flag at the main, the China Navigation Company flag[1] at the fore (indicating a joint service) and the red ensign at the stern. She is identifiable by the name on her bow. The unknown artist has a good eye for detail and the crew, in particular, are carefully drawn.

Tantalus was built in 1892 by Scott & Co. of Greenock as one of four sister ships completed that year for Alfred Holt's Blue Funnel Line.[2] They were the last ships designed solely by Holt himself. They were built as part of the rapid expansion of the company's fleet in the early 1890s which was a response to changes in the Far East trade and increased competition. In their first year these four ships alone contributed over 40% of total net earnings.[3] In 1903 *Tantalus* was transferred to the Dutch subsidiary NSMO (Oceaan), which was jointly run with J B Meyer & Co of Amsterdam who also acted as managers. She was sold to German ownership in 1922 and was broken up at Hamburg in 1924.[4]

1 China Navigation had been founded by John Swire in Shanghai in 1872. The Holts had been original shareholders and Alfred advised on ship design. See Falkus 1990, pp. 63 -70.
2 The others were *Ixion*, *Ulysses*, and *Pyrrhus*. *Tantulus* was named after the mythological Lydian king, the son of Zeus.
3 See Falkus, pp. 109-116
4 Haws Blue Funnel, p. 57.

66 *Tantalus in a storm* (page 64)

This companion to no. 65 has *Tantalus* battling against the elements in a storm. She is shown in starboard profile with the waves towering over her and crashing onto the deck as she fights to keep her bow into the wind. The artist has chosen an elevated position to provide a good view of the deck. Again the name of the vessel is on the bow but in the stormy conditions she flies no flags.

1970.173.1
Oil on canvas
44.5 cm x 59.5 cm
Prov: Miss C Spencer, Liverpool, from whom purchased, 1970.

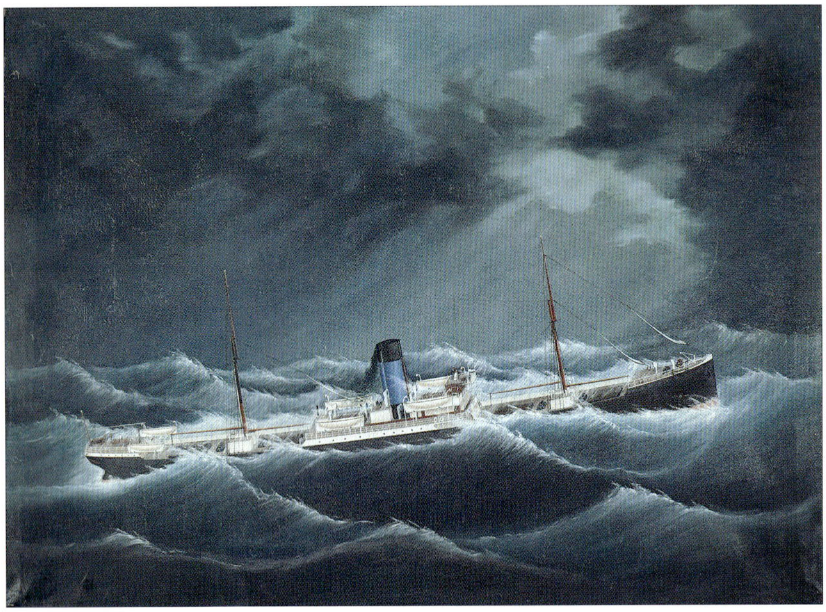

67 *The Highfields*

1955.255
Oil on canvas
61 cm x 91.5 cm
Prov: Unknown, in collections, 1955

Vessel: 291.3 ft (l), 42 ft (b), 24.5 ft (d); 2280 gross tons

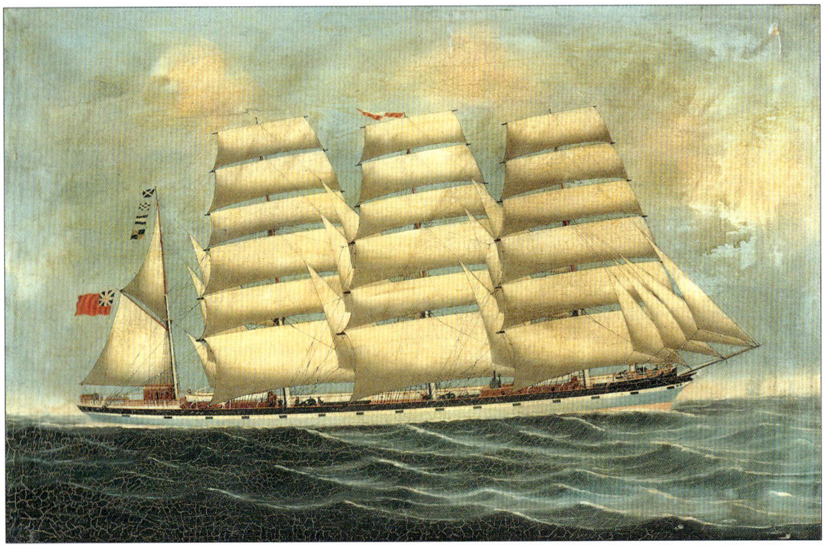

This standard Chinese School portrait shows the 4 masted steel barque *The Highfields* at sea under full sail in starboard profile. Various members of crew are depicted on the vessel's deck, including a group of men trimming the headsails. She flies a red and white check pennant, the house flag of C W Kellock, at her main mast. She is identifiable from her commercial code (M N J L) on the jigger mast and the red ensign flies at the after peak.

The Highfields was built by Richardson Duck & Co., of Stockton on Tees in 1892 and was the last sailing ship owned by the Liverpool ship brokers and valuers, C W Kellock. Although Kellocks owned few ships they were usually well built vessels and very highly regarded. On her maiden voyage *The Highfields* made the fastest run to Calcutta in that year. She was sold to MacVicar, Marshall also of Liverpool in 1899 and was lost in collision with the German steamer *Kaiser* off the breakwater to Cape Town in 1902. She sank almost immediately with the loss of 23 men.[1]

The painting dates between 1892 and 1899. There is a half-model of the vessel in the collections, accession no. 1962.343.22.

1 Lubbock Windjammers, pp. 170-1 and LCR, vol. 97, no. 38, 26 March 1892. A first-hand account of her first voyage is in a letter from Captain A W Middleton in *Sea Breezes*, vol. 11, 1951, p.456. An account of her loss is in H Ogilvie 'Wreck of the Highfields' *Sea Breezes*, vol. 11, 1928, pp. 170-1.

R S Clague (active about 1861 - about 1873)

No biographical information has been located, though it has been suggested he was a Manx artist.[1] Clague is known only from a small number of surviving works.[2]

1 Wilson, p.23.
2 DCF. His name is sometimes mis-spelt as Glague.

68 *S S Corcovado and S S Puno*

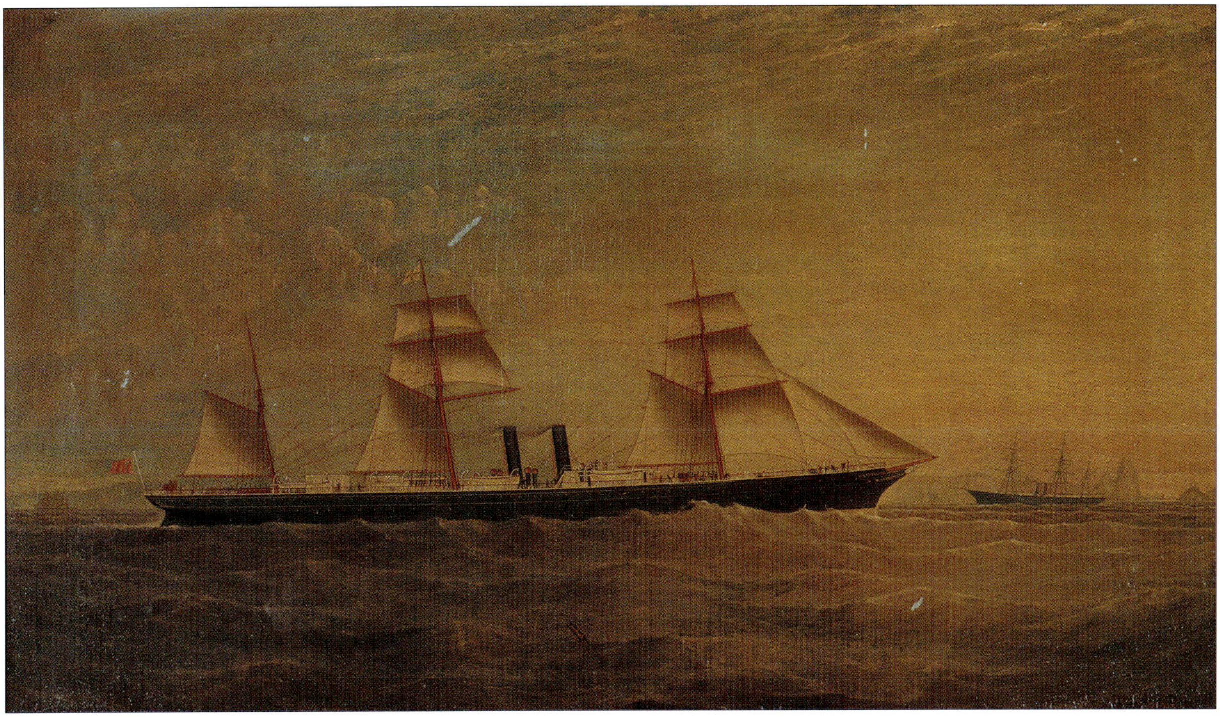

The Pacific Steam Navigation's steamer *Corcovado* is shown passing her sister ship *Puno* off the South American coast.

The barque rigged steam ship *Corcovado* is seen in starboard profile under steam and full sail except the main course. She is identifiable by her bow name. She flies the PSNC flag from her main mast. Members of the crew are shown realisticallyabout their duties. *Puno* is seen in port profile in the right middle distance with all her sails stowed. In the far right hand distance is a narrow channel, with icebergs or sheer rocky peaks, leading into a harbour where other ships are anchored. This is almost certainly intended to be off the Chilean coast.

Corcovado was named after the mountain in Chile and *Puno* after the town in Southern Peru. They were built by Lairds of Birkenhead and entered PSNC's Liverpool - Rio de Janeiro - Montevideo - Valparaiso service in 1873. With its coastal fleet, PSNC was the largest steam ship company in the world but could not sustain its growth. Forced to reduce services, both these ships were laid up in 1875 and then sold to the Royal Mail Line. *Corcovado* became *Don* and *Puno* became *Para*, both serving on the Southampton - West Indies run until 1901.[2]

This painting forms a pair with no. 69 *Santa Rosa and Colombia*.

1984.269.7
Oil on board[1]
59 cm x 102 cm
Signed and dated (br) "R. S. CLAGUE / 1873"
Prov: Pacific Steam Navigation Company, on permanent loan.

Vessel: 387.5 (l), 43.1 ft (b), 33.9 ft (d); 3805 gross tons

1 Printed label rear "HUGO LANG & CO. LTD / 19 WHITECHAPEL / LIVERPOOL"
2 Bonsor South, pp.148-9,159,160.

69 *S S Santa Rosa and S S Colombia* (page 66)

As with its pair, no. 68, the two sister ships *Santa Rosa* and *Colombia* are shown passing at sea off an unidentified coastline. *Santa Rosa* is shown in greater detail in starboard profile. She is barquentine rigged and is making use of her aft sails, jibs and fore topsail. The PSNC house flag flies from the main mast and she is identifiable from her name at the bow. The red ensign flies at the stern jack. In the right distance

1984.269.8
Oil on canvas
49.5 cm x 92.5 cm
Signed (br) "Clague" over "R. S. CLAGUE"[1]
Prov: Pacific Steam Navigation Company, on permanent loan.
Ref: A C Wardle Steam Conquers the Pacific, London, 1940, p.120 (ill).

Vessel: 308 ft (l), 38.1 ft (b), 20.5 ft (d); 1817 gross tons

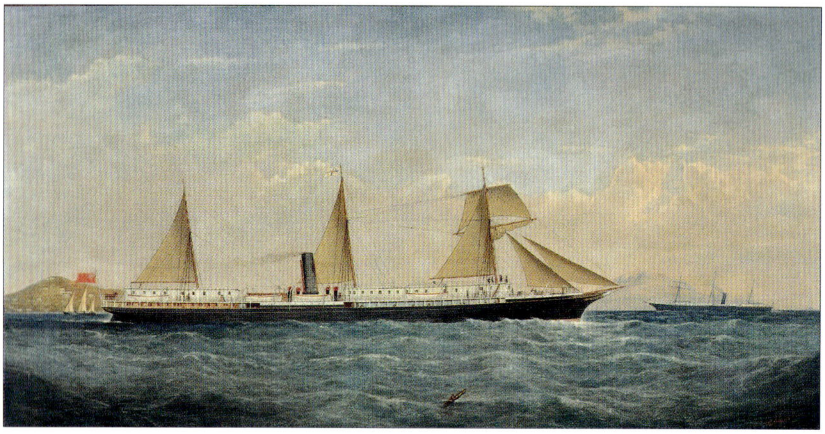

Colombia is seen in port profile with sails stowed. The vessels are shown off a coast with white houses dotted over the hillside and a large round topped mountain to the right, which is probably intended to be off the west coast of South America.
The two vessels were built by Lairds of Birkenhead in 1872 and 1873 for PSNC's west coast service between Valparaiso, Callao and Panama. They could carry 116 passengers. Both vessels were sold in 1890, *Colombia* was broken up immediately but *Santa Rosa* was employed on local coastal services around Valparaiso until 1902.[2]

1 The overwritten "Clague" appears to be in a different, probably later hand. The lower signature is identical with no. 68 and may be assumed to be original. There are indecipherable traces of a date.
2 Haws, PSNC, p 55.

William Clark (1803-1883)

The son of a seaman who later became a house painter, Clark was born in Greenock where he remained throughout his life. He mainly painted vessels based in or visiting the Clyde. There are few examples in public collections apart from the National Maritime Museum[1].

1 Archibald, p.83

70 *The Royal Mail Paddle Steamer Dee*

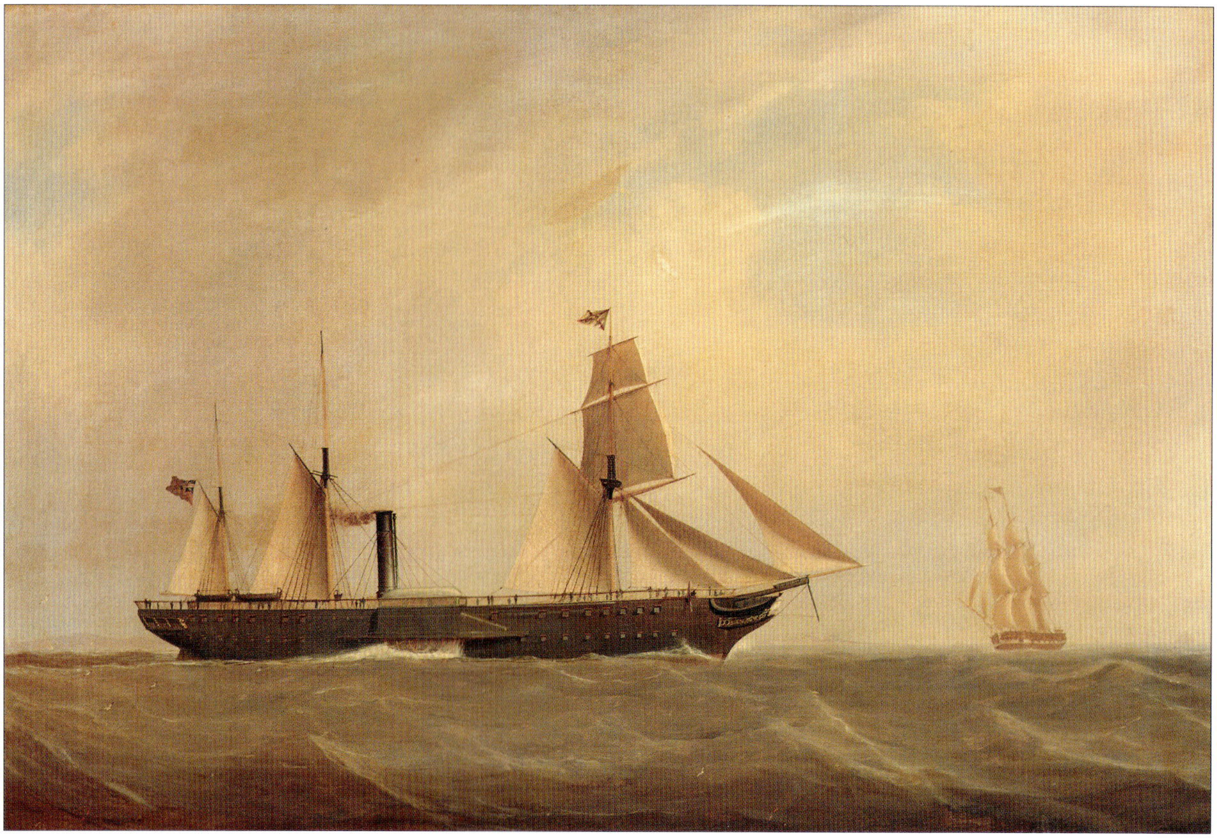

The paddle steamer *Dee* is shown in starboard profile making good progress under power and sail. She is shown off an unidentified coastline and there is an unidentified 3 masted ship heading towards her. The rather angular appearance of the paddle box is partly explained by the fact that she carried a lifeboat on top of the box. The only identifying features are the Royal Mail house flag which she flies at the foremast and the female figurehead. The red ensign is at the peak. The artist painted her at the outset of her career when she had her original barquentine rig; later the mizzen mast was removed in an attempt to reduce the uncomfortable tendency towards rolling.

Dee was built in 1841 for the Royal Mail Steam Packet Company by John Scott & Sons of Greenock. She was one of fourteen steamships built in a period of only 20 months to satisfy the terms of the mail contract to the West Indies. They were all produced to the same basic design and were named after British rivers. The mail service operated to the West Indies twice a month, calling at Corunna and Madeira for coal outward bound and Bermuda homeward bound. Initially the home port was Falmouth but she made her maiden voyage from Southampton and was transferred there in 1843. *Dee* remained in service until 1860 when she was chartered to return the so-called "Irish Brigade" from Le Havre to Cork. The brigade had been raised to fight for the Pope against Garibaldi in the Italian Wars. She was sold for demolition in 1862.[1]

The artist uses a cool palette to produce a characteristic work. A lithograph of the vessel at anchor was published by Hanhart in 1841.[2] There is a lithograph of several Royal Mail steamers of the same design as *Dee* at Southampton in December 1841, possibly including *Dee* herself.[3]

1963.137.1
Oil on canvas
76.5 cm x 112 cm
Signed and dated (bl) "W. Clark 1841"
Prov: Royal Mail Steam Packet Company, Royal Mail Line Ltd., London, who presented it, 1963

Vessel: 275 ft (l), 60 ft (b); 1849 gross tons.

1 Haws Royal Mail Line, p.29.
2 Parker & Bowen, p.89.
3 *"Assembly of the first Royal Mail Fleet at Southampton, December 1841"*, Science Museum, London. Of the four vessels depicted one is definitely *Teviot*. *Dee* made her maiden voyage from Southampton on 14 January 1842. See T A Bushell *Royal Mail*, 1839-1939, London, 1939.

Style of William Clark

71 P S Magdalena

The Royal Mail's paddle steamer *Magdalena* is shown in port profile probably off Ailsa Craig in the Firth of Clyde. Other shipping is rather sketchily indicated. The vessel is making her way under steam and with the assistance of her auxiliary sails; like other steamers in the line's service she had a barquentine rig. She wears the Royal Mail house flag on her main mast, an unidentified blue and red flag on her foremast and the red ensign at the peak.

Magdalena was one of a group of five new vessels which were built by Royal Mail when they took on an extension of the West Indies mail contract to Rio de Janeiro in Brazil. They were then the largest wooden vessels afloat. *Magdalena* was built

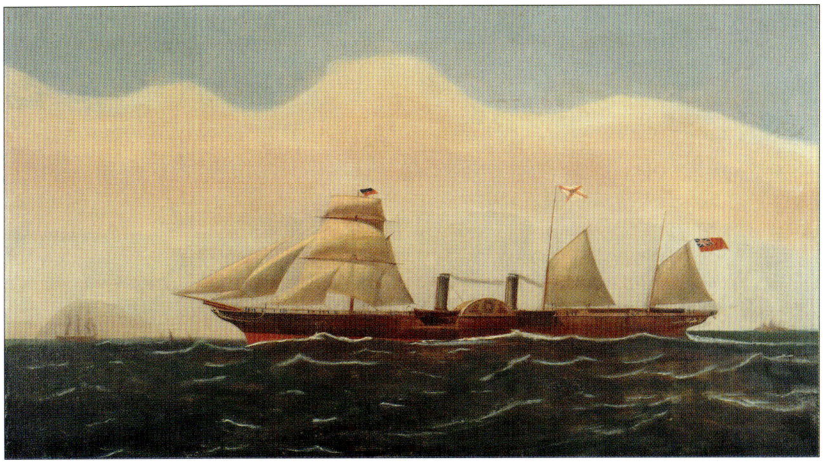

1963.137.2
Oil on canvas
107 cm x 183 cm
Prov: Royal Mail Steam Ship Company, Royal Mail Lines Ltd., London, who presented it, 1963.

Vessel: 282 ft (l), 73 ft (b), 26 ft (d); 2318 gross tons

by William Pitcher of Northfleet on the Thames in 1851 and her engines were provided and fitted by Robert Napier of Glasgow. The painting may therefore be intended to show her on her way to Southampton for her maiden voyage after the fitting of her engines. She served her career on the West Indies and Brazilian runs except for a period trooping during the Crimean War in 1854. She was broken up at Vauxhall in 1866.[1]

Traditionally this canvas has been attributed to William Clark and it is very similar in composition to his painting of the paddle steamer *Dumbarton* off Ailsa Craig, signed and dated 1864.[2] However, there appears to be considerable over-painting and an attribution to Clark is difficult to sustain with confidence.

1 Haws, *Royal Mail Line*, p.36.
2 Catalogue, Frank T Sabin, 1967, no. 113.

Charles David Cobb (b.1921)

After service in the Royal Navy during World War II, David Cobb set up as a professional artist in Cornwall in 1946. He has produced a variety of marine work including work for a number of multinational companies and also naval paintings, particularly of wartime action. There are important collections in the National Maritime Museum and the Royal Naval Museum, Portsmouth.[1]

1 Archibald, p.85. See also D. Cobb *The Making of a War Artist : the Falklands Paintings*, London, 1986.

72 *A Convoy arrives in Liverpool*

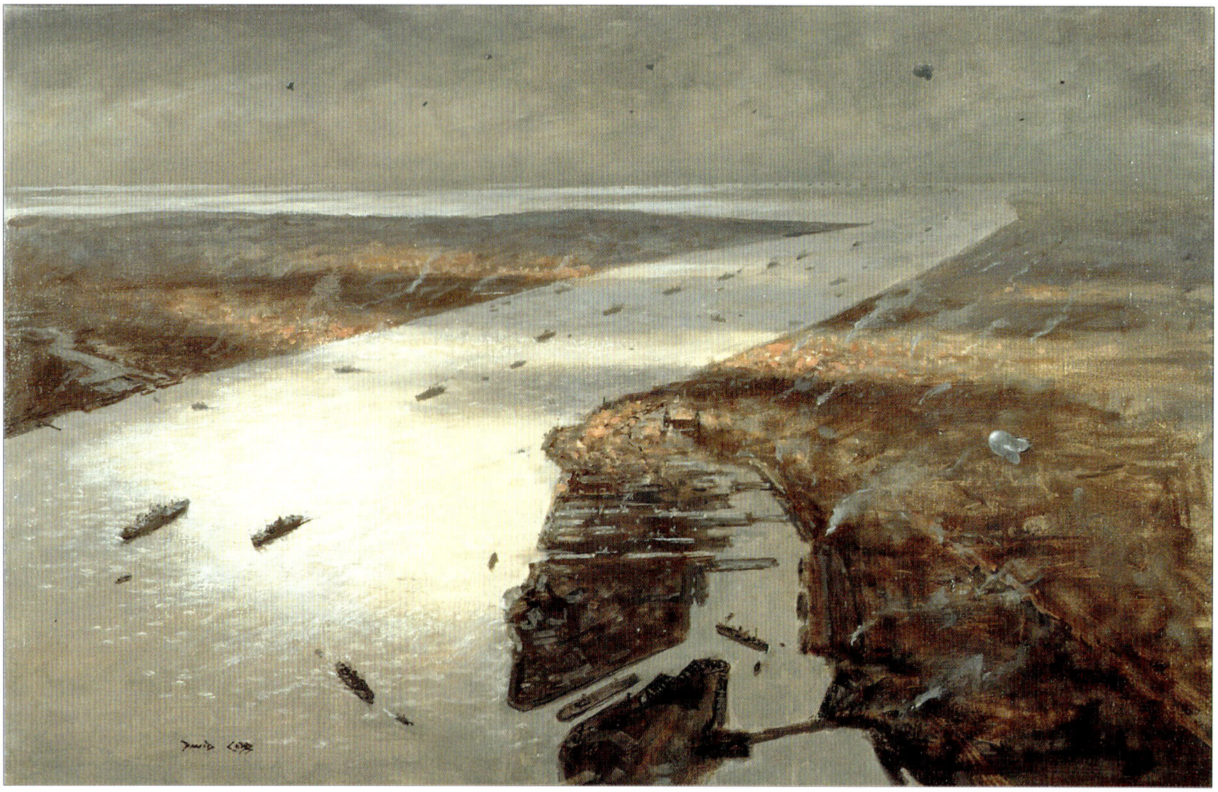

1990.48
Oil on canvas
61 cm x 91.5 cm
Signed (bl) "DAVID COBB"
Prov: Commissioned from the artist, 1990

This painting was commissioned by the Maritime Museum for its displays commemorating the 50th anniversary of the Battle of the Atlantic in 1993. This aerial view looking north from above the South Docks shows the convoy coming up the Mersey with Liverpool on the right hand bank and Birkenhead and the Wirral to the left. Liverpool Bay and the sandbanks at the mouth of the Mersey can be seen in the far distance.

The first ships in the convoy are entering Brunswick Dock at the southern end of the docks and other ships are heading for the Birkenhead Docks and the North Docks. On the Liverpool side, the Landing Stage and the Port of Liverpool Building with its distinctive cupolas are the only specific features visible. A lone barrage balloon is a reminder of the threat from air attack which was a regular feature of life in the city.

At the request of the Maritime Museum, this painting was based on an earlier canvas of the same scene commissioned by the Royal Naval Museum at Portsmouth in 1976. The artist served in the Royal Navy in the Western Approaches during the war. On completing the present painting, he commented "I can only try to relive what I saw nearly 50 years ago, which was a very sombre scene of a battered city and port."[1]

1 Letter from artist, 25 March 1990, DCF.

Charles Cockerham (active about 1900 - 1935)

Cockerham spent time at sea and also worked in Harland & Wolff's shipyard in Belfast before becoming a full time marine artist in Liverpool.[1]

1 See Davidson, 1986, p. 128-9.

73 *Pier Head, 1908*

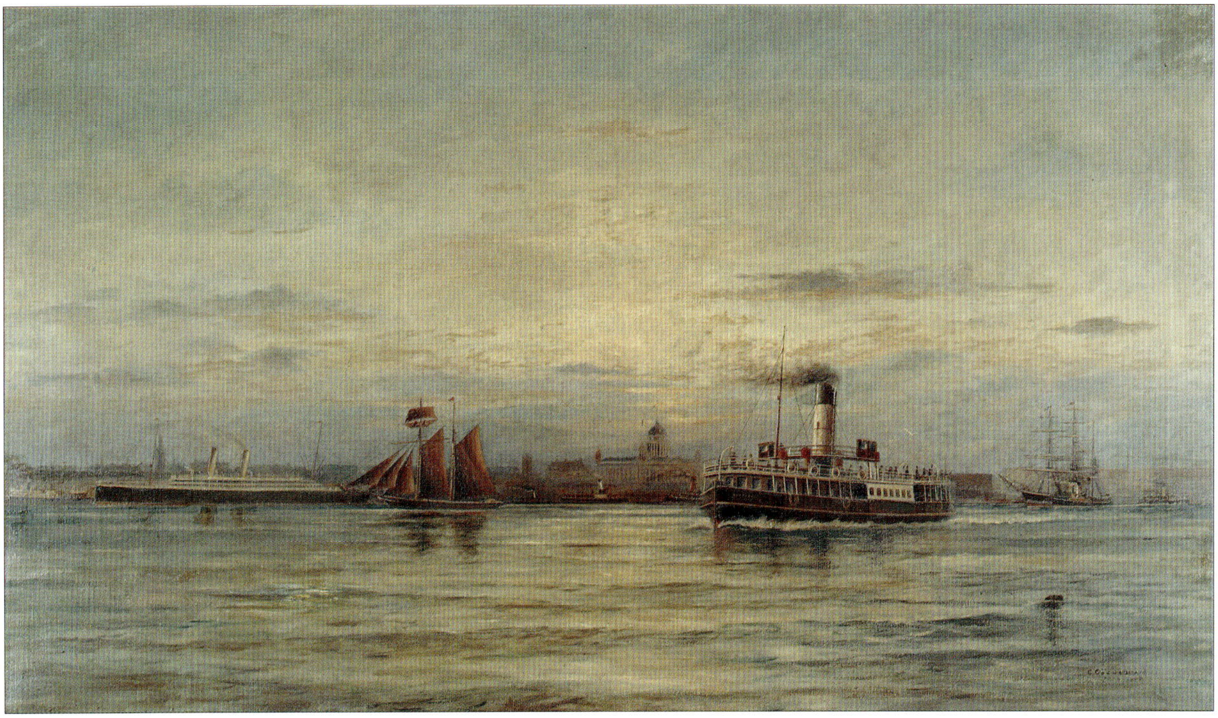

This atmospheric canvas catches the scene off Liverpool's Pier Head with the Wallasey ferry *Daffodil* centre right in port quarter view making her way across the river as the sun is setting. In the background there is a liner alongside the Landing Stage with other ferries at the southern end by the Pier Head. To the far left there is a Harrison line vessel, identifiable from its funnels. Astern of the liner, a topsail trading schooner is heading out to sea. A barque rigged vessel with a tug alongside are visible in the far right distance.

The main landmark on the waterfront is the Port of Liverpool Building, headquarters of the Mersey Docks and Harbour Board, shown in the background just to the left of the ferry. This was the first of the famous Pier Head group of buildings, completed in 1908. Other notable sights are the tower of St Nicholas behind the liner and the Albert Dock buildings astern of the ferry.

The iron paddle steamer *Daffodil* was built for Wallasey Corporation by R Stephenson & Co of Hebburn on Tyne in 1906. With her sister *Iris* she was requisitioned by the Admiralty and took part in the Zeebrugge raid of April 1918.

1951.25.2
Oil on canvas
79 cm x 132 cm
Signed and dated (br) "C. COCKERHAM / L.POOL 1908"
Prov: Mr J James, Blundellsands, from whom purchased, 1951
Exh: Liverpool 1986
Ref: Port Panorama, p.9

Vessel: *Daffodil* 152 ft (l), 40.6 ft (b), 11.2 ft (d); 465 gross tons.

After the war she returned to the Mersey and served until 1934, being broken up in 1938.[1] There is a watercolour as *HMS Daffodil* (with *Iris*) by Sam J M Brown in the collections. (Accession no 56.163).[2]

1 Duckworth, p.130, and Philip Warner *The Zeebrugge Raid*, London, 1978, pp. 101-115.
2 See Port Panorama p.8 (ill).

74 *Tarquah*

1963.16.4
Oil on canvas
92 cm x 168.5 cm
Prov: Elder Dempster Lines Ltd., who presented it, 1963.

Vessel: 360.4 ft (l), 44.3 ft (b), 14.3 ft (d); 3859 gross tons

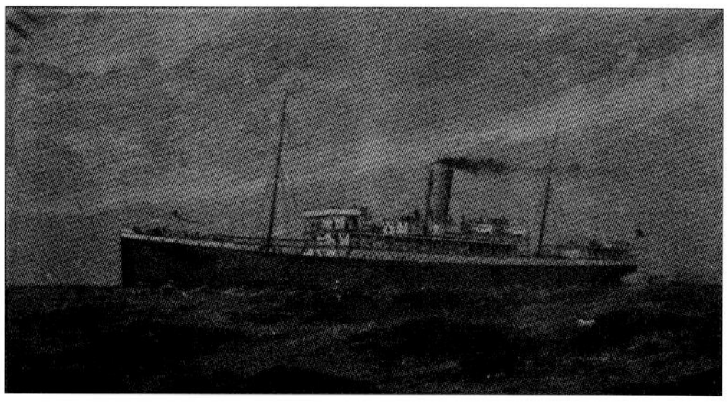

The African Steam Ship Company's vessel *Tarquah* is shown in port profile at sea with another steamer and a sailing ship in the far right hand distance. Her identification is confirmed by the name on her bow and the buff funnel. She flies the red ensign. The vessel had an open bridge and the helmsman can be seen at the wheel high up on the superstructure. Various other members of the crew and some of the passengers are shown on the decks.

Tarquah, which was named after the anglicised version of Tarkwa, a mining town in Ghana, was built by Alexander Stephens of Glasgow in 1902 for Elder Dempster, managers of the African Steam Ship Company. She had accommodation for 150 passengers and was used on the service to West Africa. She was sunk in July 1917 by a German submarine about ten miles south west of Bull Rock on a voyage to Sierra Leone. There was no loss of life.[1]

Cockerham's experience of ships ensures an accurate portrayal of the vessel. The rigging has been drawn in pencil.

1 Cowden & Duffy, p. 109.

Henry Collins (1782-1824)

Collins was almost certainly a Whitehaven man - he married there in 1808 and died there in 1824. He was highly regarded as a marine painter in his lifetime though only about a dozen works by him are currently known. Several of these feature ships in the Mersey indicating that he was a regular visitor to Liverpool.[1]

1 See Davidson, pp. 24-6.

75 *The snow Betty off Harrington*

This very detailed picture is an excellent representation of a snow at close quarters. It shows the *Betty* in two positions off the entrance to Harrington harbour with Workington and the Scottish coast is the far distance.

The main view shows the vessel leaving harbour with all her sails set, including jibs and staysails. It is unlikely she would use so much sail in this situation and the artist is taking a certain amount of licence to show the vessel's full sail plan fully hoisted. He has also chosen a view so that the details of the rigging are visible rather than being largely hidden by the sails themselves. This allows a very clear illustration of the small trysail mast abaft the main mast which is the feature that distinguishes a snow from a brig. The crew can also be seen clearly on deck, including a group at the foremast making the sails fast. Two boats are stored amidships.

In the left distance is a second port quarter view of the vessel exhibiting a more likely sail arrangements for the situation. Both main courses are furled, the trysail is scandalised (dropped) and the vessel is relying on her topsails and royals and one jib sail.

In the foreground is a charming detail of a small rowing boat heading into the harbour with two passengers in the stern, the woman shading herself with a parasol.

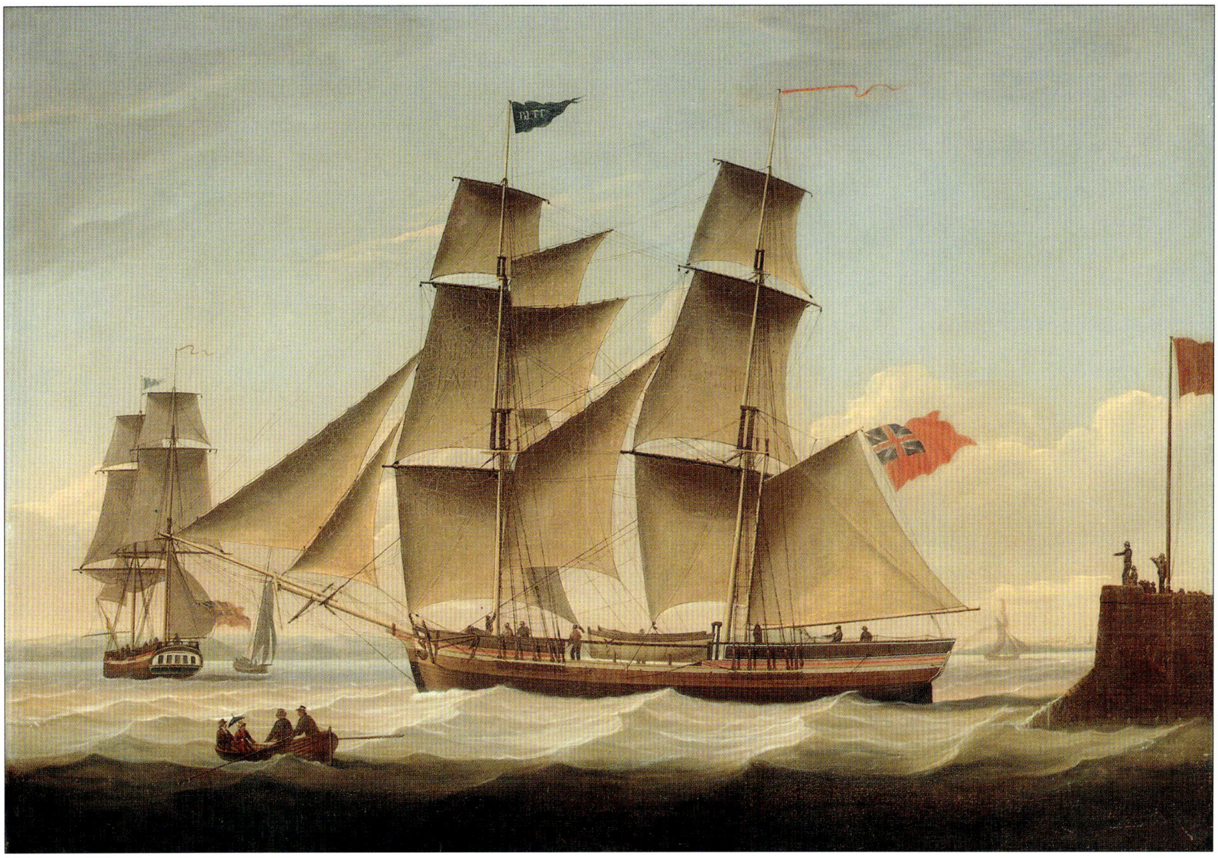

The pier at the entrance to the harbour is shown on the far right hand side with a flagpole and group of men watching the vessel leave. In the far distance between the pier and the stern of *Betty*, a large group of masts indicates the harbour at nearby Workington.
Although the vessel is recognisable as *Betty* from the name pennant on her foremast, the name is so common in the early nineteenth century that a precise identification is not possible. She flies a red ensign of the post-1801 design at her stern.

MMM.1995.50
Oil on canvas
68.2 cm x 100 cm
Signed (br) "H. Collins"
Prov: Denys Brooke-Hart; Jeremy Taylor Gallery, London, from whom purchased, 1995

W Connor (active 1915)

76 *The Hopper Dredger Miles K Burton*

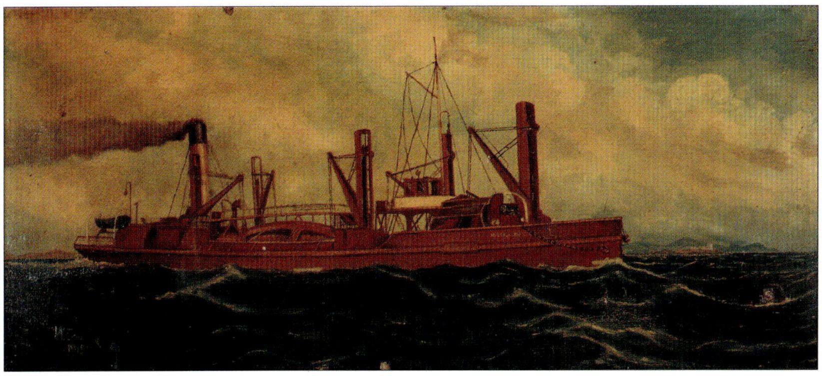

1963.317
Oil on board
30.5 cm x 70 cm
Signed (bl) "W Connor / 1915"
Prov: Mrs M Connor[1], Liverpool, who presented it, 1963

Vessel: 225 ft (l), 38.3 ft (b), 16.1 ft (d); 1202 gross tons

This amateur painting shows the Mersey Docks and Harbour Board's grab hopper dredger *Miles K Burton* in a starboard profile. Her name is on the bow. There is a No.5 navigation buoy in the right foreground, which is probably meant to be in the Crosby Channel, though the background does not conform.

1 The donor's husband was a nephew of the artist.
2 Miles K Burton (1842-1935) served MDHB for 55 years and was Secretary 1894-97 and General Manager & Secretary 1897-1912. See Mountfield, pp. 121, 199.
3 LCR, vol. 98, no. 53.

Miles K Burton was built for the Board by W Simon & Co of Renfrew in 1897. She had twin screws and triple expansion engines. She was named after the General Manager and Secretary of the Board.[2] She was mainly used for dredging the dock system rather than the river itself and remained in service until 1943 when she was sold to W H Arnott, Young & Co of Glasgow. She was broken up in 1950.[3]

H Crowther (active 1918)

77 *Runcorn Railway Bridge*

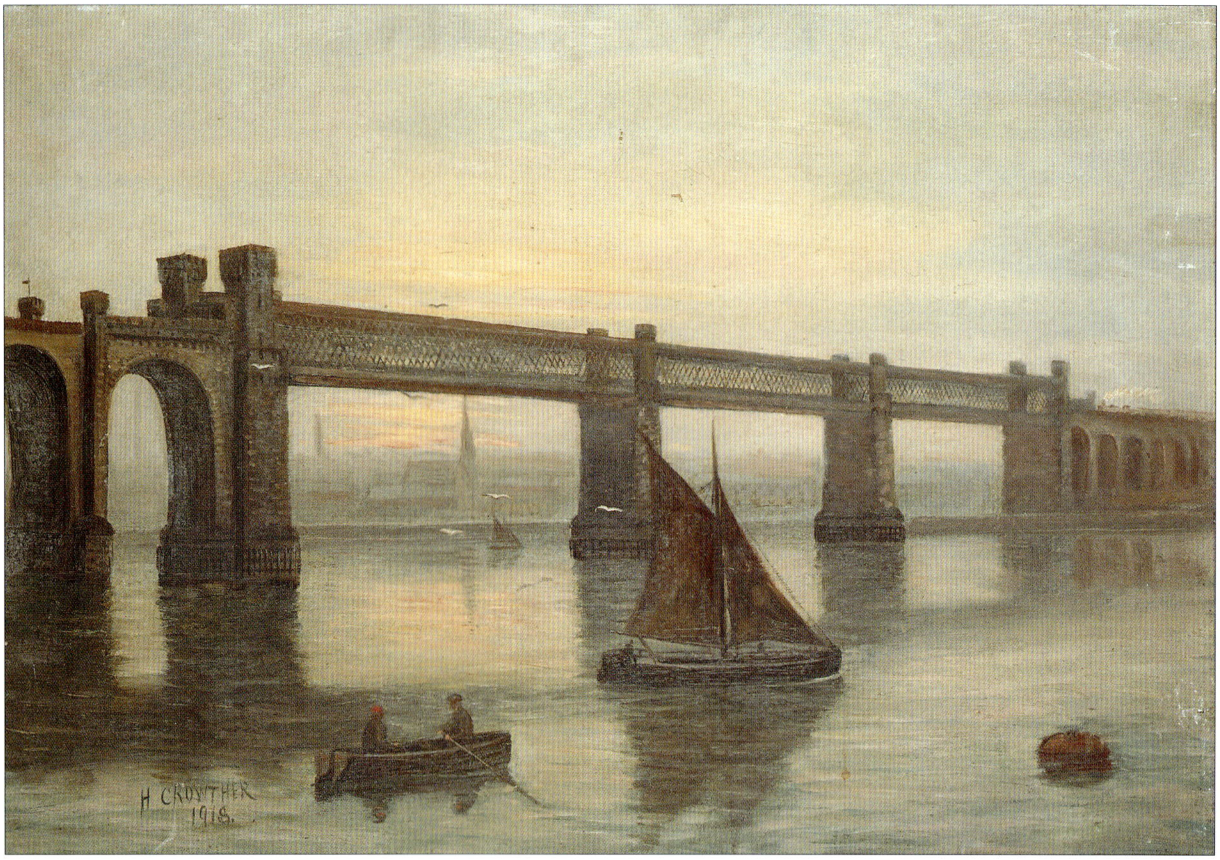

1976.62
Oil on canvas
35.5 cm x 50.5 cm
Signed and dated (bl) "H CROWTHER / 1918."
Prov: Mr J Brown, Widnes, who presented it, 1976.

1 M.K. Stammers *Mersey Flats and Flatmen*, Liverpool, 1993
2 Designed by Anthony Salvin, 1847-49, N Pevsner *Cheshire*, 1969
3 ibid.

This view of the railway bridge over the Mersey between Widnes and Runcorn is of maritime interest because it includes a Mersey flat in the foreground. Flats would still have been a (relatively) common sight on the Mersey in the early decades of the twentieth century.[1] There is also a small rowing boat in the foreground and a second flat in the distance under the bridge.

The railway bridge is seen from the Widnes West Bank and the town centre of Runcorn is visible under the arches of the bridge with the church of All Saints,[2] the only prominent feature. The bridge was built of stone and iron between 1864 and 1868 and was designed by William Baker.[3]

Salvatore De Angelis (1856 - ?)

1 Brewington 1982.

This artist was born and trained in Naples, Italy where he painted ship portraits, mainly of foreign vessels.[1]

78 *Leo*

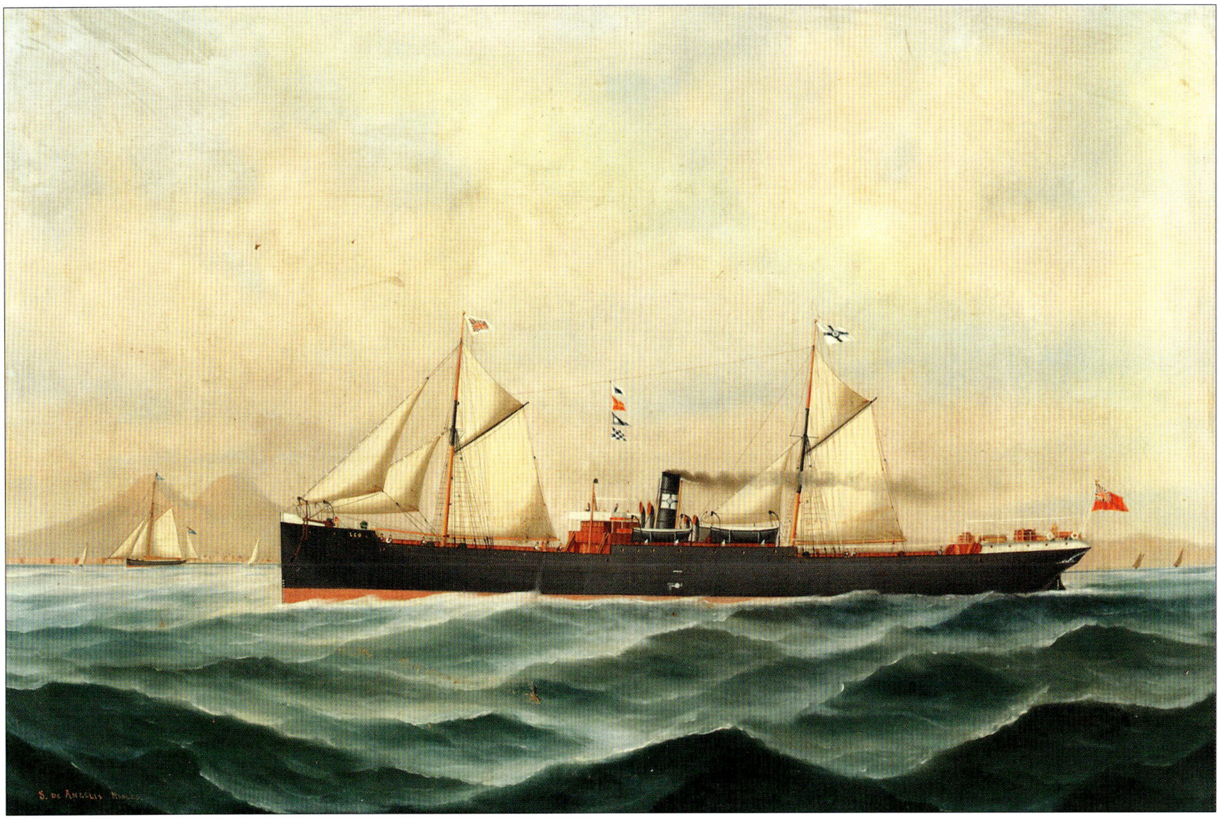

This painting shows the iron screw steamer *Leo* under sail and steam in port profile in the Bay of Naples. She flies the pilot jack at the foremast and the house flag of R B Avery on the main, the design of which is repeated on the funnel. Her name is on the hull and her flag hoist in the International code (S R D N) is suspended from a cable between the two masts. The characteristic outline of Mount Vesuvius and the coastline of the bay with parts of the city of Naples can be seen in the background. There is a small yawl rigged pleasure yacht flying a blue ensign and other craft in the far distance.

Leo was built by Swan Hunter & Co. of Newcastle in 1879 for R B Avery & Co. of the same port. They were small scale ship owners with three vessels in 1882, the largest of which was *Leo*. Towards the end of her career she was transferred to Edgar Avery and she foundered in November 1895.[1]

1963.283
Oil on canvas
49 cm x 74 cm
Signed (bl in red) "S. DE ANGELIS NAPLES."
Prov: J T Martin, Liverpool, from whom purchased, 1963.

Vessel: 285 ft (l), 35.2 ft (b), 24.5 ft (d); 1987 gross tons

1 LR 1880, 1895/6.

W Devitt (active late nineteenth century)

79 *Crown of Scotland*

The iron ship rigged *Crown of Scotland* is shown in starboard profile at sea under full sail. She flies a house flag of a red crown in a white lozenge on a blue ground at her main mast and the red ensign at the peak. Her name is visible at the bow. *Crown of Scotland* was built in 1883 by Thomas Royden of Liverpool for Robertson, Cruickshank & Co., who

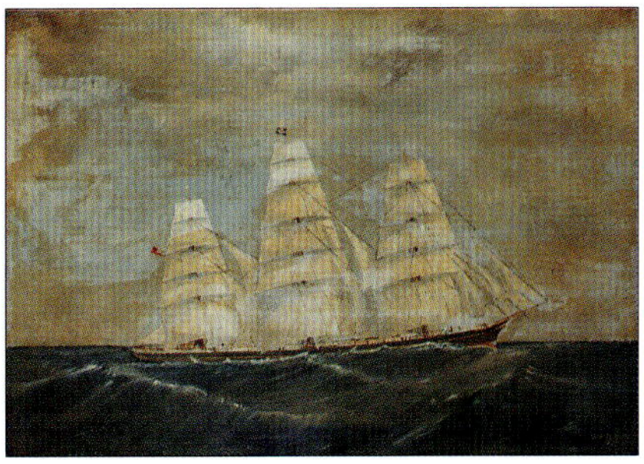

1955.148
Oil on canvas
51 cm x 71 cm
Signed (bl) "W. DEVITT"
Prov: W J Menzies, Liverpool, who presented it, 1962

Vessel: 249.7 ft (l), 38.3 ft (b), 22 ft (d); 1617 gross tons launched the Crown Line in the same year. The line had five vessels, four full-rigged ships and a 4 masted barque, trading to India, the East and Australia. *Crown of Scotland* was sold with three of the other *Crowns* to J & R Young of London in 1902. She was subsequently sold to Italian owners and renamed *Gavarone Fratelli* and then *Fortuna*. In 1912 she was hulked at Algiers and broken up in 1929.[1] Nothing is known about the artist and the naive style suggests that this is the work of an amateur but competent painter, perhaps a seaman.

1 Lubbock Windjammers, pp. 304, 482; CR no. 142, 17 September 1883.

Charles Dixon (1872-1934)

Dixon was the son of Alfred Dixon, the genre and history painter. He was an illustrator and worked for the *Graphic* and the *Illustrated London News* and was particularly interested in naval subjects. Much of his work was in watercolour.[1]

1 Brooke-Hart, pp. 97-8.

80 Alcantara in action

1963.137.4
Oil on canvas
76 cm x 127 cm
Signed and dated (bl) "Charles Dixon / 1916"
Prov: Royal Mail Lines Ltd., who presented it, 1963

Vessel: 570 ft (l); 67 ft (b), 33 ft (d); 15300 gross tons

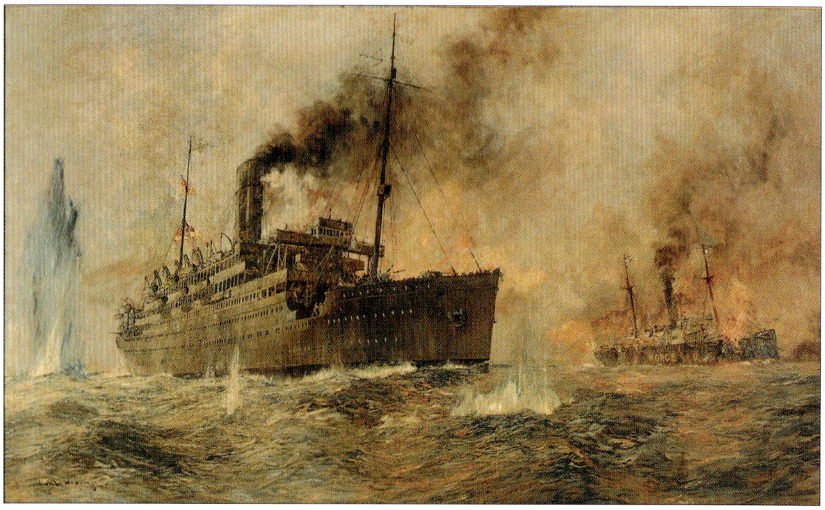

The liner *Alcantara* is shown as an armed merchant cruiser in action with the German raider *Greif* in the North Sea on 29 February 1916.

Alcantara was due to leave her patrol in the Skaggerak for Liverpool on 29 February 1916 but was ordered to intercept a disguised Norwegian merchant ship. This was, in fact, *Greif*, a German raider. *Alcantara* spotted the raider at 08.45 and was about to send a boarding party when *Greif* opened fire causing great damage to the British vessel. In the ensuing exchange, *Greif* was also hit and caught fire. As *Alcantara* listed to port, the order was given to abandon ship and she sank within two hours. *Greif* burned furiously and sank at 13.00. *Alcantara* lost 72 men and *Greif* 280.[1]

Dixon shows the action at the beginning of the encounter. He adopts a starboard quarter view for *Alcantara* which fills the centre and left of the canvas. She has been hit and smoking is pouring from her. Shells are dropping around her and a great plume of water to her stern marks a near miss. Men can be seen manning the guns at the bow. *Greif*, in the middle distance, is also in a starboard view and is on fire having sustained a hit near her bow.

Alcantara is named on her hull and carries three white ensigns. The German raider's hull is painted with two pseudo-flags in Norwegian national colours and carries the legend "Norge." However, she has raised the flag of the German Imperial Navy on her two masts.

Alcantara[2] was built by Harland & Wolff in Belfast for the Royal Mail Steam Packet Company in 1913. She made her maiden voyage to Buenos Aires but was converted to an armed cruiser in 1915.

1 T A Bushell *Royal Mail Line, 1839 - 1939*, London, 1939, pp. 213-5; Haws Royal Mail.
2 Alcantara is a town in western Spain.

Robert Dodd (1748-1815) (Attributed)

Dodd was born and lived in London. He is best known for his naval pictures, particularly commissioned battle pieces. His more general shipping scenes and paintings of single vessels are often set in heavy seas or depict an incident. Many of his works were engraved and published. The main collection of his works is at the National Maritime Museum.[1]

1 Archibald, p.95.

81 *An East Indiaman taking a pilot off Dover*

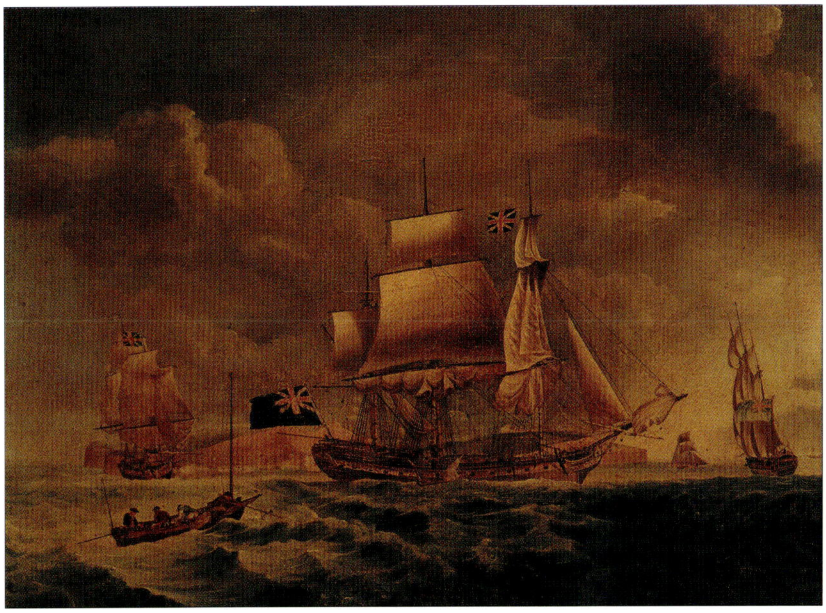

1966.12
Oil on canvas[1]
55 cm x 74 cm
Prov: Mrs L Mather, New Brighton, who presented it, 1966

This view attributed to Dodd shows an East Indiaman in three positions in the English Channel off Dover taking a pilot on board. To the left the vessel is shown in the distance in a starboard quarter view approaching the rendezvous, the main view shows her receiving the pilot and to the right hand is a port stern view as she makes her way towards the Thames. In the left foreground is a small single masted boat with four men, who are about to raise the sails.

In the centre of the canvas the vessel is shown in a starboard view, hove-to with the sails of her foremast hanging limply. The main and the mizzen courses are furled as she attempts to hold her position whilst the pilot is being taken on board from a small boat alongside. She flies a Union Jack at the foremast and the blue ensign from the stern.

The scene is set off Dover and the White Cliffs with the town just visible between the stern of the main view and the approaching vessel. The Castle can be seen behind the foremast of the main view.

An aquatint of this painting was engraved by C Morrison and published by R Pollard in London in February 1787. It is entitled "A homeward bound *EAST INDIAMAN*, Taking a *PILOT* off Dover" and was dedicated to Robert Preston MP for Dover and one of the Elder Bretheren of Trinity House.[2] A copy is in the collections (1953.41.1). In its present condition, it is difficult to tell whether this painting is the original or a copy or another version. The current impression is that this is not an autograph work of the artist.

The East India Company had a large fleet in the eighteenth century which were generally very handsome vessels. They were mostly built on the Thames for private owners and then chartered to the company. The identity of this particular vessel cannot be established, though it has a clear figurehead of a man in oriental dress.[3]

1 Relined. Label on rear stretcher for Boydell, Liverpool.
2 "A homeward bound *EAST INDIAMAN*, Taking a *PILOT* off Dover" / "To Robert Preston Esqr, a Member of Parliament for that ancient Port & one of the Elder Bretheren of the Trinity House, this Plate is most respectfully inscribed by His Obliged & Obedient humble Servant. R DODD." Published London, February 22, 1787, by R Pollard, No.7 Braynes Row, Spa Fields.
3 In 1793 the company had 76 ships. See J. Sutton *Lords of the East: The East India Company and its Ships*, London, 1981.

Thomas Dove (1811 - 1886)

Dove was born in Whitby, Yorkshire and was for a time a pupil of George Chambers. He moved to Liverpool in 1835 and had a successful career producing ship portraits and views of the port. He returned to his native Whitby in 1868 where he continued to paint until the infirmities of old age over took him.

Relatively few of his paintings are known at present and he is particularly poorly represented in public collections - there are two canvases in Whitby Museum and one in the New Brunswick Museum.[1]

1 For a full discussion of Dove's life see Davidson. 1986, pp. 72-6.

82 Combatant entering the Mersey

The ship *Combatant* is shown in two views entering the Mersey. In the main view the vessel is hove-to in port profile presumably awaiting the arrival of a pilot. Various members of the crew, in colourful clothing, can be seen about their duties on deck.

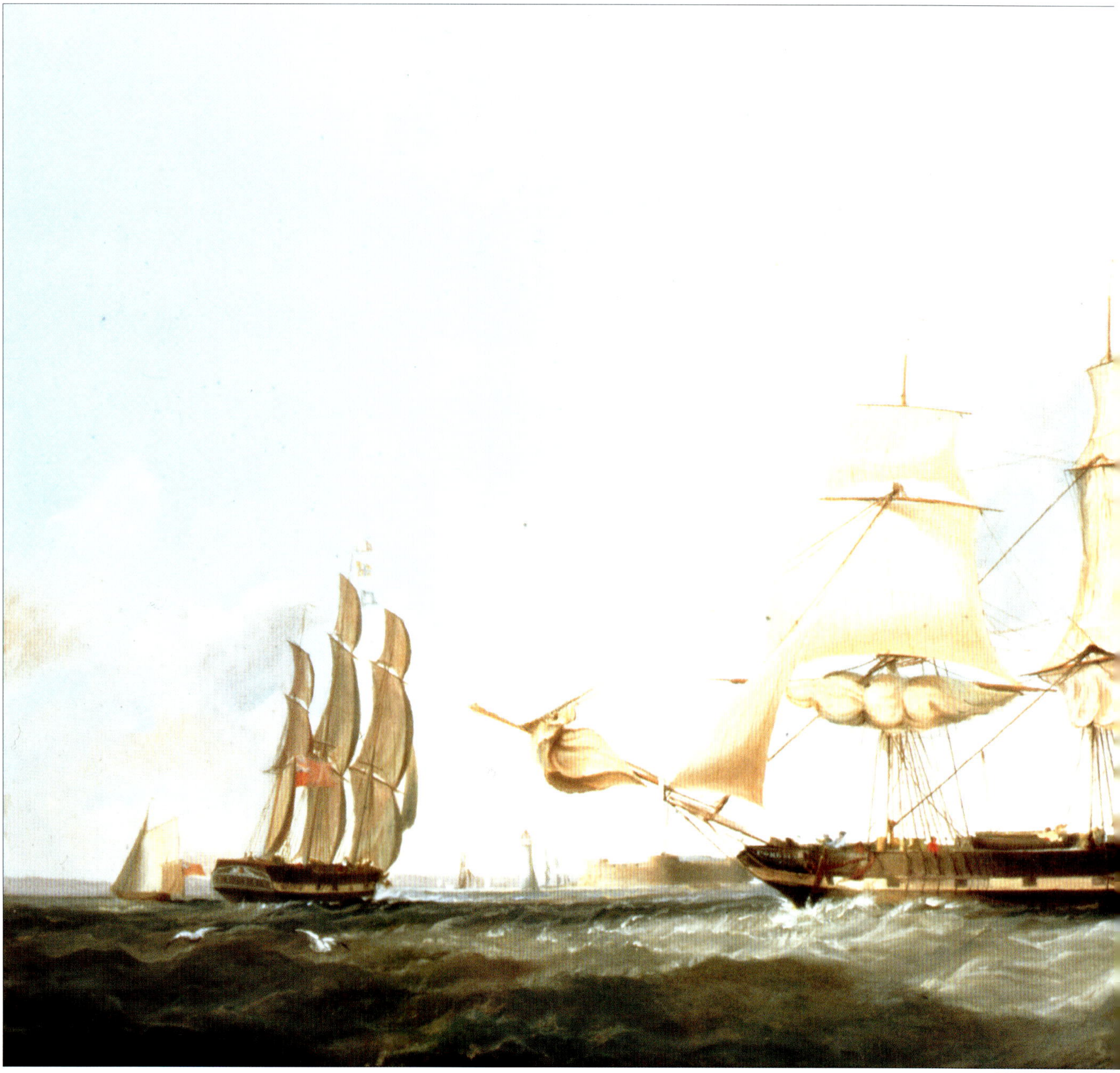

The vessel is identifiable by her name on the bow and by the Watson flag hoist (5, 3, 9) which flies from the main mast. She flies house flags of white ground with central horizontal red band at the fore and mizzen masts and the red ensign at the after peak. The second view shows the vessel from the starboard quarter under full sail, having turned and making her way into port. She wears the same flags as in the main view.

Astern of the main view is a dandy rigged vessel, which may be a Manx fishing boat. She flies a red pennant with the letter N in white on the fore mast and the red ensign.[1] The same vessel also appears off the second view. There is a lug rigged boat in the far right distance.

Combatant was built at Sutton, Holderness, Yorkshire, in 1821 and was originally owned by Stephen Gee and Thomas Loft of Hull. She was bought by Tinley and Holt of Liverpool in association with William Darby of Whitby in 1825. There were frequent transfers of shares but members of the Holt family generally

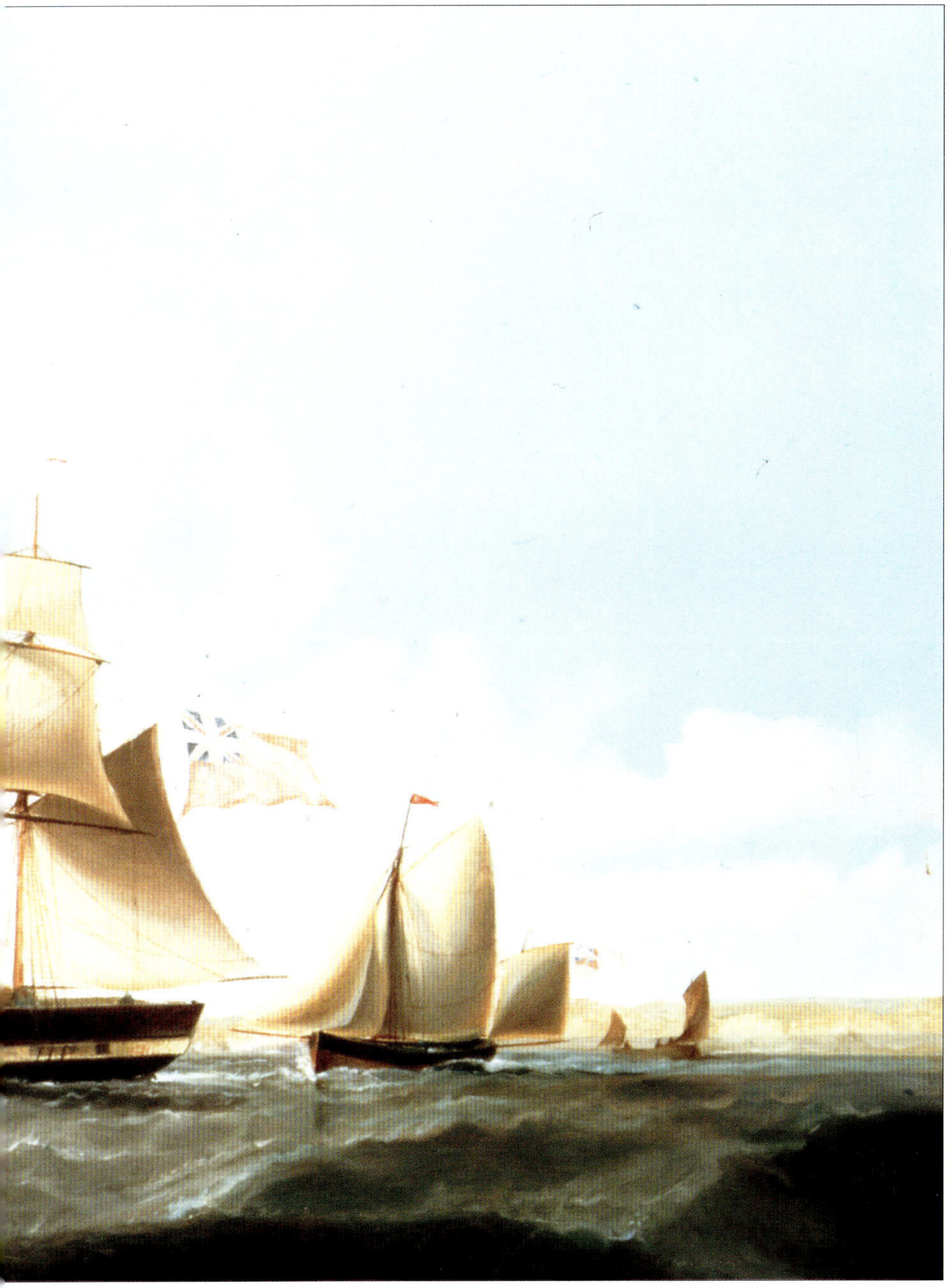

MMM.1997.110
Oil on canvas
69 cm x 116 cm
Signed and dated (br) "T. DOVE / 1837"
Prov: Purchased, Christies, South Kensington, 15 May 1997, lot 341.

Vessel: 102 ft 4 in (l), 29 ft 1 in (b), 18 ft 10 in (d); 372 gross tons

maintained the principal ownership. She was sold to Robert Hamilton, a master mariner of Liverpool in 1837 and then to George Castle, a ship owner of Limehouse in London in 1839. She was abandoned in mid-Atlantic en route for Quebec in October 1842.[2]

The familiar view of the Perch Rock fort and lighthouse appear clearly below *Combatant*'s bowsprit with the north Wirral coastline to the right.

This is one of Dove's earliest canvases and shows that he was already an artist of some competence. The composition is well-thought out and includes nice elements of detail, such as the reflection of the dandy's bow.

1 On first appearance this seems to be a white ensign but the colour is washed out and is almost certainly meant to be a red ensign.
2 LCR vol. 40, no. 77, 28 March 1825, vol. 47, no. 8, 9 January 1832, vol. 52, no. 35, 4 March 1837, vol. 53, no. 73, 10 May 1838; LL 25 October 1842.

Robert Dudley (active 1865-1891)

Dudley was a London based artist who exhibited regularly at the Royal Academy. He diversified from marine paintings in the later years of his life.[1]

1 Brook-Hart, p.346.

83 *"Canada Timber Docks, Liverpool. Towards Close of Day."*

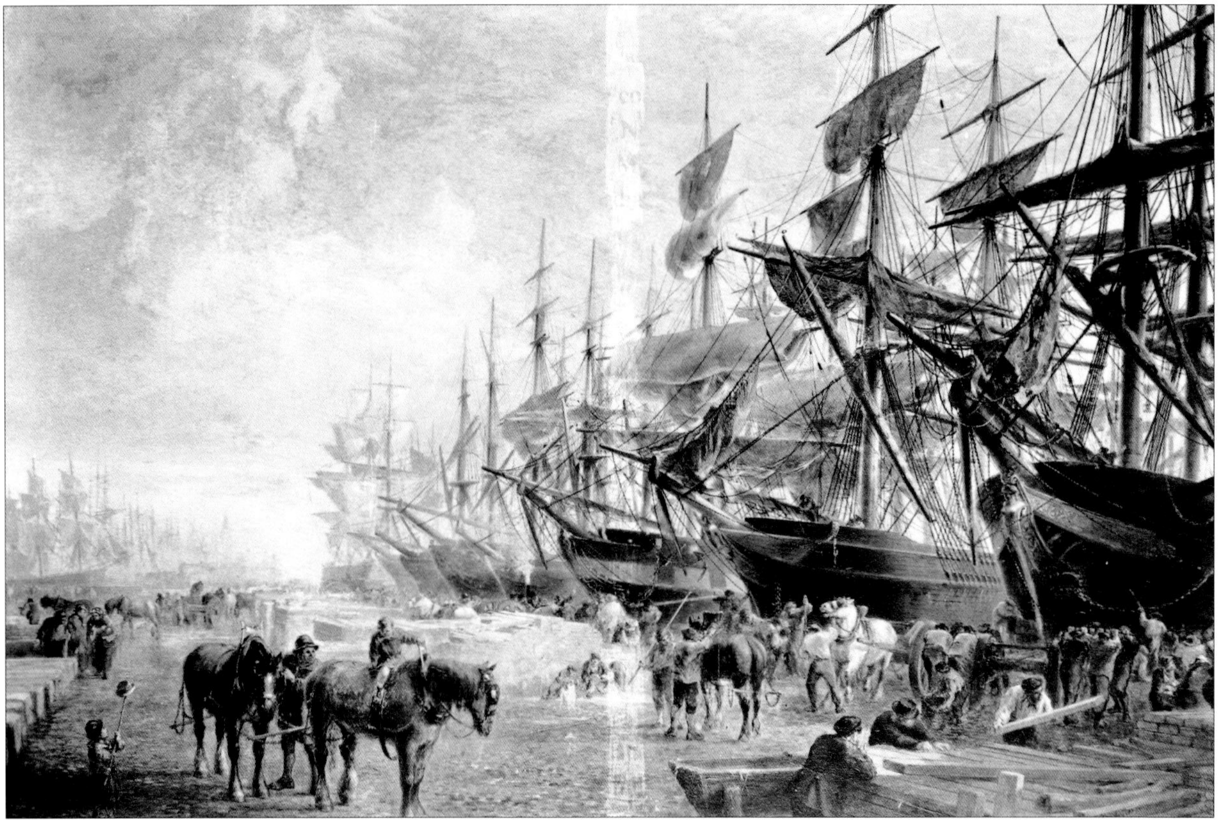

LI.1991.4.6
Oil on canvas
92.5 cm x 137.5 cm
Signed and dated (br on timber)
"R. Dudley. 1872."
Prov: Mersey Docks & Harbour Company, on permanent loan.
Exh: Royal Academy, 1872

As it's title makes clear, this is an atmospheric view of the Canada Dock which captures the hustle and bustle of the port at a time when unloading cargoes depended on physical human effort and manpower. The view looks north with the vessels lined up bow on to the quay side and a host of people, carts and horses mingling about the dock. All the vessels are typical sailing ships and though several have ornate figure heads, none are identifiable. In the foreground a number of men are moving timber and there are further piles of timber along the quay side. There is a wealth of incidental detail - the men straining at the winch or the small boy in the left foreground holding a hat on the end of a stick! In the distance to the left are further vessels and in the far distance other docks and buildings, including the tower of St Nicholas's Church, can be seen.

Canada was the last dock designed and built by Jesse Hartley and was opened in 1858. It was built to discharge and store timber taking over from Brunswick Dock in the south which was grossly overcrowded. It got its name because Canada was the major source of timber into Liverpool.[1]

1 K McCarron & A Jarvis *Give A Dock A Good Name*, Birkenhead, 1992, pp. 21-22.

Dutch School

84 Dutch Fisherman

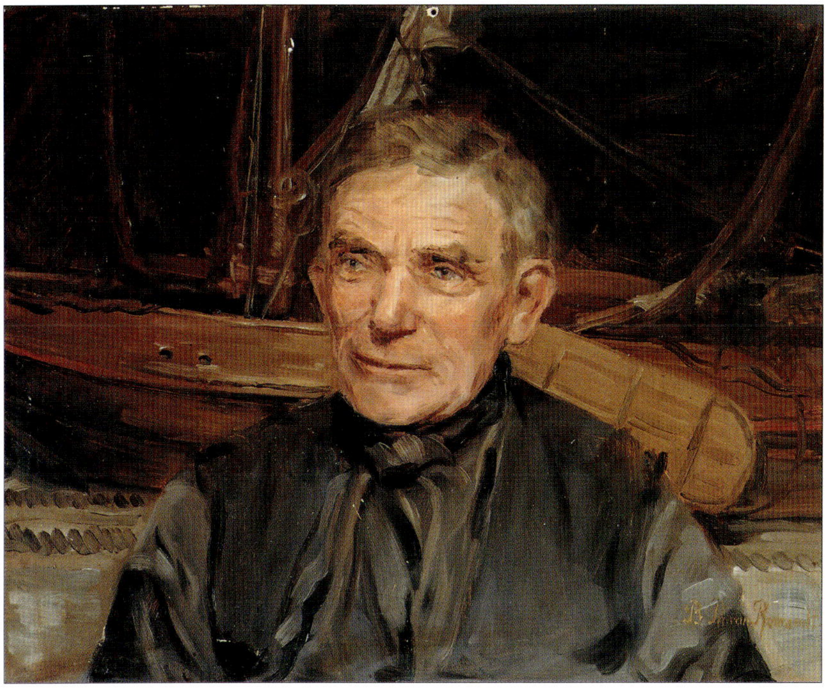

1955.710
Oil on board
40.5 cm x 49.5 cm
Signed (br) "B. Powan Roman[.......]."
Prov: Unknown; in collections, 1955.

This head and shoulders portrait shows an unidentified man with a model of a Dutch fishing boat in the background.

It has been suggested that this is a portrait of Joost Dingemanse, a model maker, who lived at Middelberg in the Netherlands, but this is insufficiently substantiated. The model in the background is probably a hoogaars or shrimping trawler. There are ten ship models by Dingemanse in the collections (1943.10).

Gordon Ellis (1921-1979)

Ellis was born and bred on Merseyside and his early career was in a printing studio and as a draughtsman with John Brown, shipbuilders. He became a full time artist in 1948 and although living in Berwick-on-Tweed, maintained a close relationship with Liverpool. He also painted landscapes and portraits.[1]

1 Davidson, 1986, pp.120-4.

85 Centaur in the tropics (page 80)

This view shows *Centaur* in port profile in tropical waters against an atmospheric pink sky. Her name is boldly shown on the bow and the funnel is painted in the house colours of the Blue Funnel Line, her initial owners.

Centaur[1] was built by John Brown & Co of Clydebank, Glasgow in 1964 for the West Australian trade of Ocean Steam Ship Company (Blue Funnel Line). She was intended to carry livestock and passengers between Fremantle and Singapore and is an example of a Liverpool registered vessel which served her time entirely in foreign

MMM.1995.108
Oil on canvas[2]
50.5 cm x 76 cm
Signed (br) "GORDON ELLIS"
Prov: Mrs E Tudor-Thomas, St Asaph, who presented it, 1995.

Vessel: 480.9 ft (l), 66.3 ft (b), 26.4 ft (d); 8262 gross tons

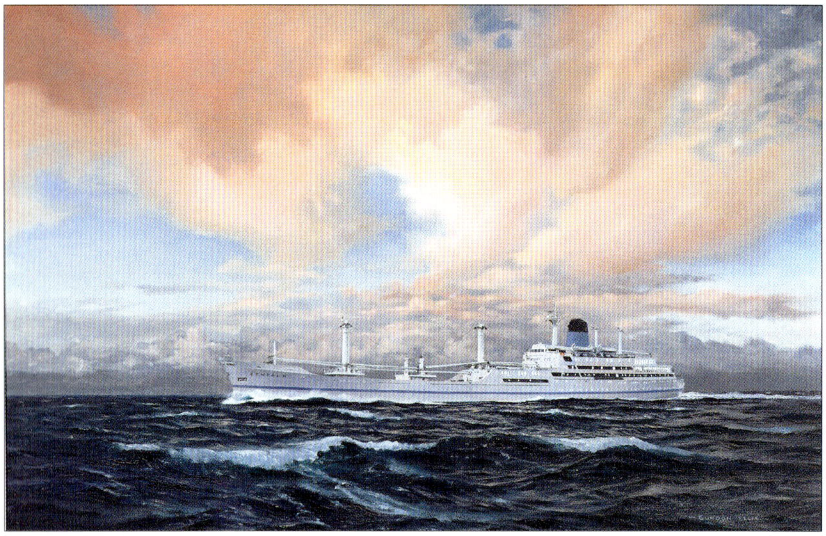

1 Centaur, a mythological beast, half man and half horse.
2 Printed label on rear stretcher for Boydell Gallery, Liverpool, with hand written addition "Original Oil Painting:- / CENTAUR IN THE TROPICS / GORDON ELLIS". The Boydell Gallery was the main outlet for Ellis's work over a long period of his career.
3 Haws Blue Funnel, pp.127-8, Falkus, pp. 326-8; still in service 1996.

waters. In management terms she was transferred between different parts of the Ocean Group and made her final voyage from Fremantle in 1981. She was sold to Shanghai Hai Xing Shipping Company in 1985 and renamed, firstly *Hai Long* and then *Hai Da*.[3]

William Garthwaite (active about 1850-1889)

A few works by this artist are known, mainly coastal shipping scenes and he also painted a version of the famous Liverpool incident, *The Burning of the Ocean Monarch*.[1] No biographical information has been forthcoming.

1 Brook-Hart, p.348. For details of the *Ocean Monarch* and paintings by Walters and Melling see Davidson, 1992, pp.141-6.

86 *Shipping off North Wales*

1959.72.4
Oil on canvas[1]
44 cm x 64.5 cm
Signed and dated (bl) "Wm Garthwaite 18[]9"
Prov: Dr D Chapman, Liverpool, who presented it, 1959.

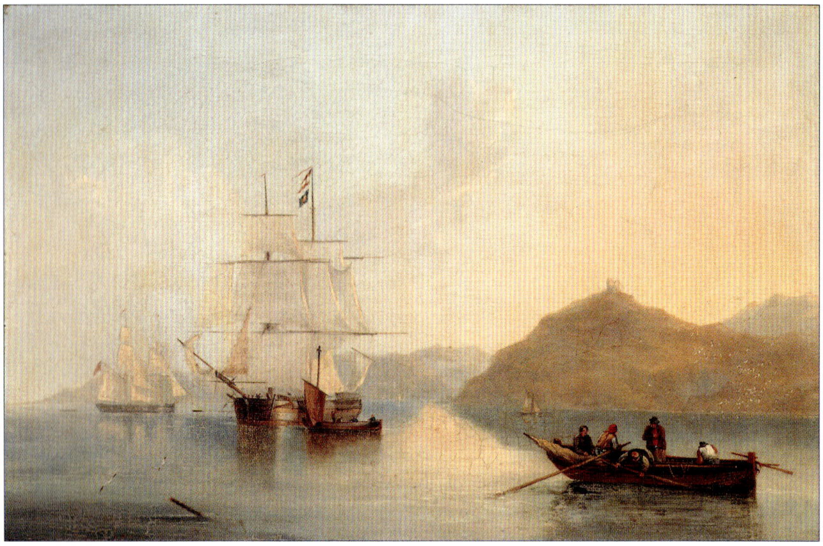

This tranquil scene is not the work of a ship portraitist and is more typical of mainstream marine painting. A brig is shown left of centre in a port quarter view under full sail but not apparently moving, with a small boat alongside. She has a studdingsail on the fore topsail and is raising another studdingsail on the port side of the vessel. There is another brig in starboard profile, again under full sail, to the left. In the right hand foreground a small rowing boat with five men is shown. There is a rocky coastline and a hillside with a castle to the right but the location is not identified. Traditionally said to be North Wales this is unlikely to be substantiated.

The ship wears a red pennant and two flags which are not standard and are probably only to add interest and colour. The painting dates from the mid-nineteenth century and the most likely date is 1849 or 1859.

1 Label on stretcher "GEORGE HUGHES / FINE ART DEALERS / BERWICK HOUSE / 50-52 PILGRIM STREET / NEWCASTLE ON TYNE."

J T Godfrey (active 1890)

87 *Stackie Barge in the Medway*

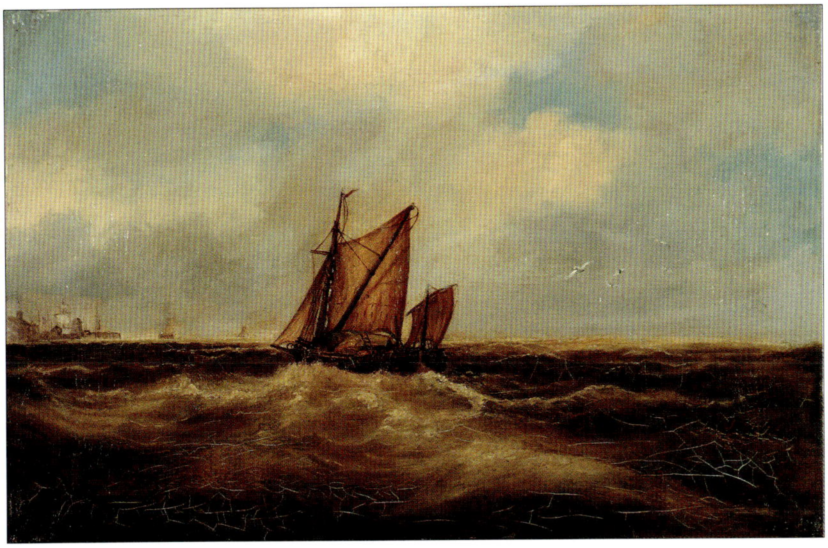

1959.72.5
Oil on canvas[1]
31 cm x 46 cm
Signed and dated "J. T. GODFREY/90"
Prov: Dr D Chapman, Liverpool, who presented it, 1959.

The "Stackie" was a name given to the flat-bottomed barge with a sprit rigged sail which was the characteristic craft of the Thames and Medway estuaries from the late nineteenth century until the 1930s. It was so named because of the huge stacks of hay which were carried into London to feed and accommodate the large number of horses required for transport purposes. The sprit rig allowed the vessel to be worked by a crew of only two.[2]

A barge is shown here in a port stern view under full sail making her way into the Medway estuary. She is loaded with hay against which a ladder is leaning. There is a unidentified quay and a group of buildings in the far left hand distance.

1 Rear canvas stamped "FROM / MILLER / 71 SAUCHIEHALL ST / GLASGOW" and attached printed label for Jackson & Sons, 13 Slater St, Bold St, Liverpool.
2 For details see E J March *Spritsail Barges of the Thames and Medway*, London, 1948

J W Green (active 1925)

88 *Outward Bound*

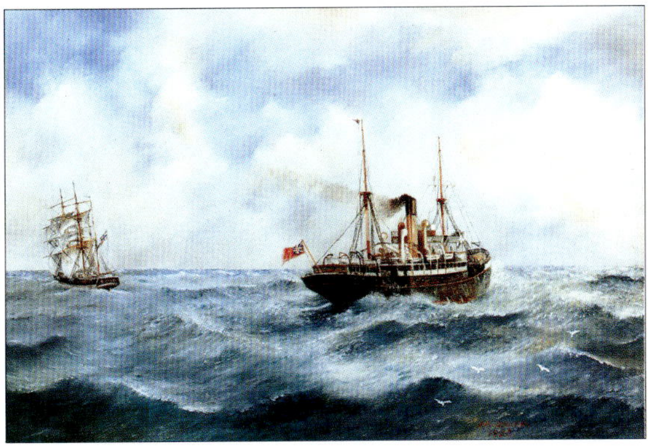

1968.201
Oil on canvas
32 cm x 47 cm
Signed and dated (br) "J. W. GREEN / 1925"
Prov: Thornton Cleveleys Urban District Council, who presented it, 1968.

A cross channel steamer is shown in a starboard quarter view in the centre right of the canvas with a port quarter view of a Norwegian registered barque in the left middle distance. The canvas is nicely composed with both vessels pulling away from the viewpoint. Neither vessel can be positively identified but the steamer wears the funnel colours of the London and North-Eastern Railway and is probably on a North Sea crossing.

Parker Greenwood (1850-1904)

Greenwood probably spent his early life at sea and only developed a second career as an artist in his early thirties, initially perhaps on a part time basis. He is listed in local directories as a "marine artist" from 1892. His subjects include liners, particularly Cunarders, and he also had a fondness for general shipping scenes in the Mersey, often in romantic light conditions. There are works in most of the main maritime museum collections.[1]

1 Davidson, 1986, pp 105-6.

89 *Anselm* (page 83)

Anselm is shown in port profile off an unknown coast. She is identified by her name on the bow but the flag hoist (beginning N W and with two indeterminate flags) does not correspond to her known code of W H B L. The vessel is under steam but some sails are assisting. There are figures, probably passengers, on the stern deck and members of the crew about their duties.

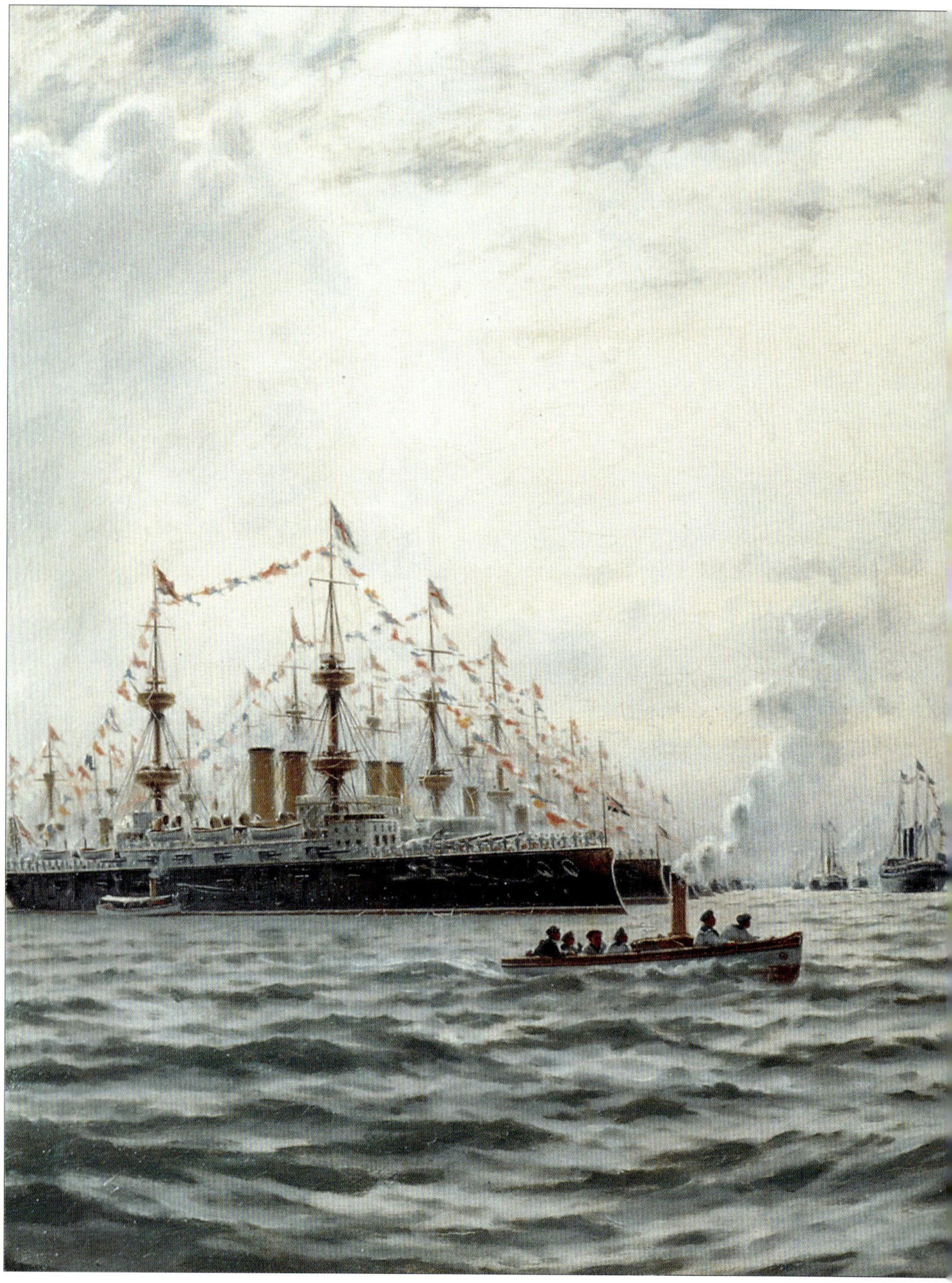

90 *Campania at the Spithead review, 1897*

(see page 84)

1968.184.5
Oil on canvas
61.5 cm x 115 cm
Signed and dated "P Greenwood / 1897"
Prov: Cunard Steam Ship Co Ltd, Private Collection, on permanent loan.
Exh: Liverpool 1986
Ref: Port Panorama, 1986, ill., p.11

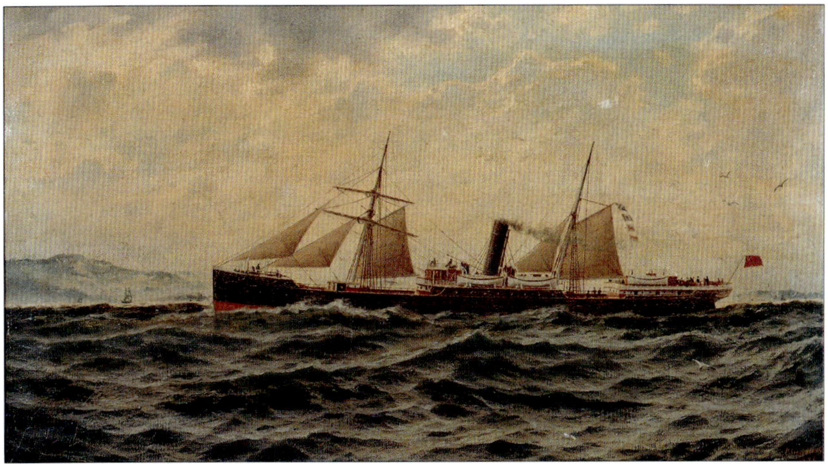

1976.232
Oil on canvas[1]
46 cm x 81.5 cm
Signed and dated (br) "P. Greenwood / 1892"
Prov: Purchased from This & That Antiques, Hoylake, Wirral, 1976

Vessel: 271.0 ft (l); 33.8 ft (b); 22.9 ft (d); 1562 gross tons.

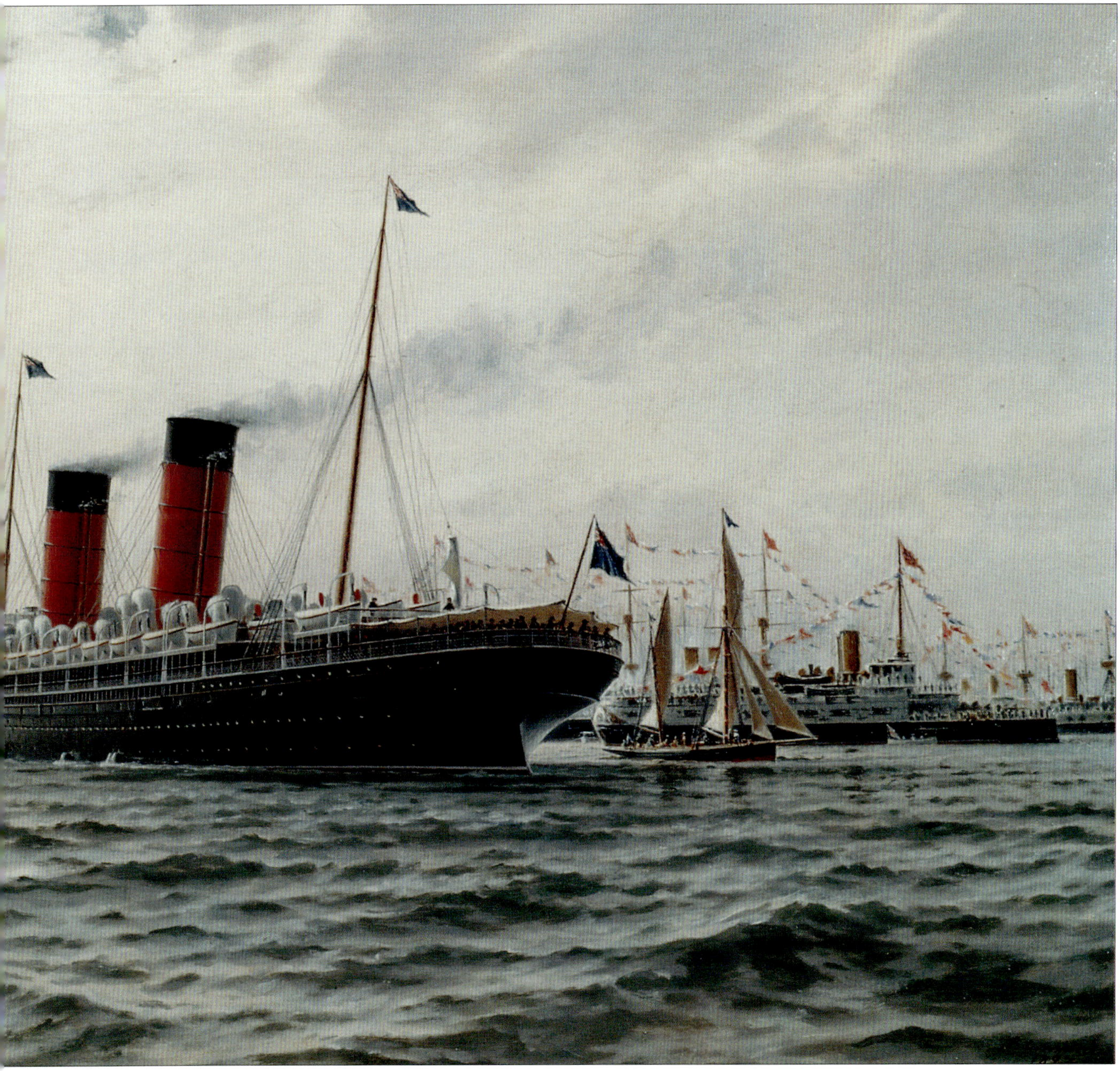

Anselm was built for the Booth Steamship Company of Liverpool in 1882 by A Leslie & Co. of Hebburn, on the south bank of the Tyne, with engines by Robert Stephenson of Newcastle. She was named after the Anglo-Saxon Church leader, in line with the company tradition of giving most of their ships the names of Early Christian Fathers. Booths were a small shipping company which operated services to the Amazon, principally for the Brazilian rubber trade. *Anselm* was built with improved passenger accommodation to cope with the increased passenger trade with was centred on Para (Belem). She remained with Booths until 1898 when she was sold. She was broken up in New York in 1908 after becoming stranded off Honduras.[2]

1 Label on rear for David T Blackburn, picture framer.
2 P M Heaton Booth Line, 1987, pp. 18, 54. CR, no. 204, 21 December 1882.

90 Campania at the Spithead review, 1897 (pages 82-83)

Vessel: 601 ft (l), 65.2 ft (b); 12950 tons

The Review of the Fleet at Spithead for Queen Victoria's Diamond Jubilee on 26 June 1897 was one of the greatest naval occasions ever held. Several famous merchant vessels attended, partly to accommodate the guests.[1] This view of the event shows *Campania*, then the pride of the Cunard fleet, steaming between the lines of the battleships. Greenwood places her in the centre foreground in a port quarter view, with other merchant vessels disappearing into the distance. She flies the blue ensign indicating that her captain and a contingent of crew are members of the Royal Naval Reserve. The battleships are dressed over all and the decks lined with their crews. A small steam pinnace with cadets is crossing in the foreground and there is a schooner rigged yacht astern of *Campania*.

Campania and her sister ship *Lucania* were ordered in 1891 as Cunard's response to the recent launches of her rivals on the transatlantic service - White Star's *Teutonic* of 1889 and the Inman liner *City of New York III*, 1888. *Campania* was built by Fairfield Ship Building & Engineering Co. of Glasgow and was launched in 1893 with claims that she and her sister ship were "the most magnificently appointed passenger liners in the world." She made 250 voyages across the Atlantic, retiring just before the outbreak the First World War. She was bought by the Admiralty and converted to an Armed Merchant Cruiser by Cammell Lairds. In 1918 she broke from her mooring in the Firth of Forth, hit *H M S Revenge* and sank.[2]

This is one of Greenwood's most impressive works, the sense of occasion bringing out the best of his talents.

1 Including White Star's *Teutonic*. For a photographic album commemorating *Teutonic's* visit see no. 133.
2 Bonsor North, pp. 97-9, 154, Haws Cunard pp. 50-51.

91 Celtic in the Mersey

1971.18
Oil on canvas
53.5 cm x 79 cm
Signed and dated (br) "P. Greenwood / 1887"
Prov: J Davey & Son, Liverpool, from whom purchased, 1971

Vessel: 437.2 ft (l), 40.9 ft (b), 31 ft (d); 3867 gross tons

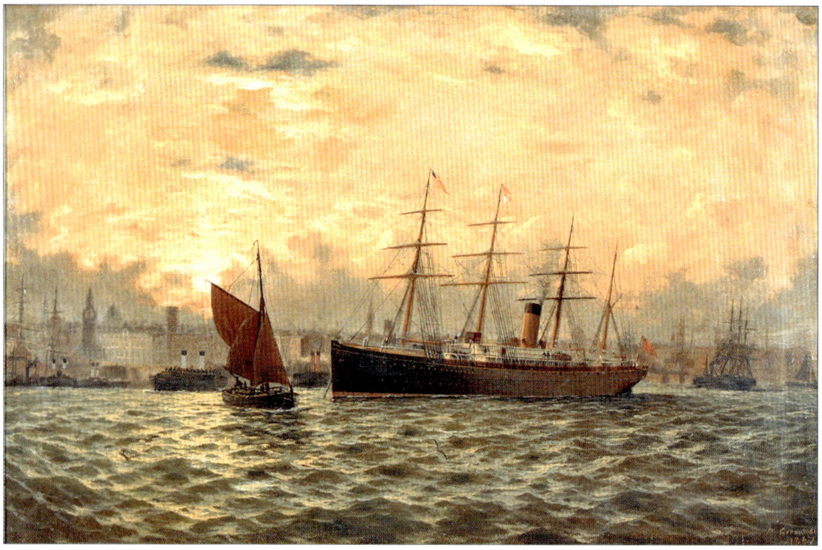

S S Celtic is shown in a port quarter view at anchor in the Mersey off the Liverpool Landing Stage. A Mersey flat is off her bow and a number of Mersey ferry boats can be seen in the left background. To the right a tug is towing a sailing ship. *Celtic* flies the Stars and Stripes, the White Star house flag and the red ensign and is preparing to depart across the Atlantic. In the background the Liverpool waterfront includes to the left of the vessel, St Nicholas Church and Tower Buildings and to the right the Albert Dock buildings.

Celtic and a sister ship *Adriatic* were built by Harland and Wolff in 1872 to add to White Star's initial fleet of four steamers on the service to New York. They were slightly longer than their predecessors but carried the same number of passengers - 166 in first and 1,000 in third class. They had a service speed of fourteen knots and were rigged as 4 masted barques, as shown here. *Celtic* served until the arrival of *Majestic* (1889) and *Teutonic* (1890) and she made her last voyage in February 1891. She was sold to Danish owners and scrapped in 1898.[1]

Greenwood was fond of using atmospheric light conditions and here uses the golden light of early morning to highlight the scene.

1 Bonsor North, pp. 756-7.

92 *A Cunarder in a storm*

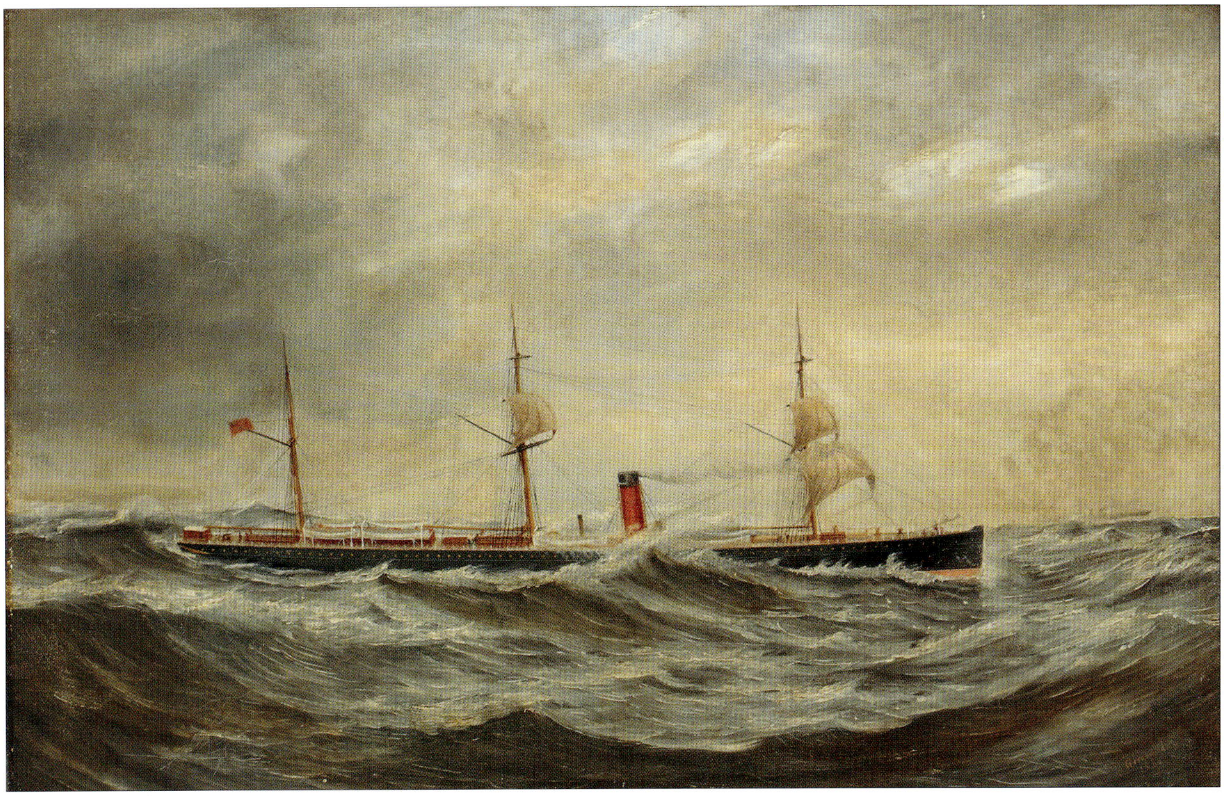

55.408
Oil on canvas
51.5 cm x 77.5 cm
Signed and dated (br) 'Greenwood / 1880'
Prov: In collections, 1955.

Vessel: *Abyssinia* 367.5 ft (l), 42.2 ft (b), 34.5 ft (d); 3376 gross tons

This early painting by Greenwood shows a Cunarder in a starboard profile in heavy conditions. Although some of the sails are set, one of the crew is busying the foresails. In line with the weather conditions there is little other activity except for the figure at the wheel on the stern deck.

The vessel is identifiable as a Cunarder from her funnel colours and she flies the red ensign at the after peak. She is one of three sister ships - *Abyssinia*, *Algeria* or *Parthia* - which were all built on the Clyde in 1870 and served on the Liverpool - Queenstown -New York service. They were quickly outclassed by the new vessels of the White Star Line which began operating the Atlantic in 1871. *Abyssinia* was acquired by her builders J & G Thomson in part payment for *Servia* and *Catalonia* in 1880 and sold on to the Guion Line. *Algeria* was sold to Red Star Line in 1881 and *Parthia* was laid up in 1883 and taken in part payment by Elders for *Umbria* and *Etruria* the following year.[1]

There is a painting of *Algeria* by Samuel Walters (no. 224) and a hull model of *Abyssinia* (1969.92) in the collections. There is also a Walters carte de visite of his painting of *Abyssinia* (Liverpool CRO).[2]

1 Bonsor North, pp. 92, 151.
2 Davidson 1992, p. 201

93 *Germanic in the Mersey*

51.25.1
Oil on canvas
40 cm x 66 cm
Signed and dated 'P Greenwood / 1886'
Prov: J James, Liverpool, from whom purchased, 1951.
Exh: Liverpool, 1986
Ref: Port Panorama, 1986, p.12.

Vessel: 455 ft (l), 45.2 ft (b), 33.7 ft (d); 5008 gross tons

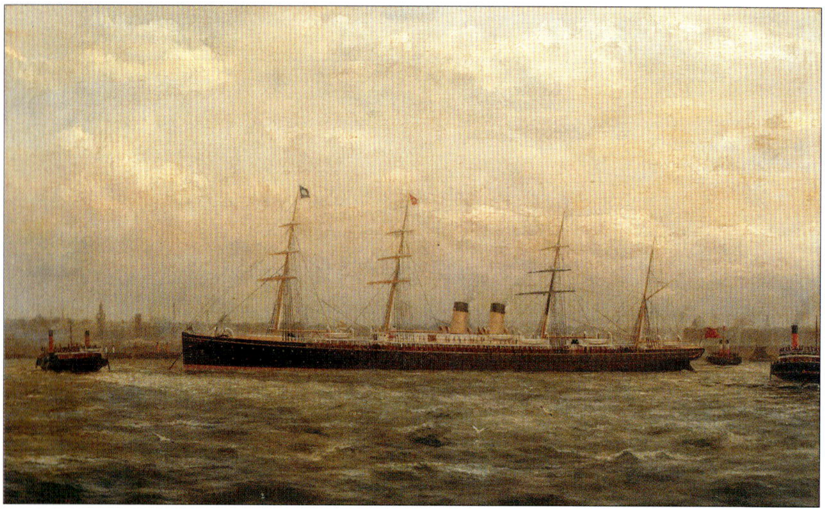

This composition is typical of Greenwood's work with *S S Germanic* shown at anchor in port profile in a busy river scene off the Liverpool landing stage. Woodside ferries are shown prominently to bow and stern with other ferries at the landing stage and a Liverpool steam tug astern in bow view. *Germanic* is flying the Ismay house flag at the main and the blue peter at the foremast, indicating she is preparing for departure.

The usual Liverpool scene is placed as a back drop behind the vessel. The landmarks visible include from the left the dome of St Paul's, the towers of St Nicholas and of Tower Buildings, the Town Hall and, astern, the Custom House and Albert Dock.

Germanic was built by Harland & Wolff in Belfast for the Oceanic Steam Ship Company (White Star Line) in 1875. Although White Star had a strong fleet of new vessels in *Oceanic* and her sisters, *Germanic* and her sister *Britannic* were commissioned to maintain the company's claim to have the fastest ships on the New York run after recent responses from her rivals. She completed several record runs and remained in service until sold to the Dominion Line in 1905. Six years later she was sold to the Turkish Ottoman-American Line and renamed *Gul Djemal*. She was not scrapped until 1950.[1]

As well as no. 94, there is another painting of *Germanic* leaving Liverpool by Greenwood, which is signed and dated 1888, in the Peabody collection[2] and he painted her entering Queenstown in 1891.[3] Samuel Walters also painted the vessel three times - at sea, off the Fastnet Rock and with her sister *Britannic*.[4]

1 Bonsor North, pp. 757-8.
2 Smith, no. 2070, p. 32, ill.
3 Signed and dated 1891, sold Sotheby's, London, 31 May 1989, Lot 274, ill.
4 Photographic print of vessel at sea (MMM.1989.239.19-20), other views on cartes de visite at LRO, see Davidson 1992, p. 202.

94 *Germanic rescuing the crew of S S Hurworth*

This action painting shows a mid-ocean rescue when *S S Germanic* went to the aid of *S S Hurworth*. Greenwood places *Germanic* in a half stern portrait just right of the centre of the canvas, hove-to and just keeping her head on in the gale force

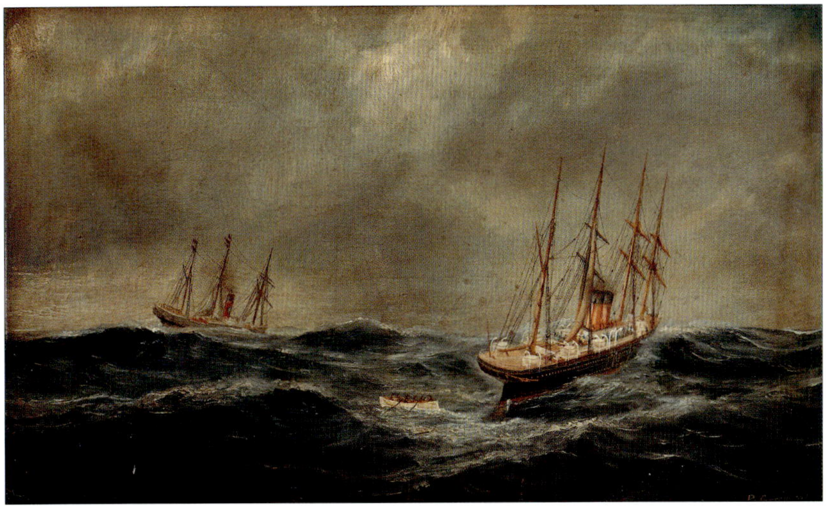

55.246
Oil on board
31.5 cm x 50.5 cm
Signed and dated (br) 'P. Greenwood / 1881'
Prov: In collection, 1955

Vessels:
Hurworth 275.8 ft (l), 34 ft (b), 24 ft (d); 2 compound inverted cylinder engines, 160 hp; 1265 gross tons
Germanic 455 ft (l), 45.2 ft (b), 33.7 ft (d); 5008 gross tons

conditions. A lifeboat with five men on board is making its way towards *Hurworth* which is shown in port profile in the middle distance.

This painting commemorates an heroic incident on 1 December 1881 when the White Star liner *Germanic*, returning to Liverpool from New York, was attracted by a distress rocket from *Hurworth*. The latter had left Montreal with a cargo of grain but had encountered foul weather losing her rudder and rudder post and had drifted for eleven days before encountering *Germanic*. A lifeboat from her rescuer, under the command of the first officer Robert Bence, made three hazardous journeys to save the 25 crew of the stricken vessel. For his bravery Bence was presented with a binocular telescope by the Liverpool Shipwreck and Humane Society.[1]

Germanic was built by Harland & Wolff for the White Star line in 1875. (see no. 93). The schooner rigged iron steamer *Hurworth* was built in Sunderland in 1878 as *Northbourne* for D P Garbutt of Hull. At the time of the event she was owned by T H Davison of Newcastle. Understandably she did not survive this incident.

1 Details of the incident were carried in *The Liverpool Mercury*, December 1881. The certificate and binoculars presented to Robert Bence, together with photographs of him and his fellow rescuers, are in the collections.

95 *Shipping in the Mersey, 1904*

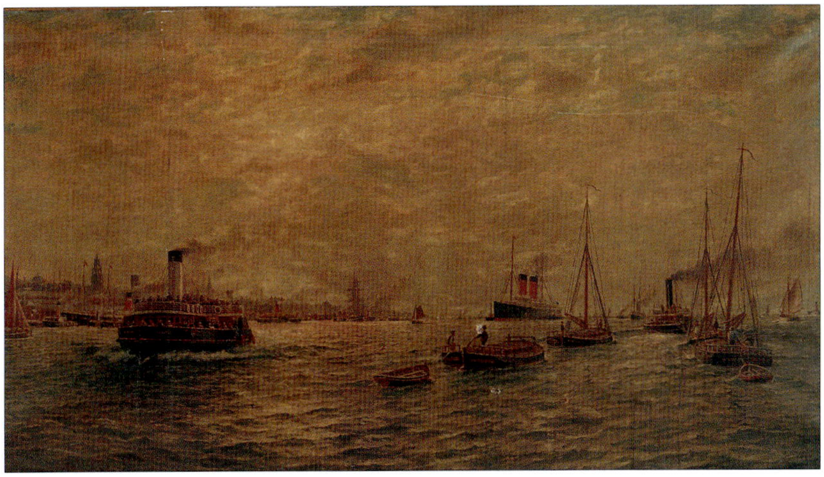

1957.13.1
Oil on canvas
64 cm x 115 cm
Signed and dated (br) 'P. Greenwood / 1904'
Prov: Miss E J Vipond, Liverpool, from whom purchased 1957.

This busy view of shipping in the Mersey is one of the last works by Parker Greenwood. He has chosen to look upstream from mid-river just below the landing stage and shows a variety of ships and boats that would have been seen in the river on a typical day. He concentrates on the everyday users - the local flats, tugs and ferries rather than the big ocean-going vessels. In the foreground to the left is the

Wallasey bound ferry *Thistle* and to the right are a group of Mersey flats being pulled upstream by a tug. The central group shows a flat towing a dumb flat and a cock boat (tender). On one of the right hand flats a woman is clearly identifiable by her white apron. In the right middle ground a Cunard liner is heading down stream; this is either *Campania* or her sister *Lucania*.[1] In the far distance various other ships and small craft can be seen, including a tug at the landing stage and centrally a 3 masted sailing ship escorted by tugs either side.

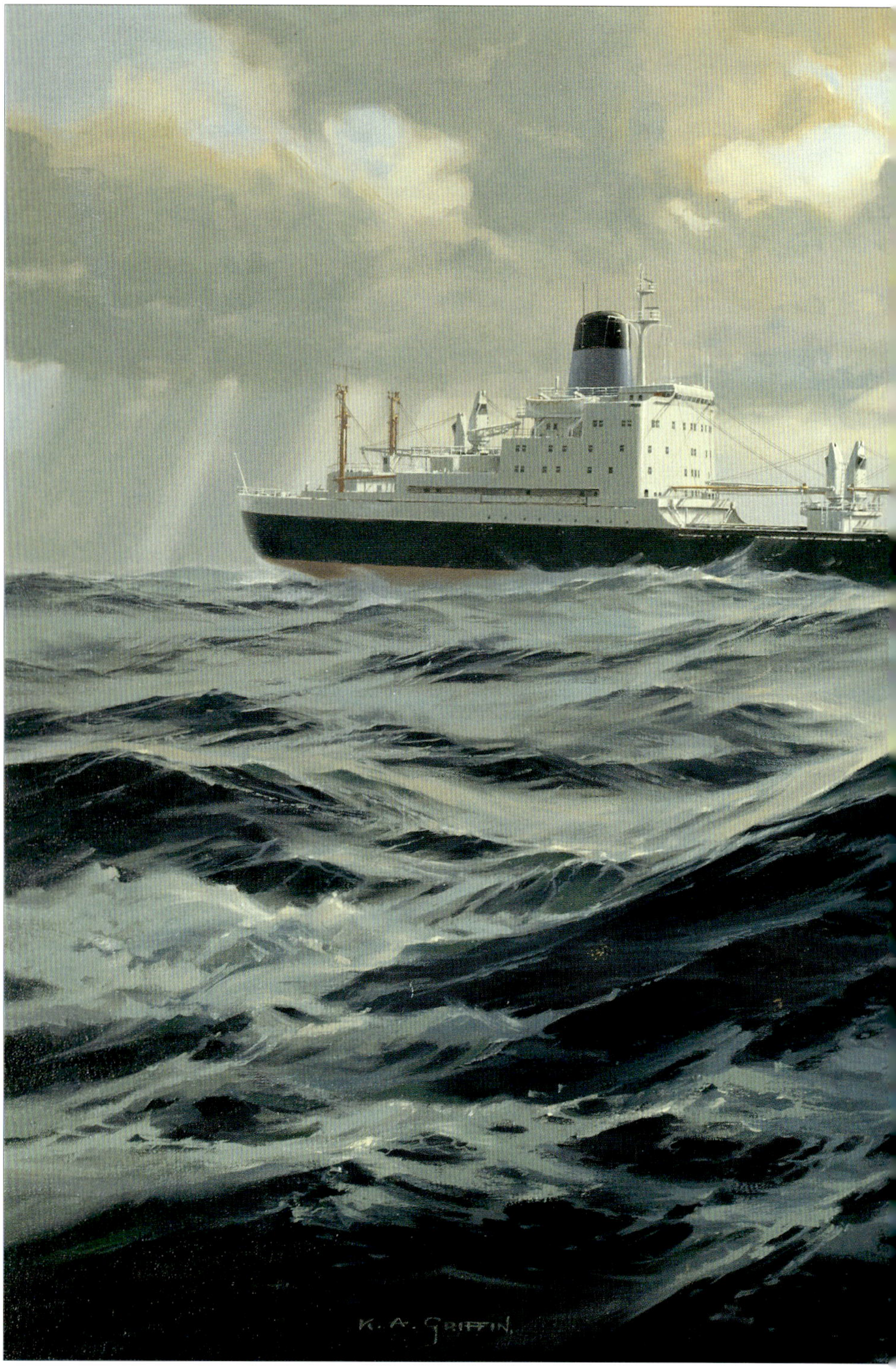

96 *Priam at sea*

(see page 90)

MMM1995.95.4
Oil on canvas
66.5 cm x 91.5 cm
Signed (bl) "K. A. GRIFFIN"
Prov: Ocean Steamship Company; P H Holt Charitable Trust, from whom purchased, 1995.

Few landmarks can be distinguished on the Liverpool shore line, apart from the landing stage and the spire of St Nicholas. The dome of the Custom House can be hazily seen. The paddle steamer *Thistle* was built by John Scott of Kirkcaldy at Kinghorn, Fife in 1891. She served on the ferry service across the Mersey for the Wallasey Local Board until broken up in 1911.[2]

This view is very characteristic of Greenwood's work with its thoughtful disposition of interesting detail across the canvas and the dark and threatening sky.

1 *Campania* and *Lucania* both built 1893 by Fairfield, Glasgow. see Bonsor North, p.154.
2 LCR vol. 97, no. 29, 6 May 1891.

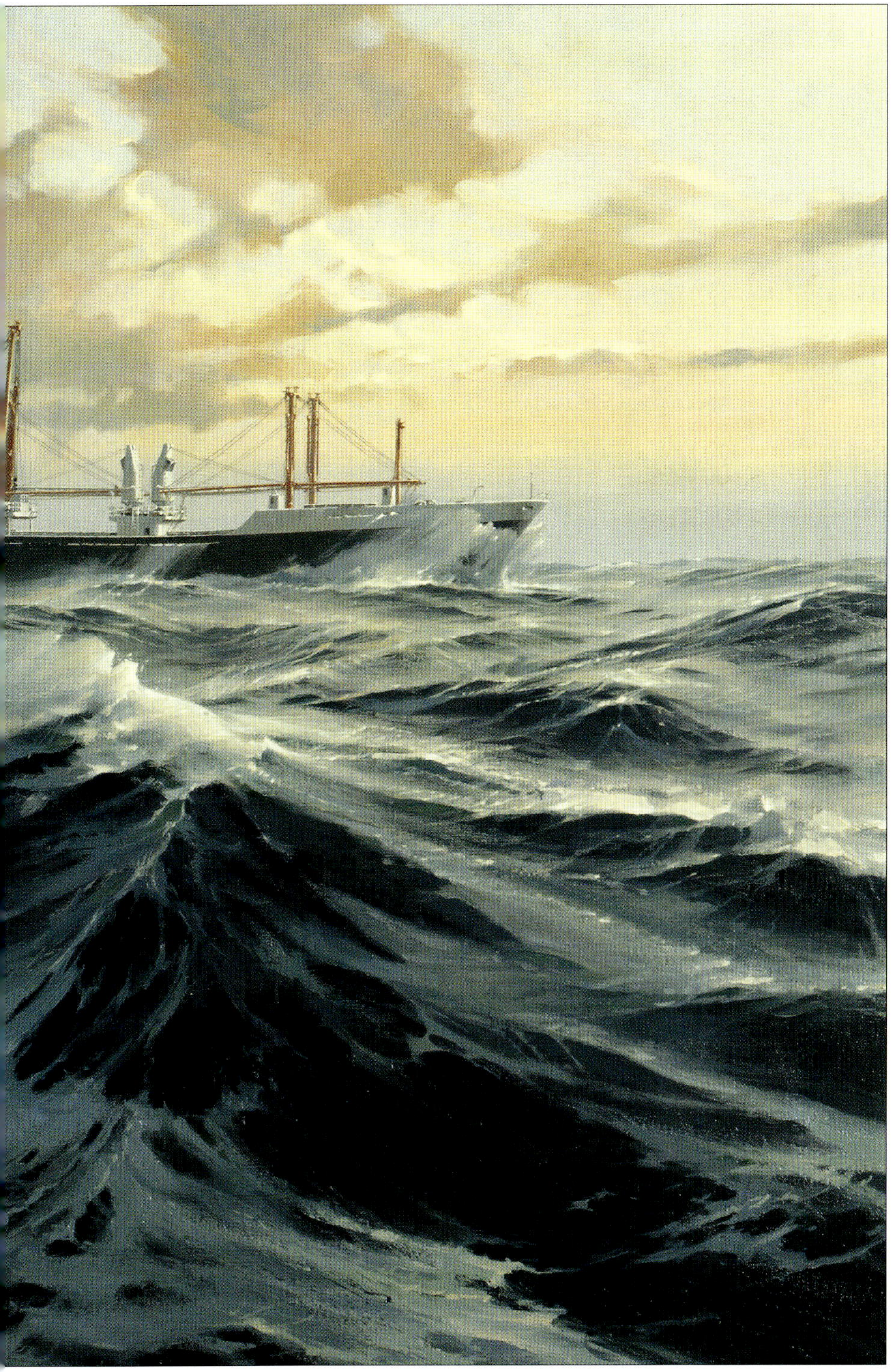

Keith A Griffin

Merseyside born and based marine artist who studied at the Laird School of Art, Birkenhead. He specialises in paintings of deep sea sailing ships and has also undertaken commissions of modern vessels.[1]

1 See catalogue *The Tall Ships: Exhibition of Marine Paintings by Keith A Griffin*, Williamson Art Gallery, Birkenhead, 28 July - 26 August 1984

96 *Priam at sea* (pages 88-89)

Vessel: 563.8 ft (l), 77.9 ft (b), 30 ft (d); 12,094 gross tons

The cargo liner *Priam* is shown in starboard profile at sea. The artist has chosen a low viewpoint to accentuate the angular waves of a heavy sea and the vessel is placed low on the level of the horizon.

Priam was built by Vickers Armstrong at Newcastle upon Tyne for the Ocean Steam Ship Company in 1966. She was the fifth Blue Funnel vessel named after the King of Troy and was the lead ship in a class of eight new ships. They were designed in the late 1950s to provide the company with some of the most technically advanced and commercially economic vessels afloat. The programme was delayed and the launch of these conventional liners virtually coincided with the introduction of containerization. After only twelve years service, *Priam* and three others in the class were sold to C Y Tung in 1978. She changed hands again and was sent for scrapping at Kaohsiung in 1985.[1]

There is an exhibition model of the vessel in the collections, accession no. 1967.218.

1 For a discussion on the Priam class ships see Falkus 1990, pp. 320-332.

John Atkinson Grimshaw (1836-1893), After

A native of Leeds, Grimshaw's early work was as a Pre-Raphaelite landscape artist. He began painting the moonlight scenes which became his hallmark in the late 1860s and some of his best known images in this genre are the dock and harbour scenes of Liverpool, London, Glasgow and several east coast ports. He had many imitators and copyists, including Walter Meegan and Wilfred Jenkins of Leeds.[1]

1 See A Robertson *Atkinson Grimshaw*, London, 1988

97 *Salthouse Dock, Liverpool*

1990.139
Oil on canvas[1]
51 cm x 76.5 cm
With signature and date (bl) "Atkinson Grimshaw / 1884"
Prov: Arthur Jefferies (Pictures); Messrs Everetts; Mrs K Jones, Birkenhead, who presented it, 1990

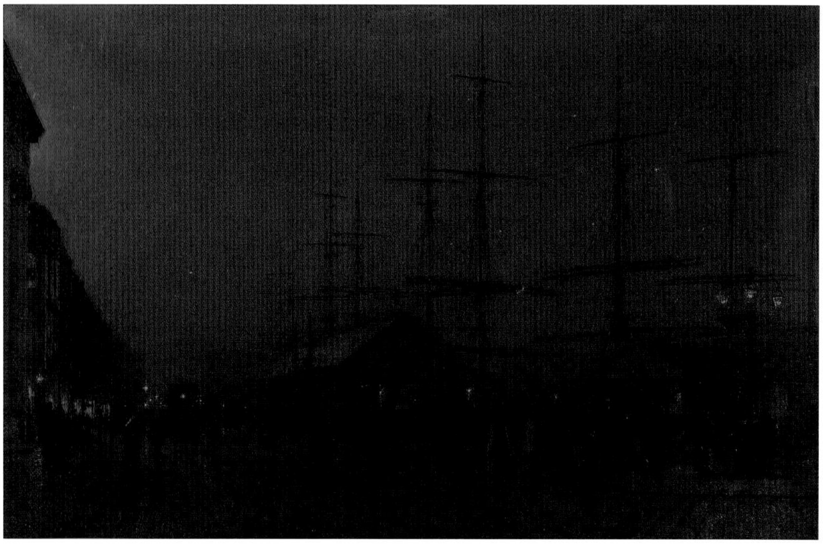

Ostensibly this is typical of Grimshaw's atmospheric paintings featuring parts of the Liverpool waterfront. An evening view makes use of the effects of the street lighting and such features as the towering masts of the sailing ships. The viewpoint is by the Custom House (of which there is a hint to the far left) looking south down Strand Street towards Wapping with brightly lit shops to the left. Salthouse Dock

1 Canvas stamped "WINDSOR & NEWTON" and inscribed "Salthouse Dock / Liverpool / Atkinson Grimshaw / 1884"; There are several labels on the rear: printed label for Alfred Stiles & Sons, Gilders and Frame Makers, Hammersmith, and (in pencil) "BD 2932"; typed label "G123/10 / ATKINSON GRIMSHAW: Salt-House Dock, Liverpool / Oil on canvas, 1884" and stamped "ARTHUR JEFFRIES (PICTURES)"; exhibition label "ARTIST: ATKINSON GRIMSHAW / Title: Salt-House Docks, Liverpool / CATALOGUE No.: 12 / PURCHASER: Messrs. Everetts"; small round label "2249" in ink; small round label "60/94" in ink.
2 See Bennett 1978, Text, pp. 106-7.

entrance is on the right with its masts and the transit sheds. People are going about their business including groups around the dock entrance, where there are some men with bill boards.
Grimshaw painted a number of views of this area, under various titles, but usually including a full view of the Custom House. Good examples are in the Walker Art Gallery and Tate Gallery, London.[2] This is almost certainly the work of one of Grimshaw's imitators.

Simon Hales (active 1917)

98 *Paddle tug approaching a sailing vessel*

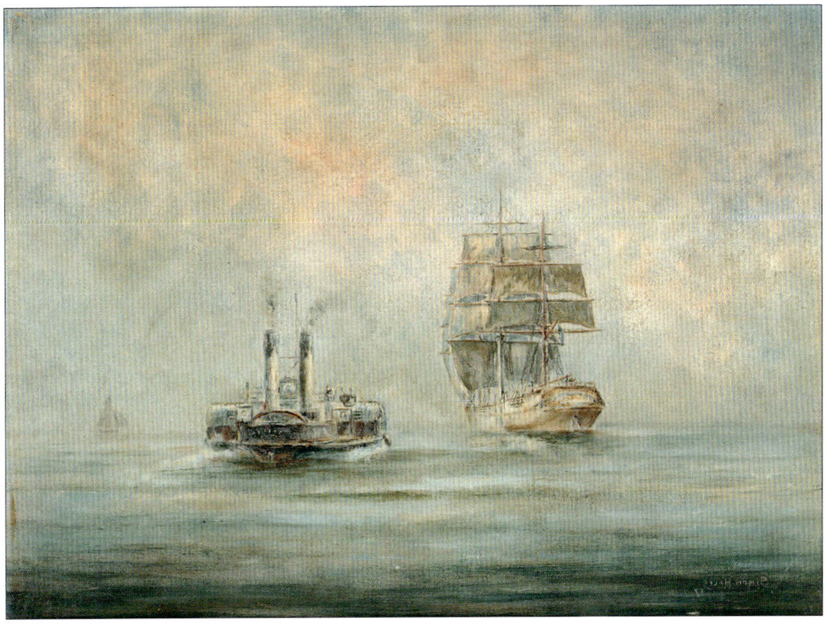

1965.197.2
Oil on canvas
46 cm x 61.5 cm
Signed and dated (bl) 'SIMON HALES / 17'
Prov: James H Lamey & Co., Liverpool, who presented it, 1965

This painting shows a paddle tug approaching a ship rigged sailing vessel. Neither vessel is identified and the artist has chosen to portray the scene atmospherically using a palette of greens and blues.
The donors, J H Lamey and Company, were tug owners in Liverpool from 1916 to 1978 but this is not one of their vessels. At the time of the painting the firm did not own any paddle tugs.[1] It is probably a pair with no. 99.

1 They only owned one vessel in 1917 - the 25 ton tug *Hero* built in 1896. See W B Hallam 'Fifty Years of Mersey Towage' *Sea Breezes*, vol. 40, 1966, pp. 849-875. Lameys were taken over by Alexandra Towing Company in 1978. See T Nicholson, *Take The Strain*, 1990.

99 *A steamer awaiting a pilot at the Bar Light Ship* (page 92)

In this atmospheric canvas, an unidentified steamer is shown waiting for a pilot at the entrance to the Mersey. The steamer herself is placed in an oblique starboard bow view, with the Bar Light Ship *Alarm* in the far distance to the right and a port bow view of the pilot boat to the far left. An indistinct flag code flies above the bridge. A small rowing boat with five men aboard is placed in the right foreground beneath the steamer's bow.
The Bar Light Ship was stationed at the mouth of the Mersey some fifteen nautical miles from the Pier Head. *Alarm* was built for the Mersey Docks and Harbour Board by Hawthorn & Company of Leith in 1912. She remained in service until replaced 1961. There is a builder's model of the light ship in the collections. (Accession number 1961.7).[1]
This painting is probably a pair with no. 98.

1DCF.

1965.197.1
Oil on canvas
46 cm x 61 cm
Signed (bl) "SIMON HALE(S)"
Prov: James H Lamey & Co. Ltd., who presented it, 1965.

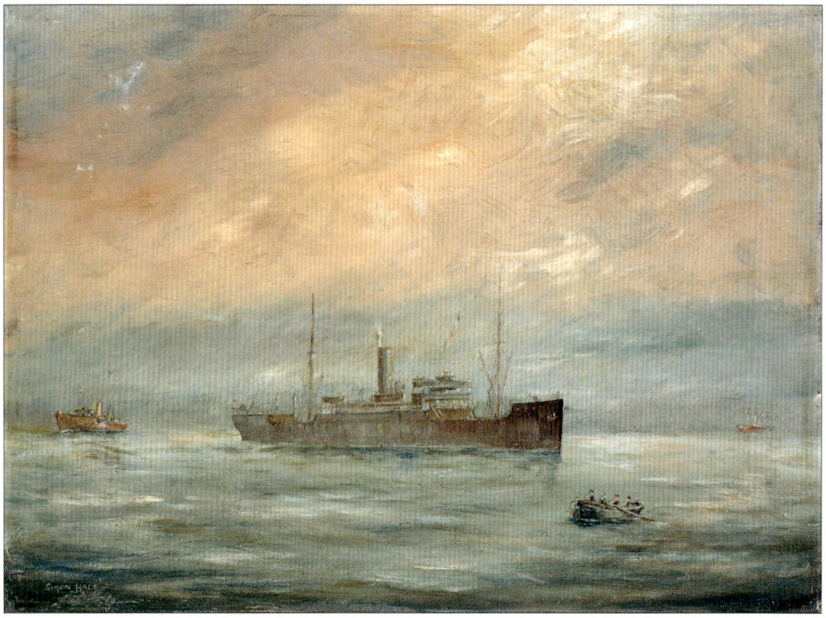

John Hall (1836/7-about 1887)

Hall is one of the least known of ship portraitists who worked in Liverpool. His principal career was as a naval architect but he is also listed as a marine artist in the directories of the late 1870s and 1880s. Few of his works are known but there are examples in the Yarmouth Museum, Nova Scotia and the New Brunswick Museum.[1]

1 Davidson, 1986, pp. 107, 111.

100 *Bessarabia*

1955.253
Oil on canvas[1]
72 cm x 108 cm
Signed and dated (bl in red) "J. Hall / 78"
Prov: In collections, 1955

Vessel: 261 ft (l), 33.6 ft (b), 23.4 ft (d); 1644 gross tons.

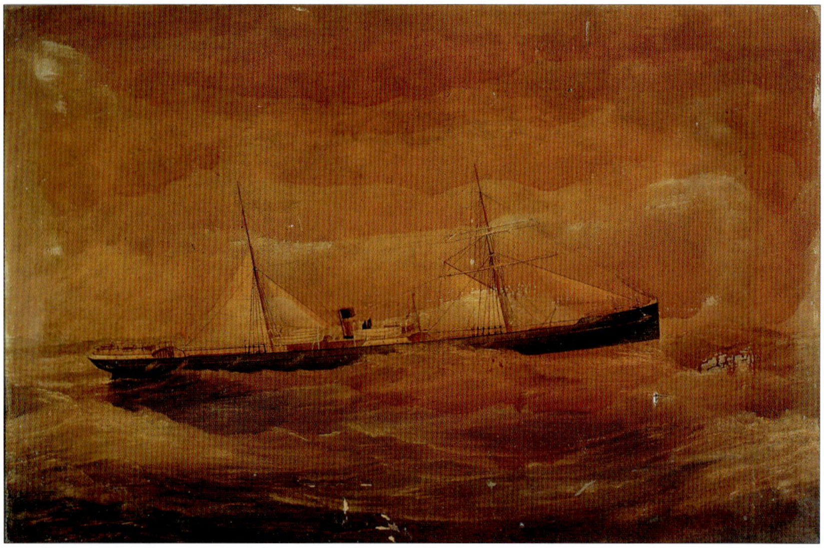

The iron screw steamer *Bessarabia* is shown in starboard profile in heavy seas. The vessel is identifiable by her name on the bow but carries no other identification. The square sails are stowed and only the fore and aft sails are set. She has an open bridge amidships with a wheel at the stern. Light hatches for the stern accommodation are clearly visible.

Bessarabia[2] was built by Gray of West Hartlepool in 1877 for Taylor, Cameron & Co a small steamship company of Liverpool. She remained in their ownership until sold to Spanish owners in 1894.[3]

1 The canvas is covered in a thick brown disfiguring varnish.
2 Old province of Russia.
3 LCR, vol. 93, no. 144, 11 December 1877.

Edwin Hayes (1819/20-1904) (Attributed)

An accomplished painter of seascapes and coastal scenes, Hayes was born in Bristol and studied in Dublin. He exhibited at most of the major exhibitions, including the Royal Hibernian Academy.[1]

1 Brook-Hart, p.10; Brewington 1982.

101 *Shipping off an East Coast Port*

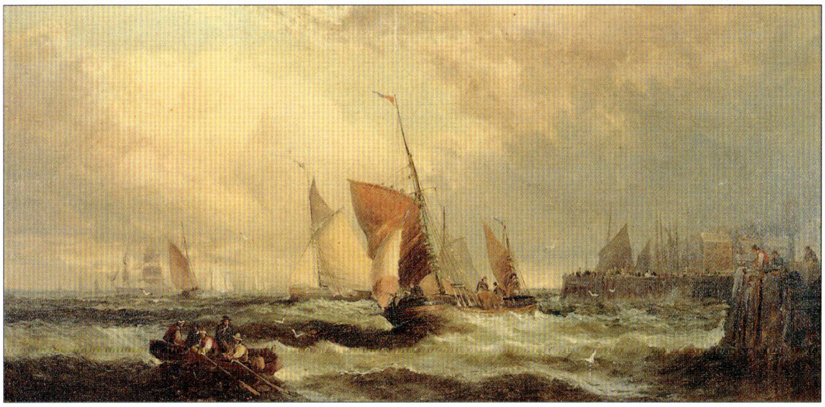

1966.301.8
Oil on canvas[1]
20.5 cm x 40.5 cm
Prov: E Cuthbert Woods, Mrs E Woods, Paignton, who presented it, 1966.

This small picture shows a number of vessels in poor weather off a harbour mouth. In the centre two fishing vessels are leaving the harbour - a yawl with a cutter behind. There is a small rowing boat manned by five men in the left foreground and in the background is other coastal shipping, including a brigantine in the left far distance.

There are two piers either side of the harbour mouth to the right, with a group of buildings, including a church on the hill in the distance, which is possibly Bridlington.

1 Label rear stretcher "HUGO LANG & CO (1831) LTD / 19 WHITECHAPEL / LIVERPOOL / Ref (in pencil) T1397"

Joseph Heard (1799-1859)

After Samuel Walters, Heard is the best known and most prolific of Liverpool ship portraitists. He was born and brought up in Whitehaven and may have had some seafaring experience before moving to Liverpool in 1833/34. Although producing many standard portraits, he also liked to depict a vessel during a particular incident, usually in a storm or being dismasted. On occasions he painted two or three pictures to tell a story, such as the two views of *Sir Henry Pottinger* (nos. 112 and 113).[1]

There are good examples of Heard's work in National Maritime Museum, Whitehaven Museum and Peabody Essex Museum, Salem.

1 For a detail account of his life and paintings see Davidson, 1986, pp. 52-57.

102 *Alliance*

Alliance is shown in port profile in a typical Heard pose which places the vessel close to the viewpoint and allows detailed depiction of this small topsail schooner. The crew can be seen about their duties with one man climbing onto the bowsprit and another securing the anchor. As well as her name on the bow, there is a name pennant at the main mast and the red ensign is at the peak. She has just passed the Eddystone lighthouse off Plymouth. A variety of unidentified shipping completes the scene including a ship rigged vessel to the right of the lighthouse and a paddle steamer and brigantine off *Alliance*'s starboard bow.

Alliance was built at Topsham on the River Exe in Devon in 1836. She was owned initially by Periam and from about 1842 by Marwood, Sons and Godwin of Liverpool, who were the main coasting traders to the West Country for more than

1945.10
Oil on canvas[1]
66.5 cm x 92 cm
Signed and dated (bl) "Josh Heard 1848"
Prov: John Marwood, Wallasey, who presented it, 1945.
Exh: Liverpool 1974

Vessel (1847): 71.9 ft (l), 16.7 ft (b), 11 ft (d); 98 gross tons

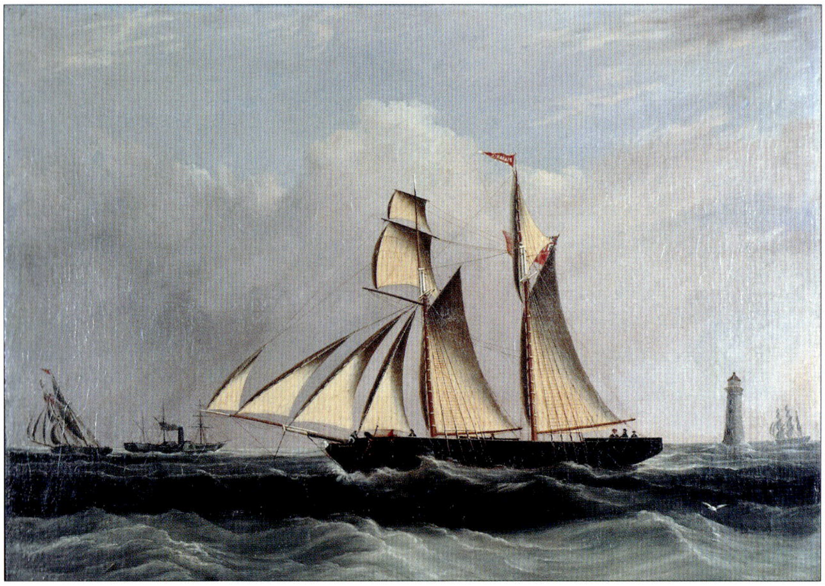

forty years.[2] She was lengthened and thoroughly repaired in 1847 and was presumed lost in March 1849 having not being heard of since 14 September 1848. Most of her career was spent coasting between the Exe and Liverpool.[3]

The Eddystone lighthouse was built in 1759 by Thomas Smeaton and was not replaced until 1882.

Given the coincidence of the donor's name and that of her Liverpool owners, this painting was presumably painted for one of the Marwoods.

1 Relined, 1973.
2 For Marwoods see Baines, pp. 460-1, GDL 1845, 1867.
3 LCR vol. 63, no. 1438, 8 May 1847. Daniel Davy of Topsham held sixteen shares. LR 1837-48 provides details.

103 *Bona Dea*

1955.243
Oil on canvas[1]
71 cm x 95 cm
Prov: John Robertson Brown, by descent to granddaughter, Mrs M E Astin, Wallasey, who presented it in memory of her grandfather, 1955.

Vessel: 122.5 ft (l), 28.9 ft (b), 19.7 ft (d); 625 gross tons

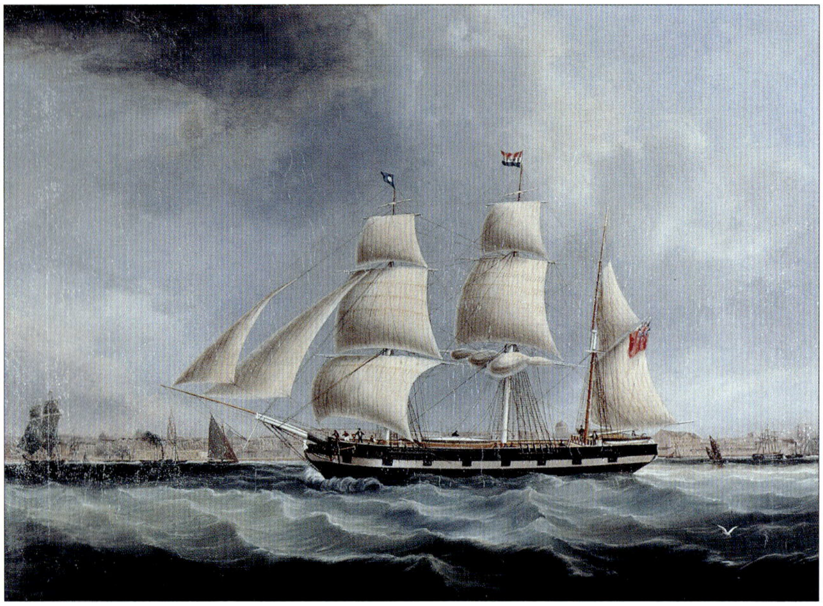

The barque *Bona Dea* is shown in port profile outward bound off the Liverpool waterfront. With a favourable south easterly wind and all sails set, except the main course, she is making good progress. She flies the red ensign at the peak, the Gibbs, Bright house flag at the main mast and the blue peter at the foremast, indicating that the vessel is about to leave port. The identity is confirmed by the name on the bow. A number of unidentified vessels can be seen in the background, including a Mersey flat under the tip of the bowsprit, a ship being towed into dock to the far right and several sailing vessels and small paddle steamers close to the shore.

Bona Dea was built in Yarmouth, Nova Scotia and launched in June 1841. The vessel was bought by the Liverpool firm of Gibbs, Bright & Co. in St John, New Brunswick, in April 1842 and remained in their ownership until July 1847 when she was sold to Thomas Froste, a Liverpool merchant. The vessel was transferred to his son, Thomas Froste junior, in July 1848 but was wrecked in mid-Atlantic in February 1854 returning from Savannah. The crew were taken off by the barque *Cuba* and the vessel was eventually salvaged. She was sold on in June 1857 to Joseph Wheeler, a ship owner of Cork.[2] During her period of Gibbs, Bright ownership she sailed mainly between Liverpool and New Orleans or Quebec.[3]

The artist has adopted an unusually oblique angle to show the waterfront. To the left are the dome of St Paul's, the tower of St Nicholas', the George's Baths and the Town Hall. The Albert Dock Buildings lie behind the vessel and to right are the Duke's Grain Warehouse and King's and Queen's Dock. Because of the oblique angle the Custom House appears oddly between the warehouses of Albert and Duke's Dock.

The attribution to Joseph Heard has been made on stylistic grounds with the vessel typically heeled slightly over to show the deck and the crew at work.

John Robertson Brown was master of *Bona Dea* from 1843 until 1847[4] and as the original owner was presumably responsible for commissioning the painting.

1 Relined.
2For details of vessel and subsequent ownership see LCR Vol. 57 no 152, 1842; Vol. 63, no. 185. 1847; Vol. 64, no. 152, 8 July 1848; TB2, p.488, 23 June 1857. For wreck see LL 16 February 1854 and *Mercantile Marine Magazine*, April 1854, p.145.
3 LL 1843-7.
4 ibid.

104 *Brigantine Centaur*

1945.11
Oil on canvas[1]
69 cm x 92 cm
Signed (on driftwood bl) 'J. HEARD'
Prov: Marwood family by descent; John Marwood; presented by his executors, 1945.

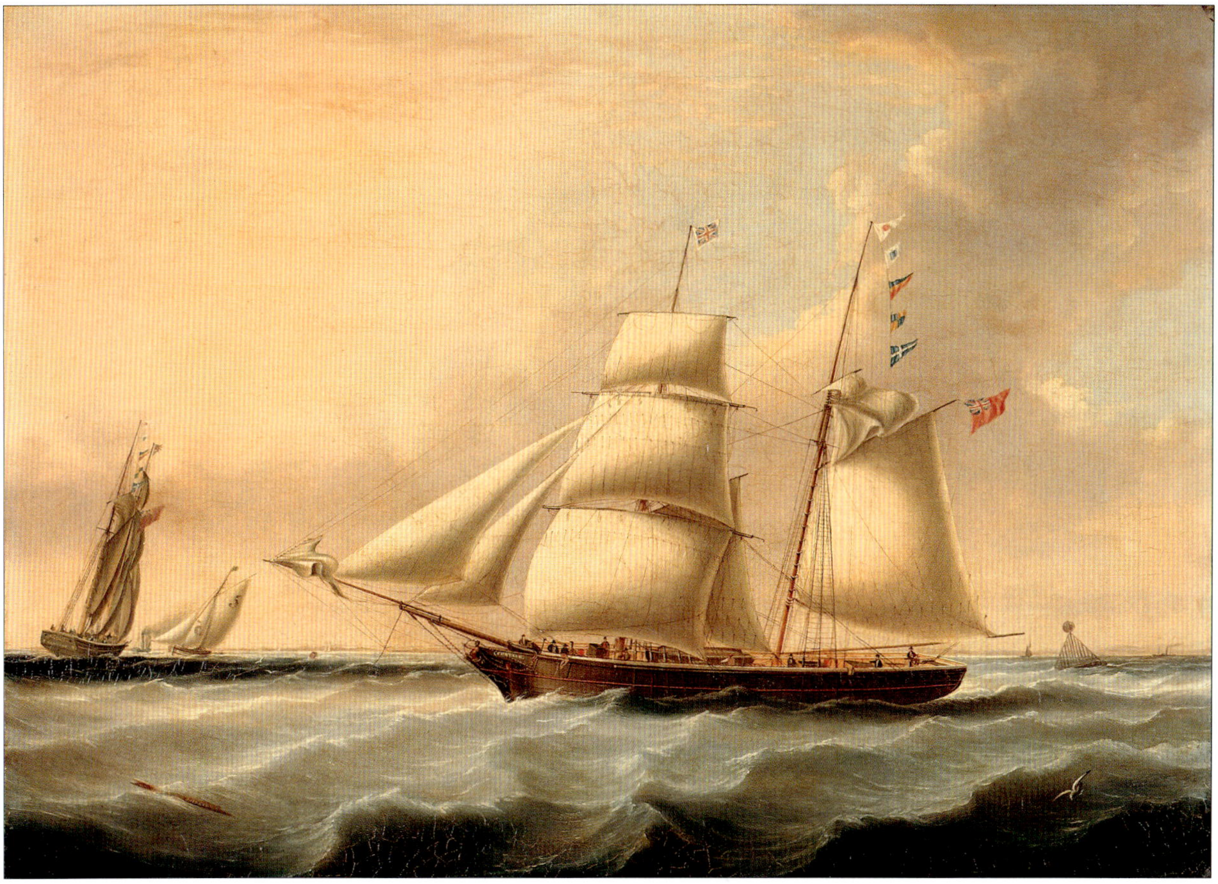

The brigantine rigged *Centaur* is shown in two views reducing sail off the Lancashire coast near Formby, in the approaches to the Mersey. The No. 5 pilot boat is

Vessel: 71.3 ft (l), 17.5 ft (b), 12 ft (d); 524 gross tons

approaching and in the far distance are a steamer and other shipping nearer the coast. In the main view she is in port profile having just passed a buoy known as the bell beacon. All the foresails are set but the topsails on the main have been reduced. The Marryat flag code (1 d.p. 1 6 9 4) flies at the main, the pilot jack at the fore and the red ensign is at the peak. *Centaur*'s identity is confirmed by the figurehead of a centaur and by the name, in the main view on the bow and on the stern in the secondary view.

In the secondary view to the left the vessel has tacked and is shown in a quarter stern view, with a similar sail pattern and flags. The No. 5 pilot boat is shown in a bow port view approaching her and there is a small manned punt astern of the pilot boat.

Centaur was built as a schooner in Liverpool by Haselden, Pearson and Broughton in 1839. She was initially owned by Wood & Co., merchants of the port but she changed hands with great regularity from 1842, her owners including William Niven Bell, Lyon & Fynney and Hughes, Cowie & Co., all of Liverpool. In August 1846 she was bought by John Sutton Marwood when she was re-registered as a brigantine. Marwood sold her to Gilbert Periam of Topsham, near Exeter in November of the same year. In the late 1850s she was converted back to a schooner and remained with Periam & Co. until wrecked in 1865.[2]

The No. 5 pilot boat is the sloop *Victoria* built by Thomas Wilson of Liverpool in 1843. She was replaced in 1856.[3]

The bell buoy was situated at the entrance to the New Cut, later Victoria Channel, which led from Liverpool Bay into the Crosby Channel. Formby Point and the long flat coast off Formby and Ainsdale can be seen in the background.

Heard used a number of different signatures, and this example, in capitals with serifs, is one of the less frequent variants.

The painting was probably painted for the vessel's one time owner John Marwood, given that it was presented to the museum with no. 102 (another Marwood owned ship) by the executors of a later John Marwood. In which case, the painting was probably commissioned about 1846, a date which would be consistent with all the other known details.

1 Relined.
2 LCR vol. 54, no. 166, vol. 57, no. 144, vol. 60, no. 157, vol. 61, no. 156; LR 1839-65. Marwood and Periam probably had good links as Marwoods had been the main coasting traders to the West Country from Liverpool for more than two decades. See also no. 102 *Alliance*.
3 Rees, p.202.

105 *The barque Charles Eyes, Captain Moss off an iceberg*

Heard shows the barque *Charles Eyes* in a typical action piece battling against heavy winds and seas. The vessel is shown close-hauled in starboard profile under shortened sail. The crew are on the yards securing the main topsail and the royals; the mizzen top mast has been struck. An iceberg is depicted astern in the middle distance and another unidentified vessel is shown to the far right of the canvas, running before the wind. The vessel only flies the red ensign at the peak but is identifiable by the name on her bow.

Charles Eyes was built in Liverpool by Thomas Royden in 1829[1] and was probably named after the merchant of the same name who was a partner in Eyes, Miller Wylie and Company.[2] She was employed in the South American trade, principally along the west coast, calling regularly at Valparaiso, Arica and Lima. In 1840 she brought the first cargo of guano into Liverpool.[3] Her first master and largest shareholder was Thomas Chapman, who was "well-known in the Trade" and was "well-acquainted round the Horn."[4] Chapman later owned and managed a number of vessels sailing mainly to South America and India. *Charles Eyes* was lost entering Vera Cruz in the Gulf of Mexico in November 1842.[5]

The painting portrays a specific incident as the inscription on the back of the stretcher makes clear. This reads "The Barque Chas Eyes, Captain Wm Moss off an iceberg,

1 LCR, vol. 46, no. 138, 1829.
2 Charles Eyes, (1786-1833), son of the surveyor Charles Eyes (1754-1773), merchant of Walton Breck and of Eyes, Miller & Co., 7 Rumford Street, Liverpool, See R Stewart-Brown 'Maps and Plans of Liverpool and District by the eyes Family of Surveyors' in *THSLC* vol. lxii (1911) and Baines, p.245.
3 Annals, 1840.
4 See, for instance, advertisements in Gores 24 May - 2 August 1832.
5 LL 3 January 1843.
6 This has previously been misread as "Captain Wallop" but no such master has been found and the Walker version has a similar inscription which reads "Wm Moss", who was master of the vessel.
7 For details of Moss as master see LCR, vol. 46, no. 138 and possible commissioning see no. 107.
8 It reads "The Barque Charles Eyes Capt. Wm Moss off an Iceberg Lat. 49.48S. Long. 48.47W / Josh Heard Pinxt / 1836".
9 No. 9382, see Penketh, p. 124.

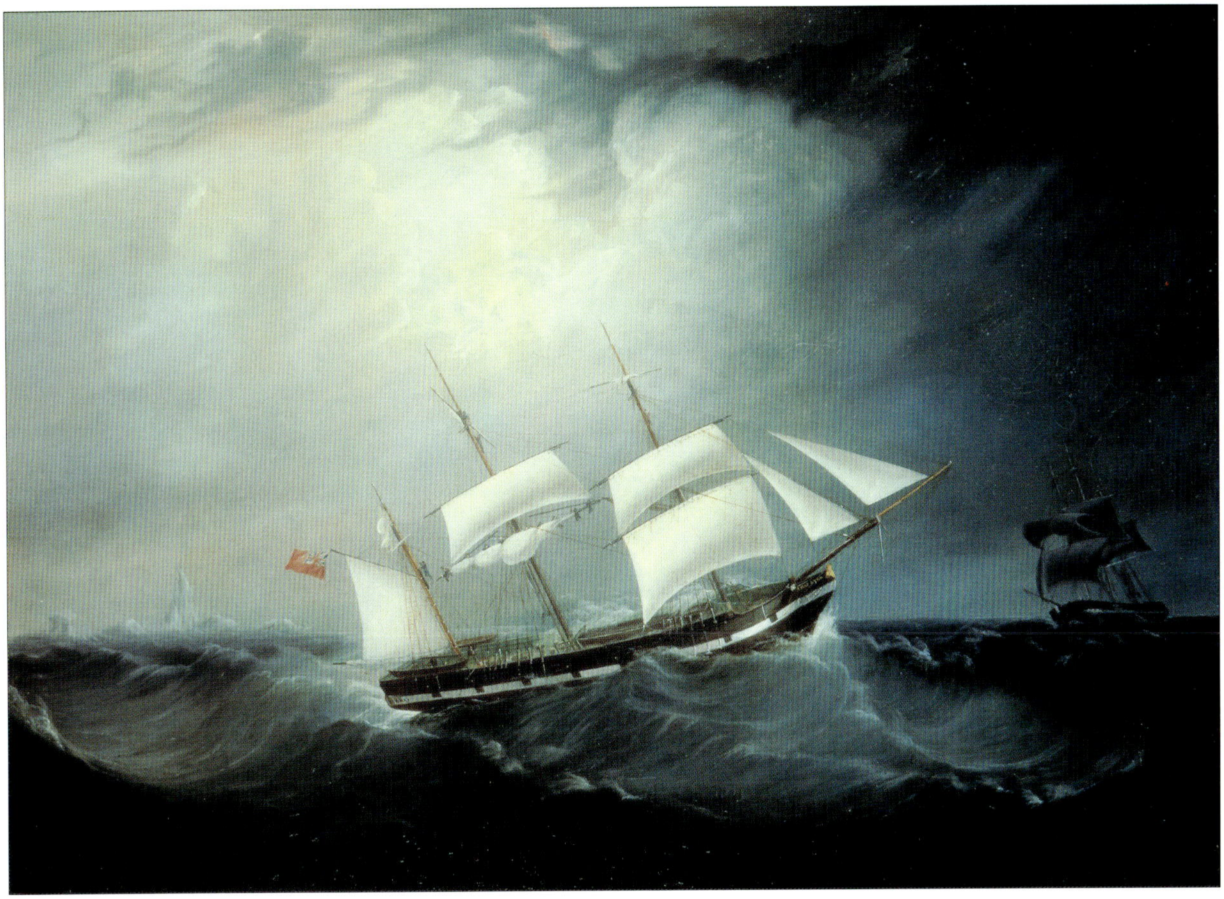

Lat. 49º 48, Long. 48º 49."[6] This location, some 40 miles or so east of the Falkland Islands, is consistent with the vessel's known voyages and the presence of icebergs. William Moss was master of the vessel from 31 January 1835 until September 1842 and may have been involved with commissioning the painting.[7] It was acquired with no. 107 which also has associations with Moss.

There is another version of this painting in the Walker Art Gallery. The same inscription is found on the stretcher but with slight variation.[8] The principal different between the two versions is that in the Walker one the vessel flies her Watson's flag code number (9 1 2) from the main mast.[9]

MMM.1990.53.2
oil on canvas
71 cm x 101.5 cm
signed (bl) 'Josh Heard / 1835'
Prov: Unidentified private collection, Ireland; Hahn Galleries, London, from whom purchased 1990.
Exh: Hahn Galleries, London, 1990.

Vessel: 94 ft 10 in (l), 24 ft 6 in (b), 17 ft 1 in (d); 255 tons

106 Damascus (page 98)

The steamer *Damascus* is shown in a starboard profile under sail and steam off Anglesey outward bound from Liverpool for the Mediterranean.

The vessel is identifiable by the name on the bow and the name pennant which flies from the main mast. The red ensign flies at the peak. All her sails are in use, except the main courses, and smoke pours from the two funnels. There is good detail on deck - for instance crewmen at the bowsprit and wheel and several passengers. A gaff rigged fishing boat is placed in the foreground far left.

The full history of this iron-hulled vessel is quite complicated.[1] She was built by Denny of Dumbarton in 1856 as *St George* but was acquired by Cunard during fitting out for their Mediterranean service. She had a single screw driven by two 2-cylinder engines supplied by Tulloch and Denny. In 1860 she was sold to the Italian nationalist Garibaldi to carry his "red shirts" to Sicily but the scheme fell through. She was chartered by the Allan Line 1862-65 and had several further changes of names and owners during her long career. She was broken up in 1912.

1956.157.1
Oil on canvas
71 cm x 91 cm
Signed (bl) "J. Heard"
Prov: A R Burstall, who presented it, 1956.

Vessel: 253.5 ft (l), 31.2 ft (b), 22.2 ft (d); 1214 tons

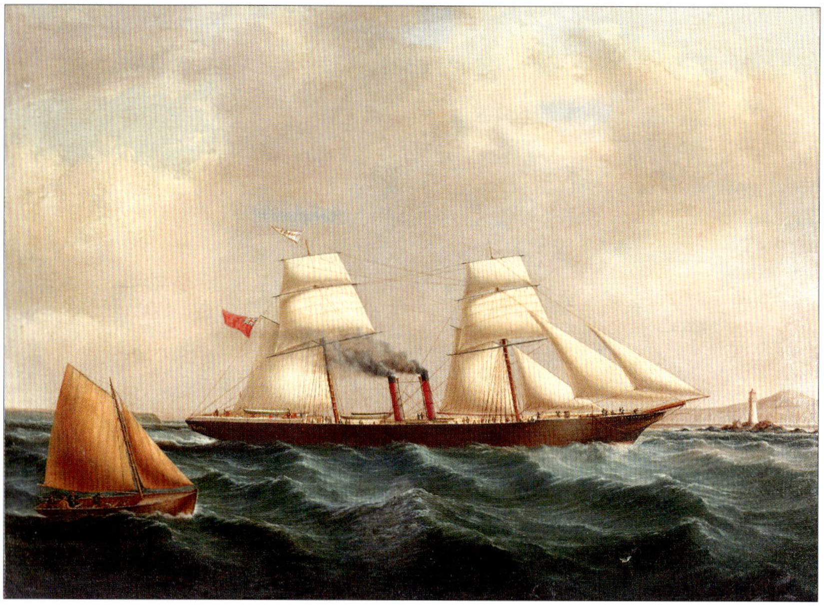

The setting is off Anglesey with the familiar landmark of the Skerries lighthouse and Holyhead Mountain to the right and in the distance to the left is Carmel Head. The painting is unusual in showing such a close and detailed view of the Skerries.

1 See Haws Cunard, pp. 32-33

107 *Elinor Chapman off Liverpool* (see pages 100-101)

MMM.1990.53.1
Oil on canvas
71 cm x 91.5 cm
Signed (bl) 'Jos[h] Heard / 1845'
Provenance: Unidentified private collection, Ireland; Hahn Galleries, London, from whom purchased 1990.
Exh: Hahn Galleries, London, 1990.

Vessel: 101.5 ft (l), 23.1 ft (l), 17.2 ft (d); 330 gross tons.

The brig *Elinor Chapman* is shown in two positions in the Mersey with other shipping off the Liverpool waterfront. In the main view she is depicted centrally in starboard profile with her guns prominently shown. The crew are reducing sail, indeed there are two men on the bowsprit. To the right she is shown in port quarter view, having tacked and taken in further sail. Her port anchor has been released ready for use. The vessel's identity can be confirmed from her Marryat flag hoist in both views (2 d.p. 4,3,1,6). The pennant at the foremast, a white ball on green ground, is almost certainly a house flag and the red ensign flies at the peak.

Elinor Chapman was built in Chepstow by Oliver Chapman in 1843. The vessel was operated by Thomas Chapman, who increased his initial small shareholding in the vessel to 24 of the 64 shares in 1849. The other shareholders were a mix of master, shipbuilders and gentlemen and merchant investors, who were regularly involved with Chapman. In October 1860 Chapman sold the vessel to James Wood, a merchant of Liverpool. She was stranded at St Martin's, New Brunswick in January 1874 and condemned and sold.[1]

The vessel was almost certainly named after a relative of Thomas Chapman and the family connection was strengthened when Thomas Hoare Chapman was appointed Master at Swansea in 1854.

Elinor Chapman's maiden voyage in 1843 was to Hong Kong but subsequently she travelled to the west coast of South America and from the mid-1860s was mainly used in the West Indies Trade.

The other vessels in the picture, including the small gaff rigged boat in the foreground and a number of small paddle steamers and flats, are typical dressing for a Mersey view. At the edge of the canvas a vessel flying the blue peter is about to leave. However, the ship rigged vessel in the far distance to the left of *Elinor Chapman*'s stern is more interesting. She carries a Marryat flag hoist (2 d.p. 4,0,1,2) which identifies her as *John Dalton*, built in 1845 by Oliver Chapman in Chepstow and again owned by Thomas Chapman and a group of investors.[2]

The inclusion of this second Chapman vessel and joint provenance with the barque *Charles Eyes*, also a Chapman ship, might indicate that a member of the family commissioned both paintings. Alternately, William Moss was in turn master of *Charles Eyes*, *Elinor Chapman* and *John Dalton* and may have been responsible for the commission.[3]

Although Heard used a setting with Liverpool as the background on relatively few occasions the viewpoint, looking north, is very similar to a number of other such views.[4] A number of features can be identified along the Liverpool waterfront. These include from the left, the dome of St Paul's, the spire of St Nicholas's, the George's Pierhead Baths, the dome of the Town Hall, the spire of St George's, the Custom House (visible between the masts) with the tower of St Peter's behind it, the nearly complete warehouses of Albert Dock and the Duke's Dock Grain Warehouse (under the bowsprit), and to the far right the spire of St. Thomas.

1 LCR, vol. 58, no. 199, 23 November 1843, vol. 65, no. 54, 6 March 1849, TB2, no. 144, LCR, vol. 81, no. 286, 14 October 1856, CR, no. 220, 29 October 1860.
2 There is a portrait of the earlier brig rigged Chapman vessel *John Dalton* (built 1843, lost 1845) attributed to British School in the Walker Art Gallery collections (9381) see Penketh, p.45
3 William Moss was master of *Charles Eyes* 31 January 1835 - September 1842, of *Elinor Chapman* 23 November 1843 - August 1845 and of *John Dalton* 30 August 1845 - December 1846. He also had a small share holding in *Elinor Chapman* and *John Dalton*. (See LCR, vol.46, no. 138; vol. 58, no. 199; vol. 60, no. 207).
4 In particular, *Bona Dea* no. 103 and *Mary Bibby* (see Davidson, 1992, p.108).

108 Jumna and other Brocklebank vessels (see pages 102-103)

This group portrait portrays a number of vessels of the Brocklebank fleet off the Company's home port of Whitehaven on the Cumbrian coast.

The ship rigged *Jumna* is shown in the right foreground in starboard profile running south before a fresh northerly breeze. On the far left is the barque *Hindoo* in port side profile hove-to. In the centre middle distance the barque *Patriot King* is shown in port quarter view outward bound under full sail. To her left the brig *Globe*, close-hauled in stern view is inward bound. To the far right behind *Jumna*'s bowsprit, the ship rigged *Hercules*, in port quarter view, is also bound for the port. A sixth unidentified Brocklebank vessel, with the distinctive broad white band on her hull and the house flag, can be detected at the harbour entrance, leaving port. A small fishing boat in the foreground is a typical artistic trick to provide balance, perspective and interest to the painting.

All the ships were built in T & J Brocklebank's shipyard in Whitehaven for their own use.[1] They fly the Brocklebank house flag at their foremasts and the red ensign at the after peak. Three of the vessels can be positively identified from their Marryat flag hoists: *Jumna* (1 d.p. 6 5 1 0), *Patriot King* (1 d.p. 9 4 0 8), and *Hindoo* (1 d.p. 5 2 4 0); the remaining two, *Globe* and *Hercules*, have name pennants.

Jumna was built in 1833 as one of a new generation of large ships with longer length and more sail area. Although her maiden voyage and most of her subsequent voyages were to Calcutta, she had the distinction of being the first vessel from Liverpool to bring home a cargo from China after the abolition of the East India Company's monopoly in 1834 in a record time of eight months and two days. She was sold in 1856 and lost in 1863.

The barque *Patriot King*, only slightly smaller than *Jumna*, was built a year earlier in 1832. Until 1856 her principal destination was also Calcutta when she transferred to the South American trade. She was sold in 1868. The barque *Hindoo* was launched in 1831 and was used exclusively to Calcutta until 1856, when she also transferred to the South American run. She was sold in 1868 when Brocklebanks were disposing of many of their older vessels.

Brocklebanks owned two vessels named *Globe* in succession, both brigs of similar dimensions. There are good reasons, discussed below, for identifying this vessel as *Globe* I built in 1822 and which operated to South America until lost off Bahia in 1835.

The oldest of the vessels depicted is the ship *Hercules* built in 1805. She was placed in government service from 1806 to 1817 and after a refit took passengers mainly to North America, until run down by a schooner in 1825.

1970.246.4.1
Oil on canvas
76 cm x 110 cm
Provenance: Cunard Brocklebank Ltd, Private Collection, on permanent loan
Exh: Liverpool, 1986
Ref: Gibson 1953, ill opp. p. 52; Port Panorama 1986, p.12; Tibbles 1988

Vessels:[7]
Jumna 107 ft 10 in (l), 27 ft 9 in (b), 18 ft 11 in (d); 364 tons
Hindoo 96 ft 8 in (l), 24 ft 11 in (b), 16 ft 11 in (d); 266 tons
Patriot King 108 ft 1 in (l), 26 ft 8 in (b), 18 ft 7 in (d); 338 tons
Globe 89 ft 8 in (l), 23 ft 6 in (b), 16 ft 6 in (d); 212 tons
Hercules 93 ft 10 in (l), 27 ft 2 in (b), 18 ft (d); 81 tons

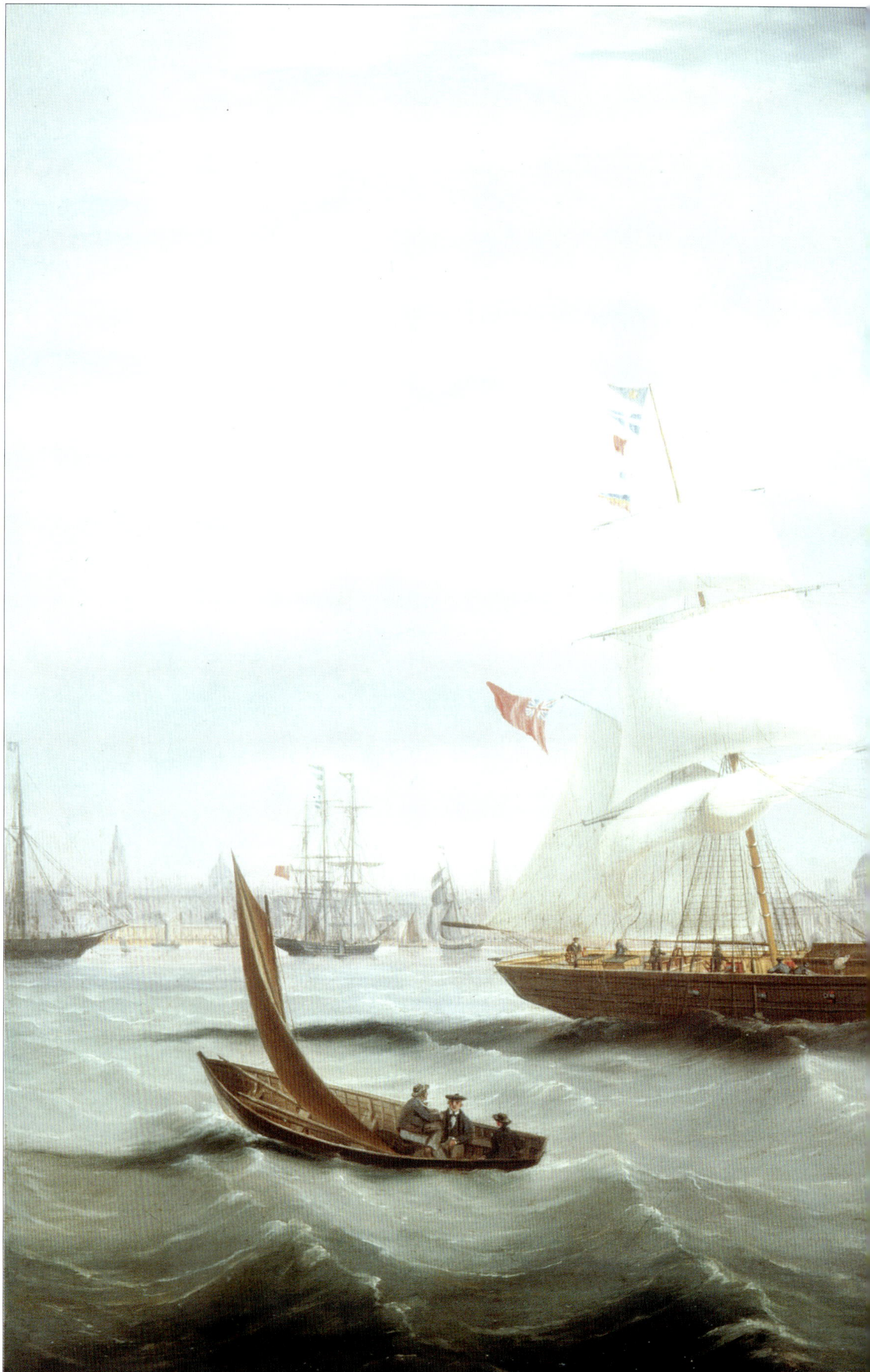

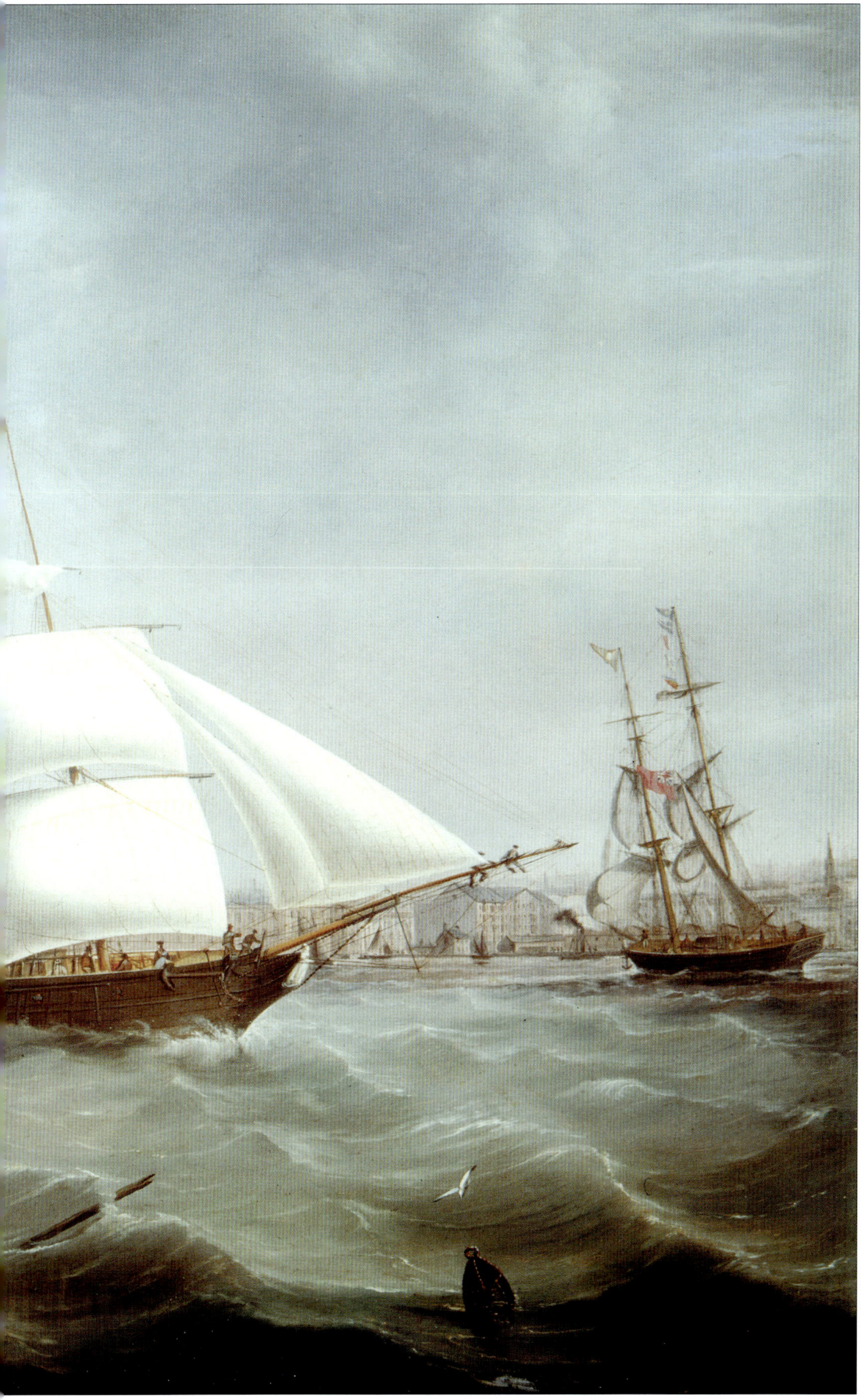

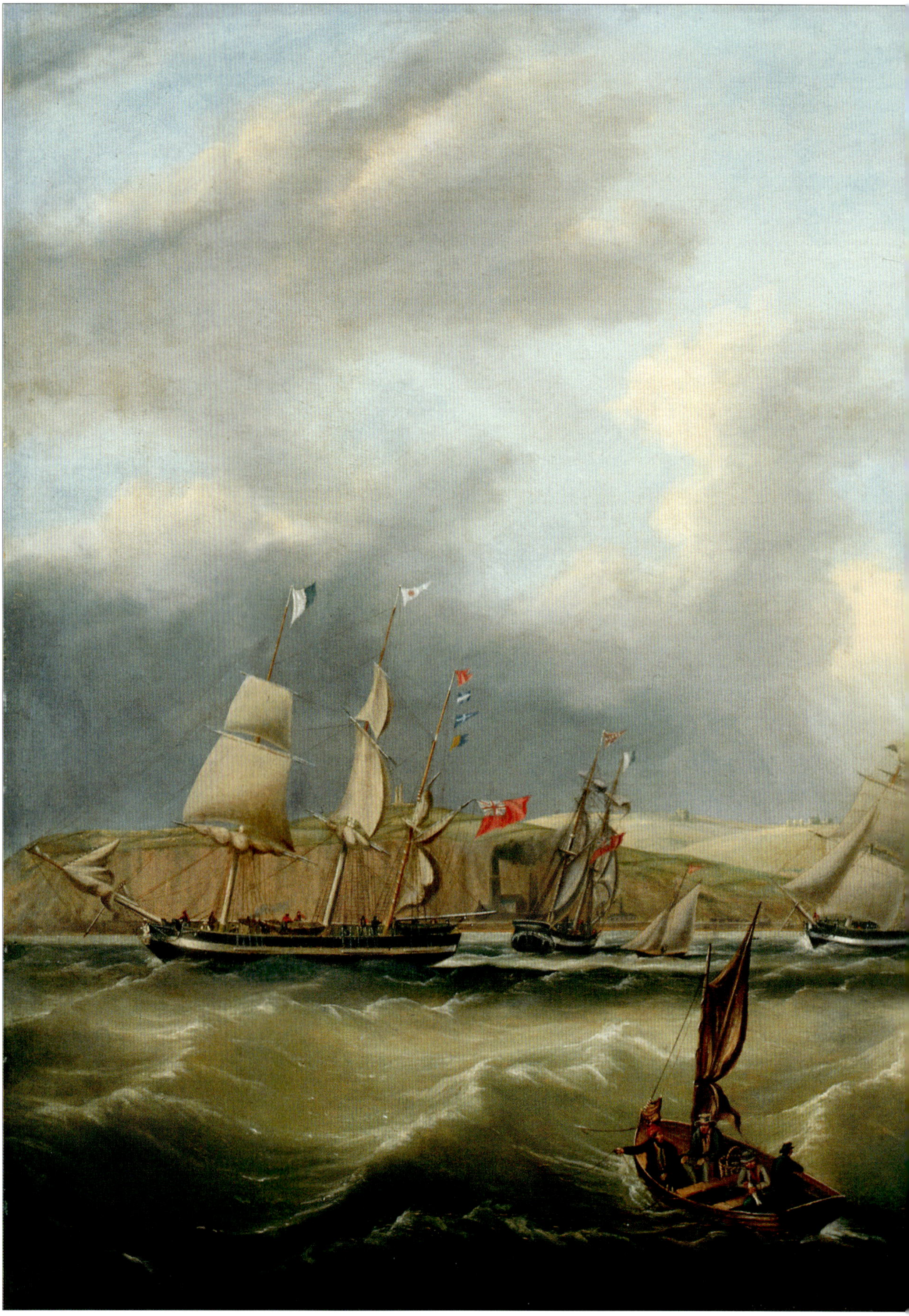

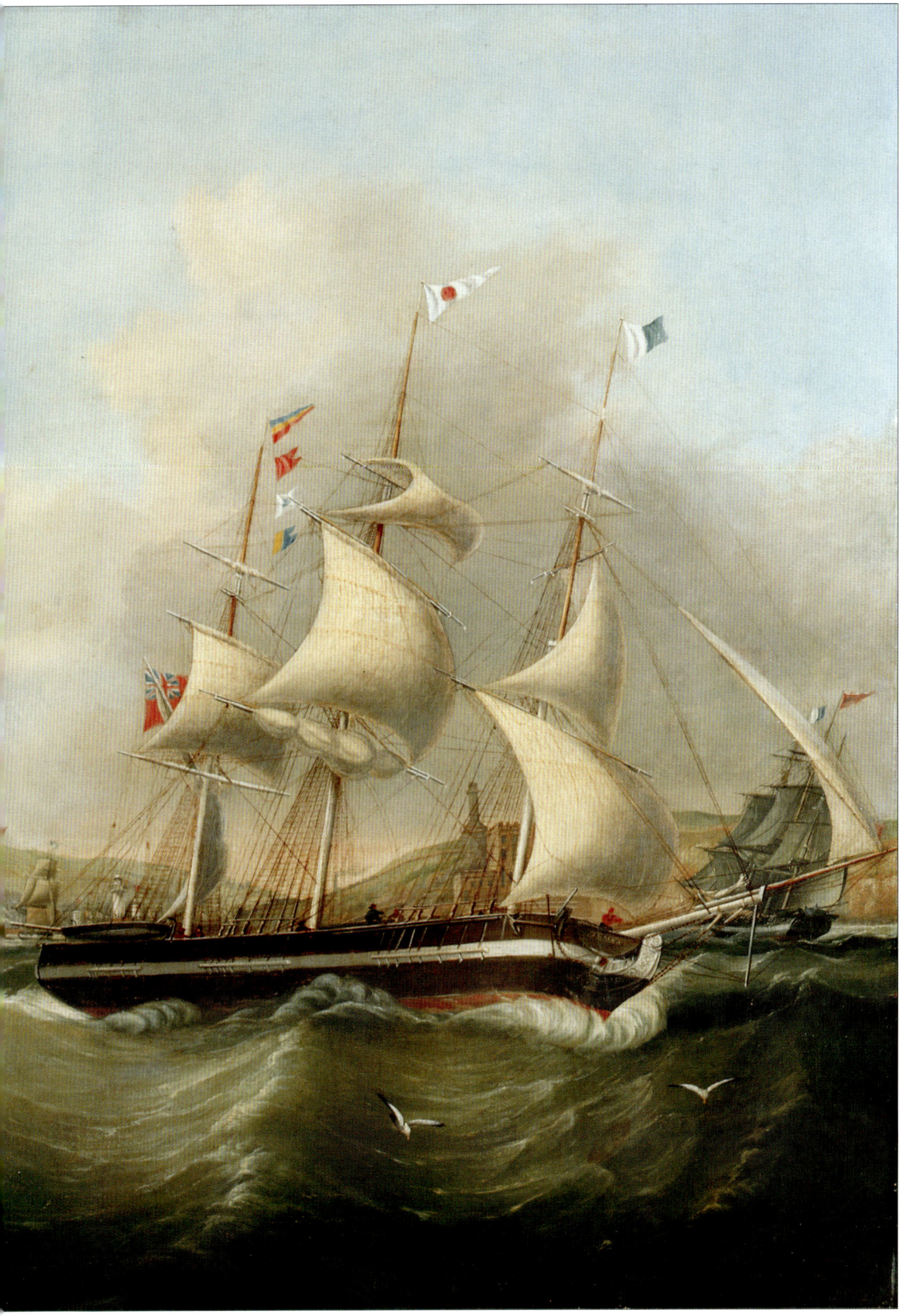

In the background Whitehaven and the neighbouring coastline can be seen between the shipping. To the left are some of the buildings of Brocklebank's Bransty shipbuilding yard. The harbour is in the centre, with the west pier and its light (completed 1838) to the right and the north pier and its light (completed 1841). The head buildings of the Wellington Pit with its distinctive "candlestick" chimney (Sidney Smirke, 1840) sunk in 1840 is visible to the left of *Jumna*'s foremast.[2]

The painting has previously been dated to about 1833[3] but the Marryat flag hoists are post-1840[4] and the inclusion of the Wellington pit head and the piers make a date at least a decade later necessary. Why then are two vessels lost in 1825 and 1835 depicted and why indeed are all the vessels which normally operated from Liverpool shown off Whitehaven?

The answer seems to lie in the career of Captain Joseph Pinder, Brocklebank's Marine Superintendent from 1836 until his death in 1850.[5] Pinder had spent his whole career with the firm. He was apprenticed in 1814 on *Hercules* and was the first master of the *Globe* in 1822 and later of *Hindoo* in 1831. The new *Patriot King* was placed in his care in 1832 and the following year he took over *Jumna*. Thus the painting encapsulates virtually his whole sea-going career.[6] The incorporation of Whitehaven rather than Liverpool suggests an element of nostalgia. The precise circumstances of the commission can only be guessed at but whether it was intended as a tribute or as a reminder of 22 years at sea, it is one of the most unusual ship portrait paintings ever completed.

1 For the detailed history and voyages of all the vessels see Gibson I, passim.
2 For Whitehaven landmarks see Daniel Hay Whitehaven, *An Illustrated History*, New ed. 1979.
3 Gibson I, ill. opp. p.52, Port Panorama (1986). *Hercules* has previously been misread as *Herculean* (Brocklebank barque built 1828).
4 See Davidson 1986, pp. 151-4. Heard is careful not to confuse matters by using his pre-1840 codes and this probably explains why the former vessels *Globe* and *Hercules* are identified by name pennants.
5 For details of Pinder's career see Gibson I, pp. 82, 96. Details of his apprenticeship on board *Hercules* are given in the Brocklebank Apprentice Book, 1809-40, MAL, 387 MD 24, f.42.
6 Only his years as master of the *Crown* are not illustrated.
7 Gibson I, pp. 198, 220, 239, 241, 243. For *Jumna* see LCR vol. 48, no. 99, 14 June 1833 and *Patriot King* see LCR vol. 47, no. 52, 27 April 1832.

109 *Maia*

1954.117.1.2
Oil on canvas[1]
67 cm x 92 cm
Signed and dated "J Heard / 1852"
Prov: Captain W Dougall, who presented it, 1954[2]
Exh: Liverpool 1986,
Ref: Port Panorama, 1986, p.12

Vessel: 96.4 ft (l), 22.4 ft (b), 16.5 ft (d); 315 gross tons.

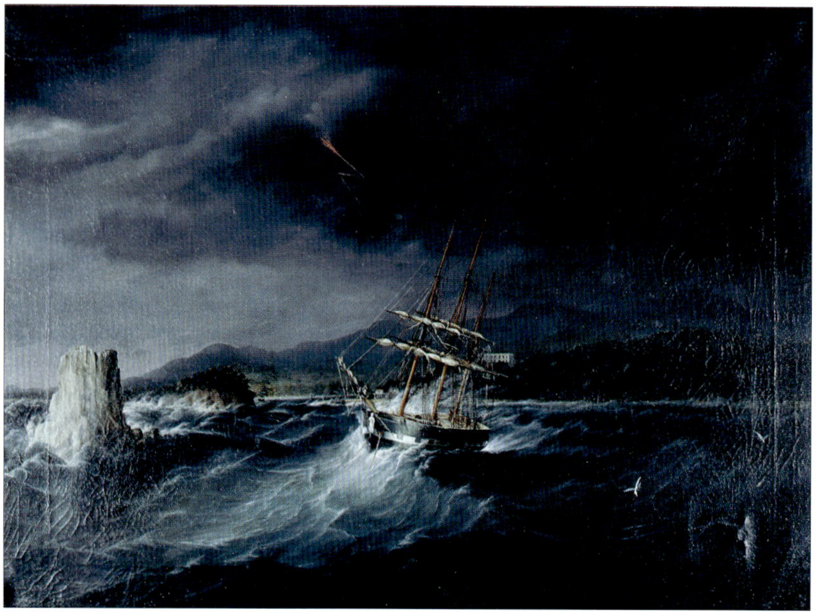

Heard depicts the barque rigged *Maia* in a quarter bow view in one of his typical action paintings. She is shown in the centre of the canvas, all sails stowed, straining at her anchors whilst riding out a tropical storm. A bolt of lightning, centre left above the vessel, illuminates the scene. Another vessel, visible in the surf under *Maia*'s bowsprit has been driven ashore. A further vessel is straining on her anchor in the bay on the left hand side of the canvas.

The identification of the vessel is based on donor information and though there is an appropriate figurehead, there is no verification on the painting. *Maia* was named after the goddess of growth and increase. She was built by Joseph Steel for Joseph

Mondel, the elder, both of Liverpool and was launched on 14 May 1839. She sailed to the Far East and in later years to South America where she was destroyed by fire off Maceio, Brazil, in January 1862.[3] William Turpin, whose name is recorded on the rear, was her master from 1847 until 1857.[4]

The unidentified background is probably off the South American coast. There is a large sheer rock and a wooded island to the left and the landscape behind the vessel is rocky and wooded. There is a large house on the hill and another one on the shore, near the beached vessel.

1 On reverse a paper label "barque *Maia* / Capt. Turpin / presented by Captain W Dougall".
2 See note 4 to no. 155 *Rapido*.
3 LCR, vol. 54, no. 121, 25 June 1839; vol. 61, no. 58, 30 March 1846; TB2, p. 303.
4 LCpR 1869. William Howlett Turpin, born Hull, 1819.

110 Rimac and Ariel

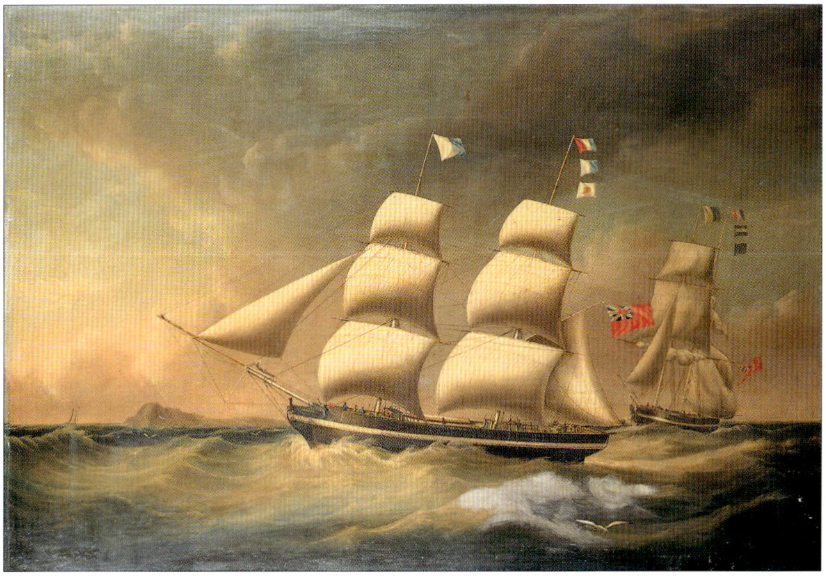

1970.246.11.1
Oil on canvas
61 cm x 91.5 cm
Signed (bl) "J Heard / 1834"
Prov: T & J Brocklebank Ltd.; Cunard Brocklebank Ltd., Private Collection, on permanent loan.
Exh: Liverpool 1986
Ref: McGregor 1984a, p. 75 (ill); Port Panorama 1986, p.13 (ill)

Vessels:
Rimac 90 ft 6 in (l), 23 ft 2 in (b), 15 ft 6 in (d); 214 gross tons
Ariel 81 ft 4 in (l), 21 ft 1 in (b), 12 ft 7 in (d); 154 gross tons

The snow *Rimac* is shown in port side profile during her maiden voyage with the brigantine *Ariel* in the middle distance to the right in port bow view off an unidentified headland. *Ariel* has taken up her fore sail and scandalised her main presumably slowing down so that *Rimac* under full sail can catch her up. *Rimac*'s name is on her bow and she has a prominent, if not attractive figurehead. She flies the Brocklebank house flag at the fore, her number in the Watson Code, 2 6 8 from the main and the red ensign at the peak. *Ariel* is also identifiable by her name and her Watson flag hoist of 2 1 4. Again the Brocklebank flag is at the fore and the red ensign at the peak.

Both vessels were built in Brocklebank's own yard in Whitehaven. *Rimac* was launched in March 1834 and was named after a river in Peru. She undertook her maiden voyage to Valparaiso, which with other ports on the western coast of South America, was to be her regular destination until her sale in 1862. She had three further owners before being wrecked in December 1874.[1]

Ariel, the third Brocklebank vessel name after the spirit in Shakespeare's Tempest, was built in 1820 and was also employed in the South American trade, though frequently combining this with cargoes for Newfoundland, the Mediterranean and Hamburg. She was the first vessel to enter Albert Dock in 1845 but was sold the same year to J Rigby of Runcorn, being lost off Bremen in 1849.[2]

The headland in the far distance under *Rimac*'s bowsprit has not been identified but would have to be off Brazil if the artist were trying to satisfy both vessels' known movements in 1834.[3] Alternatively it may be an imaginary encounter, though the reason for choosing to depict these particular vessels together can only be guessed

1 Gibson, I, p. 244; LCR vol. 49, no. 71, 17 May 1834.
2 Gibson, I, pp. 90-5, 124, 218. Annals 1845.
3 *Ariel* arrived at Rio from Newfoundland on 6 July; *Rimac* left Liverpool on 14 July arriving Valparaiso on 10 October. LL 18 July, 9 September 1834, 27 January 1835.
4 LCR vol. 49, no. 71, 17 May 1834; LR 1826.

at. One possible explanation may be that *Rimac*'s first master, Captain William Dixon also captained *Ariel* between 1826 and 1828. Unusually for Brocklebanks he also held 24 shares in *Rimac*, a significant holding which he retained until 1848, when he had retired to Whitehaven.[4] Dixon may thus have been involved in the commission.

111 The barque Rockshire off a rocky coast

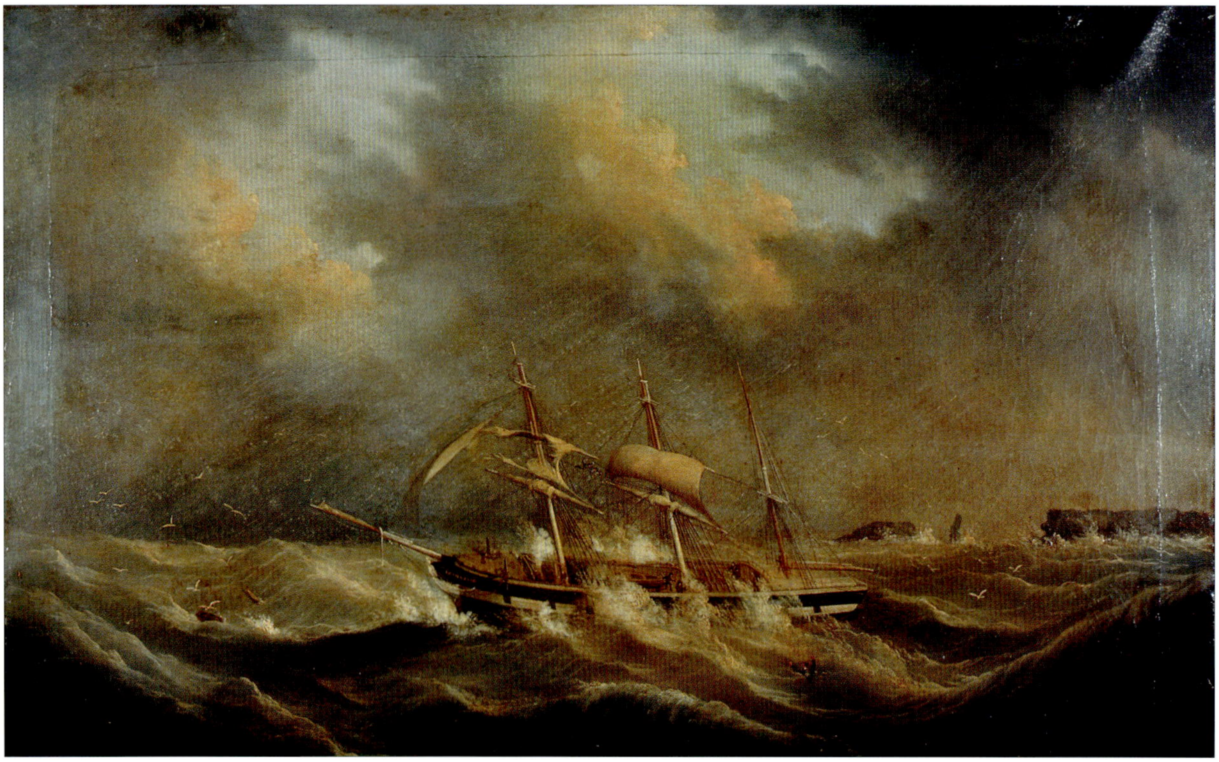

1964.194.3
Oil on canvas
61 cm x 91.5 cm
Prov: Miss May Allen, presented 1964.
Exh: Liverpool 1986
Ref: Port Panorama, 1986

Vessel: 126 ft (l), 27 ft (w), 20 ft (d); 563 tons

This dramatic depiction shows the barque *Rockshire* in port profile battling against a severe storm off an unidentified rocky coastline.

The vessel and crew are in considerable difficulty and danger. Mountainous waves are battering the vessel as she battles to survive. Although most of the sails have been stowed, the fore topsail is being ripped to shreds by the wind and rain and it is difficult to believe she will not sustained further damage. One man is in the sea and another man has lost his footing and is tumbling from the yards. Heard adopts a characteristically elevated viewpoint showing the action and crew on deck. Bad weather had been anticipated and the vessel has adopted a "winter rig" with the topgallant yards removed and the topgallant masts struck. The identity of the vessel is confirmed by the name on the bow.

The painting probably depicts an incident when the ship was damaged returning from Quebec in late 1842. Lloyd's List of 2 January 1843 reports 'The Rockshire, of Quebec, for Liverpool, totally dismasted, but making good way up the Channel, under jury-spars.' She made it to Waterford from where she was towed to Liverpool.[1] The master of *Rockshire* from 1843 to 1845 was Edward Joseph Allen, whose granddaughter presented the painting. Was he on board in January 1843 in another capacity?

Rockshire was built by William Lampson in Quebec in 1841 and was registered in Liverpool in 1844 by Thomas Froste 'formerly of Quebec but now of Liverpool'. In 1848 she was mortgaged to Richard Pope of County Waterford, Ireland, for £1755 and sold to foreign ownership in April 1851, after returning with a cargo from Savannah.[2]

The painting is in the characteristic style of Joseph Heard and is typical of his "incidents".

1 Lloyd's List, 2 January, 5 January, 19 January 1843.
2 LCR vol. 59, no. 56, 26 March 1844. For Quebec registration, see Marcil, p. 373

112 *Sir Henry Pottinger in a cyclone*

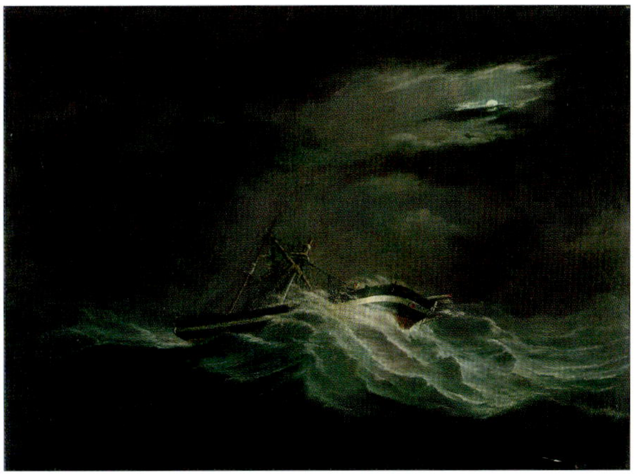

1970.244.61
Oil on canvas
71 cm x 91 cm
Provenance: T & J Brocklebank Ltd, Cunard Brocklebank Ltd., Private Collection, on permanent loan, 1970
Ref: Gibson 1953, opp. p.116 (ill)

Vessel: 102.4 ft (l), 22.7 ft (b), 17.6 ft (d); 313 gross tons.

In this typically eventful scene, Heard portrays the barque *Sir Henry Pottinger*, from the starboard side during a cyclone in the Indian Ocean on 14 January 1848. The vessel is taking the full force of the storm and has already lost her foremast and most of her main mast and bowsprit.

Sir Henry Pottinger, named after the first governor of Hong Kong[1], was built by Brocklebanks in Whitehaven in 1845 for their East India trade. She undertook seven voyages to Calcutta before being transferred to China and South America. She was wrecked in Cardigan Bay in December 1859.[2]

In January 1848 she was returning from Calcutta under the command of Captain William McWean, who later became Brocklebank's Marine Superintendent[3], when she encountered a cyclone off Ceylon. Although precautions had been taken, the severity of the storm brought down the foremast, the two upper sections of the main mast and the mizzen top mast covering the deck with a tangle of wreckage. The crew worked throughout the night to mitigate the damage. Reconstruction, utilising salvaged remains, came the following day, when it was realised that the fourteen year old apprentice had been lost. [4]

This account of the disaster is not only accurately portrayed but it is dramatically rendered with the rolling seas caught in the moonlight, in the unmistakable style of Heard.

1 Sir Henry Pottinger had been received by the East India and China Association in Liverpool in December 1844 and given a civic reception for the "favourable treaty" he negotiated with the Chinese government. *GGA*, 19 December 1844.
2 Gibson I, p.261; LCR, vol. 60, no. 213, 10 September 1845; TB2, p. 264.
3 For McWean's career see Gibson I, p.82.
4 An account of the storm is contained in D Hollett *From Cumberland to Cape Horn*, 1984, p.52.

113 *Sir Henry Pottinger under jury rig*

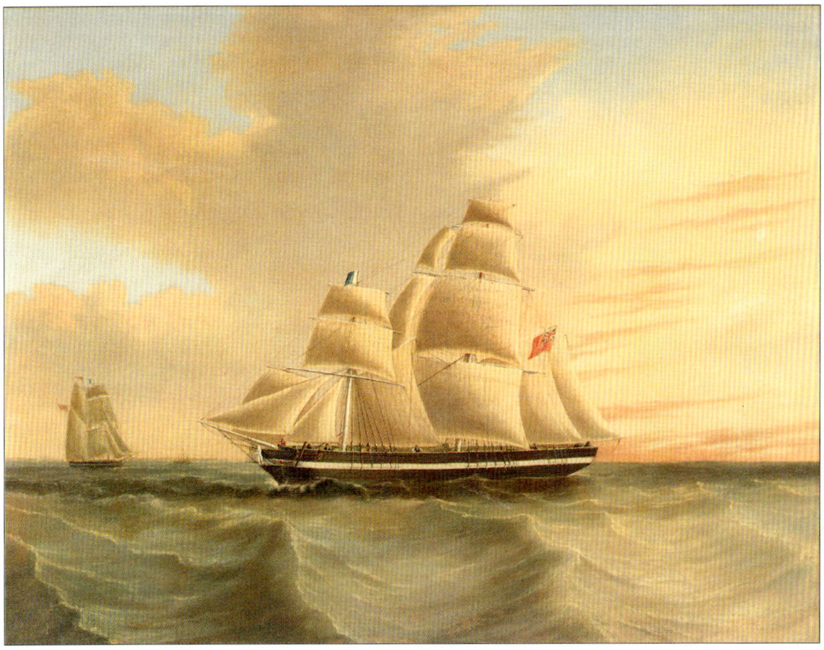

1970.246.9.1
Oil on canvas
71 cm x 91 cm
Prov. T & J Brocklebank Ltd., Cunard Brocklebank Co. Ltd., Private Collection, on permanent loan, 1970

Vessel: 102.4 ft (l), 22.7 ft (b), 17.6 ft (d); 313 gross tons.

This companion piece to no. 112 shows *Sir Henry Pottinger* in port profile entering the Mersey on 9 May 1848 on her return home following the cyclone of January that year.[1] She is under jury rig, that is a temporary rig constructed from the salvaged remains after the cyclone. The main mast has been reconstructed and the lower sections of a replacement foremast have been set up. A diminutive mizzen mast is hidden by the sails. She flies the Brocklebank house flag at her fore and the red ensign. To the far left another Brocklebank vessel, recognisable by her house flag and white hull band so distinctive of the company's ships, is outward bound. The Wirral coastline is only sketchily indicated on the horizon.

Despite the rigours of her passage, *Sir Henry Pottinger* returned to Liverpool with her cargo of sugar, rice, jute, timber and saltpetre intact.[2]

Although a seemingly tranquil scene, there is a hint of her recent misfortunes in the dramatic red sky of the setting sun.

1 LL, 10 May 1848.
2 GGA, 11 May 1848.

114 *The ship Tigris*

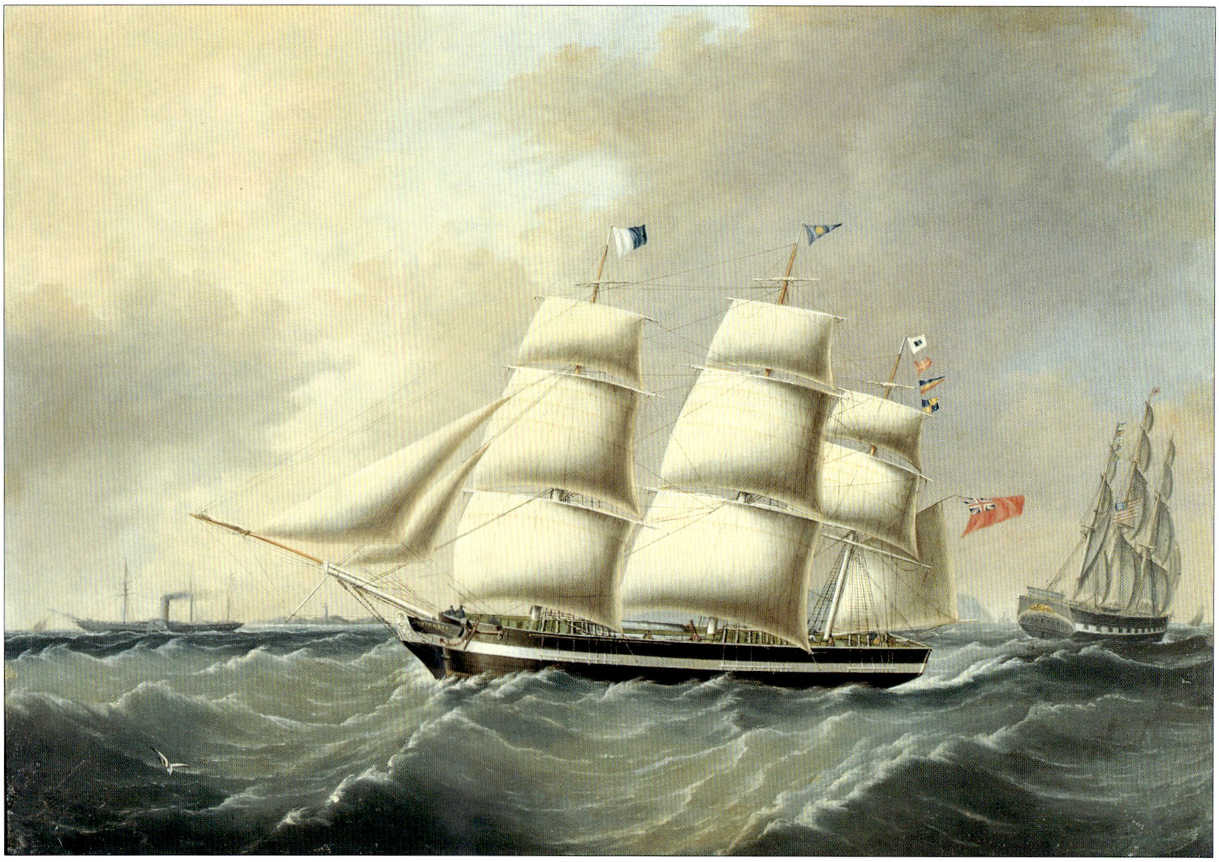

1970.246.17
oil on canvas
65 cm x 91 cm
signed (bl) "J. Heard"
Provenance: T & J Brocklebank & Co.; Cunard Brocklebank Ltd.; Private Collection, on permanent loan, 1970
References: McGregor 1984a, pp.100-1 (ill);

Vessels:
Tigris 115.7 ft (l), 28.7 ft (b), 6.8 ft (d); 423 gross tons
Guy Mannering 190 ft (l), 39.7 ft (b), 28.9 ft (d), 1419 gross tons

The ship *Tigris* is portrayed in port profile off Holyhead under full sail inward bound for Liverpool. To her right is a stern quarter view of the American ship *Guy Mannering* heading for home and in the middle distance under her bowsprit is an unidentified inward bound paddle steamer in port profile.

Uncharacteristically, Heard has made a mistake with both the name and flag hoist, which is unusually split with the distinguishing pennant on the main mast and the hoist on the mizzen. The name on the bow is "*Tigress*" and the Marryat hoist (2nd d.p. 1,7,6,9) is also for *Tigress* (*Tigris* is 1,7,8,0). However, the vessel's identification as *Tigris* cannot be doubted given the Brocklebank house flag on the foremast and the painting's provenance.

Tigris was built in Whitehaven in 1835 by Brocklebanks for use in their East Indies trade and the majority of her voyages were to Calcutta. She was wrecked in Manila in 1865.[1]
Guy Mannering was built by William H Webb in New York in 1849 for Williams and Guion's Black Star Line. Their house flag flies at the main mast, her Marryat code (2 d.p. 6,1,8,9) is at the mizzen and the Stars and Stripes are at the after peak. A portrait of *Guy Mannering* entering the Mersey by John Hughes (1806-78) is in an American private collection.[2]
In the background are the mountains of Anglesey behind Holyhead with the South Stack lighthouse visible between the sterns of the two sailing ships and the Skerries lighthouse can be seen in the distance under *Tigris*'s bowsprit.

1 LCR, vol. 51, no. 224, 31 December 1835, Gibson I, p. 246.
2 Exhibited 1995-6, see 'Across the Western Ocean: American Ships by Liverpool Artists', *Peabody Essex Museum Collections*, vol. 131, no. 1, 1995, p. 57 (ill).

115 *P S Windsor towing Siam*

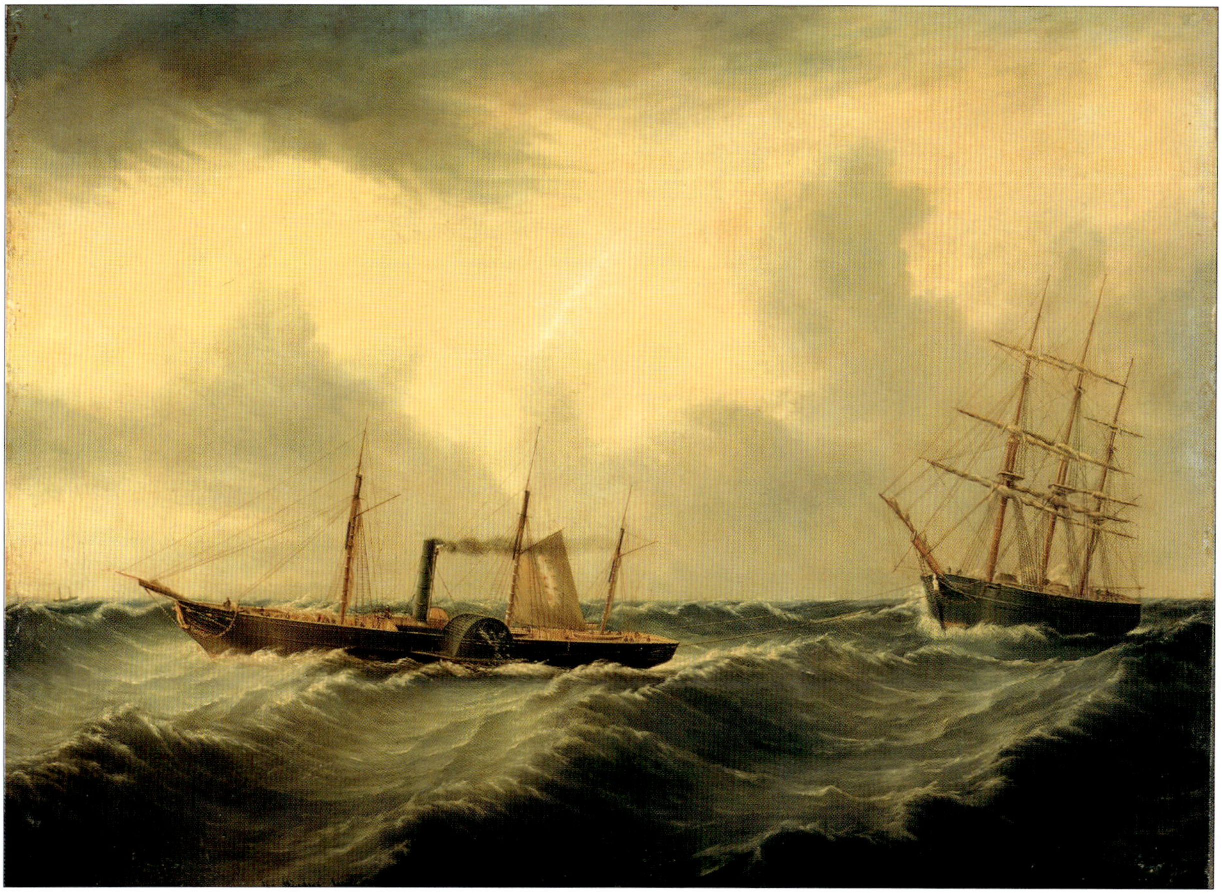

This view shows the paddle steamer *Windsor* towing the ship rigged *Siam* in heavy weather off the Owers Light Ship, on station in the English Channel south-east of Selsey Bill, Sussex.
The lightship is on the horizon to the extreme left so the vessels are making their way down the Channel against an adverse tide. It is clear *Siam* is not being salvaged: she has all her sails furled and appears to be undamaged with her rigging and masts intact. The explanation is that she has sought assistance to get under way against the gale force winds which are obviously blowing. The waves crashing over the starboard side of both vessels indicate that the wind is now coming from the north-west and that the situation will improve once the tide turns.
In fact, *Siam* had left Gravesend under Captain Wilson bound for Constantinople on 23 October. A gale had been blowing in the Channel for some days and many ships had been forced back into port.[2] It would seem *Siam* went into Deal on 24

3.12.26
Oil on canvas[1]
71 cm x 102 cm
Signed (bc) "The Windsor Isaac Davies Commander towing the Ship Siam off the Owers Light Ship 26th October 1855. / Josh Heard painter"
Prov: Robert Gladstone, who presented it, 1926
Exh: Crosby, 1951, no. 99; Liverpool, 1986
Ref: Handbook, 1935, p.50; Port Panorama, p.14; A S Davidson "Narrative Marine Painting" in *The Antique Collector*, March 1988, p.104

Vessels:
Siam 182 ft (l), 30 ft (b), 18.6 ft (d); 743 gross tons
Windsor 205 ft (l), 700 gross tons

October to seek assistance before venturing further against the weather. She left the same day "in tow of the *Windsor* (s[teamer])".[3] By 26 October the gale was abating.[4] Thus the details of Heard's composition are confirmed.

The identification of both vessels is confirmed on their bows. The iron paddle steamer *Windsor* was built in Liverpool in 1845. She operated on the Liverpool-Belfast passenger service for the City of Dublin Steam Packet Company from 1846 to 1851.[5] There is a painting of *Windsor* off the Mersey by Joseph Heard in the Peabody Collection.[6]

Siam was built in Ipswich in 1855, the year of this painting, for the Middlesborough Dock Company and initially operated between London and the Crimea. Later she was in the China trade. She was abandoned at sea by 1872.[7]

Isaac Davies may be the master mariner listed as living at 2 Virgil Street, Liverpool in 1851.[8] He was presumably responsible for commissioning the painting from Heard.

1 Relined. Stretcher label for J Davey, Liverpool.
2 On 21 October "Most of the outward bound that sailed yesterday" had put back into Deal, LL 22 October 1855.
3 LL 25 October 1855. Another vessel, *Figli Seteri* also left Deal under tow of a steamer on 24 October, ibid.
4 "gale abated", LL 26 October 1855.
5 McNeill 1969, pp. 52, 194.
6 Brewington PM, no. 637, illus.
7 LR 1856-72.
8 GDL 1851.

Associate of Joseph Heard ["Old Ensign"][1]

Paintings by this artist are initially very similar to those of Joseph Heard in terms of composition and style. Characteristically they feature a red ensign of the pre-1801 design, i.e. without the red diagonals of the St Patrick's Cross, with a regularity that cannot be unintentional. Occasionally, the artist depicts the union flag correctly (as in no. 117, *Borneo*) and the old ensign must be a specific "hallmark". He often makes other mistakes, in spelling with *Borneo* and *Bosphorus* (no. 118), or in the flag code, again in *Borneo*. It is surprising these errors were not corrected for the discerning patrons who commissioned them. The artist almost certainly worked closely with Joseph Heard. Davidson has suggested that he may be identified as Isaac Heard, brother of Joseph, who is known as a ship portraitist but for whom no signed works are known.[2]

1 I am grateful to Sam Davidson for first setting me on this trail.
2 Davidson, 1992, p. 113, discusses *Kingston* off the Skerries which bears the characteristics and which he attributes to Isaac Heard. The artist is known as a portrait painter and signed examples of his work in this medium are known in private collections.

116 *Amity in the Mersey*

This conventionally composed portrait of the barque *Amity* in two positions in the Mersey includes a good view of Liverpool and a wealth of other shipping in the distance.

In the centre of the canvas *Amity* is shown in a full port profile with all sails set, except the main course. The name of the ship, shown on the bow, is confirmed by the Marryat hoist on the mizzen (1 d.p., 3,0,8). An unidentified pennant of a blue cross on a white background flies from the main mast and on the foremast the blue peter shows that the vessel is about to leave port. A pre-1801 red ensign flies from the peak.

The second view to the left shows *Amity* in a quarter stern view having reduced sail further. She flies the same pennant and ensign as in the main view. To the far right, again in a quarter stern view, is the No. 1 pilot cutter *Liverpool*, built by William Dickinson of Liverpool in 1834 and in service until 1856.[1] The pilot boat flies a blue peter, which in this case indicates that a pilot is available.

The Liverpool waterfront is depicted across the background with most noticeably the George's Baths, St Peter's and the Custom House visible between the two views of *Amity*. The spire of St Michael's can be seen between the fore and main masts in the principal view and astern are Queen's Dock, St James' church, Parliament Street and the windmill at Mill Street. The view trails away towards Garston. A variety of small coastal craft, including a rowing boat astern of the main view, and various paddle steamers and tugs are depicted along the waterfront.

Amity was built in Whitby by Barricks in 1818 for the Chapman Brothers, a leading Quaker family of merchants, ship owners and bankers.[2] She was generally employed in trading from London to a variety of distant destinations, including Bombay, The

1 Rees, p.202.
2 see R Weatherill *The Ancient Port of Whitby and its Shipping*, 1908; *Amity* was originally ship rigged but was later lengthened and converted to barque rig.
3 LCR, vol. 58, no. 104, 27 May 1843, and vol. 60, no. 189, 11 August 1845.
4 Davidson 1986.
5 Davidson 1986, p.47, follows previous attribution to Walters and *Port Panorama* p.4 proposes Dove.
6 LCR, vol. 58, No. 104, 11 August 1845.

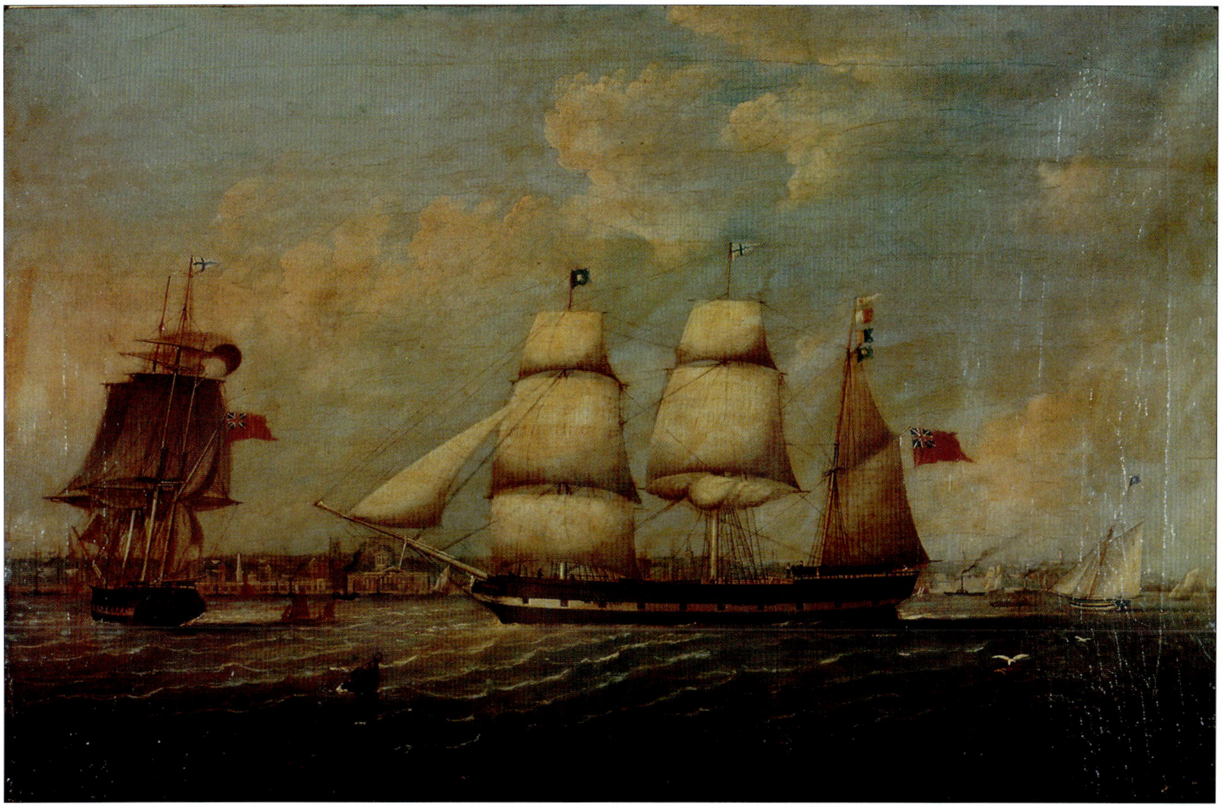

Cape and Quebec. She was bought by the Liverpool firm of Chapman and Willis in May 1843 and was abandoned at sea in October 1848 returning from New Brunswick with a cargo of timber.[3]
The painting must date from after 1837 because of the Marryat code hoist[4] and presumably was completed during her Liverpool ownership of 1843-48. Earlier attributions to Samuel Walters and Thomas Dove cannot be sustained.[5] The pre-1801 ensign and general composition and style suggest this is one of the works by the anonymous artist "Old Ensign".
Edward Joseph Allen was Master of *Amity* from 1845[6] and it was his granddaughter who presented the painting, along with nos. 111 and 117.

1964.194.1
Oil on canvas
61 cm x 91.5 cm
Prov. Captain E J Allen, by descent to Miss May Allen, who presented it, 1964.
Exh. Liverpool 1986
Ref: Port Panorama, 1986 p.4 (ill)

Vessel: 105.1 ft (l), 25 ft (b), 19 ft (d); 435 gross tons.

117 Borneo (page 112)

Borneo is depicted in two views in Beaumaris Bay, off Anglesey. In the main view, placed centrally in the canvas, the ship is shown in port profile with the crew clewing up her main course as she prepares to heave to and await a pilot for her inward journey to Liverpool. Unusually the second view shows the vessel astern in starboard quarter profile outward bound. There is some nice detail in the main view, such as the shadows from the foresails falling across the mainsails.
To the left of the main view a pilot cutter is heading to rendezvous with the vessel. The blue peter indicates she is in service and has a pilot on board. In the distance, under the bowsprit a ship is shown in port profile and astern a steamer and other sailing ships are visible. The familiar outline of Parys Mountain with Point Lynas to the right can be seen in the far distance under the bowsprit.
The evidence for the identification of the vessel is not consistent. The name on the bow is *Borneo* but *Bornea* on the name pennant on the main mast. This is presumably a careless mistake but one that could have been rectified easily. She flies a Union Jack at the foremast and a pre-1801 red ensign from the peak. More perplexing is

1964.194.2
Oil on canvas
61cm x 91.5 cm
Prov: Miss May Allen, presented 1964.

Vessel: 120.5 ft (l), 29 ft (b), 6.2 ft (d); 458 gross tons

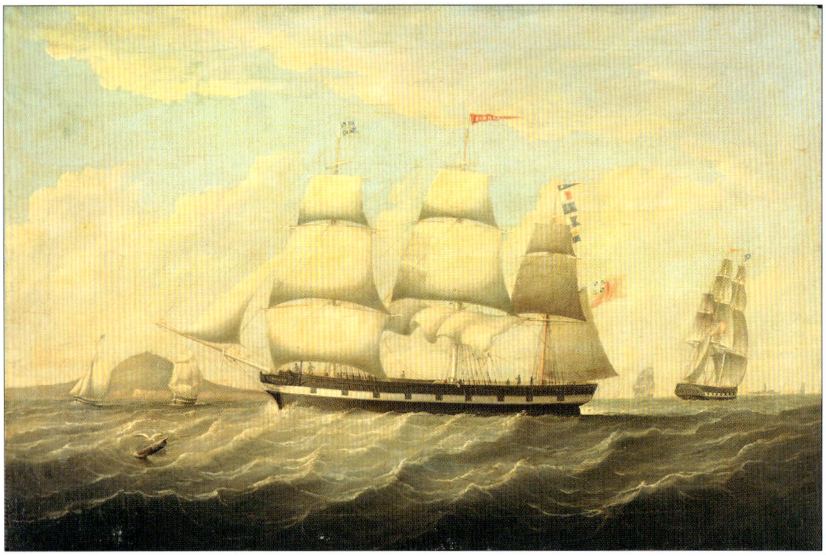

that the flag hoist (2 d.p. 3,8,0,9) signifies the barque *Rockshire*.[1] This is hardly likely to be a random choice on the part of the artist. It cannot be a coincidence that this painting (with Nos. 111 and 116) came from the granddaughter of Captain E J Allen who was master of *Rockshire* (no. 111) from August 1843. Did Allen serve on *Borneo* before getting his master's ticket?[2] So what is going on?

The ship rigged *Borneo* was built in Quebec by John Bell in 1835 for James Logan, a Liverpool merchant. She was re-registered in Limerick in 1836 and was owned by F Speight in 1845. She sailed between Ireland and Quebec until she was lost on a return voyage in the Straits of Belle Isle in July 1846.[3]

There is strong evidence for attributing this painting to "Old Ensign". It bears all the hallmarks of this artist - a similarity of style with its close affinity to Joseph Heard, the pre-1801 ensign and an inaccurate name and flag code. An almost identical composition of the ship *Oregon* (built St John, New Brunswick, 1846) is in the New Brunswick Museum.[4]

1 The correct number for *Borneo* in the post-1840 code was 2 dp 3 6 1 4.
2 Edward Joseph Allen was born 1819, so *Rockshire* was almost certainly his first command. See LR 1850. He died on a run to Melbourne in 1863. (R Anderson *White Star*, 1964, p.35).
3 LCR, Vol. 51, No. 138; LR 1845. For loss see LL 29 August 1846. For Quebec registration see Marcil, p. 372.
4 See R S Elliot & A D McNairn *Reflections of an Era*, New Brunswick Museum, 1987, No. 8. There attributed to John Hughes (1806-1878).

118 Bosphorus

1931.212
Oil on canvas
61 cm x 91.5 cm
Prov: Robert Gladstone, who presented it, 1931
Exh: Crosby 1951, No. 89
Ref: Handbook 1932, p.40; M K Stammers *The Passage Makers*, Brighton, 1978, (ill p.366); Tibbles 1988 (ill.); Nottingham 1992, pp. 62-3 (ill.)

Vessel: 217.5 ft (l), 39.8 ft (b), 23 ft (d); 1346 gross tons.

The ship rigged *Bosphorus* is shown in port profile entering the Mersey with an impressive amount of sail. However, the top royals and the lower sheets of the fore and main masts are being furled as the vessel enters the hazardous approaches of the river. The No. 5 pilot boat is visible under the bowsprit with the familiar Perch Rock Lighthouse and Fort in the far left-hand distance. A Mersey flat can be seen on the horizon to the right.

The vessel is identifiable by her Marryat flag code of 1 d.p. 1, 0, 7, 8. A blue name pennant flies from the main mast but the artist misspells her name as *Bosphorous* (though he gets it right on the hull). At the foremast is the Rathbone house flag of an "R" on a white band between two red bands. She flies a pre-1801 red ensign at the peak.

Bosphorus was built of wood in St John, New Brunswick, Canada in 1855 and was acquired by Rathbone and their associates from Francis, Thomas and Joseph Ruddock of New Brunswick in December of that year. She sailed mainly to India, in particular Bombay. Rathbones sold her to James Stoddart of Liverpool in 1863 and she was transferred to London owners in February 1869.[1]

The No.5 pilot Boat is the schooner *Victoria and Albert* built by Michael Ratsey in West Cowes in 1856. She collided with the barque *Governor* under tow three miles off the Bar light vessel in May 1888 and sank with the loss of one pilot.[2]

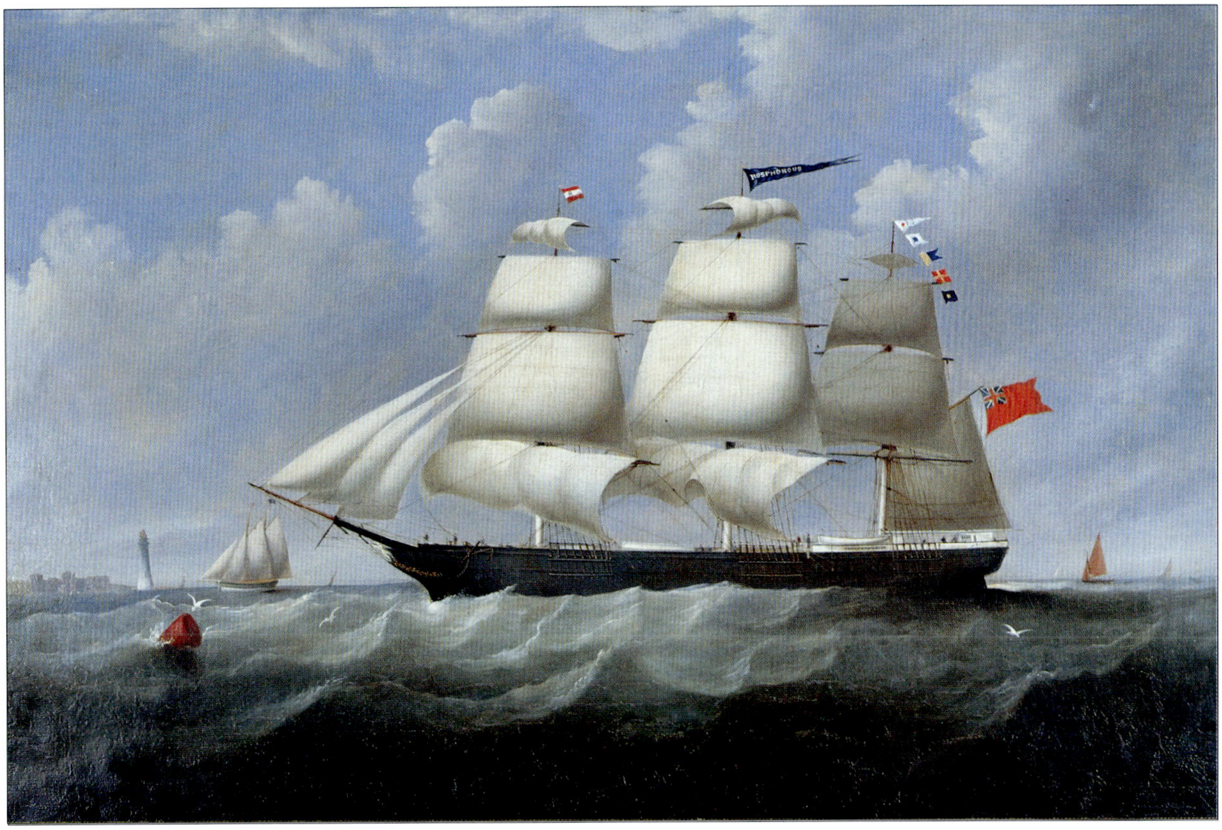

The painting has previously been attributed to an Associate of Joseph Heard but it bears the style and hallmarks of "Old Ensign", including the misspelling of the name pennant.

A gouache and watercolour version of this painting was offered for sale in 1996.[3] It follows the same composition and the principal difference is the cloud formation of the sky. The name on the pennant is correctly spelt but the old ensign maintained. It is signed "A E S".

1 LCR vol. 80, no. 415, 17 December 1855; vol. 85, no. 385, 28 September 1863.
2 Rees, p.203.
3 Northeast Auctions, New Hampshire, 18 August 1996, lot 684.

119 *Salacia picking up a pilot* (page 114)

The ship rigged *Salacia* is shown in two views in Beaumaris Bay off Point Lynas picking up a pilot. In the main view the vessel is depicted in port profile hove-to with the small pilot punt alongside ready for the pilot to climb aboard for the passage into Liverpool. The secondary view to the left of the canvas shows the ship under way in a stern view having turned towards the coast and all her sails set except the main course. The unidentified pilot boat is on the far right in the middle distance. She is shown from the stern in a half port profile and flies the blue pilot jack.

Salacia is identifiable from her name on the bow and on the port side near the stern. She flies a pre-1801 Union Jack at her fore, the house flag of Gibbs Bright & Co. at her main, a pre-1840 Marryat flag hoist (1 d.p. 4,9,7,5) for *Salacia* from the mizzen and a pre-1801 red ensign from the peak.

The vessel was built in St Andrews, New Brunswick, Canada in 1848 for Edward and John Wilson also of New Brunswick. She was bought in May 1849 by Samuel Bright of Liverpool and George Gibbs and Robert Bright of Bristol, trading as Gibbs, Bright & Company of Liverpool. They sold her on in 1853.[2]

The familiar outline of Parys mountain and Point Lynas on Anglesey can be seen under the bowsprit of the main view, with a 3 masted steamer making for Liverpool.

1 Relined.
2 LCR vol. 65, No. 127, 14 May 1849.
3 born 1814, LR 1850.
4 The post-1840 number is 2 dp 5, 6, 7.
5 Brewington, no. 1305, p.333, ill.

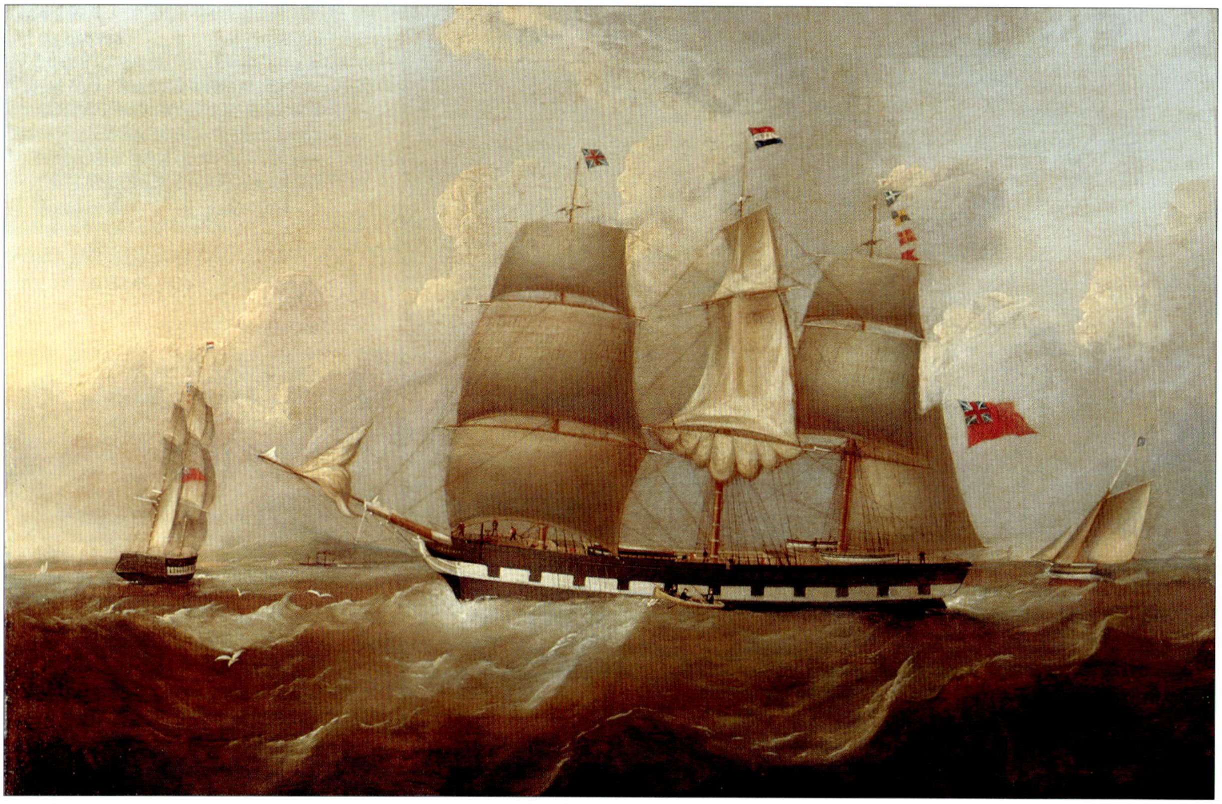

1955.147
Oil on canvas[1]
61 cm x 91.5 cm
Prov: John Robertson Brown, by descent to granddaughter, Mrs M E Astin, Wallasey, who presented it in memory of her grandfather, 1955.

Vessel: 145.8 ft (l), 29.6 ft (b), 21.7 ft (d); 844 gross tons

The painting must date from the period 1849-53 when she was in Gibbs Bright ownership and this would seem to be confirmed by the provenance of the painting from her master at this time, John Robertson Brown.[3] However, the artist has made a significant mistake in using the pre-1840 Marryat code for *Salacia* rather than the code that would have been applicable at the time of the painting.[4] It is intriguing that if this was painted for the captain he did not object to this obvious error. Did he perhaps acquire it later in life when a correction was no longer possible?

The style, with the pre-1801 flags and the inaccurate code, bears all the hallmarks of "Old Ensign".

There is a watercolour of *Salacia* attributed to W F Settle in the Peabody Collection.[5]

120 Sea Flower

1955.251
Oil on canvas
61 cm x 91.5 cm
Prov: Unknown, in collections, 1955

Vessel: 181.5 ft (l), 36.4 ft (b), 24.2 ft (d); 1072 tons

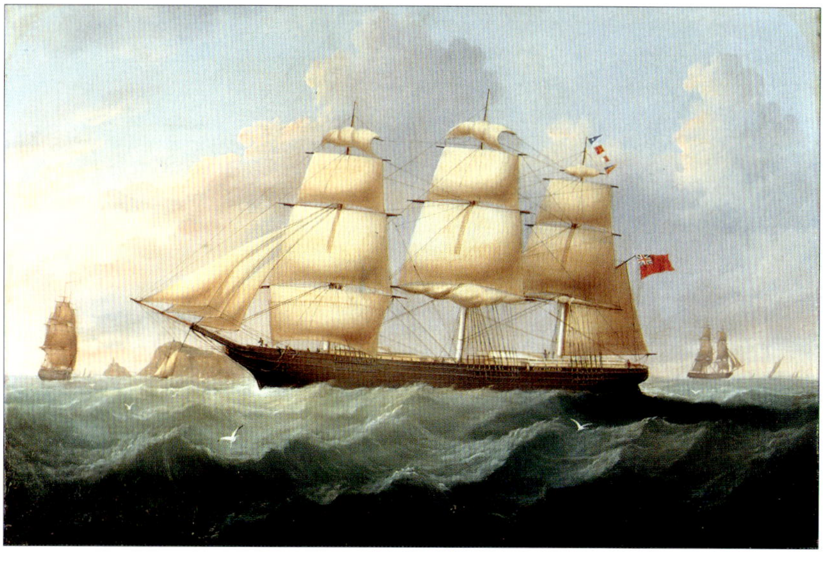

The ship rigged *Sea Flower* is shown in port profile off South Stack Lighthouse and Anglesey with other shipping in the far distance. All her sails, except the main and mizzen course, are set. All her topsails feature a central panel indicative of the Cunningham patent reefing system which allowed the sails to be reefed from the deck.[1] Her name is painted on her port stern and the Marryat flag code (2 d.p. 7, 3, 6) on the mizzen confirms her identity. She flies a pre-1801 red ensign at the peak. An unidentified pilot boat can be seen under the bowsprit displaying her blue peter. There is a brig in a starboard profile outward bound off the stern and a ship rigged vessel in a quarter bow view to the far left.

The wooden ship *Sea Flower* was built at Mudford in the United States in 1853. She was purchased by James Jackson, Robert Honan and George McCorquodale, all Liverpool merchants in 1863 and remained in their ownership until sold to a Sunderland shipbuilder, Thomas Oswald in 1868. She was later sold to Richard Muir of Greenock, converted to a barque in 1880 and was condemned and hulked in 1883.[2]

The style is very similar to other works attributed to "Old Ensign" and bears the indicative pre-1801 ensign.

1For a description of the system, patented in 1850, see Underhill, pp. 127-130, 156.
2 LCR vol. 85, no. 106, 28 March 1863; Beard.

S G P Heath (active 1901)

121 *S S Manchester Merchant*

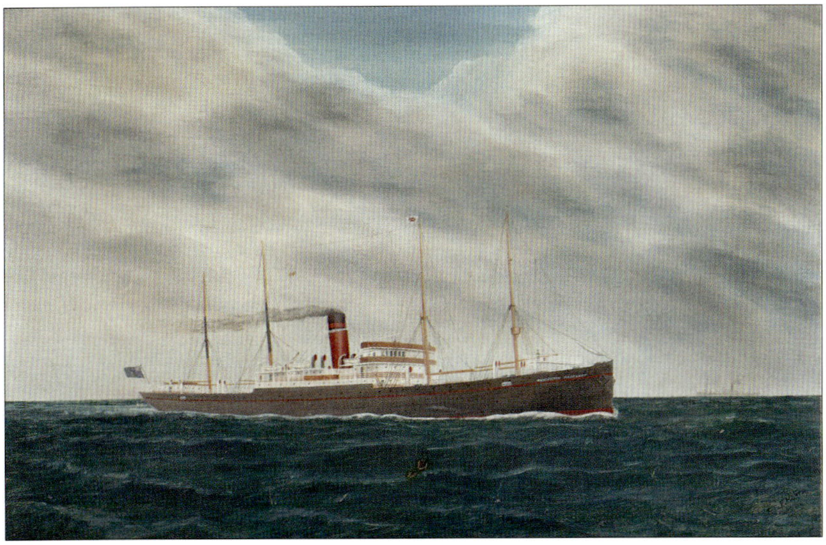

1972.174.1
Oil on canvas
51 cm x 76.5 cm
Signed and dated (br) "S. G. P. HEATH / 1901"
Prov: Mrs H J Chubb, Wirral, who presented it, 1972

Vessel: 452 ft (l), 52.2 ft (b), 28.3 ft (d); 5657 gross tons

This starboard view of the steamship *Manchester Merchant* shows the vessel at sea during her period as a transport ship during the Boer War. She is painted in the house colours of her owners, Manchester Liners, and flies their house flag on her second mast. The blue ensign, flying from her stern, indicates her temporary naval role and her troopship number "No.92" is painted on the hull. A similar steam vessel is shown on the horizon in the far right distance.

Manchester Merchant was built by Palmers & Co. of Newcastle in 1900. She was chartered by the Admiralty and made five voyages as a transport vessel to Table Bay and Natal during 1901.[1] She was scuttled on fire in Dingle Bay in January 1903 on a passage from New Orleans to Manchester.[2]

1 LL Index, 1901.
2 See *Sea Breezes*, vol. 26, 1958, pp. 34-46.

Harry Taylor Hoodless (1913 - 1997)

Harry Hoodless was born in Yorkshire and trained in Leeds and at the Royal College of Art. He was appointed to the Laird School of Art in Birkenhead in 1939 and served in the Royal Navy, 1941-5. In 1946 he returned to the Laird retiring in 1976. The majority of his paintings are of boats and dock scenes. A retrospective exhibition was held at the Williamson Art Gallery in 1993.[1]

1 See illustrated catalogue, *Harry Hoodless*, Williamson Art Gallery & Museum, Birkenhead, 13 June - 11 July 1993.

122 Waiting The Tide

MMM.1996.16
Oil on hardboard[1]
68 cm x 97 cm
Signed and dated (br) "Hoodless / 1954"
Prov: Boydell Galleries, Liverpool; S Wood, Wimborne, who presented it, 1996.

Vessel: 515.5 ft (l), 68.3 ft (b), 35.2 ft (d); 10,109 gross tons

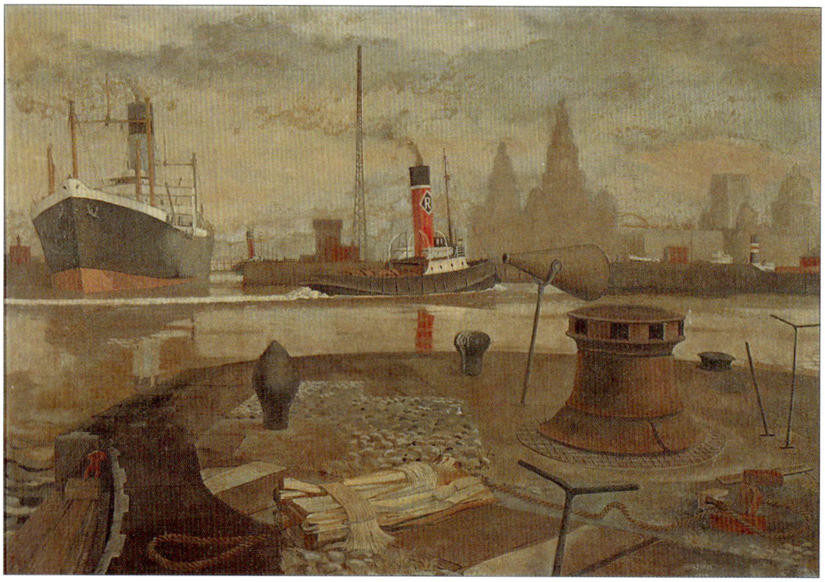

This painting shows a Blue Funnel Liner tied up against the quay in the Alfred Dock, Birkenhead, waiting for the tide, presumably prior to her departure. The vessel, which may be *Philoctetes*[2] is portrayed in a bow view in the left middle distance and there is a Rea Company tug in starboard profile in the centre of the canvas. Another Rea tug is in the distance and the funnel of a T & J Harrison tug (identifiable by its black, red and white funnel) can also be seen behind the dock wall. The vantage point is from the central island of the gates leading into the Wallasey Dock. The Liverpool waterfront, with the famous Pierhead buildings and the ventilation tower for the Mersey tunnel, is in the background.

The composition is typical of Hoodless with a strong foreground featuring dock furniture and various ropes and equipment prominently.

Philoctetes was built by Vickers, Armstrong of Newcastle for use by the China Mutual Steam Navigation Company, a subsidiary of Ocean, in 1950. She was broken up in 1973 in Taiwan.[3]

1 There are a series of labels on the rear: 1) hand-written "WAITING THE TIDE / No. I"; 2) printed Boydell Galleries, Liverpool; 3) hand-written "No. I. ~~PHILOCTETES~~ / WAITING THE TIDE / H. T. HOODLESS / 41, GRAFTON DRIVE / UPTON WIRRAL / CHESHIRE" added in pencil "35 gns"; 4) printed label for James Bourlet & Co., G16218. An inscription on the board reads "Artist - H. T. HOODLESS / 41, GRAFTON DRIVE / UPTON WIRRAL / CHESHIRE / Title - (blank) / No. - I"
2 This name is crossed out in a label, see above. Philoctetes was an archer in the Trojan wars.
3 Haws Blue Funnel, p. 119

John Hughes (1806-1880)

Born in Liverpool in 1806, Hughes was self-taught. His earliest works date from the mid-1830s. He was patronised particularly by American captains and owners and there are few of his works in British collections. There are good examples at India House, New York, South Street Seaport Museum, New York and Bath Museum, Maine.[1]

1 For details see Davidson, 1986, pp. 76-9, 88-9.

123 *Pilot Cutter No. 11*

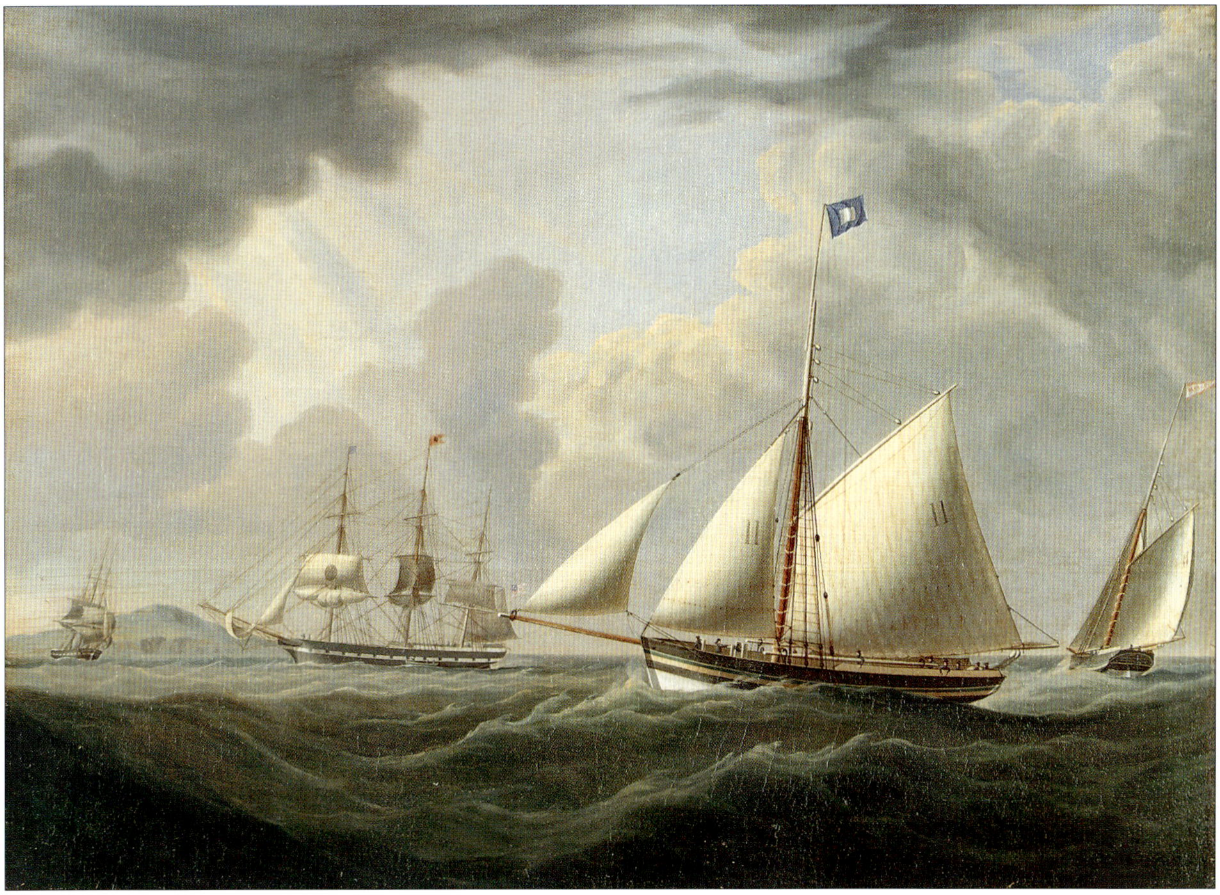

The No. 11 Pilot Cutter is shown in two views off Point Lynas, Anglesey, in the process of putting a pilot on board a packet ship, which is making her way into Liverpool. The scene is dramatically lit with sunlight streaming from behind the dark clouds in the top left-hand corner of the canvas.

The pilot boat is portrayed centre right in port profile with a further port quarter view to the right. She flies the blue peter to indicate she has pilots available for boarding. The packet ship, also in port profile, is shown in the middle distance hove-to and the pilot punt is alongside boarding the pilot for the inward run. There is other unidentified shipping closer to the coast. A fresh easterly wind is blowing and all vessels are well reefed, the gaff of the pilot boat has been lowered almost halfway down the mast and the normal jib has been replaced by a smaller one.

The exact identity of the pilot boat cannot be precisely established. She is either *Mersey*, built by Mottershead & Heyes in 1816 and sold in 1847, or *Mersey*, built by Thomas Royden in 1847 and replaced in 1878. Both were square sterned and of similar dimensions.[2] The packet ship belongs to the American Black Ball Line, as indicated by the characteristic black circle on the fore topsail.

The vessel is shown in Beaumaris Bay off the coast of Anglesey with Point Lynas and Parys Mountain in the background. Incoming vessels often sheltered from the westerly winds here whilst awaiting a pilot.

The picture has been attributed to John Hughes on stylistic grounds and a similar painting with the same location is in an American private collection.[3]

1976.322.1
Oil on canvas
48 cm x 67 cm
Prov: Mrs L B Ward, London, from whom purchased 1988[1]

Vessel:
(built 1816) 48.1 ft (l), 16.3 ft (b), 6.3 ft (d); 52 gross tons
(built 1847) 55.7 ft (l), 14.6 ft (b), 8.7 ft (d); 47 gross tons

1 The painting was offered with a certificate and notebook belonging to James Durrant (1823-1877), a pilot on no. 11 boat, suggesting a possible provenance. Documents in DX 1044 (MAL). Information on Durrant see Tebay 1991 and pilotage records, MAL.
2 Rees, pp. 201-2.
3 *Great Western* in Beaumaris Bay, see Finamore, 1995, no. 27.

Stanley J Hugill (1906 - 1992)

Born on the Wirral, Stan Hugill spent 26 years at sea. He was an amateur artist but is best known as a collector and singer of sea shanties and as an author.[1]

1 S J Hugill *Sailortown*, London, 1967.

124 Garthpool

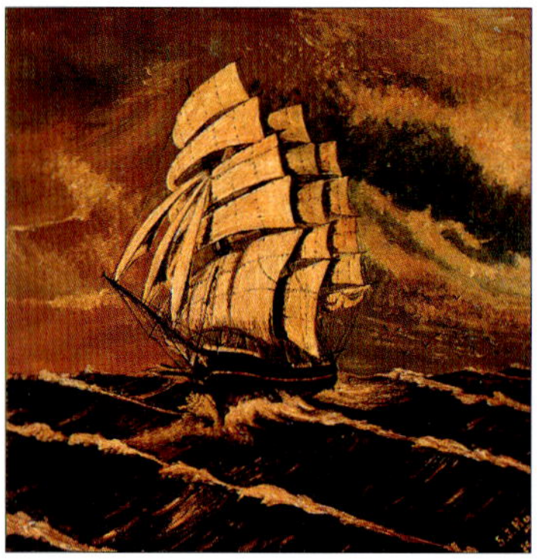

1981.733
Oil on plyboard[1]
61 cm x 61 cm
Signed and dated (br) "S. J. Hugill / 1930"; inscribed rear "Presented to E Louis / ("Doc") / In Remembrance of the / British 4 masted Barque "Garthpool" / Last British Windjammer / Wrecked November 11th 1929 on / Ponta Reef, East Sandhead / Boa Vista / Cape Verde Islands / Painted by S. J. Hugill A.B. & Chanteyman / En Recuerdo."
Prov. Mr E Louis, by descent to son, Mr A E Louis, Bootle, who presented it, 1981
Ref: George Harrison, 'The Mersey Wall', in *Liverpool Echo and Evening Express*, 6 October 1966.

Vessel: 310 ft (l), 45 ft (b), 25.1 (d); 2842 gross tons.

The 4 masted barque *Garthpool*, which was the last deep sea British sailing ship under full sail, is shown in port quarter profile. It is a typical sailing ship pose - the vessel has all her sails set and is proudly pulling through the sea. The artist has included a painted border to look like a mount for the painting.

Garthpool was built by W B Thompson in 1891 as *Juteopolis* for Barrie & Co. for the Dundee to Calcutta jute trade. Within a few years sailing ships were pushed out of the jute trade and *Juteopolis* was sold to the Anglo-American Oil Company in 1901. She was sold to George Windram & Sons of Liverpool in 1911 for £6500 and was transferred to Sir William Garthwaite's Marine Navigation fleet in 1918 and renamed *Garthpool*. She was employed in deep sea trades, particularly the grain trade from Australia. She was lost off the Cape Verde Islands in 1929.[2]

The painting was given to the donor's father who was employed as the cook on *Garthpool*.[3]

1 The plyboard is split in the top right hand corner.
2 Lubbock Windjammers, II, pp. 149-150. *Juteopolis* is illustrated opp. p.144. Full details of her loss are in A A Hurst *Square Riggers - The Final Epoch*, 1972, pp. 277-279.
3 *Liverpool Echo and Evening Express*, 6 October 1966.

William Jackson (active about 1770 - about 1803)

Jackson is listed as a painter in the Liverpool directories from 1777 to 1803 and exhibited in the town in 1774, 1784 and 1787. He was also a painter of porcelain ship bowls, possibly from 1754 and is almost certainly responsible for a group of bowls dating from 1770-1790. Currently only two signed paintings and a handful of attributed works are known.[1]

1 For a summary of Jackson's career and full details of his work on ship bowls see Watney, B. 'William Jackson of Liverpool', *Transactions of the English Ceramic Circle*, vol. 15, part 1, pp. 122-133.

125 A Liverpool Slave Ship, about 1780

Jackson portrays an unidentified 16-gun ship of about 1780 in port profile centrally placed in the canvas. A second view of the vessel is sketchily shown in a port quarter view in the middle distance to the right and in the far distance on the left hand side a wooded coastline is indicated.

The ship is shown in some detail in the main view, including the decorated topsides which are painted with flags and trophies and the figurehead in classical dress. In addition to the guns, there is a small swivel gun at the bow. There is a great deal of activity on board the vessel with her master in his tricorn hat and other officers giving orders: the sails are being furled, preparations are being made to drop anchor and one of the boats is about to be launched. She flies the pilot jack at the stern and a union flag at the end of her bowsprit. Despite the detailed figurehead there is insufficient information to allow the vessel to be identified.[1]

The vessel is almost certainly involved in slaving as the four ventilation ports in her lower hull confirm. Three small boats are approaching the ship from the shore. Each boat is being rowed by a number of Africans, who all use a standing position. The coastline, which is reminiscent of tropical climes, is almost certainly intended to be West Africa. There are huts in the trees and various Black figures, including a man with a stick, children and women with bundles, can be seen on the shore.

The approaching small boats and some of the figures on the shoreline had been

1 Williams 1897, Appendix IV, lists at least 21 vessels of sixteen guns for the period 1775-83. Jackson exhibited a painting in 1784 under the title "Tartar Sloop Sea Piece". The only Liverpool registered vessel of this name, although ship rigged, did not possess a figurehead and carried eighteen guns. Craig & Jarvis, p.102; Williams, p.237.
2 NMGM Conservation Report, 25 August 1995, DCF.
3 See Watney, op. cit..

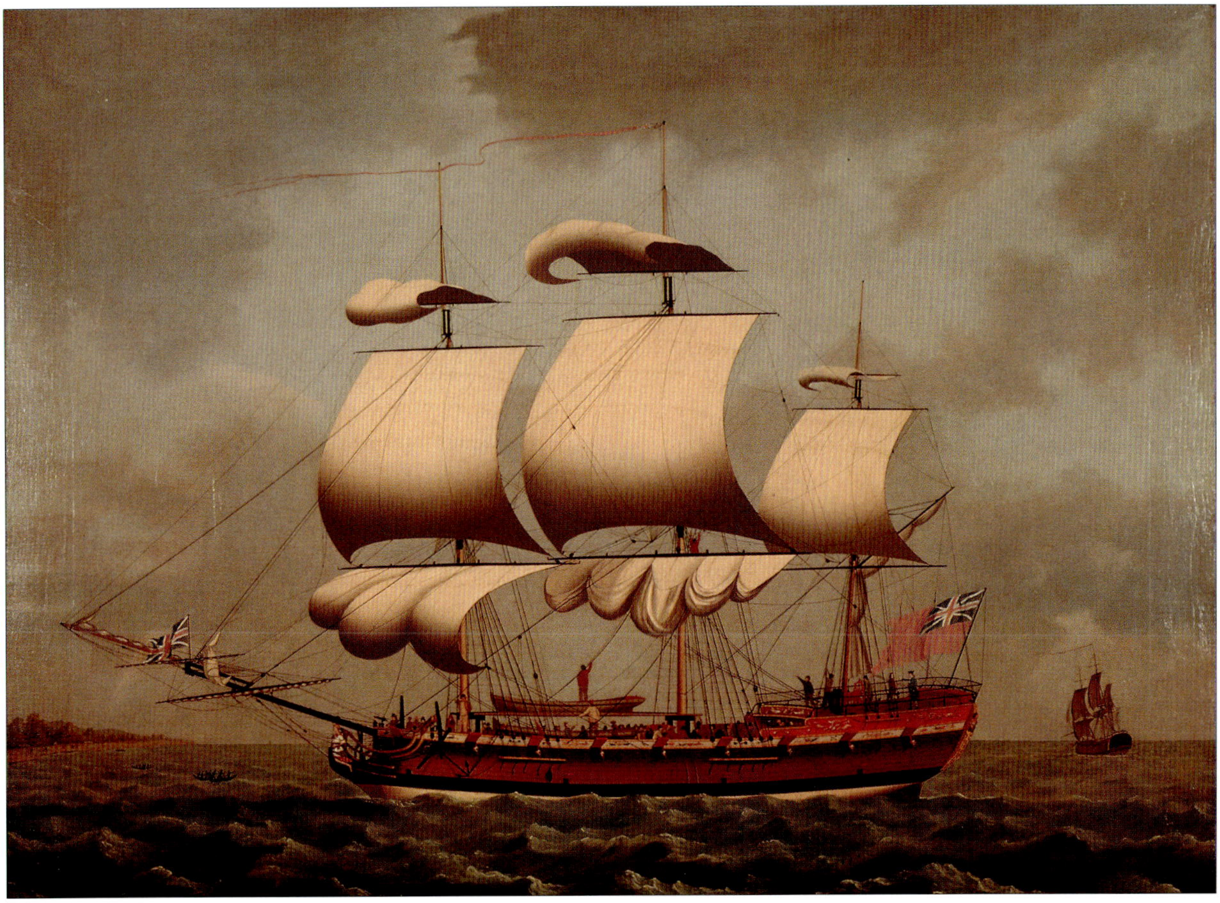

painted over prior to the painting's acquisition by the museum and were only revealed as a result of conservation treatment in 1994.[2]
The stylised sails are typical of the few works by Jackson which are known at present.[3]

1964.227.2
Oil on canvas
102 cm x 127 cm
Signed 'W Jackson Pnx'
Prov: Transferred from the Manx Museum, Isle of Man, 1964.
Exh: Liverpool, 1986
Ref: Port Panorama 1986, p.14 (ill); Anthony Tibbles (ed.) Transatlantic Slavery, 1994, no. 87, ill. p. 41.

126 *Watt*

The ship rigged *Watt* is shown in three positions off an unidentified coast in this fine portrait. In the centre of the canvas the vessel is shown centrally in port profile with a stern view in the left middle distance and a starboard quarter view to the right which is at odds with the perspective. The main view shows her making progress through the water with all sails set, except the headsails and mizzen course and the main sail is clewed up. She displays a fine classical warrior as her figurehead and painted and decorated galleries. Her crew are disposed about the deck undertaking a variety of duties and the master can be identified in front of the mizzen issuing orders through a speaking trumpet. She flies a long pennant from the main mast and the post-1801 red ensign at her stern in all three views.
Watt was built by Edward Grayson of Liverpool in 1797 for the local merchant firm of Watt and Walker. The *Advertiser* noted the launch of this "remarkable fine three-decked ship" and reported that "a large band of military music" was on board to entertain the spectators.[1] She was equipped with 22 guns and was built for the Jamaica trade, where Richard Watt also had an estate. She was sold to two Liverpool merchants, Morrall and Boland, in association with members of the Scott shipbuilding family of Greenock in 1809. She continued in the West Indies trade, principally carrying sugar, until 1812.[2]

1 Quoted in Williams, pp. 354-5.
2 LCR vol. 12, no. 11, 27 February 1897; vol. 14, no. 202, 15 December 1798; vol. 27, no. 327, 30 December 1809.
3 Label rear details DCF.
4 Illustrated R Stewart-Brown, *Liverpool Ships in the 18th Century*, Liverpool, 1932 p. 125.
5 On loan from Williamson Art Gallery, Birkenhead; illustrated in Anthony Tibbles *Transatlantic Slavery*, HMSO, 1994, p.39.

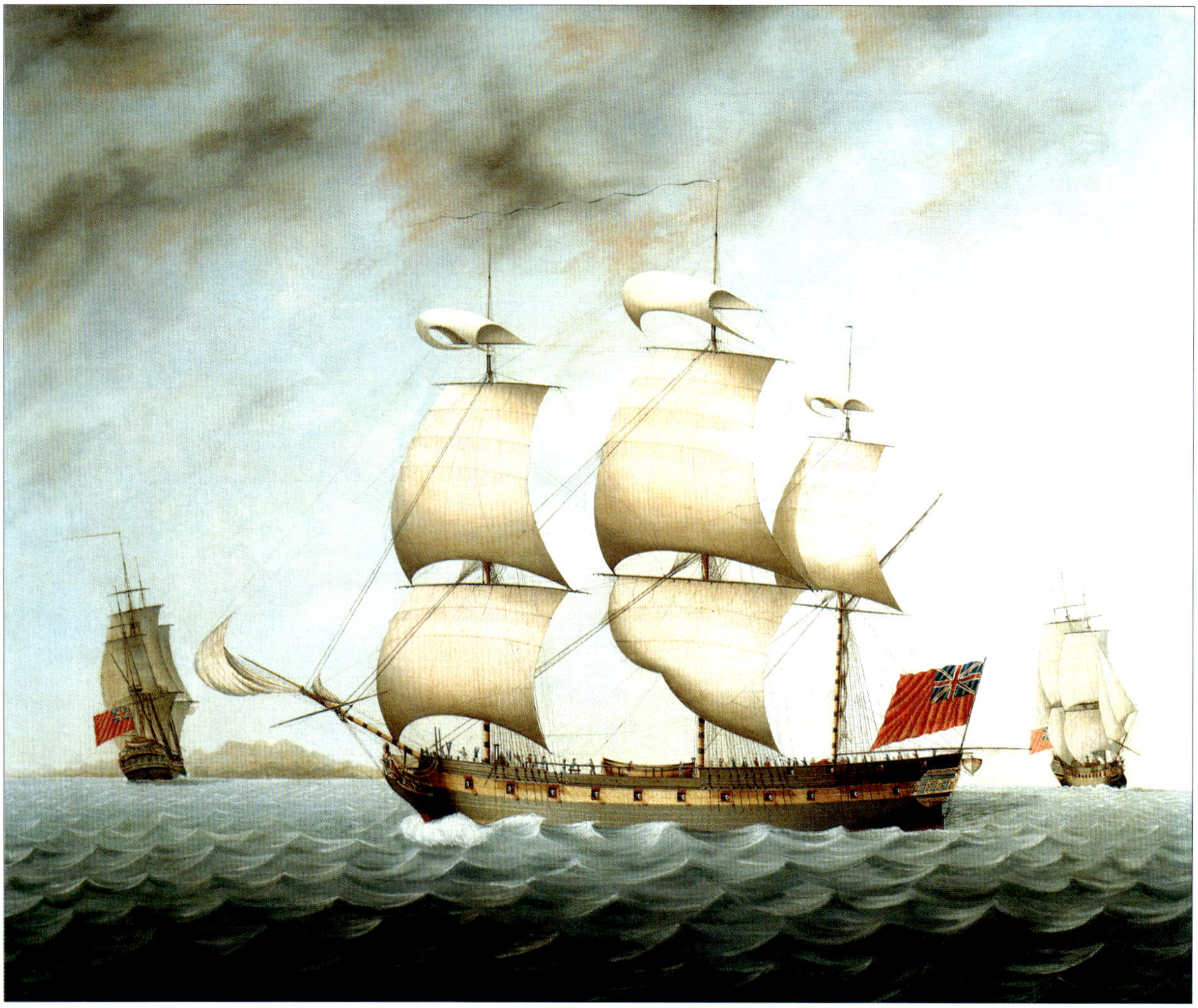

MMM.1996.195
91 cm x 117 cm
Oil on canvas
Prov: probably Captain W Kilpatrick, by descent in family; sold Bearne's, Torquay, 7 March 1995, lot 611; Lane Fine Art, London, from whom purchased, 1996.

Vessel: 122 ft (l), 33 ft (b), 6 ft 2 in (d); 564 gross tons

The painting has been attributed on stylistic grounds to William Jackson, particularly because of the distinctive treatment of the sails. It is one of the finest canvases so far known by his hand and is also a late work, completed in the last two years of his life.

The painting has probably descended in the family of Wilfred Kilpatrick, captain of the vessel from 1802 until 1805.[3]

There is a drawing of the vessel by J T Serres dated 27 March 1797 (formerly Liverpool Central Libraries)[4] and a contemporary builder's hull model in the collections (Accession no. L1982.186).[5]

Antonio Nicolo Gasparo Jacobsen (1850-1921)

Jacobsen was born in Denmark but emigrated to New York in 1873. He was perhaps the most prolific of all ship portraitists and produced more than 6,000 works during his lifetime. He mainly painted vessels that visited New York harbour and painted some of them many times. The majority of his paintings conform to a very standard format but he could be more inventive on occasions.[1]

The principal collection of his work is at Mariners' Museum, Newport News. Peabody Essex Museum, Salem and most other major museums have examples.[2]

1 For a detailed critique see Sniffen, 1994.
2 A complete list of his works are in Sniffen Checklist.

127 *Belle of Arvon*

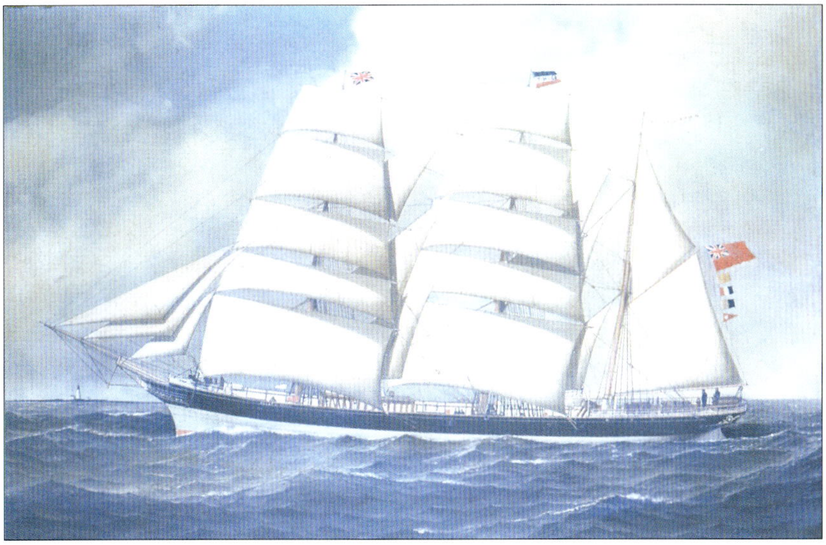

1960.161
Oil on canvas
56 cm x 91.5 cm
Signed "A Jacobsen"[1]
Prov: Mr L Stephenson, Anglesey, who presented it, 1960

Vessel: 193.1 ft (l), 33.2 ft (b), 20.6 ft (d); 946 gross tons

The three masted barque *Belle of Arvon* is shown in port profile probably off Anglesey. She has all her sails set and is making good progress. She has her name on the hull, on her wheel box and flies a name pennant from the mizzen mast. She also flies the pilot jack at the fore, her owner's house flag (blue, white and red bands with the initials T H & Co in the centre) at the main and her commercial flag code Q T K F below the red ensign at the after peak.

The lighthouse and adjacent buildings on rocks in the far distance under her bowsprit is probably intended to be the Skerries.

Belle of Arvon was built by Osbourne, Graham & Company of Hylton, Sunderland in 1876. She was initially owned by two Welshmen, William Griffiths and Edward Thomas, and then from 1885 by Tomlinson, Hodgetts & Co. of Liverpool. Throughout her career she had a large number of small scale Welsh shareholders, at one point there were 29 of them. Indeed she has one of the longest entries of any vessel in the Liverpool registers. *Belle of Arvon* was wrecked off Huara on a passage from Galapagos to Leith with a cargo of guano in 1899.[2]

There is a signed sketch of *Belle of Arvon* by Jacobsen in Mariners' Museum, Virginia, dated 1897, which is a study for this painting.[3]

1 DCF shows that the painting was indistinctly dated 1897 but this is no longer visible.
2 LCR vol. 92, no. 108, 5 September 1876 and subsequently TB5, pp. 438, 529, TB8, p.29, TB9, pp. 130, 540, TB11, p.60.
3 Sniffen Checklist, p.44-45.

128 *City of Berlin*

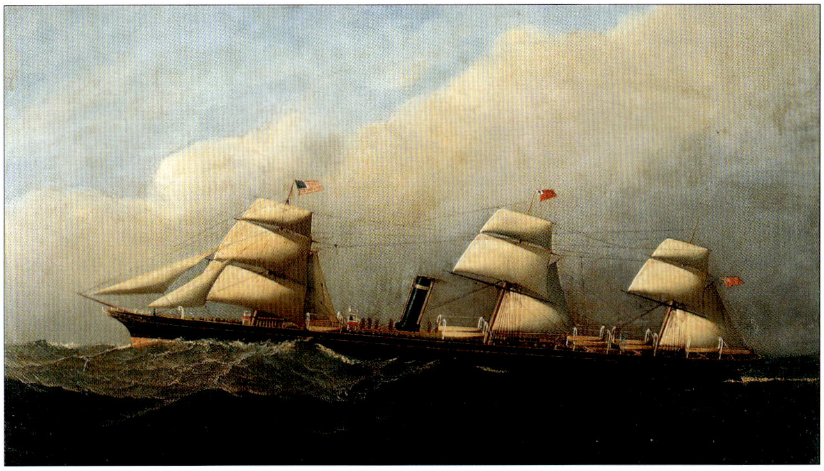

1955.256
Oil on canvas[1]
56 cm x 91.5 cm
Signed and dated (br) "Antonio Jacobsen / 257 8 Av NY / New [?] 23. [?7] 81"
Prov: Unknown, in collections, 1955.
Ref: Sniffen Checklist as *City of Chester*, p.68-9.

Vessel: 488.6 ft (l), 44.2 ft (b), 34.9 ft (d); 2 compound inverted direct action engines, 850 hp; 5491 gross tons.

City of Berlin is shown in a typical Jacobsen portrait. She is portrayed in port profile, slightly tilted to show her decks where substantial groups of people can be seen standing near the bow and aft deck. She is making good use of her auxiliary sail. At her foremast she flies the Stars and Stripes, indicating she is bound for New York. The Inman Line house flag is on the main mast with the red ensign at the peak. The funnel is painted in the Inman colours of black with an upper white band.

The name on the bow is given as *City of Chester* but this must be incorrect as the vessel of this name, built for Inmans in 1873, had two funnels not one as portrayed here. The deck layout, particularly the disposition of lifeboats, corresponds with *City of Berlin* and not with *City of Chester*.

City of Berlin was built for Inman by Caird & Co of Greenock in 1874. She was the first liner with interior electric lighting and had accommodation for 1770 passengers, 1500 of them in third class. She had a long career, outlasting the Inman Line, and completed her life as the US Government ship *Meade*. She was finally scrapped in 1921.[2]

There is another version of this painting in the Peabody collection which has also been incorrectly identified as *City of Chester*.[3] There are at least nine other paintings of *City of Berlin* by Jacobsen, including one in the Mariners' Museum and one at Mystic Seaport.[4] A carte de visite of a painting by Samuel Walters exists.[5] There is a coloured lithograph of the vessel by A L Palethorpe in the collections (55.256.1).

1 Relined, 1981.
2 Bonsor North, pp. 230-2, 243.
3 Brewington, no. 691, p.152.
4 Sniffen Checklist, pp. 68-9; the Mariner's painting is illustrated in Sniffen Painted Ships, fig. 56, p.70; for the Mystic painting see Brewington 1982, no. 186, p.69 (ill).
5 See Davidson, 1994, p. 202.

129 *City of Rome*

1934.63
Oil on canvas
56 cm x 91.5 cm
Signed and dated (br) "A. Jacobsen. 1885. / 705 PALISADE AV. WEST HOBOKEN. N.J."
Prov: G E Welsh, Liverpool, who presented it, 1934.
Ref: Handbook, 1935, p.61; Finch 1983, p.133 (ill); Sniffen Checklist, p.74, no. 3

Vessel: 560.2 ft (l), 52.3 ft (b), 37 ft (d); 8415 gross tons

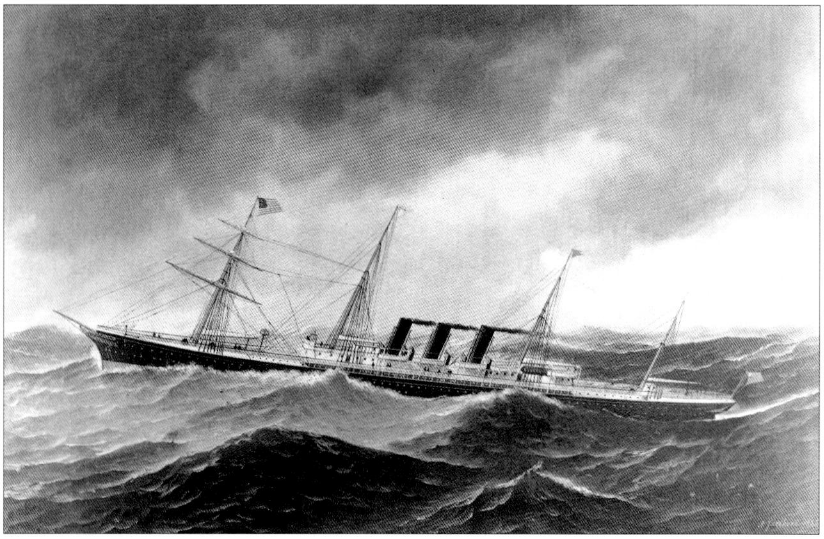

The famous liner *City of Rome* is shown in port profile in heavy seas in the Atlantic, making her way towards New York under full steam with no assistance from her auxiliary sail. A flag or pennant flies from each of four masts, in order from the bow these are the Stars and Stripes, the Anchor Line house flag, a red swallow tail[1] and a name pennant. The red ensign flies from a jack at the stern.

The iron screw steamer *City of Rome* was built by the Barrow Shipbuilding Co. in 1881 for the Inman Line. Although a very fine ship, her speed and freight capacity were disappointing and after only five voyages, she was handed back to her builders and transferred to the Anchor Line in 1882. She continued on the transatlantic service from Liverpool to New York for her new owners but her home port was moved to Glasgow in 1891 after deepening of the Clyde. She made her last voyage in 1901 and was scrapped in Germany in 1902.[2]

1 Probably indicating that she is carrying the mail.
2 See Bonsor North, pp. 233-4, 243, 437-8.
3 Sniffen Checklist, pp. 73 -74, these are all in collections in the United States; one of these is illustrated in Sniffen Painted Ships, p.9, fig. 6.
4 Location of painting not known but carte de visite photographic print in LRO, see Davidson, 1992, p. 202, illus. p. 203. Also ill. in Maginnis, p. 63.

Jacobsen often painted multiple versions of the same ship and Sniffen lists fourteen paintings of *City of Rome* and two sketches.[3] Samuel Walters also painted the vessel.[4] The collections also contain a sailor made picture model of the vessel (Accession no. 1952.39.1).

130 *Marathon*

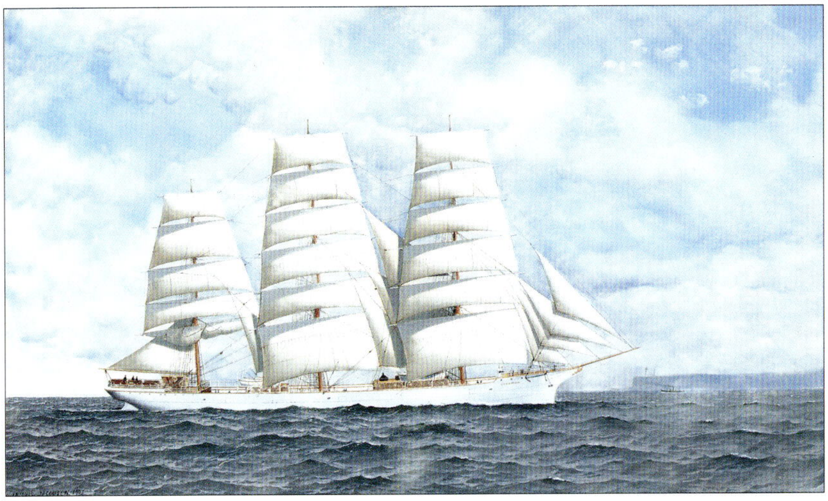

1970.220.1
Oil on academy board
56 cm x 91.5 cm
Signed and dated (bl) "ANTONIO JACOBSEN. 1907"
Prov: A J Grenville Jarvis, purchased from executors, 1970
Ref: Sniffen Checklist 1994

Vessel: 260.6 ft (l), 40 ft (b), 23 ft (d); 1988 gross tons.

Although a standard Jacobsen portrait, this depiction of the 3 masted steel barque *Marathon* is one of a small minority of the artist's work where he adopts a starboard profile. The vessel is identifiable by her name on the bow. She is shown in full sail off the approaches to New York, with the headland of the Atlantic Highlands and its twin towers in the far distance under the bow.

Marathon[1] was built in 1893 by Russell of Greenock for W Thomson & Co of Liverpool. She was sold to R Thomas & Co. in 1903 and spent much of the period 1905-8 trading between New South Wales and the west coast of South America returning to Antwerp in July 1908. She was then renamed *Denbigh Castle* and went missing with a cargo of guano from Lobos d'Afuera to Antwerp, in November 1912.[2]

There is an earlier painting of the vessel by Henry Loos of Antwerp dating from 1894 in the New Brunswick Museum[3]

1 The battle of Marathon of 490 BC also gave its name to the long distance race.
2 For history of vessel see *Sea Breezes*, vol. 21 (n.s.), 1956, p.26.
3 Elliot & McNairn, no. 39.

131 *Teutonic*

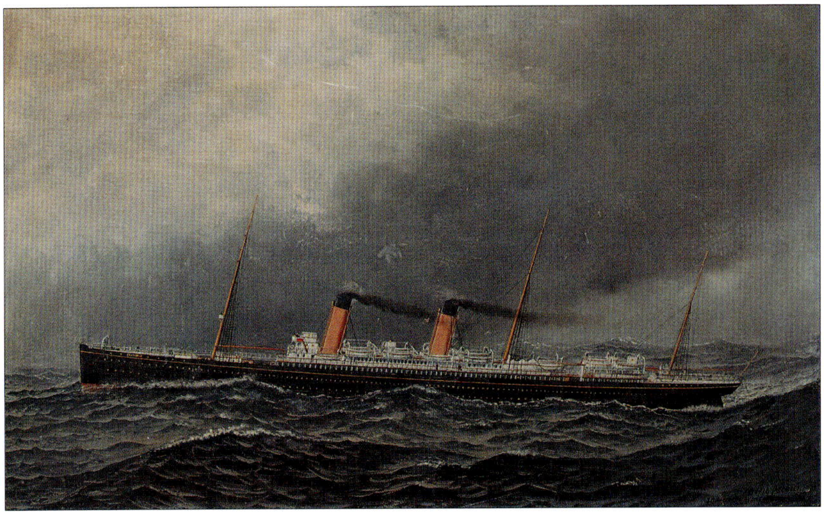

1980.113.6
Oil on board
56 cm x 91.5 cm
Signed and dated (br) "ANTONIO JACOBSEN. 1908 / 31 PALISADE AV: WEST HOBOKEN. N.J."
Prov: Mercantile Marine Services Association, who presented it, 1980.

Vessel: 565.8 ft (l), 57.8 ft (b), 39.4 ft (d); 9984 gross tons

The screw steamer *Teutonic* is shown in port profile in heavy seas. She was the first transatlantic liner to abandon auxiliary sail and she is shown here relying only on her engines. As in many of Jacobsen's views, the vessel is tilted slightly towards the observer to give a good view of the decks and the equipment. A few people have braved the weather to take a turn on deck.

Teutonic was built by Harland and Wolff in Belfast for the White Star Line in 1889. She was the first vessel built as an armed merchant cruiser and before making her maiden voyage, she attended the Naval Review at Spithead on 4 August. She served between Liverpool and New York until 1907 when she was transferred to Southampton. In 1911 with the arrival of *Olympic*, she returned to Liverpool to serve on the Canadian route to Quebec and Montreal. In 1914 she took up cruiser duties with the Admiralty and from 1918 acted as a troopship until laid up at Cowes in 1921 and scrapped the same year.[1]

There are three other representations of *Teutonic* by Jacobsen.[2] Other paintings of the vessel include two canvases by W L Wyllie including an impressive view of the 1889 Naval Review.[3] There is a volume of photographs of this Review privately printed for the Ismay family, a similar volume for the 1897 Diamond Jubilee Review printed for private circulation in 1898 and a builder's model in the collections (MMM Archives and 1933.167).

1 Bonsor North, p. 759.
2 Sniffen Checklist, p.284-5; Sniffen 1994, pp. 134, 137 (ill).
3 'The steamship *Teutonic* leaving Liverpool', NMM, Concise NMM, p. 470 (ill) and 'Spithead, 4th August 1889' with *Teutonic* being inspected by the German Kaiser and Prince of Wales, sold Sotheby's, London, 30 May 1990, lot 611 (ill).

132 *Wisconsin*

5.10.15.3
Oil on canvas
56 cm x 91.5 cm
Signed and dated (br) "Antonio Jacobsen/. N.Y. 1875"
Prov: Mr W. Honour, who presented it, 1915
Ref: Sniffen Checklist pp. 304-5

Vessel: 366 ft (l), 43.2 ft (b), 26.6 ft (d); 3238 gross tons

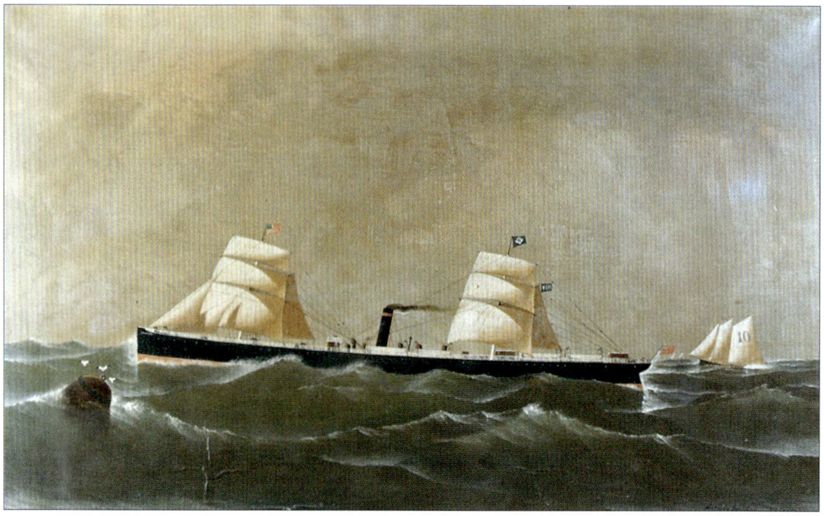

The transatlantic passenger steamer *Wisconsin* is depicted in port profile at sea, approaching New York, as indicated by the inclusion of the buoy in the left foreground and a pilot boat in the right distance. She is under full steam and is also making full use of her auxiliary sail. The vessel is identifiable from her name on the bow and the Guion Line house flag at her main mast and the house colours on her funnel. She flies the Stars and Stripes at the foremast together with United States Mail pennant at the after peak.[1] These indicate that she is bound for an American port with the mail on board. Astern is the No. 10 pilot schooner which is shown under full sail in port profile.

Wisconsin was built by Palmer Brothers of Newcastle upon Tyne in 1870 for The Liverpool and Great Western Steamship Company, universally known as The Guion Line after its founder Stephen Guion. She was the first transatlantic steamer designed with compound engines and could carry 800 third class and 176 other passengers, emphasising the line's principal trade in emigrants. Her last voyage was made in

October 1892 and she was scrapped at Tranmere in 1893, only months before the final demise of line itself.[2]

The schooner rigged pilot boat with the number 10 on her sail and a black hull is in the New York pilot service.

1 Blue ground with letters USM.
2 Bonsor North, pp. 702, 709 and CR no. 95, 7 June 1870.

Henry Freeman James (active 1803 - 1823)

James was a minor artist who was engaged in a range of artistic activities in Liverpool - he was a drawing master, draughtsman, surveyor, teacher of French and art auctioneer and dealer. He moved to Manchester about 1815 and established a lithographic business, which was inherited and developed by his son.[1]

1 See Davidson, 1986, pp. 29-31.

133 A view of Liverpool

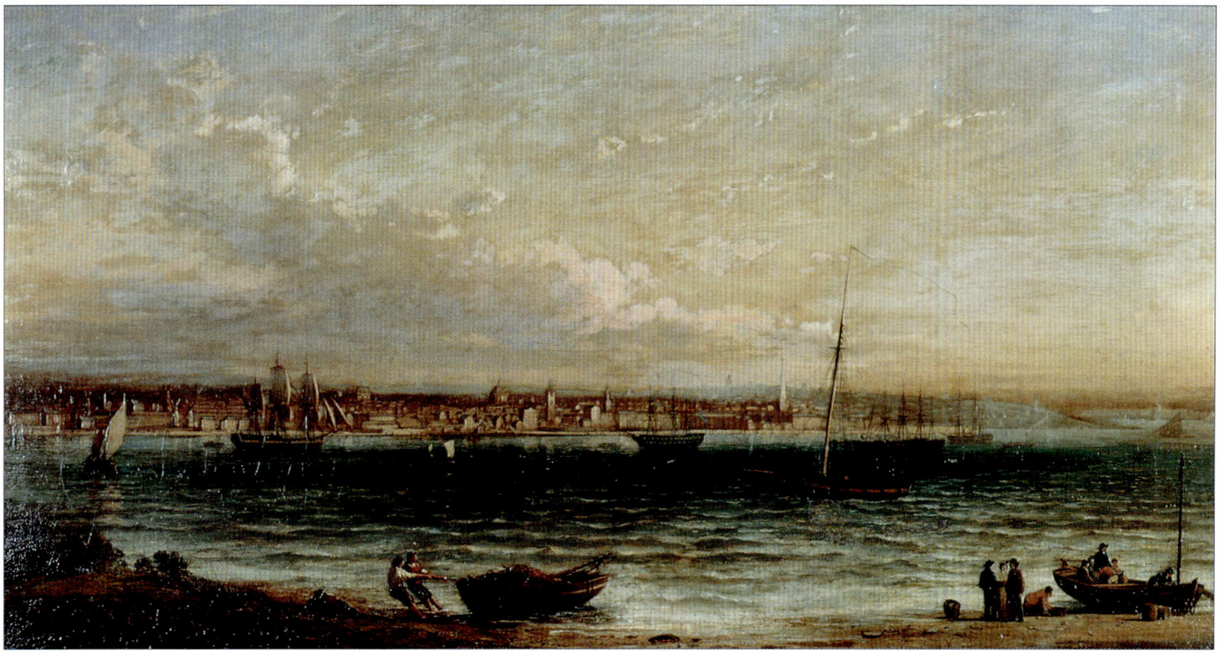

This view of the Liverpool waterfront across the River Mersey from the Cheshire shore shows a busy and thriving scene. A variety of different shipping is depicted including fishing and ferry boats on the shore in the foreground, a revenue cutter at anchor in the middle distance to the right of centre and in the far distance nearer the Liverpool shore from left to right the most obvious are a 3 masted ship making its way up river, a man of war at anchor, and a group of other anchored vessels. A number of small boats, some carrying animals, ply their way through the shipping and a small early steam vessel is to the right of the anchored group of ships.

The viewpoint, from the common at Seacombe, allows a particularly detailed view of the Liverpool shore to be included. It begins at the north end of the town, where a few warehouses are starting to appear alongside the windmills of this still rural area, continuing to the town itself with its rows of warehouses and clearly visible the domes of St Paul's and the Town Hall, the tower of St Nicholas, the Goree Warehouses, the spire of St George, then probably the spire of St Thomas and to the south the still mainly rural areas along the Toxteth shore stretching down towards Garston.

This painting is almost identical to "A View of the Town and Harbour of Liverpool" published by H F James in Manchester in 1817.[1] The fishing boat in the foreground is missing and two small boats have been included and there are a few other minor differences. However, the painting is probably the original for the engraving.

1955.411
Oil on canvas
44 cm x 80 cm
Prov: Unknown, in collections 1955
Exh: Liverpool 1986
Ref: Port Panorama 1986, p.14 (ill); Davidson 1986, pp. 29-30

1 "A View of the Town and Harbour of Liverpool. / Taken from a North West Station on Seacomb Common. / Begun in 1810: impeded in its progress by the fall of St Nicholas Steeple 1811. / Published by H F James, Manchester, Oct. 1817.", "Drawn by H F James", "Engraved by W J Bennett" (Copies in National Maritime Museum and Liverpool City Libraries, see Liverpool Prints, 1907, p. 36). Davidson includes details of a handbill advertising the engraving which attributes it to "H F JAMES, PROFESSOR OF FINE ARTS, / (Assisted in the Shipping Department by the ingenious Artist, Mr. Anderson, of London.)".

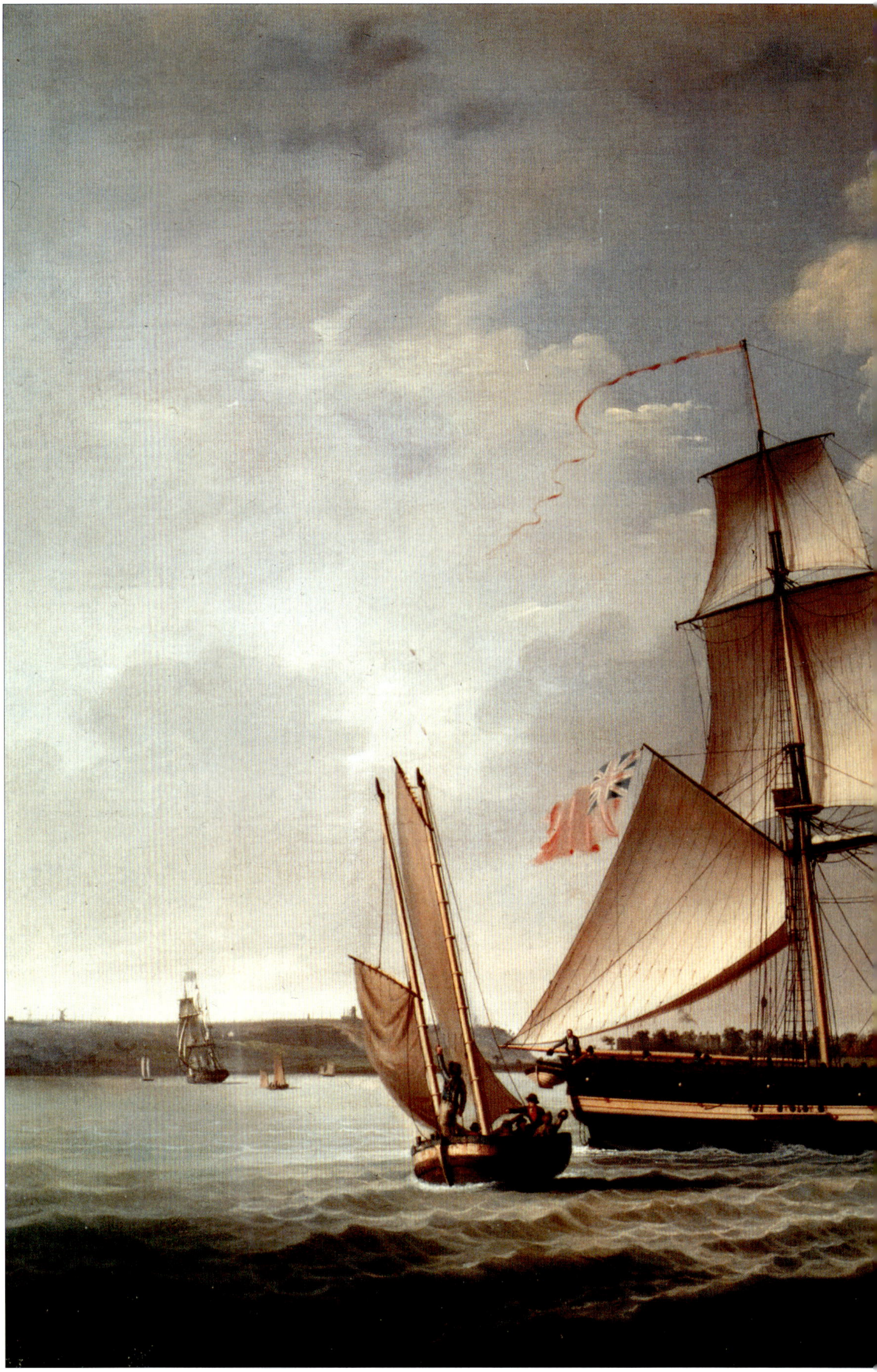

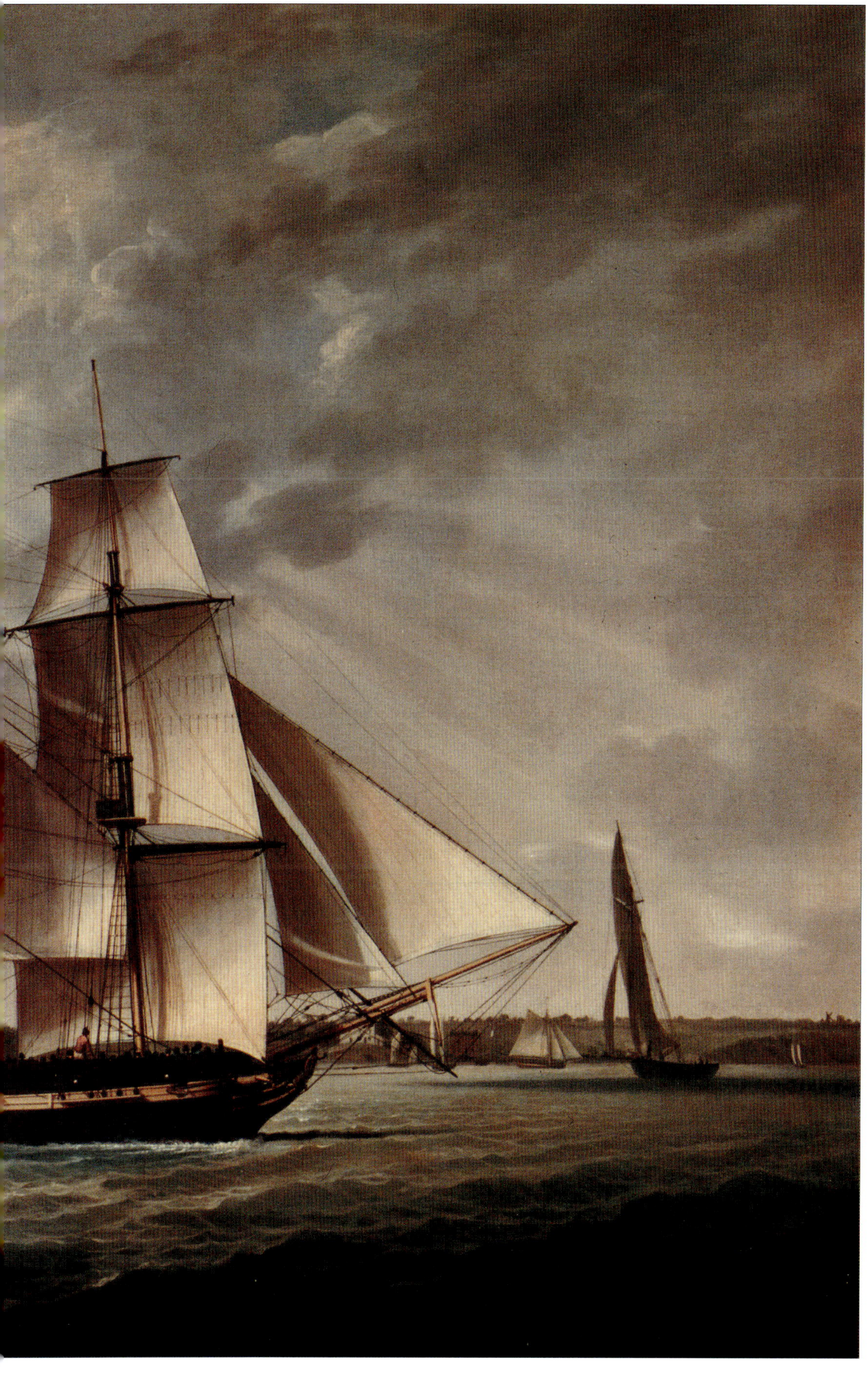

John Jenkinson (active about 1800 - 1821)

Despite the fact that Jenkinson is an important Liverpool artist very little is known about his career. He is listed as a "marine and portrait artist" from 1816 to 1821 in he Liverpool directories and works by him were shown at the Liverpool Academy between 1810 and 1814. Many of his works are not signed or the signature is hidden, as in no. 134. His work has frequently been attributed to Robert Salmon (q.v.).[1]

1 See Davidson, 1986, pp. 26-9.

134 28 Gun Ship In The Mersey

1962.257
Oil on canvas
79.5 cm x 131.5 cm
Signed (stern of boat, br) "J. Jenkinson / Liverpool"
Prov: G D Lockett, Cheshire; presented in 1962 in memory of members of the Lockett family[3] of Grassendale House, Liverpool.

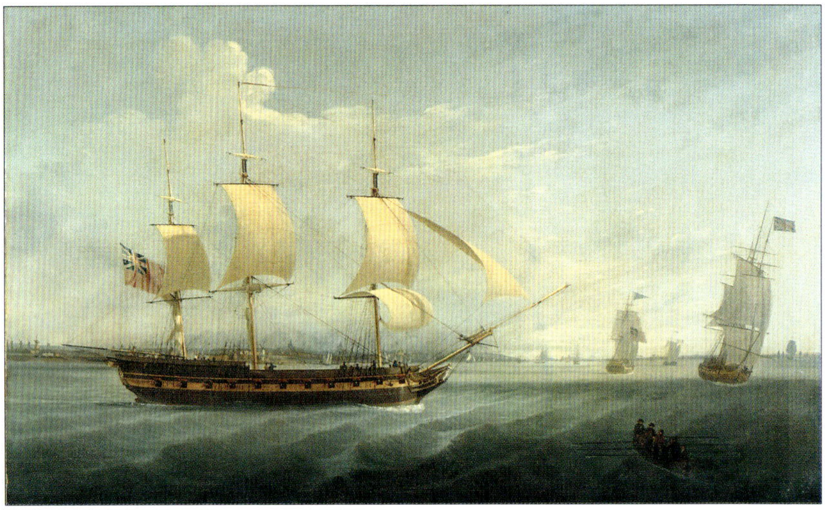

This impressive canvas shows a 28-gun ship in the Mersey with a distant view of Liverpool and other shipping in the river.

The vessel is shown in starboard profile to the left of centre. Her topsails are set and the main forecourse is clewed up. She flies a red ensign at the stern and a long pennant from her main mast. Although there is a clear female figurehead, the ship is unidentified. She may be a naval frigate, involved in patrol and defence work during the uncertain years of the Napoleonic Wars with France, or she may be a well-armed privateer.

The two other main vessels depicted are a stern view of a 3 masted ship with red ensign and blue pennant moving up the Mersey and a starboard quarter view of another with a male figurehead and union jack at the fore, both under full sail. There is a rowing boat with eight men aboard in the right foreground. A large number of other coastal and deep sea vessels are included in the distant reaches of the estuary.

In the background is a view of the north bank with to the far left a group of windmills at Bootle and the North Fort on the foreshore at Hog's Head Nook.[1] The mill[2] on the north shore is just forward of the main mast and the domes of St Paul's and the Town Hall are both visible. Immediately forward of the foremast on the shore is the Old Fort with behind a group of spires probably of St Nicholas, St George and St Thomas. Groups of figures can be seen walking or riding along the north shore.

The painting dates from after 1803 (when the North Fort was built) and is probably one of Jenkinson's earliest surviving works, completed before about 1815.

1 Hog's Head Nook was at the junction of what later became Clarence Dock and Collingwood / Salisbury Docks.
2 Known as Taylor's Mill at this period, see GDL 1790, 1805, 1813.
3 John Hilton Lockett (1799-1873) and John Lockett (1881-1957).

135 Armed Vessel in the Mersey off Birkenhead (see pages 126-127)

This fine example of Jenkinson's work shows an armed vessel departing from the Mersey with a view of the Wirral coastline near Birkenhead in the background. The vessel is shown in a starboard profile from the leeward side with all her sails, except the main course, set. She is rigged as a snow and the leeward view provides a very clear depiction of the small auxiliary mast which supports the aft sail. This sail is clewed up. She flies a long red pennant from her main mast and the red ensign from the stern. The hats of approximately 40 members of the crew are visible along the length of the vessel and there are two standing figures. One of these at the stern is presumably the master who has removed his hat as a gesture of farewell to the small boat which has just pulled away. This small boat is similar to the small ferry boats which were found on the Mersey at this period and which has probably been used as a tender. One of the crew is just raising the fore sail of this boat while the passengers wave to the main vessel.

The vessel has a female figurehead and fourteen guns but this is insufficient to allow identification. She is mostly likely to be a merchantman and may have been built as a guineaman or slave ship.[1] Although differently rigged, she is similar in overall appearance to the slaver *Kitty* which was painted by Robert Salmon.[2]

There is other shipping depicted in the river including, in the far distance under the bowsprit, what appears to be a pilot boat judging by the cutter rig and the green and yellow livery of the hull. To the left is another substantial square rigged sailing vessel and other local coastal craft.

The view in the background shows the Wirral coastline with the entrance to the former Wallasey Pool behind the stern of the main vessel. To the left of this, on the hillside in the distance (by the sail of the small tender), is the Bidston Lighthouse and signal station. To the right is a wooded area north of Seacombe with a number of large residences overlooking the river. The land again rises to the far right towards Egremont.

MMM.1991.5
Oil on canvas
81 cm x 112 cm
Signed (bl) "J. Jenkinson"
Prov: Private Collection, Cheshire; sold Christies, London, November 1983, lot. 51; Lane Fine Art, London, from whom purchased, 1991.
Ref: *Catalogue of Marine and Landscape Paintings*, Lane Fine Art, London, 1990, no. 27, ill.

1 "The Guineamen here, are in general the handsomest ships; being every way modelled after the Frigates, and rather more ornamented." [W. Moss] *Liverpool Guide*, 1796, p.51.
2 Formerly Parker Gallery, London. Illustrated in D MacGregor 1980, p.64.

136 *Frigate and Sloop in the Mersey*

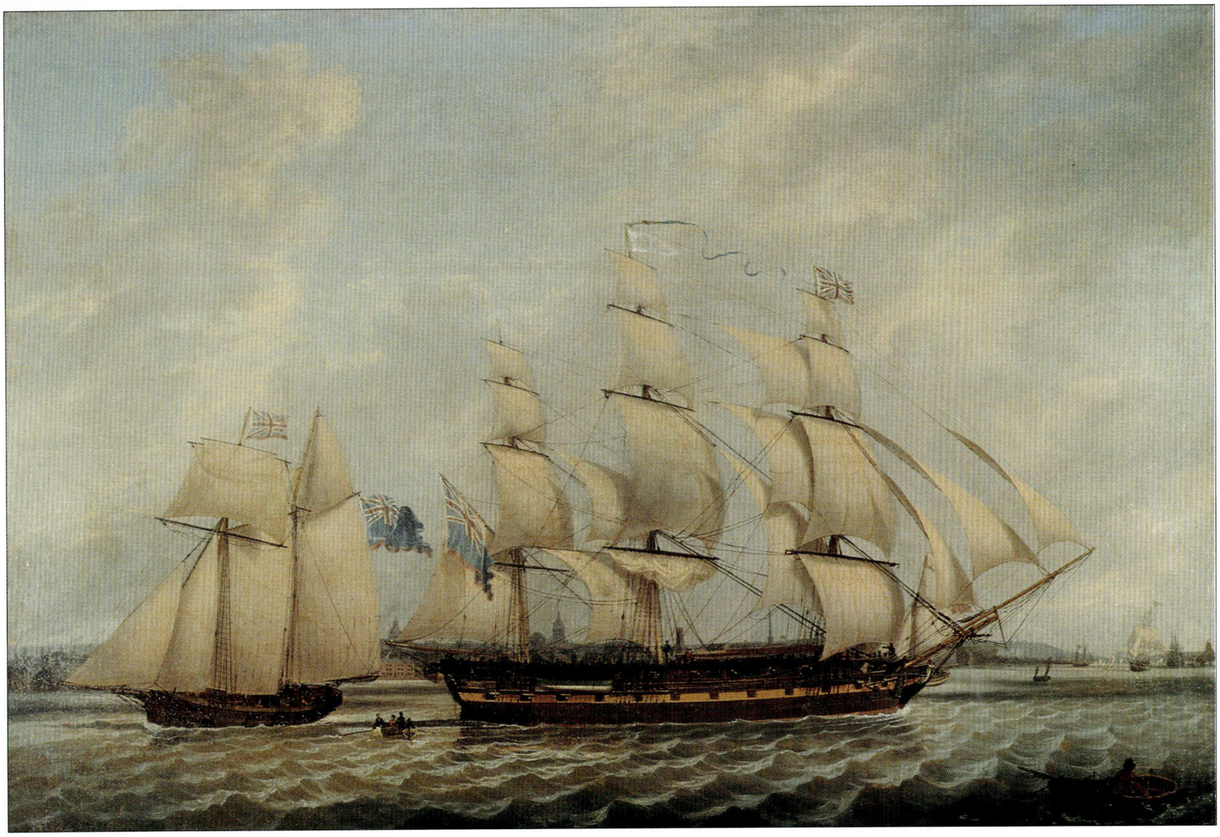

1948.30
Oil on canvas
90 cm x 132 cm
Signed (br) "J. Jenkinson"
Prov: Robert Bunting, Liverpool, from whom purchased, 1948.
Ref: Tibbles 1988, ill.

This view shows two naval vessels in the Mersey with the Liverpool waterfront in the background.

To the centre right a ship-rigged frigate of 24 guns is shown in starboard profile under virtually full sail making her way up river. The second vessel, passing to her stern, is a topsail schooner-rigged sloop of twelve guns in a port quarter view. A man on board the sloop is communicating with a man on the stern of the frigate by means of a speaking trumpet.

Neither vessels bears any identifying marks and the situation is further complicated by the flags being worn. The frigate flies the Union flag, with a red lower border, at the foremast, a long pennant and a normal sized white pennant with central red ball at the main and a blue ensign with red lower border at the gaff. The cutter has the Union flag at her foremast and blue ensign at the gaff, again both with lower red borders. Under normal circumstances, the union flag would not be flown from the masthead and especially not the foremast.[1] The pennant on the frigate's main mast is probably that of a commodore.[2] The significance of the lower red borders on the flags has not been established and does not conform to known naval practice.[3] The most likely explanation is that some, as yet untraced, local usage is being depicted. Although the precise role of these two vessels is not clear, they would have formed a formidable pairing with their armaments. They may perhaps be a small detachment under the command of a commodore undertaking patrol duties in the Irish Sea to protect Liverpool bound merchantmen from the activities of French privateers.

In the foreground between the two vessels is a small rowing boat with a number of occupants. In the bottom right foreground a small boat is anchored with a solitary fisherman. Behind the bow of the frigate the distinctively painted hull of a pilot boat can be observed and there is other shipping further upstream.

In the background various local landmarks can be spotted including the dome of St Paul's Church between the two naval vessels and between the masts of the frigate the dome of the Town Hall, the tower of St Nicholas and the spire of St George.

The painting is undated but must have been completed after 1800 (when the Union flag changed) and probably after 1806 when the commodore's pennant was introduced. The cessation of the Napoleonic Wars is likely to be the latest date. It may possibly date from the period around 1812-15 when war with the United States brought a renewed fear of attacks on the port from the Americans.

1 The use of the Union flag was normally reserved for Admirals.
2 In 1806 Commodores were allowed a distinguishing pennant. See T Wilson *Flags at sea*. London, 1986, p.31.
3 The blue ensign with a red border also appears in other Jenkinson paintings, such as *The Irish Packet*, sold Sotheby's, 15 July 1988, lot 64.

137 A view of Liverpool

Jenkinson painted several views of Liverpool across the Mersey from the Wirral shore. In this painting he uses a number of vessels to frame the central subject of a distance view of the main town and the north shore. To the left a three masted ship in quarter stern view fills the side of the canvas with a second ship crossing her bow in the middle distance; to the right the framing is provided by a short stretch of shore with a couple of coasters, including a beached schooner, her masts angled to draw the eye into the centre of the picture. A number of small boats are being rowed across the river and other shipping lies off the area of the old dock. A particularly nice compositional touch is the figure of a shrimper with his net and basket, accompanied by a young boy and his dog, in the foreground at the water's edge.

The principal landmarks of the town are shown beginning at the left with the domes of St Paul's and the Town Hall visible behind the warehouses and the Old Fort on the waterfront, the spire of St George and as the main focus the prominent tower of St Nicholas and then the spire of St Thomas and the south end disappearing behind the off shore shipping.

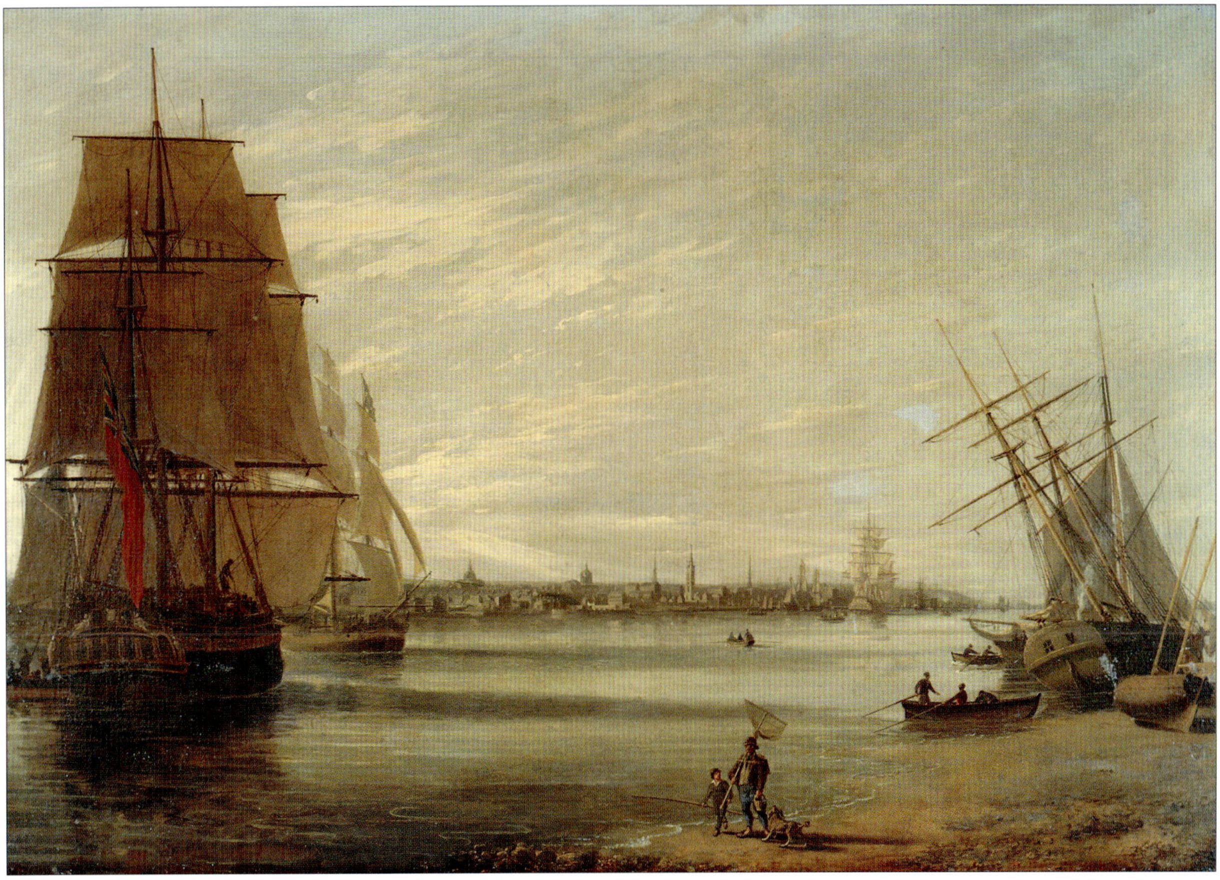

The painting has been known as "Liverpool from Seacombe" for many years but the oblique view of the town makes a location further north necessary. There are two other surviving works which use the same vantage point, "A View of Liverpool with the Isle of Man Packet", signed and dated 1813 (Private Collection) and "Liverpool Harbour" (Peabody Museum of Salem).[1] The Peabody painting includes a vessel with the name "*Magazine*" on her stern and a location known as Magazines, between Egremont and New Brighton where gunpowder was stored, seems likely for all three paintings.

Both these other views are very similar to each other and although less obviously framed than the present picture, are clearly variations on a theme. They use the device of a foreground group, but substituting a small ferry boat with passengers paying the ferryman, for the shrimpers. There is an engraving of another painting by Jenkinson of 1816, entitled "A View of the Town and Harbour of Liverpool from Seacombe", which shows the straighter view of the town which is gained from this location.[2]

The painting probably dates to about 1815 but is certainly before 1817 when the Old Fort was demolished to make way for the new Prince's Dock. For many years it was wrongly attributed to Jenkinson's better known contemporary Robert Salmon.[3]

1955.259
Oil on canvas
91 cm x 127 cm
Signed (on transom of ship to left)
"J Jenkinson"
Prov: Unknown, in collection 1955.
Exh: Liverpool 1986
Ref: Port Panorama 1986, p.15 (ill.); Davidson 1986, p.29; Tibbles 1988 (ill.)

1 For details see Davidson 1986, pp 22-23, 29.
2 Engraved by T Dixon and published in Liverpool by Henry Fisher in 1820. Copy in MMM collections, 1953.41.11.
3 See DCF.

J E Johnston (active 1894)

138 *Macedonia*

The iron screw steamer *Macedonia* is shown towards the end of her career in port quarter profile at sea. She is under steam and has some sail on the fore mast and headsails. The wind is coming from the port stern, as indicated by the red ensign at the stern and the smoke from her funnel. The wind conditions are confirmed by the

1955.252
Oil on canvas
51 cm x 76.5 cm
Signed and dated (br in red) "J E Johnston / 1894"
Prov: Unknown, in collections, 1955

Vessel: 288.6 ft (l), 35.3 ft (b), 22.9 ft (d); 1732 gross tons

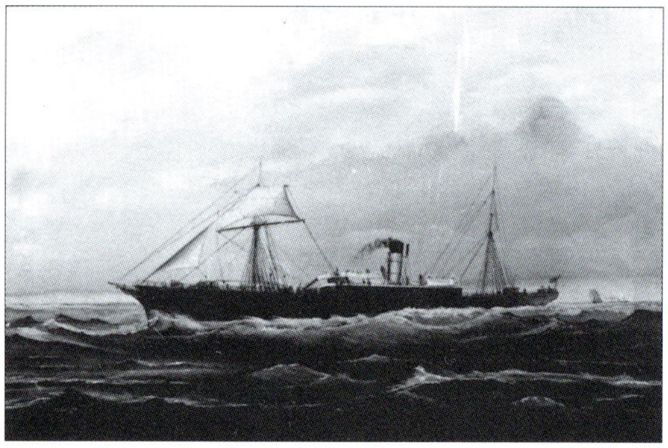

steamer and ship in the background. Various members of the crew are on deck and much of the detail of the deck with its windlass, deckhouses and derricks are clearly visible. The vessel is identifiable by the name on her bow and the funnel is painted in the pink and black house colours of her owners, Papayanni of Liverpool.

Macedonia was built by Thomas Vernon and Son of Seacombe, Wirral for the Papayanni Brothers in 1867. The Papayanni Line was involved in the Eastern Mediterranean trade and during the American Civil War began shipping cotton from Egypt. They maintained a fleet of about nine vessels until taken over by Ellerman in 1901. *Macedonia* was lengthened by some 60 ft in 1881 and was taken out of service and broken up in Italy in 1899.[1]

1 Haws Ellerman, pp. 28-29, 31-32. Confirmed CR no. 91, 29 March 1867.

C Kensington (active about 1880 - 1920)

This artist is known for a number of works, including oils and particularly watercolours, mainly in The British Mercantile Marine Memorial Collection and in the Bergen Maritime Museum, Norway. No biographical information is available but Finch suggests he is a London artist.[1]

1 Information in DCF; Brewington 1982; Finch 1983.

139 Sierra Estrella

1950.29.1
Oil on canvas
51 cm x 69 cm
Signed and dated (bl) "C. Kensington. 1884"
Prov: R B Read, Liverpool, who presented it, 1950
Exh: Crosby, 1951, no. 102.

Vessel: 238.6 ft (l), 38 ft (b), 22.7 ft (d); 1500 gross tons

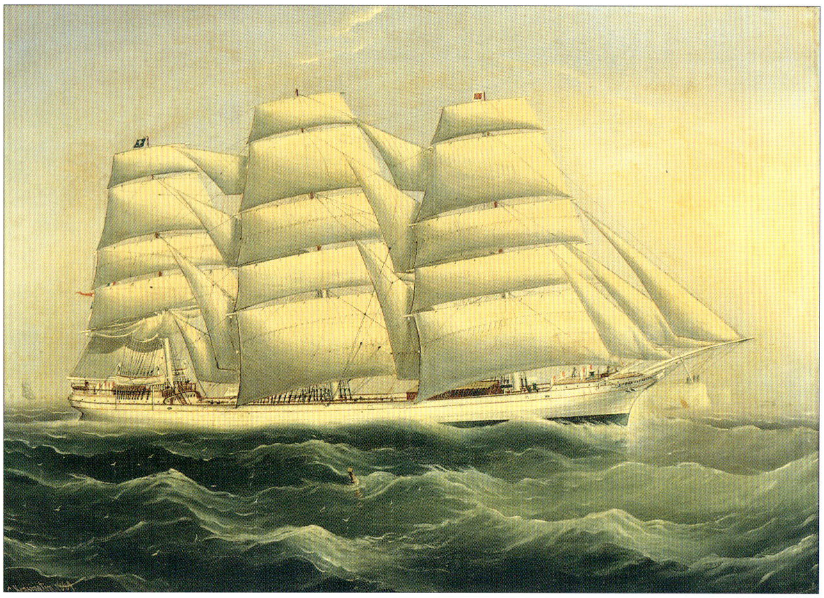

The iron ship *Sierra Estrella* is shown in starboard profile off two headlands under full sail. She has her name on the bow and flies the Thompson Anderson house flag from the mizzen and the pilot jack at the foremast. A partially hidden signal code (T F [P] [S]) flies from the after peak. The background is probably intended to be the entrance to Dover harbour, though rather stylised and inaccurately depicted.[1]

Sierra Estrella was built in 1880 by Richardson, Duck & Co. of Stockton-on-Tees for Thompson Anderson's Sierra Line.[2] She was involved in deep sea trades to San Francisco and the East. She was sold in 1899 to G Gallo of Genoa, Italy and had various Italian owners before being hulked in 1927 and broken up the following year.[3]

1 The headlands appear to have buildings and a ship is sketchily shown between the two.
2 For reference to Sierra Line and *Sierra Cordova* see no 64.
3 CR, no. 42, 21 May 1880 and Beard.

William Calcott Knell (active 1848-1879)

Probably the son of William Adolphus Knell (about 1808-1875), also a marine artist. He lived and exhibited in London, showing mainly coastal scenes. Like his father, he was heavily influenced by the Dutch tradition of marine painting.[1]

1 See Brook-Hart, p.51.

140 Shipping Scene with Dutch Fishing Vessel

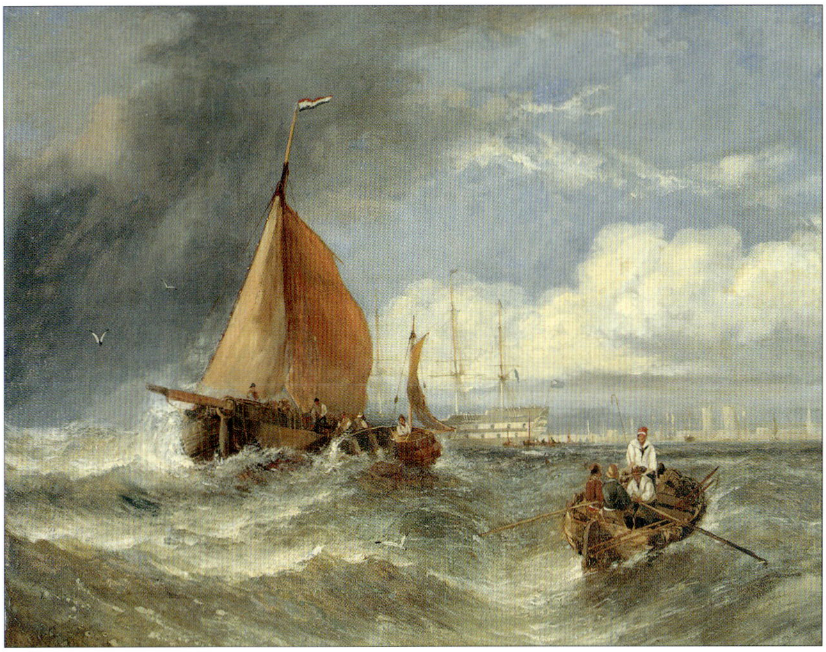

1971.14.2
Oil on canvas
54 cm x 69.5 cm
Signed and dated (bl) "W C / Knell / 1855"
Prov.: Cunard Brocklebank Ltd., Private Collection, on permanent loan, 1971.

This energetic scene shows a Dutch fishing vessel in a bow view off the harbour at Portsmouth. In the heavy waves, the crew are struggling with their cargo, perhaps preparing to unload into the small single masted double ended boat that has come alongside. In the foreground is a small rowing boat with two sailors and a couple of passengers heading for the shore.
The naval vessel in the background is probably intended to be Nelson's flagship *Victory* which was moored in the harbour from 1835.

Kwong Sang (active 1890-1894)

A Chinese artist based in Calcutta who produced ship portraits on commission for Western clients. He generally signs his painting in red. His style is very similar to Lai Fong who also worked in Calcutta.

141 4 masted ship Liverpool (page 134)

The 4 masted iron ship *Liverpool* is shown in starboard profile under plain sail, except for the course on her jigger mast. The image of the ship virtually fills the canvas but a No.5 pilot boat can be spotted in the far distance under *Liverpool*'s bowsprit. The crew can be seen straining to trim the sails as she gets under way. The vessel flies the pilot jack at the fore, the house flag of R W Leyland & Co of Liverpool and her flag hoist in the commercial code ([L] B F K) just visible at the after peak. The red ensign is at the stern.
Liverpool was built for R W Leyland at Port Glasgow by Archibald Russell & Co. in 1889, the largest sailing ship in the British fleet. Although intended for the Calcutta jute trade (she could stow 26,000 bales of jute), she spent much of her time in other

1981.527
Oil on canvas
97 cm x 153 cm
Prov: Calder family; "Long John Silver" Collection, Cutty Sark Society, who presented it, 1981.[4]

Vessel: 333.2 ft (l), 47.9 ft (b), 36.5 ft (d); 3396 gross tons

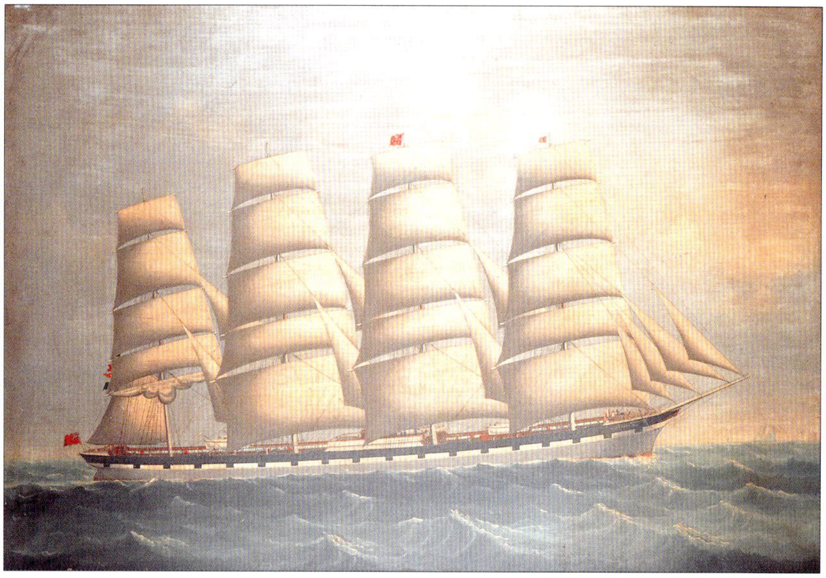

trades - her first two voyages were to Australia.[1] The vessel was lost after hitting rocks off Fort Hommeaux Florians on Alderney in fog in 1902 when bound from Antwerp to San Francisco with a cargo of cement girders and marble.[2]
The painting is attributed to Kwong Sang on general stylistic grounds and in particular on the characteristic and distinctive way in which he painted his figures. Her first captain was Thomas Calder who presumably commissioned the portrait given the later provenance.[3]

1 See D Walker *Champion of Sail: R W Leyland and his shipping line*, London, 1986, pp. 140-8; Lubbock *Windjammers*, I, pp. 276-7, II, 25-28.
2 For details of the loss and salvage operation see Victor Coysh 'The Loss of the "Liverpool"', *Sea Breezes*, vol. 34, pp. 242-3.
3 CR no. 3, 17 January 1889.
4 Information from Sir Patrick Bayley, 20 February 1980, see DCF.

142 *Windermere*

1951.25.10
Oil on canvas
64 cm x 89 cm
Signed and dated (br) "Kwong Sang / Calcutta. 1894"
Prov: J James Esq, Blundellsands, who presented it, 1951

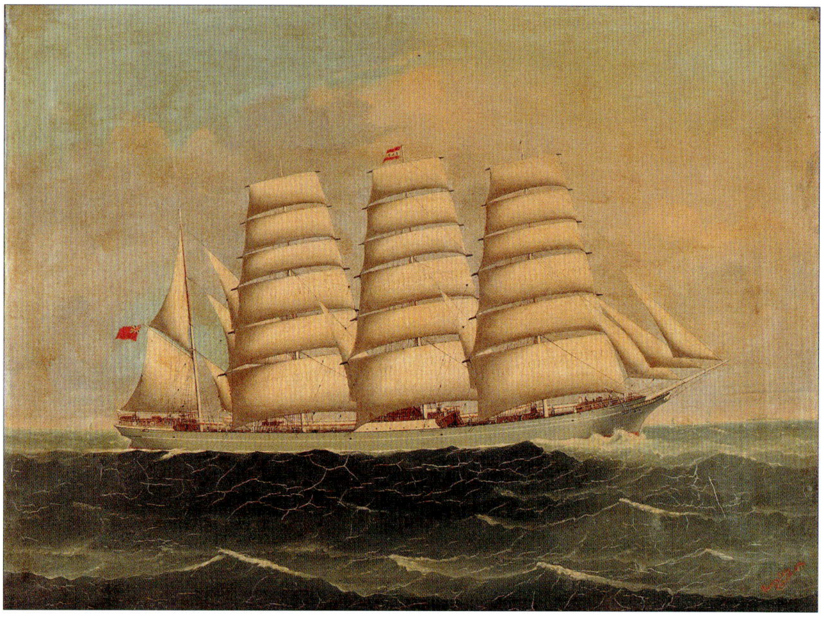

The 4-masted iron barque *Windermere* is shown in standard starboard profile with all her sails set cutting through the waves. There is a clear view of the deck and various members of the crew can be seen, including the helmsman aft and the officer of the watch with his telescope on the raised midship accommodation. This latter is joined to the fo'c'sle and poop deck by an elevated catwalk. On the main mast the vessel flies a house flag , "F & S" in black on a white band between red bands, for Fisher & Sprott of London. There is other unidentified shipping in silhouette under the bowsprit.

Fisher & Sprott were small scale ship owners operating with a handful of vessels. *Windermere* was their largest vessel, built in 1892 by T R Oswald & Co. of Milford Haven. She voyaged from London or Hamburg to India, Australia and the Pacific. She was sold to R C Rickmers of Bremerhaven in 1897 and renamed *Paul Rickmers*. She went missing in July 1907.
The vessel was in Calcutta in June 1894 when the painting was probably commissioned.[1]

1 LL 1, 9 June 1894.

Lai Fong (active 1870-1905)

This Chinese artist was based in Calcutta where he painted ship portraits on commission for western artists. His style is very similar to Kwong Sang who also worked in Calcutta.

143 *Milton Stuart*

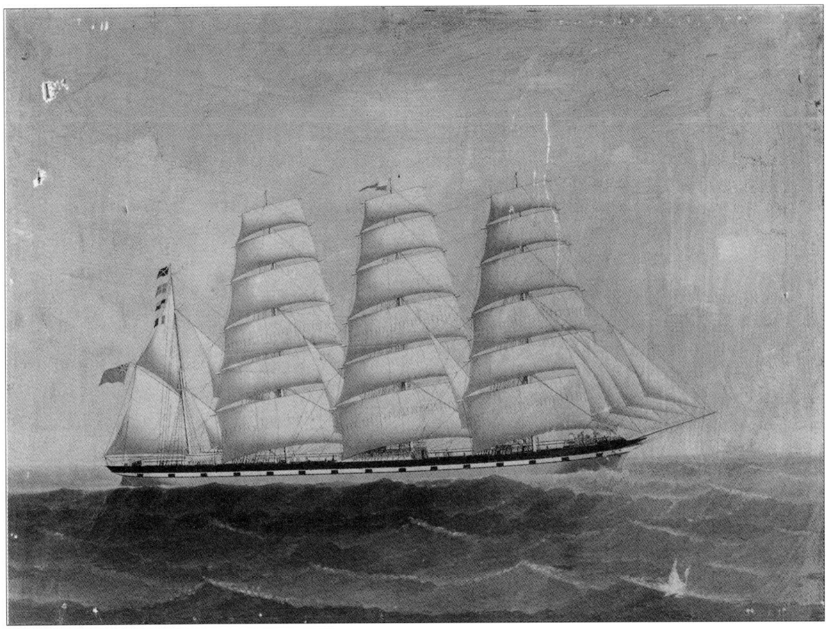

1955.231
Oil on canvas
66 cm x 89 cm
Signed and dated (br) "Lai Fong / Calcutta / 1898"
Prov: In collections, 1955

Vessel: 327.2 ft (l), 46.6 ft (b), 25.8 ft (d); 3224 tons.

In this typical composition by Lai Fong, the 4 masted steel barque *Milton Stuart* is shown in starboard profile close-reefed on a port tack with all her sails set. She flies the house flag of C W Kellock from the main mast, her international code (M R L T) at the mizzen and the red ensign at the peak. Under the bowsprit an unidentified steamer is silhouetted on the skyline.
Milton Stuart was named after the eponymous owner and was built by Swan Hunter & Co. at Wallsend on the Tyne in 1892. She was the largest of the small fleet of sailing ships operated by Stuart and Douglas of Liverpool in the India trade.[1] Kellocks managed her from November 1896 and two years later she was sold to G H Siemers & Co. of Hamburg and renamed *Thekla*. She was lost in the Le Maire Straits, Argentina, on a voyage from Cardiff to Valparaiso in July 1911.[2]
The vessel was in Calcutta from January to March 1898[3] when the painting was presumably completed.
There is a builder's half model of this vessel in the collections (1962.343.3)

1 The first master of the vessel was Frank Norman, who had been master of *Polestar* (see no. 5) in the mid-1880s.
2 LCR, vol. 97, no. 85, 1892.
3 LL, 18 January, 26 March 1898.

Lai Sung (active 1850-1885)

A Chinese painter based in Hong Kong who produced ship portraits on commission for the Western market. There are six paintings of American ships in the Peabody Essex Museum at Salem.[1]

1 Brewington 1982, Crossman, p.145.

144 Scawfell off Hong Kong

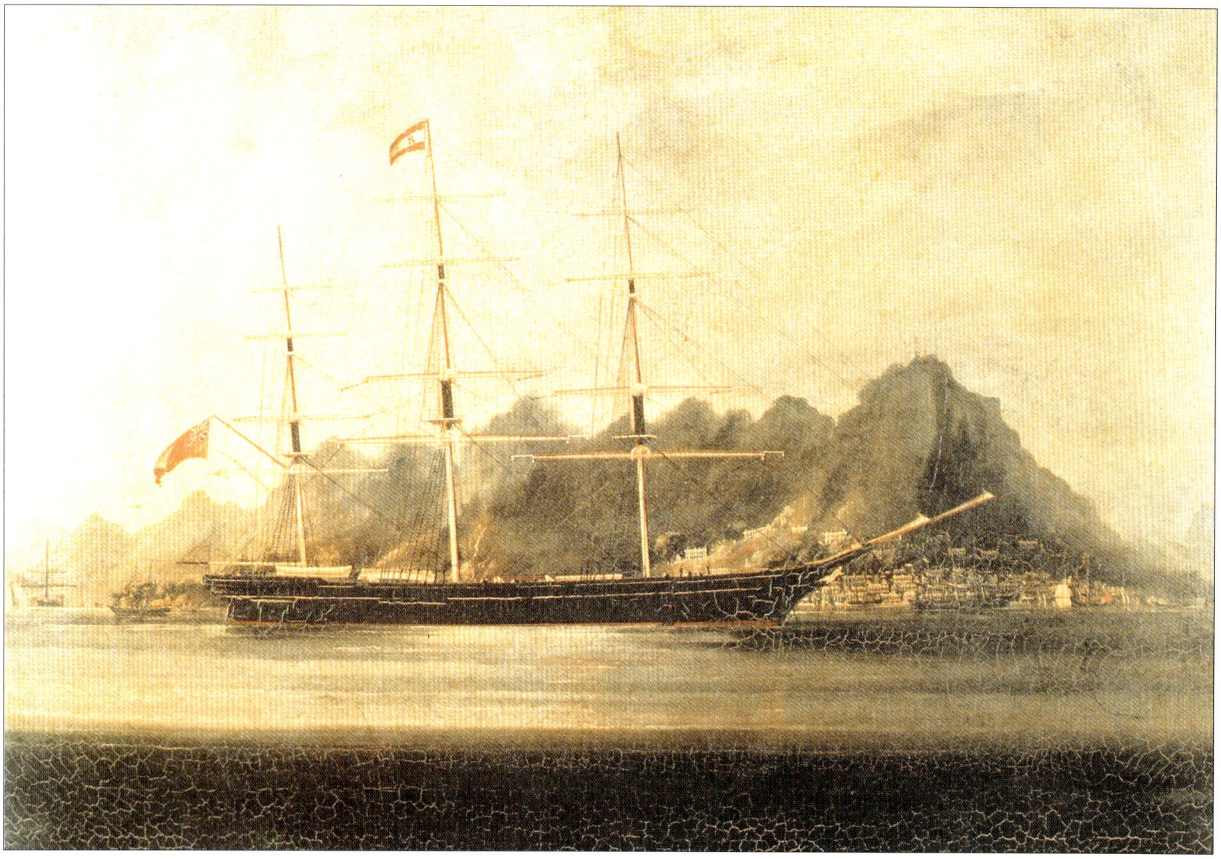

1950.29.3
Oil on canvas[1]
59 cm x 77.5 cm
Prov: Captain Thomson by descent to R B Read, Liverpool, who presented it, 1950
Ref: MacGregor 1983, pp. 115-6 (ill); Nottingham 1992, pp. 62-3 (ill)

Vessel: 198 ft (l), 32.6 ft (b), 21.8 ft (d); 826 gross tons

The famous tea clipper *Scawfell* is shown at anchor with all her sails stowed in starboard profile off Hong Kong. On her main mast she flies the house flag of Rathbone Brothers, a red R on a white band between two red bands, together with the red ensign at the peak. In the background are the sharp mountainous peaks of Hong Kong while the town nestles at their feet under the vessel's bowsprit. Other shipping, including local junks, can be seen closer into the shore. This composition was a view frequently adopted by artists.[2]

Scawfell was built in 1858 by Charles Lamport & Co. of Workington for Rathbone Brothers of Liverpool who were major participants in the China trade in the 1850s and 60s. Although not one of the largest vessels at 826 tons, she was one of the fastest and made several record voyages. She held the record for the fastest voyage between Whampoa and Liverpool of 88 days in 1861. *Scawfell* remained in Rathbones' ownership until 1872 when she was sold to Wilson & Blain of South Shields following a fire in the holds when she was returning with a cargo of cotton, coir and cocoa nut fibre from Colombo the previous year. She was later sold to W Hutchinson and was abandoned during heavy gales in 1883.[3]

Throughout her career with Rathbones' the vessel was captained by Robert Thomson, whose letters to his wife survive in the Maritime Museum Archives.[4] From 1871-81 he commanded Blue Funnel's *Agamemnon*.

1 There is part of a printed label on the rear stretcher "......Daguerreotypes..... / Hongkong Queens Road / No. 414". The majority of Lai Sung's paintings are stencilled or labelled on the rear, usually "LAI SUNG / PORTRAIT PAINTER / HONGKONG" see Brewington, pp. 52-3.
2 For instance the painting of *Corriemulzie*, 1864, reproduced MacGregor 1983, p.111.
3 MacGregor 1983, pp. 115-6; LCR vol. 82, no. 133, 24 May 1858.
4 Collection D/RT.
5 I am grateful to Dr Lee Minton for first suggesting this attribution. For *Shirley* see Brewington 1981, pp. 52-3.
6 The model scales to slightly different dimensions, see MacGregor 1983, p.116.

The painting has been attributed to Lai Sung on stylistic grounds and strong similarities can be seen with *Shirley* (M208, Peabody Museum of Salem)[5] and a work in a private collection. It can be dated to after 1861 when the telegraph on Victoria Peak was erected.
The collections include another painting of *Scawfell* (no. 180) and a half-model, (accession no. 1950.29.5)[6]

William J Leathem (active 1840 - 1855)

Leathem was based in Brighton, Sussex, but exhibited in London from 1840 to 1855. He specialised in storms and dramatic sea scenes. There are works in Brighton Art Gallery and the National Maritime Museum.[1]

1 Archibald, p. 130

145 *The President as last seen signalling with the Brig Pearl*[1]

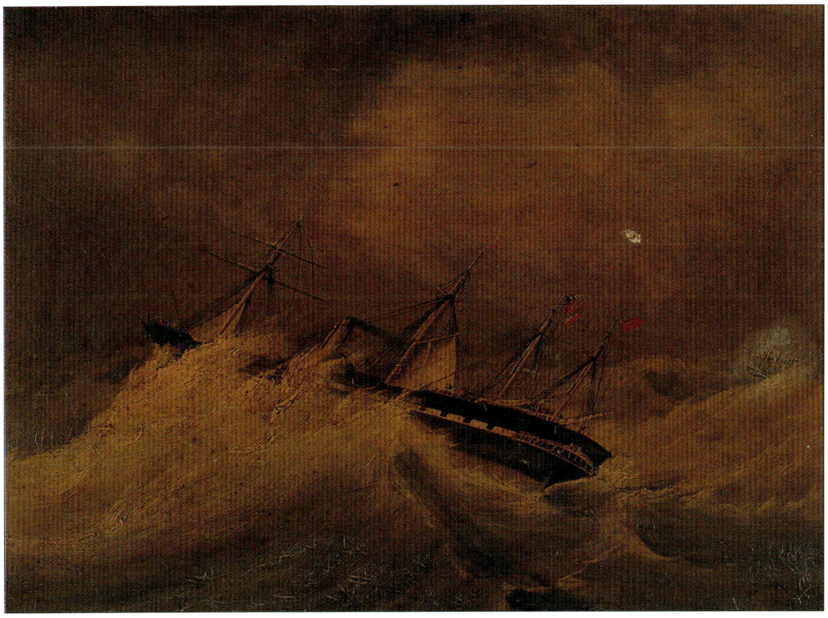

1960.118
Oil on canvas[2]
44.5 cm x 58 cm
Inscribed on rear of canvas "W J Leathem delt 1841"
Prov: Mr L K Foster, Suffolk, who presented it, 1960

Vessel: 243 ft (l), 41 ft (b); 2366 gross tons.

This dramatic view of the Paddle Steamer *President* shows the vessel on her last voyage from New York to Liverpool in March 1841, when she was lost without trace. The artist portrays her in port quarter view being hit by a huge wave. Her bowsprit has broken but there are still groups of people shown at the stern and the bow. She has hoisted three flags on her mizzen to signal to the Brig *Pearl* which is shown in the far distance on the right hand edge of the canvas, partially hidden by the waves. The meaning of this hoist has not been identified (and may be artistic invention).[3] The painting has been cut down at some stage in its existence, altering the composition.
Whether this painting represents an authentic encounter is open to question. According to contemporary sources *President* was last seen by Captain Cole of the *Orpheus* on 12 March.[4] No specific reference to the brig *Pearl* has been found.[5]
President was built in 1839 by Curling & Young of Limehouse, London, with engines by Fawcett Preston & Co of Liverpool, for the British and American Steam Navigation Company. She made her maiden voyage in August 1840. With this ship and *British Queen*, the company was the first to start a regular service across the Atlantic. These ships were the largest and most spectacular of their day, attracting admiring crowds wherever they went. However, the company was dogged by bad luck, which culminated in liquidation following the loss of the *President*.[6]

1 Paper label attached to rear of stretcher "The President as last / seen signalling with the Brig "Pearl / GRC / (indecipherable figures)" GRC stands for G R Cooper, an ancestor of the donor. DCF.
2 Canvas stamped "BROWN / & CO. / HIGH HOLBORN / LONDON".
3 The flags do not conform to known codes. They are from the top blue ground with vertical yellow stripes, red ground with yellow cross and white above red.
4 For a discussion on the loss of *President* see Pond, E. L., *Junius Smith: A biography of the father of the Atlantic liner*, New York, reprinted. There is a print based on Cole's evidence to the enquiry, see Parker & Bowen, 1938, p.239.
5 There are a number of vessels called *Pearl* but none appear to have been in the North Atlantic at this time.
6 Bonsor North, pp. 54-9.
7 For details of the prints, and the paintings from which they were taken, see Parker & Bowen 1938, pp. 238-9. A painting of *President* in the Mersey by Walters is illustrated in Davidson, 1992, p. 90
8 Information from Lars Scholl.

Despite her short career, *President* was painted by several artists including Samuel Walters and a number of prints were produced. Leathem painted another version of *President* in an earlier storm in November 1840.[7] There is another painting showing the vessel sinking by Andreas Achenbach in the Altonaer Museum in Hamburg.[8]

Liverpool School

The following unsigned and unattributed paintings are likely to be the work of artists working in Liverpool.

146 Aconcagua

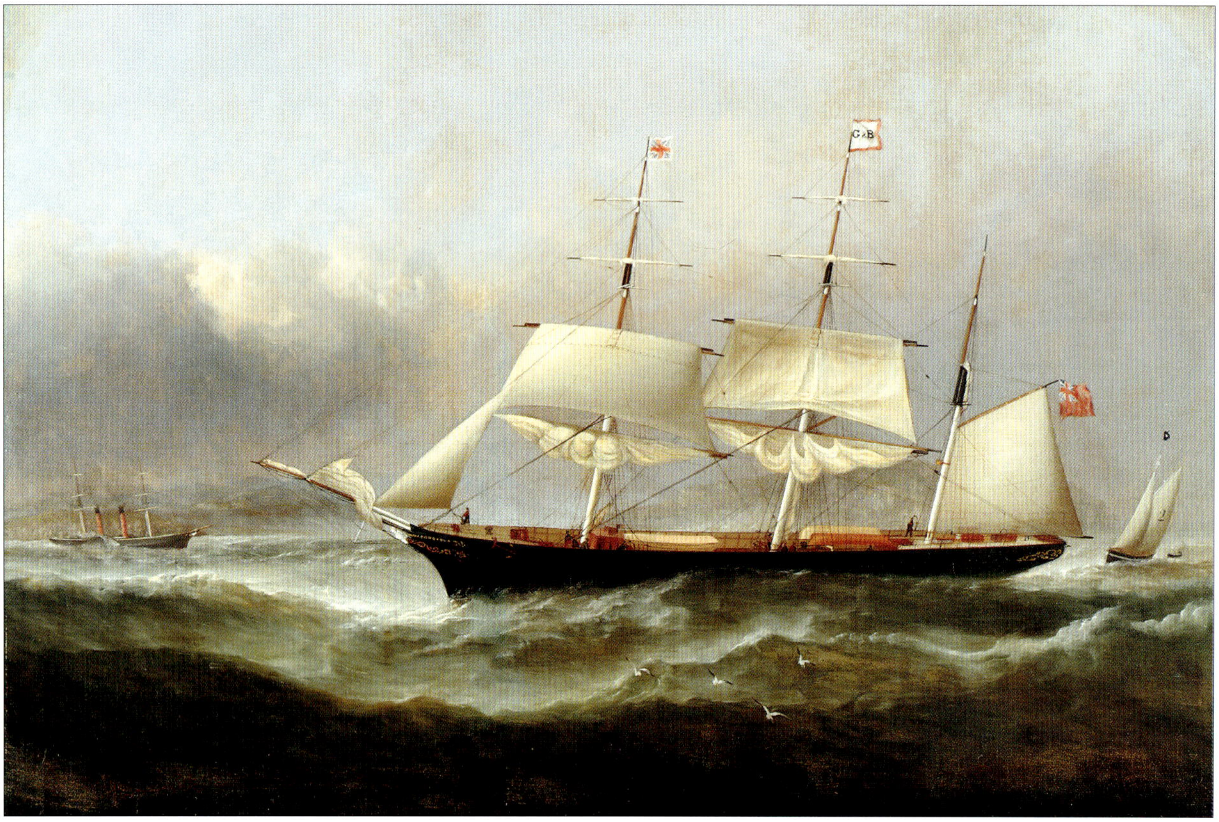

1955.250
Oil on canvas[1]
66.5 cm x 102.5 cm
Prov: In collection 1955.

The iron barque *Aconcagua* is shown hove-to in port profile, awaiting a pilot from the No.2 boat which is approaching from her stern. In the far left distance is a starboard view of a Cunard steamer[2] against a mountainous background, which is probably intended to be Parys Mountain on Anglesey.

Aconcagua flies the pilot jack at the foremast and at the main is a house flag with the legend "G & B", denoting the owners, Gardner and Broomhall of Liverpool. Both her topsails are fitted with Cunningham's Patent Reefing a system which allowed the sails to be rolled round the yard from the deck.[3] The crew are mainly grouped around the masts and the captain is visible by the mizzen. The pilot boat, which tows her punt, flies the blue peter indicating she is ready to put a pilot on board.

Aconcagua, named after the highest mountain in South America,[4] was built by John Jones Junior (later Jones, Quiggin) of Liverpool in 1859.[5] She was owned by James Gardner and Edward Broomhall, listed as ship owners, ship store deliverers and importers of wines and spirits,[6] who were initially in partnership with two other small-scale ship owners. She was sold to J Walmsley also of Liverpool in 1878 and she worked out of Mauritius from 1892 until abandoned in 1904.[7]

1 Relined; label on reverse "Richard Jeffreys, 188 Bold Street [Liverpool]
2 Probably meant to be either *Persia*, built 1856, or *Scotia*, built 1862.
3 For a description of the system see Underhill, pp. 127-130, 156.
4 6980m, in the Andes, on the Chilean-Argentine border north east of Santiago.
5 See Jones Quiggin Specification Book, f.152 (MAL, DX 154).
6 GDL, 1867.
7 LCR, vol. 83, no. 251, 30 November 1859.
8 Rees, p.203.

The No.2. pilot boat is the schooner *Leader* built by Thomas Harvey and Sons of Ipswich in 1856. She was withdrawn from service in 1896.[8]
Although attributed to Heard on entering the collection, this seems unlikely on stylistic grounds and the fact that Heard died in November 1859.

147 *Alchymist*

1955.235
Oil on canvas
66.5 cm x 101.5 cm
Prov: In collections, 1955

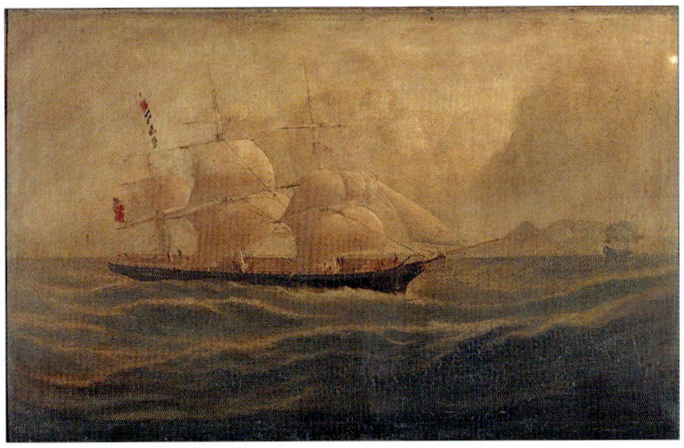

The ship rigged *Alchymist* is shown in starboard profile off an unidentified coast. She is seen from an elevated viewpoint to show the deck; the crew are reducing sail and already her royals and mizzen course are furled. She flies a Marryat flag code (1 d.p. 5 2 9 8) which should be 2 d.p. for her name. To the far right is a starboard bow view of a ship, which may be intended to be the same vessel.
Alchymist was built in Robbinston, Maine in 1854 as *Oswingo* but was bought by James Beazley and other partners of Liverpool in March 1855. She was wrecked off the Laccadive Islands in the Indian Ocean in April 1858. Beazley remained her master throughout her short career.[1] Stylistically the painting is similar to work by artists of the Liverpool School but the treatment of certain areas is rather coarse, particularly the sails which have little detail.

1 LCR vol. 78, no. 111, 19 March 1855.

148 *Alliance*

1955.232
Oil on canvas
46 cm x 61 cm
Prov: Unknown, in collections 1955.

Vessel: 52.6 ft (l), 16.9 ft (b), 10 ft (d);
79 gross tons

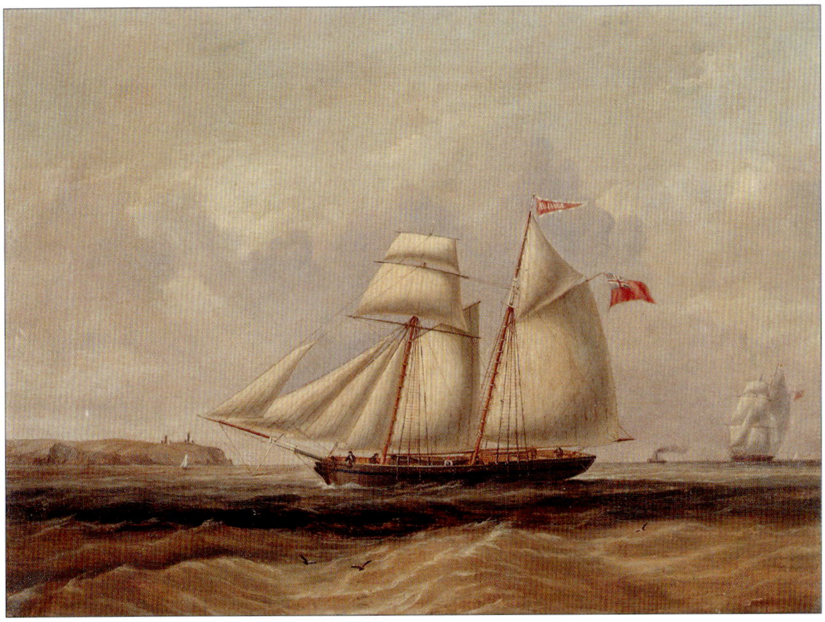

The topsail schooner *Alliance* is shown in full sail in port profile running before a stiff breeze possibly off Kinsale Head, Ireland. She wears a red ensign at the after peak and a name pennant on the main mast. To her stern in the distance is a quarter stern view of an unidentified brig with the beginning of a flag code (1 d.p., 1) and there is a steamer in the far distance between the two sailing vessels.

Alliance is typical of the small sailing vessels which carried out a thriving coastal trade until driven out of business by the competition of the railways and road transport in the present century. She has been identified previously as the same vessel as no. 102, but there are small structural details, such as the shorter coaming round the after deck, which suggest that they are different. She may, therefore, be the 72 ton schooner built in 1834 at Kelvin, Glasgow, and owned by Strong & Co. of Liverpool from 1837 until lost at sea in 1844.[1]

Certain characteristics are reminiscent of Heard, such as the bow wave and the elevated view showing activity on deck. However, these are insufficient to allow an attribution to Heard without further evidence.

In the background to the left is a headland with two towers, which is possibly the Old Head of Kinsale, on the south-west coast of Ireland.

1 LR 1844; LCR Vol. 53, no. 208, 28 November 1837.

149 *Baboo overset in Canning Graving Dock*

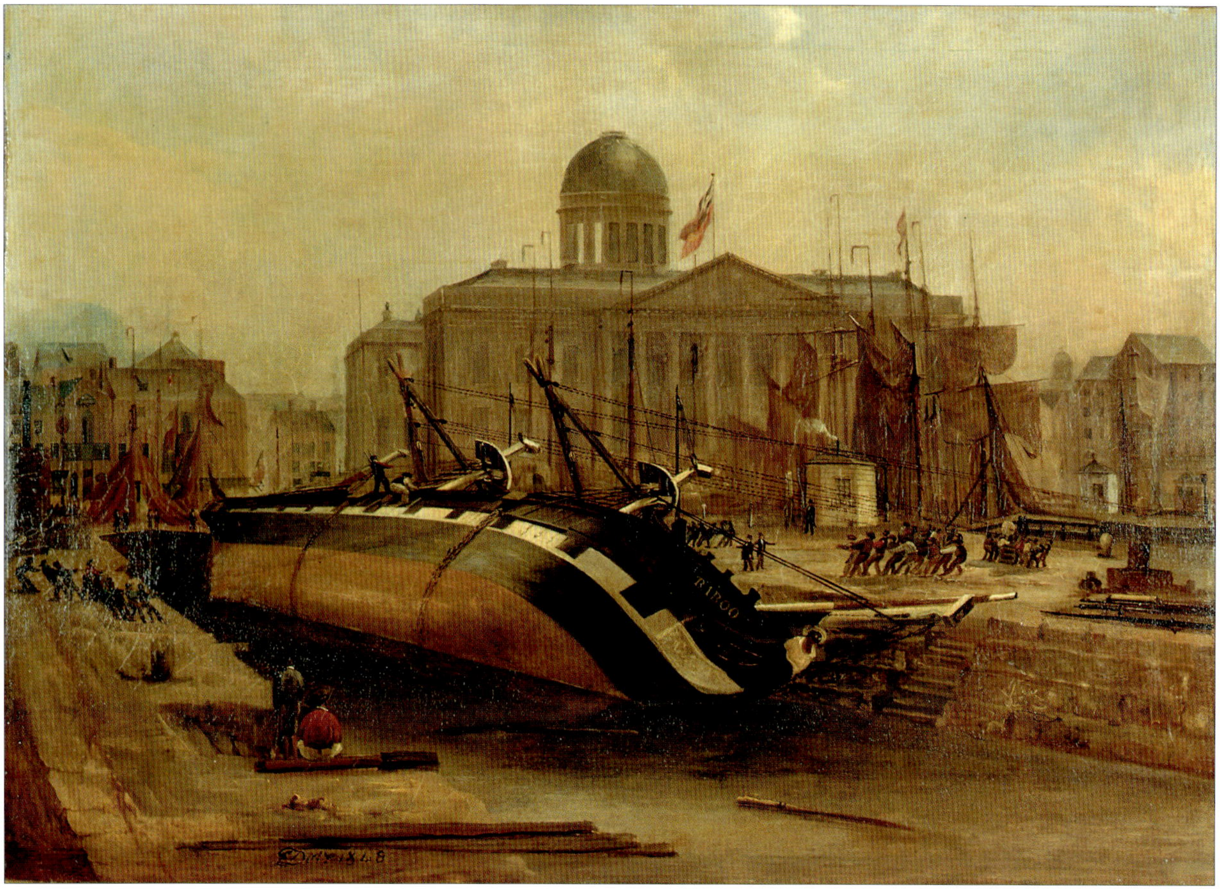

LI.1987.248
Oil on canvas
64 cm x 91 cm
Signed and dated "E D M Y 1848"
Prov: Liverpool Underwriters' Association, on permanent loan, 1987.

This painting depicts an incident on 22 February 1841 when the barque *Baboo* capsized in the Canning Graving Dock as the water level was being raised. The operation to right her is beginning and there are chains round her hull and groups of men on the quay sides are straining on the ropes. On the south side of the dock two men are directing and there is a third gentleman in the background watching the proceedings. The warehouses and shops of the Strand are in the background, though the impressive facade of the Custom House dominates the scene. To the right is the entrance to the Canning Dock, where the masts of other berthed ships can be seen. She had arrived in Liverpool from the East in January 1841 with a cargo of sugar, linseed, saltpetre, jute, rum, flour and chutney[1] and had entered the dry dock to be repaired and coppered. As *Gore's General Advertiser* recorded this "novel accident occurred........On Monday she was ready to take in cargo, and was about to leave the graving dock for that purpose. Unfortunately she was not sufficiently ballasted, and, as the water rose upon her, she suddenly sprung up and immediately fell over on her beam ends. The ballast that was in her hold slipped over, which, with the water which rushed into her, contributed to fix her with increased firmness in her awkward position. None of the workmen or sailors sustained any injury, and active measures were immediately resorted to, to replace the vessel in her natural position."[2] She sailed for Bombay and China on 3 April.[3]

Baboo[4] was built in Calcutta in 1835 for the China trade, and during her career she sailed to India, China and Australia. She was owned by T. Kincaid of Greenock and made her last voyage from Shanghai to London in 1850.[5]

1 GGA, 21 January 1841.
2 GGA, 25 February 1841.
3 GGA, 8 April 1841.
4 Baboo or babu was an Indian clerk who could write English; it is now regarded as a derogatory term.
5 LR, 1835-1850; arrived London 30 January 1850, LL 30 January 1850. There are no further entries in LL.

150 *Countess of Lonsdale*

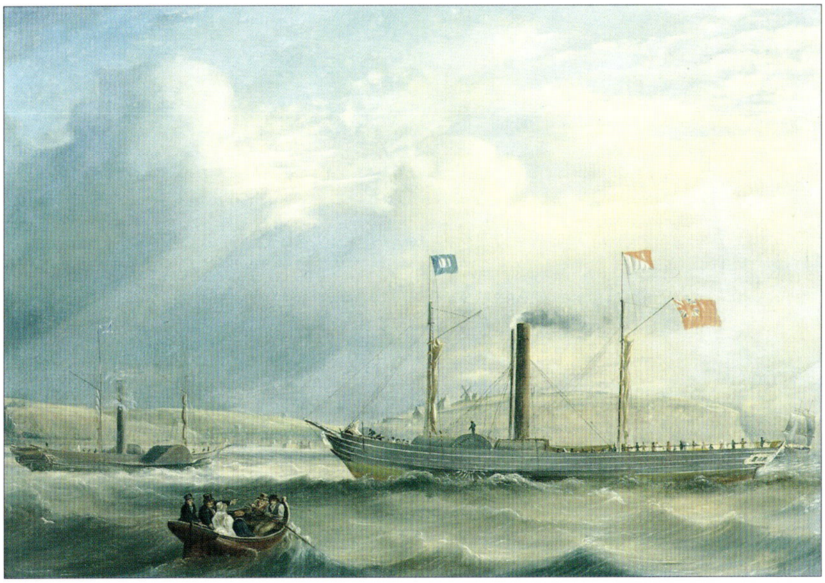

1970.246.12
Oil on canvas[1]
52.5 cm x 75 cm
Prov: T & J Brocklebank Co Ltd., Cunard Brocklebank Ltd., Private Collection, on permanent loan.
Ref: Gibson, ill. opp. p.68

Vessel: 127 ft (l), 20 ft (b), 13 ft (d); 120 h.p.; 241 gross tons

The paddle steamer *Countess of Lonsdale* is shown in port profile under steam with sails furled as she approaches her home port of Whitehaven. One member of the crew is standing on the port paddle box and another one is at the anchor; various passengers can also be seen on the after deck. She flies the blue peter at her foremast and a red and white flag, diagonally split, at the main. The meaning of these flags is not clear.[2] The red ensign flies from a gaff. A second paddle steamer shown in starboard quarter view is also heading towards the harbour. She wears an indistinct flag at the main mast. This has previously been regarded as a second view of *Countess of Lonsdale* but this vessel has her paddle boxes mounted externally, rather than contained within the hull as shown in the main view. This must represent another paddle steamer.

A small punt with a group of well-to-do citizens is in the foreground heading towards the main view of vessel. Astern is a distant brig and there is other shipping in the vicinity of the harbour which can be seen between the two paddle steamers. It appears that the west pier is still under construction - there is scaffolding and a group of men at its seaward end, where the lighthouse was built in 1832.

Countess of Lonsdale was the first paddle steamer built by Brocklebanks and was commissioned by the Whitehaven Steam Navigation Company (in which Brocklebanks had shares) in 1827. She had sleeping accommodation for 20 to 30

1 Relined.
2 The blue peter normally meant that a vessel was about to sail.
3 Gibson I, pp. 78, 229.
4 Haws, Brocklebank, p.30.

passengers and began a twice weekly passenger service between the port and Liverpool.[3] Later transferred to the weekly service to Belfast, she was replaced in 1848 and broken up in 1854.[4]
This canvas is reminiscent of the work of Joseph Heard and could possibly be an early work, perhaps before he left Whitehaven for Liverpool about 1833.

151 *George Canning, Pilot Cutter No.7*

1987.310
Oil on board
61 cm x 45 cm
Inscribed rear "Liverpool Pilot's Cutter No.7, Rowlands Master, year 1859"
Prov: Goffey Collection, sold Outhwaite & Litherland, 26 September 1979, lot 201; Sotheby's, 3 June 1987, Lot. No. 282, where purchased.

Vessel: 54 ft (l), 15 ft (b), 9 ft (d); 43 gross tons.

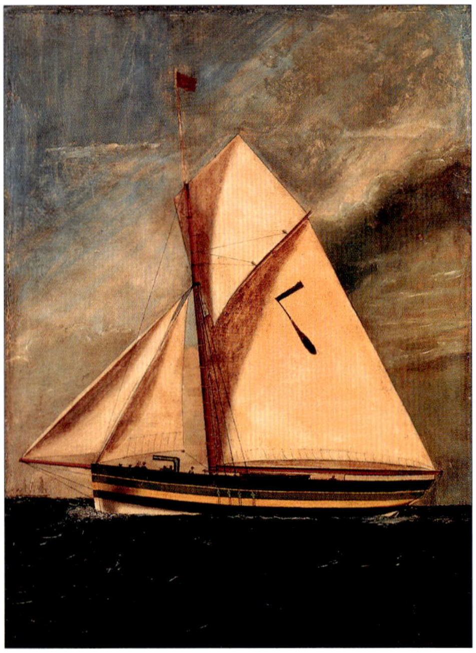

This painting shows the No.7 Pilot Boat in port profile with all her sails set and details of her rigging. She flies a red flag, number 7 in Watson's code. On board members of the crew can be seen looking over the side, including two pilots in their top hats near the bow. Another prominent feature is the chimney of a galley stove. A sailing ship is shown close-hauled, probably awaiting a pilot, under the cutter's bow.
George Canning[1], the No.7 boat was built by Peter Cato of Liverpool in 1844. She remained in service until 1863 when she was replaced. Her subsequent history is not known.[2]
"Rowlands master", referred to on the rear is William Rowlands, who gained his pilot's licence in 1829 and retired in 1878. He seems to have had an unblemished career over a period of 49 years.[3]

1 George Canning (1770-1827), politician and MP for Liverpool, 1812-23.
2 Rees, p.202.
3 Tebay 1991.

152 *Tug Lion off the Great Orme*

MMM.1997.72.2
Oil on canvas[1]
43 cm x 60 cm
Prov: W & T Jolliffe & Co., Alexandra Towing Company, H B Bicket, who presented it, May 1997.
Exh: Liverpool, 1987b

Vessel: 116.3 ft (l), 20.5 ft (b), 11.3 ft (d); 163 gross tons.

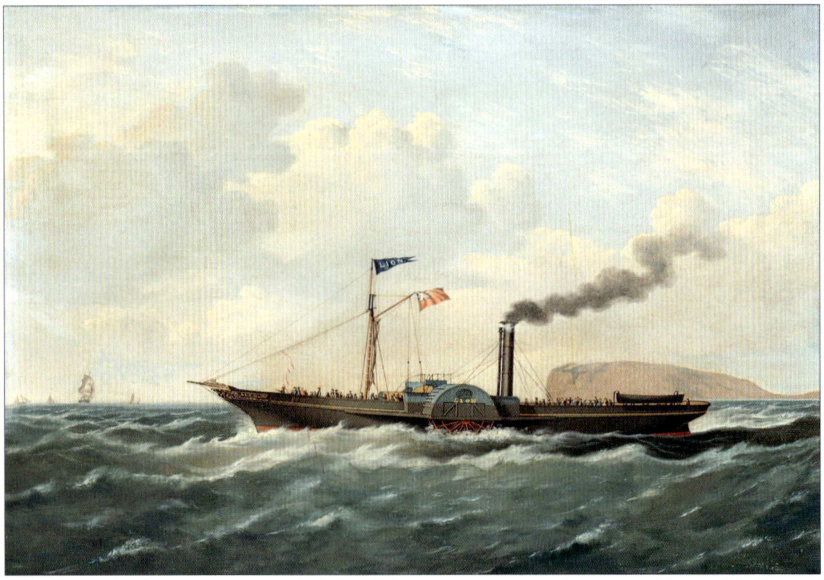

The steam tug *Lion* is shown in port profile off the Great Orme, on the coast of North Wales. This iron plated tug has a single funnel with a clipper bow and shield figurehead. The single mast is placed forward of the paddle boxes and the sail is furled. She is flying a blue name pennant from the mast and a red ensign at the gaff. The name is also carried on the bow and paddle box. The vessel is in fact carrying a significant number of passengers, between 50 and 60, perhaps on an inaugural trip; there is a lifeboat towards the stern. Other unidentified shipping can be seen to the left in the far distance.

The scene is set in Beaumaris Bay off Conwy with the outcrop of the Great Orme's Head in the background.

Lion was built in 1856 at South Shields, County Durham, for William and Thomas Jolliffe, tug owners of Liverpool. The vessel was changed to schooner rig in 1858 and sold to Fenton, Maugnall, merchants and manufacturers of Manchester in 1860. She was taken off the register in December 1884 and broken up.[2]

The painting was presumably completed in her early days in Liverpool and before the rig alteration in 1858. The style is reminiscent of John Hughes (1806-78).

1 Relined

2 CR, no. 14, 17 January 1857, CR, no. 236, 19 November 1860. Jolliffe's owned another vessel called LION, built 1859 in South Shields but this was schooner rigged with 2 masts. See CR, no. 130, 20 May 1859.

153 *Marco Polo*

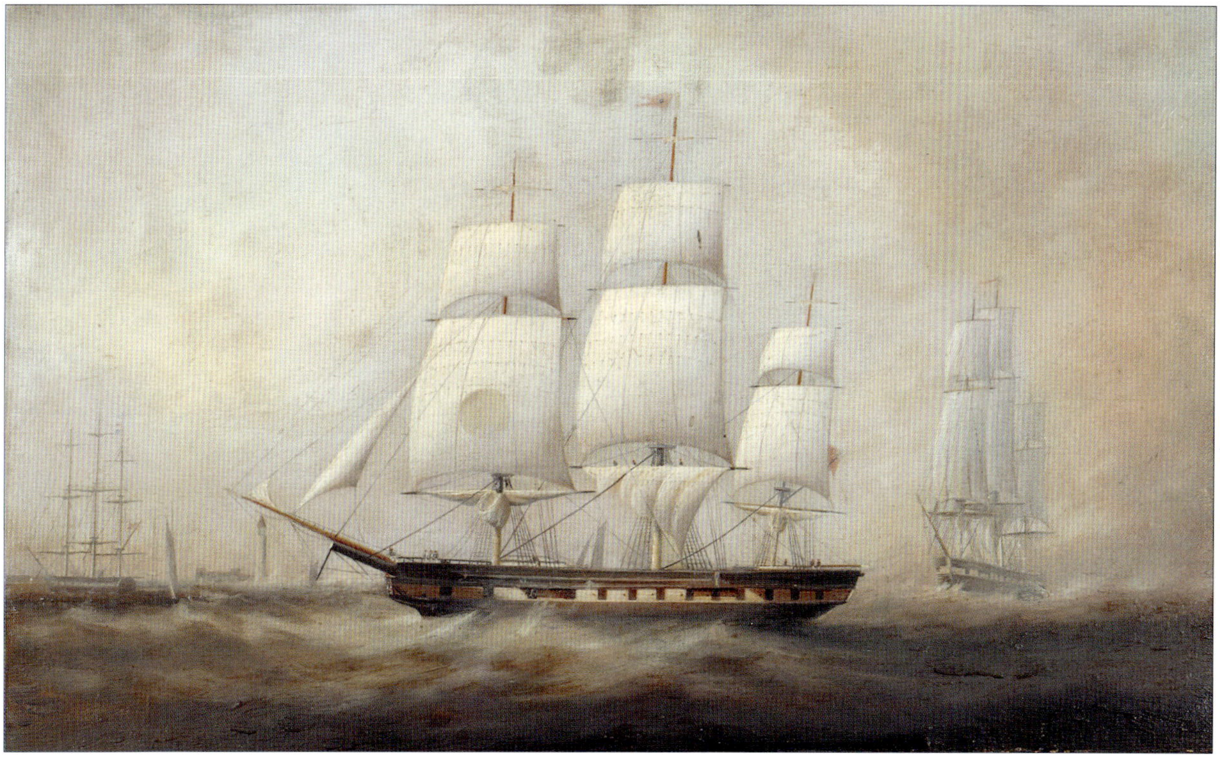

Marco Polo is probably the best known of the Liverpool-based Black Ball Line packet ships which ran passenger services to Australia in the mid-nineteenth century. Here she is shown in three views at the entrance to the Mersey with the Perch Rock Fort and Lighthouse in the far distance under the bowsprit of the main view.

To the right she is shown approaching in a port bow view with all sails set except the fore and mizzen courses and the main which is clewed. The main view in the centre shows her in port profile reducing sail and with men on the main yard arms. The left hand view shows her in the far distance in a port stern view stationary with all her sails furled. The vessel is identifiable as a Black Ball liner from the main view where the fore course has the distinctive black ball and the house flag flies on the main mast. The other views have indistinct flags.

Although the vessel is generally depicted in a competent manner, the height of the masts and sails are exaggerated, particularly in the right hand view.

The ship rigged *Marco Polo*[1] was built by James Smith in Marsh Creek, St John,

1961.130.22
Oil on canvas
31 cm x 51 cm
Prov: J A Howard-Watson, Liverpool, who presented it, 1961.

Vessel: 185 ft (l), 35 ft (b), 29 ft (d); 1625 gross tons

New Brunswick and launched in 1851. She was bought by James Baines of Liverpool for his Black Ball Line in June 1852 and was refitted in opulent style to attract passengers, particularly emigrants, travelling to Australia. *Marco Polo* was a fast ship. On her first voyage both passages were made in 76 days at a time when the average run was 120 days or more. She consistently made fast voyages and remained on the Australia run until she failed her passenger survey in 1867. She was then employed by Baines in general cargo carrying but was sold in 1871. She changed hands regularly until she ran aground on Prince Edward Island in 1883 where she broke up.[2]

Several other paintings of *Marco Polo* survive, including a port profile painted for her first master (Yarmouth Museum, Nova Scotia),[3] another port profile at sea by Captain Tom Robinson (State Library of Victoria, Australia),[4] and a view of her drying her sails in the Mersey, attributed to Thomas Dove, (Private Collection).[5] There is a coloured lithograph of her entering the Mersey, taken from an untraced painting by Thomas Dove (New Brunswick Museum)[6] and an illustration of her hove-to off the Liverpool waterfront in the *Illustrated London News* taken from a painting by Samuel Walters, which again is untraced.[7]

The collections include an exhibition model of the vessel (1935.122) and two pieces of replica stern carving featuring a recumbent Marco Polo and an elephant (1981.528). The original carving of Marco Polo is in the New Brunswick Museum and the other carving, together with other items rescued from the wreck are on Prince Edward Island.[8]

1 Marco Polo (1254-1324), Venetian traveller.
2 For a full history of the vessel see M K Stammers *The Passage Makers*, Brighton, 1978, pp. 364-382.
3 Illustrated in colour, Stammers, op. cit., p.365.
4 Illustrated, Stammers, op. cit., p.377 and MacGregor, 1988, p.187.
5 Sold Christies, 2 November 1995, lot 590 (ill).
6 Illustrated Davidson, 1986, p.75.
7 23 February 1853, illustrated, Stammers, op. cit., p.237 and Davidson, 1992, p.87.
8 The Marco Polo carving is illustrated in Stammers, op. cit., p. 381. George MacBeath 'The Marco Polo, the most famous ship ever built in New Brunswick' in *Maritime Advocate and Busy East*, May 1951, p.22.

154 *Northern Monarch*

1970.152.1
Oil on canvas
46 cm x 59.5 cm
Inscribed (bc) "NORTHERN MONARCH"
Prov: Miss Sumner, Old Colwyn, who presented it, 1970.

Vessel: 227.4 ft (l), 36.6 ft (b), 21.7 ft (d); 1280 gross tons

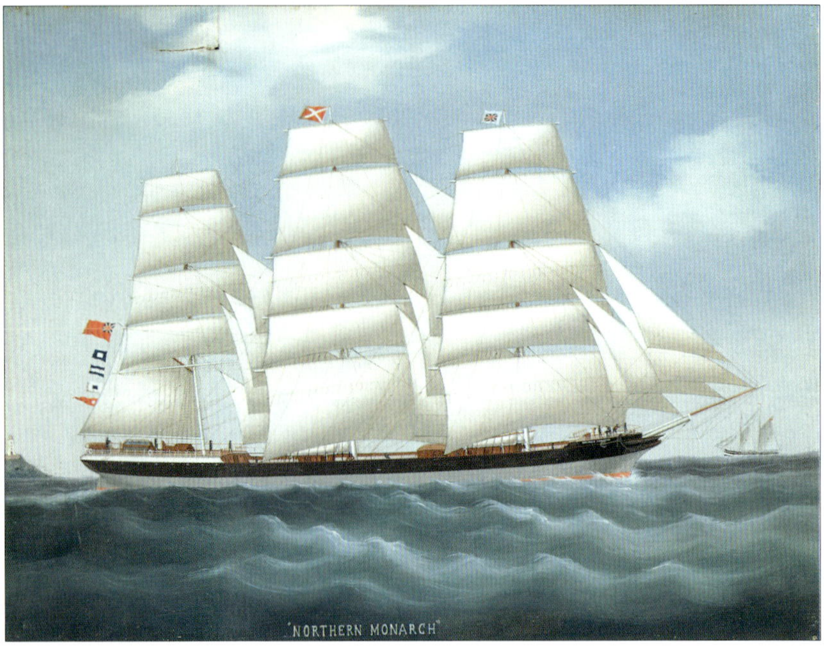

The sailing ship *Northern Monarch* is shown in starboard profile from the leeward side under all plain sail. Various members of the crew can be seen on the decks, including a group at the bow adjusting the sails. She flies the pilot jack at the fore mast, the house flag for Edgar and Co. (red ground with white St Andrews cross) at the main and at the after peak her commercial flag code (P J S F) below the red ensign. The No. 1 Liverpool pilot boat is shown in port profile under the bowsprit and presumably the scene is set off Anglesey. However, the lighthouse to the far left is not an accurate depiction of any of the neighbouring lights.

The iron hulled *Northern Monarch* was built by McMillan and Son of Dumbarton in 1876 for the Royal Exchange Shipping Company of London. With two other "*Monarchs*" she was employed in the emigrant trade to Australia and New Zealand.[1] She was bought by J Edgar & Co. of Liverpool in 1887 and was converted to barque rig in 1897. She was lost off the New Zealand coast on a passage from Newcastle, New South Wales to Callao, Peru, with a cargo of coal in November 1903.[2]
The Liverpool pilot boat is the schooner rigged *Queen* built in 1856 by Michael Ratsey of West Cowes and withdrawn from service in 1898.[3]
The painting presumably dates from the period 1887 to 1897.

1 *Western Monarch* (1875) and *Eastern Monarch* (1874), see Lubbock, Windjammers, I, pp. 170-171.
2 LCR vol. 96, no. 74, 8 November 1887, TB9, p.291, TB11, p. 131; Beard; Lubbock, op. cit., pp. 171-2, there is a photograph of her smashed wheel opposite p.9.
3 Rees, p.203.

155 *Rapido*

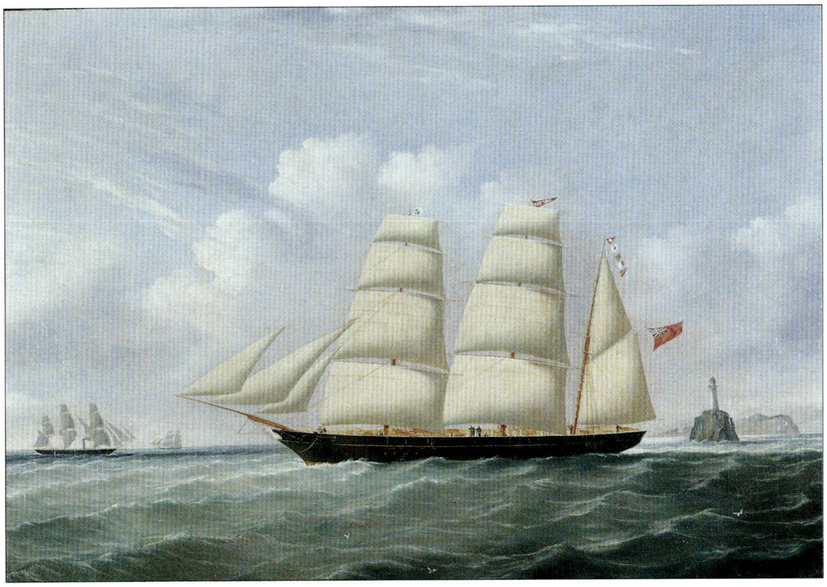

1954.117.1
Oil on wood panel[1]
65.5 cm x 91.5 cm
Prov: Captain W Dougall, Birkenhead, who presented it, 1954[2]
Exh: Liverpool 1986
Ref: Port Panorama, 1986, p.6

Vessel: 128.3 ft (l); 25.5 ft (w), 16.1 ft (d); 299 tons

The outward bound barque *Rapido* is portrayed centrally under full sail in port profile passing the Fastnet Rock, off the south-west corner of Ireland. A homeward bound transatlantic steamer is passing in the distance at the far left hand side of the canvas and there is an outward bound brigantine in the distance. *Rapido* flies a red ensign at the peak, her Marryat code of 2 d.p. 1, 9, 3, 6 from the mizzen, a name pennant from the main and the Mondel house flag of a blue anchor on a white ground from the foremast.
Rapido was built by R Williamson in Harrington, Cumberland, in 1855 and was owned by Joseph Mondel of Liverpool. She was sold in 1865 and had a number of Liverpool owners before finally passing to Chatfield of Auckland, New Zealand in 1885. She was abandoned ashore at Port Darwin, Australia in 1886.[3]
Astern of the vessel is the Fastnet Rock with its lighthouse, built in 1854, and in the distance is Cape Clear at the south eastern most tip of Ireland.
Captain James Dougall, whose name appears on a label on the rear, was master of *Rapido* from 1868 and was presumably an ancestor of the donor.[4]
This is almost certainly the work of an artist of the Liverpool school.

1 A label on the rear reads "Rapido / Capt. J. Dougall".
2 No. 109 *Maia* was also presented by Capt. Dougall. *Maia* and *Rapido* were both initially owned by Mondel & Co. and Captain W H Turpin was master of *Maia* 1847-57 and of *Rapido* 1857-8. The provenance of these paintings is undoubtedly linked but the exact situation is by no means clear.
3 LCR, vol. 80, No. 233, 11 July 1855 and No. 307, 22 September 1855, Transaction Book, p.165; Beard.
4 James Dougall, b. Peterhead 1842, certificate gained 1866. LCpR, 1869. *Rapido* was his first command.

156 *Tugs off New Brighton* (page 146)

This scene shows two tugs towing a dismasted vessel into the Mersey off New Brighton, Wirral. The main action is set in the middle distance across the centre of the canvas with the two tugs assisted by four Mersey flats acting as "camels" on either side of the incapacitated vessel, which has been left with only the stumps of

1971.276.26
Oil on canvas[1]
45 cm x 67 cm
Prov: C W Kellock Ltd, Liverpool, on permanent loan, 1971
Exh: Liverpool 1907, no. 20 "Old Liverpool Steam Tugs Towing the Dicky Sam"

Vessels:
John Bull 93.5 ft (l), 16.9 ft (b), 9.7 ft (d); 45 tons
Robert Burns 84.6 ft (l), 15.8 ft (b), 9.4 ft (d); 41 tons
Dickey Sam 96.3 ft (l), 22 ft (b), 15.8 ft (d); 305 tons

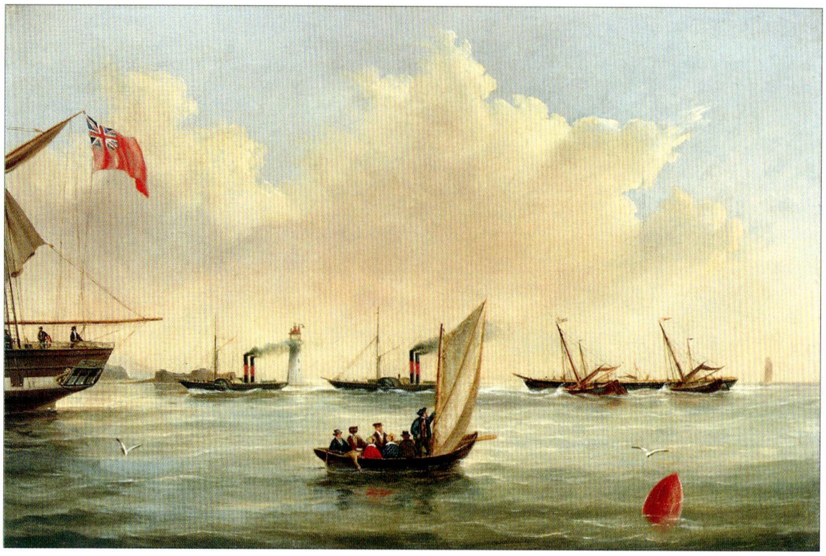

her masts.[2] In the foreground a group of passengers in a small boat is watching the proceedings and to the far left is the stern of an unidentified sailing ship, flying a red ensign at the after peak.

The two tugs are driven by paddle engines and have twin black funnels with a broad central red band. The tug to the far left has part of a name visible on its paddle box (JOHN ?U??) and there is a hint of two names on the second tug's box. They are probably meant to be *John Bull* and *Robert Burns*[3] which were employed on the Mersey between 1853 and 1859 by John Watkins Jnr., son of the founder of the more famous London firm.[4] *John Bull* was built at Mill Wall in 1849 and *Robert Burns* at South Shore, Gateshead in 1837. They were both sloop rigged wooden planked vessels.[5]

Traditionally the dismasted vessel has been identified as *Dickey Sam*, though there is no corroboration in the painting. Indeed, the vessel depicted is too long in relation to the tugs and the figurehead appears to be female rather than male. The barque rigged *Dickey Sam*[6] was built in Liverpool by William Seddon and launched in February 1841. The vessel was owned by John Thompson and a group of investors trading to India and South America. She was sold to James Poole & Co in 1853, then to Luis Isac Santa Maria, both of Liverpool. In 1856 she was sold to Alexander King & Co of Glasgow[7] and was lost in the English Channel in 1866.[8]

In the background behind the tugs are the familiar landmarks of the Perch Rock Fort and Lighthouse.

1 Relined, 1985.
2 For flats used as camels and a similar painting showing flats assisting in the salvage of the barque *Valparaiso*, see M K Stammers *Mersey Flats and Flatmen*, Liverpool, 1993, pp. 182-3 (ill.).
3 The other possibility is *Uncle Sam*, built Westham, Essex, 1839, see LCR vol. 72, no. 285, 27 June 1853.
4 See F C Bowen *A Hundred Years of Towage. A History of William Watkins Ltd 1833-1933*, Gravesend, 1933, pp. 25, 33. A painting of *John Bull* in NMM, (Illustrated T Nicholson, *Take The Strain*, 1990, p.23), is not the Watkins vessel. The tug *John Bull* was a small sloop rigged vessel, the NMM one has a barquentine rig and is a larger and more sophisticated vessel.
5 For *John Bull* see LCR, vol. 72, no. 272, 18 June 1853 and TB3, p.128; for *Robert Burns* see LCR, vol. 74, no. 577, 29 November 1853 and TB3, p.145. John Bull was a nickname for an Englishman from the eighteenth century. Robert Burns, Scottish poet, (1759-96).
6 The name Dicky (Dickey) Sam was applied to Liverpudlians born within the sound of the bells of St Nicholas's Church. There was one earlier vessel of this name (built 1831, see LCR, vol. 47, no. 93, 26 July 1831).
7 LCR vol. 56, no. 49, 2 March 1841; vol. 60, no. 143; vol. 72, no. 154, 8 April 1853; vol. 77, no. 661, 16 November 1854; TB2, p.225, 3 October 1856.
8 LL, 5 November 1866.

157 Vision

The clipper ship *Vision* is shown in starboard profile off the north end of the Liverpool waterfront on her way into port. She is reducing sail and many of the main sheets are already furled and there are crew taking in the sails at the bowsprit. She wears a house flag on her main mast and her number in the Marryat Code (2 d.p. 9 5 1 4) on her mizzen mast. The red ensign is at the after peak.

There is other shipping in the background including an unidentified paddle steamer making her way downstream under *Vision*'s bowsprit and there is a small boat in the foreground. The scene is set off the Salisbury Dock with its distinctive Victoria Tower (completed 1848) clearly visible in the right hand distance. The tower of St Martin's church can be seen behind the dock. Further north, the river wall and warehouse buildings near Huskisson Dock can be seen. The various windmills that can be seen are a reminder that dock development along the river was faster than development inland.

Vision was built by Hall & Co. of Aberdeen for James Beazley & Company of Liverpool in 1854. She was one of the last vessels built by Hall with their distinctive

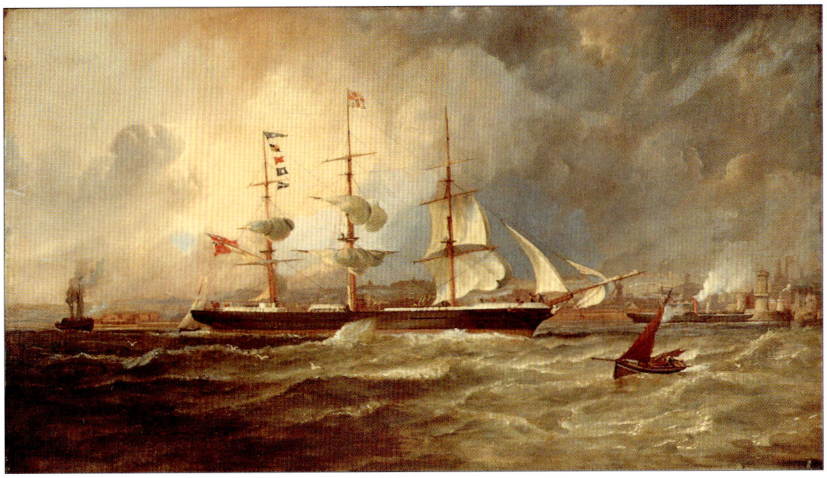

1970.259
Oil on canvas[1]
63.5 m x 107 cm
Prov: B Glasier, Liverpool, who presented it, 1970

and influential Aberdeen bow and which gave added speed and sailing capabilities.[2] On her maiden voyage in 1854 she was the first ship to arrive home with the new teas from Whampoa. She capsized in 1857 in the Min river on her way to Foochow through pilot error and became a total wreck.[3]

A painting of *Vision* off Anglesey by Samuel Walters was formerly owned by Gracie, Beazley & Co. and there is a constructional half model in the collections.[4]

1 Relined.
2 For a discussion of the Aberdeen bow see McGregor Tea Clippers, 43-47.
3 See McGregor Tea Clippers pp. 63-4 (ill).
4 The painting is illustrated in McGregor Tea Clippers, p.63; the half model is Accession no. 31.86.2.

158 *William Jolliffe*

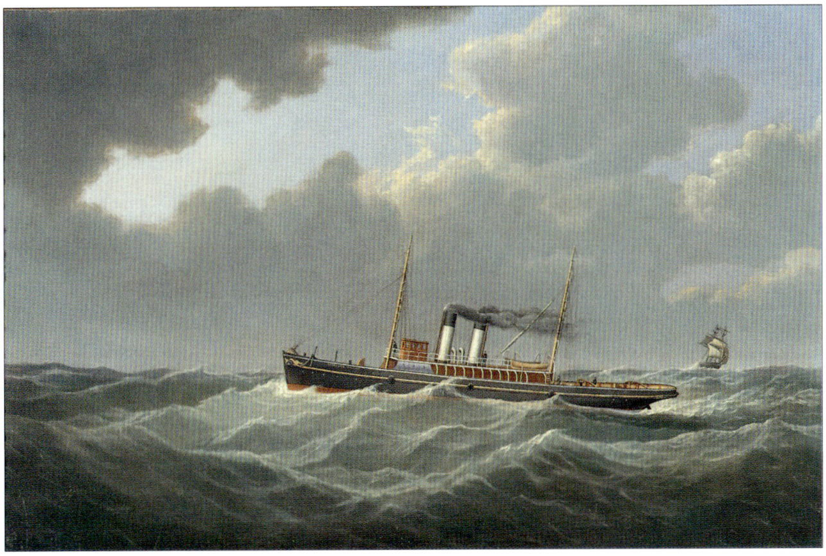

MMM.1997.72.1
Oil on canvas[1]
56 cm x 92 cm
Prov: W & T Jolliffe & Co., Alexandra Towing Company, H B Bicket, who presented it, May 1997.
Exh: Liverpool, 1987b

Vessel: 148.4 ft (l), 26.2 ft (b), 13.9 ft (d); 329 gross tons

The steam screw tug *William Jolliffe* is shown in port profile at sea. She was one of the largest and most powerful tugs of her generation undertaking towing at sea as well as duties around the Mersey. Indeed, she is shown here battling against heavy seas. She was schooner rigged though the sails are shown furled and she has a bridge house. The two funnels are in the Jolliffe livery and she is named at the bow. In the far left distance is a quarter starboard view of an unidentified brig.

William Jolliffe was built by John Readhead & Co., of South Shields in 1885 for T A Jolliffe of W & T Jolliffe, tug owners of Liverpool. She remained with Jolliffes until sold to new owners in Vancouver, Canada in April 1914.[2] An almost identical vessel of the same name was also built by Readhead a few months earlier in 1885 but was purchased by the Admiralty for Naval use.[3]

Although unattributed, the painting could perhaps be the work of Joseph Witham (1832 - 1901).

1 Relined; label on rear stretcher for C Atkinson, Liverpool.
2 CR, no. 107, 17 October 1885.
3 CR, no. 27, 19 March 1885.

Gothic Scroll (active about 1875- about 1890)

This pseudonym describes an artist who generally paints Liverpool registered ships on a metal panel. Almost all the views feature a local background. Many of the paintings include details of the vessel and captain in Gothic script on a scroll at the bottom of the painting. Other features are the stick-like depiction of people and the characteristic way in which rigging, rails and flags are shown. The artist also has a habit of including single letter flags which do not generally relate to known usage of the time.

There are some affinities with the work of the Chinese School and this has given rise to the suggestion that he may have been an expatriate Chinese artist working in Liverpool. There is a possibility that the artist may be connected with R Wareing (active about 1912), who is known from a couple of paintings of similar style.[1] There are several examples in The British Mercantile Marine Memorial Collection.[2]

1 See *Karina*, signed and dated R Waring, 1912, lot 952, N E Auctions, Portsmouth, New Hampshire, USA, 19 August 1996.
2 I am grateful for comments on this artist from Sam Davidson.

159 R M S Britannia

1984.269.9
Oil on white brass[1]
41.5 cm x 76 cm
Inscription "The Pacific. Steam. Navigation. Cos. R. M. S. "Britannia." of L.pool. C. C. Brough. Commander."
Prov: Pacific Steam Navigation Company, on permanent loan.

Vessel: 411.5 ft (l), 43.8 ft (b), 33.8 (d); 4129 gross tons

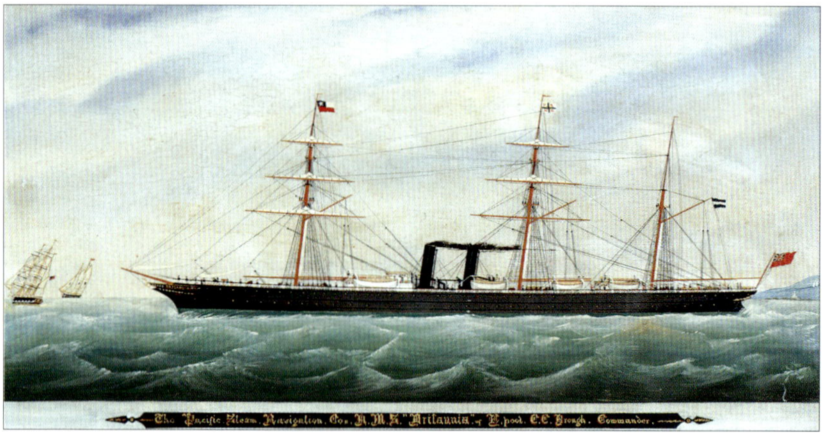

The Pacific Steam Navigation Company's *Britannia* is shown in port profile off Anglesey under steam with her auxiliary sails stowed. She is barque rigged with two funnels. There are various crew on deck and a few passengers on the stern deck. She flies the PSNC house flag on the main mast and the Chilean national flag at her fore, together with letter J in the Commercial Code at the after peak.[2] The red ensign is at the stern jack. In the far left distance are the outlines of the No. 5 Liverpool pilot schooner and an unidentified barque. The Skerries lighthouse is shown in the right background.

The iron steam ship *Britannia* was built by Laird Brothers of Birkenhead in 1873 for the PSNC mail service from Liverpool to Valparaiso via Rio and Montevideo. In 1885 she was requisitioned as an armed cruiser during the Afghan crisis with the Russians but was not used. In the same year she was rebuilt with improved accommodation and a simplified rig. She was grounded leaving Rio harbour in 1895 but was refloated and sold for local coastal use. She was scrapped at Preston in 1901.[3]

No. 5 Liverpool Pilot schooner is *Victoria and Albert* built by Michael Ratsey of Cowes in 1856 and was in service until foundering in May 1888.

There is no reference in official or PSNC sources to a Captain Brough but Charles Curtis Bray was master from May 1877 to June 1881.[4] Is this a simple mistake? This painting is clearly one of the series produced by "Gothic Scroll" with his characteristic style and gothic inscription. Samuel Walters also painted *Britannia* leaving the Mersey on her maiden voyage.[5]

1 Support assumed same as no. 160 *City of Cambridge*. Printed label rear "HUGO LANG & CO. LTD / 19 WHITECHAPEL / LIVERPOOL".
2 The significance of this flag is not clear.
3 Bonsor South, p.160 and CR no. 132, 20 August 1873.
4 See CR 1873.
5 Offered for sale, Phillips, London, 12 December 1995, lot 29.

160 S S City of Cambridge entering the Mersey

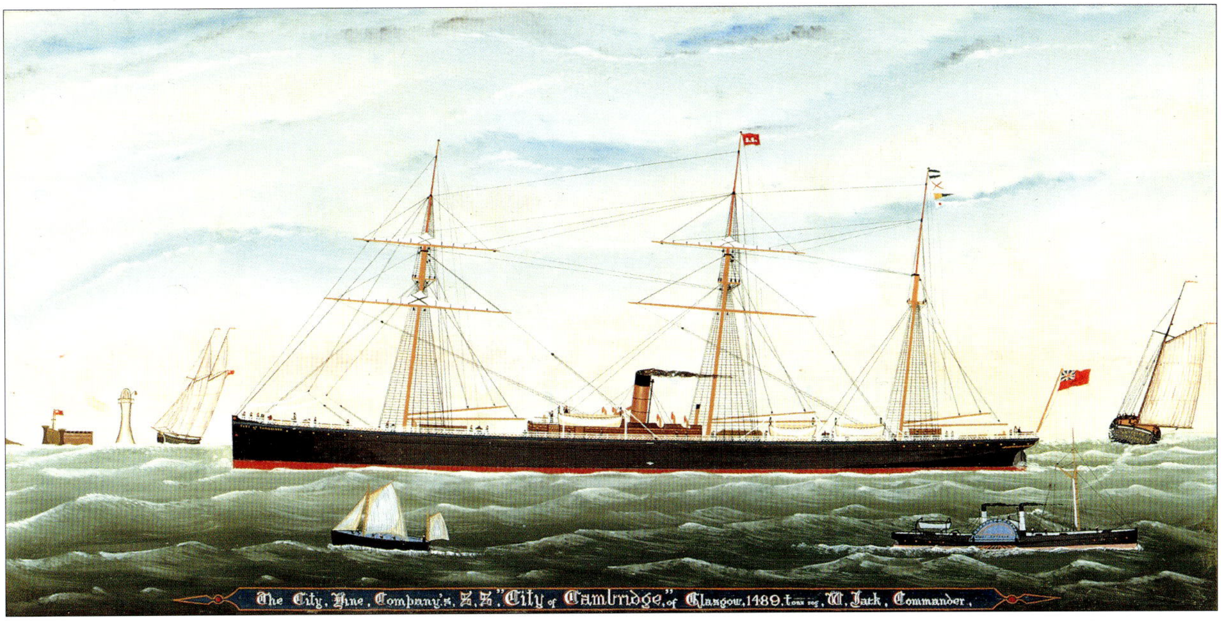

The iron screw 3 masted barque *City of Cambridge* is shown in port profile entering the Mersey. On the left is the Perch Rock Fort and Lighthouse, with a schooner rigged vessel about to pass the lighthouse. In the foreground, totally out of scale with the main portrait is a Mersey gig boat and the steam tug *Great Emperor*, named on the paddle box, in port profile. To the right of the canvas is a stern view of a cutter, identified by her stern lettering as *Activity* of Liverpool. She flies two red pennants.

City of Cambridge flies the City Line house flag from the main mast and her commercial code number (J V G C) from the mizzen. She was one of four vessels built in 1870 by Barclay Curle & Co. for George Smith & Sons of Glasgow to take advantage of the opening of the Suez Canal the previous year for their Indian service. She was sold to Clan Line in 1881 and renamed *Clan Maclean* and was wrecked off Cape St Vincent, Portugal in 1903.[2]

The iron steam tug *Great Emperor* was built at Wellington Quay, Newcastle upon Tyne in 1864 and owned by William & Thomas Jolliffe of Liverpool. She was broken up in 1899.[3] There is a wash drawing of the tug by Gilbert Stevens in the collections. (1984.69.17a).

The inscription in Gothic style lettering on a ribbon records details of the vessel, including the captain, W Jack. He was master of the ship from 1876 to 1879, providing an approximate date for the painting.[4]

51.25.7
Oil on white brass[1]
43.5 cm x 83.5 cm
Inscription "The City. Line. Company.'s. "S.S. City of Cambridge." of Glasgow. 1489 tons reg. W. Jack. Commander"
Prov: J James Esq of Liverpool, from whom purchased, 1951

Vessels:
City of Cambridge 326.5 ft (l), 36.1 ft (b), 27.7 ft (d); 2329 gross tons
Great Emperor 145.7 ft (l), 23.1 ft (b), 11.8 ft (d); 251 gross tons

1 Analysed 1990.
2 Haws Ellerman, pp. 90-1
3 LCR, vol. 86, no. 317, 20 July 1864.
4 Probably William Jack, b. Glasgow, 1838, master's certificate Glasgow 1863.

161 Gaboon (page 150)

Although on first appearance this painting is different from other portraits by this unknown artist, the variations are almost certainly due to later overpainting. In particular, the sea appears to have been "replaced" with a more naturalistic effect and the scroll inscription lost. However, in all other respects, particularly the treatment of the rigging and figures on deck, it is clearly part of the series and the composition is close to *Britannia* (no. 159).

Gaboon is shown in port profile off Anglesey under steam with all sails stowed. She is now only identifiable from her bow name and flag code (R H M D). She flies the house flag of her owners at the main mast, the pilot jack at the fore and the red

1933.119
Oil on white brass[1]
41.5 cm x 76 cm
Prov: Mr T Bremner, Liverpool, who presented it, 1933.
Ref: Handbook 1935, p.61

Vessel: 302.2 ft (l), 34.2 ft (b), 23.6 ft (d); 1863 gross tons

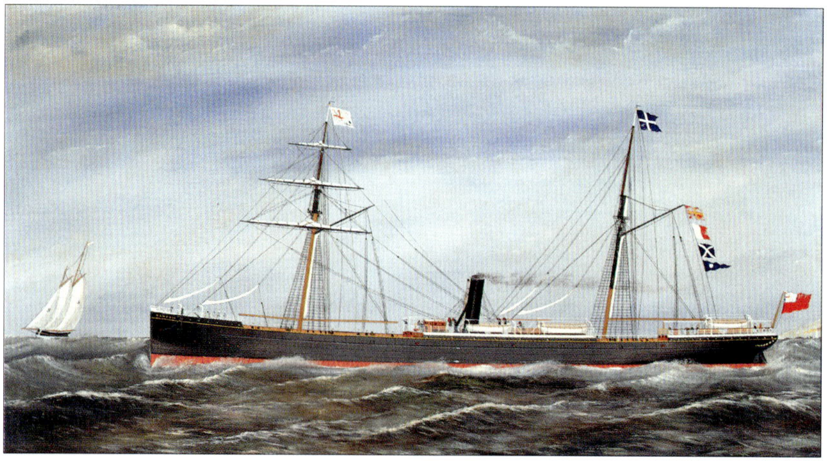

ensign at the stern.[2] The No. 5 Liverpool pilot boat is visible in a port quarter view in the distance off her starboard bow and the Skerries lighthouse can be seen astern.
The brigantine rigged iron screw steamer *Gaboon* was built by John Elder & Co. of Glasgow for the Liverpool-based British and African Steam Navigation Company in 1878. She remained in service until transferred to the African Steamship Co. (also managed by Elder Dempster) in 1897.[3] She was sold to the Bank of Athens in the following year and renamed *Galaxidion*, remaining in Greek ownership until scrapped in 1912.[4]
The No. 5 pilot boat is the schooner rigged *Victoria and Albert* built in 1856 by Michael Ratsey of Cowes and sunk in May 1888.
The painting was completed in the period between 1878 and 1888.

1 Part of printed label on rear for J Davey, 44 Duke Street, Liverpool and printed label for Ocean Archive, indicating that the painting was on loan to Ocean Transport & Trading Co. 1968-79.
2 Some of the detail of her flags have been lost during restoration before entering the collection.
3 For a description of a voyage on the vessel by James Deemin in 1883 see P N Davies *Trading To West Africa*, 1976, also repr. in Cowden & Duffy, see below n.3.
4 J E Cowden & J O C Duffy *The Elder Dempster Fleet History 1852-1965*, 1986, pp. 62-3.

162 *S S Magellan*

1960.63.2
Oil on canvas
43 cm x 84 cm
Prov: Mrs Crawford, Liverpool, who presented it, 1960.

Vessel: 359.6 ft (l), 41 ft (b), 26.1 ft (d); 2856 gross tons

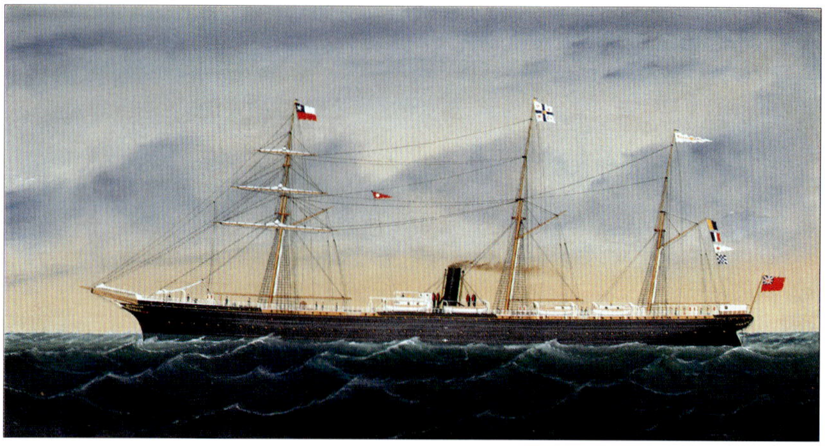

The steamship *Magellan* is shown in port profile under full steam at sea with all her auxiliary sails stowed. Members of the crew and some of the passengers can be seen on deck. She flies the Chilean national flag at the fore mast, the house flag of the Pacific Steam Navigation Company at the main mast, a "Royal Mail" pennant at the mizzen and the flag hoist (K T C N) at the after peak. The artist has made an error here because her signal flags were H T C N. Another flag, F in the Commercial Code, flies from a cable between the fore and main masts.[1]
Magellan was the first of four steam ships built by Randolph, Elder & Co. of Glasgow in 1869 for PSNC's new through service from Liverpool to Chile. Named after the first circumnavigator of the world, she could carry 520 passengers. After the problems of over-capacity in the mid-1870s, *Magellan* and her sisters were sent

to the River Plate in 1877 and later were fitted with refrigeration equipment to participate in the Argentine meat trade. She was sold in 1890 and broken up in the Thames in 1893.[2]

Although painted on canvas, and without the usual inscription, all the other characteristic features of the artist are present. It was painted before 1889 when the barque rig shown was altered to schooner rig.[3]

1 The significance of this flag is not clear.
2 Bonsor South, p.157.
3 CR no. 53, 8 March 1869.

163 S S Michigan

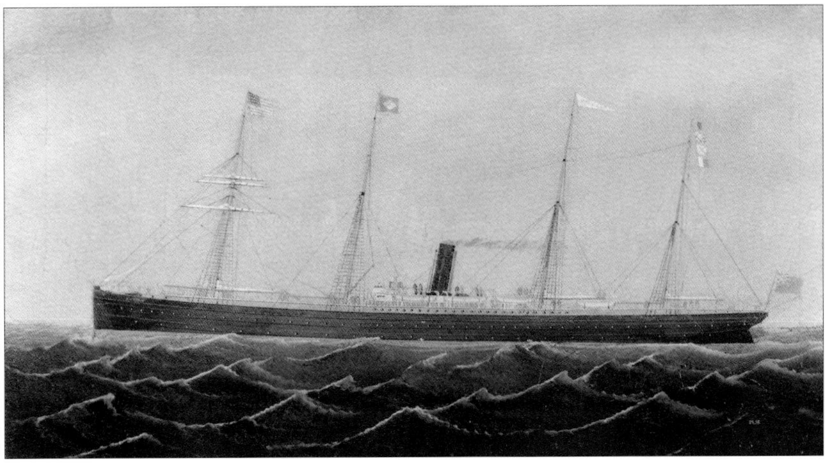

1928.18
Oil on canvas
43 cm x 83 cm
Prov: Captain Ritchie, who presented it, 1928

Vessel: 400.4 ft (l), 47.2 (b), 26.2 (d); 4979 gross tons

The Warren Line's *S S Michigan* is shown at sea in starboard profile under steam with her auxiliary sails furled. She flies a variety of flags which include, from the bow, the American Stars and Stripes, signifying her destination; the house flag of the Warren Line (a white diamond on a red ground - a reminder of the company's origins as the White Diamond line of sailing packets); her name pennant; the vessel's signal flags (K N V H) and the red ensign at the stern.

Michigan was built by Harland & Wolff in Belfast in 1887. She was the Warren Line's first steel ship and the first to be fitted with triple expansion engines and spent her career on the Liverpool to Boston run. In 1914 she was bought by the Admiralty and became a dummy battleship. The Warren Line was one of the smaller companies working the transatlantic passenger trade and in 1912 joined Furness Withy.[1]

This painting bears all the characteristics of "Gothic Scroll", apart from an inscription itself. It is one of the few painted on canvas by the artist.

1 Bonsor North, pp.678-9, 685-6; CR no. 67, 5 October 1887.

164 S S Sardinian leaving the Mersey (page 152)

The steamship *Sardinian* is shown in starboard profile off New Brighton as she leaves the Mersey. She flies the American Stars and Stripes at the fore, a red swallow-tail[2] at the main mast, the Allan Line house flag below a red pennant[3] at the mizzen, the letter L at the peak and the red ensign at the stern. An interesting feature is the pole compass, a wooden tripod keeping the compass away from the effects of the metal hull, which is sited in front of the funnel.[4]

A number of other vessels are portrayed in the foreground, though they are all at a different scale to the main view. They include from left to right an unidentified brig, the Allan Line tender *Mersey*, the steam vessel *Trader* and a schooner rigged boat. The Wirral coast in shown in similarly naive terms with the buildings outlined as boxes, though two are identifiable as churches. To the far right the Perch Rock Fort and Lighthouse are shown.

It is not entirely clear what is going on in this scene. The rails of both the main

1 Analysed 1990.
2 Probably indicating that she is carrying the mail.
3 The house flag was the same as the French tricolour but was always flown beneath a red pennant.
4 See H Pasch *Illustrated Marine Encyclopaedia*, Antwerp, 1890, p.203.
5 Bonsor North, p.234.
6 Letter B, under both national and local codes, would normally mean she is loading or discharging gun powder but this seems unlikely in the circumstances.
7 There is a contemporary description of the vessel in *The Allan Line of Royal Mail Steamers. Official Guide* [1877], pp. 4-7.
8 Bonsor North, p.314-5.
9 Mercantile Navy List, London, 1877.
10 Joseph Ebenezer Dutton, b. Cumberland 1828, master certificate Liverpool 1855 see LCpR, 1869. He was well-known for his "muscular Christianity", see T E Appleton *Ravenscrag: The Allan Royal Mail Line*, London, 1974, pp. 126-7.

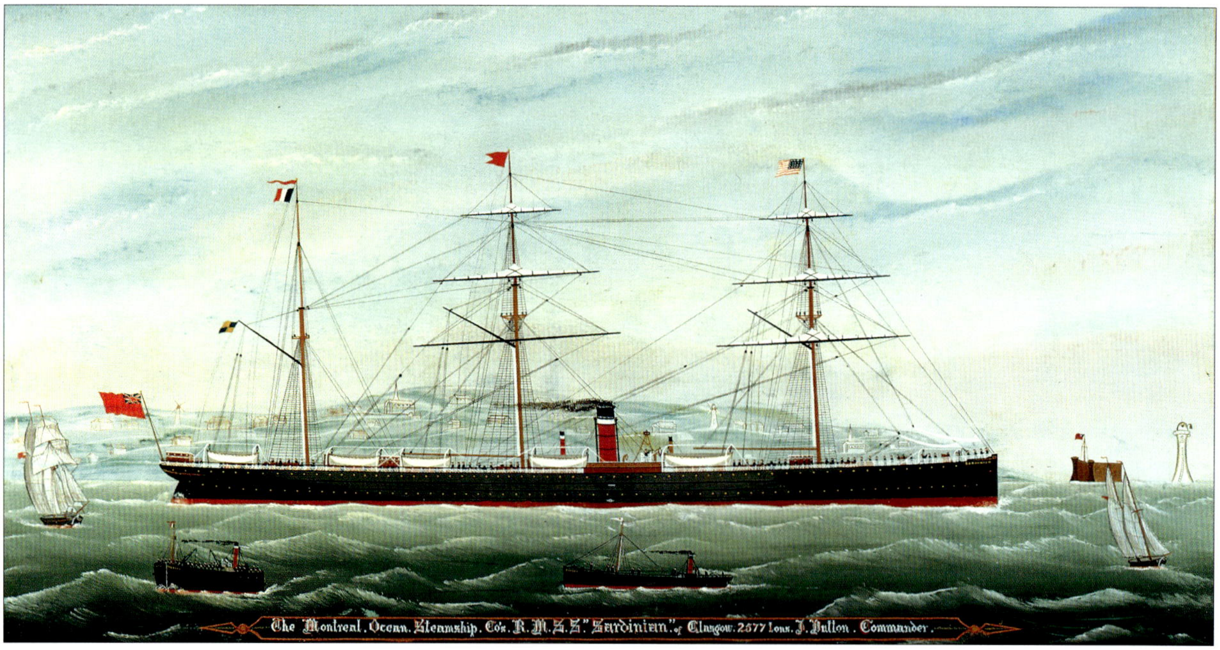

55.254
Oil on white brass[1]
43.5 cm x 83.5 cm
Inscription "The Montreal. Ocean. Steamship. Co's. R.M.S.S. "Sardinian." of Glasgow. 2577 tons. J. Dutton. Commander."
Prov: In collections, 1955

Vessel:
Sardinian 400 ft (l), 42.3 ft (b), 34.6 ft (d); 4400 gross tons
Mersey 132 ft (l), 23.1 ft (b), 10 ft (d); 227 gross tons
Trader 83.6 ft (l), 19.5 ft (b), 8.2 ft (d); 87 gross tons.

vessel and the tender are lined with members of the crew, suggesting that this may represent some occasion. There are also some anomalies with the flags. *Sardinian* voyaged to Canada, so why is she flying the Stars and Stripes indicating her destination is an American port? One explanation may be related to the fact that she was chartered to the Inman Line in 1883 for two voyages to New York.[5] The meaning of the single letter flags is unclear.[6]

Sardinian was built in 1875 by R Steele & Co. of Greenock for the Montreal Ocean Steamship Company, popularly known as the Allan Line.[7] She was an unlucky vessel, catching fire, being scuttled and refloated in 1878, then later losing a rudder in mid-Atlantic and colliding with a schooner. However, she was a stalwart of the Liverpool-Canada service until 1897 when she was transferred to other transatlantic voyages. She was also very long lived making her last voyage in 1919 and spending a further period as a hulk at Vigo before being scrapped in 1938.[8]

The iron screw steamer *Mersey* was built for Allans by Cunliffe and Dunlop of Port Glasgow in 1872. The wooden hulled *Trader* was built at Winsford, Cheshire in 1873 and owned by Robert Heath of the Biddulph Valley Iron Works of Newcastle-on-Tyne.[9]

The inscription in Gothic style lettering on a ribbon records details of the vessel, including the name of the Captain, J Dutton.[10] He was the first master of the ship serving until 1885, providing an approximate date for the painting of 1875-85.

"Ribbon artist"(active about 1800 - about 1825)

This anonymous artist has a very distinctive style of the naive, folk art type which makes his painting readily recognisable. He also includes ribbons in the sky bearing the name of the subject of the painting. Many of his works, including all those in the collection, have a Liverpool connection which may indicate that he lived in the town for some while. He was probably active in the first two decades of the nineteenth century.

Other works by him include *Princess Amelia*, in the National Maritime Museum,[1] *Waterloo* of Nevin (Private Collection)[2] and *Seahorse* and *Druid* (formerly Judkyn Pratt Collection, Bath).[3]

1 See Concise NMM.
2 Illustrated Davidson, 1992, p.8.
3 Sold Christie's, London, 8 November 1995, Lots 99 and 100.

165 "Success to the James of Liverpool"

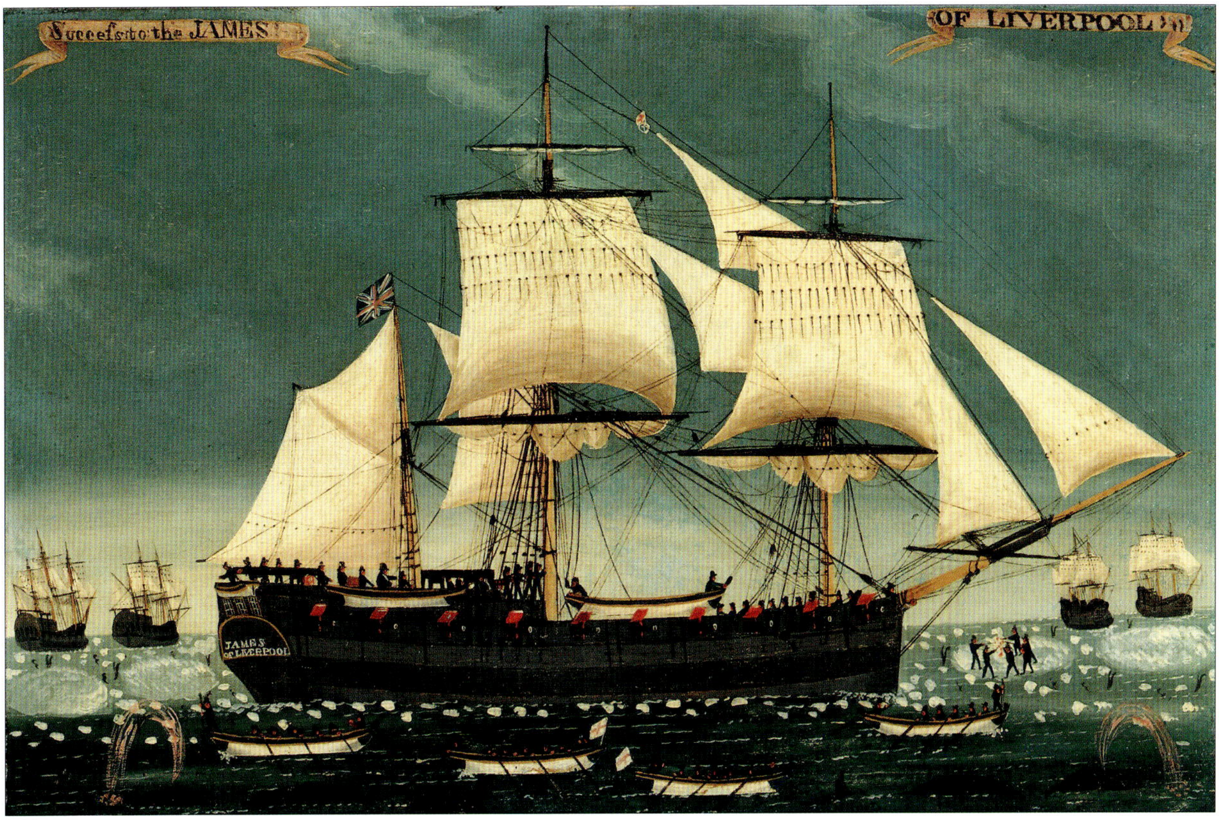

This large and detailed painting shows the Liverpool owned barque rigged *James* whaling off Greenland. The vessel is shown in the centre of the canvas in a starboard profile but, in a characteristic feature of the artist, the stern (bearing the legend "JAMES / OF LIVERPOOL") is also visible. She is under sufficient sail to maintain her position but the main course and fore course are furled. A number of men are shown on deck, including at the aft the master, who is larger and more prominent than his crew. Two men are in the boat amidships, preparing to drop it into the water. She flies the Union Jack at her mizzen and above the aft sail between the fore mast and main mast is a curious object which looks like a sphere with a flag[1] attached. There are four other whalers in the background, two under the bowsprit and two astern. Four whaling boats are in the water in the foreground each with a man at the stern, five men rowing and a marksman with a harpoon at the bow. Two of the marksmen are standing and about to throw their harpoons. Several whales are depicted, the two at either side are most visible by the spouts of water coming from their blow holes. Under the bowsprit of *James* is a group of six men on an ice floe who look as though they are killing a seal. There are smaller ice floes and pieces of ice floating in the water and the tails of seals can be seen diving into the depths.

At the top of the painting are the two characteristic ribbons with the inscription "Sucfess : to : the JAMES :-" and "OF + LIVERPOOL".

The 20-gun ship rigged *James* was a prize which had been taken from the French in 1781 and was initially owned by the Ansdell Brothers of Liverpool and then from 1795 by John Tarleton junior in partnership. In July 1800 she was bought by Jonas Bold and registered as a barque. She was bought by Hurry & Co. in 1808 and in her final years from 1817 was owned by Hurry & Gibson & Co.[2] She made her first whaling voyage in 1801 and this and subsequent voyages are documented in *Lloyds List* and the local *Gore's Advertiser*, often with details of the catch.[3] By this time,

MMM.1996.63.1
Oil on paper covered board
57 cm x 87.5 cm
Prov: Sold Holloway's, Banbury, 5 December 1995, lot 441; Patrick and Gillian Morley Antiques, Warwick, from whom purchased, 1996.

Vessel: 82 ft (l), 29 ft (b), 5 ft 5 in (d); 234 tons

1 Probably meant to be the English national flag.
2 LCR, vol. 4, no. 82, 16 March 1787 (Reprinted in R Craig & R Jarvis *Liverpool Registry of Ships*, Manchester, 1967); LCR, no. 30, 12 February 1801; LCR no. 149, 3 October 1808; LCR no. 30, 28 March 1817.
3 LL 21 July 1801; in 1802 she returned with the 'produce of 15 whales and 2 unicorns', GGA, 15 July 1802.
4 A detailed contemporary account of a whaling voyage by *Baffin*, also owned by Hurry & Gibson can be found in W Scoresby *A Voyage to the Whale Fishery*, 1822, reprinted Whitby, 1980.
5 Accession no. 29.4.75.7. For details see B M Watney and C Roberts 'Liverpool Porcelain Ship Bowls in Blue-and-White' *Transactions of the English Ceramic Circle*, vol. 15, pt. 1, 1993, pp. 6-7 (ill), 22. There is also a teapot featuring *Polar Star* in the National Maritime Museum Collections, see R Prentice *A Celebration of the Sea*, London, 1994, p. 73 (ill. 114c).

only two or three ships a year were going whaling from Liverpool. Bold, Hurry and Gibson, together or with various other partners, were the main participants in the whaling trade from Liverpool in these years.[4]

This is the only painting so far encountered of a Liverpool whaler or of the port's whaling activity and as such is an important historical document. There is a porcelain ship bowl of the whaler *Polar Star* of about 1776 in the Liverpool Museum.[5]

166 A Liverpool Pilot Boat [No.9]

MMM1990.165
Oil on canvas[1]
61.5 cm x 91.5 cm
Prov: Sotheby's, 30 May 1990, Lot 117; Purchased from L Swerdlow Esq, Wirral, October 1990.
Ref: Davidson, 1992, p.9 (ill)

Vessel: 46.1 ft (l), 15.3 ft (b), 9 ft (d); 42 gross tons

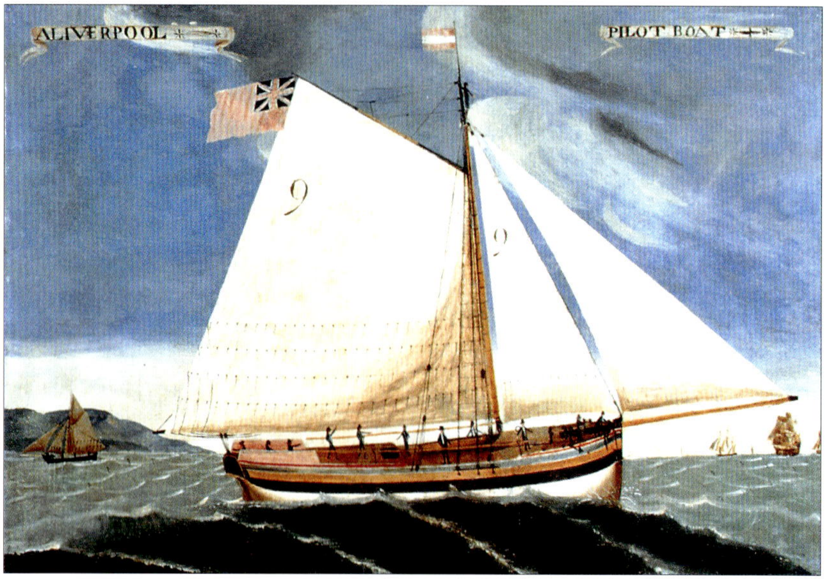

This very early depiction of a Liverpool pilot boat, shows the No.9 boat in starboard profile in the centre of the canvas, off an unidentified coast, probably North Wales. There is a cutter to the left and other unidentified vessels under the bowsprit to the right. Twelve members of the crew, who will include pilots and apprentices, are shown about the deck, with a further crewman at the top of the mast as a look-out. The significance of the flag, on the main mast, a red field with a central white band is not known[2] (is it an identification for a pilot vessel or a sign that the boat has pilots available?) The red ensign flies at the peak. In the sky at the top of the canvas, two ribbons, in a distinctive feature of the artist, bear the legend "A LIVERPOOL" and "PILOT BOAT".

Despite the inclusion of the "9" painted on the sail, it is not possible to identify the pilot boat with certainty. It is most probably the first pilot boat to bear that number, which was built by Grayson and Fearon in 1796 and entered the pilot service in July 1799. It hit the rock perch, a wooden pole with vanes which marked the Black Rock, in February 1821 and was replaced in 1822.[3] Both it and its successor were square-sterned, carvel-built sloops, which accords with the vessel depicted.[4]

Although naively handled, the boat itself is well depicted from a technical point of view and details of rigging and sail position are accurately shown. As one of the earliest depictions of a Liverpool pilot vessel, it is of great interest.

1 Extensively restored 1990, restoration removed and painting conserved for NMGM, 1991.
2 Pilot boats later hoisted a red and white flag as an indication that they were ready to board a pilot.
3 Rees, p.83.
4 Rees, p.200. The later No.9 boat was built by Clarke & Nickson in 1822 and was replaced in 1846. She was 49 ft 10 in long, 15 ft 10 in and 8 ft 4 in. She is the subject of no. 222.

167 Mary of Liverpool

The barque rigged *Mary* is shown in port profile in the centre of the canvas under full sail. Typically the stick like crew are shown on deck, in the yards and on the bowsprit. She flies a red ensign and long pennant. To her stern is the No.10 Liverpool

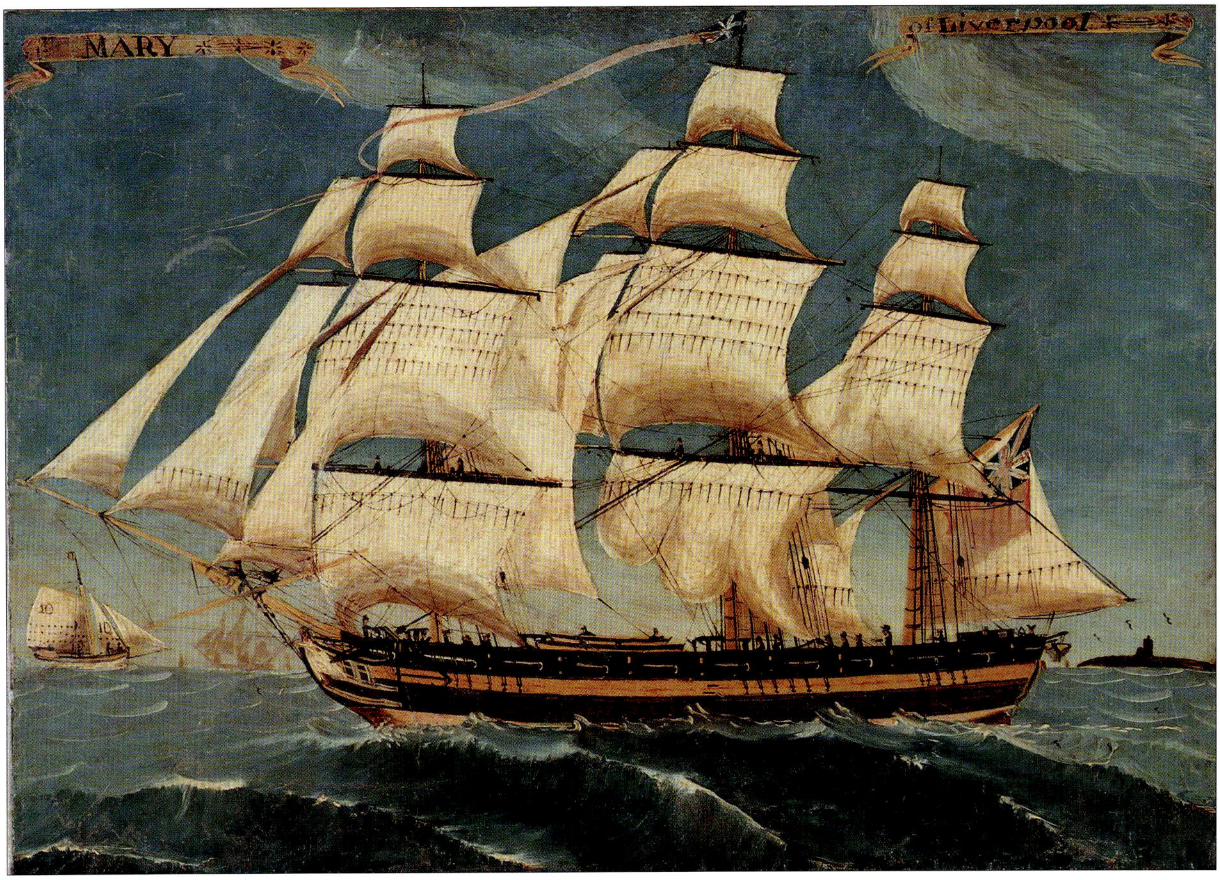

pilot boat in a starboard profile. The background to the right is probably intended to represent The Skerries. The characteristic ribbons in the sky bear the legend "MARY" and "of Liverpool".

Mary was one of the most popular names for a ship in the eighteenth and early nineteenth centuries and it is virtually impossible to identify the particular vessel depicted. There was no No.10 pilot boat between 1770 and 22 March 1811 when the sloop *Prince Regent* entered service under that number. She was built by Mottershead and Hutchinson and was replaced in 1835.[2]

This painting dates from after 1811 and probably from the period about 1815 to about 1820.

1961.237.2
Oil on card stuck on canvas[1]
40 cm x 57 cm
Prov: presented by the family of Alderman Henry Bloor, Birkenhead, 1961

1 Relined 1978.
2 Rees, pp. 199-201.

168 The Nancy of Amlwch (page 156)

The brig *Nancy* is shown in port profile reducing sail as she nears the coast and moves towards her destination. There is appropriate activity on board with men in the yards, at the bowsprit and on deck reducing the jibs, the forecourse and the main course. Two men are preparing to launch a small boat from amidships. The master is on the aft deck and is giving orders to the crew through a speaking trumpet. The vessel carries no identification apart from a red ensign at the stern and a long red pennant with union flag at the main mast head.

The vessel is placed off a headland with a square tower which may be intended to be a lighthouse. It is not sufficiently detailed to identify the location but may be intended to be in Liverpool Bay or off North Wales. To the right is a port quarter view of an approaching ship and there are other vessels silhouetted in the background.

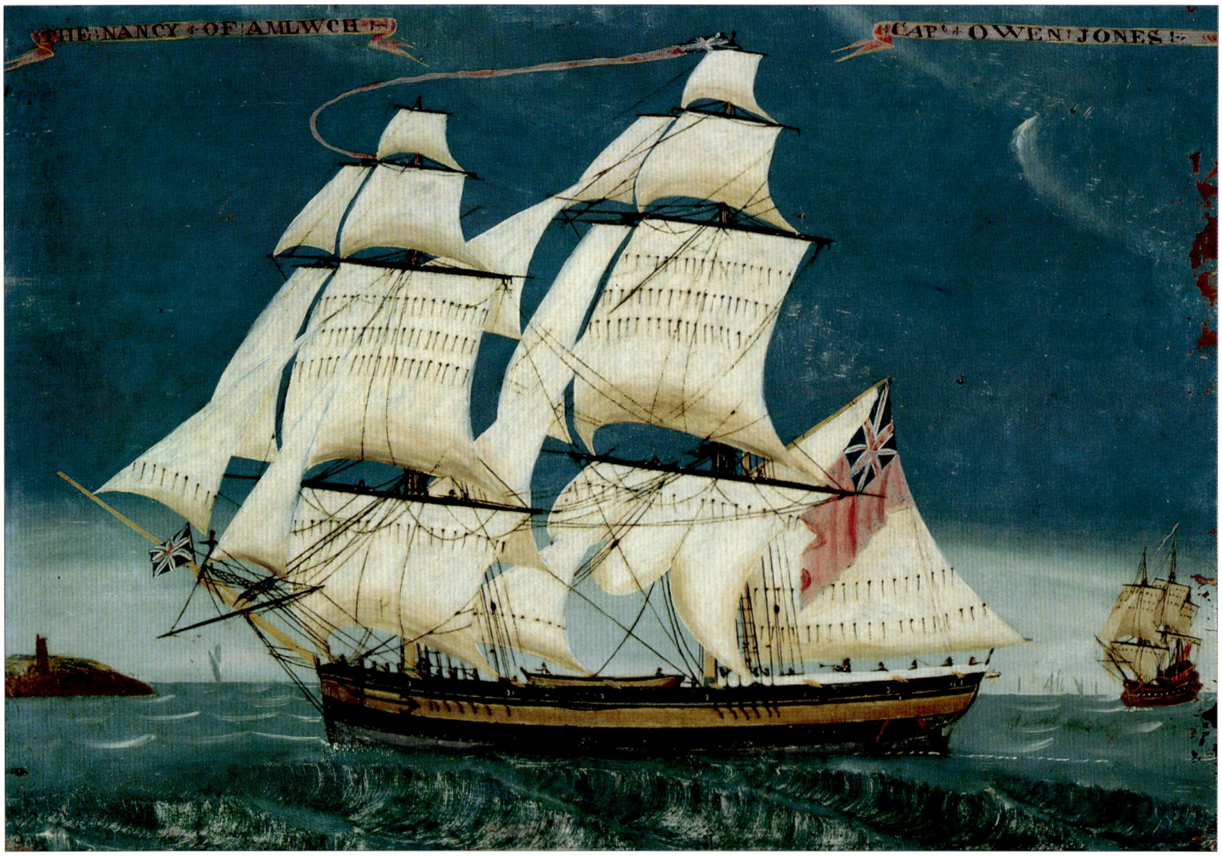

MMM.1996.63.2
Oil on paper covered board
60.5 cm x 86 cm
Prov: Sold Holloway's, Banbury, 5 December 1995, lot 441; Patrick and Gillian Morley Antiques, Warwick, from whom purchased, 1996.

In the sky are the characteristic ribbons which identify the vessel. These read ":THE: NANCY + OF : AMLWCH —" and "CAP^{T} + OWEN : JONES —". Despite this detail the name *Nancy* is too common to establish exactly which vessel is being depicted. The painting probably dates from about 1815-20.

J Livingstone (active 1840s)

169 *P S Europa*

16.1.25.1
Oil on canvas
65.5 cm x 104.5 cm
Signed and dated (bl) "J. Livingstone 1840"
Prov: D Blackburn, Liverpool, from whom purchased, 1925

Vessel: 251 ft (l), 35.2 ft (w), 25 ft (d); 1834 gross tons

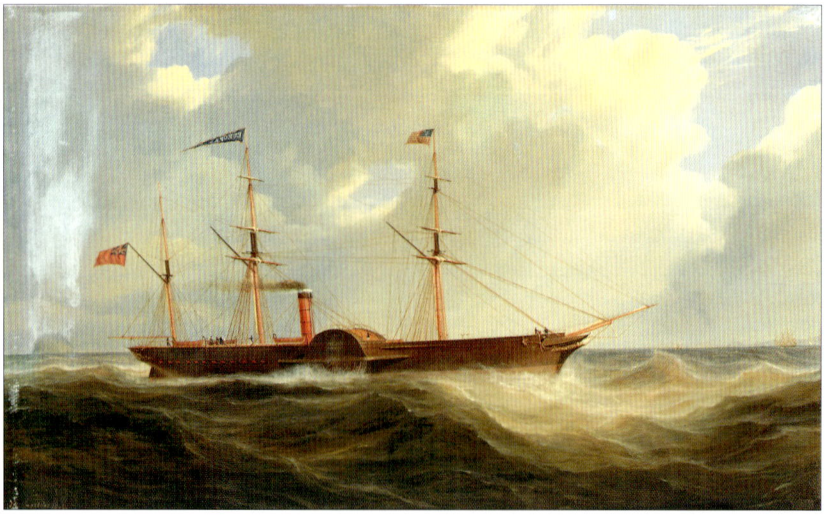

The early Cunard paddle steamer *Europa* is shown in starboard profile leaving the Clyde where she was built, ready to undertake her maiden voyage. She is flying the Stars and Stripes confirming that she is sailing to take up her transatlantic duties.

She is barque rigged but all her sails are stowed. The mizzen mast was removed in 1853. A series of open ports aft probably indicate the saloon. She is identifiable by her name pennant on the main mast and she displays the well-known Cunard livery on her single funnel. The master is shown between the paddle wheels, there are crew at the windlass at the bow and there is a small group of visitors on the after deck. The vessel is shown leaving the approaches to the Clyde with the island of Ailsa Craig astern to the left and to the far right the Ayrshire coast, towards Bennane Head and Ballantrae.

Europa was one of four new ships added to the Cunard fleet in 1848, which allowed the establishment of a weekly service across the Atlantic from Liverpool to Boston and New York. All four were commissioned from Robert Napier of Glasgow who subcontracted the hulls to other shipbuilders, in the case of *Europa* to John Wood of Port Glasgow. Napier provided the engines. She held the Blue Riband briefly in 1848. She had two unfortunate collisions during her career - in 1849 when 135 lives were lost from the US emigrant ship *Charles Bartlett* and in 1858 with Cunard's own *Arabia* when there was no loss of life. She was sold in 1867.[1]

Although the painting is clearly inscribed 1840, this is obviously a mistake and should read 1848 or 1849.

Samuel Walters and William Clark also painted portraits of the vessel in about 1848.[2]

1 Bonsor North, p.142; Spratt, pp. 47-48.
2 Walters painting exhibited Bootle, 1959, no. 23; at that time owned by Cunard Steam Ship Company. A lithograph of the Clark painting is noted in Parker & Bowen, p.108.

Duncan McFarlane (1818-1865)

McFarlane's early life is not known but he is listed as a marine painter in the Liverpool directories from 1848. He was particularly popular with American patrons and many of his paintings are now in the United States.[1] There are works in the National Maritime Museum, Mystic Seaport and Peabody Essex Museum.

1 Davidson 1986.

170 Sardinia

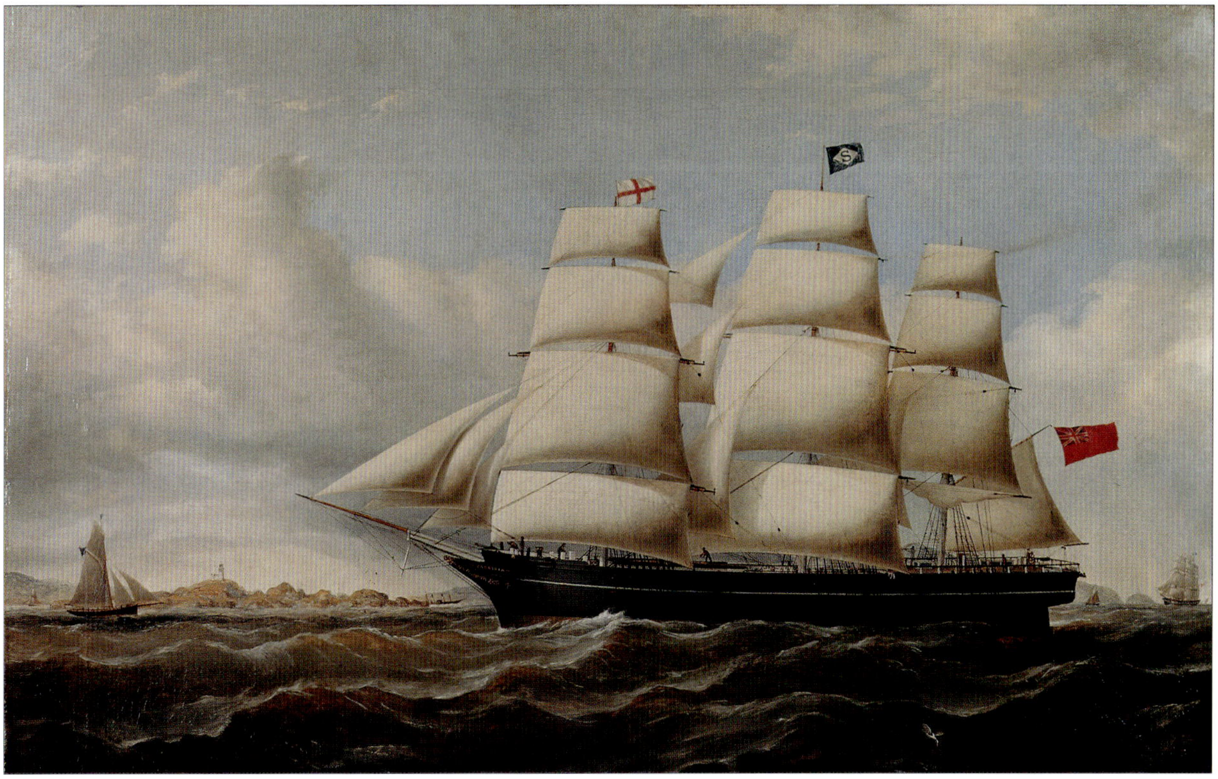

1989.227
Oil on canvas
60.5 cm x 91.5 cm
Prov: City of Hull Museums, on long-term loan, 1990.

Vessel: 183.6 ft (l), 36 ft (b), 21.6 ft (d); 969 gross tons

The ship rigged *Sardinia* is shown in port profile under all plain sail off Anglesey inward bound for Liverpool. *Sardinia* is identifiable by her name on the bow. She flies the red ensign at the after peak, the Sinclair house flag at the main and, unusually, the English national flag at her foremast. An outward bound steamer is emerging on the far side of the rocks, visible under *Sardinia*'s bowsprit. In the far distance astern is South Stack and what initially appears to be a second view of the vessel. Although flying the Sinclair house flag this vessel has painted ports on her hull. A cutter is approaching *Sardinia* in the left foreground. The blue peter at the top of the mast would seem to indicate that this is a pilot boat. However, the mast and rig are taller than one would expect for a pilot vessel and the blue ensign flying from the stern makes it more likely to be a revenue cutter. The significance of the blue peter is unexplained.

The vessel is very close in to the Skerries and allows the artist to depict the rocky terrain and lighthouse in unusual detail. The signal station on Holyhead Mountain can be seen just fore of the mizzen mast where the captain stands with his telescope. *Sardinia* was built at Miramichi, New Brunswick in 1856 and was owned by Sinclair & Co. of Belfast. She voyaged mainly to India and was sold to Josias Milford of Liverpool in February 1867. She put into Manila in January 1869 damaged by a storm and was condemned as unseaworthy.[1]

Although superficially similar to compositions by W G Yorke,[2] the attribution to McFarlane is made on general stylistic grounds, in particular the degree of detail of his figures and the treatment of the sea.

1 CR, no. 55, 20 February 1867.
2 *Lord Palmerston*, signed and dated 1863, in New Brunswick Museum (See Elliot and McNairn) and *Mobile*, signed and dated 1862, *Spirit of the Sea*, Catalogue of Vallejo Gallery, 1993, p. 41

H McLeod (active 1850-1870)

Probably a part time artist, who is only known from a handful of signed works.[1]

1 Davidson 1986.

171 *The Rock Ferry Paddle Steamer Sylph*

1961.130.21
Oil on canvas[1]
43.5 cm x 71.5 cm
Signed and dated (bl) "H. MacLeod. / 1851"
Prov: J A Howard Watson, Liverpool, who presented it, 1961
Exh: Liverpool 1986
Ref: Port Panorama 1986, p.16 (ill)

Vessel: 112.8 ft (l), 16.8 ft (b), 8.8 ft (d); 128 gross tons, 60 h.p.

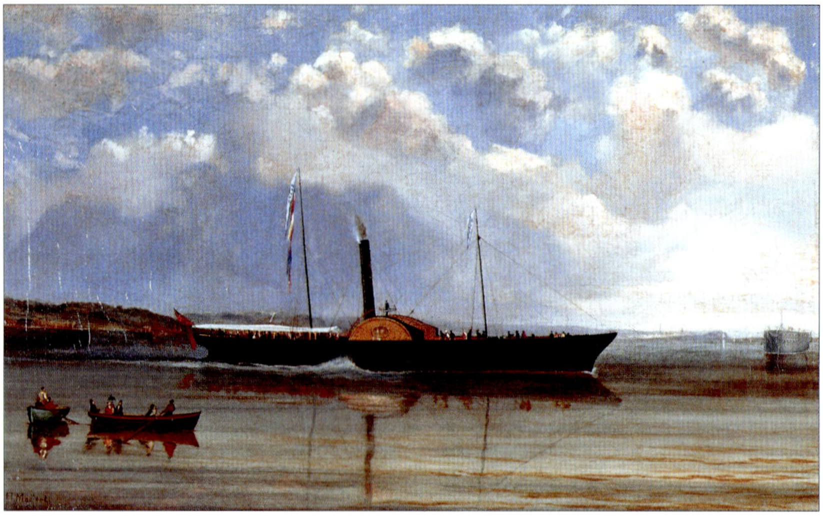

The iron paddle steamer *Sylph* is shown in starboard profile on a calm summer's evening departing from Rock Ferry on the Wirral side of the Mersey bound for Liverpool. Most of the passengers are under the awning on the stern deck but a few are standing admiring the view from the fore deck. In these placid conditions the name and other indistinct pennants on her masts hang down limply. The vessel is identifiable from the name pennant and the lettering on the bridge "Rock Ferry 2." There are two small rowing boats in the left foreground and the hulk of a quarantine vessel can be seen in the distance on the far right of the canvas.

The pier and part of the small village of Rock Ferry is shown on the left hand side of the canvas and in the further background the coastline fades away towards the then developing Birkenhead. A ferry had operated from the shore at Rock Ferry since the seventeenth century. A slipway was built in 1820 and steamer services began in the 1830s. *Sylph*[2] was built in Liverpool for the Royal Rock Ferry Steam Packet Company in 1845 and remained in service until 1854.[3] The hulk is probably the former *HMS Akbar* which had been a quarantine ship in the Mersey since 1829.[4]

1 Relined, 1985.
2 Spirit of the air.
3 For history see Duckworth & Langmuir 1956, pp. 35, 116.
4 In 1855 she was acquired by the Liverpool Juvenile Reformatory Society and became a reformatory ship. See John Smart 'Reformation Afloat: The Story of the "Akbar"' in *Transactions of the Liverpool Nautical Research Society*, ix, 1963, pp. 90-5.

William Kimmins McMinn (1820-1898)

Born in Workington, Cumberland, McMinn had settled in Liverpool by the time of his marriage in 1841. He is generally described in the directories as a "marine artist and draughtsman". There are very few of his paintings in public collections but Peabody Essex Museum, Salem, has two examples.[1]

1 See Davidson 1986, pp. 82-84, 89.

172 *The Barque Esther off the Skerries*

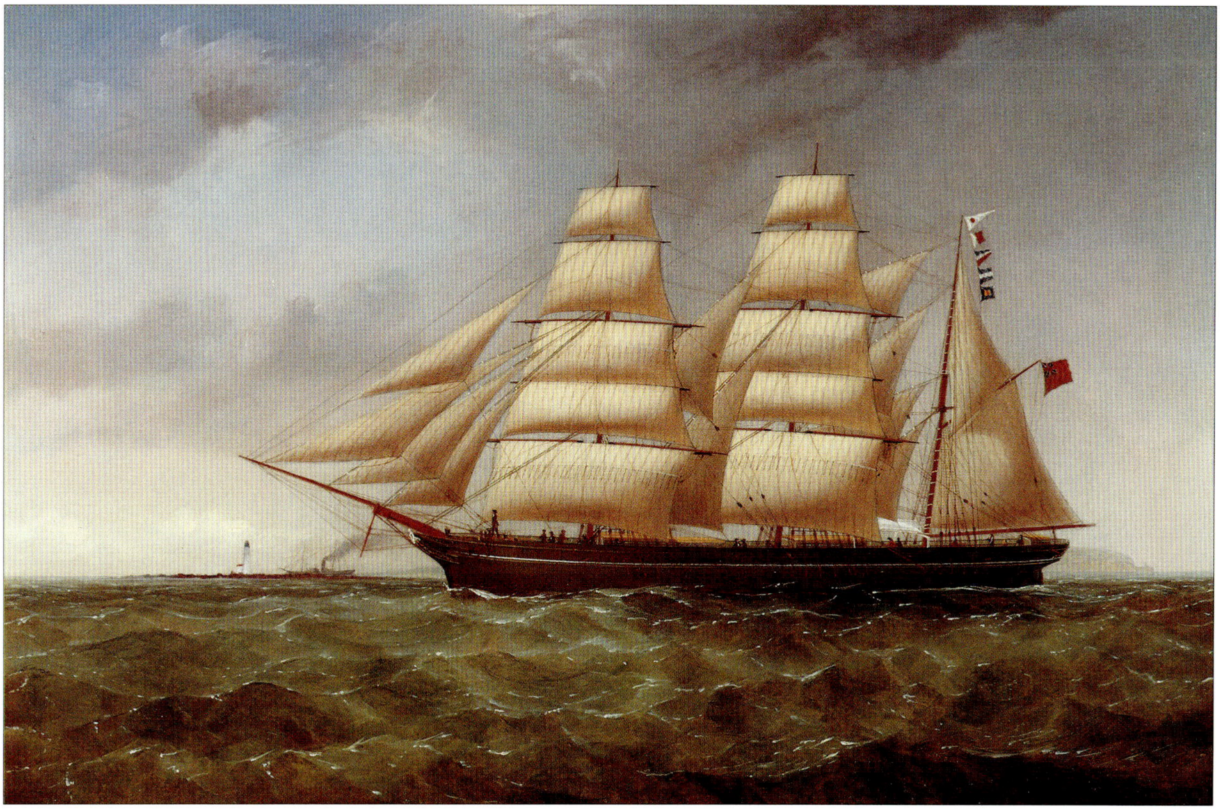

The barque *Esther* is shown in port profile on her way into Liverpool off the Skerries rock and lighthouse, Anglesey. The vessel is shown under full sail and is identifiable by her Marryat flag code on the mizzen mast of 1 d.p. 3, 6, 2, 8. The red ensign flies at the after peak. The topsail of the vessel is fitted with Captain Howe's patent reefing system which includes an extra yard at the lower mast cap. By letting go the halliards, the sail is automatically close-reefed.[1] She is shown slightly to the right of centre and in the distance under her bowsprit a paddle steamer is passing the other side of the Skerries, no doubt also bound for Liverpool. To her stern in the misty far distance is the South Stack lighthouse.

Esther was built in 1854 by Rennie Johnson and Rankin of Liverpool and was owned by William Miles Moss in association with other Liverpool investors. She

1988.4
Oil on canvas
49.5 cm x 74.5 cm
Prov: Sotheby's, London, 1987, lot no. 301, attributed W H Yorke; N R Omell Gallery, 1988, from whom purchased with the support of the Friends of the Merseyside Maritime Museum, 1988.
Exh: N R Omell Gallery, 1988
Ref: Tibbles 1988 (ill.)

Vessel: 113.7 ft (l), 19.9 ft (b), 15 ft (d); 280 tons

was sold to Walsh & Duckett, of Liverpool, in 1874 and finally to the Sulymah Trading Company, also of Liverpool in 1881. She was wrecked on the west coast of Africa in 1885.[2]

This painting is typical of the work of McMinn with its draughtsmanslike depiction of the vessel and the treatment of the sea is particularly characteristic with its olive green colour and the choppy waves outlined in white along their tops.

1 Introduced by the American Captain Frederick Howe, see McGregor 1988, p. 149. For further details see Underhill, pp. 133, 163. The lack of complicated mechanical gear was a particular attraction.
2 LCR vol. 75, no. 327, 9 May 1854; TB4, p.60; TB7, p.57.

173 Pilot Schooner Pioneer

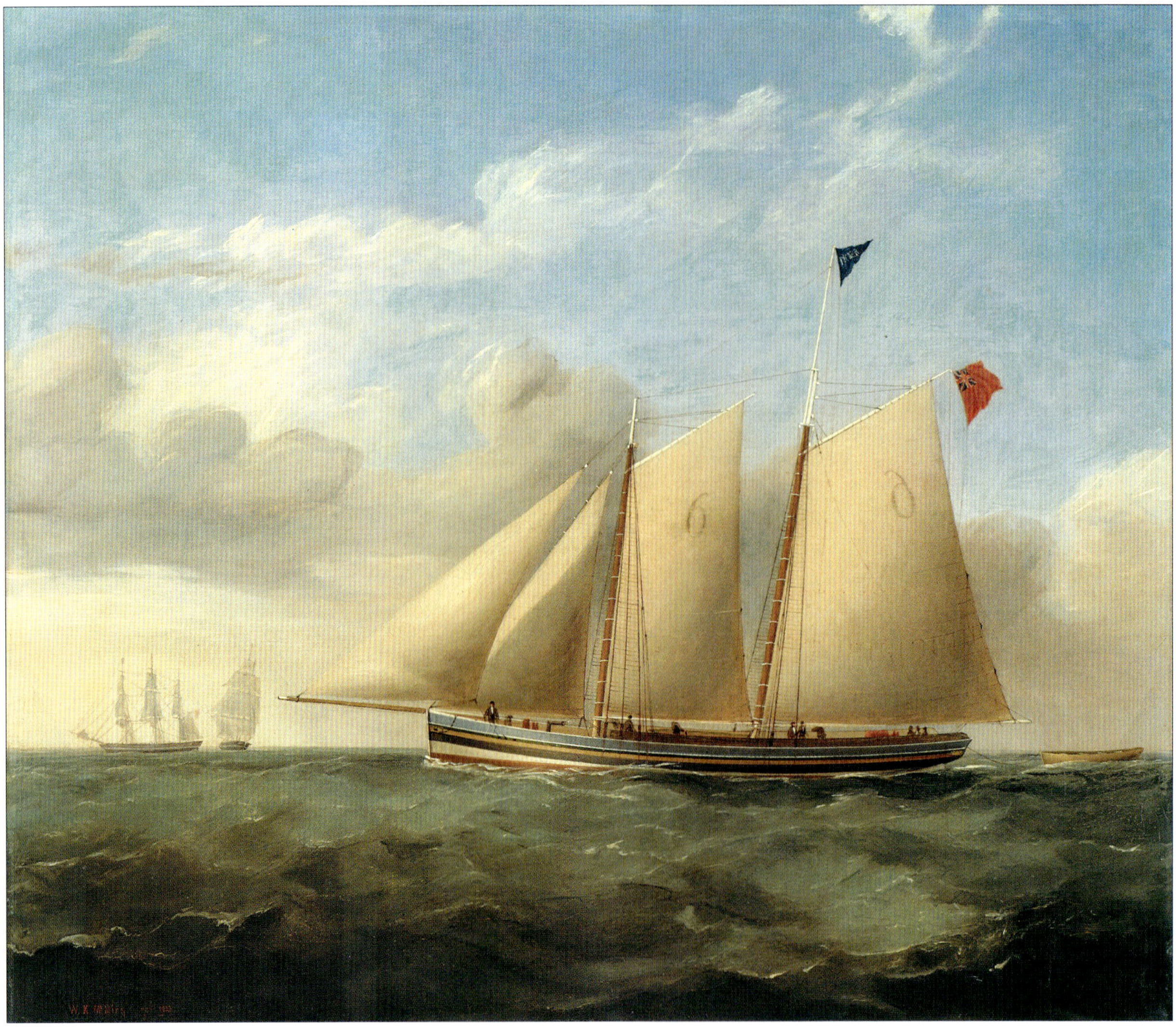

LI.91.4.3
Oil on canvas
56.5 cm x 66.5 cm
Signed and dated (bl) "W. K McMinn Jany 1853"
Prov: Mersey Docks and Harbour Company, on permanent loan.

Vessel: 68 ft (l), 15.7 ft (b), 7.6 ft (d); 53 gross tons.

This very detailed view of the No. 6 pilot boat *Pioneer* shows her in port profile towing a punt. She is schooner rigged and has all her sails set. She is fully identified with the number "6" painted on her main sails and she flies a blue name pennant from the main mast. The red ensign is at the after peak. The boat's hull colours are shown in particularly good detail, though they do not entirely correspond with other paintings of pilot boats of the same period.[1] In the distance to the left are two vessels - a ship in port profile, close hauled and presumably awaiting a pilot, with astern a ship under full rig in a port quarter view. The location is almost certainly the pilot station at the mouth of the Mersey.

Pioneer was built by Buckley Jones of Liverpool in 1852. She was the first schooner rigged boat employed in the Liverpool pilot service. She was sold in 1879 and sailed to Dakar where she was wrecked.[2]

This is one of McMinn's earliest surviving canvases with his characteristic treatment of the sea.

There is another view of *Pioneer* in the collection (no. 188) painted by Ogilvy some fifteen years later.

1 From the top the bands are narrow white, broad blue, narrow white, green, yellow, grey, white and red. See Ogilvy's depiction of *Pioneer* no. 188.
2 Rees, p.203.

Arthur Joseph Meadows (1843-1907)

Arthur Meadows was a member of a family of marine artists which included his father, James, and two brothers James Edwin and William. He was influenced by Clarkson Stansfield and painted general shipping and harbour scenes.[1]

1 Brook-Hart, pp. 45-6.

174 French Luggers

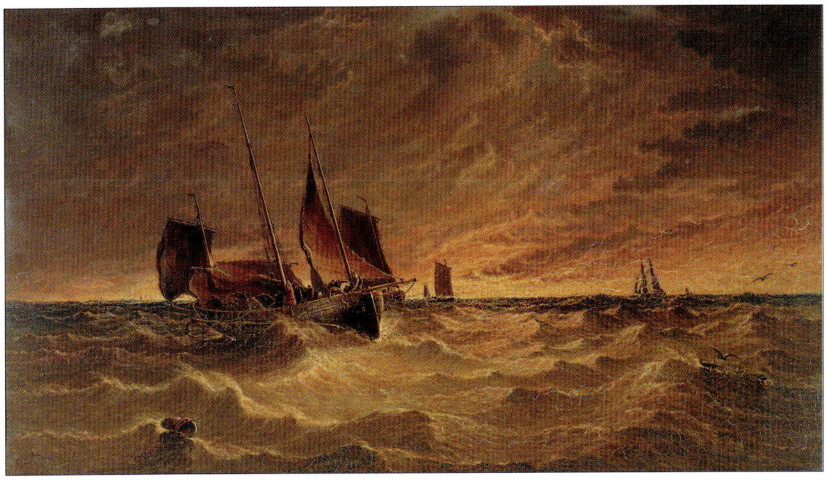

1966.13.1
Oil on canvas[1]
61 cm x 107 cm
Signed and dated (bl) "Arthur J. Meadows / 1873"
Prov: Mr D Fell, Ulverston, who presented it, 1966.

A group of French fishing vessels is shown at sea suffused in the golden light of the setting sun. The main vessel is shown left of centre in a starboard quarter view. She has a lug rig, favoured by many continental fishing and coastal craft and carries a beam trawl. Originally luggers were two masted, but many carried an addition mizzen as shown here. On board more than 20 crew can be seen straining to raise the vessel's sails. She carries a registration mark "Sot 91" on her bow. Two further two masted luggers can be seen in the distance and on the horizon is a schooner in port profile.

1 Rear canvas stamped "PREPARED BY / BRODIE & MIDDLETON / 79 LONG ACRE LONDON".

Henry Melling (1808-1879)

Although Melling studied art in Liverpool and London, his early career was probably in optical and navigational instruments. He set up studios in Liverpool in 1841. He was very fond of sailing and was Honorary Secretary of the Royal Mersey Yacht Club (1844-79).[1]

1 See Davidson, pp. 133-4.

175 The "Dry Bason" (page 162)

This busy, atmospheric view shows the Dry Dock and entrance to the Old Dock at the heart of the Liverpool Dock system filled with shipping. The viewpoint is from the south quayside on the Dry Dock with the entrance and gates to the Old Dock on the far right and the river is out of sight to the left. The observer is looking north and to the left of centre is the tower of St Nicholas Church and to the right of centre the spire of St George's Church. Parts of various warehouses and buildings which line the quaysides can be seen in the background and names are occasionally painted on the warehouse walls.

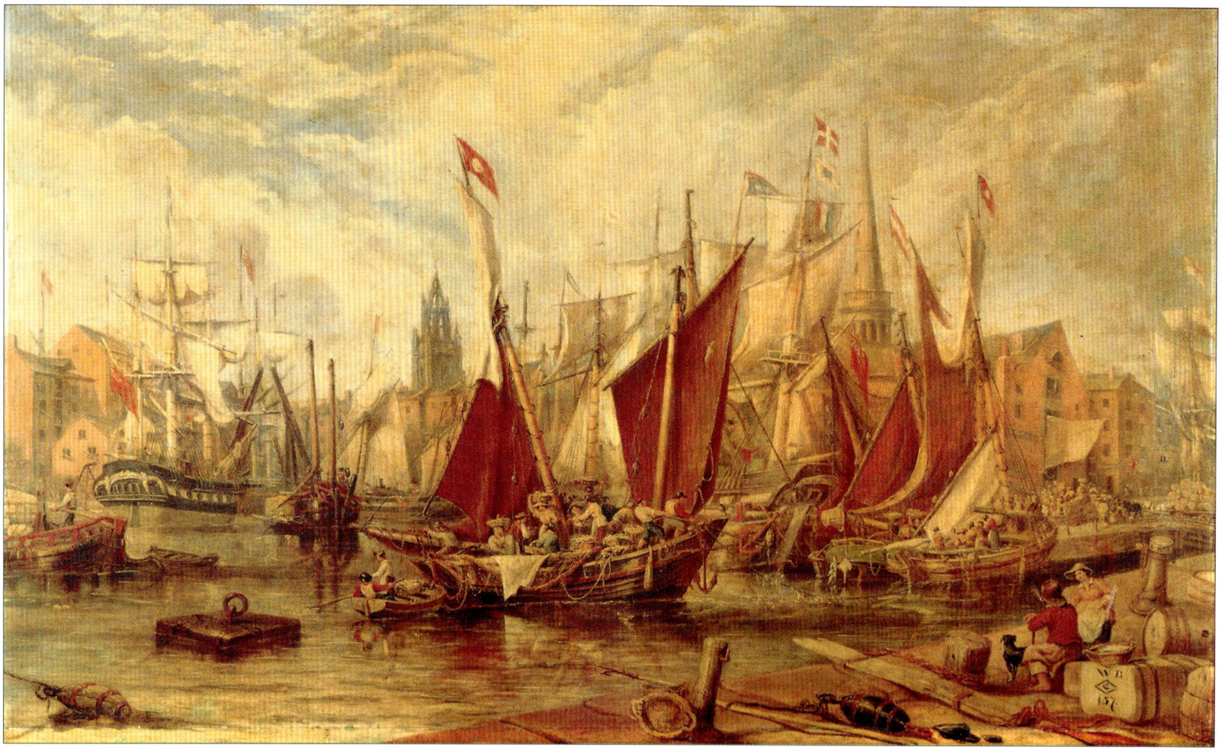

Vessels fill the dock to such an extent that it is not possible to distinguish them all. From the left there is the stern of a flat named *Winnington* in the foreground and a starboard stern view of the ship identified on the stern as "*Gen(eral) Gascoyne* of Liverpool". In the centre is a small lug-sailed fishing vessel from which women are unloading a cargo of fish and there are various vessels behind including the ship rigged *Mary* identifiable by a name pennant. To the right is the flat *Ramsey* which is again unloading fish from an adjoining vessel, identified on the stern as "*William (and) Mary* / No.4?". There is insufficient detail to identify any of these vessels more fully.[1]

The Dry Dock was created about 1740 as part of changes to the tidal basin entrance to the Old Dock (opened in 1715). It was converted into a wet dock and renamed Canning Dock in 1829.[2]

The painting gives a very good impression of the hustle and bustle of the docks and is a useful visual reminder of the significant role that women played in the work and life of the docks in the early nineteenth century.

LI.91.4.4
Oil on canvas
110 cm x 182 cm
Signed and dated (br - on piece of wood) "Henry Melling 1821"
Prov: Sir Alfred Jones KCMG, who presented it to the Mersey Docks and Harbour Board, 1906, on permanent loan, 1991.

1 Names such as *Mary* and *William and Mary* are too common to identify. The only vessels registered as *General Gascoyne* and *Wlinnington* were both built in 1831.
2 Ritchie-Noakes, pp. 19, 41.

Charles K Miller (1836-1907)

Charles Keith Miller was born in Dundee and went to sea, gaining his master's certificate in 1862. He moved to Glasgow on marrying in 1866. His paintings date from the early 1870s though he continued to spend some time at sea until at least the early 1880s. A ship portraitist of modest standing he enjoyed a local reputation for painting Scottish registered ships, often off Dundee or in the Clyde.[1]

1 I am grateful to Patricia Bouchier for information on Miller. Her research on the artist has been deposited with the Mitchell Library, Glasgow.

176 Terra Nova

Although built as an arctic whaler *Terra Nova* is better known as a polar expedition ship. She is shown outward bound in starboard profile passing the Bell Rock lighthouse off the Firth of Tay. She is a barque rigged steamer and is under her full auxiliary sail. A wooden hulled vessel, her bow has been reinforced for cutting through ice. She flies an unidentified flag at the fore,[2] the house flag of the Dundee

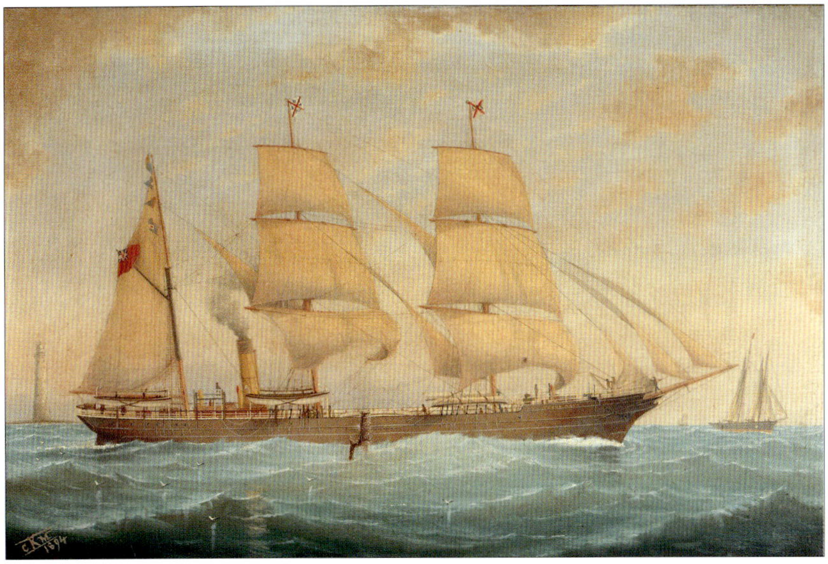

1970.119.1
Oil on canvas[1]
61 cm x 91.5 cm
Signed and dated "CKM" between horizontal lines, "1894"
Prov: Mr J Simpson, Blundellsands, who presented it, 1970.

Vessel: 187 ft (l), 31 ft (b), 19 ft (d); 744 gross tons

Arctic Fisheries Company at her main mast and the red ensign at the after peak. Her commercial flag code (K D G W) is just decipherable at the mizzen and her identity is confirmed by her bow name.

An unidentified brigantine rigged vessel is shown in the distance to the right. To the far left is the Bell Rock lighthouse which is located on a reef some 27 miles east of Dundee and was erected between 1808 and 1811.[3]

Terra Nova[4] was built by Alexander Stephens & Company of Dundee in 1884 and was then the biggest whaling ship afloat. She was employed initially by her builders but from 1894 she was operated by the Dundee Arctic Fisheries Company, managed by D Bruce & Company.[5] She worked mainly off Newfoundland, frequently taking large numbers of seals.[6] From 1894 to 1897 she served the Jackson-Harmsworth expedition to Franz Josef Land in the Arctic. C T Bowring of Liverpool acquired her in 1899.[7] In 1903/4 she accompanied *Morning* to the Antarctic to relieve Scott's *Discovery* and joined the Admiralty to take Scott's fatal expedition to the Antarctic in 1910.[8] She reverted to Bowring's ownership in 1914 and continued her career in seal fishing off Newfoundland and in coastal trading until she sank off Greenland in September 1943.

There is another painting of the vessel off the Bell Rock by Miller dating from 1903 (Kendall Whaling Museum). This is a rather more accomplished painting but again shows the vessel outward bound in starboard profile with other coastal shipping.[9] There is also a painting by Miller of *Discovery* in an almost exact composition off the Bell Rock in a private collection.[10]

1 Inscribed on top stretcher in pencil "S. S. Terra Nova (Whaler) By C. K. Miller Glasgow 1894".
2 This may relate to her expedition duties.
3 J S Wry *British Lighthouses*, 1913, pp. 182-185.
4 meaning new land.
5 LR 1893-4, 1895-6.
6 See B. Lubbock *Arctic Whalers*, London, 1937, for details of her voyages.
7 For her service with Bowring see D Keir *The Bowring Story*, London, 1962 (though he mistakenly assumes the vessel was built for and operated by Bowring from 1884).
8 T Willis *The Frozen World*, London, 1971, pp. 92-3; Captain R F Scott *The Voyage of The Discovery*, London, 1907, pp. 239-87.
9 Brewington KWM, no. 30 (ill).
10 DCF.

John Henry Mohrmann (1857-1916)

Mohrmann was born in Estebruegge and was a sailor for eighteen years from the age of 13. He received some ad hoc artistic training and set up as a ship portraitist in Antwerp in 1886. He moved with his family to Alberta in Canada in 1913. There is a good collection in the Nationaal Scheepvaartmuseum, Antwerp.[1]

1 See Jan van Beylen 'John Henry Mohrmann, scheepsportrettist', *Mededelingen van de Marine Academie*, Antwerp, 1965, pp. 67-99.

177 *S. S. Galileo* (page 164)

The brig rigged iron steamer *Galileo* is shown in starboard profile under both sail and steam at sea. The vessel is making good progress as the almost horizontal smoke from her funnel shows. She is identifiable from her name on the bow and the Lamport and Holt colours of her funnel. There is a sailing vessel in the far right distance.

1972.74
Oil on canvas
40.5 cm x 63 cm
Signed and dated (br) in red
"H Mohrmann / 1886"
Prov: Captain R Yaxley, by descent to Mrs E D McKay, Isle of Man, from whom purchased, 1972

Vessel: 343.2 ft (l), 35.1 ft (b), 27.7 ft (d); 2263 gross tons

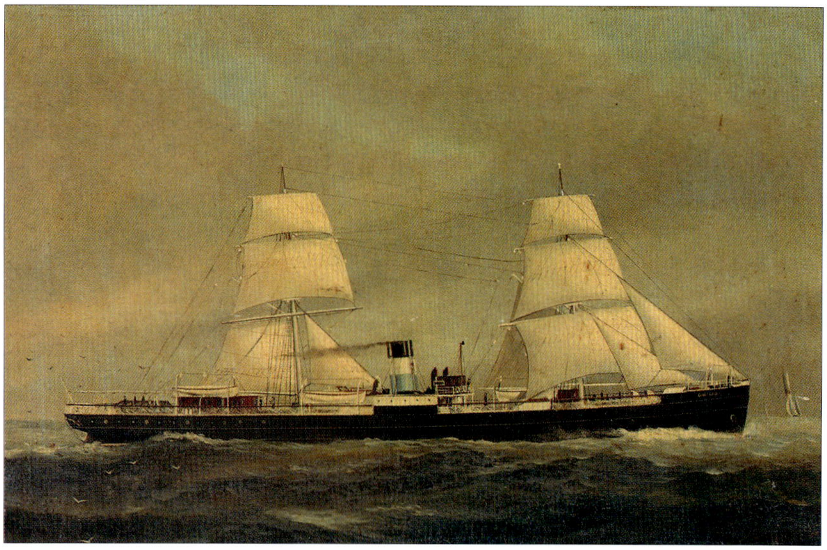

Galileo[1] was built by A Leslie & Co of Hebburn, Newcastle upon Tyne for Lamport and Holt of Liverpool in 1873. She had a single compound inverted engine by Maudsley Son & Field of London. In 1885 the vessel was transferred to the company's Belgian subsidiary, Societe Anonyme de Navigation Royale Belge Sud-Americaine, which ran services from Antwerp to South America. She returned to Lamport's own flag in 1897 and was broken up in August 1899.[2]
Mohrmann took a passage to Montevideo on *Galileo* as "garcon" in the spring of 1886, as a way to get to Independencia (now Fray Bentos) to marry.[3] The donor's grandfather, Robert Yaxley, was captain of the vessel at this time[4] and presumably acquired the painting from the artist. In fact the captain appears to be depicted standing in front of the aft deckhouse faced by another figure, possibly the artist?[5] There is a smaller painting of this vessel by Mohrmann in a private collection.[6] Joseph Witham also painted a portrait of the vessel entering the Mersey.[7]

1 Galileo Galilei, Italian astronomer, 1564-1642.
2 CR, no. 22, 21 February 1873; Heaton, p.112; photograph of vessel, ibid, ill 6.
3 See Beylen, op. cit., n.6. Personal details about Mohrmann in a note from his grand-daughter, 20 January 1999, DCF.
4 Yaxley was captain from 1881. See CR, op. cit.
5 The second figure appears to be holding a round object, could it be an artist's palette?
6 DCF.
7 Parker Gallery catalogue, 1996, no. 8, (ill. p.8).

178 Saint Mildred

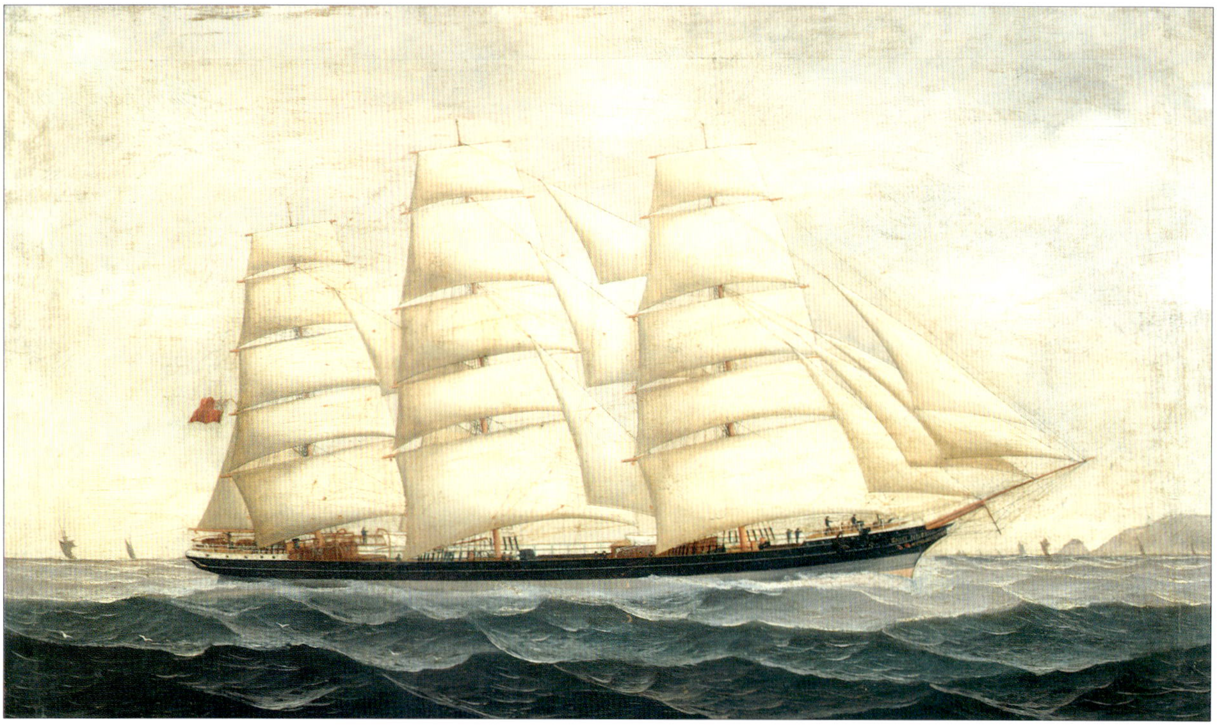

The full rigged ship *Saint Mildred* is shown in starboard profile off an unidentified coast under full sail. Members of the crew can be seen around the deck - a man at the wheel, two leaning over the port side and two others adjusting the jibs. She flies the red ensign at the after peak and is identifiable from her bow name. There are other unknown sailing vessels in the far distance. The unidentified background includes a conical island off a headland with a lighthouse on the upper slope.

Saint Mildred[1] was built of iron in 1877 by Richardson, Duck & Co at Stockton on Tees for Rankin, Gilmour of Glasgow (later of Liverpool). She was sold to Eugene Cellier of Hamburg in 1897 and renamed *Brunshaven*. She was lost on fire in 1901.[2]

1959.72.6
Oil on canvas
60 cm x 99 cm
Signed (br in red) "H Mohrmann"
Prov: Dr D Chapman, Liverpool, who presented it, 1959.

1 St Mildred, Anglo-saxon abbess, died c.700.
2 Beard; for a history of Rankin, Gilmour see J Rankin *A History of Our Firm*, Liverpool, 1921.

Robert Edward Morrison (1851 - 1924)

Morrison was born at Peel in the Isle of Man and came to Liverpool at 18. He studied in Liverpool, London and Paris before settling in Liverpool where he specialised as a painter of civic and public figures. There is a good selection of his work in the Walker Art Gallery.[1]

1 See Bennett, pp. 150-2.

179 Hamilton Boswell Gilmour

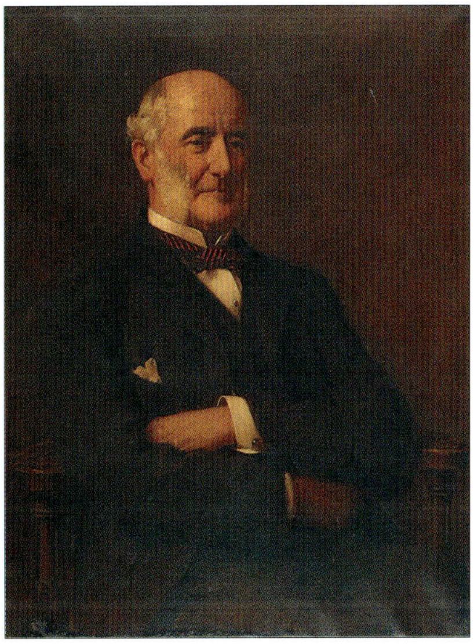

Hamilton Boswell Gilmour (1825 - 1903) was an East India merchant, who also had banking and insurance interests.[2] He was a partner in the firm of Finlay, Campbell & Co. and was also Chairman of the North Western Bank, the Liverpool & London & Globe Insurance Co., and a director of Union Marine Insurance and other companies. After his retirement from the shipping business in the early 1870s he devoted "much of his attention to charitable and philanthropic work in Liverpool."[3] He served on the boards of various local educational establishments and hospitals and was Chairman of the Liverpool Royal Infirmary from 1877 to 1893.

This portrait of Gilmour was presented to him on behalf of the Royal Infirmary by Mrs A H Brown, wife of the Treasurer, Colonel A H Brown M P, on 27 October 1892.[4] It hung in the boardroom of the Infirmary until 1983.

1983.3079.2
Oil on canvas[1]
92 cm x 71 cm
Signed and dated "R. E. Morrison 1892"
Prov: Liverpool Royal Infirmary; presented by Liverpool Health Authority, 1983
Ref: Orchard 1893, pp. 324-325; ill. plate 69
Exh: Walker Art Gallery, Spring Exhibition, 1893

1 Part of printed label on rear stretcher for Liverpool Exchange Art Gallery Dale Street.
2 For biography of Gilmour see Orchard, 1893, and obituaries in *Liverpool Daily Post* 26 and 30 January 1903.
3 B.G. Orchard, *Liverpool's Legion of Honour*, Birkenhead, 1893, p.323.
4 *Ibid* pp.324-5.

Namcheong (active about 1845-1875)

A port painter who worked in Whampoa and Hong Kong, generally producing ship portraits on commission for Western clients and port scenes.[1] There are examples at Fogg Museum, Harvard; Peabody Essex Museum at Salem and Kendall Whaling Museum.

1 Crossman, pp.67-73, 252.

180 Scawfell (page 166)

In this view of the tea clipper *Scawfell*, the vessel is shown in starboard profile with all sails set, probably approaching the Chinese coast. The helmsman can be seen at the wheel taking her towards the mountainous coastline behind the bowsprit. Other unidentified shipping can be seen in the background. She flies the Rathbone house flag of a red R on a white band between two horizontal red bands at the main mast her Commercial flag code (N G M Q)[1] on the mizzen mast and the red ensign at the after peak.

1950.29.2
Oil on canvas
52 cm x 65 cm
Inscribed on rear of canvas 'Capt. Robert Thomson / China Tea Clipper Scafell' (sic)
Prov: Captain Robert Thomson, by descent to R B Read, who presented it, 1950.

Vessel: 198 ft (l), 32.6 ft (b), 21.8 ft (d); 826 gross tons

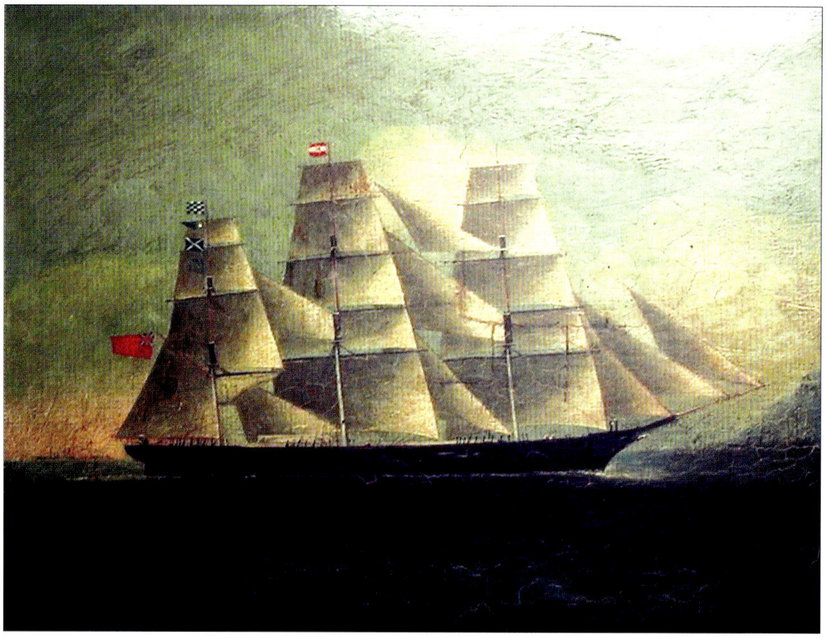

The history of this vessel is given in no. 144, the painting of *Scawfell* by Lai Sung. As well as the inscription on the reverse, the canvas also has a partially covered portrait of an unknown man. The painting has been attributed to Namcheong on stylistic grounds.[2]

1 The 'G' flag is inaccurate in having a white ball in the yellow field.
2 I am grateful to Stuart Frank, Director of the Kendall Whaling Museum, Massachusetts, for suggesting this attribution.

George Alexander Napier (1827/8-1869)

Napier was born in Montrose, Scotland and lived and worked as a railway superintendent in Glasgow before becoming a ship portraitist.[1]

1 Archibald, p. 150.

181 Russia

1968.184.13
Oil on canvas[1]
91.5 cm x 165.5 cm
Signed (bl) "G Napier"
Prov: Cunard Steam Ship Co Ltd; Private Collection, on permanent loan

Vessel: 358 ft (l); 43 ft (b); 2960 tons

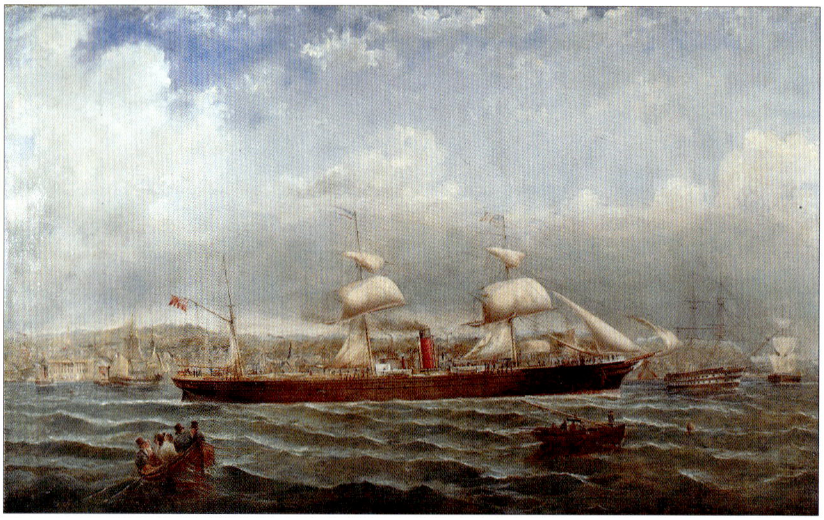

The Cunarder *Russia*, nicknamed "Rolling Russia", is shown in starboard profile off Greenock, leaving the Clyde for her maiden voyage from Liverpool across the Atlantic. She is making her way down river under steam with a minimum of sail. Groups of passengers can be seen on deck and around her is a busy shipping scene. Astern is a brig and three paddle steamers. There is a brig behind her bow and further right a three quarters starboard profile of a 72-gun warship, another paddle steamer and a brig. In the left and centre right foreground are two small boats with groups of passengers probably being ferried across the river.

Russia had an auxiliary barque rig and her topsails were fitted with Cunningham's patent reefing system, allowing them to be rolled round the spars from the deck.[2] She flies the red ensign at the after peak, the Stars and Stripes at her foremast and on the main mast the house flags of Burns & MacIver, a blue pennant with white saltire cross above a red pennant. Members of the Burns and MacIver families were partners of Samuel Cunard, and this firm acted as agents for the Cunard Line.

Russia was built by J & G Thomson & Co. of Glasgow as a partner for the paddle steamer *Scotia* in 1867. She was the last Cunard ship built with a clipper bow and figurehead and had accommodation for cabin passengers only. She held the east bound Blue Riband for one voyage in 1867. She made her final voyage for Cunard in 1878 and was sold to the Red Star Line and completely rebuilt in 1880 as *Waesland*. She sank following a collision in fog off Holyhead in 1902.[3]

The warship is probably intended to be *HMS Lion*, a second rater of 1847 which was on coast guard service in the Clyde from 1865. However, she only had 60 guns.[4] In the background is Greenock, with the classical Custom House (built William Burn, 1819) to the far left, and the rest of the town stretching downstream along the south bank of the Clyde.

There is a print of this painting with slight variations.[5] Samuel Walters also painted *Russia* on two occasions, once off Fastnet and also in a northerly gale. Though the present locations of these pictures are not known, there are two photographic carte de visite prints in the Liverpool Record Office. [6]

1 Relined.
2 For a description of the system see Underhill, pp. 127-130, 156.
3 Bonsor North, pp. 149-150.
4 Navy List, 1865, 1867.
5 Illustrated in G A Godden, ed., *Thomas E Beaumont : A "Constitutional" Voyage Round The World: 1870 - 1871*, London, 1971, between pp.82-83; print then with Cunard Steam Ship Company.
6 See Davidson, 1992, p.201. The view off Fastnet is illustrated in Maginnis, p. 39.

George Hall Neale (c.1870-1940)

Neale was born in Liverpool and was initially a genre painter before concentrating on portraiture. He moved to London about 1914 but retained a studio in Liverpool. He was married to Maud Rutherford, also a portrait painter. There are examples in the Walker Art Gallery including a self-portrait and portrait of the artist W J J C Bond.[1]

1 Bennett pp.157-8.

182 Ralph Brocklebank

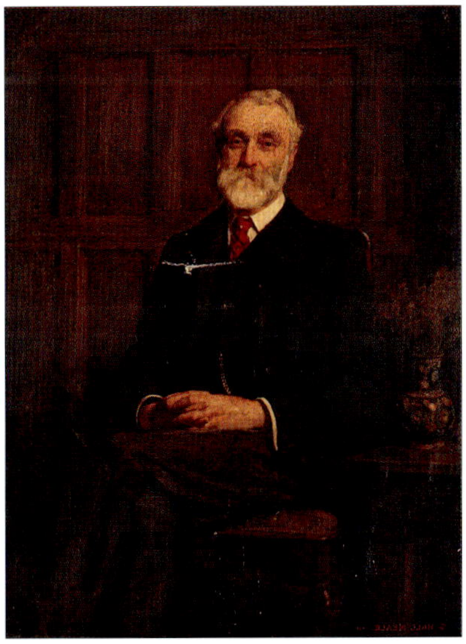

1983.3079.1
Oil on canvas
137 cm x 102.5 cm
Signed (bl) "G. HALL. NEALE. 1903"
Prov: Royal Liverpool Infirmary; presented by Liverpool Health Authority, 1983

Ralph Brocklebank (1840 - 1921) of the famous ship owning family is shown seated on a chair against wood panelling with a vase of flowers to his left.

Ralph Brocklebank was the son of Ralph Brocklebank (1803-1892)[1]. Although he was a partner in the family firm for some years, his main business interests were as a Director of the London & North Western Railway and Chairman of the Thames and Mersey Marine Insurance Company.

He was an assiduous supporter of the Royal Liverpool Infirmary serving as Honorary Treasurer from 1879 to 1909 and Chairman of the Board in 1898-99. He was also a significant personal benefactor.[2] This portrait came from the hospital's boardroom.

1 Ralph Brocklebank Senior is well-known not only as a partner in the family firm but as a leading member of the Mersey Docks and Harbour Board which he served for 32 years, six as Chairman. See Rees Brocklebank
2 ibid. Quoting *Liverpool Post and Mercury*, 21 December 1921.

183 *Sir Alfred Read*

1972.198
Oil on canvas
143.5 cm x 90.5 cm
Signed (br) "G. HALL NEALE"
Prov: Coast Lines Ltd., Liverpool, who presented it, 1972.

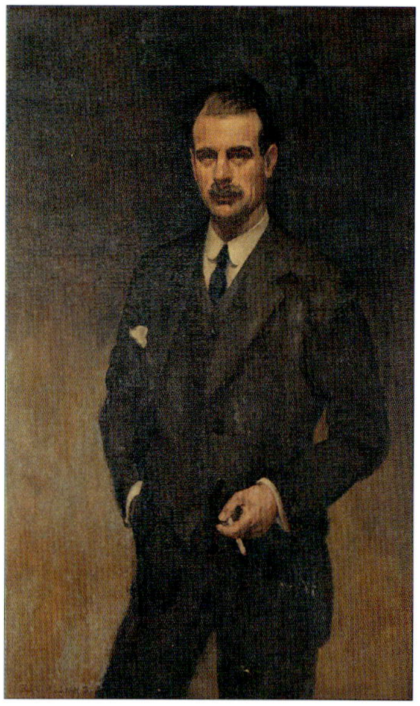

Sir Alfred Read (1871-1955) began his career with Anchor Line but in 1893 at the age of only 22 he became a partner in F H Powell & Co., a relatively small coasting firm, where his father was also a partner. Read effectively took control in 1895 and built up the business. In 1912 he formed a new company amalgamating the fleets of two other small companies, John Bacon and Samuel Hough, trading as Coast Lines. For more than three decades, Coast Lines was the largest group of coastal traders between British and Irish ports. In 1917 the firm became part of the Royal Mail Steam Packet Company with Read effectively remaining in charge. Coast Lines survived the collapse of Royal Mail in 1931 and Read served as Chairman from 1931 until his retirement in 1950 at the age of 79.[1]

Amongst his many other activities he was a member of the Mersey Docks and Harbour Board, 1904-20, Chairman of the Liverpool Steamship Owners Association, 1913, Director of Home Trade Services at the Ministry of Shipping, 1917-19, a member of the Port of London Authority, 1934-41 and President of the Institute of Transport, 1936.

The portrait shows Read in relaxed mood, with a cigarette in his hand.

1 The only biography of Read is an unpublished account, John Winter-Lotimer *Alfred Henry Read - Shipowner* (copy MAL 541/1/PM). For Coast Lines see N L Middlemiss *Coast Lines*, Newcastle-upon-Tyne, 1998.

Neapolitan School

184 *Hannibal entering Naples Bay*

1955.234
Oil on canvas
51 cm x 74 cm
Inscribed (centre bottom of canvas) "HANNIBAL, S^{T}. IVES ENTERING NAPLES BAY HANNIBAL THOMAS MASTER"
Prov: Unknown, in collections, 1955

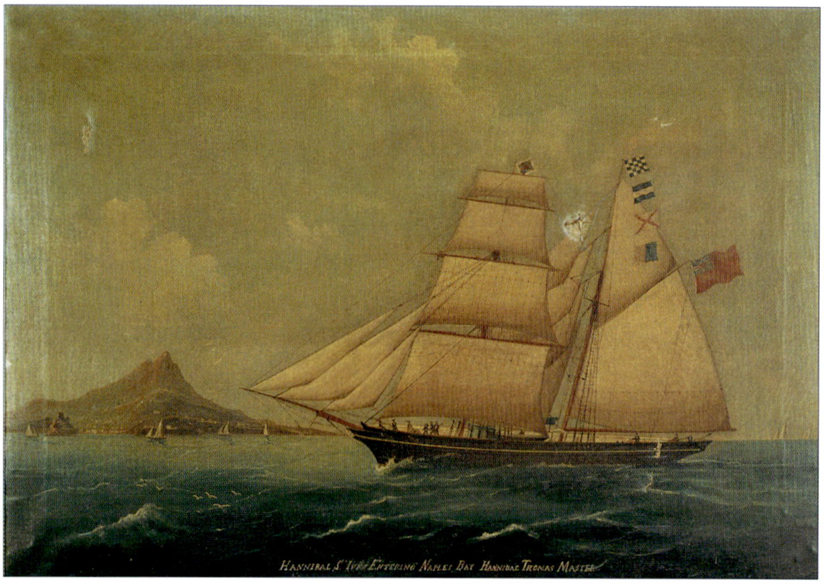

The brigantine *Hannibal* is shown in a port profile under full sail entering the Bay of Naples on the west coast of Italy. This engaging view shows the vessel accurately and eight members of the crew are on deck about various duties. She flies her commercial flag code (N J V K) from the main mast along with the red ensign at the peak and the pilot jack from the fore mast.

In the background is the conical outline of Mount Vesuvius and there are various small coastal craft and yachts in the distance.

Hannibal was built in Rye, East Sussex, in 1858. At that time there were a number of builders of small coastal vessels in the town.[1] *Hannibal* was owned by Hannibal Thomas of St Ives and spent much of her career in the fruit trade between the Bristol Channel ports and the Mediterranean. She was sold to London owners in 1867[2] and disappears from the registers in 1872.[3]

1 See John Collard *A Maritime History of Rye*, Rye, 1985, which also illustrates a similar vessel, *Marian Zagury*, described as a clipper schooner, p.67.
2 Although LR 1867 gives her port of registry as Liverpool, she is not listed in LCR.
3 for history see LR 1859-1872.

W. Nicholson (active 1835)

185 Captain Grayson

This portrait is reputedly of Captain Grayson, who may be related to the Grayson family of ship builders of Liverpool. He is obviously a man of means as his dress and small items of jewellery, such as the pin in his shirt and the ring on his watch chain, make clear. He holds a smoking cigar in his right hand and his left arm rests on and covers a chart[2].

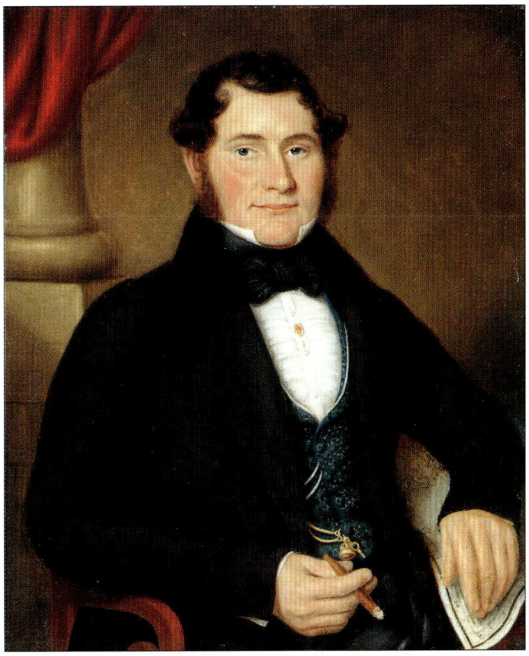

1965.246
Oil on canvas[1]
76.5 cm x 63.5 cm
Signed and dated (rear canvas) "Painted W. Nicholson / Dec. 24th. 1835 / Liverpool"
Prov: J H Seel, Southport, who presented it, 1965.

1 Relined.
2 Given the latitude and longitude visible in the corner, the chart should cover an area off the St Lawrence River, Canada.

Orlando Norie (1832-1901)

Principally a military artist, Norie was born in Scotland but worked for most of his life in England, mainly in Aldershot.

186 Canning Half Tide Dock, Liverpool[1] (page 170)

This view of the Canning Half-Tide Dock is inaccurate in a number of respects. The vantage point is near the entrance to the dock in front of what is now the reconstructed Piermaster's House. The observer looks towards the town and apart from the vessels in the dock, the most prominent feature is the Custom House to the right and on the far side of the canvas is part of the Albert Dock warehouse. In the foreground are capstans and the box for winding gear to open the Rennie bridge which can be seen to the right. To the left, more vessels can be seen in the main Canning Dock.

However, the quay side has been foreshortened and one would expect to see more of the Albert Dock warehouse itself on the right hand side from such a straight angle. The Custom House has also been inaccurately portrayed. Its width has been truncated, with a bay missing on either side of the portico. The portico has been squashed resulting in a narrower and higher pediment than existed.

1960.287
Oil on canvas
53.5 cm x 70 cm
Signed (br) "[O] NORIE 1852"
Prov: Sir Ernest Royden, Hill Bark, Wirral; purchased from sale of contents of Hill Bark, Talbot, Wilson & Co., 19-21 December 1960.
Exh: Liverpool, 1957.

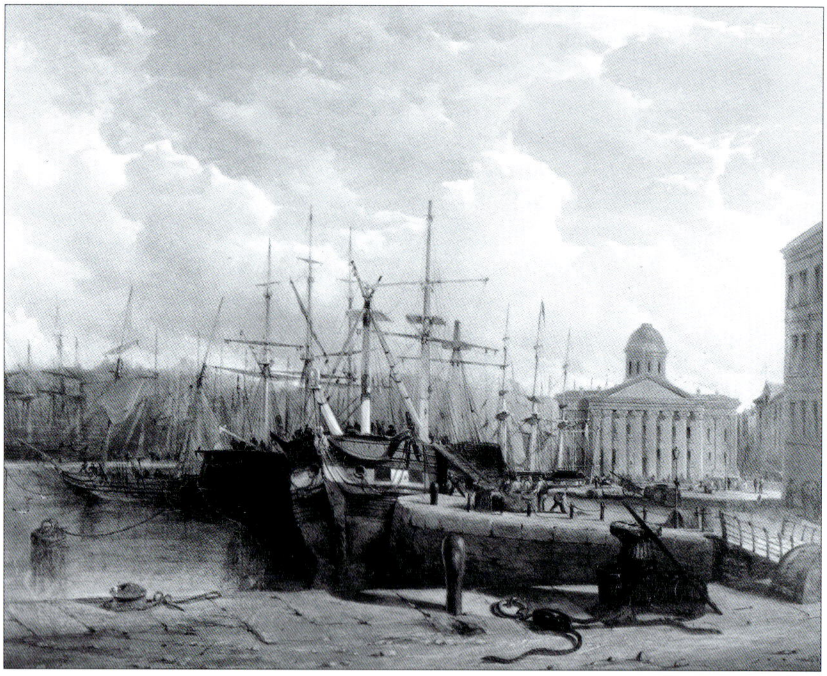

The Canning Half Tide Dock was created in 1845 as part of the Albert Dock construction works of 1843-46. It had formerly been a tidal basin providing entrance to the Old Dock and Salthouse Dock but was fitted with gates in 1829. The Custom House designed by John Foster (1759 - 1827) was built between 1827 and 1839 on the site of the Old Dock.[2]

None of the vessels portrayed are identifiable but they are typical of the deep sea sailing ships using the port in the 1840s and 1850s. The artist shows plenty of activity around the docks with groups of men on the quayside, many examples of the ubiquitous barrel, a cart and other equipment necessary to the life of the docks.

1 The painting was acquired with a plaque incorrectly identifying the scene as Salthouse Dock.
2 Ritchie-Noakes, pp.22, 51-52.

Henry Frederick Oakes (1818 - 1849)

187 Laying the Foundation Stone of Birkenhead Docks, 23 October 1844

LI.91.4.5
Oil on canvas
67.5 cm x 107 cm
Signed and dated (br) "OAKES 44"
Prov: Mersey Docks and Harbour Company, on permanent loan, 1991.

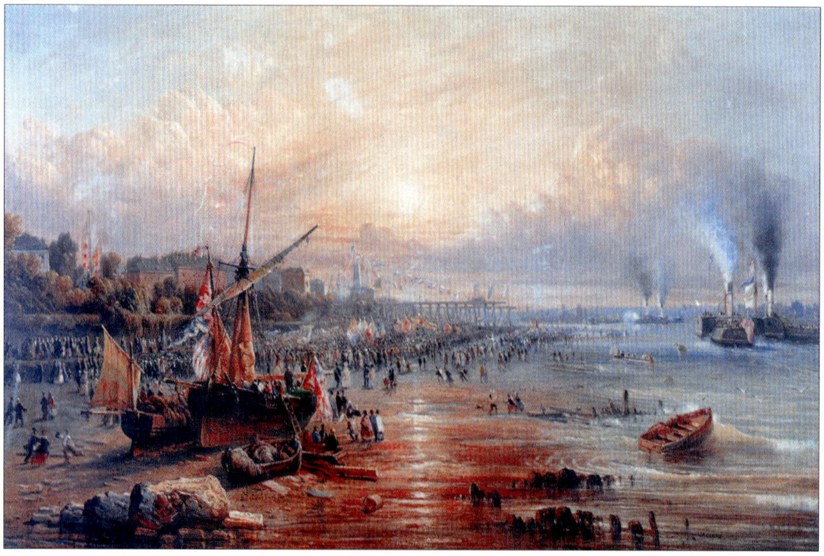

This busy scene shows the laying of the foundation stone for the Birkenhead Docks on 23 October 1844. The view is looking north up the Mersey with the inlet of

Wallasey Pool on the left hand side and the Liverpool shore in the far right background. In the centre foreground two wooden jetties protrude into the river and towards the far end of these jetties the foundation stone is being lower to the ground from a platform. On the hillside above are some large villas and buildings with the chimney of a factory or works to which the lines for the flags of the jetties have been attached. A large crowd of people is gathered on the shore, and there is a line of people waving large flags. Off shore are two groups of paddle steamers crowded with other onlookers, some of them standing on the paddle boxes for a better view. In the foreground a group of beached wooden coastal vessels also provide a vantage point to view the proceedings.

There is little real sense of what is going on and the main action, although at the centre of the canvas, is so far away that the immediacy is lost. In fact, the foundation stone for the docks was laid by Sir Philip Egerton, MP for South Cheshire. There was a procession through the town and a dinner for 200 invited guests and bonfires and fireworks took place in the evening.[1]

Several other views of this event are known. There is another painting attributed to H Oakes in the Williamson Art Gallery, Birkenhead. Another view by John Wright Oakes (1820-1887) shows a similar scene but from the north looking up the Mersey. The same basic components of crowds, jetties and activity are present though the act of lowering the stone is rather clearer.[2] Another view from the same direction is provided by Edward Duncan in a painting in the Walker Art Gallery which gives a more detail view of the actual ceremony.[3]

1 See Hilda Gamlin *Memoirs or the Chronicles of Birkenhead*, 1892, pp. 16-17.
2 Formerly Racquets Club, Liverpool. Sold Phillips, Chester, 13 September 1994, lot 213.
3 WAG No.31 Illustrated in P. Aughton *Liverpool: A People's History*, Preston, 1990, p.112.

Charles Ogilvy (1833-c.1890)

It seems likely that Ogilvy maintained a joint career as a seafarer and marine artist. He appears in a number of Liverpool directories over a period from 1868 to 1884 listed as a "marine artist." Only a small number of paintings by him are known.[1]

1 Davidson, 1986, pp. 86-7.

188 No.6 Pilot Schooner Pioneer

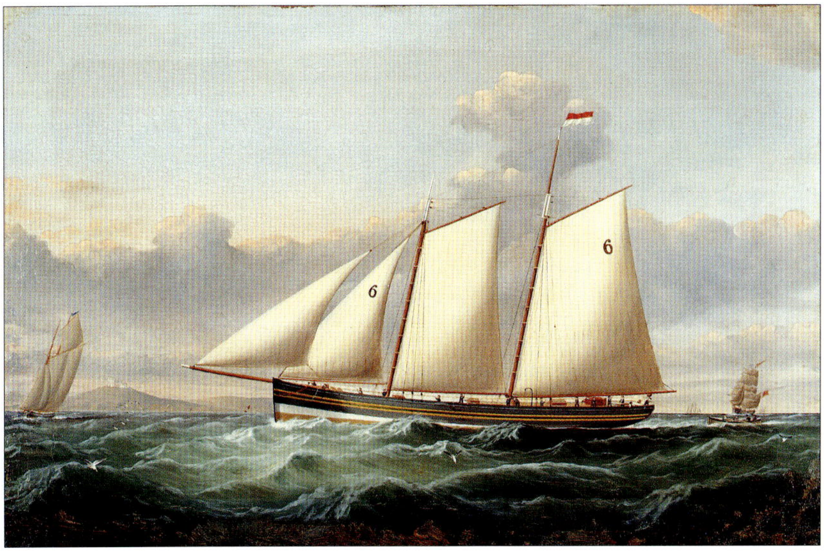

1933.120
Oil on canvas
61 cm x 91.5 cm
Signed and dated C Ogilvy, 1868[1]
Prov: Mr H Jones, Liverpool, from whom purchased, 1933
Exh: Crosby 1951, no. 90; Liverpool 1986
Ref: Handbook 1935, Sea Breezes, 1935, Port Panorama, 1986, p. 17, Youde 1994 ill. p.49

Vessel: 68 ft (l), 15.7 ft (b), 7.6 ft (d); 53 gross tons.

The No.6 Pilot Schooner *Pioneer* is shown off Point Lynas, Anglesey in port profile under full sail. A line has been thrown to the punt at her stern and a pilot will be about to come back on board. Two other vessels, a schooner and a British registered brig, are shown in the far distance. The pilot flag being flown from the main mast is upside down. Although this could be an error by the artist, it also happens in the other Ogilvy painting in the collection, *Queen* (no. 189). In both instances, the pilot boat is about to pick up a returning pilot and one suggestion may be that it indicates that the boat is temporarily unavailable.

The pilot boat is painted in the service's characteristic colours with on the upper hull a narrow green band between narrow yellow bands and broad grey-blue bands; the lower hull has a broad white above a yellow band.

Ogilvy chooses the less popular north-east corner of Anglesey to place his painting and includes a good representation of Point Lynas, the pilot station and lighthouse, on the cliff top just east of Parys mountain.

Pioneer was built by Buckley Jones of Liverpool in 1852. She was the first schooner rigged boat employed in the Liverpool pilot service. She was sold in 1879 and sailed to Dakar where she was wrecked.[2]

There is another painting of *Pioneer* by McMinn in the collections, no. 173.

1 Removed during restoration, 1949-50 (DCF).
2 Rees, p.202; for a first hand account of the voyage to Dakar, see D S Forbes 'Liverpool Pilot-Boat' in *Sea Breezes*, vol. 19, June 1935, pp. 200-3.

189 No. 1 Pilot Schooner *Queen*

1972.147.1
Oil on panel
28.5 cm x 46.5 cm
Signed and dated (br) "C.O. / 1865"
Prov: N Morrison Esq, Caldy, who presented it, 1972
Exh: Liverpool 1986
Ref: Port Panorama 1986, p.17 (ill)

Vessel: 79.4 ft (l), 17 ft (b), 9.7 ft (d); 61 gross tons

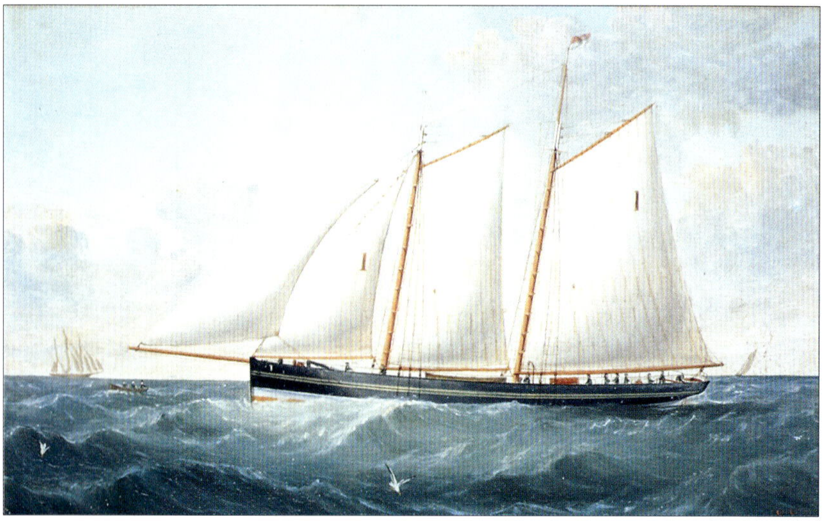

The schooner rigged No.1 pilot boat *Queen* is shown in port profile with all her sails set. She is probably just about to pick up a pilot who can be seen sitting in the stern of the small punt which is depicted just below the pilot boat's bowsprit. The pilot is at the tiller and two other crew are at the oars. He may have come from the sailing ship which is sketched on the horizon. The pilot flag on the main mast is being flown upside down, as discussed in no. 188. (*Pioneer*).

Queen was built by Michael Ratsey of West Cowes in 1856. Her most notably episode occurred in May 1891 when she was in collision with *S S Sailor Prince* in the Crosby channel and sank. She was raised and remained in service until 1898 when she was sold to A and M Smith, fish merchants of Aberdeen and Leith. She continued as a fishing vessels for owners in the Faroes and was wrecked off Iceland in April 1933.[1]

1 For the vessel's career see Rees, pp.176, 183-4, 202.

Joseph Parry (1756-1826)

Parry was the son of a Liverpool pilot. He trained as a house painter but became a successful artist. He moved to Manchester in 1790 and painted genre, landscapes and portraits. He was known as "the father of art in Manchester".[1]

1 See J C P Burleigh 'Joseph Parry, artist: dates and origins' in *THSLC*, vol. 140, 1991, pp. 229-232.

190 Liverpool privateer returning with a prize

This is the earliest known Liverpool ship portrait and shows a privateer returning home with a French prize.

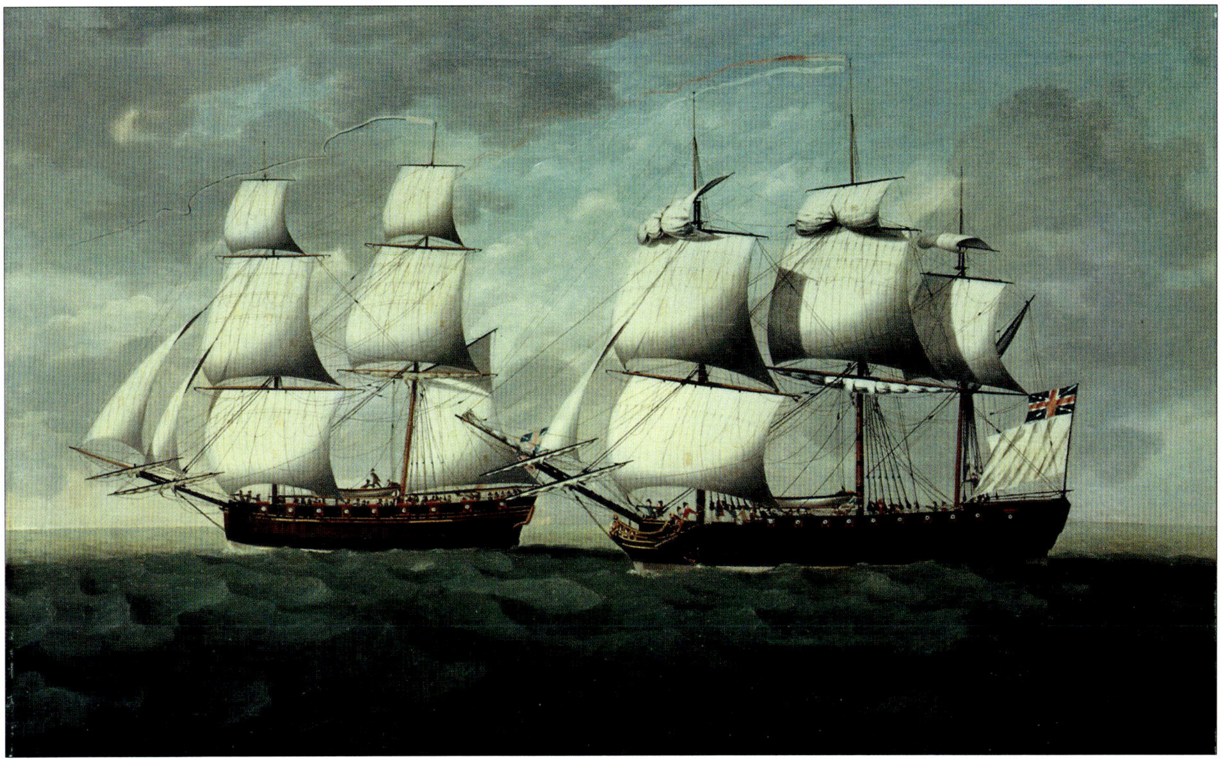

1987.377
Oil on canvas[1]
62 cm x 99 cm
Signed and dated "Jo^s Parry. Pinx. Liverpool / 1781"
Prov: Rutland Gallery, London, 1968; Purchased at Sothebys, 11 November 1987, lot 3

To the left of the canvas is the privateer, an 18-gun brig, in port profile. She has begun reducing sail and there is a lot of activity on board with men on the bow and a small group about to launch a tender. She flies a long pennant of red, white and blue bands from her main mast and the red ensign at the stern. On board the prize, a larger ship rigged vessel, there is commensurate activity and further sail has been reduced with the main and mizzen courses furled and the royals being shortened. She flies two long pennants from her main mast and the union jack at the stern. Both ships show signs of the action and careful repairs to shot holes have been made to a number of the sails.

The privateer has a serpent figurehead and the vessel may well be *Viper* of 160 tons owned by Birch and Co. and under the command of Captain Cowell. She held a privateering licence and captured a number of vessels during her career.[2] She was employed mainly in the Jamaica trade. The French prize has not been identified. She is a ship of 20 guns and has a male bust figurehead wearing armour, including a plumed helmet and shield.

This is one of Parry's only two known ship portraits and though the vessels are accurately and well painted, the sea is rather stylised and there is little feeling of the vessels moving through the water.[3]

A smaller modern copy of this painting appeared in the sale rooms in 1991.[4]

1 Relined.
2 Gomer Williams, pp. 236, 669.
3 The other is *Mentor*, Parker Gallery Catalogue, 1980, no. 25.
4 Bonhams, 15 August 1991, lot 296; Cato Crane, Liverpool, 17 October 1991, lot 433.

J Pearson (active 1819)

191 Perseverance (page 174)

The ship rigged *Perseverance* is shown in two views off Whitehaven. In the main view the vessel is shown in the centre of the canvas in port profile. She has only her upper sail set including her topsails and the top gallants on the main and fore masts. She flies the early Brocklebank house flag[1] together with a long red pennant, probably denoting her departure and a red ensign at the peak. She has eighteen guns and a male figurehead with a helmet.

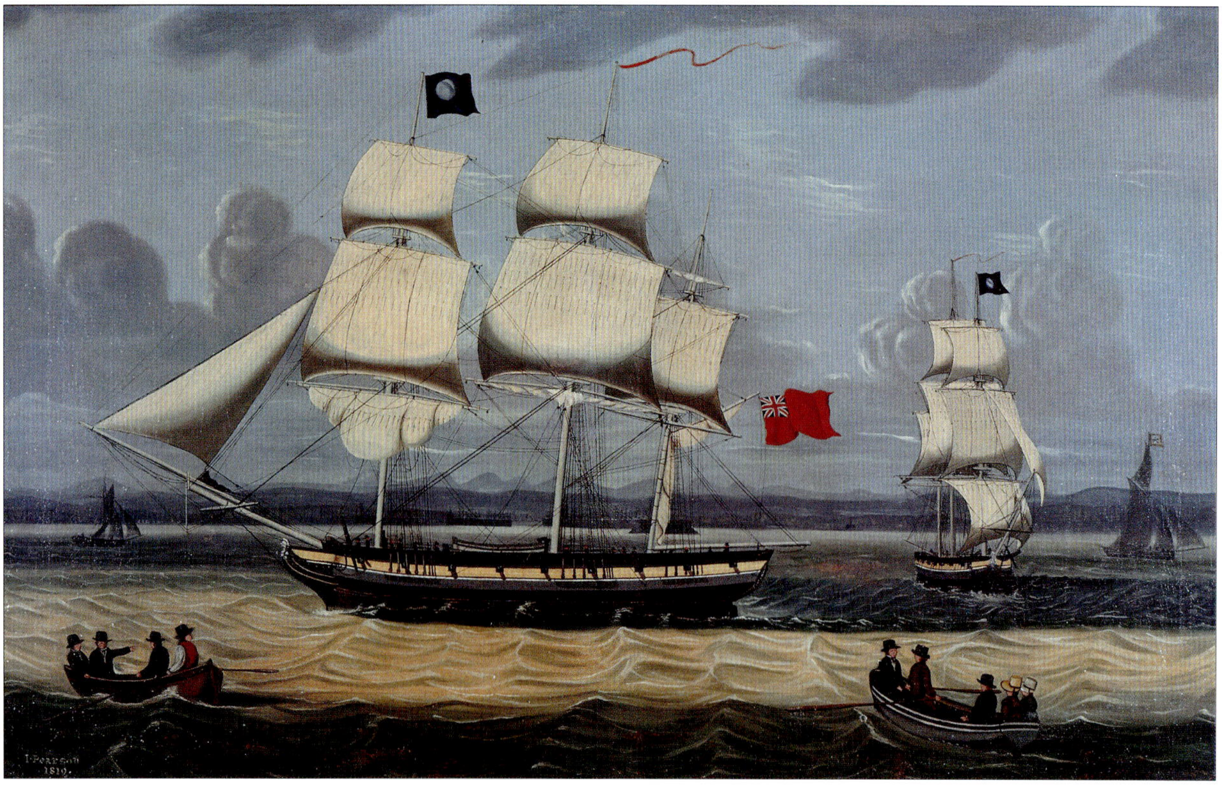

1970.246.15
Oil on canvas[2]
60 cm x 94 cm
Signed and dated (bl) "I. Pearson / 1819."
Prov: T & J Brocklebank Ltd; Cunard Brocklebank Ltd., Private Collection, on permanent loan.
Ref: Chandler Liverpool Shipping, ill. No. 40

Vessel: 123 ft (l), 30.5 ft (b), 18.5 ft (d); 513 gross tons

In the second view to the right she is shown in starboard quarter profile with all her sails set except the main course on the main and mizzen masts. The same house flag and pennant are included. In the foreground to each corner are two small rowing boats and in the far right hand distance is a topsail schooner with an unidentified flag of a five pointed star on a white ground with red border.

The vessel is depicted off Whitehaven, the firm's home port, and the entrance to the harbour can be seen behind the main mast in the central view. Neighbouring Parton and Lowca can be seen to the far left.

Perseverance was built by Brocklebanks in Whitehaven in 1819 as a companion ship for *Princess Charlotte* in the India trade which they had recently entered. She was a finely built ship and had excellent accommodation for passengers and carried a surgeon on board. She sailed from Liverpool to Calcutta calling at Madeira, Cape Town and Madras. In fact she was wrecked approaching Madras in March 1829.[3]

No other work by this artist is known. He seems to have some nautical knowledge from the generally accurate portrayal of the vessel though the stylistic handling of the sea is even more simplistic than other ship portraitists of the period.

1 From 1820 blue and white halved.
2 Relined.
3 Rees Brocklebank, pp. 58-59, Gibson I, pp. 81, 216.

Heinrich Andreas Sophus Petersen (1834-1916) and Peter Christian Holm (1823-1888)

These two ship portraitists worked in Altona and Hamburg, Germany. They often worked jointly and Holm also collaborated with Peterson's father, Lorenz (1803-1870). There are examples of work by all these artists in the Altonaer Museum, Hamburg and the Peabody Essex Museum, Salem.[1]

1 See H Poulson *Danske Skibsportraetmalere*, Copenhagen.

192 S S Gothland

S S Gothland is shown under full sail and steam in a port profile off an unidentified harbour, perhaps in north Germany. She flies the red ensign at her stern and the Donald Currie house flag from her main mast.

Gothland was an iron-hulled single screw steamer built for the Leith, Hull and

1 Printed label on rear stretcher for David T Blackburn, Picture Frame Maker, 16 Wood Street [Liverpool].1 Printed label on rear stretcher for David T Blackburn, Picture Frame Maker, 16 Wood Street [Liverpool].

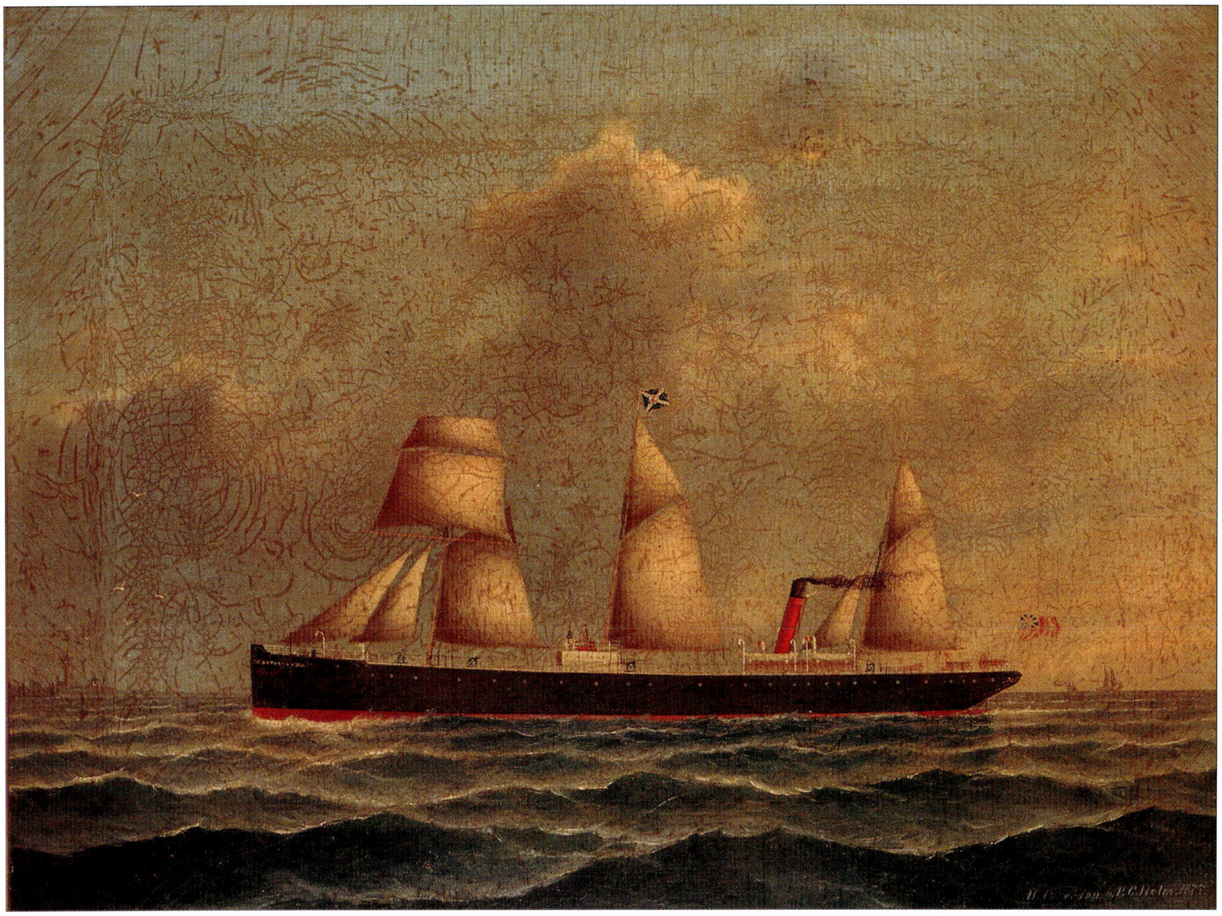

Hamburg Steam Packet Co. by J & G Thomson of Glasgow in 1871. She was chartered by Donald Currie, founder of the Castle Line, for his first service to the Cape and was transferred to his Liverpool - Hamburg Line in 1877, the date of this painting. She continued in this trade until sold to the Admiralty in 1915 for use as a blockade ship, though she was not used. After further sales, she was broken up in Germany in 1924.[2]

George Ruxton was captain of the vessel on many voyages in the late 1870s and 1880s including a voyage in 1877.[3]

The painting is a typical product of the two artists and *S S Sutherland* (no. 193) is by the same hands. George Ruxton captained both *Gothland* and *Sutherland* and the paintings came to the museum from the same owner, indicating a linked provenance.

1951.81.1
Oil on canvas[1]
47 cm x 65 cm
Signed and dated (br) "H Petersen + P C Holm / 1877"
Prov: J H Davies, Dyserth, Flint, who presented it (with no. 193), 1951

Vessel: 251.6 ft (l), 32 ft (b), 16.6 ft (d); 150 hp engines, 1482 tons

2 For Currie and history of Gothland see M Murray *Ships and South Africa*, Oxford 1933, pp. 41-46, 294 and G Somner "Hamburg Steam Packets (1)" in *Sea Breezes*, vol. 36, August 1964, pp.114-123, 126.
3 CR, no. 75, 21 May 1878.

193 *S S Sutherland*

The iron-hulled steamer *Sutherland* is shown in central port profile passing Heligoland as the inscription makes clear. The vessel was schooner rigged and is making use of her sails as well as her engines. She flies the red ensign at her stern and the house flag of Donald Currie. There is other unidentified shipping in the far distance.

Sutherland was built for James Cowan of Glasgow by Barclay Curle & Co. in Glasgow in 1866 but was sold to Donald Currie & Co. early in 1867. Currie was best known for his later Castle Line services to South Africa but also had trading interests with Germany and the Baltic through the Liverpool & Hamburg Steamship Co.. It was in this trade that *Sutherland* spent her career until sold to French owners in 1904. The vessel was lengthened in 1871 and re-engined in 1878.[1]

1951.81.2
Oil on canvas
47 cm x 65 cm
Signed and dated (br) "H Petersen + P C Holm 1873", inscribed (bl) "S S Sutherland, Geo. Ruxton Commander, Passing Heligoland, Apil [sic] 2. 1872."
Prov: J H Davies, Dyserth, Flint, who presented it (with no. 192), 1951

Vessel: 252.1 ft (l), 30.1 ft (b), 16.5 ft (d);140 hp engines; 959 tons

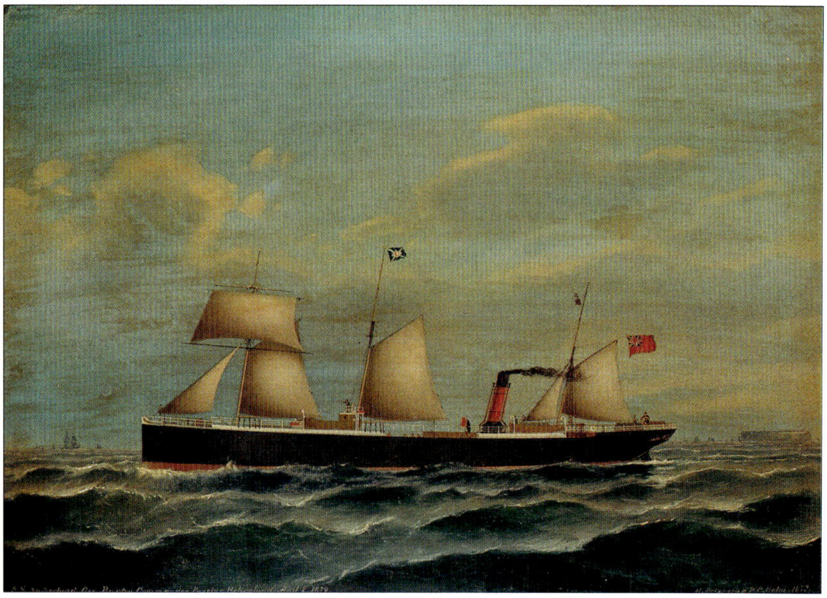

The rock island of Heligoland lies in the North Sea about 40 miles north west of the mouths of the Elbe and Weser rivers. The sheer face of the island can be seen and what appears to be the lighthouse.[2]
George Ruxton was captain of *Sutherland* from March to June 1872.[3] The connection with no. 192 *Gothland* has already been noted.

1 CR, no. 246, 9 October 1866, no. 21, 17 January 1867, no. 123, 2 August 1871.
2 Heligoland was under British control from 1807 until ceded to Germany in 1890. It was a popular resort for German visitors.
3 CR, no. 123, 2 August 1871.

Burnett Poole (active 1919)

194 *Mauretania in dazzle paint*

1968.184.6
Oil on canvas[1]
82 cm x 122 cm
Signed and dated "Burnett Poole. / London. June 1919."
Prov: Cunard Steam Ship Company, Private Collection, on permanent loan.
Exh: Liverpool, 1974

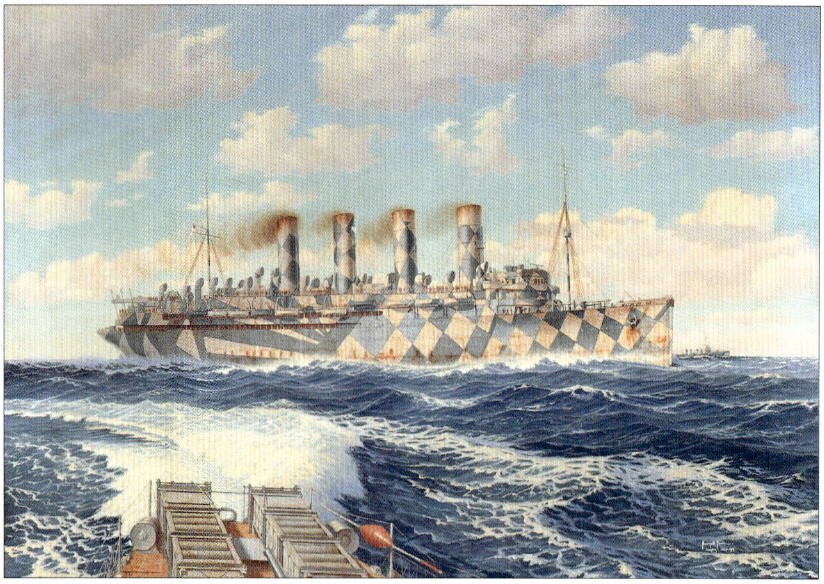

During the First World War the Royal Navy used dazzle paint as a means of confusing enemy raiders. Here the requisitioned transatlantic liner *Mauretania* is shown painted in this way. She is portrayed in starboard profile from the stern of an accompanying destroyer. The dazzle paint is obviously ageing and rust marks are showing through at the tops of her funnels and on her hull. She carries guns at her stern and on her bow deck. There is a second four funnel vessel also in dazzle paint in the distance behind her bow.

The idea for dazzle painting was suggested and developed in 1915 by the marine artist Norman Wilkinson, then serving as a Lieutenant Commander in the Royal Navy.[2] *Mauretania* was built by Swan Hunter and Wigham Richardson of Newcastle in 1907 for Cunard. With her sister *Lusitania* she offered both speed and comfort on the Liverpool - New York service. Her war service began in 1915 when she took troops to the Dardanelles. Later that year she was converted for use as a hospital ship but was laid up at Greenock and dazzle painted. She completed her wartime duties carrying Canadian and American troops. She resumed her normal duties in 1919 but was transferred to Southampton in 1920. She remained in service until 1935.[3] Cunard issued a poster of *Mauretania* in her dazzle paint, though a more strident palette is used including bright red, yellow and blue.[4]

1 Canvas stamped "WINDSOR & NEWTON ......LONDON"
2 See his pamphlet on the subject, Norman Wilkinson *The Dazzle Painting of Ships*, NE Coast Institute of Engineers and Shipbuilders, 1919. For a general discussion on camouflage techniques see D Williams *Liners in Battledress*, London, 1979.
3 Bonsor, North, pp. 109, 157. Haws Cunard, p.58.
4 Entitled *On War Service - On Peace Service*. It is illustrated on the cover of Williams, op. cit.

W F Preston (active 1885-1895)

W F Preston is listed as an artist living in Birkenhead in Gores Directory of 1895. A similarity of signature would strongly suggest that he is the William Preston who was working in Hull in the previous decade. The scarcity of signed or attributed works makes it very difficult to draw any firm conclusions.[1]

1 For William Preston see Credland, p.209, with illustration of signed painting of steam yacht *Eira*, 1888.

195 *The Liverpool Landing Stage*

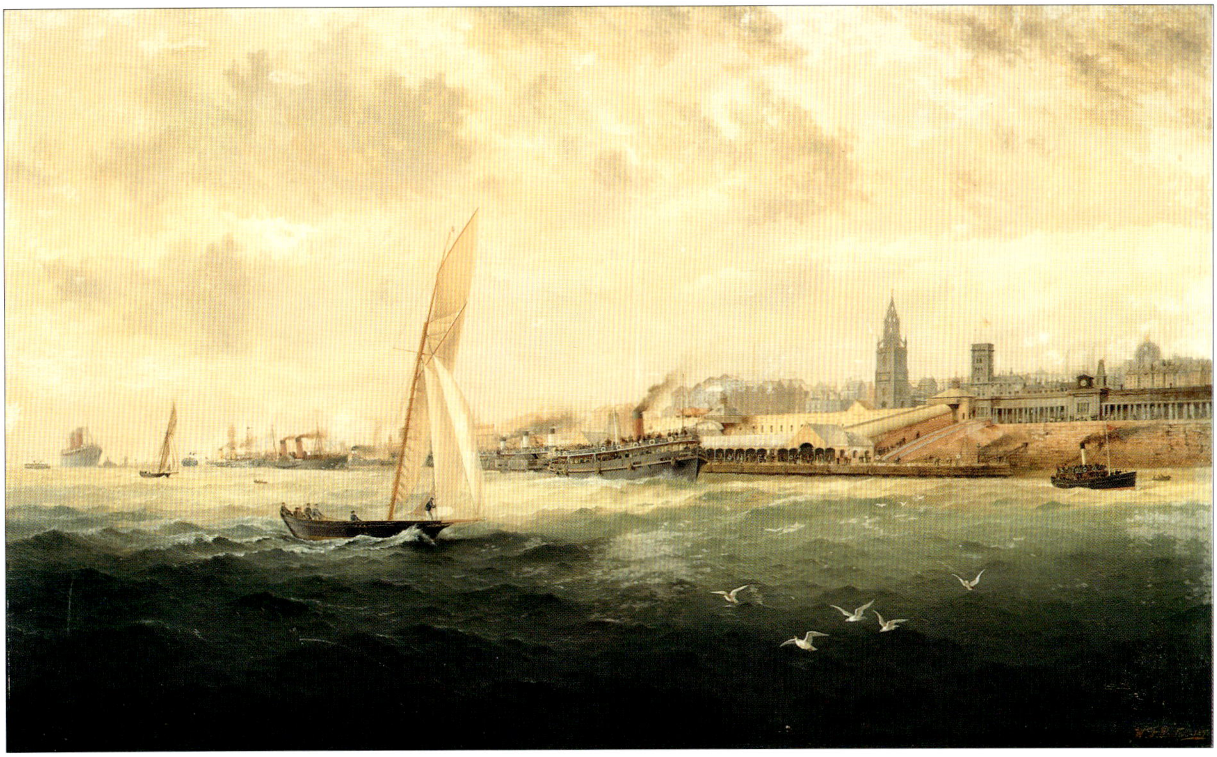

This oblique view of the Liverpool landing stage provides an impressive scene of the waterfront looking down the Mersey. The principal subject is the floating landing stage and its covered bridges and walkways where an array of ferry boats are berthed. There are other ferries in the river, a couple of cutter rigged yachts in the centre and in the far left distance a Cunard liner is approaching. There are two steam paddle tugs of the Liverpool Screw Tug Company with their black, white and red funnels. Behind the landing stage is the Riverside station with St Nicholas Church[2] and the Public Baths to the right and, behind, the dome of the Town Hall and Tower Buildings. On the top of this building a flag and inverted cone fly from poles, the latter a warning of high winds. Moving downstream are warehouses, the masts of

LI.90.14
Oil on canvas[1]
77 cm x 127.5 cm
Signed and dated (br) "W. F. Preston. 1893"
Prov: Ocean Group, on loan from the P H Holt Trust, 1990.

Vessel: *Mersey* 145.1 ft (l), 32 ft (b), 10.4 ft (d); 308 tons.

ships in Prince's Dock and the final landmark is the Victoria Tower at Salisbury Dock in the far distance.

The only named vessel is the ferry *Mersey*[3] at the southern end of the landing stage. She was one of two twin screw boats built of steel in 1890 by J Jones & Co. for Birkenhead Corporation and remained in service between Liverpool and Woodside until 1925.[4] The other vessels are not individually identifiable but include two Wallasey ferries (with white and black funnels) immediately behind *Mersey* and further along an Isle of Man and a North Wales paddle steamer (identifiable by their red and black and yellow funnels respectively).

The Floating Landing Stage was rebuilt in 1876 after a fire in 1874 had destroyed the previous floating piers. These had been erected from 1847 to cope with the problem of the Mersey's great tidal range.[5]

1 Relined.
2 The ship weather vane can be seen on top of the tower.
3 The name on the bow is shown in script, an unusual feature characteristic of Woodside ferries from about 1890.
4 Duckworth & Langmuir 1956, p.114.
5 Ritchie-Noakes, p.30.

G. Reid (active about 1910-15)

196 S S Comic passing Formby Lightship

MMM.1996.36
Oil on canvas
23 cm x 40.5 cm
Signed (br) "G. Reid"; inscribed (bc) "S S COMIC. CAPT. McMURTRY. MASTER / - PASSING. FORMBY. LIGHTSHIP. -"
Prov: Unknown, in collections, 1962

Vessel: 236.3 ft (l), 31.2 ft (b), 15.3 ft (d); 935 gross tons

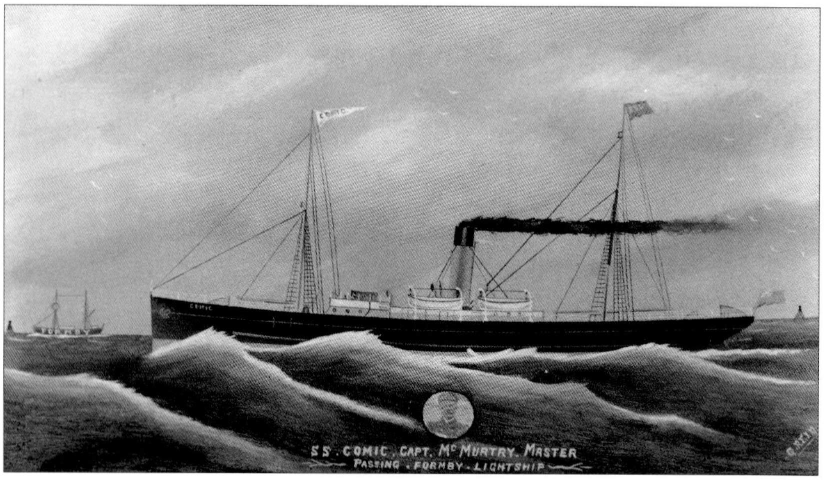

The steamer *Comic* is shown in port profile passing the Formby Lightship and a buoy which is in the background to the left. She flies a name pennant, the house flag of the Belfast Steam Ship Company and her funnel is painted in the company colours.

Above the inscription is a small circular cut-out photograph which is presumably J. McMurtry, who was captain of the vessel from 1909 until 1915[1] and for whom it must have been painted.

The steel screw steamer *Comic* was built in 1896 by Harland and Wolff for the Belfast Steam Ship Company. She served on the Derry to Liverpool service, maintaining their twice weekly sailings single handedly. In 1921 she was transferred to the Laird Line serving on the Belfast to Ayr service until 1929 under the name *Cairnsmore*. She then went to the British and Irish Steam Packet Company and was renamed *Lady Kerry*. She was broken up in Liverpool in 1934.[2]

The Formby Lightship was located near the entrance to the Queen's Channel[3] which led into the Crosby Channel and was the main approach into the Mersey.

1 LR 1910-1915.
2 R C Sinclair *Across The Irish Sea, Belfast-Liverpool Shipping Since 1819*, 1990, pp. 44-45.
3 A lightship was established here in 1834 and was removed during World War II.

Dorothy Rimmer (active 1940)

Dorothy Rimmer was an amateur artist who worked for the Liverpool firm of T & J Brocklebank. A handful of works by her are known.[1]

1 DCF.

197 *S S Marwarri*

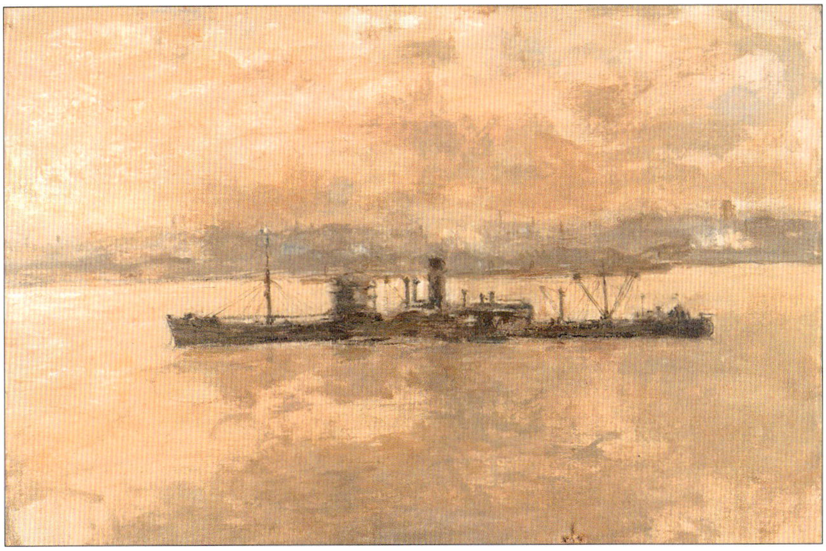

1985.497.1
Oil on canvas
50 cm x 64 cm
Signed and dated (bl) " D Rimmer 1940"
Prov: Mr & Mrs Philip E Bates, Hampshire, who presented it, 1985[1]

Vessel: 471 ft 6 in (l), 62 ft 6 in (b), 34 ft 10 in (d); 8031 gross tons

This amateur painting of *Marwarri* was painted by Miss Dorothy Rimmer who worked as a secretary for the vessel's owners T & J Brocklebank. The vessel is seen in the Mersey from the window of Miss Rimmer's office in the Cunard Building at the Pierhead; Birkenhead is in the background. She flies the blue and white Brocklebank house flag.

Marwarri was built by William Hamilton of Port Glasgow in 1935. She was named after a caste of Indian traders. She had a speed of fourteen knots and made her first voyage to Calcutta in 24 days. At the outbreak of war she was requisitioned for carrying motor transport but in October 1939 on her way back from Belfast, where she had collected stores, she was badly damaged by a magnetic mine off the Scarweather Lightship. She was beached at the Mumbles and then towed to Swansea. She was repaired and re-engined and after further service, took part in the D Day landings in Normandy.[2] She returned to normal duties with Brocklebanks and was broken up in Hong Kong in 1963.

There is an exhibition model of the vessel in the collections, accession no. L1970.246.10

1 Philip Bates was Managing Director and Deputy Chairman of Cunard.
2 Gibson I, pp. 50, 158-166, 182.

198 *The Mersey*

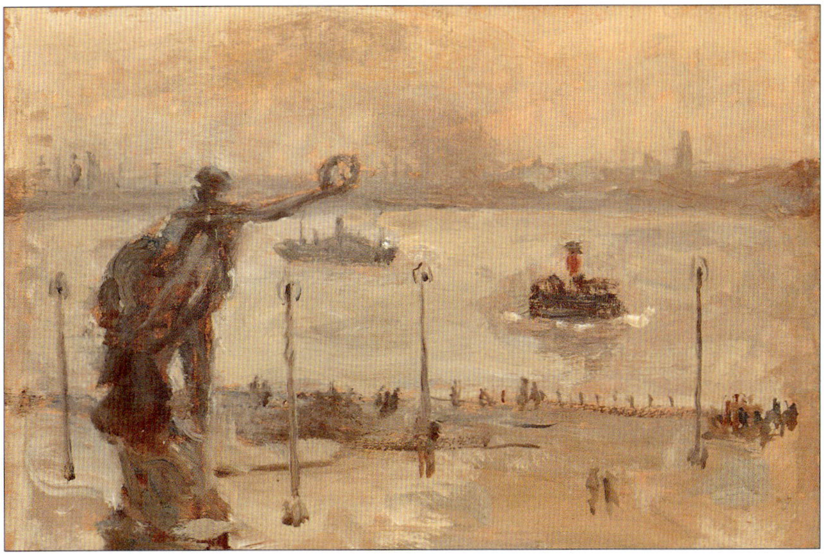

1985.497.2
Oil on canvas[1]
24 cm x 33 cm
Prov: Mr & Mrs P E Bates, Hampshire, who presented it, 1985

As with the other painting in the collection by Miss Rimmer (no. 197), this view of the Mersey was painted from her office in the Cunard Building overlooking the Pier Head, Liverpool. A statue on the building itself fills the left foreground and a Mersey ferry and probably a naval vessel can be seen in the river with the Wirral shore and Birkenhead in the background. It depicts the scene at the beginning of the war in September 1939.

1 Handwritten note on rear "The Mersey / Dorothy Rimmer / September 1939"

Harry Hudson Rodmell (1896-1984)

Rodmell was born in Hull and lived there throughout his life. He studied art locally 1911-14 and became a very successful poster artist in the inter-war years, producing work for many of the great shipping companies. After World War II he continued commercial artwork but also undertook a wider range of marine subjects in oil, acrylic and pen and ink. The Town Docks Museums, Hull, have a representative collection of his work.[1]

1For full details of Rodmell's life see Credland, pp. 134-143.

199 *Innisfallen*

1971.67.1
Oil on canvas[1]
71 cm x 107 cm
Signed (br) "HARRY / HUDSON / RODMELL" and international code flag H
Prov: Coast Lines Ltd., who presented it, 1971.
Ref: E R Reader 'Some Famous Little Ships' in *Sea Breezes*, vol. 4, 1947, p.127 (ill.)

Vessel: 321 ft (l), 45.7 ft (b), 15.2 ft (d); 3019 gross tons.

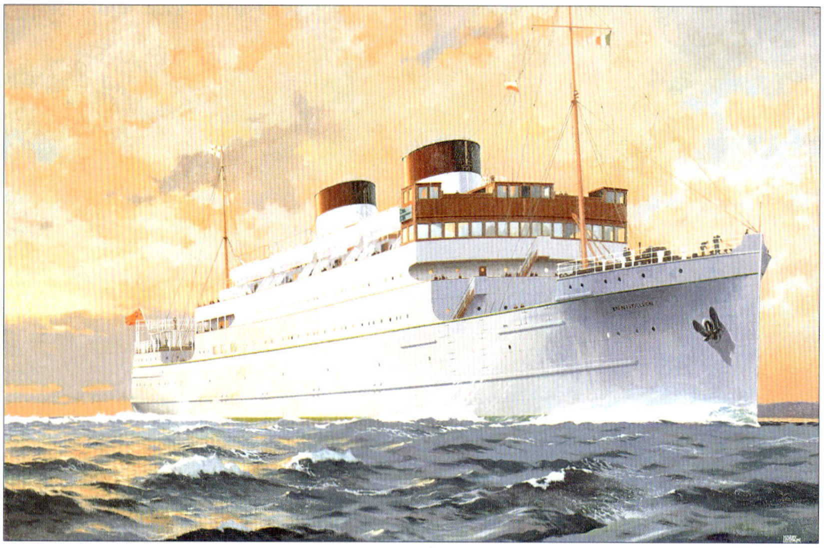

The Irish passenger steamer *Innisfallen* is shown in a close starboard quarter view at sea. She flies the Irish tricolour and a pilot flag at her foremast and the company house flag at the mast on her stern.

TSMV *Innisfallen* was built by Harland and Wolff in Belfast for the City of Cork Steam Packet Company, then part of Coast Lines, in 1930. She served on the Cork to Fishguard route but the service was transferred to Liverpool at the outbreak of war in 1939. The vessel was lost in an air raid in Liverpool in December 1940 when two crew men and two cattle men lost their lives. All 143 passengers were saved.[2] The strong bold colours and composition are a reminder that much of Rodmell's work was for shipping posters.[3] The composition is very similar to no. 200 and they may be considered a pair, probably produced for publicity purposes.

1 Stamped "WINDSOR & NEWTON / PREPARED CANVAS / ROMAN / LONDON ENGLAND".
2 McNeill 1971, pp. 116, 204.
3 Credland, pp. 134-143.

200 *Lady Munster*

Lady Munster is shown against a greyish blue sky in starboard bow view at sea. She flies the Irish tricolour at her foremast, the pilot flag above her bridge and the house flag of the British & Irish Steam Packet Company at the mast on the stern.

Lady Munster had an eventful career and also underwent several name changes.

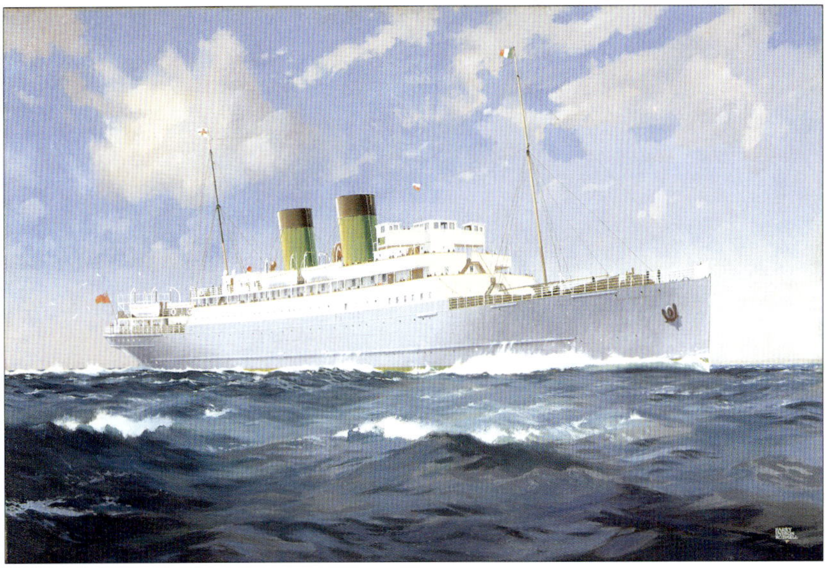

1971.67.2
Oil on canvas
56.5 cm x 71.5 cm
Signed (br) "HARRY / HUDSON / RODMELL" and international code flag H
Prov: Coast Lines Ltd., who presented it, 1971.

Vessel: 320 ft (l), 41 ft (b), 16 ft (d); 1871 gross tons.

She was built as *T S S Graphic* for the Belfast Steamship Company[1] by Harland & Wolff in 1906. She worked on the Belfast - Liverpool route from 1906 until 1929 when she was given an extensive overhaul and fitted with a second dummy funnel. Under her new name of *Lady Munster* she worked for the British & Irish Steam Packet Company from Dublin to Liverpool. In 1938 she was renamed *Louth* and returned to the Belfast - Liverpool service in 1945 as *Ulster Duke*. She was withdrawn from service in 1951 and foundered in the Bay of Biscay on her way to being broken up in Italy.[2]
The overall composition is similar to no. 199 and the two may be a pair intended for publicity use. The painting shows her after 1929 in the British & Irish livery as *Lady Munster*.

1 Later taken over by Coast Lines, McNeill 1969, p. 50.
2 McNeill 1969, pp. 60-61.

J.E. Rooney (active 1950s)

201 *City of London under tow*

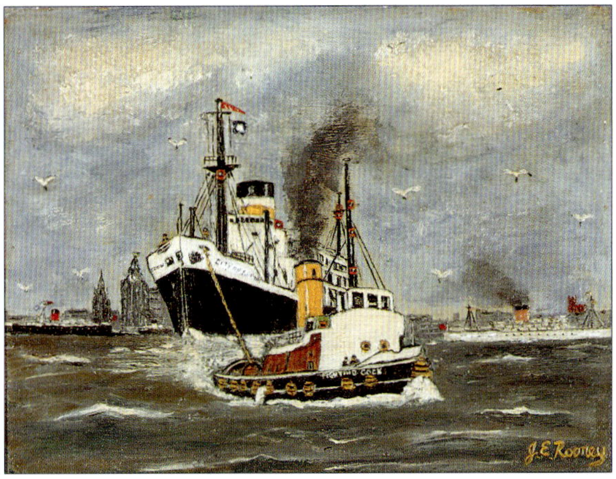

1985.48
Oil on plyboard[1]
22 cm x 29 cm
Signed "J. E. Rooney"[2]
Prov: In collections, 1984

City of London is shown in a bow view under tow by the tug *Fighting Cock* off the Liverpool waterfront. There is a starboard view of a liner in the distance to the right.
City of London was built in 1947 by Swan Hunter, Wigham and Richardson of Wallsend. She carried cargoes of oil, vegetable oil or latex for Ellerman Bucknall Steam Ship Company. She was sold to Greek owners in 1967 and scrapped the following year.[3] The tug *Fighting Cock* was built by Cammell Laird for the Liverpool Screw Towing and Lighterage Company in 1953.

1 The name on the bow has been completed in biro.
2 Signature on rear "J. E. Rooney / 1966"
3 Haws Ellerman, p.189.

202 *Laconia off the Landing Stage*

1985.49
Oil on plyboard
27 cm x 32 cm
Signed (bl) "J. E. Rooney"[1]
Prov: In collections, 1984.

Vessel: 600.7 ft (l), 73.8 ft (b), 40.7 ft (d); 19695 gross tons.

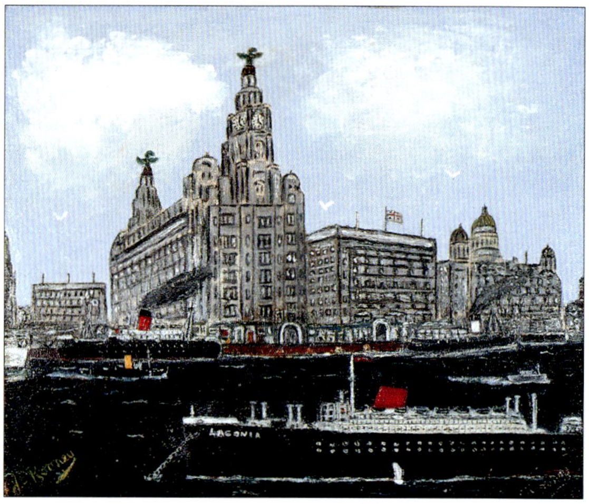

This simple painting of *S S Laconia* off the Liverpool Landing Stage. It shows the vessel at anchor with other craft, such as a tug and ferry against the background off the three famous Pierhead Buildings.

Laconia[2] was built for the Cunard Line in 1922 by Swan Hunter and Wigham Richardson of Wallsend. She sailed mainly Liverpool to New York. She was fitted out as an armed merchant cruiser in 1941 and was torpedoed and sunk by U156 in the South Atlantic in 1942.[3]

1 Also signature on rear "J. E. Rooney / Liverpool".
2 Laconia or Sparta in ancient Greece.
3 Bonsor, North, p. 164.

G Ross (active 1916)

203 *The topsail schooner Maude*

1965.197.3
Oil on canvas[1]
51 cm x 71.5 cm
Signed and dated (br) "G. ROSS / APPLEDORE N.D. / 4/2/1916"
Prov: J H Lamey Ltd, Liverpool, who presented it, 1965.

Vessel: 87 ft (l), 21.3 ft (b), 8.8 ft (d); 93 gross tons.

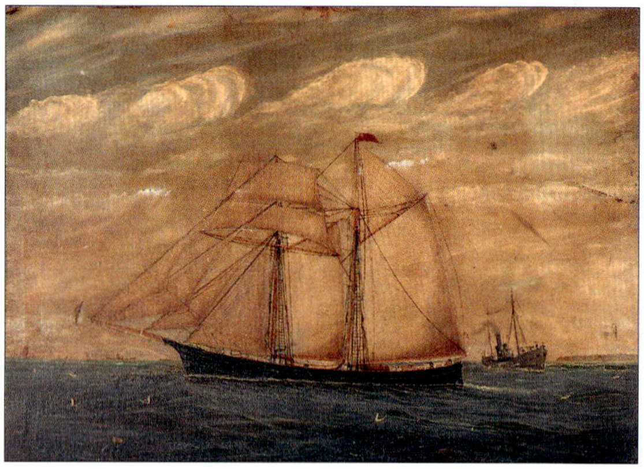

The topsail coasting schooner *Maude* is shown centrally in port profile with all her sails set. She has a rounded stern and flies a red ensign from her main mast. The wartime setting is indicated by a small armed trawler, shown in starboard quarter view off *Maude*'s stern. In the far distance to the right is an unidentified headland which is probably intended to represent the north Devon coast. There is other shipping on the horizon.

Maude was built by Ferguson & Baird of Connah's Quay, Flintshire, in 1894. Her first owner was W H Hancock of Hawarden but she changed hands before coming into the ownership of J H Lamey in 1915. Originally from a family of small-scale ship owners in Appledore, north Devon, Lamey moved to Liverpool and in 1916 began a towing company which grew into a substantial business.[2] At the time of the painting (1916) he also owned the schooner *Irish Minstrel*, represented by a Reuben Chappell watercolour in the collection (1965.197.5). *Maude* operated in the coastal trade and is listed in Lloyds Registers until 1920.[3]

The painting is rather crude and the vessel gives little impression of moving through the water.

1 The canvas is stamped "[ ] RATHBONE PLACE / LONDON"; inscribed in pencil on rear canvas "W. LAMEY." W H Lamey was the eldest son of J H Lamey.
2 See R Craig el al 'Some aspects of the business of Devon shipping in the nineteenth century' in *New Maritime History of Devon*, II, Exeter, 1994, p.107, and T Nicholson *Take The Strain*, Liverpool, 1990, pp. 128-9, 137, 228. The firm was taken over by Alexandra Towing in 1968. (Nicholson, op. cit., p.228).
3 For details of vessel see LR 1895-20.

Rowlson (active about 1840)

204 *P S Royal William*

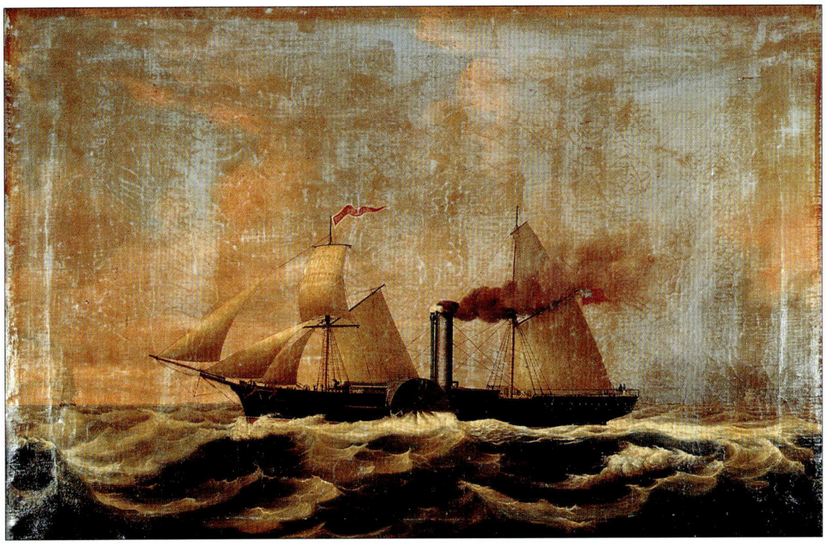

13.9.13.1
Oil on canvas
66.5 cm x 102 cm
Prov: Bradley, Pass & Co., who presented it, 1913
Exh: Liverpool 1986
Ref: Handbook 1932, p.51; Port Panorama 1986, p.18

Vessel: 175 ft (l), 27 ft (b), 17 ft 6 in (d); 276 hp engines; 617 tons

Although built to compete with the Admiralty mail steamers on the Liverpool - Kingstown service, *Royal William* in fact initiated the Liverpool - New York liner service with the paddle steamer *Liverpool* in 1838. She is depicted in a detailed port profile under power and sail in moderate seas. She flies her name pennant from the foremast. There are unidentified sailing ships in the far distance to left and right of the steamer.

The wooden paddle steamer *Royal William* was built by Thomas Wilson of Liverpool for the City of Dublin Steam Packet Company in 1837. Her 276 hp engines were supplied by Fawcett Preston of Liverpool. At this time there was frenzied competition to establish steam services across the Atlantic and the Company accepted an offer from the newly formed Transatlantic Steamship Company to charter the vessel. She made three return voyages across the Atlantic before resuming her duties across the Irish Sea. She was scrapped in 1888 after some years as a coal hulk.[1]

The assumption has always been that Rowlson is depicting *Royal William* on her first voyage across the Atlantic. However, there is some evidence that the painting may originally have been of *Royal Adelaide*, another company vessel built of iron in 1838.[2] The name on the pennant has been changed from *Royal Adelaide* to *Royal William* and the vessel depicted appears to be iron rather than wooden hulled.

There is a lithograph by Samuel Walters of *Royal William* during her first transatlantic voyage "on the 14th of July 1838 ..... from a sketch taken at the time."[3]

1 See Kennedy, pp. 73-75 and Bonsor North 1, pp. 67-8.
2 The iron hulled steamer *Royal Adelaide* was built at Paisley in 1838. See McNeill 1971, p. 188.
3 For details of lithograph see Davidson 1992, p.195; ill. in Kennedy, p.74. There is a copy in the collections, MMM.1992.39.3.

Robert Salmon (1775-c.1845)

Salmon was born in Whitehaven in 1775 but little is known of his early life. He was probably in London by the early 1790s and spent time in several ports, including Greenock, North Shields, and Southampton. He was in Liverpool in 1806-11, 1822-5 and briefly in 1828. He moved to New York in 1828 and settled in Boston where he prospered. It is thought he returned to Europe in 1842 and probably died about 1845. There is a transcript of a lost manuscript catalogue of his paintings, principally from 1828 to 1840, in Boston Public Library. His name was originally spelt "Salomon" but he changed it in 1828. There are works in the Walker Art Gallery; National Maritime Museum and most of the major collections in USA.[1]

1 Wilmerding, which includes the transcript and a checklist of works in public collections.

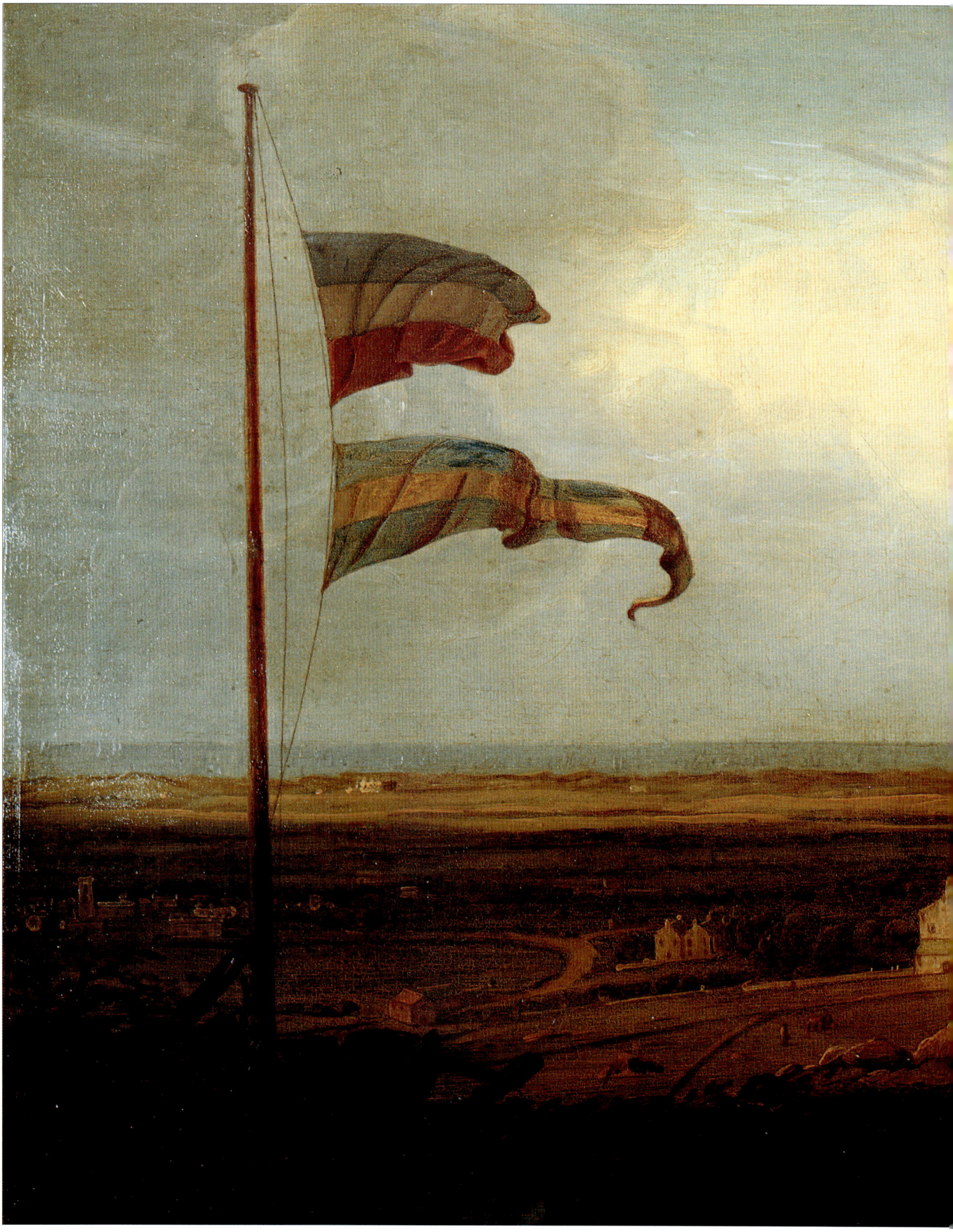

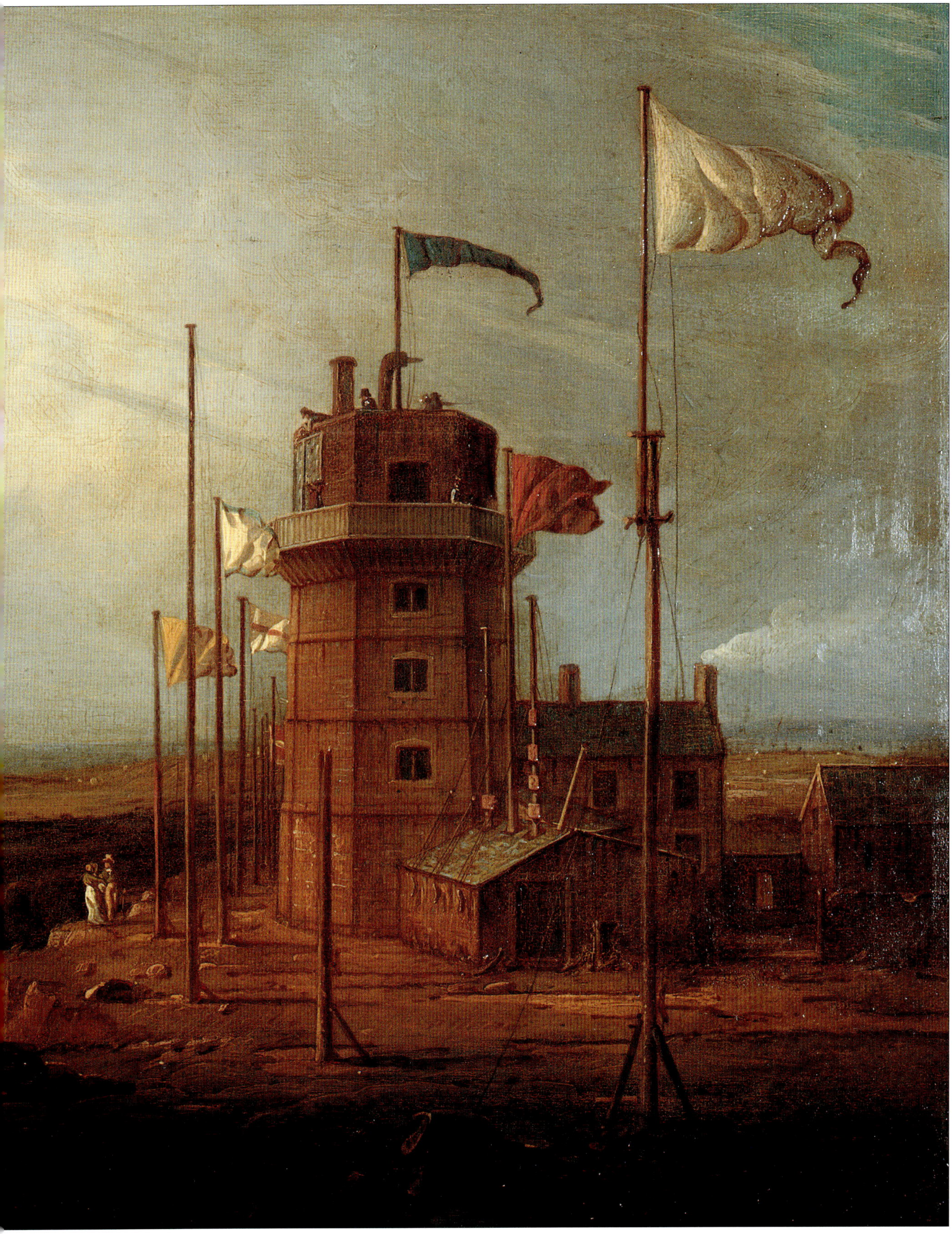

205 Bidston Old Lighthouse and Flagpoles (pages 184-185)

1961.43
Oil on panel
46 cm x 73.5 cm
Signed and dated ." R.S. 1825"'
Prov: Royden family by descent; Sir Ernest Royden; Purchased Christie's, 24 February 1961, lot no. 45.
Exhibited: Liverpool, 1907, No. 111; Liverpool, 1931, No. 407;
References: (Sir Ernest Royden) *Thomas Royden and Sons, Shipbuilders, 1818-1893*, Liverpool, 1953, illus. between pp. 39 and 40.

This is one of a number of surviving works by Robert Salmon which is not a ship portrait. It depicts the Bidston lighthouse from the south, with the northern part of the Wirral peninsula and Liverpool Bay in the background.

The Bidston lighthouse was erected by the Liverpool Corporation in 1771 as a navigational aid for vessels in the Rock Channel, at that time the principal approach to the Mersey. It also acted as a look-out and signal point. Bidston Hill, on which the lighthouse stands, was clearly visible from Liverpool and also commanded excellent views over Liverpool Bay. It provided a marvellous vantage point to spot vessels approaching the port and convey news of their arrival to their owners in the town. A flag or shape was allotted to each owner at a specific point on a specified flagpole. This was raised when one of the owner's ships was identified. By 1825 there were some 50 flagpoles stretching both north and south of the lighthouse, as can be seen in the painting.[1]

Further information to aid identification of incoming vessels was provided by the poles on the single storey outbuilding adjoining the lighthouse. Metal shapes were raised on the poles corresponding to the number of vessels in sight according to their rig. A flag was flown when the number exceeded three. From the lighthouse the poles indicated in order: snows, brigs and ships. The pole at an oblique angle on the end of the building was used to indicate a vessel in distress in the Rock Channel by means of flying a flag at half-mast.

Salmon portrays various observers on top of the lighthouse, whilst below a lady and gentleman are taking a stroll. On the distant shore, to the right of the left-hand flagpole, the castle and lighthouse at Leasowe are just visible and to the far left is the village of Bidston.

Another smaller painting by Salmon which just shows the lighthouse and flagpoles without the landscape elements is in a private collection in the United States. It adopts the same viewpoint but includes rather more activity on the ground and around the flagpoles.[2]

Flag sheets illustrating the lighthouse and its signals together with a key were published from about 1780 until the 1830s when the semaphore had established itself. The lighthouse and signals also appear on items of Liverpool pottery of the same period.[3]

1 For Bidston and signals see A C Wardle "Liverpool Merchant Signals and House-flags" in *Mariner's Mirror*, vol. 34, 1948, pp. 161-3.
2 See Davidson, 1986, p.22, ill. 23f.
3 Flag sheets and ceramics are found in a number of maritime collections. Examples of flag sheets are in LRO and of pottery in decorative art collections, NMGM (see ed. E M Brown and T A Lockett *Made in Liverpool. Liverpool Pottery and Porcelain, 1700-1850*, Liverpool, 1993, nos. 181,183).

John Scott (1802 - 1885)

Scott spent his early career at sea but came ashore permanently in 1834 and worked as a grocer in order to look after his family. He worked as an artist from the 1850s and painted mainly ship portraits with north-east coast backgrounds, particularly North Shields.

206 Tug Tiger off North Shields

The paddle steam tug *Tiger* is shown in port profile off the entrance to the Tyne with the coast of North Shields in the background.

The vessel has an open bridge between central paddle boxes and two funnels. A single mast forward of the bridge carries a furled sail and at its top a name pennant with the legend *Tiger* in white on a blue ground with red edging. The name is also repeated on the bow and paddle box. The union flag flying on a stay above the bow indicates that there is a pilot on board. He is one of the three figures on the bridge. Immediately astern is a brig in starboard view under full sail, except her main course. She flies an illegible name pennant and the blue peter. There is a small rowing boat

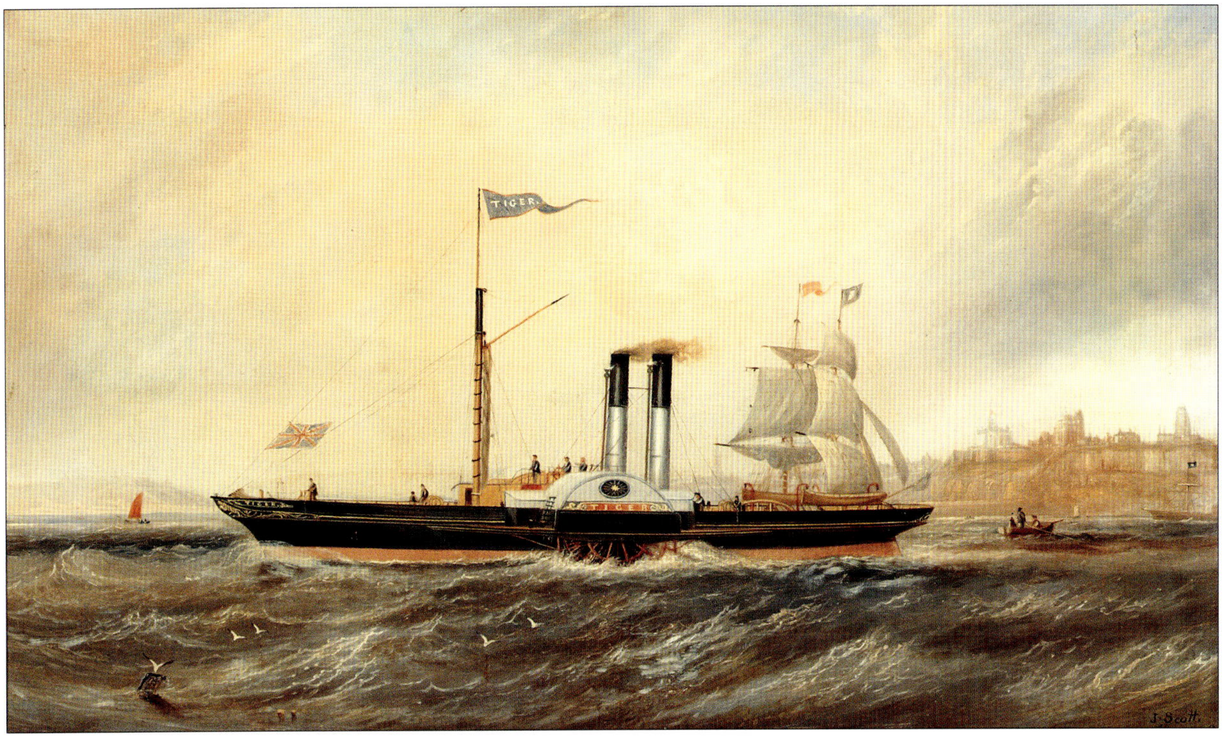

astern and another small boat with an orange sail to the left. Another paddle steamer flying a blue peter is visible in outline to the far right.

The scene is placed off the mouth of the River Tyne. The town of North Shields is visible immediately behind the funnels and to the far right are the cliffs with the famous landmarks of Tynemouth castle, priory, church and lighthouse. To the left of the canvas is the southern shore and the outskirts of South Shields.

Tiger was built at Billington Quay, Northumberland, in 1863 for William and Thomas Jolliffe, steam tug owners of Liverpool.[2] In fact, they sold the vessel to foreign ownership within a few months and ordered another vessel of similar dimensions which they also called *Tiger*. This was delivered in 1864.[3]

MMM.1997.3
Oil on canvas[1]
51 cm x 84 cm
Signed and dated (br) 'J. Scott / 1863'
Prov: W & T Jolliffe & Co., Alexandra Towing Company, H B Bicket, who presented it, May 1997.
Exh: Liverpool, 1987b

Vessels: 120.6 ft (l), 20.5 ft (b), 10.4 ft (d); 157 gross tons

1 relined; label on rear for J. Davey of Liverpool
2 CR, no. 104, 27 March 1863.
3 CR, no. 264, 11 June 1864. Converted into a coal hulk in 1904.

Max Sinclair (active about 1870 - about 1890)

Although his paintings appear regularly in the sale room, nothing is known about Sinclair's life. As well as these Mersey views, he also painted atmospheric views of shipping particularly off English east coast ports and landscape views of North Wales.

207 *In The Mersey* (pages-188-189)

This is one of the most evocative scene of the River Mersey off the Liverpool waterfront showing it bustling with a variety of shipping, typical of its period.

The main vessel featured is the recently launched Inman liner *City of New York* which is shown in port profile just beginning to get underway on her voyage across the Atlantic. In the foreground is a starboard quarter view of the Birkenhead ferry *Lancashire* with a few passengers on board. To the left of the liner is the iron barque *Lord Clyde* in port bow view raising her anchor with another unidentified barque with a green hull anchored alongside but partly hidden. In the foreground of these two vessels is a steam tug, *Queen Bess*, and in the distance a starboard view of the paddle steamer *Wellington* and a Cunard liner, only identifiable by her funnel colours. To the right a group of three Mersey flats and a gig boat are making their way up river.

1967.62
Oil on canvas[1]
114.5 cm x 183 cm
Signed and dated (br) "Max Sinclair / 1889"
Inscribed, verso, "Copyright Reserved / Apr. 20th 1889 / IN THE MERSEY / Inman Liner "City of New York" ready to leave"[2]
Prov: Boydell Galleries, Liverpool, from whom purchased, 1967
Exh: Liverpool, 1974

Vessel: *City of New York* 527.6 ft (l), 63.2 ft (b), ;10499 gross tons

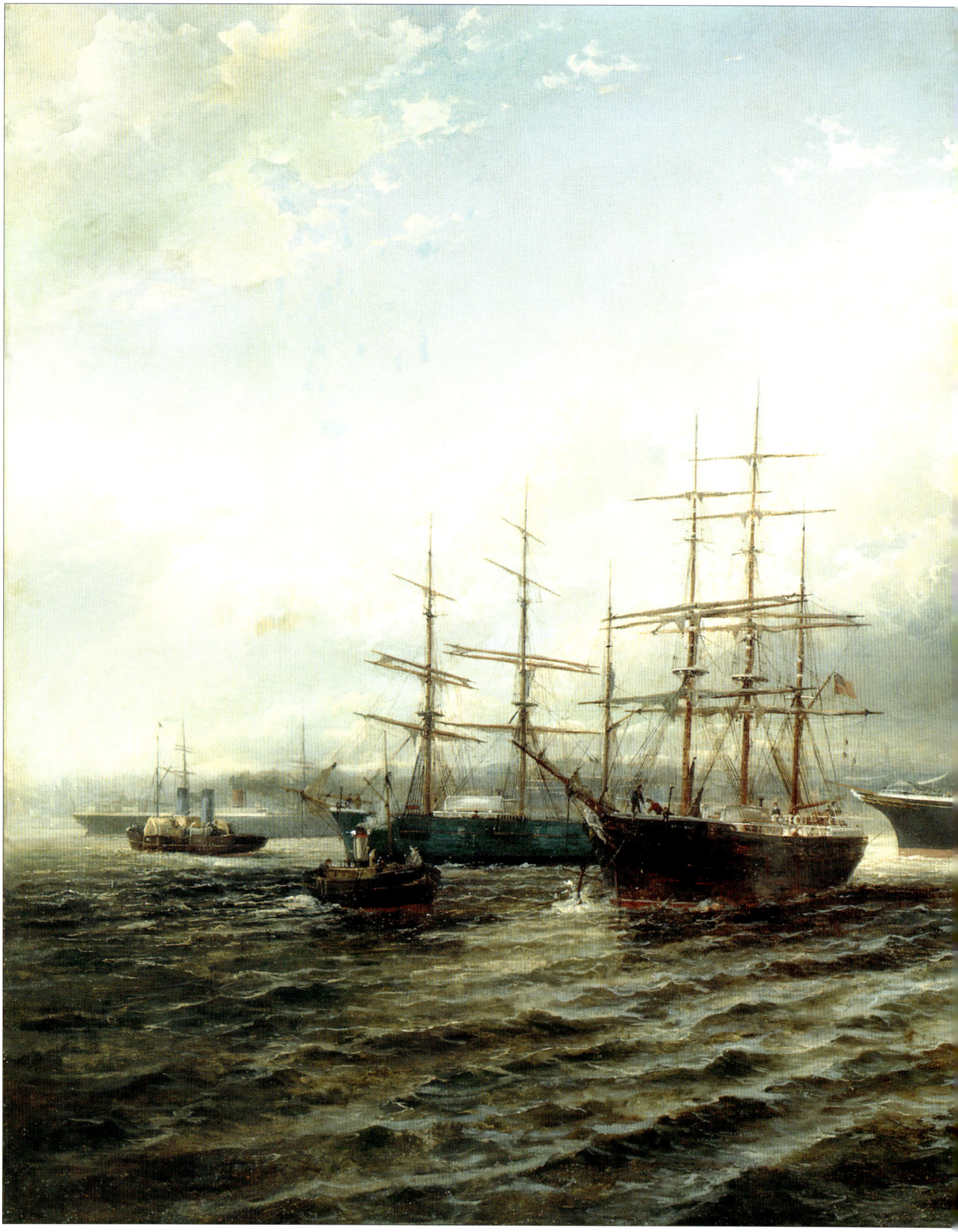

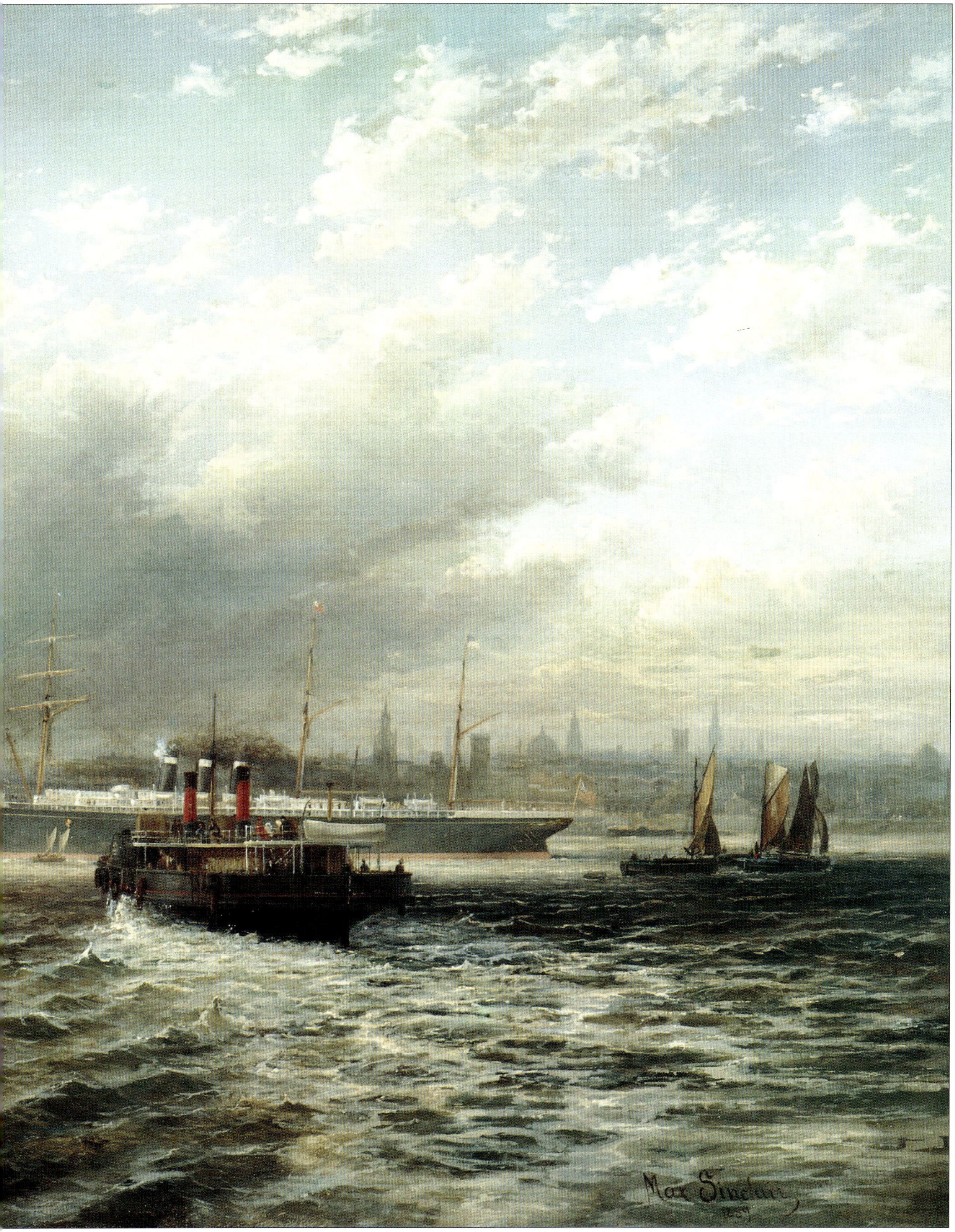
Max Sinclair

The three funnelled *City of New York* was built by J & G Thomson of Clydebank in 1888 for Inman. She was for a time the largest steamship afloat and was the first of the express transatlantic steamer to be fitted with twin screw propellers. Inman had been in financial difficulties for some time and in 1893 became the American Line under the United States flag. *City of New York* was renamed *New York* remaining on transatlantic voyages to Southampton and Liverpool. She was used for trooping during the first world war and was scrapped in Genoa in 1923.[3]

Interestingly, *City of New York* appears to fly the original Inman Line flag (red ground with black diamond on white in top left hand corner) on her main mast rather than the post-1886 version. This may indicate that the artist used sketches from before 1889 to compose the picture, particularly as the paddle steamer *Wellington* was only registered in Liverpool between 1884 and 1887.

The iron paddle steamer *Lancashire* was built by C J Mare and Co., of Northfleet, in 1865 and was employed on the Liverpool-Woodside route until 1891.[4]

The iron barque *Lord Clyde* was built by Alexander Stephens & Co. of Glasgow in 1875 for L Tulloch of Swansea.[5]

Although there was more than one paddle steamer named *Wellington*, this is probably the one built in Gravesend in 1876 and owned by Sylvester Mattison of Liverpool from 1884 until sold to owners in Jersey in September 1887.[6] The funnel colours of *Queen Bess* shows that she belongs to the Hercules Steam Tug Company, one of the smaller tug owners operating on the Mersey.

In the background the familiar Liverpool waterfront is visible, particularly the stretch from the Landing Stage and George's Dock along to the Custom House, with the towers and domes of St Nicholas, Tower Buildings, the Town Hall and Municipal Buildings prominent on the skyline. The northern docks on the left hand side are less immediately visible.

1 Canvas stamped "WINDSOR & NEWTON".
2 In fact, *City of New York* and *Lord Clyde* had both sailed on 17 April, LL 18 April 1889.
3 Bonsor North, p.244.
4 Duckworth and Langmuir, p.113.
5 LR 1889.
6 LCR, no. 38, vol 95, 18 March 1884.

208 *In The Roads*[1]

1955.99.1.2.3A
Oil on canvas[2]
30 cm x 41 cm
Signed (bl) "M. Sinclair 85"
Prov: In collections, 1955

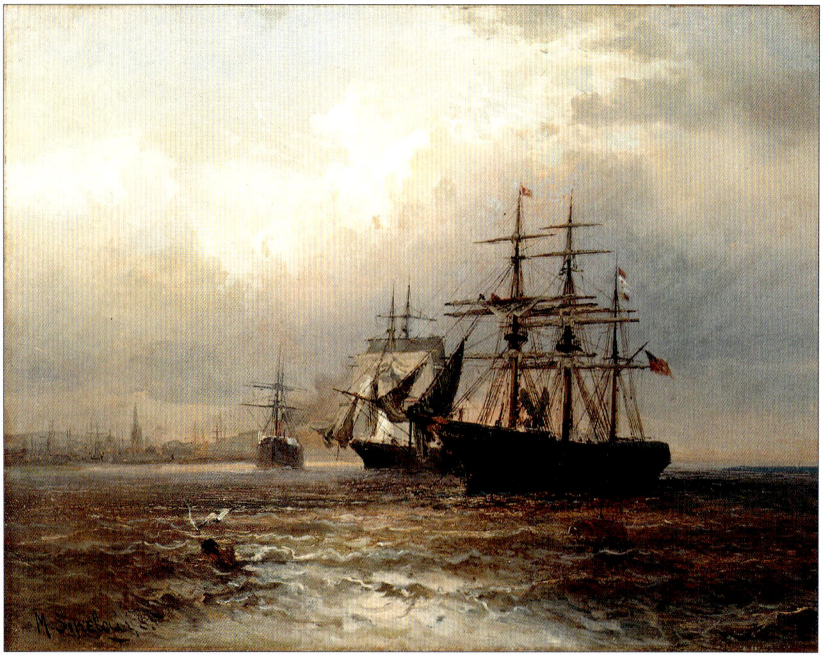

This atmospheric canvas forms a pair with no. 209 *Outside The Bar*. It shows a typical off shore scene with a ship rigged vessel anchored in port profile with all sails furled. Some of the crew are on the yards to let out the fore course. Although the vessel flies a flag code and house flag these are not identifiable and are probably fictitious.[3] A second vessel is passing on the starboard side and is partially hidden

behind the first. In the distance a brig is approaching bow on.
The tower and spire of St Nicholas church is the only identifiable landmark on the Liverpool waterfront in the far distance but an array of masts in the docks and other buildings are indicated.

1 Rear canvas "In The Roads".
2 Relined, 1990.
3 The letter C is wrongly repeated as the second and third flags in the hoist.

209 Outside The Bar[1]

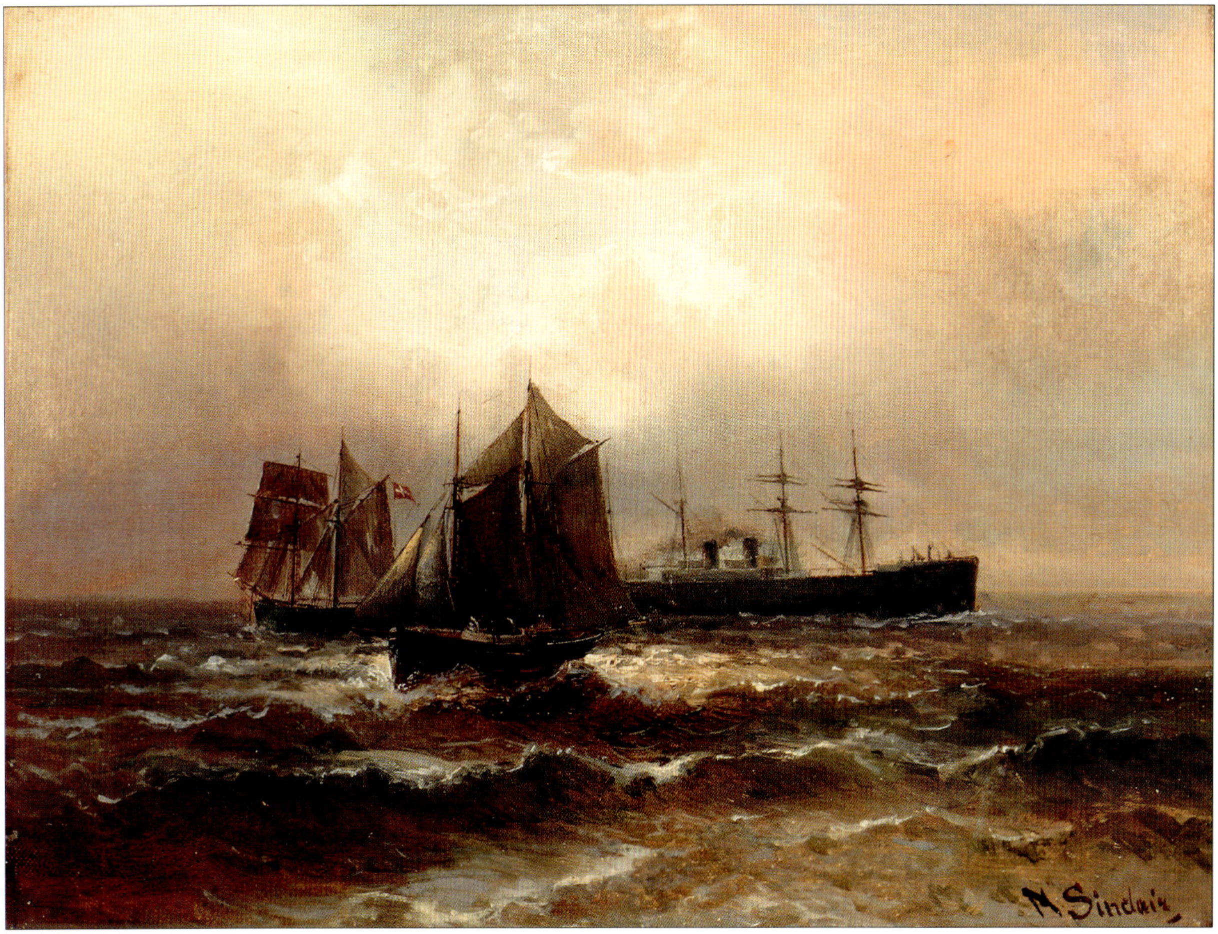

Like its pair, no. 208, *In The Roads*, Sinclair shows a small number of vessels in an atmospheric grouping beyond the bar at the entrance to the Mersey. The main vessel portrayed is a 4 masted steamer with two funnels in starboard profile. This may be intended to be a White Star liner judging by the funnel colours. To her stern is a topsail schooner, heading away in a half stern view. She flies the Danish national flag. In the foreground, a small schooner rigged vessel is coming towards the observer.

1955.99.1.2.3B
Oil on canvas[2]
30 cm x 41 cm
Signed (br) "M. Sinclair"
Prov: In collections, 1955

1 Rear canvas "Outside the Bar".
2 Relined, 1990.

Richard B Spencer (active 1850-1880)

Spencer was a London-based artist who painted standard ship portraits frequently showing vessels under full sail. He generally used south coast backgrounds, in particular Dover with its readily recognisable cliffs and castle. There are more than a dozen works in the National Maritime Museum.[1]

1 Brook-Hart, p.20; Concise NMM.

210 Barque off Dover

This unknown barque is shown in starboard profile reducing sail passing Dover on her way up the Channel. The viewpoint provides a good view of the deck and various members of the crew can be seen adjusting the sails. Although she flies a red ensign at the stern and a house flag of a white crosslet on a red ground, this is

1955.244
Oil on canvas
51cm x 76.5cm
Prov: Unknow; in collections, 1955

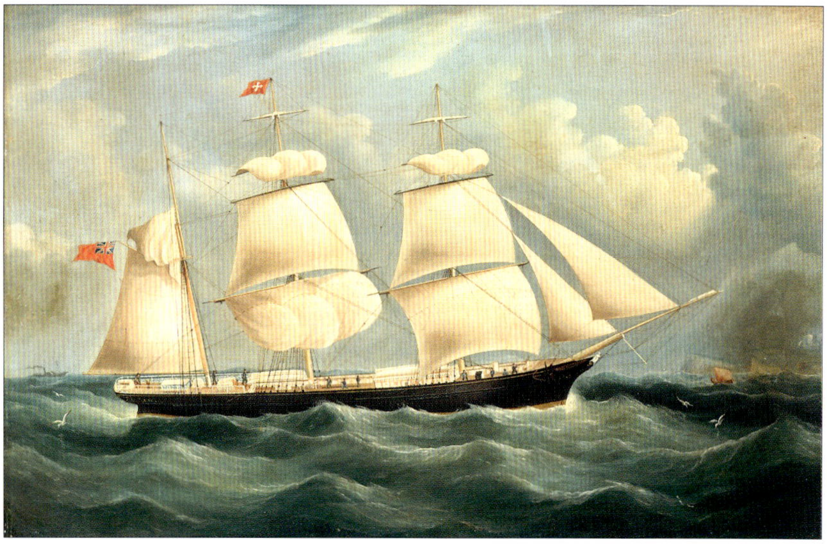

insufficient to provide an identification. She appears to be an iron vessel of the 1850s or 1860s. Unusually for this date there are no reefing points on the topsails and there are chains and what appears to be iron fittings at the ends of the spars. This is compatible with Colling & Pinkey's self-reefing and furling system, first patented in 1862.[1] Astern in starboard profile is a paddle steamer and to the right a small lug rigged fishing boat.

The background is one frequently used by Spencer and shows the outline of the castle and cliffs at the entrance to Dover harbour.

Although attributed to Joseph Heard on entering the collection, it is stylistically more consistent with the work of R B Spencer.

1 For details of its operation see Underhill, pp. 130-3, 162.

Anthony Carey Stannus (active 1862 - 1903)

A genre, landscape and marine painter he exhibited in London 1862-1903.

211 A Thames Bawley

1955.181
Oil on canvas[1]
76.5 cm x 122 cm
Prov: Unknown, in collection, 1955.

This unconserved canvas is in poor condition and is very dark and dirty. A Thames fishing smack or bawley is shown from the starboard stern wrestling against poor conditions. Two men are on board and a boiler and trawl are visible. In the left foreground are two further men in a small rowing boat. There is other shipping in the background.

The name of the bawley can be partially discerned on the stern as "PETE[ ]" or PETR[ ]" and her home port is given as "LEIGH". On her bow her registration number appears to be "MN64" (Maldon, Essex) and this is repeated on the sail.

The bawley was a small fishing vessel restricted to the Thames estuary. They were mostly used for oyster dredging though craft from Leigh chiefly brought in shrimps. They were cutter rigged with a short mast and a main sail set without a boom.

1 Label on stretcher "G B RAIM / CARVER AND GILDER / Looking Glass and Picture Frame Manufacturer / 62 MARYLEBONE LANE LONDON W"

P C Stevens (active mid-twentieth century)

212 Waterfront Scene

This unidentified scene shows a passenger liner leaving port. The liner, which is shown in a port quarter profile, has buff funnels with black tops but no other identifying marks. There are two tugs in the far distance with red funnels and black tops. A small boat in the centre middle ground has the name *Imro.* There are a number of distinctive buildings in the background including a tall tower topped by a dome and two over low domed shaped buildings which are reminiscent of the Eastern Mediterranean.

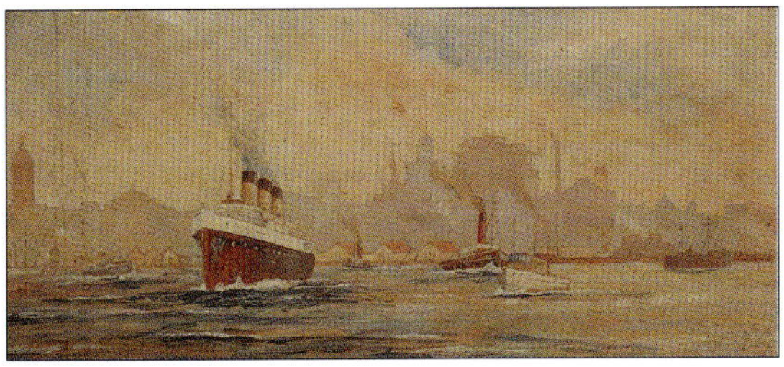

1955.238
Oil on canvas
25.5 cm x 55 cm
Signed (br) "P. C. Stevens"
Prov: Unknown, in collections, 1955.

Walter Thomas (1894-1971)

Thomas worked as an artist-designer of posters and other liner ephemera for the Liverpool Printing Company from about 1927. He produced nearly all the Blue Funnel's artwork and posters for Cunard and other liner firms survive.[1]

1 See Davidson, 1986, p.138.

213 Perseus off Gibraltar

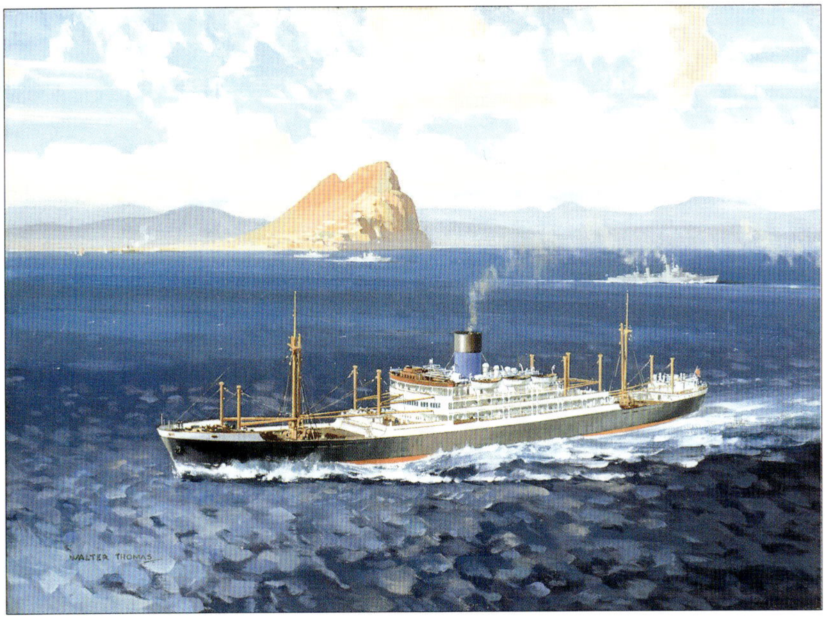

MMM1995.95.5
Oil on canvas
52.5 cm x 71.5 cm
Signed (bl) "WALTER THOMAS."
Prov: P H Holt Charitable Trust, from whom purchased, 1995

Walter Thomas chooses an aerial perspective to depict *Perseus* from her port side in the straits of Gibraltar. There are various naval vessels in the background with the dominant feature of the Rock in the centre left of the picture.

Perseus was one of five 18 knot 10,000 ton vessels built in 1949-51 as part of Holts' post-war rebuilding of the Blue Funnel fleet. They were intended to sustain a monthly cargo liner service from Birkenhead to Singapore, calling at Rotterdam. *Perseus*[1] was built by Vickers Armstrong & Co. at Newcastle and undertook her maiden voyage in April 1950. After an undramatic career, she was sent for scrapping at Kaohsiung in 1973.[2]

A colour print of the painting was produced by the company.

1 Greek mythological hero, son of Zeus.
2 For career see Haws Blue Funnel, p.120; for general history of class see Falkus 1990, pp. 262-4, 301-2.

214 Voltaire (page 194)

This very evocative canvas was the original artwork from which a poster and other publicity material were reproduced. It shows *T S S Voltaire* in a starboard bow view at anchor off Madeira. The vessel is painted in white cruising colours and the funnel is in the distinctive Lamport and Holt livery. One of the company's tenders is just leaving the vessel with a group of passengers and there are other small boats

1964.198
Oil on canvas
76 cm x 60 cm
Signed (bl) "WALTER / THOMAS"
Prov: E Simmons, Liverpool, who presented it, 1964
Exh: Liverpool 1986
Ref: Port Panorama, 1986, p.22 (ill, p.23)

Vessel: 510.5 ft (l), 64.3 ft (b), 39.3 ft (d); 13,248 gross tons

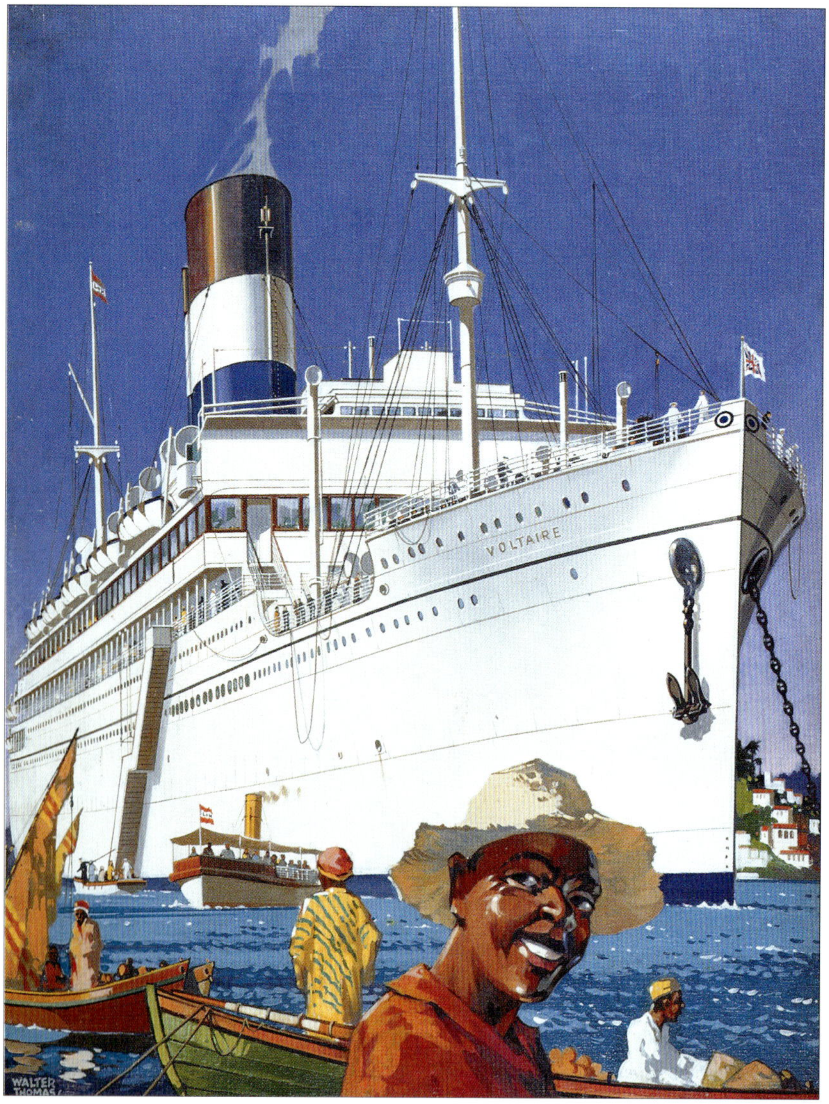

alongside and in the foreground. A prominent feature is the figure of the Black man in a hat in the foreground.

Voltaire[1] was built in Belfast in 1923 by Workman Clark & Co. for the Liverpool firm of Lamport & Holt, managing owners of the Liverpool, Brazil and River Plate Steam Navigation Company. She was initially employed on the company's fortnightly service to New York but was laid up in 1928 as a result of the effects of the world economic situation. Lamport & Holt, in fact, went into receivership in 1930 and many vessels in the fleet were sold. Under a reconstituted company, *Voltaire* was brought back into service, cruising in the Mediterranean, the Atlantic Islands, the Caribbean and the Baltic. At the outbreak of war she was requisitioned by the Royal Navy and refitted as an Armed Merchant Cruiser. She was sunk on convoy duties in April 1941.[2]

The painting dates from the period of *Voltaire*'s cruising in the 1930s. A poster was produced from this painting and it was also used for other publicity and souvenir material, including a jigsaw puzzle.

1 Francois Marie Arouet de Voltaire, French writer, 1694-1778.
2 Heaton, pp. 54-60, 130.

Alfred William Vincent Trant (1867-1934)

A career sailor for more than 50 years, Trant was also an amateur artist. He spent many years with the Frederick Leyland Line on the Liverpool to Boston run and was torpedoed in the Company's *S S Devonian* in 1917. For the rest of the war he was a liaison officer between the Royal and Merchant Navies. He spent the last years of his career with the Red Star Line, retiring in 1932.[1] The only other known painting by Trant is in The British Mercantile Marine Memorial Collection.

1 Notes in SAS 23A/11/6, MAL.

215 S S Drumpark

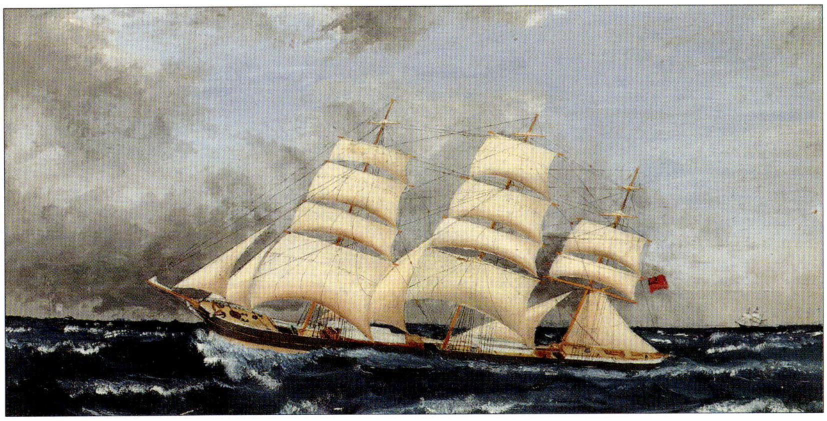

MMM1990.161
Oil on artist's board[1]
23 cm x 46.5 cm
inscribed on reverse "S S Drumpark Painted by Capt. A. W. V. Trant who sailed in this ship on his first voyage as a ship's boy, to Australia from Salthouse Dock, Liverpool in 1883".[2]
Prov: Captain A W V Trant by descent to son; bequeathed to neighbour, Mr I Williams, from whom purchased, 1990.

Vessel: 243.6 ft (l), 37.9 ft (b), 22.6 ft (d); 1551 gross tons.

This piece of sailor's art shows the ship rigged *Drumpark* in port profile under full sail. The iron-hulled *Drumpark* was built in Liverpool in 1877 by W H Potter & Sons for James Gillison & Joseph Chadwick, founders of the "Drum" Line of generally medium sized sailing ships. *Drumpark* was the second in the small fleet and was one of only two ship rigged vessels. She was sold to Genoese owners in 1897 and was broken up in 1918.[3]

Trant's artistic activities are not documented but one other work is known, a rather more accomplished oil of *City of Sparta* on a properly stretched canvas signed with the initials "AWVT" in an arc and dated 1908.[4]

Trant left *Drumpark* in 1886 as third mate. The NMGM collections also include medals awarded to Trant for service during World War I and two life saving certificates awarded in 1910 and 1913.[5]

1The frame bears a torn label which partly reads "[Jackson] 3 Slater Street, Bold Street, Liverpool".
2 In pencil.
3 Lubbock Windjammers, pp. 256-7, 473; LCR vol. 93, no. 176, 25 August 1877; LCR TB9, p.282.
4 Details in letter in DCF, 26 March 1993.
5 MAL Accession No. 1976.71 (DX/711).

Charles E Turner (1883-1965)

Principally known as a designer of posters and other shipping company artwork, Turner was also an illustrator for the *Illustrated London News*. He produced many illustrations of naval encounters during World War II.[1]

1 Archibald, p. 188.

216 S S Saxonia (page 196)

This unusual aerial view of *Saxonia* is a reminder that the majority of Turner's output was produced as marketing material for Cunard and other shipping companies and that bold, imaginative images were needed to catch the public's eye. *Saxonia* is seen from an imagined vantage point above her port side looking towards the bow with the funnel and lifeboats prominently displayed. Passengers are shown in typical pursuits on deck – promenading, talking in small groups and sitting in deck chairs. The vessel is shown in the St Lawrence River with the Quebec Bridge in the background.

Saxonia was built for Cunard by John Brown & Co. of Glasgow in 1954. She was one of four vessels which provided the Canadian service to Quebec and Montreal.

1987.313
Oil on canvas[1]
81 cm x 71.5 cm
Signed (bl) "C. E. TURNER"
Prov: Ernest Wardle & Co.; R Bramley, Southwell, from whom purchased, 1987.[2]

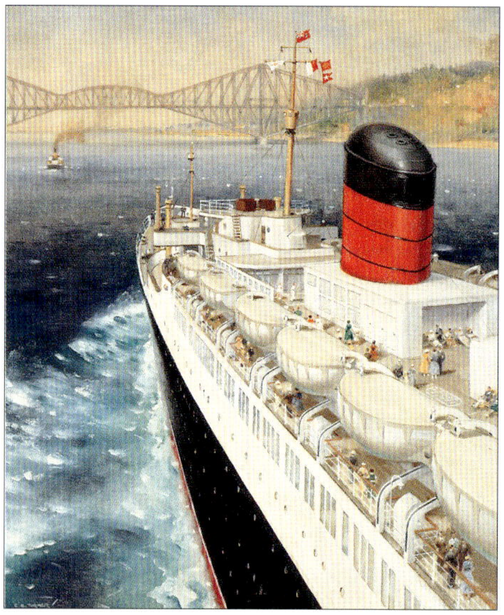

Saxonia mainly sailed from Southampton or London until 1963 when she was refitted and renamed *Carmania*. She subsequently undertook cruises in the Mediterranean and Caribbean and went aground in the Bahamas in 1969. Although refloated and repaired, she was laid up in 1971 and sold to Russian owners as *Leonid Sobinov* in 1973.[3]

This paining almost certainly follows an advertising image for the vessel, though associated material based specifically on this work has not been located. Given that much artwork was required for advanced publicity, the painting was probably completed before the vessel was launched in 1954.

1 Canvas stamped on rear "'KENTON' / prepared by / WINDSOR & NEWTON / LONDON ENGLAND".
2 Ernest Wardle produced advertising material for Cunard. This painting was presented to the donor on his retirement from the company.
3 Haws Cunard, pp.92-3

Unknown

217 Liverpool in 1680

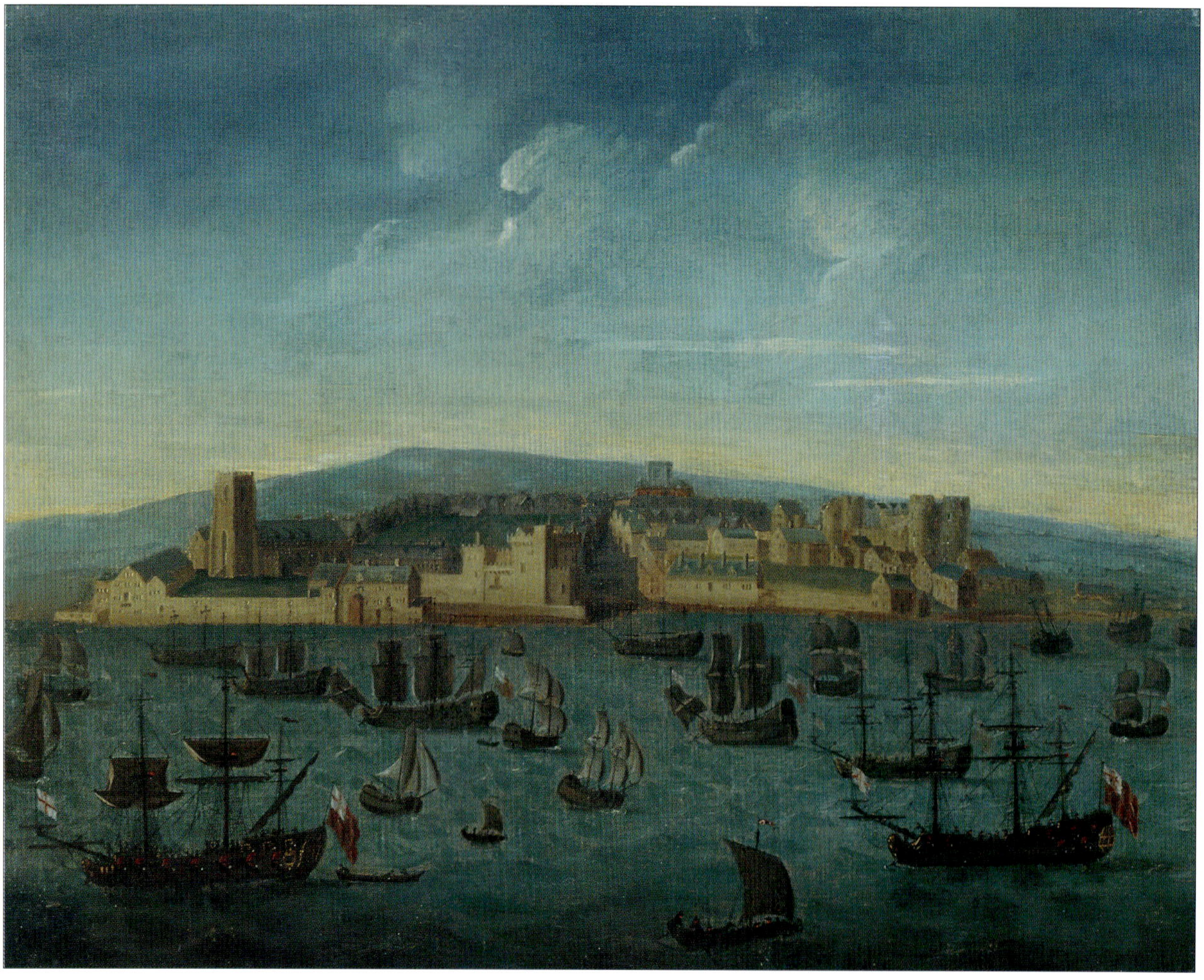

This is almost certainly the earliest known painting of Liverpool and shows a significant part of the waterfront and town about 1680 with a large number of vessels in the river. There is no reason to think that this is not an authentic contemporary representation and the physical condition of the painting is consistent with a late seventeenth century date.[2]

The painting has a long history.[3] It was presented to the Town Council in 1818 by Ralph Peters III (1775-1838) and was certainly in his father's possession in 1766 when John Eyes produced an engraving "*The West Prospect of the Town of Liverpool, as it appeared about the year 1680. Taken from a painting in the possession of Ralph Peters Esqr.*" Family history maintains that it originally belonged to Ralph Peters I (1675-1742). Because of this provenance, the painting is frequently referred to as the `Peters painting'.

The painting shows the main part of the town between St Nicholas Chapel in the north and the area around the entrance to the Pool to the south. A number of key features and buildings are visible.[4] Starting at the left is St Nicholas Chapel, (from 1699 the parish church) with the former Chapel of St Mary del Key, at this time a school, to its left nearer the river; the Earl of Derby's former town house, the stone castellated building known as the Tower and built before 1540, is prominent on the quayside. Behind these buildings is the Common Garden bounded by Chapel Street, High Street and Water Street. Immediately to the right of the Tower is Water Street which leads up into the town and slightly to the right and on the horizon is the tower of the Town Hall, completed by 1675.

On the south side of Water Street along the waterfront is the Custom House (identifiable by its four chimneys and three gables) and its adjoining yard. This was a new building, leased to Customs from 1680. At the far end of the Customs Yard is Moor Street (laid out 1665) and James Street (laid out about 1676), with the Castle behind. Built about 1235, the castle was various repaired and extended throughout the Middle Ages but by this stage had probably fallen into disrepair.

A report that the painting was once dated 1680[5] cannot now be substantiated but the buildings shown do suggest a date of about this period. The painting cannot date to before about 1675/6 when James Street was laid out and the Town Hall newly built. The Castle was referred to as the "remaining ruins" in 1704-5 and had presumably been deteriorating for some years rather than as a result of a sudden change. Liverpool was also expanding rapidly in the last years of the seventeenth century and an earlier date is most likely.

The artist also shows a wealth of shipping in the river. This includes vessels for deep sea trading as well as coastal and local river craft. Of the larger vessels, there is a group of three ships to the left off St Nicholas and the Tower which are beginning to make sail and head down river. Another ship in the left foreground is also shown raising sail. To the right hand side off the Custom House are a further three ships, all as yet with their sails furled. Across the middle distance, in the river between the Tower and the Castle, are five brigs and a barque, all with their sails set. One of these brigs, off the Custom House, has a very high poop deck and may be a Dutch vessel. There are two further vessels beached to the right of the Castle.

Amongst the smaller craft there is a coastal vessel, astern of the ship in the left foreground, which may be a hoy or possibly a Mersey flat. If the latter, this would be the earliest representation of a flat in the Mersey. There are two small single masted gig or ferry boats off the Tower and in the right centre foreground is a larger ferry boat. This is almost identical to the boat identified as "The Rock house Ferry Boat" in the key which accompanies *The South West Prospect of Liverpool* by Samuel & Nathaniel Buck of 1728.

1931.211.2
Oil on canvas[1]
59.5 cm x 74 cm
Prov: Ralph Peters (1675-1742), Town Clerk of Liverpool 1710-42; Ralph Peters (1728-1807); Ralph Peters (1775-1838) who presented it to the Town Council, 1818; transferred to the Museum, 1931.
Exh: Town Hall, Liverpool, various periods nineteenth century; Liverpool, 1907, no. 101; Wembley, 1924, 'Liverpool about 1670'; probably Crosby, 1951, no. 104 'Peter's "View of Liverpool"'.
Ref: [J Wallace] A General and Descriptive History of Liverpool, 1795; Troughton, T. Troughton *The History of Liverpool, 1810* (ill) 1810; E W Cox 'Liverpool Castle' in *THSLC*, vol. 6, new series, 1890, pp. 214-5; Touzeau, 1910; R Stewart-Brown 'An Account of the Oil Painting "Liverpool in 1680" with notes on the Peters family of Platbridge and Liverpool' in *THSLC*, vol. 60, 1909, pp. 35-71.

The vessels depicted on this canvas appear to be authentically reproduced and in keeping with a late seventeenth century date. For instance, the ship rigged vessels are consistent with the drawings in the Journal of Bryan Blundell, in particular *Mulberry* of 1696.[6]

Whilst the depiction of such a large number of vessels in the river may relate to artistic composition, the inclusion of so many ship and brig rigged vessels may indicate a significant event, such as a fleet about to depart for North America, the principal long-distance destination at this period.

The identification of the artist has not been determined, though it has previously been thought to be the work of a Dutch painter.[7]

This painting, probably through the medium of the Eyes engraving of 1766, has been the inspiration for many prints, drawings and watercolours over more than two centuries.[8] There is also an obviously close relationship with no. 29, which is discussed in detail.

1 Relined and restored, 1908; restored 1962.
2 Report by NMGM Conservation, November 1995. The report concludes that despite overpaint and considerable wear from over zealous cleaning, the major details appear to be original and there is nothing to suggest that the painting may not date from the late seventeenth century.
3 See R Stewart-Brown, op. cit.
4 See ibid.; Nicholson.
5 R Stewart-Brown, op. cit., p.41.
6 Journal of Bryan Blundell, Lancashire Record Office (DDBb).
7. R Stewart-Brown, op. cit.
8 The main items are listed in *Catalogue of Liverpool Prints and Documents in Liverpool Public Library*, Liverpool, 1907, p.31; additional items listed R Stewart-Brown, op. cit., Appendix A, p.69.

E D Walker

Ted Walker is a contemporary Merseyside artist who specialising in ship paintings and marine subjects.

218 Lively Lady rounding the Horn

1984.508
Oil on canvas
51.5 cm x 76 cm
Signed (br) "E. D. WALKER"
Prov: Purchased from the artist, 1984

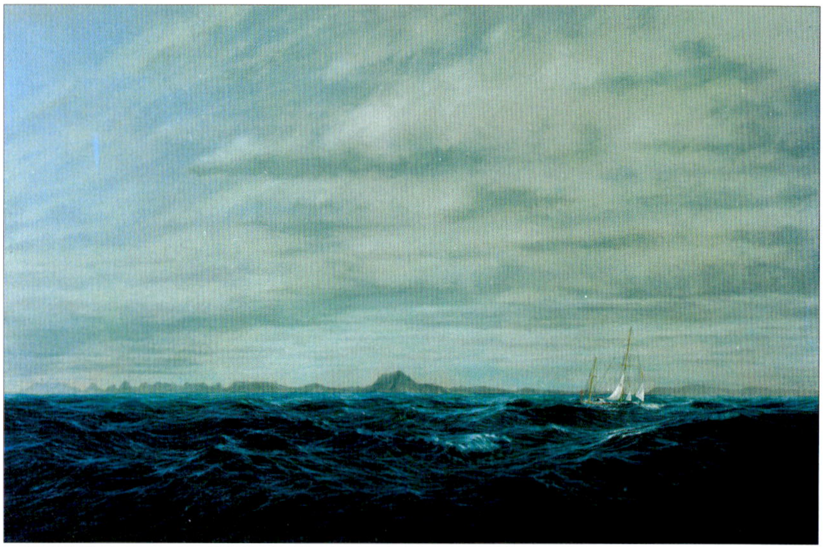

Lively Lady was the yacht in which Sir Alec Rose (1908-1991) made his single handed circumnavigation of the world in 1967-8. She is shown running before the wind under a minimum of sail with the rocky coast of Cape Horn in the background. The battle with the forces of nature is emphasised by the small scale of the yacht against the expanse of hostile water and rocks.

Alec Rose bought *Lively Lady* in 1963. She had been built by S J P Cambridge in Calcutta in 1948 to a modified design of Frederick Shepherd. Rose sailed her in the 1964 single-handed transatlantic race and came fourth. He added a mizzen mast for the circumnavigation which he completed in 318 days.[1] She was acquired by the Maritime Trust in 1975 and was on display at the Merseyside Maritime Museum 1982-86. She has been on display at Portsmouth since 1986 and was transferred to Portsmouth City Council in 1995.[2]

1 See Alec Rose *My Lively Lady*, London, 1968.
2 *The Maritime Trust Annual Report and Accounts for 1995.*

Joseph Walter (1783-1856)

Walter was born in Bristol and lived and worked there all his life. On his death he was described as "marine portrait painter" and although much of his work was of ship portraits in and around Bristol, he also painted some contemporary and historical marine events. There are paintings in Bristol City Art Gallery and the National Maritime Museum.[1]

1 Archibald, p.196.

219 *S S Great Britain*

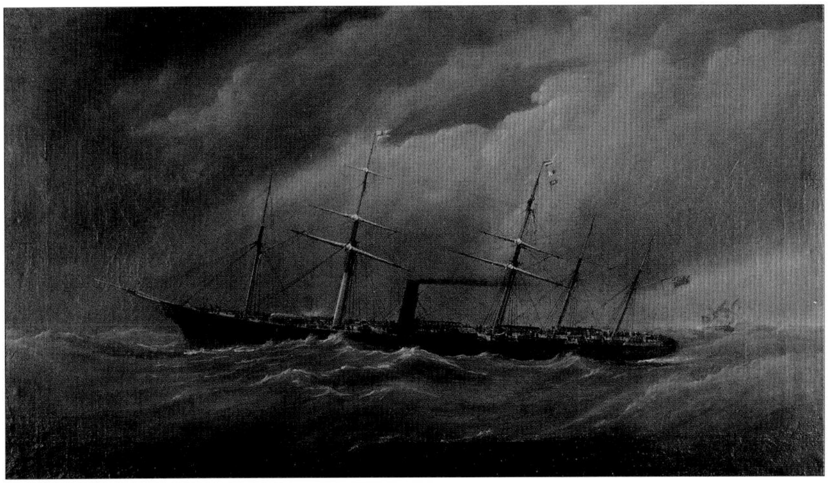

28.89.2
Oil on canvas
46 cm x 76 cm
Prov: H. Cox, Liverpool, from whom purchased, 1928
Exh: Liverpool 1974; Liverpool 1986
Ref: Finch 1983, p.136 (ill); Port Panorama 1986, p.22

Vessel: 289 ft (l), 50.5 ft (b), 32 ft (d); 1040 gross tons

The place of *S S Great Britain* in history is assured. She was the first ocean-going iron steamship, the first significant vessel to be fitted with a screw propeller and the first iron screw steamer to cross the Atlantic.[1]

Walter portrays her in port profile with all sails stowed steaming into the wind. The swell is not sufficient to prevent passengers being on deck and they can be seen leaning over the rail and promenading. Their main interest appears to be an unidentified sailing vessel which is astern to starboard and is shown close reefed and close hauled. The vessels are communicating and *Great Britain* is displaying the message "has been adopted" (2,3,8 in the Marryat Code) but the hoist on the other vessel cannot be distinguished. On the cross-trees below the hoist a crew member is adjusting the yard. There is an indistinct flag on the second mast which may be the captain's personal flag.

Great Britain was built in 1843 by Patterson of Bristol to a design of I K Brunel for the Great Western Steamship Company. After fitting out and trials she made her maiden voyage from Liverpool to New York in July 1845 at a disappointingly average speed of 8.5 knots. She underwent an overhaul in the winter of 1845/46 when bilge keels were fitted, a 4-bladed propeller substituted and her masts reduced from six to five. In 1846 on only her seventh voyage she went aground at Dundrum, Ireland and was subsequently laid up. She was sold to the company's Liverpool agents, Gibbs, Bright & Co. in 1850 for 20% of her original cost. After extensively rebuilding she served on the Liverpool - Australia route until 1876. In 1882 she was sold to Antony Gibbs and her engines were removed. She suffered damage off Cape Horn in 1886 and she spent the next 50 years of her career as a wool and coal hulk in the Falkland Islands. A campaign to preserve the vessel resulted in *Great Britain* being brought back to Bristol in 1970 where she is now a major visitor attraction.[2]

Walter painted the vessel on a number of occasions. Two early versions, one in the Peabody collection, shows her in starboard profile with six masts under steam and sail.[3] Here he portrays her with five masts thus dating the depiction to 1846.

1 For a history of the vessel see Ewan Corlett *The Iron Ship: The Story of Brunel's Great Britain*, Wiltshire, 1975.
2ibid.
3 Peabody version, see Smith, no. 2286, p.107. For the other version see *Bygone Liverpool*, 1913, plate 40.
4 Details of 25 engravings are given in Parker & Bowen, pp. 130-2. See also Corlett, op. cit.
5 For details see Davidson 1992, pp. 92, 190 (Walters), p. 112 (Witham). There is also a Walters carte-de-visite see Davidson 1992, p. 203.

Great Britain was also painted by several other artists during her career and was also the subject of many engravings.[4] Of particular interest in a Liverpool context are views by Samuel Walters, of her return to Liverpool after her maiden voyage, 1845, (Private Collection) and a pair of engravings of 1852. Joseph Witham also painted her later in her career.[5] One of the most interesting canvases depicts her against the Liverpool waterfront in the company of that other great Brunel vessel, *Great Eastern*. (Mitchell Library, Sydney, Australia).
There is an exhibition model in the collections, Accession no. 34.93.

Miles Walters (1773-1855)

1 For details of Miles Walters see Davidson, 1992, pp. 15-24, 51-76.

Miles Walters was the son of John Walters (1748-c.1826) a carpenter and part time artist in north Devon. He was apprenticed as a shipwright and spent time at sea before setting up in Limehouse, in the dockland area of London and beginning his artistic career. He moved to Liverpool about 1828/9 where he spent the rest of his life. The earliest surviving London paintings date from the early/mid 1820s and there is a group of Bristol Channel paintings from 1826 and 1827. From 1827 onwards many paintings were produced jointly with his son Samuel (q.v.) and Miles Walters seems to have painted nothing after 1832. Most of the paintings use one of a number of standard backgrounds. In his remaining years he appears to have concentrated on carving and gilding frames.[1]

220 *Antigua Packet*

1970.246.13
Oil on canvas
47 cm x 78.5 cm
Provenance: T & J Brocklebank Ltd, Cunard Brocklebank Ltd, Private Collection, on permanent loan
Exh: Liverpool 1986
Ref: Port Panorama, 1986, p.24 (ill)

Vessel: 95 ft 9 in (l), 25 ft 4 in (b), 18 ft (d); 272 tons

The ship *Antigua Packet* is shown in two positions entering the Mersey in one of the standard compositions by Miles and Samuel Walters which Davidson has christened the "Egremont group".[1]
To the right of centre a port profile of the vessel under full sail fills the canvas. In the second view to the far left she is shown in starboard quarter profile, turning head into the wind. All her courses are up, her fore and main sails are loose and

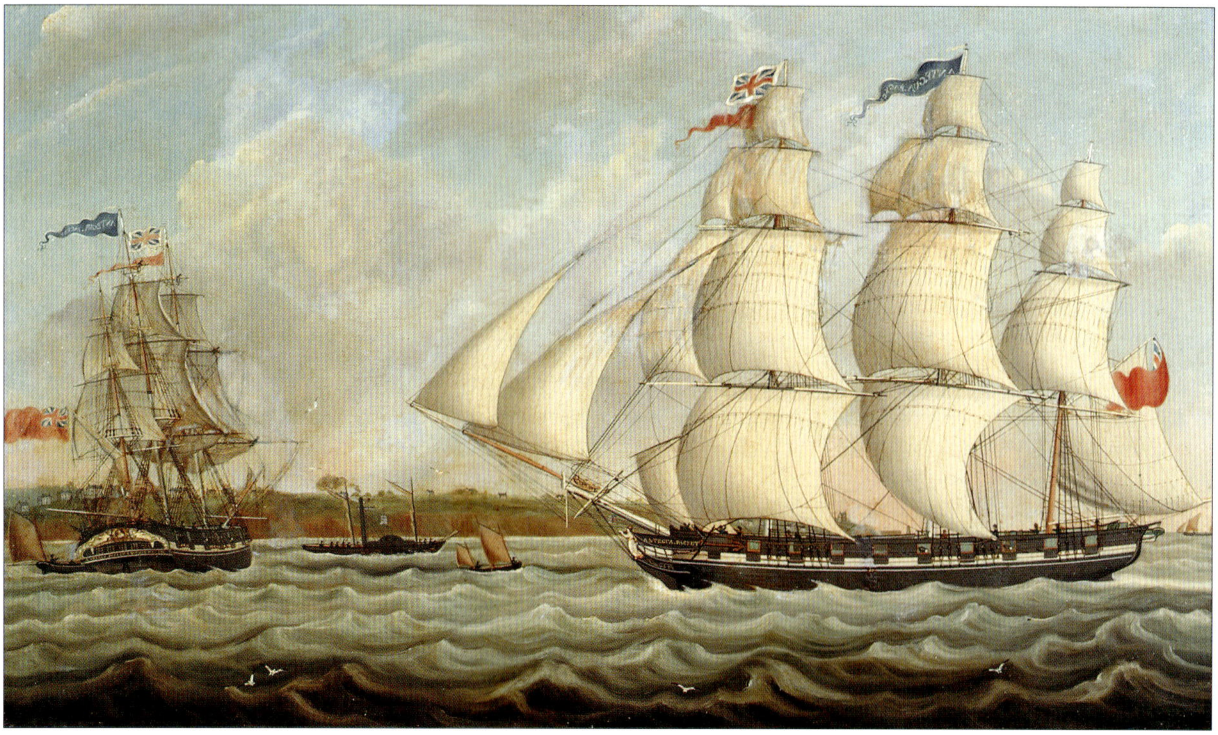

only the mizzen sails are drawing. Men are in the yards taking in the stunsail yards. There is a small boat on her port side. Between the two views in starboard profile is a small paddle steamer heading up river and a gig boat in the middle distance.
The ship is identifiable by the inscription "ANTEGUA PACKET, WHITEHAVEN" on the painted stern in the second view and the blue name pennant, edged in white, on each of the main masts. The red ensign flies at the after peak. The flags on the foremast, a white edged Union Jack and a red pennant, are part of a local code devised by William Henry, Lloyd's agent in Liverpool, which indicates that the ship requires an anchor of 12-14 cwt weight.[2]
In the background is the Wirral coast by Egremont. The Perch Rock Fort and Lighthouse are depicted by simple blocked outlines, probably during construction. *Antigua Packet* was built by T & J Brocklebank at Whitehaven in 1815.[3] Although intended for their own use, she was sold almost immediately on completion to one Captain Dawson and spent her career in his family's ownership, mostly voyaging to the West Indies.[4] She had a long career, eventually being wrecked off Workington in 1863.[5]
This is likely to be one of the earliest works in the "Egremont" group and by the hand of Miles Walters alone. The handling of the sea is similar to other signed and dated works of about 1827-8 including *Eagle* (Private Collection, U.K.) and *Feejee* (Private Collection, U.S.A.).[6]

1 Davidson 1992, pp. 60-1
2 ibid. p.60
3 Gibson I, p.212.
4 LR 1818-1863.
5 Gibson I, p.212.
6 Davidson 1992, pp. 54,74

Miles and Samuel Walters

A number of paintings between 1827 and 1832 are the joint work of father and son and are signed "Walters & Son". The increasing influence of Samuel can be seen over this period as the naive elements are played down, the treatment of the sea becomes less mechanical and the overall treatment more accomplished. They generally use one of a number of standard backgrounds, for instance the Mersey paintings are almost always off Egremont, New Brighton or Everton.[1]

1 For details see Davidson, 1992, pp. 51-76.

221 The Snow Arab (page 202)

This is unmistakably another of the so-called "Egremont" group of compositions in which the snow *Arab* is shown in two views entering the Mersey.[1] The ship is identifiable by the inscription on the stern in the secondary view which reads "ARAB / LIVERPOOL" and by the Watson's flag code of "144" included on the main mast in both views.
The main view is a port profile of the 14-gun vessel placed in the centre of the picture. All sails, except the main and forecourses are set and drawing. In the secondary view the vessel has turned to starboard and is shown in the quarter stern position heading towards the coast. Sail has been reduced and men on the yards are in the process of securing the topgallants. The small boat from the stern is now in the water astern on the port side.
Between the two views are a number of small sailing craft and to the right of the canvas several vessels are shown, including a paddle steamer and a brig, which could be another view of *Arab*. It also has fourteen guns, two of which (the near port gun and the farthest starboard gun) are being fired. There is a small boat with lugsails in the right foreground.
The scene is set against the Wirral coastline, opposite Egremont and the Perch Rock Fort and Lighthouse are visible to the right of the main mast.
There are two similar ships with the name *Arab* registered at Liverpool at this period. The vessel depicted was built in Liverpool by William Haselden for his relative, John Haselden, a Quaker merchant, in 1819 and can be identified by her scroll

1 Davidson 1992.
2 LCR, vol. 35, No. 47 , 2 June 1819. The other *Arab* built 1825, also by Haselden for Gouthwaite of Liverpool had a man's bust figurehead (LCR, vol 41, No. 147, 21 July 1825) Watson's Code 144 was re-allocated in 1832. (The Gouthwaite *Arab* survived until at least 1848 when she was re-registered at Belfast - LCR, vol. 52, No. 155, 6 November 1848).
3 Described as "square sterned brig", LCR, vol. 36, no. 128, 1820.
4 LCR, vol. 39, no. 7, 10 January 1824; LR 1819-1830.
5 Davidson, 1992; illustrated in F E Hyde *Shipping, Enterprise and Management 1830-1939: Harrisons of Liverpool*, 1967.
6 Incorrectly identifies vessel as Gouthwaite *Arab*, see above n.2.

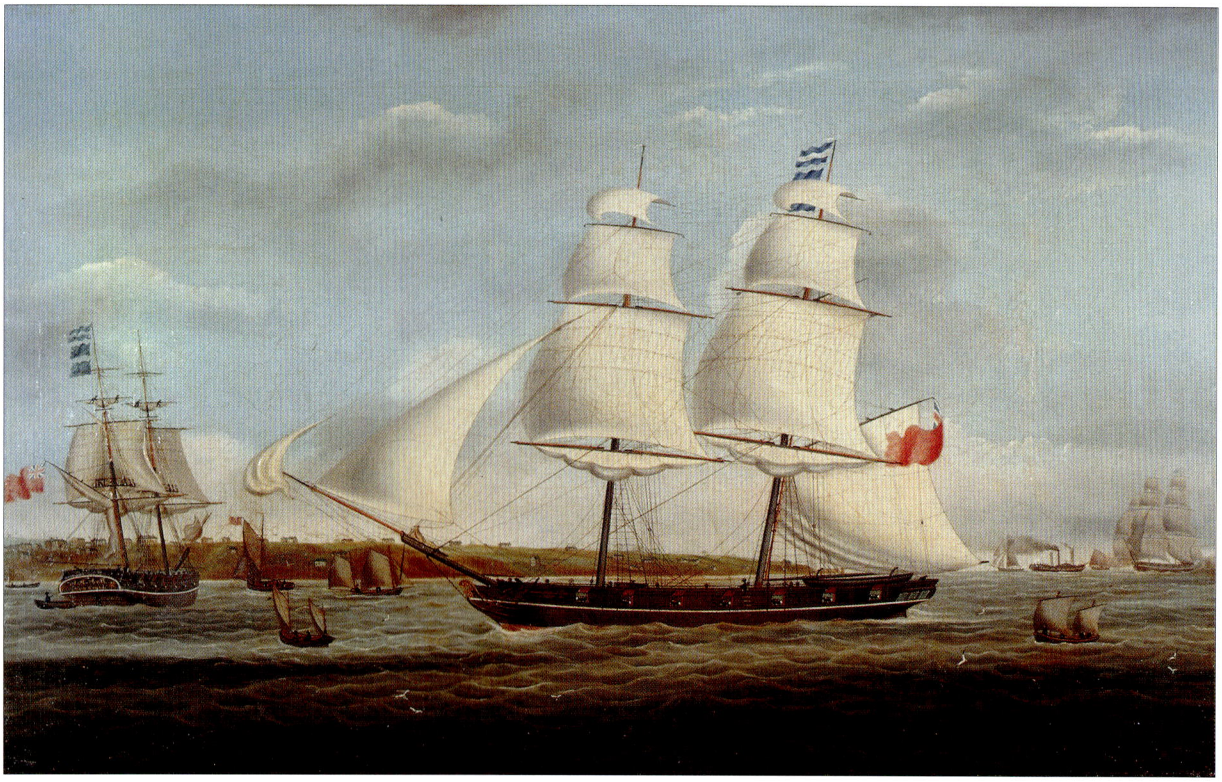

1953.84
Oil on canvas
58.5 cm x 86.5 cm
Signed (br) "WALTERS & SON" between two horizontal lines
Provenance: Miss Buchanan, Liverpool, who presented it, 1953
Exh: Liverpool, 1974; Liverpool, 1986
Ref: Port Panorama, 1986, p.24 (ill)[6]

Vessel: 85 ft 4 in (l), 23 ft 1 in (b), 11 ft 7 in (height in hold); 175 gross tons

billet figurehead.[2] Initially rigged as a schooner, she was changed to a snow in 1820.[3] She traded mainly to Smyrna and then Valparaiso and was re-registered in Scarborough in 1822 before returning to Liverpool ownership in 1824, when she was bought by G F Dickson. She left Liverpool in December 1830 bound for Vera Cruz, Mexico, but was never heard of again.[4]

Although the painting bears the inscription Walters and son, the principal hand must be that of Miles. It is one of no less than sixteen similar compositions of the Egremont group completed by Miles and Samuel in the period 1827 to 1831. Although the wave forms of the sea have been modified from the angular shapes of earlier canvases (see *Antigua Packet*, no. 220), they are still stylised and monotonous in their regularity. In its overall treatment and handling of the sea, it closely resembles *Mariote* and *Margaret*, signed and dated 1829 (Private Collection, U.K.).[5]

222 No.9 Pilot Sloop Liver

The No.9 Liverpool pilot boat *Liver* is shown here in two views off the South Stack and Holyhead mountain.

In the main view, which fills the right hand side of the canvas, the pilot boat is seen from her port side under full sail making good progress through the water. As well as the numbers on her sails she also has a small "9" flag at the top of the mast. The blue peter indicates she is on station with pilots available. An apprentice, wearing his distinctive red woollen hat, is at the rudder and a top hatted pilot can be seen near the mast. Three further members of crew, which may include another pilot can also be seen on deck. This is an excellent close-up view of a pilot boat of the period clearly showing for instance the distinctive colour bands of the hull. Under the bowsprit is an outward bound paddle steamer, probably en route for one of the southern Irish ports.

The second view shows the pilot boat on the opposite tack at the left hand side of the scene. In the foreground is a small two masted boat which may contain an agent awaiting the arrival of a vessel.

1 Rees, p.201.
2 Formerly N R Omell Gallery, London. See Davidson 1992, p.72 (ill).

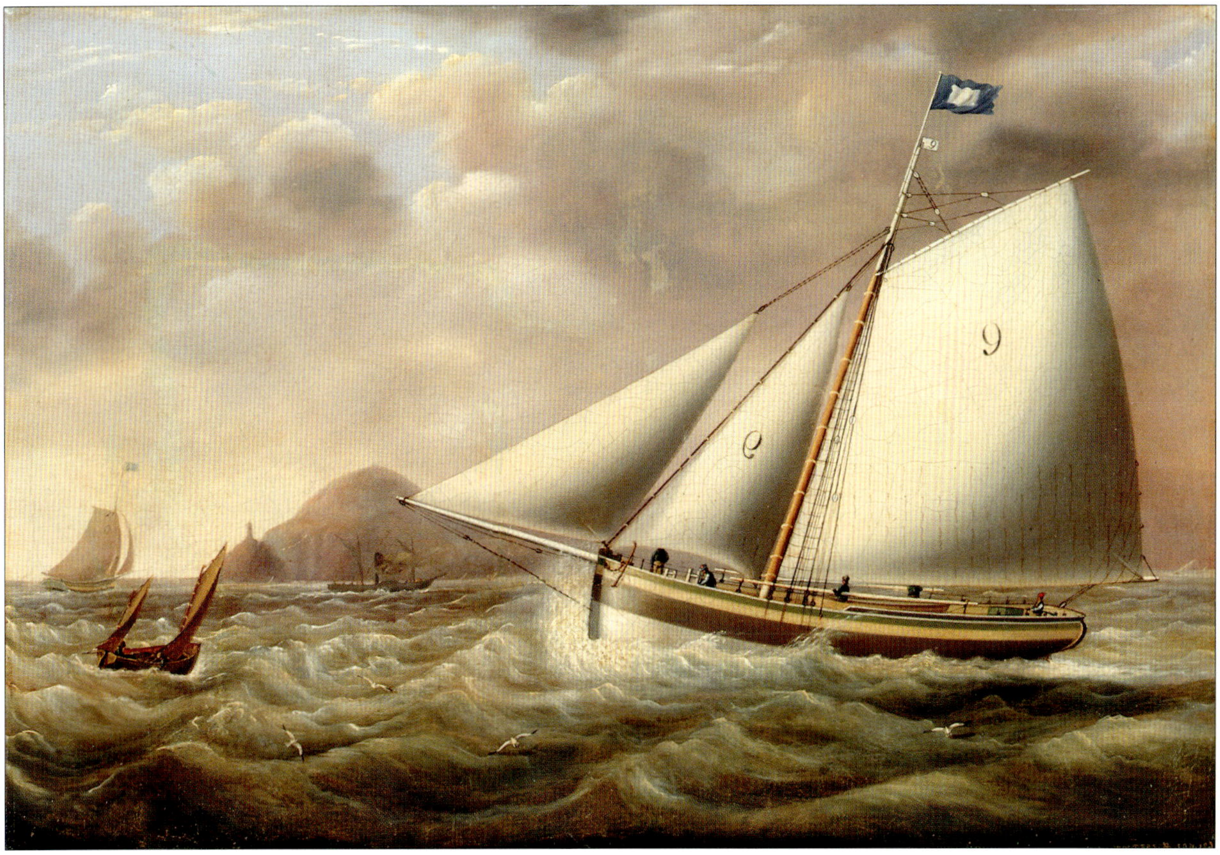

In the background the lighthouse on South Stack can be clearly seen against the sky with the mass of Holyhead mountain on the north-west corner of Anglesey rising behind it.

Liver was built by Clarke & Nickson in Liverpool in 1822 and remained in service until she was replaced in 1846.[1]

There is a similar Walters and Son canvas of the No.4 boat also painted in 1830.[2]

1987.109
Oil on canvas
41 cm x 61.5 cm
Signed and dated (br) "WALTERS & SON / 1830"
Prov: Purchased at auction, Eldon Worrall, Liverpool, 11 December 1987, lot 228
Ref: Davidson 1992, p.72 (ill)

Vessel: 49 ft 10 in (l), 15 ft 10 in (b), 8 ft 4 in (d); 59 gross tons.

Samuel Walters (1811-1882)

Samuel Walters is probably the best known and most accomplished of all the ship portrait artists who worked in Liverpool. He was the son of Miles Walters (q.v.) and was brought up in the docklands area of London before moving to Liverpool with his family about 1826. He initially worked in his father's studio and studied at the Liverpool Academy School. He was a prolific artist and painted a large number of ship portraits, usually with local backgrounds, mainly for British and American patrons. Many of his paintings were produced as engravings and he also experimented with photographic reproductions from the 1860s. He produced some seascapes and coastal scenes which were exhibited at the Royal Academy (1842-61) and in Liverpool (1830-65).

Other important collections of his paintings are at National Maritime Museum; Peabody Essex Museum, Salem; Mariner's Museum, Newport News.

See the major biography, A S Davidson *Samuel Walters: Marine Artist*, Coventry, 1992.

223 C S S Alabama

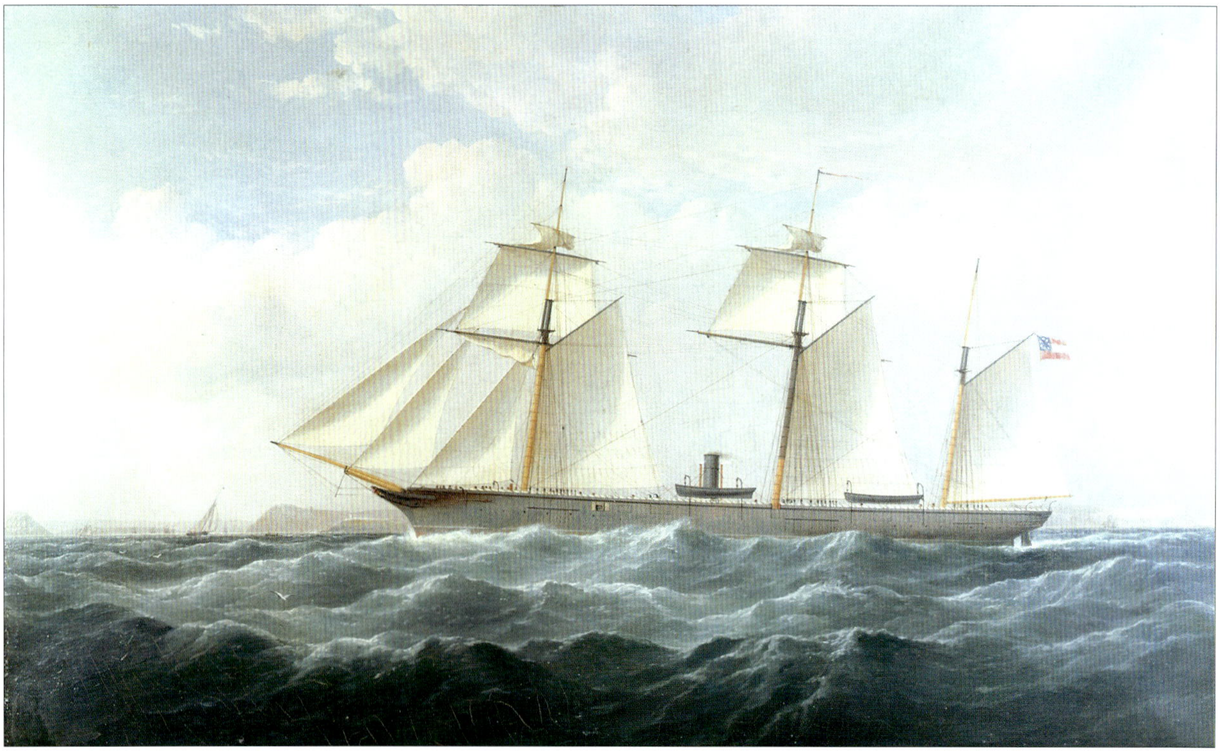

1940.22.2
Oil on canvas
49.5 cm x 79.5 cm
Signed and dated (bl) "S. WALTERS / 1862"
Prov. Mrs Maxwell, who presented it, 1940.
Exh. Bootle 1959, No.6; Liverpool 1974; Liverpool 1986
Ref: Port Panorama 1986, p.24 (ill.); Tibbles 1988, ill.

Vessel: 220 ft (l), 31.6 ft (b), 17.6 ft (d); 1050 gross tons.

The Confederate steamship *Alabama*, one of the most famous ships built at Laird's yard in Birkenhead, is portrayed in port profile under steam and sail off Cork. She was wooden hulled and had an auxiliary barque rig with single funnel. The vessel is flying the Confederate flag at the after peak and a Confederate pennant from the top of the main mast.

In the background to the left is the entrance to Cork harbour with Roches Point and lighthouse immediately under the bowsprit.

The history of *Alabama* is well known.[1] There was much sympathy for the Confederate cause in Liverpool and the vessel was built secretly at Laird's, known only by her job no. 290. Despite Britain's neutrality in the war and official concern about the role of the vessel now called *Enrica*, she left the Mersey on 28 July 1862 supposedly for further sea trials. Instead she sailed to the Azores where she was fitted out with armaments and ammunition. During her career as a commerce raider she sank 68 federal vessels and was herself sunk by *U S S Kearsarge* after being trapped in the harbour at Cherbourg in June 1864.[2]

The collections contain a photographic print of this painting entitled "Screw Steamer No. 290", the only difference being the absence of the confederate flag.[3] This supports the likelihood that the painting was completed before the vessel left the Mersey. In fact, she travelled round the north of Ireland and did not pass Cork. There is another painting of *Alabama* by Walters off the Tuskar Lighthouse in the Williamson Art Gallery, Birkenhead.[4] Two Hull artists depicted *Alabama*. James Wheldon shows her off Gibraltar (Private Collection)[5] and Reuben Griffin painted a pair of panels of the final encounter with *Kearsarge* (Town Docks Museum, Hull).[6] There is an exhibition model of the vessel in the collections, accession no. 1963.140.1.

1 For history of vessel see R Lester *Confederate Finance and Purchasing in Great Britain*, 1975, pp. 72-77, 214-216 and Chronology, VI, pp. 191-193.
2 The site of the wreck was discovered in 1984, see C M Robinson *Shark of the Confederacy: the story of the C S S Alabama*, London, 1995, epilogue.
3 Accession Number 1955.240.
4 See Davidson, 1992, p.215.
5 Credland, pp. 107, 109 (ill.).
6 Credland, pp. 54-5 (ill.).

224 *Algeria*

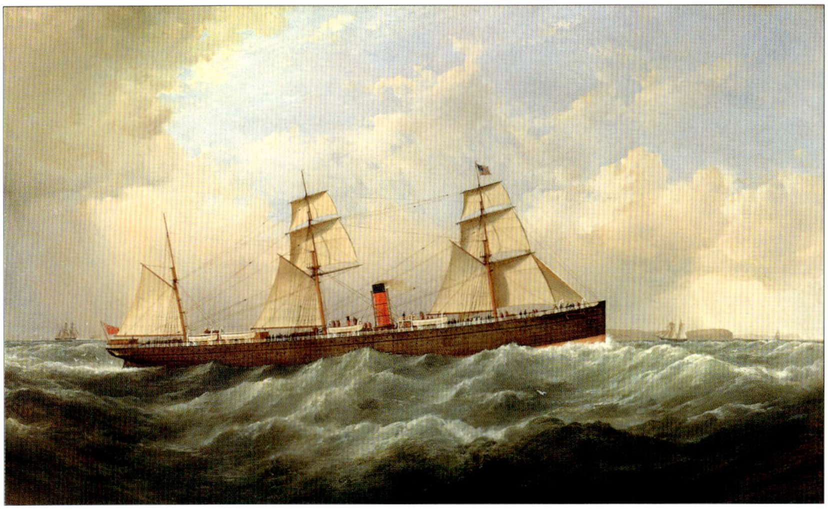

1968.184.9
Oil on canvas[1]
77 cm x 126.5 cm
Signed and dated (bl) "S. WALTERS / 1873"
Prov: Cunard Steam Ship Company, Private Collection, on permanent loan.
Exh: Bootle 1959, no. 21
Ref: Davidson, 1992, p. 133, illus.

Vessel: 367.2 ft (l), 42.2 ft (b), 34.5 ft (d); 3428 gross tons

S S Algeria is shown in starboard profile under steam and sail in a fresh northerly wind off the North Wales coast on her way to New York. She is shown using her auxiliary sails which help economise on coal as well as offering a measure of stability. She flies the red ensign at her stern and the Stars and Stripes at her foremast. Small groups of crew and passengers can be seen on the decks. To her left are an unidentified barque and a paddle steamer and there is a brig in the distance on the right hand side of the canvas. In the background is the Great Orme with Anglesey in the right far distance.

The iron screw steamer *Algeria* was one of two sister ships built by J & G Thomson of Glasgow in 1870 for Cunard's transatlantic service. She could carry 200 first and 1054 third class passengers plus 1600 tons of cargo. She remained in service until 1881 and was sold to the Red Star Line and renamed *Pennland*. She spent most of her later career on the Antwerp - New York route and was scrapped in 1902.[2]

Walters also produced another painting of *Algeria* probably off Cape Race (present whereabouts unknown) and a photographic print of this survives.[3]

1 Relined.
2 Bonsor North, p.151.
3 MAL, (1989.239.5-7), illustrated Davidson, 1992, p. 201 (ill. 203).

225 *Baltic*

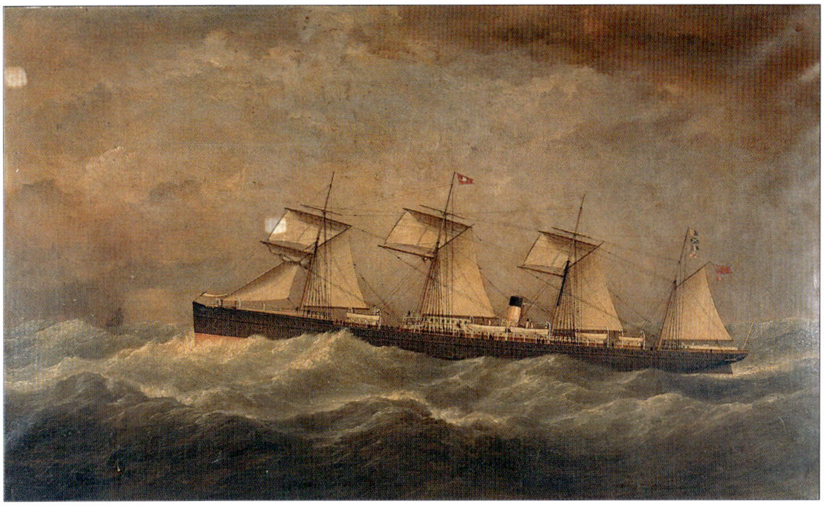

1951.25.11
Oil on canvas
66 cm x 107 cm
Prov: Mr J James, Blundellsands, from whom purchased, 1951.

Vessel: 420.4 ft (l), 40.9 ft (b), 31 ft (d); 3707 gross tons.

The White Star liner *Baltic* is shown in port profile making her way through heavy seas on a passage across the Atlantic. She is under the power of her engines but a significant amount of auxiliary sail, except the main courses, is in use. There are various passengers and members of the crew on the decks. She flies the White Star house flag and her commercial flag code (K M T V). The red and white banded pennant below the red ensign at the after peak indicates she is answering another vessel and explains why she is flying her identifying code in mid-Atlantic. There is, in fact, a sailing vessel disappearing over the horizon beyond the bow of the main view.

S S Baltic was one of four sister ships with which Thomas Ismay entered the highly competitive express passenger trade across the Atlantic in 1871. One of Ismay's partners was the financier Gustavus Schwabe who had shares in Harland & Wolff and whose nephew was the junior partner. Schwabe insisted that the ships were built by Harland & Wolff, as all future White Star commissions were to be. *Baltic* was the third vessel to be launched and entered service in September 1871. These vessels were significantly in advance of their rivals, not only in economy of coal consumption, but in the degree of comfort offered to passengers. Most of the cabins were double the average size then available and nearly all of them had a port hole. The saloon extended the width of the ship and the whole atmosphere was one of airiness. *Baltic* made a record run from New York to Queenstown in 1883. She was sold to the Holland America Line in 1888 and renamed *Veendam*. She foundered in the North Atlantic in 1898.[1]

A lithograph of *Baltic* at sea was published in New York by James Sutton & Company.[2] There is painting of the vessel by Jacobsen in the National Maritime Museum.[3]

1 Bonsor North, 732-4, 756 and for White Star generally, Anderson.
2 Signed "J.A.", Parker & Bowen, p.28.
3 Concise NMM, p.226 (ill).

226 P S Banshee

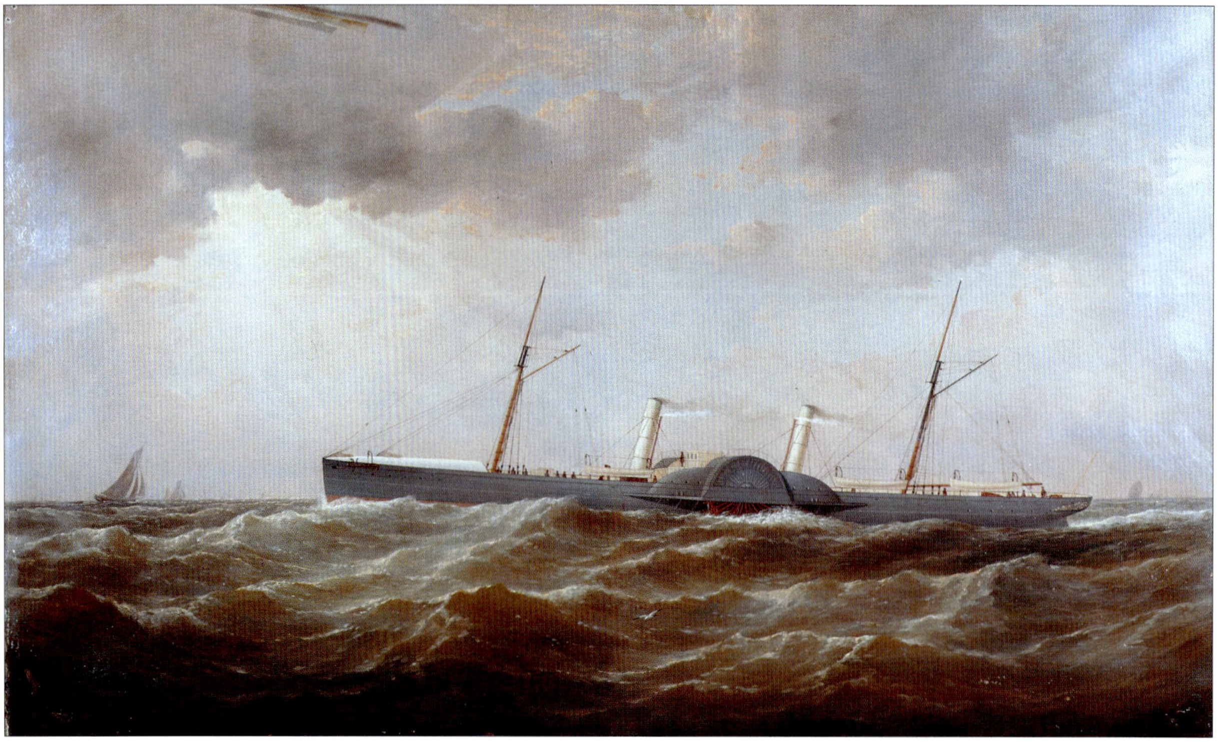

The American Confederate schooner rigged paddle steamer *Banshee I* is shown at sea in a port profile under full steam with all sails furled. The controversial role of the vessel may explain why there is no name or identifying flags included in the painting.

There were two almost identical vessels named *Banshee*, both built by Jones, Quiggin & Co. of Liverpool for the Anglo-Confederate Trading Company.[1] *Banshee I* was the first of a number of fast steel-hulled steamers built to beat the blockade of Confederate ports imposed by the Federal Navy. She was completed early in 1863 but had problems. Captain Thomas Taylor described her as a frail vessel "ill-constructed and ill-engined."[2] She was captured on her ninth voyage near Cape Hatteras, North Carolina, in November 1863 and became a Federal vessel. After the war, she was renamed *J L Smallwood* and carried cattle in the Gulf of Mexico. *Banshee II* was built in 1864 as a replacement blockade runner with finer lines than her predecessor and some forty feet longer. She also survived the war without mishap.[3]

The painting has generally been thought to portray the earlier vessel. This is likely given that the painting was commissioned by William Quiggin, the builder, who might well have wished to remember the first steel built vessel to cross the Atlantic.[4] Although placed centrally on the canvas, the long low profile of the vessel makes it an almost subservient element of the picture. The eye is caught by the rough, murky sea and the brilliant sunlight breaking through the dark and brooding storm clouds. There is a builder's model of *Banshee I* in the collections, accession no. 16.9.27.1(A),[5] and also a half-model of the same vessel, accession no. 1962.343.2. There are watercolours of both vessels in the St George's Museum, Bermuda.[6]

1968.5.2
Oil on canvas
49.5 cm x 79.5 cm
Signed and dated (bl) "S. WALTERS / 1864"
Prov.: William Quiggin, by descent to grand-daughter, Mrs M Stevenson, from whom purchased, 1968.
Exh: Bootle, 1959, No. 40; Liverpool, 1986.
Ref: Bootle Catalogue; Port Panorama, p.25 (ill); H P Spratt (1980)

Vessel: 214.8 ft (l), 20 ft (b), 11.3 ft (d); 324 gross tons.

1 But registered to local owners. *Banshee I* was registered to John Toulmin Lawrence of E Lawrence & Co. of Liverpool. See LCR, no. 58, vol. 80, 1863. A banshee was a female spirit whose wail portends death.
2 Thomas E Taylor *Running The Blockade*, London, 1912, p.70. He covers her full career, pp. 33-85.
3 For history of *Banshee I* see Spratt, 1980; Jones Quiggins Specification Book, f.364-7, MAL, DX 154. Quiggins built more than a dozen other blockade runners. See Civil War Chronology and Lester, appendix.
4 However, Davidson 1992 identifies her as BANSHEE II. For ownership see letter from Mrs M Stevenson, 7 April 1967, DCF.
5 See Handbook 1935, p. 55-56.
6 Illustrated, with others, in Civil War Chronology, pp. 338-9.

227 *Baroda*

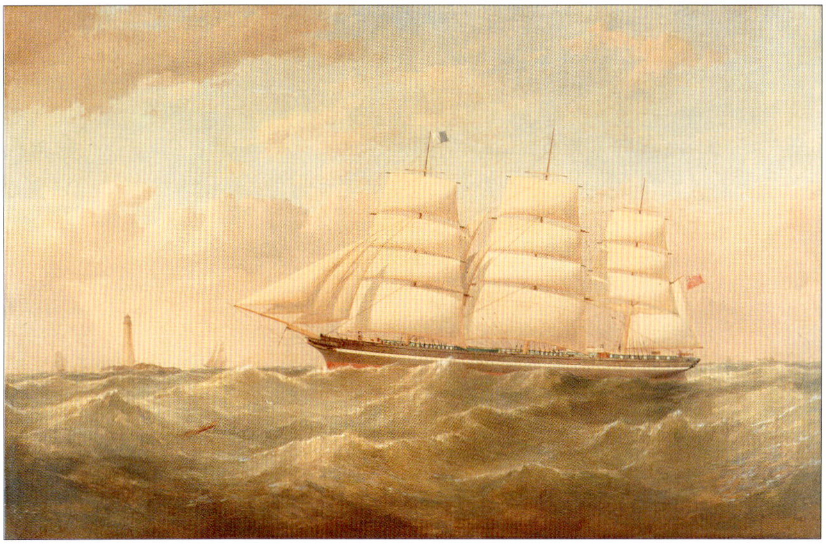

1970.246.14
Oil on canvas
70 cm x 105.5 cm
Signed and dated (bl) "S. WALTERS / 1864"
Prov: T & J Brocklebank Ltd., Cunard Steam Ship Co. Ltd., Private Collection, on permanent loan
Exh: Liverpool 1986
Ref: Port Panorama 1986, p.26; Tibbles 1988 (ill.)

Vessel: 231.5 ft (l), 36.5 ft (b), 23.7 ft (d); 1364 tons

The ship rigged *Baroda* is shown in port profile under full sail off the Tuskar Rock and lighthouse at the south eastern tip of Ireland. She is identifiable from her name on the bow. At the foremast she displays the blue and white house flag of T & J Brocklebank and has the firm's characteristic broad white band on the hull. She is carrying all sail, except royals, and the topsails are divided into upper and lower as was more convenient with smaller crews. (Her complement of crew was 32).[1] There are other vessels, including a steamer, in the distance.

Baroda[2] was built in Belfast by Harland & Wolff in 1864. She was only the second iron hulled vessel ordered by Brocklebank's, who were moving away from wooden

1 Gibson I, p. 276 and LCR vol. 86, no. 269, 14 June 1864.
2 Baroda, now Vadodara, a town in Gujerat, India.
3 Gibson, op. cit. For detailed information see wreck file in MAL, MBHC/WR/7.

ships and in fact closed their Whitehaven shipyard the following year. *Baroda* made 23 voyages to Calcutta before sinking in the Mersey after a collision with *Buccleuch* in November 1887.[3]

This composition is almost identical to Walters' *Domitila* (no. 228).

228 *Schooner Domitila*

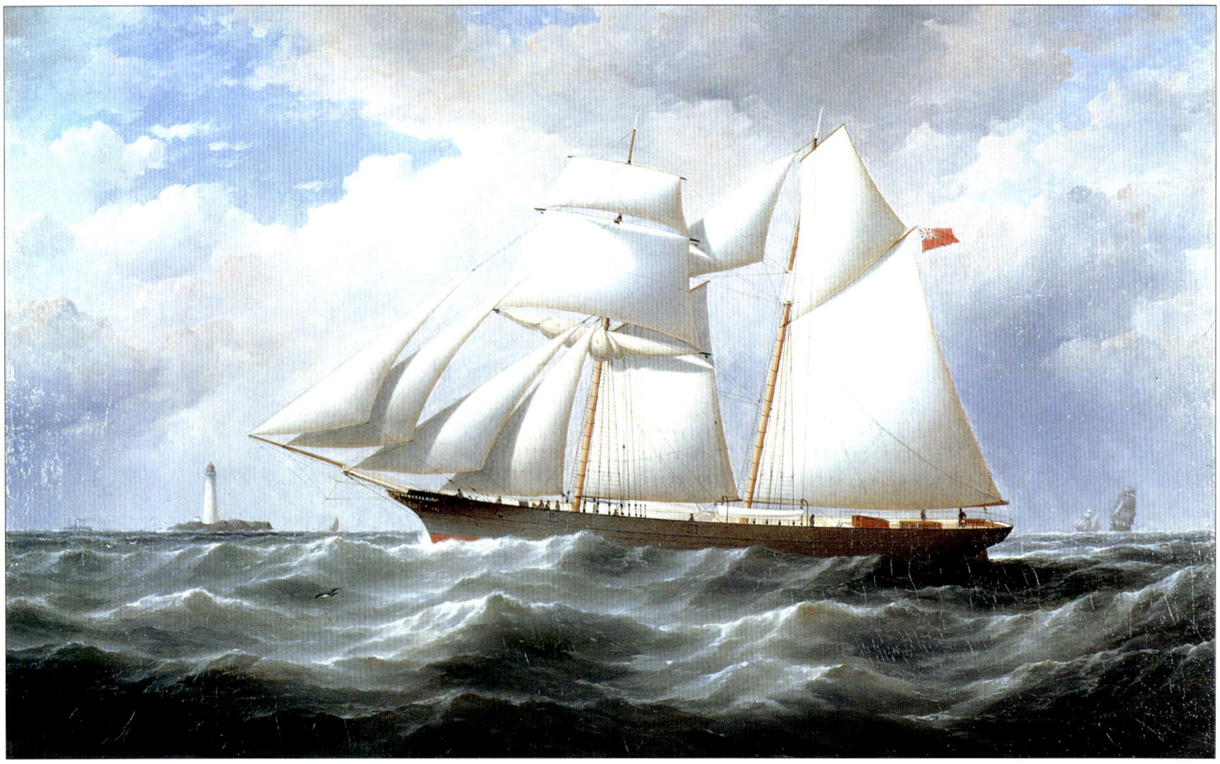

1968.5.1
Oil on canvas
49.5 cm x 79.5 cm
Signed and dated (bl) "S WALTERS / 1863"
Prov: William Quiggin, by descent to granddaughter, Mrs M Stevenson, from whom purchased, 1968
Exhibited Bootle, 1959, No. 39; Liverpool, 1986
Ref: Bootle Catalogue; Port Panorama, p.26; Davidson 1992, p.158

Vessel: 115.6 ft (l), 22 ft (b), 11.8 ft (d); 206 gross tons

The topsail schooner *Domitila* was one of the earliest steel hulled vessels to be built in Liverpool. She is shown here in the centre of the canvas in port profile off the Tuskar Rock off the south eastern tip of Ireland. The vessel is identifiable from her bow name. She flies the red ensign at the after peak.[1] Other unidentified craft in the far distance include a paddle steamer and two sailing vessels.

Domitila was built by Jones, Quiggin for R. C. Janion and others of Liverpool in 1863.[2] She was named after the niece of the Emperor Domitian and had a steel hull and lower masts. She was sold to John Hargrove of Liverpool in 1867 and "capsized on her way down from Runcorn to Liverpool and became a total wreck" in October 1874.[3] The painting is interesting because it shows Cunningham's patent reefing fitted on the lower topsail. This allowed the sail to be rolled around the spar from the deck.[4]

The composition is very similar to Walters' *Baroda* (no. 227) which uses the same location and dates from a year later. The painting of the sea is particularly fine.

William Quiggin retained a small shareholding in this vessel until 1867 (as did his partner Josiah Jones) which may explain why he owned a painting of her.[5]

There is a photographic carte de visite print of the painting in the collections also presented by the donor.[6]

1 The ensign is inaccurate, missing the red diagonals of the union flag. There is no reason to doubt the authenticity, despite this characteristic of artist here described as Associate of Joseph Heard, Old Ensign.
2 Iron Registry, 1863-64; There is a specification for the vessel in Jones Quiggin Specification Book, ff. 406-412, MAL, DX 154. R C Janion was a merchant and district manager of Northern Assurance. He was in partnership with a number of Liverpool engineers with ship owning interests. See LCR, vol. 85, no. 122, 8 April 1863, TB4, p.416.
3 TB4, p. 416.
4 For a description of the system see Underhill, pp. 127-130, 156.
5 LCR, as above n.1.
6 MMM, 1968.5.1a. Printed on back in shield "S. WALTERS / Publisher of / MARINE / PHOTOGRAPHS" in garter with legend "3 FALKNER CRESCENT. BOOTLE. LIVERPOOL." and below "COPIES MAY BE HAD AT ANY TIME".

229 *Paddle Steamer Ethiope off the West Coast of Africa* (pages 210-212)

MMM1990.182
Oil on canvas[1]
58 cm x 91.5 cm
Provenance: Sothebys, 30 May 1990, lot 86 (ill); N R Omell Gallery, from whom purchased 1990.
Exh: N R Omell Gallery, 21st Annual Exhibition, 1990, No. 25 (ill).

Vessels:
Ethiope 95.5 ft (l), 16.9 ft (b), 8.4 ft (d); 80 tons (burthen)
Warree 78.7 ft (l), 18.0 ft (b), 10 ft (d); 148 tons

The Paddle Steamer *Ethiope* is shown in starboard profile off the coast of West Africa, probably in the Bight of Biafra, under full steam and with all sail set. In the background to the right of her bow is a schooner, also full set, and there are a number of small local craft along the coast.

Ethiope was built by Thomas Wilson of Liverpool in 1839.[2] She was schooner rigged with three masts and was fitted with "a condensing engine of the first class, thirty horse power, by Messrs Fawcett and Co "and her furnaces are so constructed to burn either coal or wood."[3] She was built for Robert Jamieson, a Liverpool merchant with various trading interests, including in West Africa,[4] for the express purpose of finding a route via the Benin River to the main Niger River "and at the same time to endeavour to establish a commercial intercourse with the interior."[5]

Ethiope left Liverpool in September 1839[6] and in April 1840 began the ascent of the Benin River under the command of John Beecroft, an experienced trader and government agent.[7] Initially frustrated in their aim, a second attempt via the Warree River, a tributary of the Benin, took them into the main Niger River and more than 400 miles up the river. However, sickness and death amongst the European crew convinced Beecroft and Jamieson that "commerce on the Niger can only be followed by means of steam-vessels manned entirely by native Africans, under the direction of European officers and engineers well inured to the climate."[8]

In October of the following year *Ethiope* helped rescue the surviving colonists of the government's ill-fated Niger Expedition to settle the interior and assisted H M Steamer *Albert* back to Fernando Po. Later in 1841 and in 1842, she explored the Old Calabar or Cross River but found it "quite unimportant."[9]

Ethiope returned to Liverpool in July 1843 and was immediately put up for auction, described as "a first-rate sea-boat, and a very fast sailer under canvas as well as when propelled by steam. Has unusually airy and spacious cabin accommodation, rendering her eligible for a pleasure yacht, a passage packet or a trading vessels in tropical climates."[10] She did not sell and in August 1844 returned to West Africa.[11] In 1845 Beecroft again took her up the Niger as far as Rabba.[12] She was back in Liverpool in May 1847.[13]

Ethiope had a mixed crew of "fifteen Europeans, including officers, medical men an engineer, and seamen, with a full compliment of blacks, or Kroo-men, besides interpreters."[14] A number of the black crew are depicted in the painting. Also clearly visible on the foredeck is the "nine-pound swivel gun" and other unspecified guns can be seen from some of the gun ports. Such armament was a necessary precaution in areas where Europeans were viewed with suspicion and hostility.[15]

The ship flies a red ensign at the after peak, a name pennant at the main mast and an unidentified blue pennant with a white O at the foremast, presumably a house flag.

Ethiope was sold by Jamieson in 1853 to Wilson, her original builder, and then quickly to another Liverpool shipbuilder before she was acquired by Joseph Brown, a Liverpool merchant. Brown re-registered her in 1854 as "a sailing vessel" having removed her engines. She subsequently passed through three further owners between 1855 and 1858 when she was bought by the Dutch firm, Kerdyk & Co. of Rotterdam, and renamed *Biaffra*. She disappeared from Lloyds Registers in 1867.[16]

The topsail schooner in the background is almost certainly Jamieson's *Warree*. She flies the same blue pennant as *Ethiope*. Her description in 1843 when offered for sale is consistent with the vessel depicted.[17] Built in 1837 by Thomas Wilson, she was also used for exploration in West Africa from 1838 until at least 1846.[18] She was sold about 1856 and was used as a coaster in Northern Ireland before disappearing from Lloyds Registers in 1867.[19] (continued page 212.)

1 Relined, 1990.
2 LCR, Volume 54, certificate no. 141.
3 GGA, 14 September 1843.
4 For Jamieson see DNB.
5 JRGS (1841), p.184.
6 GGA, 19 September 1839.
7 JRGS (1841), p.184. For Beecroft see K O Dike 'John Beecroft, 1790-1854', *Journal of the Historical Society of Nigeria*, vol I, pt. I, 1956, pp. 5-14.
8 JRGS (1841), p.189.
9 ibid, p.189; a detailed account of the expedition is in JRGS (1844), pp. 260-283.
10 GGA, 14 September 1843.
11 She sailed on 25 July but was forced to put back "leaking in her upper works, and pumps choked with coal" and finally sailed on 12 September. GGA, 1 August, 8 August, 19 September 1844.
12 Burns, A., *History of Nigeria*, 1972, 8th edition, p.96.
13 GGA, 13 May 1847. She brought back a cargo of palm oil.
14 JRGS (1841), p.184. Kroo-men are inhabitants of present-day Liberia. See Burns, op. cit., pp.109-110.
15 GGA, 14 September 1843.
16 LCR, volume 54, certificate no. 141, LR.
17 GGA, 14 September 1843.
18 ibid and DNB, JRGS (1841), p.190.
19 LR.
20 For sightings see GGA, 20 March and 3 April 1845.
21 Oil on canvas, 22.5" x 35.5", Sold Sotheby's 29 August 1971, attrib. W J Huggins; Sabin Gallery, Catalogue 1973, No. 13, attrib. S. Walters.

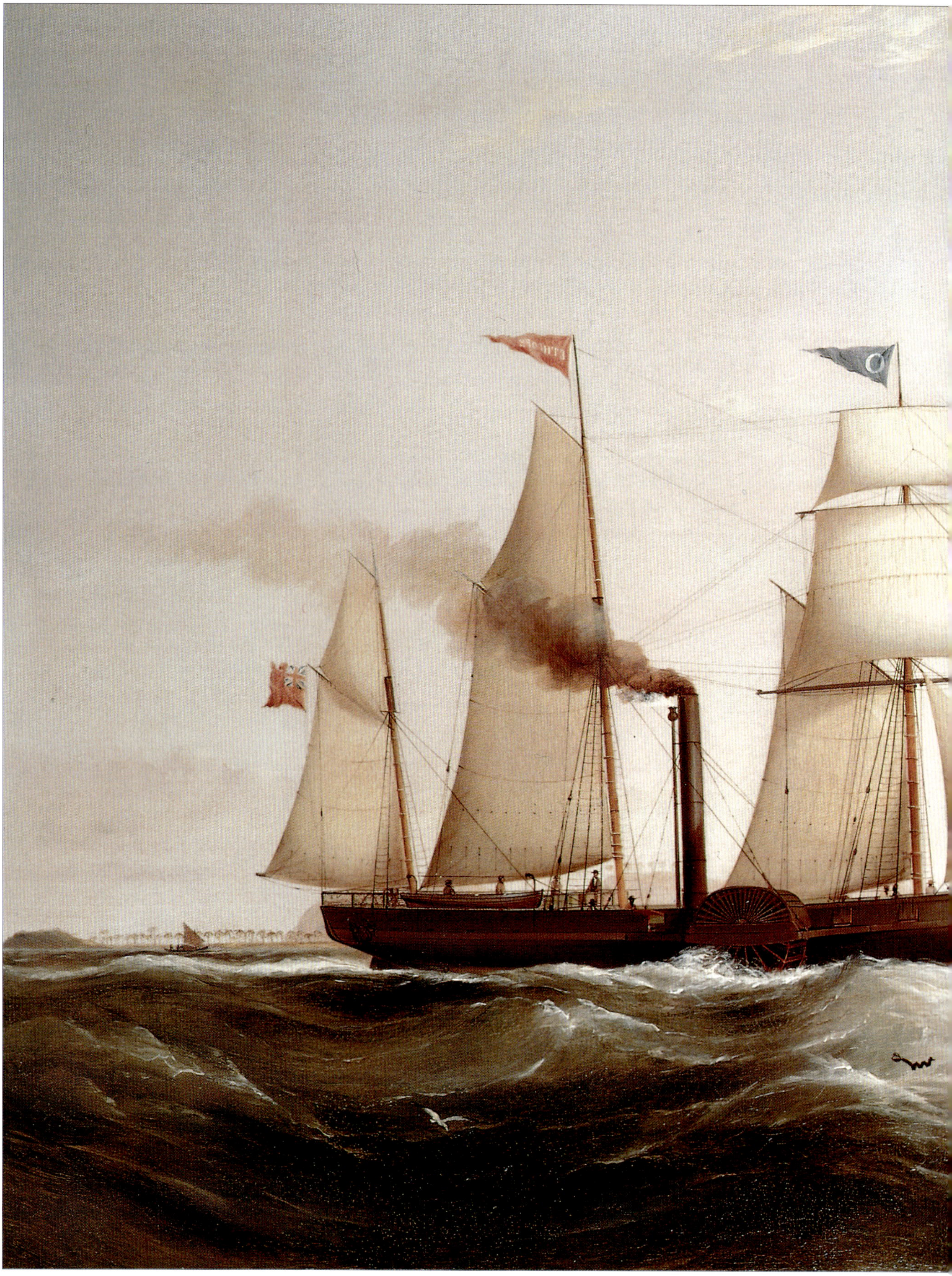

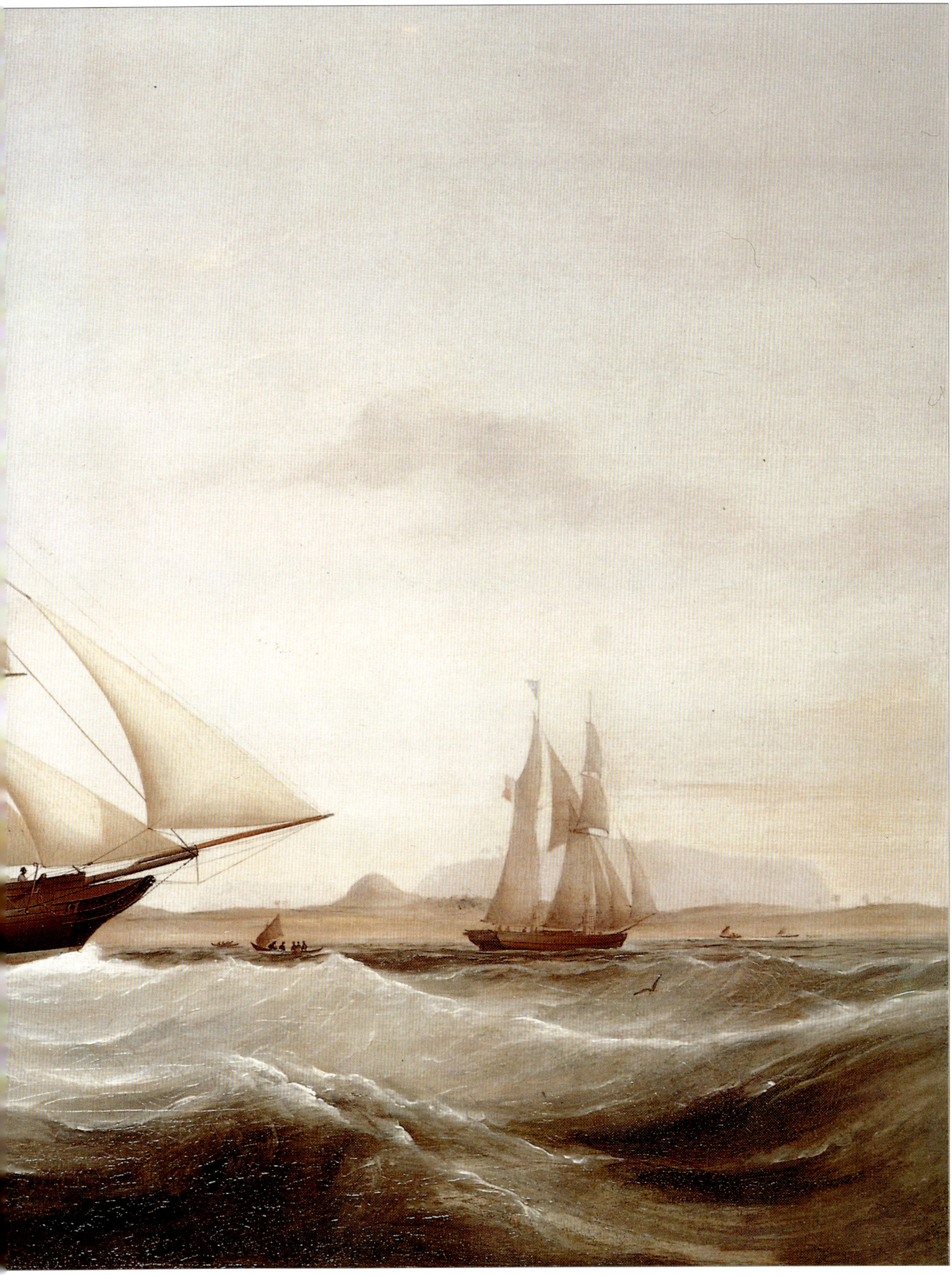

The location has not been precisely identified but the only hills near the Niger Delta and adjoining coastline are the Cameroon mountains, near the mouth of the Cross River, or on the island of Fernando Po where *Ethiope* was sighted in 1844.[20] There are a number of local coastal craft in the background.

Although attributed to Heard on entering the collection, the high quality of the painting, and in particular of the figures, together with the treatment of the sea suggests that this is more likely to be the work of Samuel Walters. The painting probably dates from about 1840-45. Another version of the painting exists with slight variations to the background and with the schooner positioned to the left of *Ethiope*.[21]

230 C S S Florida

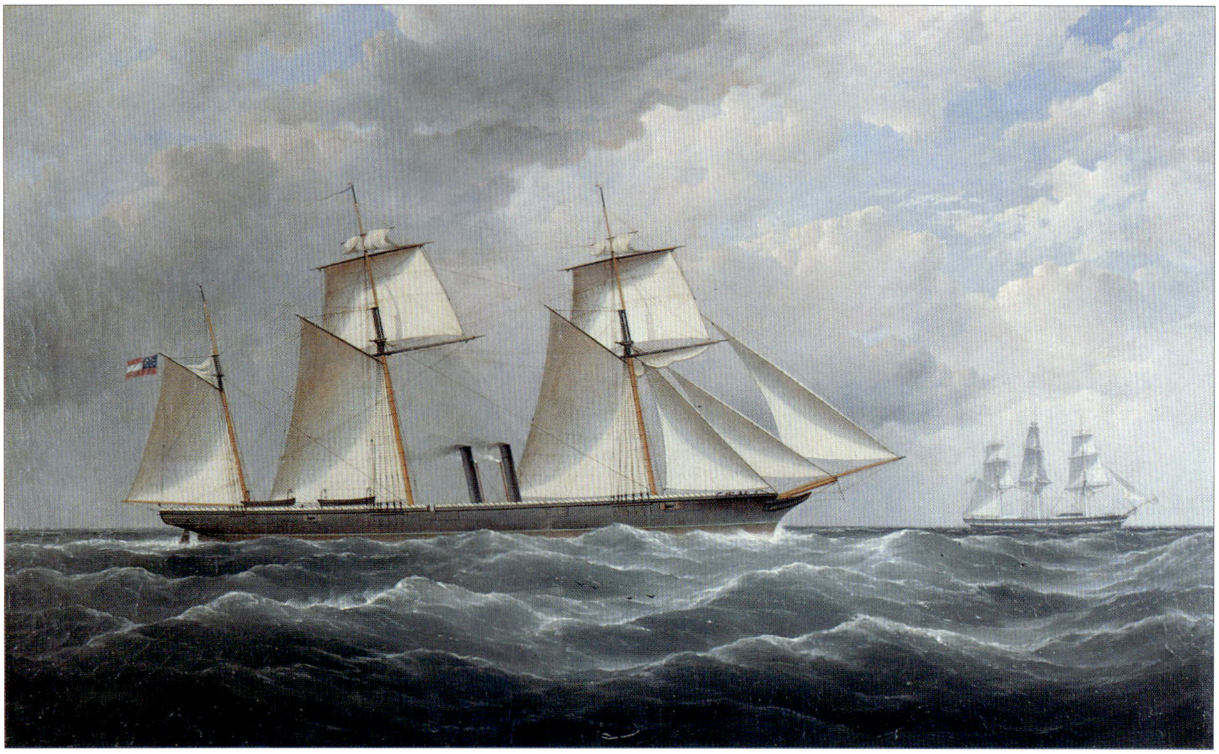

1940.22.1
Oil on canvas
51 cm x 82 cm
Prov. Mrs Maxwell, presented 1940.
Exh. Bootle 1959, No.7; Liverpool 1986
Ref: Finch 1983, p.139 (ill); Port Panorama 1986, p.26-7 (ill)

Vessel: 191 ft (l), 27.1 ft (b), 14 ft (d)

The confederate raider *S S Florida* is shown in full starboard profile under sail and steam with an unidentified Union merchant ship which has been forced to heave-to and is no doubt about to be boarded. She flies the Confederate flag at her after peak and a Confederate pennant from the main mast. The scene is undramatic. The accurate portrayal of *Florida* is the artist's principal concern and the captured vessel is shown in a standard starboard profile in the middle distance.

The wooden hulled *Florida* was built by William C Miller & Son of Toxteth Dock, Liverpool, and was fitted with engines by Fawcett, Preston & Company. During construction the pretence was maintained that she was destined for an Italian owner under the name *Oreto*. Despite official doubts, which included an inspection, she was able to leave the Mersey in March 1862 and sailed for Nassau. Again her confederate ownership was investigated but in January 1863 she escaped to sea fully armed and began her career as a raider. She sank 36 Union ships before being captured illegally in the neutral Brazilian port of Bahia by the Union warship *Wachusett* in October 1864. She sank in Hampton Roads, Virginia, in suspicious circumstances the same year.[1]

Although not signed, perhaps because of the political considerations involved, this painting is clearly the work of Samuel Walters.

1 See R Lester *Confederate Finance and Purchasing in Great Britain*, 1975, pp. 66-72, 212-213 and Chronology, VI pp. 228-229.

231 *Helen of Liverpool arriving in the Mersey*[1]

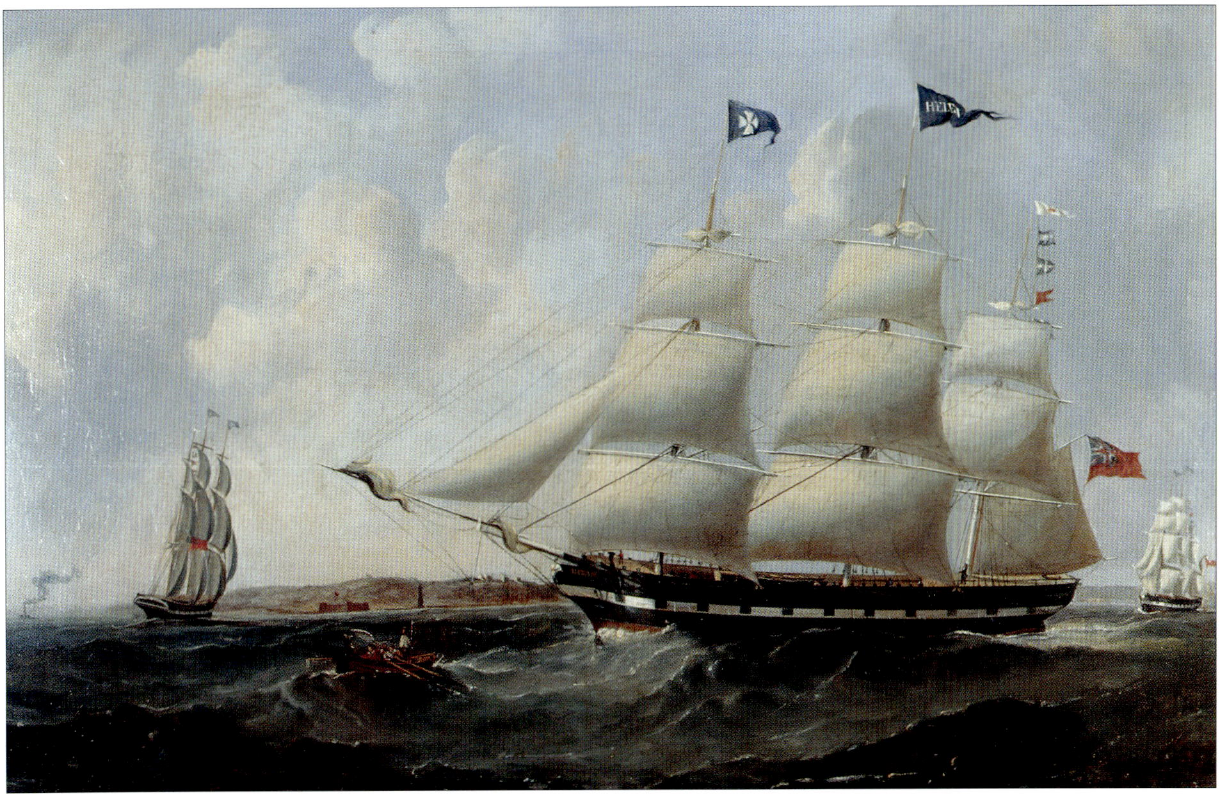

Unusually this portrait of the ship rigged *Helen* shows the vessel in no less than three views arriving in the Mersey. The principal view, which fills the right hand of the canvas, depicts the vessel in port profile in the Crosby Channel under full sail. The secondary views are both in the middle distance; astern is a port bow view of the vessel approaching and to the left of the canvas a starboard quarter view as the ship tacks towards the Wirral side of the river. A small boat has rowed out from the shore to greet the vessel and perhaps receive early messages.

Although the pennant giving the name *Helen* flies at the main mast, the Marryat flag hoist on the mizzen does not correspond to either of the known codes for *Helen*. The hoist as depicted in all three views reads 1 d.p. 2 4 5 followed by a partially obscured flag which is either 8 or 9. The 1837 number for *Helen* was 2159 and from 1841 was 4987.[2] The unidentified flag of a white cross on a blue background on the foremast is probably the Sharples house flag. The red ensign flies at the after peak.

In the far distance under the bowsprit of the main view, the Perch Rock Fort and Lighthouse can be seen against the Wirral coastline.

The vessel was built as *Helen Sharples* in Quebec in 1840 but was registered as *Helen* on her arrival in Liverpool in August of that year. Her owners were two Liverpool timber merchants, Henry Sharples and Owen Jones, trading as William & Henry Sharples & Co.. In 1854 she was bought by Nicholas Treweek of Amlwch, Anglesey but returned to Liverpool ownership the following year when she was purchased by Richard Wainwright, a merchant. *Helen* was abandoned at sea, waterlogged in mid-Atlantic, in September 1859.[3] She had a varied career, voyaging to Australia, the east coast of the United States and South America.[4]

The composition very closely follows an 1835 canvas by Walters of the ship *John Bagshaw*, formerly at the Peabody Essex Museum, Salem.[5]

1983.455
Oil on canvas
63 cm x 97.5 cm
Prov: Sotheby's Chester, 1983
Exh: Liverpool, 1986
Ref: Port Panorama 1986, p.28 (ill.); Marcil, p.150 (ill.)

Vessel: 133.9 ft (l), 31.5 ft (b), 22.1 ft (d); 861 gross tons

1 Inscribed on label on stretcher.
2 The situation is slightly confused because no copy of the 8th edition which was published between 1837 and 1841 has been located to date.
3 LCR, Vol. 54, No. 165, 24 August 1840 and Vol. 80, No. 238, 12 July 1855. For Quebec registration see Marcil, p. 373.
4 LR, 1843-50, 1855-59.
5 Brewington PM, no. 1716, p.446 (ill).

232 *No.6 Pilot Sloop Irlam*

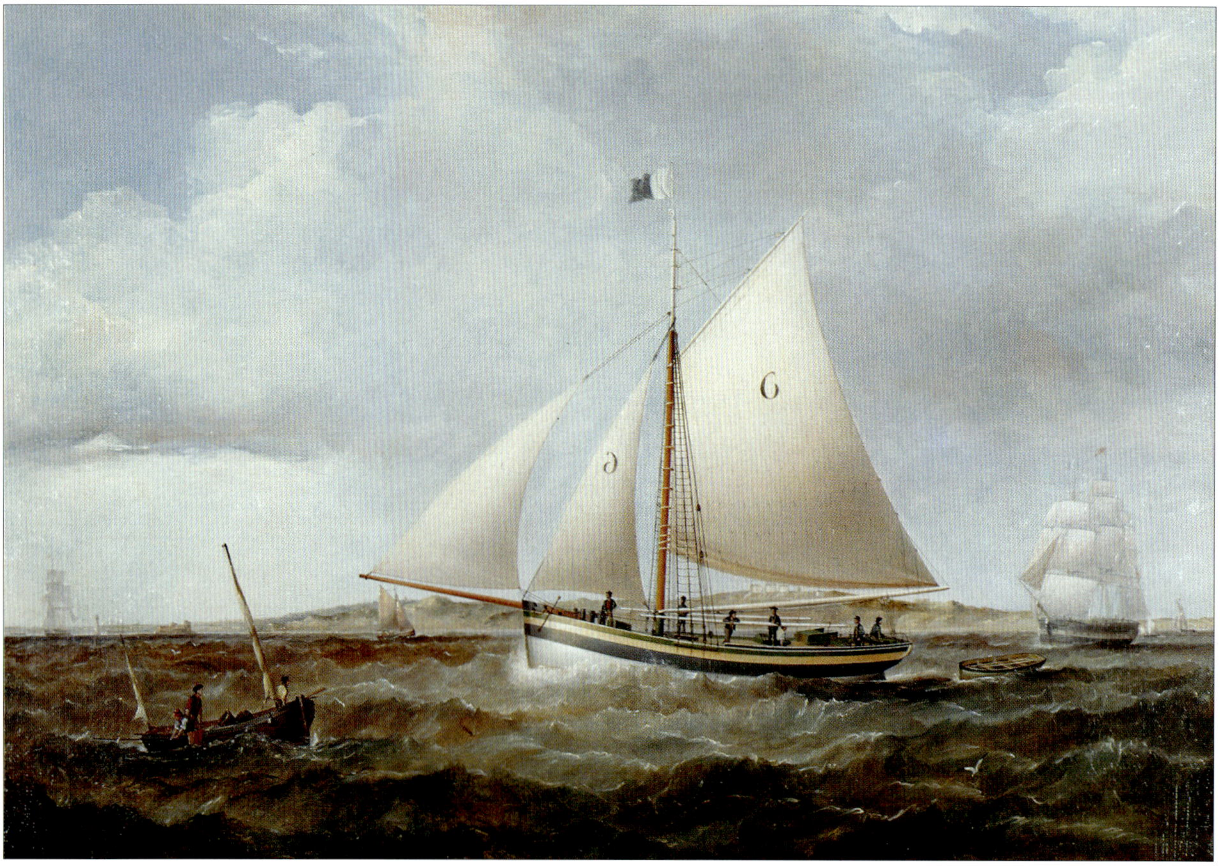

1948.21
Oil on canvas
68.5 cm x 98 cm
Signed and dated (br) "S. WATERS / 1834" (sic)
Prov: Miss Jones, from whom purchased, 1948
Exh: Crosby 1951, no. 93; Liverpool, 1957; Liverpool 1986
Ref: Finch 1975, p.105 (ill); Port Panorama, 1986, p.29 (ill); Davidson 1992, p.153 (ill, detail).

Vessel: 49.3 ft (l), 16.3 ft (b), 8.3 ft (d); 53 tons

This painting of the No.6 Pilot sloop *Irlam* is one of the most detailed portraits of a pilot vessel, providing valuable evidence of the equipment and layout of a pilot boat of this period. She is shown off the north Wirral coast on station awaiting vessels inward bound for Liverpool.

The pilot boat fills the centre of the foreground of the canvas providing a very detailed view of the vessel. On board are eight pilots in their top hats and other crew can be seen in relaxed poses on the look out for approaching shipping. She flies the blue peter, indicating she has pilots available, and a small square flag inscribed "6" at her masthead. She tows a small punt used for placing pilots on boat ship. Astern an unidentified ship approaches under full sail. In the left foreground a small fishing boat is depicted and there are other vessels in the far distance including a sloop (visible under *Irlam*'s bowsprit) in the Rock Channel.

Irlam, named after the Lancashire village, was built by Mottershead & Hayes of Liverpool in 1831. Although described as a sloop she is almost identical to the vessels termed cutters, though there may be some variation in hull design, the cutter being proportionately narrower and deeper. At one time sloops had bowsprits which could be withdrawn, as opposed to the fixed one of the cutter. Unlike modern usage, both terms include vessels with two head sails. *Irlam* was sold out of the pilotage service in 1852 and was wrecked when driven ashore near Warren Point, Northern Ireland, later that year.[1]

The sand dunes in the distant background correspond with the area of present-day Harrison Drive and to the far left the Perch Rock lighthouse and fort can be seen.

This is one of Walters' most accomplished early paintings when he has developed his handling of the sea and there are indications of the creamy coloured sea, which is very characteristic of his work in the mid and late 1830s.

1 Rees, p.201.

233 *P S Liverpool*

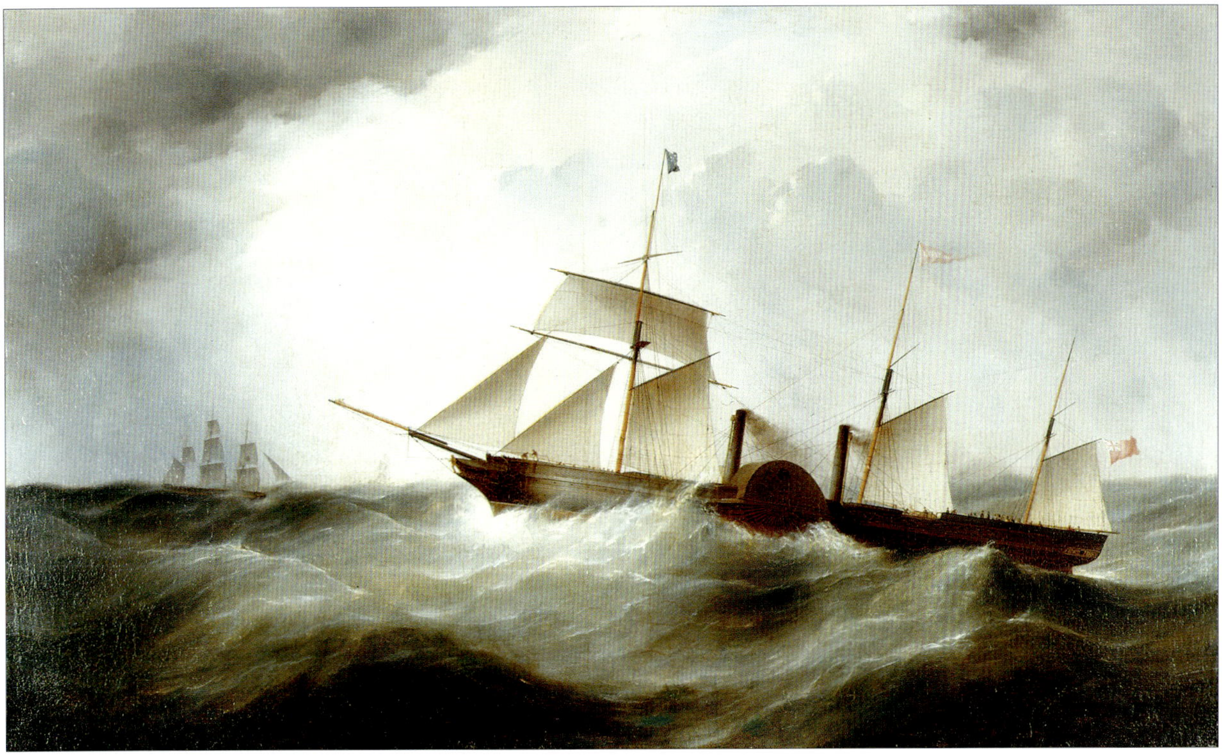

The paddle steamer *Liverpool* is shown in port profile on her maiden voyage from Liverpool to New York in 1838.[2] She is making good progress to windward, close-hauled on a port tack under engine and reefed sails. The vessel is shown battling against the elements using both the power of her paddles and full sails. Groups of passengers can be seen on the after deck. She flies a name pennant from her main mast, the United States jack at her fore to denote her destination and the red ensign at the peak. On the horizon is a packet ship of the American Black Ball line, identifiable by the symbol on her fore main course; with a favourable wind she is making good headway under full sail.

Liverpool was built in wood by Humble and Milcrest of Liverpool, with side lever engines by G Forrester & Co., for Sir John Tobin, one of the port's leading merchants.[3] However, she was purchased before completion by the Transatlantic Steamship Co. (in which Tobin was also a partner). She was the first two funnel steamer on the Atlantic service. She left Liverpool on 20 October 1838 but was forced back to Cork by violent storms in which she lost her figurehead. She eventually reached New York on 23 November.

It might be thought that this painting would have been completed after the maiden voyage. However, *Gore's General Advertiser* for 25 October 1838 not only carries the announcement of the vessel's departure but a note that "a spirited engraved portrait" of *Liverpool* has been published based on "the original by Mr S. Walters."[4] His commercial acumen no doubt told him that interest in the vessel would be at its height during this first voyage.

The Transatlantic Steamship Co. was dissolved in July 1840 and *Liverpool* was sold to the Peninsular and Oriental Steam Navigation Company. Her new owners renamed her *Great Liverpool*. She was lost off Cape Finisterre in 1846.[5]

1924.26.11.2
Oil on canvas[1]
81.5 cm x 132 cm
Prov.: D Blackburn Esq, Liverpool, from whom purchased, 1924.
Exh: Crosby 1951, no. 101; Liverpool, 1986.
Ref. Griffiths 1985, ill. p.107; Port Panorama (1986) ill. p.29

Vessel: 212.9 ft (l), 28.5 ft (b), 19.3 ft (d); 581 tons (burthen)

1 Relined 1983.
2 There is an almost identical print entitled "The Transatlantic Steamship Liverpool Lieutenant R A Fayrer RN Commander on her first voyage to New York, 1838" in NMM see Parker & Bowen 1928, p.180, plate xciii.
3 LCR vol. 53, no. 59, 20 April 1838.
4 GGA, 25 October 1838.
5 Spratt (1980), pp. 33-4.

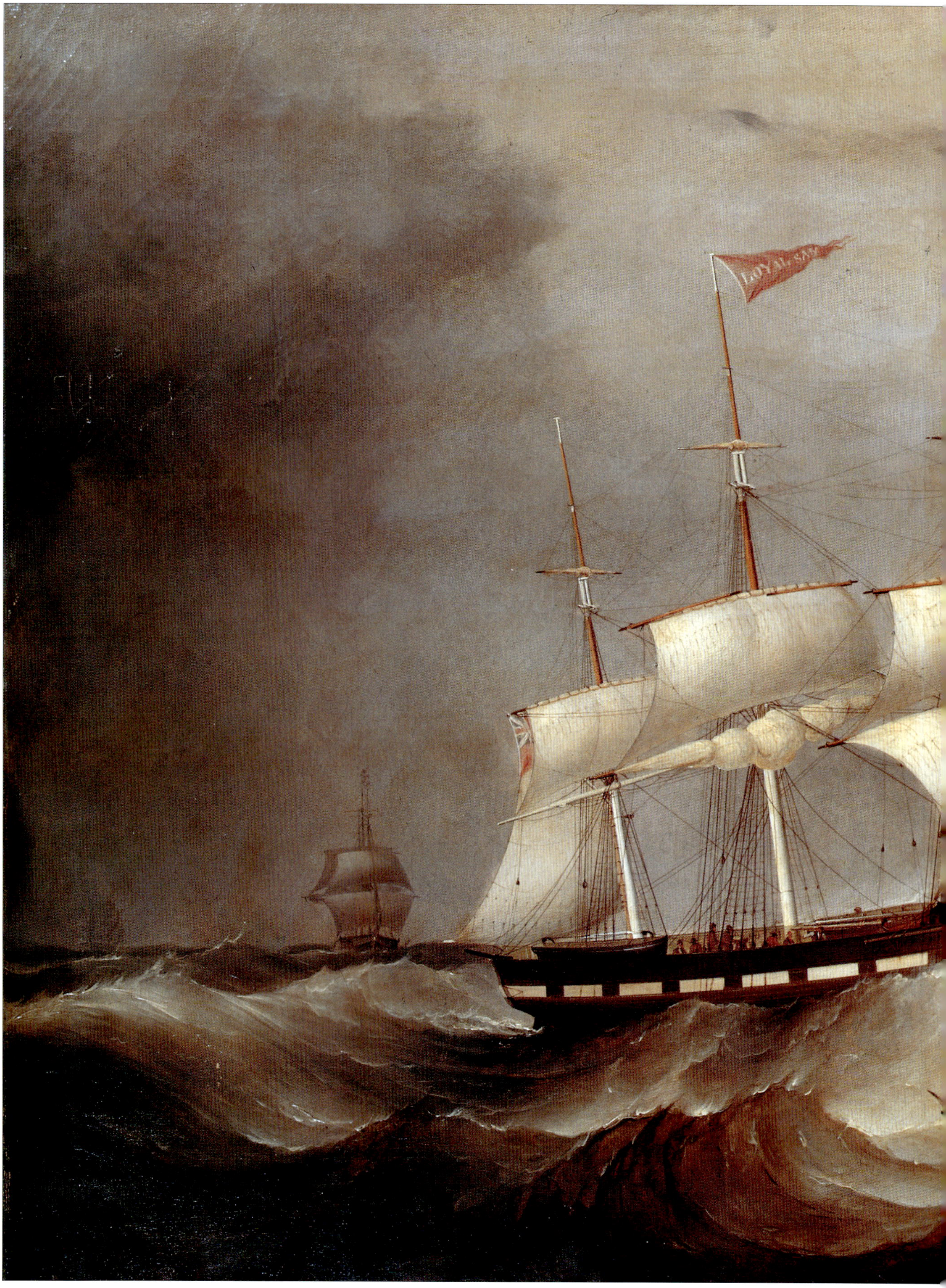
LOYAL SAM

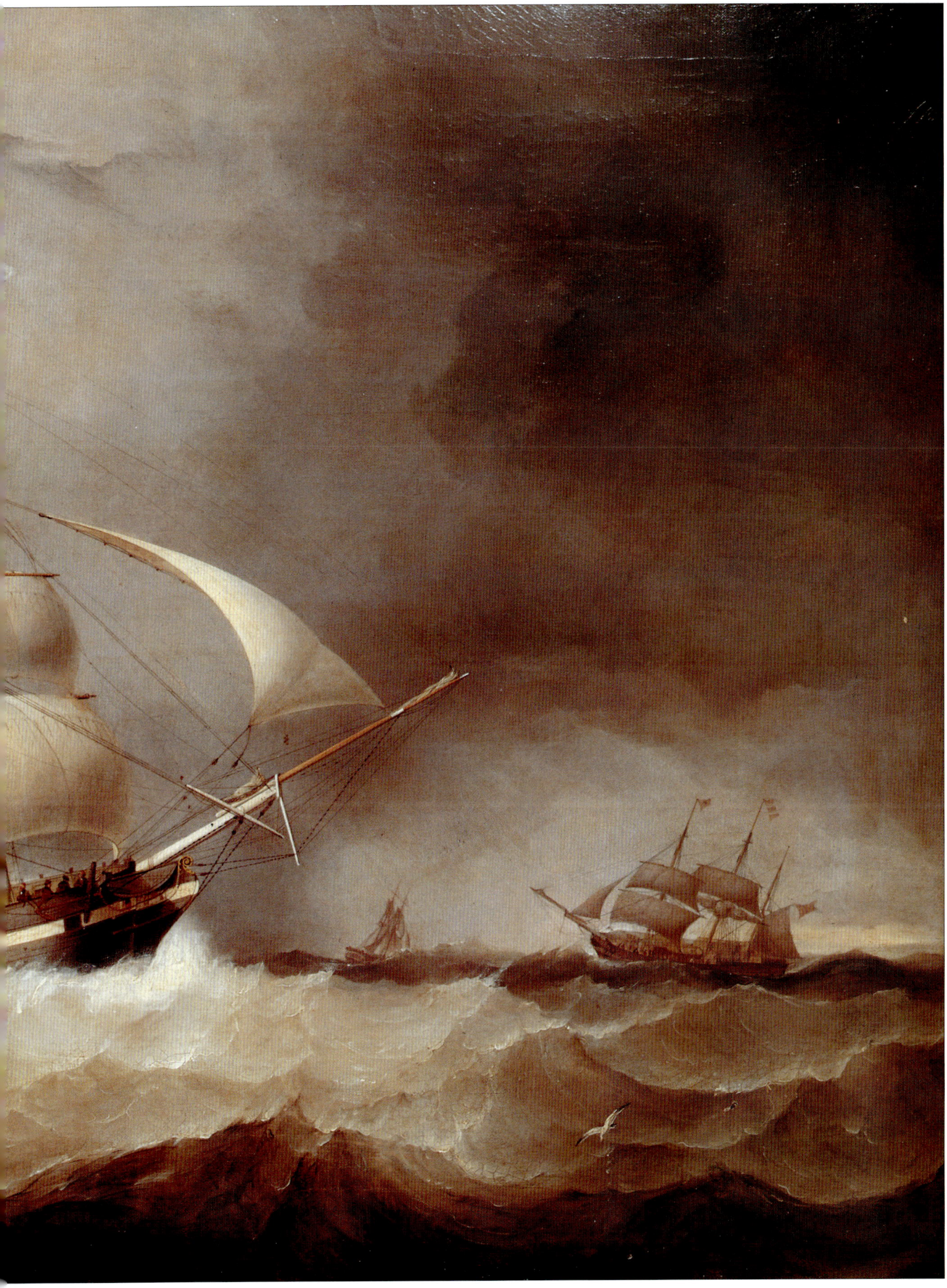

234 *Loyal Sam* (pages 216-217)

1962.152
Oil on canvas
71 cm x 107 cm
Signed and dated (br) "S. WALTERS / 1836"
Prov: Mrs M Cowan, Liverpool, who presented it, 1962
Exh: Arts Council, 1965, no. 36; Liverpool, 1986
Ref: Archibald, no. 36; Port Panorama 1986, (ill. p. 31)

Vessel: 95 ft 3 in (l), 25 ft 3 in (b), 16 ft 2 in (d); 239 tons (burthen)

Ostensibly a simple portrait of the ship rigged *Loyal Sam*, this is one of Walters' most accomplished and interesting canvases. In the centre, identified by a name pennant on the main, *Loyal Sam* is portrayed in starboard profile in strong winds and following seas, with her sails matched to the conditions. The main course is furled and the other sails reefed, with the exception of the foremast course and the staysail which keep the ship's head before the wind. To the right is a barque in port profile travelling on a parallel course in the opposite direction. Her topgallant spars have been taken down suggesting a winter rig. Although she wears a house flag at the fore, a three flag signal at the main, and red ensign at the peak, these have been painted indistinctly and were presumably not intended to identify a particular vessel. Between the two views a close-hauled brig is almost disappearing over the horizon. Astern of *Loyal Sam*, two other unidentified vessels are shown in bow view.

If there had been a connection between the vessels, Walters would have almost certainly have made this plain by the use of pennants and flags. He may be taking the opportunity to portray a number of different vessels from varying points of sail. *Loyal Sam* was built in Bermuda in 1806 and passed through various owners before she was bought by the Mather Brothers of Liverpool in 1823. She was sold to Joseph Nickels in September 1826 and it is his house flag which is flown at the foremast. She was lost near Maceio, Brazil, on 30 January 1830, with a cargo of cotton.[1]

The vessel is, therefore, portrayed retrospectively and the gap of six years is unusual and unexplained. The creamy hollow of waves in the foreground is characteristic of a number of Walters paintings at this period.

1 The vessel's early history can be traced in LR. The Liverpool ownership details are in LCR, Vol. 38, No. 57, 4 July 1823, Vol. 39, No. 38, 23 February 1824 and Vol. 43, No. 239, 25 September 1826. LR indicates changes to the rig in the years 1824-29 but these are not supported in LCR. For loss see LCR and LL 16 April 1830.

235 *Mail Packet from Liverpool to Glasgow*

1969.152
Oil on canvas
63.5 cm x 86.5 cm
Prov: Parker Gallery, London, from where purchased, 1969.
Exh: Liverpool, 1987a
Ref: Davidson 1992, p.105 (ill).

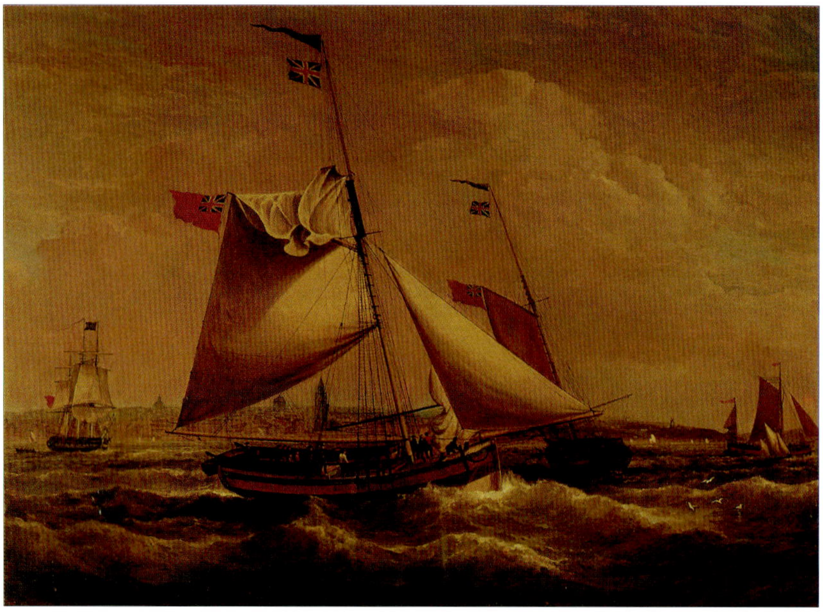

This is a copy of a painting *The Mail Packet from Liverpool to Glasgow, 1805*, by Robert Salmon.[1]

Until the mid-nineteenth century travel by sea was often more convenient and quicker than land transport and vessels known as packets carried the mail, passengers and cargoes on regular services between various ports around the British coast and indeed to Ireland and overseas. There were several traders serving Liverpool and Glasgow at this period, with a boat at least every ten days.[2]

In this painting, the arriving mail packet is portrayed in two views off the Liverpool waterfront. In the centre of the canvas the vessel is shown in starboard profile partially obscuring the second starboard quarter view behind the jib where she has turned towards the shore. She flies a blue pennant over the Union Jack, probably indicating her official business, and the red ensign is at the peak. The main sail is triced up, incidentally allowing a fuller view of the town. In the distance, to the left, a ship is close-hauled and to the far right is probably a Dutch vessel with a characteristic rounded hull.

As Wilmerding points out, the original painting is an unusual example of Salmon's early work with its free execution, loose brushwork and low point of view. Walters follows Salmon very closely in the composition but in copying the detail, lacks the crispness of the original. In particular, many of the buildings along the waterfront are only shown in outline and Walters takes an independent line by placing St Nicholas' church much more prominently behind the main view and increasing its size. He also abandons Salmon's stylish treatment of the sea adopting a more natural approach.

Although the general lack of technical adroitness suggests a youthful work, the treatment of the sea is consistent with a later date, probably in the 1860s.[3] We can only guess at the reasons for producing this copy.

1 In the collection of Dr & Mrs A Kulin, Waltham, Massachusetts (1971), see Wilmerding, 1971, pp. 60 (ill), 77.
2 GDL, 1805, p.20 and addenda.
3 A comparable sea is *Baroda* (no. 227). Davidson, 1992 suggests this is a late work

236 *S S Morocco*

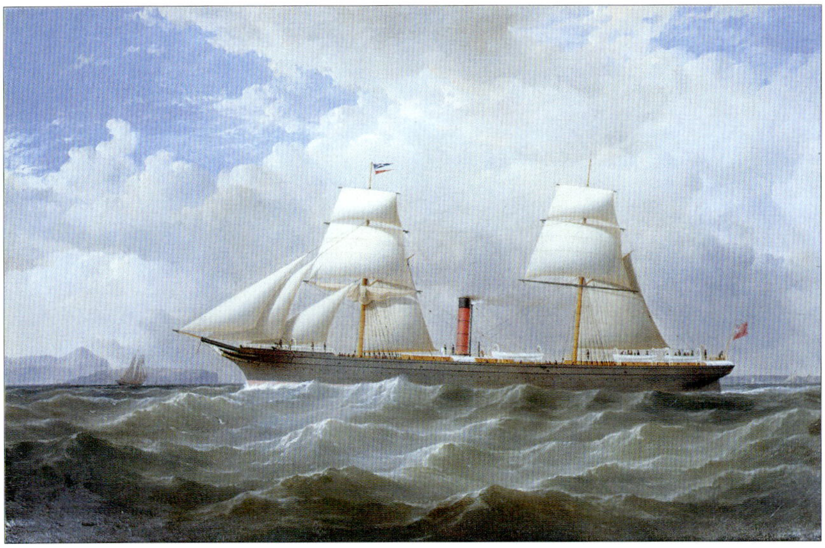

1928.89.3
Oil on canvas
67 cm x 106 cm
Signed and dated (bl) "S. WALTERS / 1862"
Prov: H. Cox, Liverpool, from whom purchased, 1928

Vessel: 275.5 ft (l), 36.3 ft (b), 25.7 ft (d); 1855 tons

The iron hulled *S S Morocco* is shown in port profile, off the North Wales coast. She is rigged as an auxiliary brig and is inward bound for Liverpool under power and sail. At her foremast she displays the pennants of Burns and MacIver, agents of the Cunard Company - a white saltire on a blue ground above a plain red one. The red ensign flies at the stern. There is good detail on the deck with the anchor being made ready and the bell visible alongside. A pole compass, lifted away from the effects of the metal hull by a wooden tripod, is alongside the officer on the raised after deck.[1] A number of passengers can be seen promenading on the aft deck, including a woman with a parasol. Other unidentified shipping, including a schooner and paddle steamer to the left, can be seen in the far distance.

Morocco was built in 1861 by William Denny & Bros. of Dumbarton as one of seven ships for the British and Foreign Steam Navigation Company, Cunard's Mediterranean arm. She was fitted with engines by Tulloch & Denny. Unlike her sister ships, who ended up on the North Atlantic run, she was employed for the whole of her career in the Mediterranean service. She could carry 70 cabin

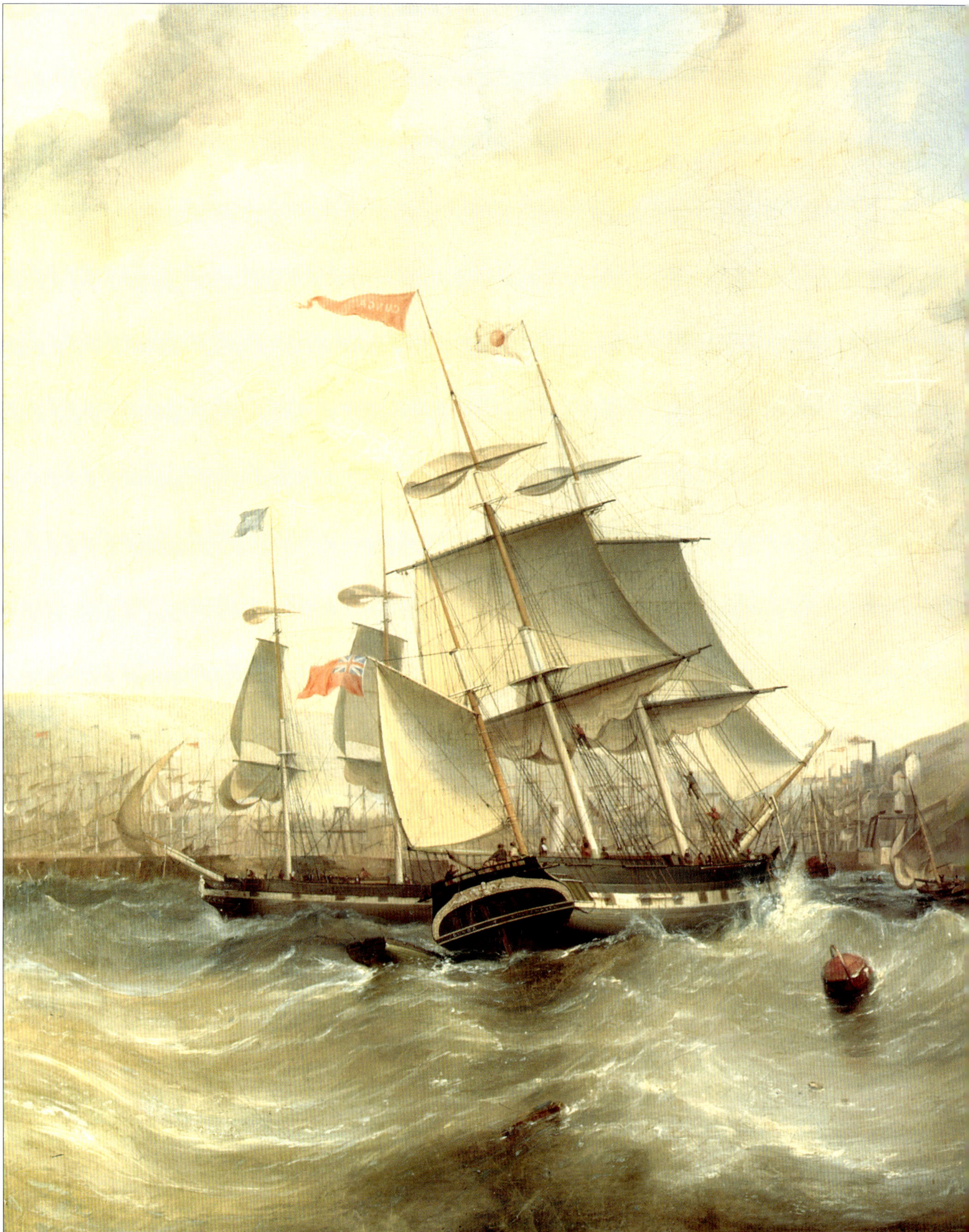

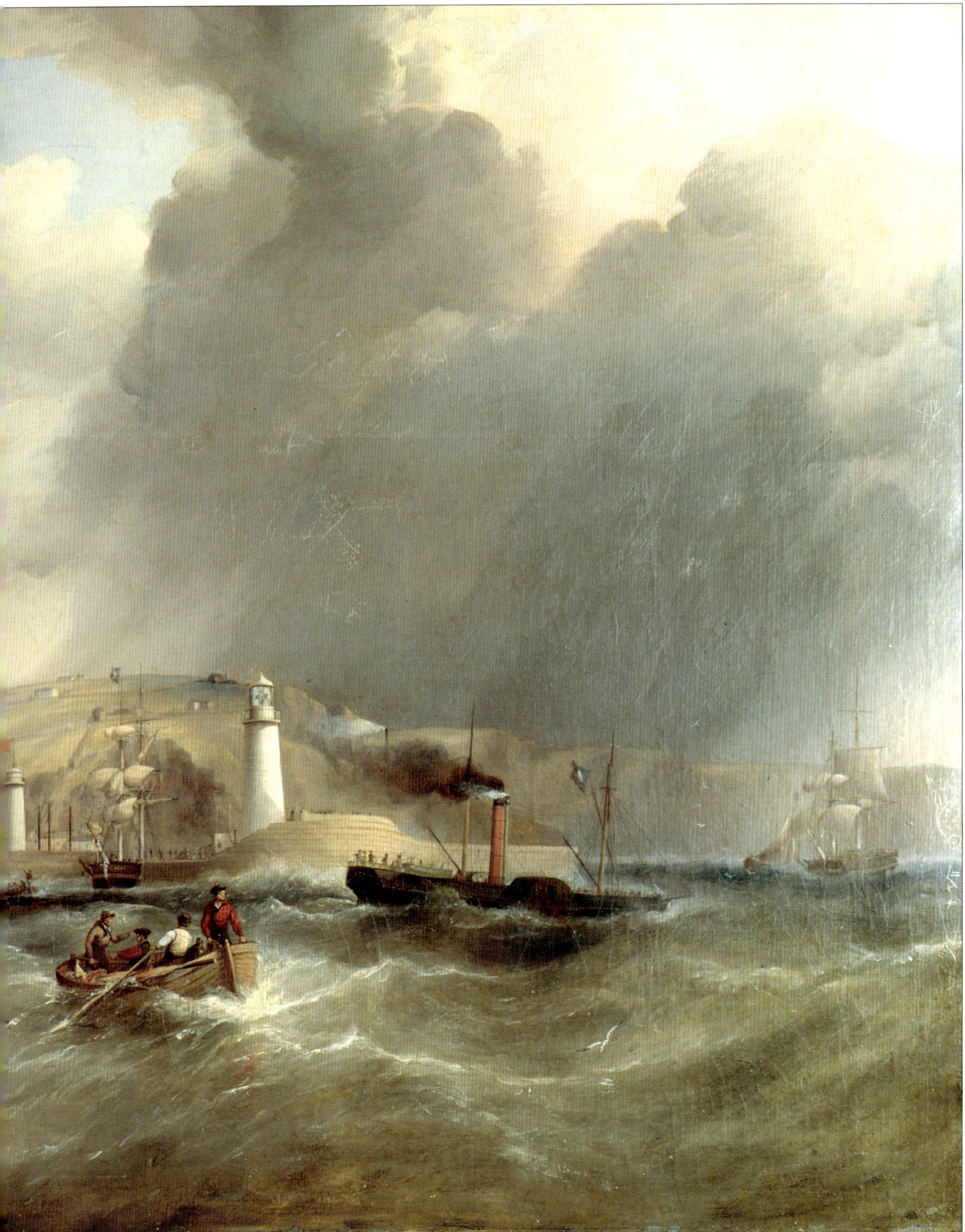

passengers and 800 steerage and she acted as a feeder for the transatlantic emigrant trade. She was sold for scrap in 1897.[2]

In the background is the North Wales coast with the headland of the Great Orme and a sketchy outline of Llandudno to the left; the Anglesey coastline is visible astern of the vessel.

1 See H Pasch *Illustrated Marine Encyclopaedia*, Antwerp, 1890, p.203.
2 Haws Cunard, p. 35.

237 The Port and Harbour of Whitehaven (pages 220-221)

1955.257
Oil on canvas[1]
84 cm x 139 cm
Signed (br) "S WALTERS"
Provenance: J F Younghusband Esq.; unknown; in collections before 1939.
Exh: Liverpool 1974
Ref: Davidson, 1992, (ill) p.178

Vessels:
Gunga 98 ft 5 in (l), 25 ft 2 in (b), 17 ft 2 in (d); 227 tons
Calder 88.3 ft (l), 22.3 ft (b), 15.3 ft (d); 200 tons

This busy scene off the entrance to Whitehaven harbour shows a variety of shipping, including three vessels owned by Younghusband and Co. who were based in the town. The picture was painted for J F Younghusband and was completed before December 1840 when a print after the painting was published.[2]

The principal vessel shown in starboard quarter profile to the left of centre is the barque *Gunga*, clearly identifiable with her name and port of registration on the stern. She is making for the harbour under reduced sail and her crew are going aloft to make further adjustments as she nears the entrance. She flies the red ensign from the peak, a name pennant from her main mast and presumably house flag, of red ball against a white ground, from the fore. To her left the brig *Calder*, identifiable from her name on the bow, is outward bound. She flies the blue peter from her foremast. Emerging from behind the west pier is another brig, which is probably *Bleng*, though only part of the name is legible on the bow.[3] Again she flies the blue peter. A number of small boats occupy the centre of the canvas and to their right is a paddle steamer, possibly the Brocklebank-built *Earl of Londsdale*, of the Whitehaven Steam Navigation Company.[4] To the extreme right is an unidentified brig making for port.

The three Younghusband vessels were all built in the town and were employed in the company's trade to the Americas and the Far East. *Gunga* was built in 1834 by John Scott and remained in Younghusband's ownership until lost in the Madras Roads in 1850.[5] *Calder* was built by L Kennedy in 1837, was sold to Liverpool owners in 1856 and disappears from Lloyds Register in 1870.[6] *Bleng*, built in 1836 also by Kennedy, sank in 1840.[7]

The harbour is crowded with ships and a number of landmarks in and around the town are portrayed including on the right, the west pier (completed 1838) and to the left of Gunga's mast, the lighthouse on the north pier completed in 1841, probably under construction.[8]

Compositionally this is one of Walters' most interesting and adventurous canvases. It is not a normal ship portrait. None of the Younghusband vessels is shown in full profile and they are made part of the overall scene. In many ways this approach is more reminiscent of Walters' academic paintings. Was this an attempt to encourage a less rigid form of portraiture? It does not seem to have been a development liked by Walters' clients because there are no similar forays in this direction.

1 Relined.
2 "PORT AND HARBOUR OF WHITEHAVEN......from a picture painted for J F Younghusband Esq." for full details see Davidson 1992, p.196.
3 The names appears to be BLON? but could be read as BLENG.
4 W Sawyers *List of Whitehaven Vessels corrected to February 1840*,(reprinted Moon, 1975).
5 LCR 63, no. 184, 7 July 1849; Sawyers, op. cit..
6 LCR 81, no. 327, 25 November 1856; TB4, p. 452; Sawyers, op. cit..
7 LR, 1840, 1841; Sawyers, op. cit..
8 For details of Whitehaven landmarks see Hay.

238 The Port of Liverpool, 1836 (pages 224-225)

LI.91.4.1
Oil on canvas
106.5 cm x 152.5 cm
Prov: Sir Ernest B Royden; who presented it to the Mersey Docks and Harbour Company, 1931; on permanent loan.
Exh: Liverpool, 1931, No. 405.

This famous view of the port shows a number of vessels in the Mersey battling against a northerly gale during the high water of a spring tide.

To the left the ship rigged *John Bagshaw* and a ketch are running up river before the gale force winds. The ship is just about identifiable from a now rather rubbed name pennant which reads "JOHN BAGS[HAW]". She is shown in a starboard view with her crew up in the yards working hard to bring in the forecourse and the main topsail. The ketch, which flies a Dutch national flag, is heeling over towards the other vessel in a starboard quarter view.

The other main vessel depicted, on the right, is the ship *Maria Brandt* which is shown in port bow view straining at her anchor. She has already lost her bowsprit and again her crew are in the yards taking in the forecourse and the main course. In the foreground some brave salvagers are attempting to recover part of a mast with grappling hooks from a small rowing boat. Other vessels in the background are battling against the conditions including a ship with Dutch flag to the far left, a paddle steamer in the centre, which is probably bound for the Isle of Man, and other small coastal craft.

The fine view of Liverpool includes, from the left, the long wall of Princes Dock with the masts of numerous ships safely berthed in the dock itself, the dome of St Paul's Church, various warehouses, the tower and church of St Nicholas on the waterfront, with George's Dock and George's Baths to the right and the dome of the Town Hall behind.

John Bagshaw was built in Liverpool in 1835 by Robert Clarke and William Nickson for their own use. She was employed in the China trade, mainly sailing from London, and was lost off the Cape of Good Hope in September 1842.[1] The 850 ton *Maria Brandt* was built in Archangel for W Brandt of the same port in 1829. She worked between Liverpool and Archangel until about 1838 when she disappears from Lloyds Registers.[2]

The painting was engraved by R G Reeve and published by Henry Lacy in Liverpool in 1836 and produced in a number of editions as both a coloured and a monochrome aquatint.[3]

A painting of *John Bagshaw* entering the Mersey by Walters, dated 1835, was formerly in the Peabody Museum.[4]

Vessels:
John Bagshaw 115 ft 3 in (l), 28 ft 2 in (b), 19 ft (d); 416 gross tons.
Maria Brandt 850 gross tons

1 LCR, vol. 50, no. 65, 13 April 1835; LR 1835-1841.
2 LR 1830-1838.
3 Copies in MMM, coloured aquatint 1953.41.5, monochrome aquatint 1971.246.24, 1966.301.6, 1982.861.
4 Brewington PM, no. 1716, p.446 (ill).

239 *Pride of Liverpool leading vessels into the Mersey during the Great Storm of 1866*

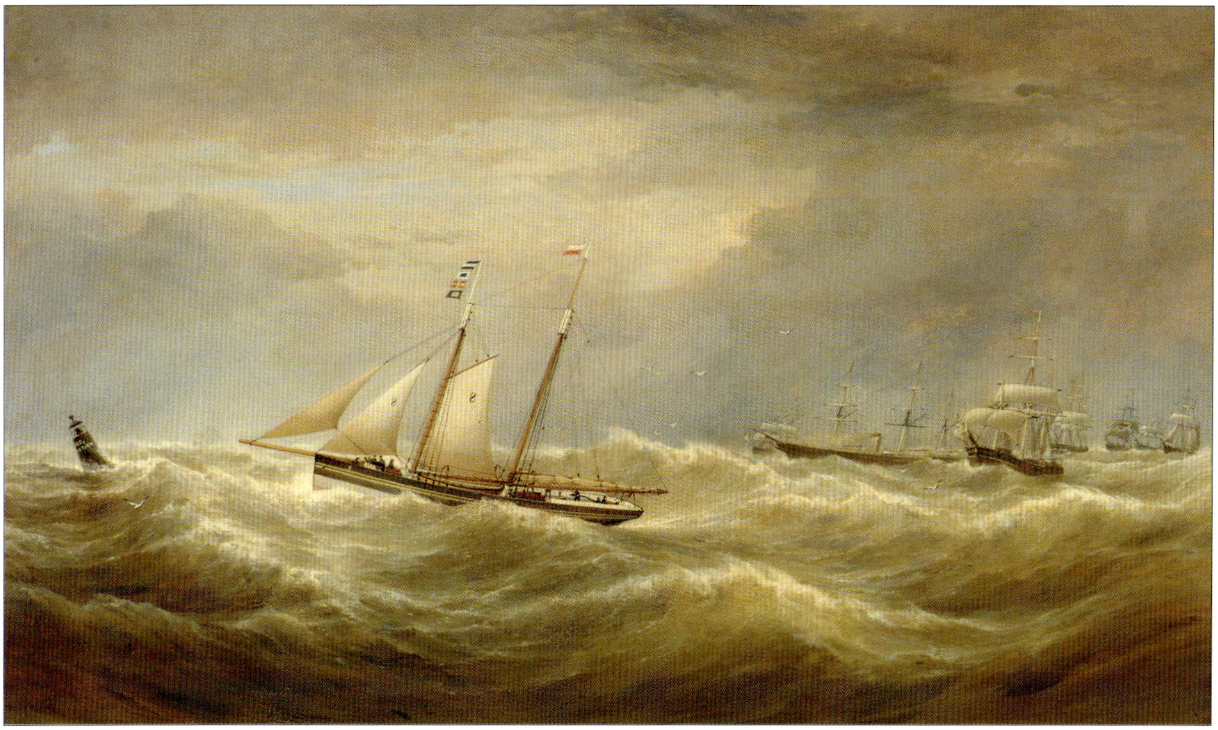

This is one of the famous "Follow Me" incidents when a pilot boat led a group of vessels into the Mersey during storm conditions. Here Walters is portraying the occasion on 9 January 1866 when the No. 8 Pilot Boat *Pride of Liverpool*

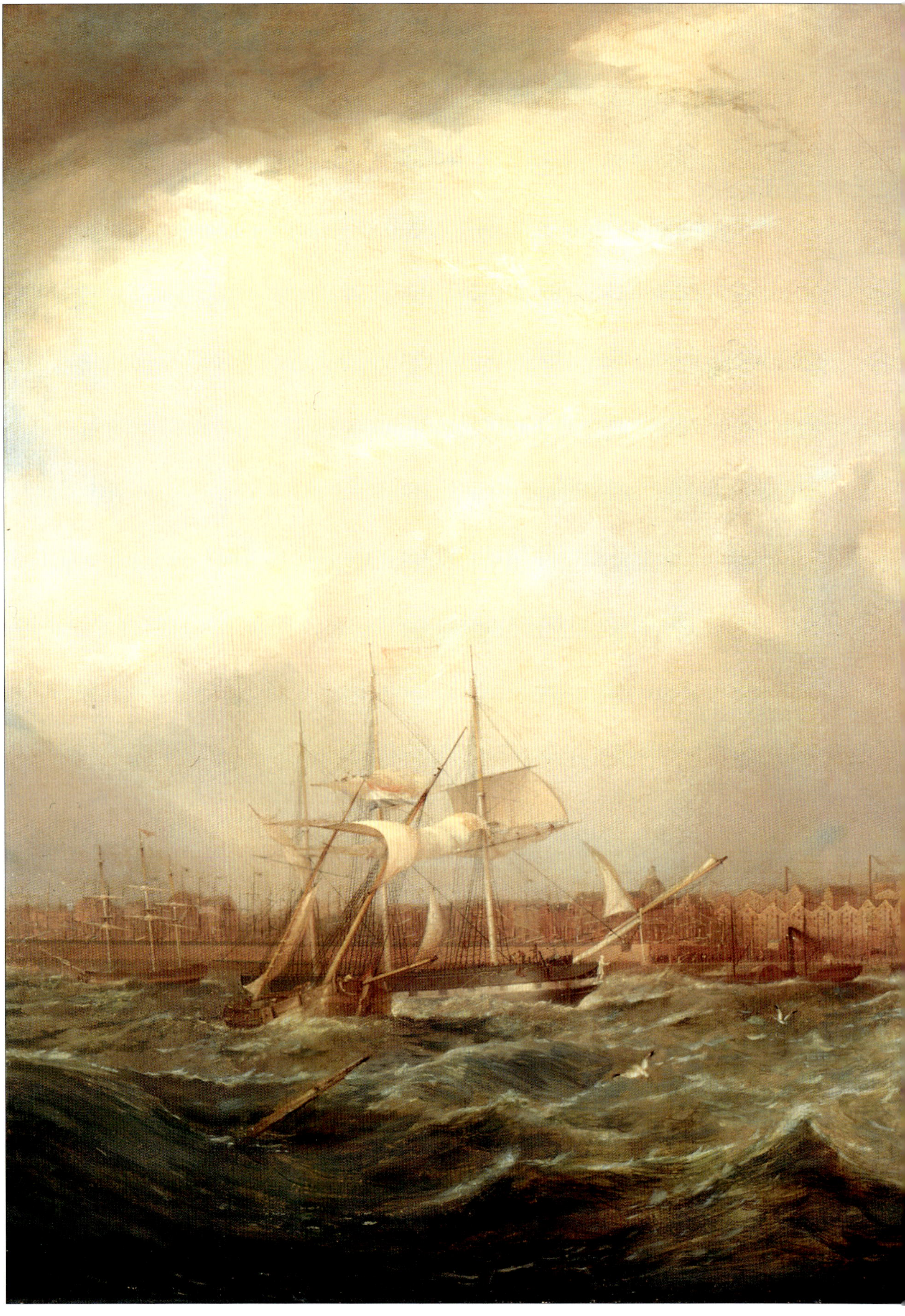

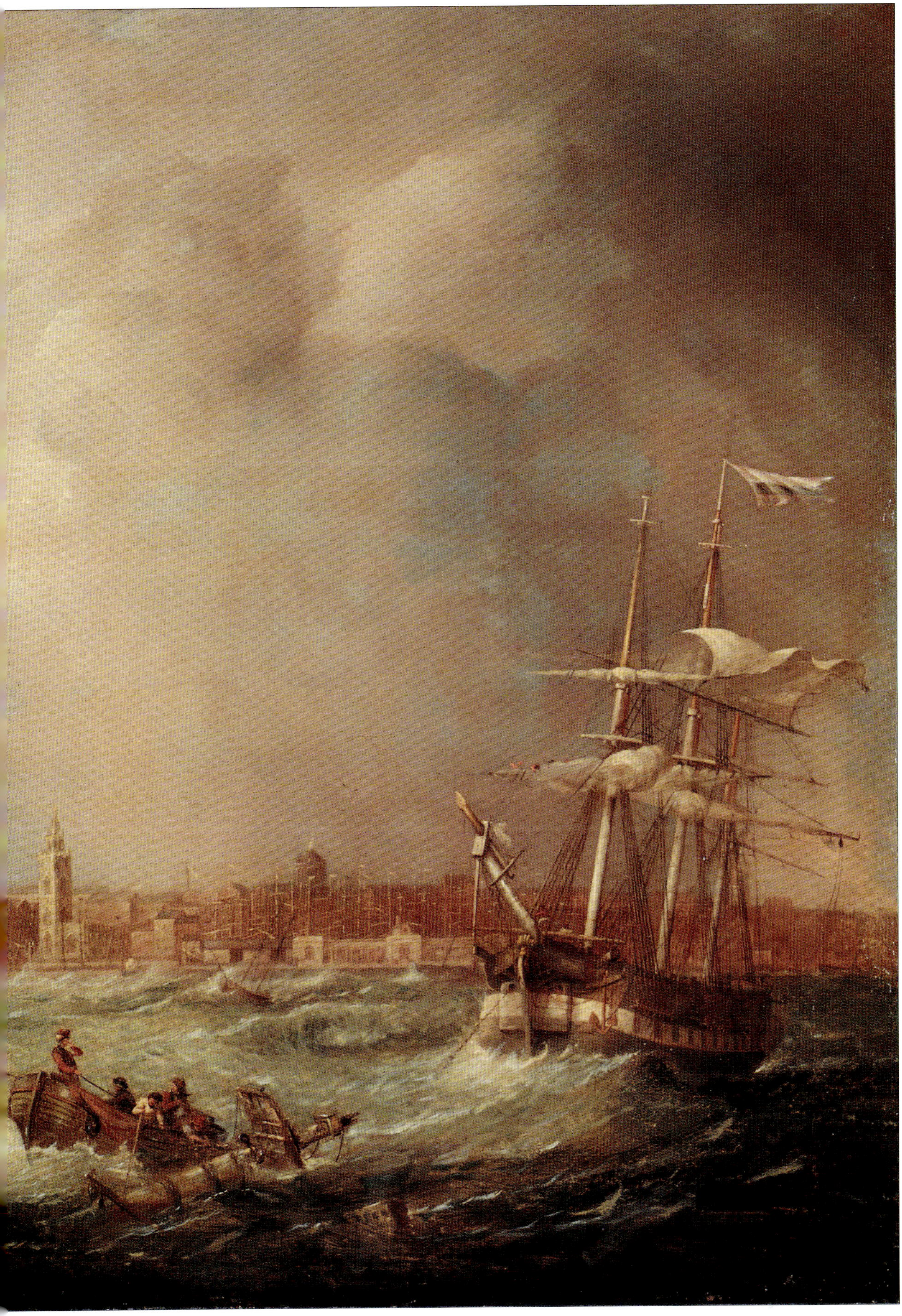

LI.91.4.2
Oil on canvas
72.5 cm x 121 cm
Signed and dated (bl) "S. WALTERS / 1871"
Prov: Presented to Samuel R Graves MP by the Liverpool Master Pilots Association, January 1871; by descent to W S Graves, who presented it to the Mersey Docks and Harbour Board, January 1931; on permanent loan.
Ref: Rees, p. 155.

Vessel: 80 ft (l), 17.6 ft (b), 9.7 ft (d); 64 tons

brought in twelve vessels from beyond the Mersey Bar and led them up the Crosby Channel to the safety of the port.
The schooner rigged pilot boat is shown in the centre ground in a port profile battling against the gale conditions using only her fore sails. She is heeled over towards the viewer and the pilots and other crew can be seen in various parts of the boat. She is flying the pilot flag from her main mast and the signal "Will you follow me" at the fore mast. In the distance to the right is the group of vessels following her. A steamer, probably *Athenian*, is just at their head and the majority of vessels are ship rigged. Although there are various flags depicted it is not possible to identify all the vessels individually and Walters has chosen only to show seven of the twelve assisted.[1]
To the far left a buoy is shown at the entrance to the channel. In the far distance between the pilot cutter and the buoy another ship is shown on the horizon.
Pride of Liverpool was built in 1861 by Thomas Royden & Sons of Liverpool. She remained in service until sunk off Point Lynas by *S S Rydal Water* in February 1890 without loss of life.[2]

1 The incident is described in Rees, pp. 154-155.
2 Rees, p. 203

240 *Brig Robert Quayle*

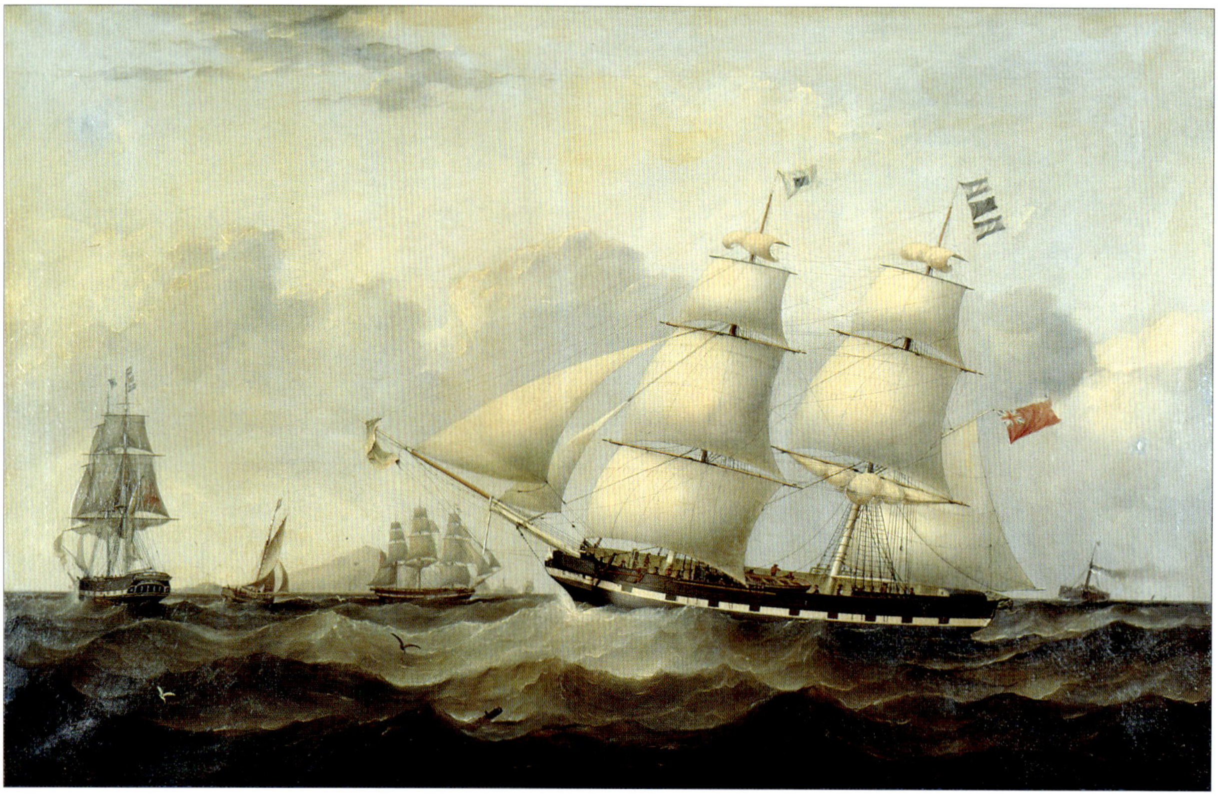

1962.151
71 cm x 107 cm
Oil on canvas
Provenance: T S Thearle, New Brighton, who presented it, 1962

Vessel: 101 ft 8 in (l), 28 ft 10 in (b), 14 ft 1 in (d); 356 tons burthen.

The brig *Robert Quayle* is shown in two views off Anglesey, picking up a pilot on her inward journey to Liverpool. The main view is placed slightly to the right of centre where the vessel is shown in port profile, shortening sail. The viewpoint allows a good view of the deck and crew about their business. The narrative continues to the left where the vessel is shown hove-to in port quarter profile about to drop anchor, awaiting the pilot who is on board the small punt coming alongside. The pilot cutter is manoeuvring, presumably to rendezvous with the returning punt. She flies the blue peter to show she is on station. An unidentified 3-masted ship can be seen in the middle distance under *Robert Quayle*'s bowsprit and astern a paddle steamer is shown approaching.

The vessel is identified by her Watson's Code flag hoist of 141 on the main mast in each view and the name on the stern in the second view. The flag on the foremast, central blue square on white ground, also appears on *Loyal Sam* (no. 234) and is presumably a Nickels house flag. The red ensign flies from the after peak.

Robert Quayle was built in Liverpool in 1814 by James Page & Co. and was owned by various groups of local merchants. In 1830 she was bought by Joseph Nickels, probably as a replacement for the recently lost *Loyal Sam.*[1] The vessel was re-rigged as a barque in 1834 and was re-registered in London. She disappears from Lloyds Registers after 1838.[2]

The pilot cutter is identifiable as *The Prince of Wales* from the number '8' on her main sail. She was a square-sterned sloop built by Finlay Wilson & Co. of Liverpool in 1819 and replaced in 1846.

In the background between the two views of *Robert Quayle* is the familiar profile of Anglesey's Holyhead mountain with the Skerries to the left and the South Stack lighthouse to the right.

The busy composition with plenty of activity placed well forward on the canvas is typical of Walters' early work, as is the lighter colour of the hollowed sea. Presumably this dates from about 1833, just prior to the vessel's re-rigging.

1 Joseph Nickels is described as ship owner of Harrington, Lancashire, although he was living in Mill Street, Liverpool. He founded the famous Liverpool firm of sail-makers.

2 LCR, 32, No. 135; 34, No.7; 35, No. 58; 43, No. 43; 47, No. 108. She is last mentioned in LL 31 October 1838.

241 *S Y Said*

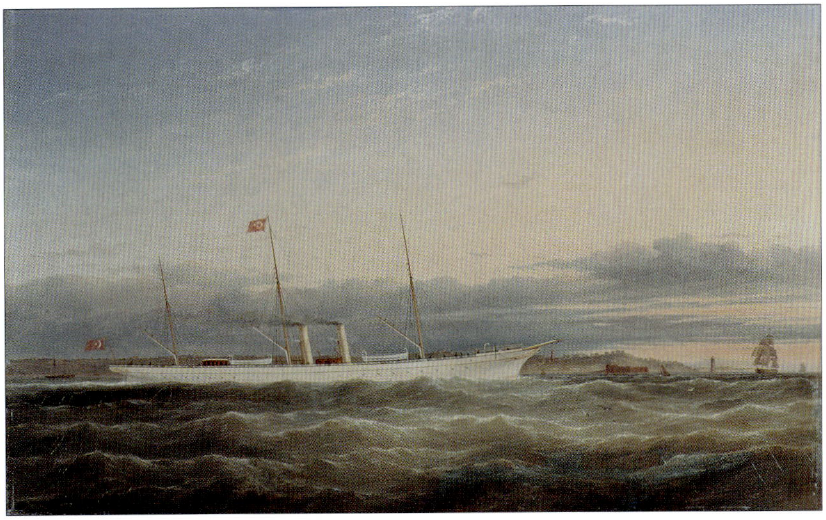

26.11.24.23
Oil on canvas
61cm x 97.5 cm
Signed (bl) '[S] WALTERS / [1858]'
Prov: D Blackburn Esq., Liverpool, from whom purchased, 1924
Exh: Bootle 1959; Liverpool 1986
Ref: Handbook 1935; Bootle 1959; Port Panorama 1986

Vessel: 234.5 ft (l), 128.7 ft (w), 16.6 ft (d); 607 tons

The steam yacht *Said* is shown in starboard profile leaving the Mersey with the Perch Rock Fort and Lighthouse in the background.

Said was an iron schooner-rigged steam screw yacht built by John Jones Junior & Co. (later Jones, Quiggin) of Liverpool for Said Pasha, Viceroy of Egypt.[1] Her two oscillating 250 h.p. engines were supplied by George Forrester of Vauxhall Foundry, Liverpool. According to the specification of the vessel, dated 24 June 1857, the hull and fittings were to be "painted and packed ready for shipment" and "delivered alongside a ship in one of the Liverpool Docks" for re-erection abroad.[2] There was obviously a change of plan and the vessel was completed in Liverpool. She was registered in July 1858 under the ownership of William Fergus McGregor.[3]

No expense was spared in fitting out the vessel. The masts and spars were highly varnished and polished, the deck woodwork was polished teak and oak and the metalwork polished brass. The interior was equally elegant. The saloon 40 ft by 20 ft had a fountain, settees of blue damask silk and a papier mache floor.[4]

The yacht sailed from the Mersey for Alexandria on Friday 15 October 1858 and that is the occasion on which Walters depicts her.[5] She flies the Egyptian flag of a

1 Mehemet Said, Khedive of Egypt, 1854-63.
2 Jones Quiggin Specification Book, ff.80-4, MAL, DX 154.
3 LCR, vol. 82, No. 165, 8 July 1858. McGregor was presumably acting in some agency capacity. The register records the actual sale to the Pasha on 1 March 1859.
4 ILN, 30 October 1858, pp. 401-2; GGA 21 October 1858.
5 GGA, 21 October 1858.

white crescent and star against a red background at the stern and a similar flag with three stars on the main mast.

The Wirral coastline behind the Perch Rock Fort and Lighthouse is particularly well depicted with a nice view of the villas above an incipient New Brighton and the spire of George Gilbert Scott's recently built St James, Victoria Road.

There is a builder's model of this vessel is in the collections, accession number 55.142

242 *P S Scotia*

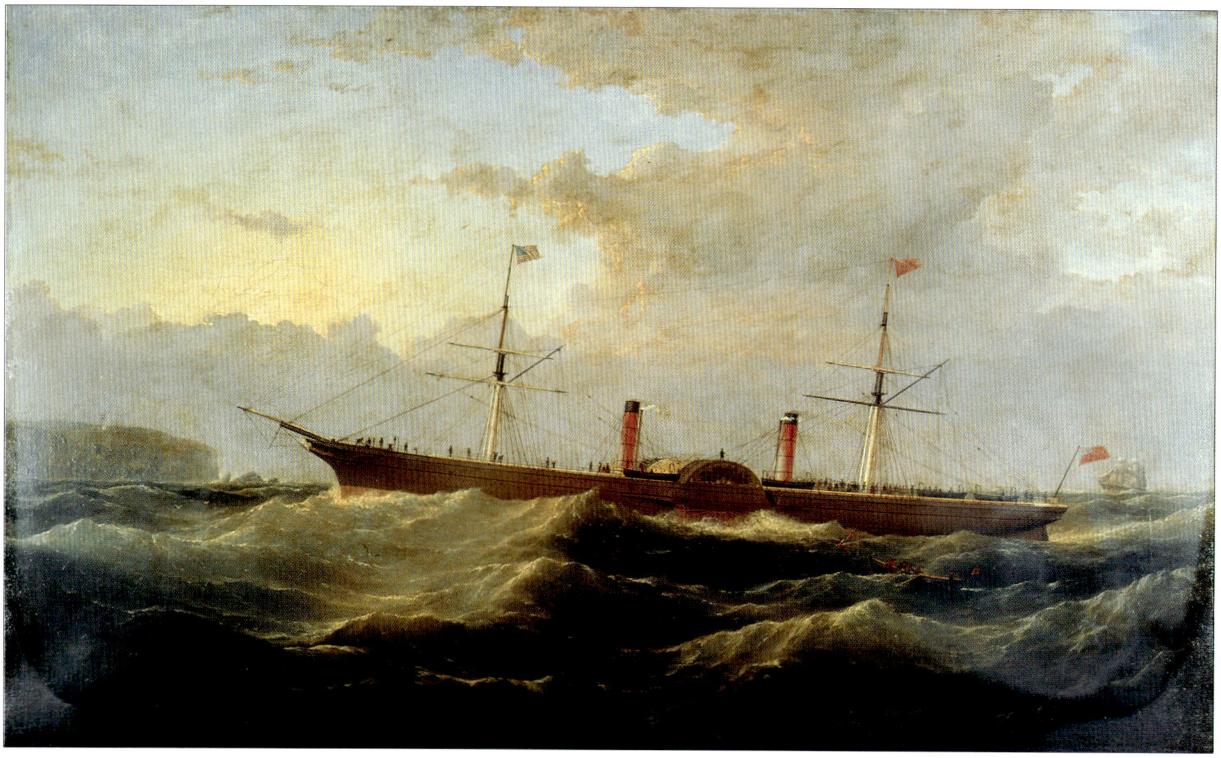

1928.89.1
Oil on canvas
79 cm x 127.5 cm
Signed and dated (bl) "S. WALTERS / 1863"
Prov: D & C MacIver; H. Cox, Liverpool; from whom purchased, 1928
Exh: Liverpool, 1907, No. 136(?); Crosby 1951, no. 100; Bootle, 1959, no. 13; Liverpool, 1986.
Ref: Bygone Liverpool, 1913, plate xli; Port Panorama 1986, p.32 (ill)

Vessel: 379.4 ft (l), 47.8 ft (b), 30.5 ft (d); 3871 gross tons.

Cunard's last paddle steamer *Scotia* is shown in port profile off Cape Race throwing overboard the Associated Press mail for New York, thus allowing important news to be telegraphed ahead.[1] A small rowing boat in the right foreground is moving to collect the canister which is floating between the boat and the steamer. The sailor who has placed the canister in the water is watching from the sponson, overseen by an officer on the apex of the paddle wheel. Many of the passengers have lined the rails to view this ceremony. *Scotia* flies the Stars and Stripes at her foremast, the red ensign[2] at the stern and a red swallow-tailed flag on the main mast, no doubt a signal relating to the mail. The canister carries the same red flag and the rowing boat also flies a red flag with a black circle at the stern.

Scotia was built at Govan on the Clyde by Robert Napier for the Cunard Steam Ship Company. She was launched in June 1861 and went into service in the following year. After the *Great Eastern*, an unusual and commercially unsuccessful vessel, she was the world's largest ship when built. She held the Blue Riband for the fastest crossing of the Atlantic from 1862 to 1867. She had accommodation for 300 passengers and could carry 1400 tons of cargo. She was sold in 1878 to the Telegraph Construction and Maintenance Company and was converted to a twin screw cable-laying ship. She was wrecked at Guam, in the Pacific, in 1904.[3]

In the background is the headland of Cape Race, at the south-eastern corner of Newfoundland, with its lighthouse and the poles of the telegraph. Cape Race is the

1 The specific incident can be identified from the inscription on a print of the painting, "Off Cape Race, Throwing overboard the New York Associated Press parcel", S Walters del. Published by Currier & Ives, New York. Copy in NMM see Parker & Bowen, 1928, p.267, plate cxlix.

eastern most point of the North American continent and was generally the first sight of land for vessels crossing the Atlantic. In the far right distance is a sailing ship with an indistinct Marryat flag code.

An engraving of this painting was produced by Currier & Ives and it was also reproduced as a photographic carte de visite.[4] Walters painted *Scotia* again in 1866 in a view off the Skerries. (N R Omell Gallery, 1978)[5]. He also produced an oil sketch of the vessel running before a gale (Atkinson Art Gallery, Southport)[6] and there is an almost identical oil portrait of this sketch in the Peabody collection. This is unattributed but may also be by Walters.[7]

2 The ensign is inaccurate, missing the red diagonals of the union flag. There is no reason to doubt the authenticity, despite this characteristic of artist here described as Associate of Joseph Heard, Old Ensign.
3 Spratt, pp. 67-8.
4 For the engraving see note 1 above. The carte de visite is in LRO, Accession no. 4569, see Davidson, 1992, p.201.
5 N R Omell Gallery, Catalogue, 1978.
6 Davidson, 1992, p.122 (ill.).
7 Smith, no. 2162, p.73.

243 *Steam Paddle Ferries off New Brighton*

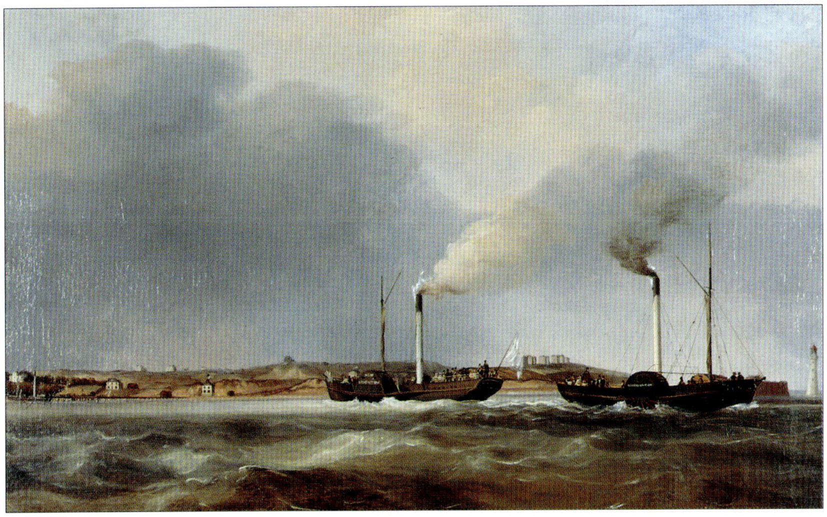

1928.90
Oil on canvas
54 cm x 89 cm
Prov: William Donovan, Rock Ferry, from whom purchased, 1928
Exh: Crosby 1951, no. 103; Liverpool, 1957; Liverpool 1986
Ref: R Cuthbert Woods and P Culverwell Brown *The Rise and Progress of Wallasey*, 1929, ill. opp. p.106; *Handbook* 1935, p.46; Maritime Exhibition Catalogue, 1957, plate x; *Port Panorama* 1986, ill., p.32

Sir John Moore: 103 ft 7 in (l), 16 ft 6 in (b), 8 ft
8 in (d); 50 hp engines, 92 tons.

In this view Walters depicts two ferry steamers off the north Wirral coast. In the centre the paddle steamer *Sir John Moore* is shown in port profile making for the New Brighton pier with a second boat to the right on her way to the Liverpool shore. Each vessel has a good complement of passengers. A third steamer can be seen to the left in the far distance, moored at the end of the pier. Both the main vessels have "NEW BRIGHTON" painted on the paddle box. *Sir John Moore* can be identified from the name on her stern but the second vessel is unidentified. *Sir John Moore* flies a white ensign at the stern, though why this should be is a mystery.[1]

The Liverpool - New Brighton ferry was established in 1833 by James Atherton to serve the holiday and residential area which he had begun to develop on 170 acres of land bought in 1830. *Sir John Moore*[2] took up her duties in March 1834. She had been built in 1826 by J Lang and Denny of Dumbarton, with engines by Murdoch & Cross, for service on the Clyde. The Post Office ran her as the mail packet to Kingstown under the name *Jonathan Hulls* between 1827 and 1833. She continued as a ferry until 1846 when she became a houseboat on the shore at Tranmere.[3]

The detailed background shows to the far left the original wooden pier at New Brighton with a small cluster of houses, including the New Brighton Hotel, just above the shore. Between the two steamers a group of houses is depicted on the hillside, though their odd shape is more reminiscent of modern tower blocks! To the far right the Perch Rock Fort and Lighthouse are shown.

The attribution to Walters is on stylistic grounds consistent with his work in the second half of the 1830s. He painted an unidentified New Brighton ferry towing a brig off the Perch Rock Fort in 1835 (Private Collection, UK).[4]

A model of the vessel (scale 1:48) was made for Wallasey Corporation by Capt. N. Kennedy in 1933.[5]

1 Although legally reserved to the Royal Navy, the white ensign was occasionally used unofficially by merchant vessels. See Wilson, p.34.
2 Named after Sir John Moore (1761-1809), soldier and a native of Glasgow.
3 Duckworth & Langmuir 1956 p. 42; LCR, vol. 49, no. 35, 11 March 1834, vol. 53, no. 31, 1838, vol. 60, no. 200, 1845; her later use as a house-boat is referred to in a letter from the owner's great grandson, in DCF.
4 DCF
5 N W Kennedy *Records of the Early British Steamships*, Liverpool, 1933, p.2 (ill).

244 No.3 Pilot Schooner The Duke

1948.22
Oil on canvas
50 cm x 76 cm
Signed (bl) "S. WALTERS / 1853"
Provenance: Miss Jones, from whom purchased 1948.
Exh: Crosby, 1951, No. 94; Bootle, 1959, No.10; Liverpool, 1986
Ref: Davidson 1986, p.47; Port Panorama, 1986, p.33

Vessel: 69 ft (l), 15.7 ft (b) and 9 ft (d); 62 gross tons.

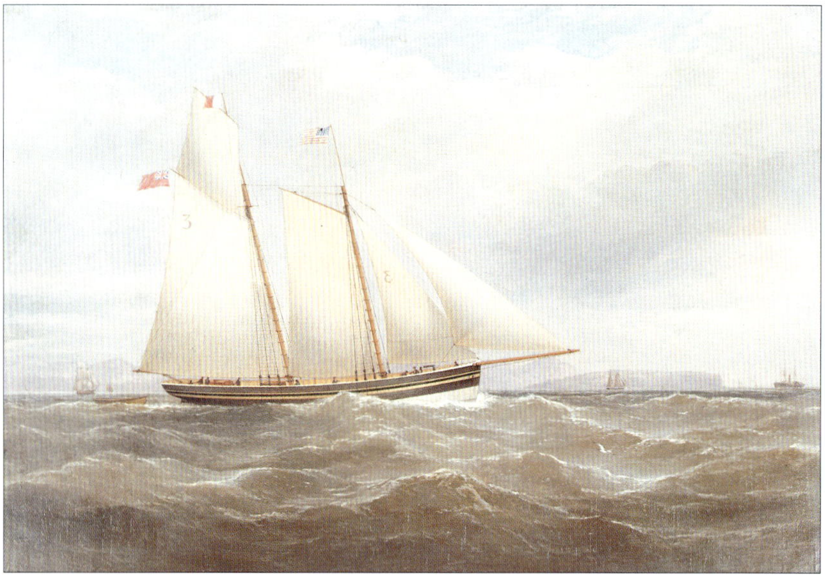

The schooner-rigged pilot boat *The Duke* is shown in starboard profile towing her punt, close-reefed with topsail set, off North Wales. She is identifiable from "3" on her sails and she flies the number 3 flag in the Marryat code at her main mast. The red ensign flies at the peak. The Stars and Stripes being flown at her foremast indicates that she is ready to put a pilot on board an American vessel, probably the Collins Line paddle steamer,[1] which can just be identified by her funnel colours, approaching from the far right-hand distance almost on the edge the canvas.

The Duke was built in 1852 by Buckley Jones of Liverpool as the No.3 boat for the Liverpool Pilot Service. She remained in service until 1894 when she was sold to Danish owners and became a fishing vessel.[2]

In the distance is the North Wales coast with the distinctive headland of the Great Orme beneath *The Duke*'s bowsprit.

1 This will be one of the first four ships built - *Atlantic, Pacific, Arctic* or *Baltic*. They were built with three masts but had the mizzen removed about 1853. See Bonsor North pp. 206-7.
2 Rees, p.203.

245 The snow Trinculo

1932.90
Oil on canvas
60 cm x 87 cm
Prov: C T Bowring & Co., Liverpool; purchased, 1932
Exh: Liverpool 1931, No. 425; Crosby, 1951, No. 95; Liverpool 1986
Ref: Handbook 1935, p.17; Port Panorama 1986, p.32 (ill)

Vessel: 89 ft (l), 24.5 ft (b), 16.8 ft (d); 253 tons burthen

The snow *Trinculo* is shown in port profile hove-to off the Perch Rock Fort and Lighthouse, on the extreme north-east corner of the Wirral peninsula, at the entrance to the Mersey. The vessel, named after the jester in Shakespeare's *The Tempest*, is identifiable from the flags on her foremast, 1, 2, 9 in the Watson Code. The finely painted figurehead is also reminiscent of a jester. She flies a red pennant with a white capital T (probably for *Trinculo*) on the main mast and the red ensign at the after peak.

Around her is a lively scene. A small boat is shown in the foreground and the two top hatted men may be the owner and agent rendezvousing with the ship. Beneath *Trinculo*'s bowsprit an early paddle steamer tug can be seen and a small cutter lies off the fort. Between the fort and lighthouse is an unidentified sailing vessel in bow view which is actually in the Rock Channel and will pass seaward of the lighthouse before coming into the Mersey. Two further ships are depicted in the far distance approaching the same channel.

Trinculo was built at West Cowes on the Isle of Wight in 1833 by Thomas White for Francis Gouthwaite and partners of Liverpool. Her early voyages were to Bombay and Singapore. In October 1839 she was sold to Barton, Irlam and Higginson who

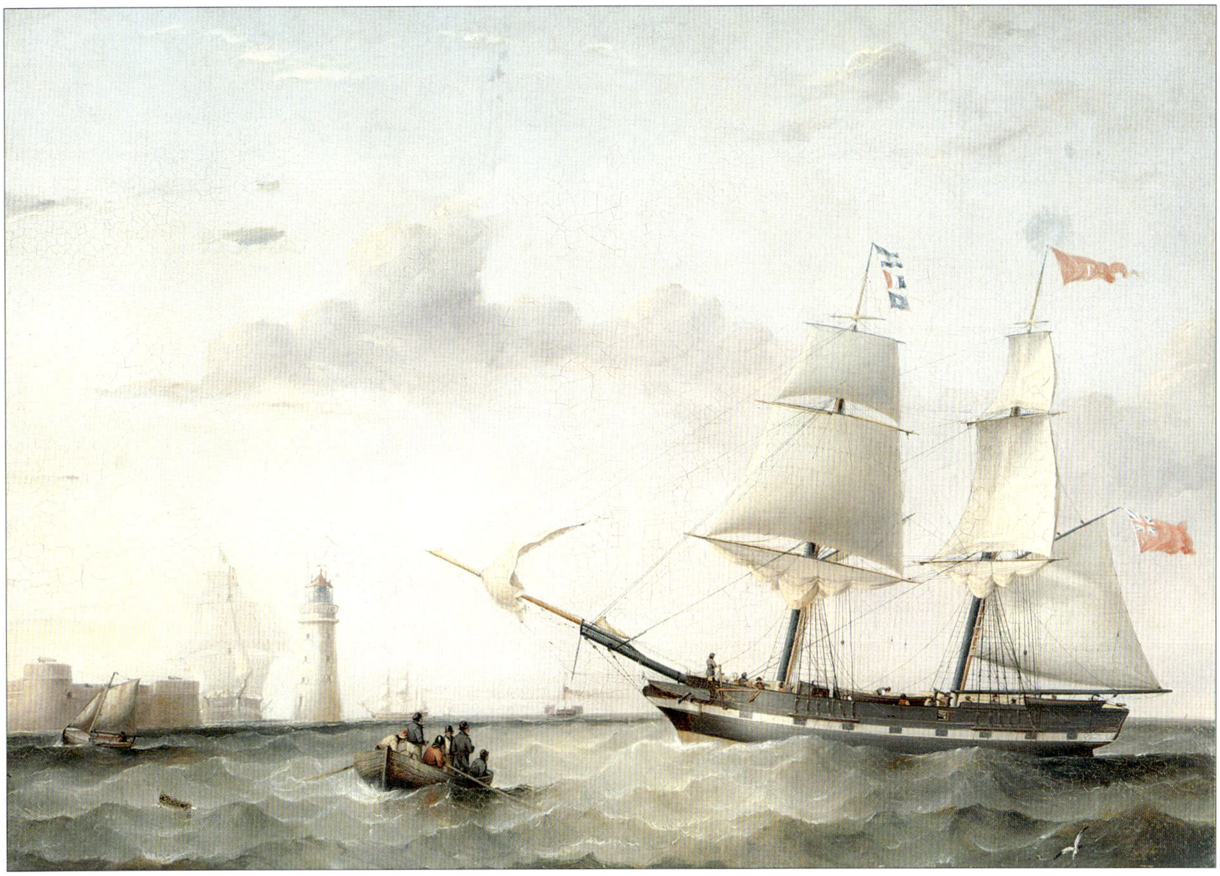

traded between Liverpool and Barbados.[1] She was lost at sea returning from Nassau in 1843.[2]

Like many of Walters' early paintings, this is interesting in compositional terms. The vessel is placed off centre with a good view of the deck and the eye is also attracted by the small rowing boat in the foreground and the background detail. The fort and lighthouse are prominently shown, including the pivot guns on the towers. The creamy sea is typical of the artist's work in the mid to late 1830s.

1 LCR, 48, no. 117, 22 July 1833; LCR, 52, no. 259, 30 September 1836. She made the return voyage to Singapore in eight months in 1838. See advert in GGA 25 October 1838.
2 LCR, 55, no. 203, 31 October 1839.

246 *P S Victory* (page 232)

The paddle steamer *Victory* is shown in port profile approaching Cork under both power and sail to combat the heavy sea conditions. The vessel had three masts and was schooner rigged. The fine figurehead of a lion is prominently depicted. She is identifiable by the name pennant on her main mast and the name on the bow. The flag on the foremast, which features a horse and rider on a white ground with blue border, indicates she is carrying mail for the Post Office. No evidence for the official green ensign at the after peak is known but it may relate to the fact that the company was Irish based. The emblem of St George on her paddle box indicates the ownership of the St George Steam Packet Company. A number of passengers are on deck.

Victory was built by John Wilson & Son of Liverpool in 1832 for the St George Steam Packet Company of Cork. She was one of a number of paddle steamers operating services between various ports in England and Ireland, in particular Cork and Bristol. In 1844 she was sold to the Cork Steam Ship Company and the following year transferred to the Waterford Steam Navigation Company. She foundered off Barrel Rock, Wexford in September 1853.[1]

15.4.10.5
Oil on canvas
33 cm x 63 cm
Signed (br) "S WALTERS 1838"
Exhibited: Wembley, 1924; Bootle, 1959, No.15, Liverpool, 1986
Provenance: John Lecky, Esq., who presented it, 1915
Ref: Finch 1983, p.143 (ill) incorrectly attributed to Heard; Port Panorama, p.34 (ill); Davidson 1992

Vessel: 152 ft 9 in (l), 24 ft 2 in (b), 16 ft (d); 256 gross tons.

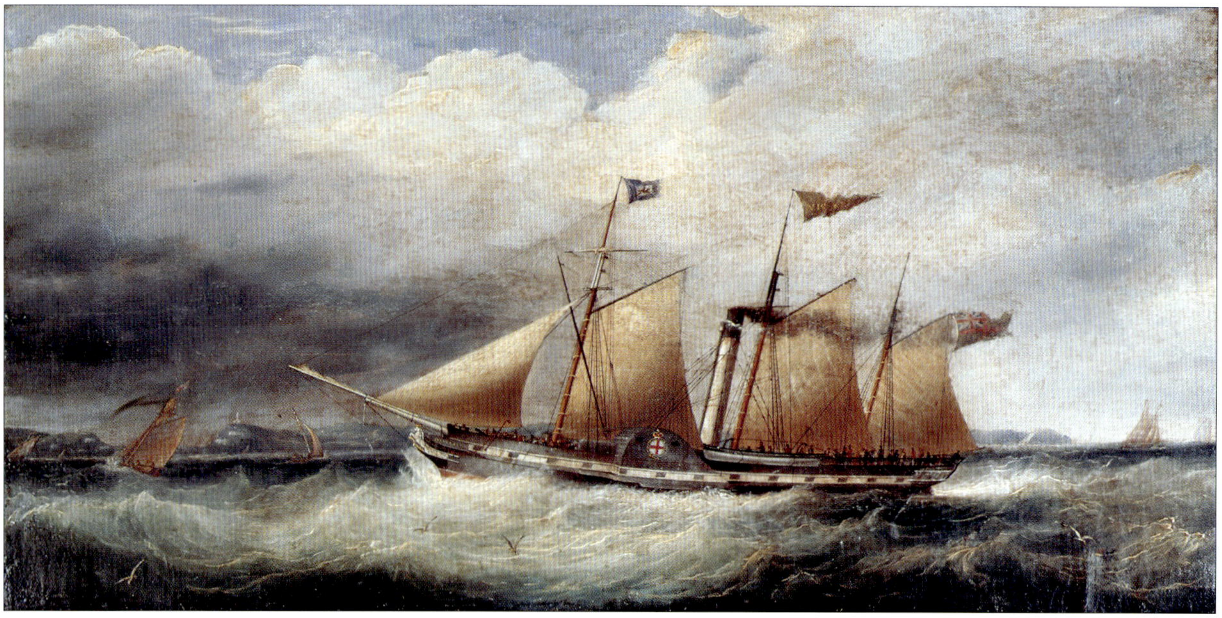

In the background is the Irish coast, off Cork, with the entrance to the port and Roches Point and lighthouse to the left. There are other coastal craft in the distance. Two handwritten notes, formerly on the back of the painting, record details of the vessel's initial ownership including an extract from the registration certificate.[2]

1 R Greenwood and F Hawks *The Saint George Steam Packet Company, 1821-1843*, Kendal, 1995.
2 Handwritten notes on rear of frame (a) details of ownership from JL 1906, vol. 3, p.20 and (b) quoting reminiscences of James Murphy writing in 1888 about PS Victory and Samuel Walters.

247 *The Pleasure Yacht Zephyr*

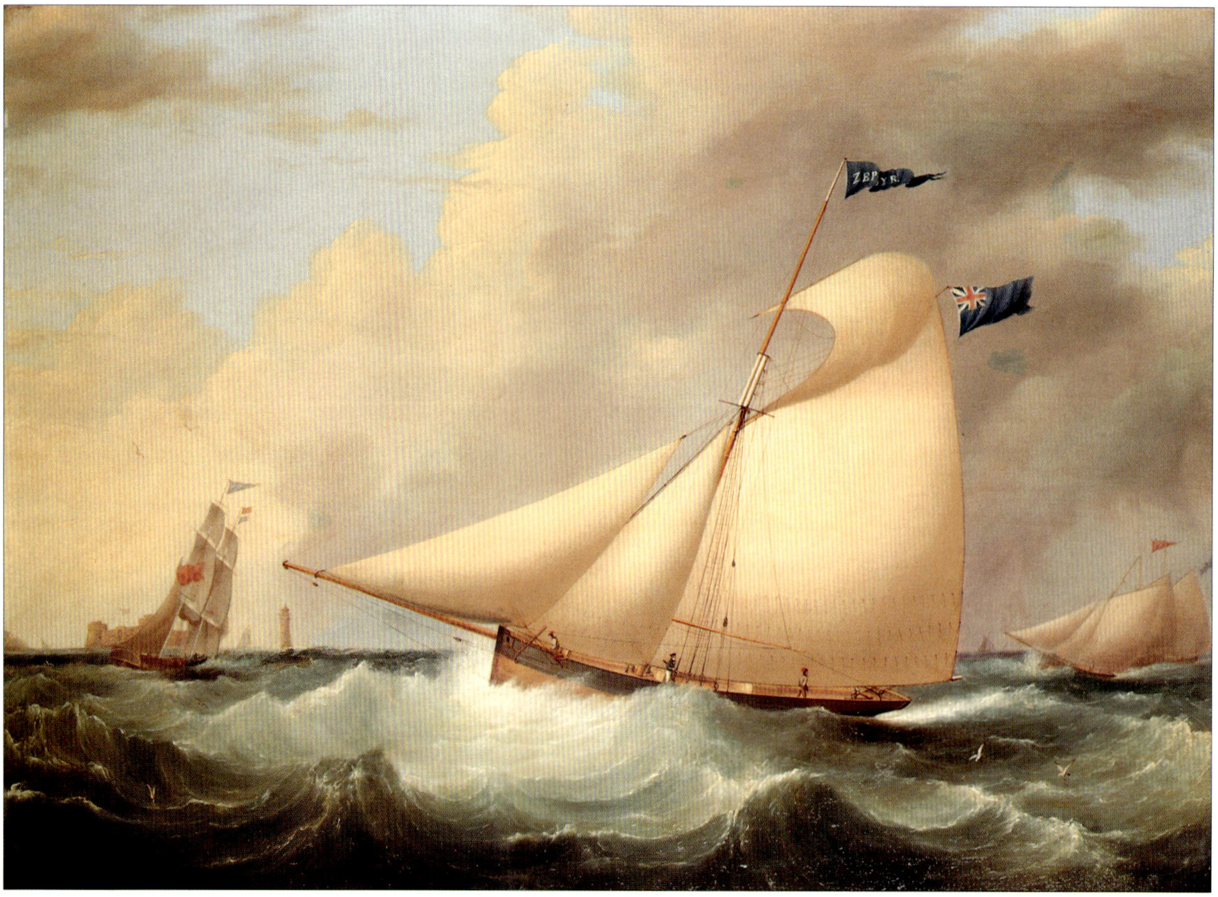

The pleasure yacht *Zephyr* is shown in port profile in the Mersey off the Perch Rock Fort and Lighthouse during the course of a race. Two other unidentified yachts are shown astern and the brig *Victory* is in the middle distance off her starboard bow.
The scene is probably set during the Mersey Regatta of 1832. At first sight *Zephyr* appears to be winning the race but one of her crew is in the process of lowering the topsail yard, probably prior to tacking as she approaches the Wirral shore. The outcome of the race cannot be assured and she could be overtaken by the following yacht during these manoeuvres.[1]
Zephyr was built in 1832 by John Wilson and Sons of Liverpool[2] for James Watson, a Liverpool merchant.[3] She was carvel built with a square stern and was sloop rigged with a running bowsprit. She is typical of the lighter designed yachts then being built, which retained many of the basic features of the revenue cutters from which they had developed. She was appropriately named after the west wind of classical mythology.
Zephyr was immediately successful in her first season winning three prestigious races, including the Greenock Challenge Cup at the Clyde Regatta in July[4] and the Gold Cup, presented by the Duchess of Kent, at the Beaumaris Regatta in early September.[5] She remained in Watson's ownership until wrecked off the Isle of Wight in 1840.[6]
Her owner James Watson was also part owner from 1832 to 1835 of the eponymous paddle steamer *Zephyr* which ran a service from Liverpool to Dublin.[7]
The exact identity of the brig cannot be established. Although she flies a name pennant for *Victory* there is no other identification except a red ensign and what may be a partial flag code. Perhaps it is the artist playing on words in view of the racing composition?[8]
The original attribution to Miles Walters cannot be sustained[9] and virtually every aspect of the painting confirms that it is the work of Samuel. Whether the canvas should be identified with that exhibited at the Liverpool Academy in 1832 is open to question.

MMM.1991.370
Oil on canvas
75.5 cm x 102 cm
Signed (br) "Walters 1832"
Prov: Frank Sabin Gallery, London, purchased by Liverpool City Council, 1959, from whom purchased, 1991.
Ref: Davidson, 1992, pp. 76-7, (ill).
Exh: ? Liverpool Academy, 1832 (324)

Vessel: 49 ft 3 in (l), 14 ft 9 in (b) 7 ft 10 in (d); 41 tons (burthen)

1 See Davidson 1992, p. 76 for a full assessment of the situation.
2 LCR vol. 47, cert. no. 63 (22 May 1832).
3 Probably James Otley Watson, solicitor of Greville St, Liverpool (GDL).
4 GGA, 2 August 1832.
5 GGA, 6 September 1832.
6 LCR, op. cit.
7 LCR, vol. 48, cert. no. 5, 11 January 1833.
8 There is no appropriate Liverpool registered vessel named VICTORY at this time. LR lists several possibilities.
9 Bennett, p. 209.

W H Walton (active 1901)

248 *A Sea Captain*

This head and shoulders portrait shows an unknown sea captain in his top coat supposedly on the bridge of his ship. There is no clue as to the identity of the sitter.

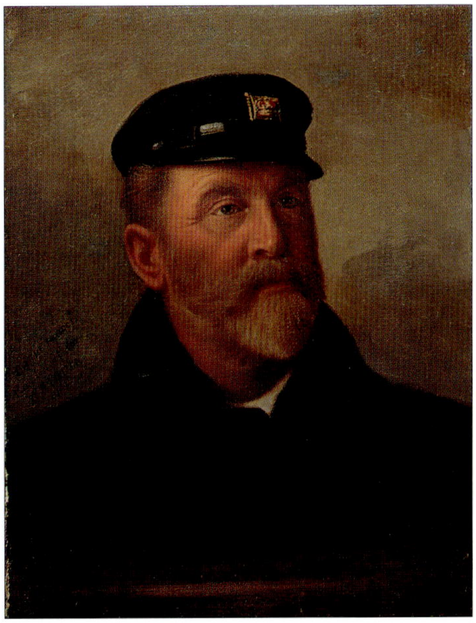

MMM.1997.29
Oil on canvas[1]
38 cm x 29 cm
Inscribed (left side) "ON THE BRIDGE / Painted at Sea / W. H. WALTON / 1901"
Prov: Unknown, in the collection 1995.

1 Relined.

W J Wickholm (active 1980s)

249 *The steam yacht Gondola*

1982.1206
Oil on plyboard
40 cm x 52 cm
Signed (br) "W J WICKHOLM (LAC)"; inscribed rear "W J Wickholm LAC / Neston 1980"[1]
Prov: presented by the artist, 1982.

Vessel: 84 ft (l), 14.2 ft (b), 3.1 ft (d); 42 gross tons

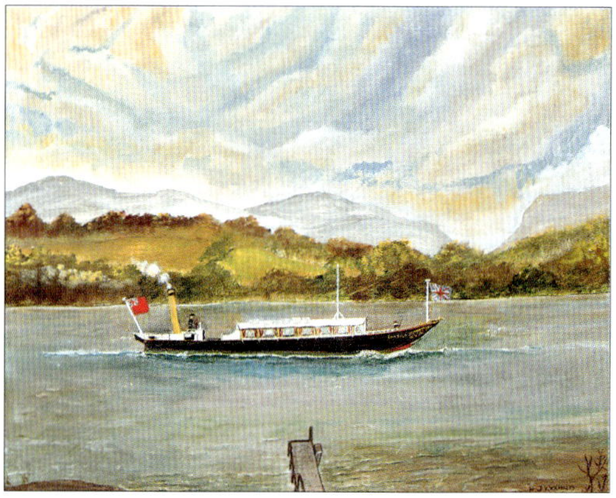

The steam yacht *Gondola* is shown under steam on Lake Coniston. Described as "a cross between a submarine and a cucumber", she was built by Jones, Quiggin of Liverpool in 1859 for the Barrow and Lake District Section of the Furness Railway Company. She provided passenger services for many years before being mothballed, converted to a house boat in 1946 and scuttled in 1960. She was raised and restored by the National Trust and put back into service in 1980.[2]

1 LAC - Liverpool Art Club
2 Early history and quotation in C Duckworth & G Langmuir *Railway & Other Steamers*, Glasgow, 1948, pp. 29-30, ill. opp. p.30. The specification of the vessel is in MAL, DX 154, ff.186-187.

Norman Wilkinson (1878-1971)

One of the most important marine artists of the twentieth century, Wilkinson is best known for his shipping and railway posters. He was also commissioned by many shipping companies to produce portraits of their ships. Born in Cambridge, he studied at Portsmouth School of Art. He served in the Royal Naval Volunteer Reserve during the first world war and was responsible for suggesting the use of dazzle painting as camouflage.[1]

1 Archibald, p.200.

250 *Aragon*

1963.137.3
Oil on canvas
87 cm x 140 cm
Signed (cr) "NORMAN WILKINSON"
Prov: Royal Mail Lines Ltd., who presented it, 1963
Exh: Liverpool 1986
Ref: Port Panorama, p.35

Vessel: 513.2 ft (l), 60.4 ft (b), 30.7 ft (d); 9588 gross tons

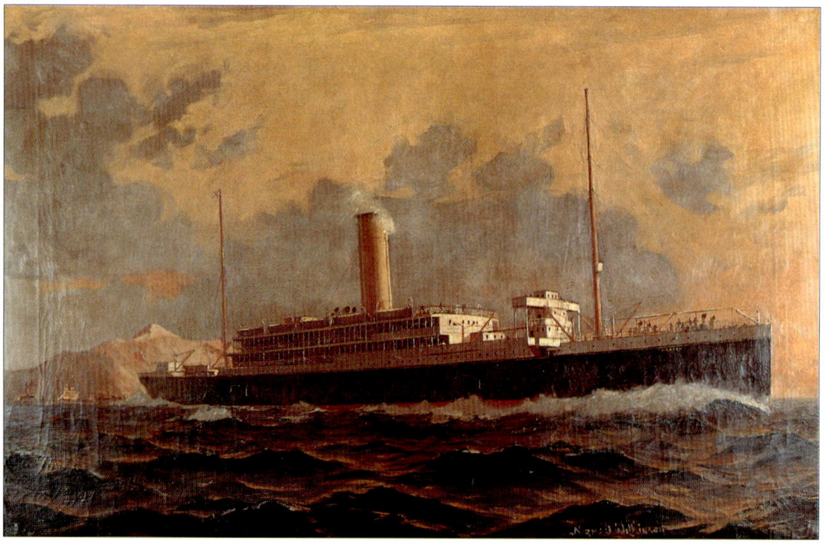

Wilkinson uses the late summer evening sunshine to show the passenger liner *Aragon* in starboard bow view passing St Vincent in the Cape Verde Islands at full cruising speed. Other unidentified shipping is shown in the left distance.

Aragon[1] was built by Harland & Wolff in Belfast in 1905 and was the first twin screw vessel built for the Royal Mail Line. She was also the first of the line's "A" class liners designed for the passenger service from Southampton to Brazil and the River Plate and providing new standards of speed and luxury on this route. Her accommodation consisted of 306 first, 66 second and 632 third class berths. At the outbreak of war in 1914 she was requisitioned as a troopship and was used in the Dardenelles campaign. She was torpedoed and sank off the harbour at Alexandria in December 1917.[2]

1 Former kingdom, now region of Spain.
2 Haws Royal Mail, p. 63; Bonsor South, pp. 27-8.

251 *S S Baltic*

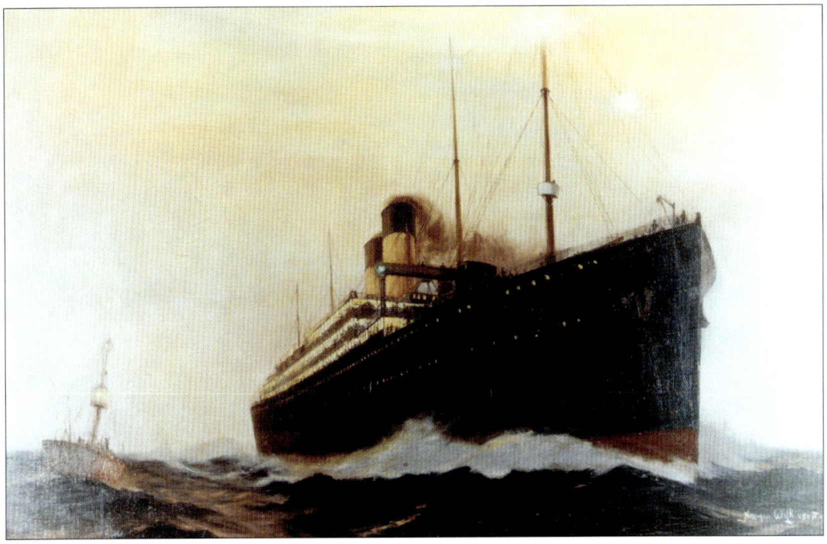

1968.184.1
Oil on canvas
75 cm x 100.5 cm
Signed and dated "NORMAN WILKINSON / 1904"
Prov: Cunard Steam Ship Co. Ltd.; Private Collection, on permanent loan, 1968
Exh: Liverpool, 1986
Ref: Port Panorama, 1986, p. 35, ill.

Vessel: 709.2 ft (l), 75.6 ft (b), 52.6 ft (d); 23,884 gross tons

The huge physical size and presence of the transatlantic liners of the Edwardian period is captured in this dramatic painting of *S S Baltic*. The ship, shown in starboard bow view ploughing through the Atlantic, dominates the canvas and a lightship in the left foreground. The scene is set at dusk with the deck and navigation lights sparkling against the encroaching darkness. There is a hint of land in the far distance.
Baltic was built by Harland & Wolff in 1904 as the third of four sister ships for the Liverpool - New York service of the White Star Line, at that time part of the recently established International Mercantile Marine Company. As well as providing passenger accommodation, particularly in third class, she had a very large cargo capacity. During the First World War she remained in service but contributed to the war effort by carrying troops and large amounts of cargo, including fuel oil. She was retired in 1932 and scrapped the following year.[1]
There is a watercolour of *Baltic* by R H Neville-Cummings in the Peabody Museum[2] and a sketch by Jacobsen in the Mariners' Museum.[3]

1 Anderson, p.208.
2 Smith, no. 2031, p.18.
3 Sniffen Checklist.

252 *RMS Queen Mary* (page 236)

Queen Mary must be one of the most famous ships ever built and is celebrated for her service as a transatlantic passenger liner. This painting captures her in a less familiar role as a troopship during World War II when she made an invaluable contribution to the Allied war effort.
Wilkinson shows the vessel in her wartime colours in port profile at anchor in the Clyde with steam up. In the right foreground is a Clyde steamer in bow port view, her decks crowded with troops. Other shipping includes an aircraft carrier in the far right distance, other naval vessels to the left and a couple of launches.
The history of *R M S Queen Mary* is well known.[1] She was built for the Cunard Line in 1934 by John Brown & Co. of Clydebank for the passenger service to New York. She was laid up in New York at the outbreak of war but in 1940 sailed to Sydney and began trooping between Australia and Suez. When the United States

1 See J Steele, *Queen Mary*, London, 1995; for her wartime service see William H Miller & David F Hutchings *Transatlantic Liners at War: The Story of the Queens*, Newton Abbot, 1985.
2 C L D Duckworth & G E Langmuir *Clyde River and other steamers*, Glasgow, 1937, pp.30-1.
3 'The Passenger liner Queen Mary raising steam', Concise NMM, p. 454 (ill).

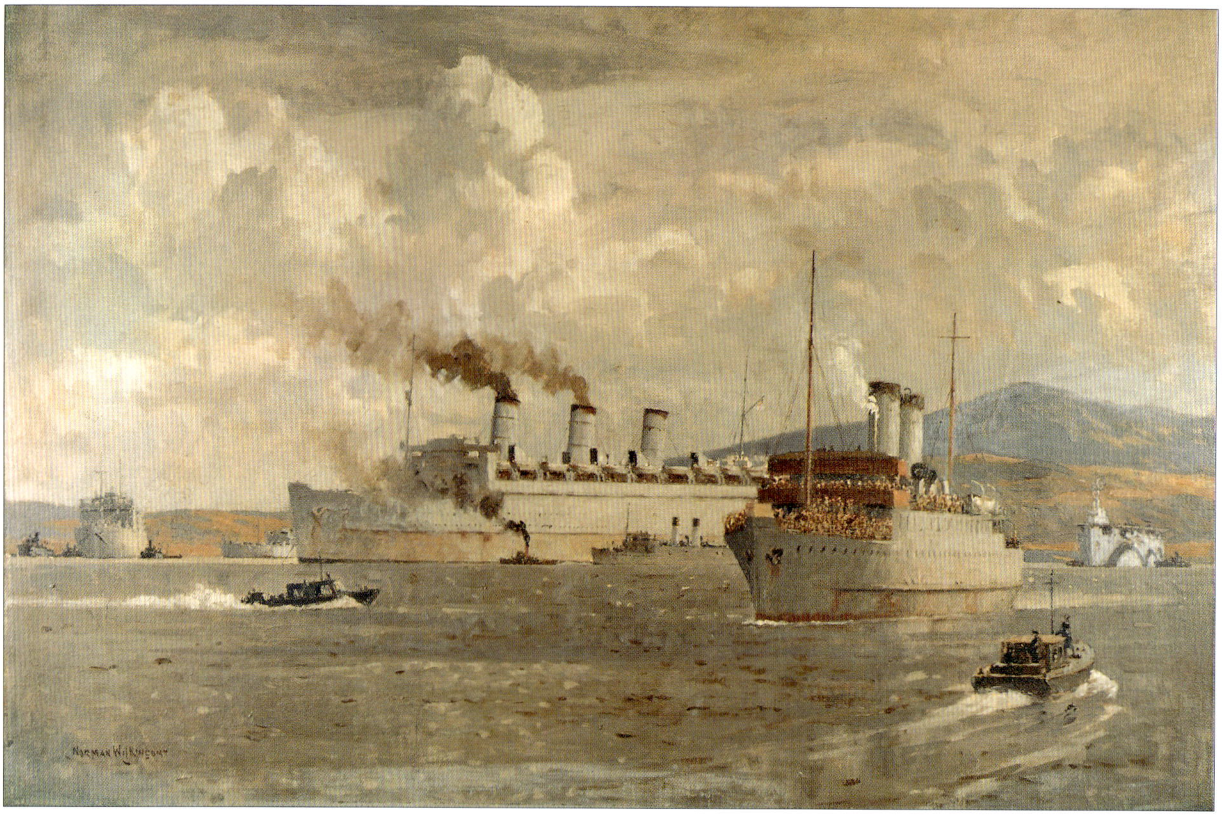

1963.30
Oil on canvas
76.5 cm x 114.5 cm
Signed (bl) "NORMAN WILKINSON"
Prov: Cunard Steam Ship Co. Ltd., who presented it, 1963.
Exh: Liverpool 1974

entered the war, she brought American troops to Europe docking in the Clyde. She was seriously damaged in a collision in the Clyde in October 1942. During her war career she carried nearly 800,000 military and other personnel.
The steamer is one of two sisterships of the Caledonian Steam Packet Company - either *Duchess of Montrose*, built in 1930 by William Denny of Dumbarton, or *Duchess of Hamilton*, built by Harland & Wolff at their Govan yard two years later. They were built for cruising and excursion on the Scottish west coast.[2]
There is another version in the National Maritime Museum Collection.[3]

W Williams (active 1874)

253 *City of Paris*

1970.174
Oil on canvas
53.5 cm x 82 cm
Signed and dated (on barrel bl) "W. WILLIAMS / 1874"
Prov: B G Foster, Knutsford, on permanent loan, 1970

Vessel: 358.7 ft (l), 40.4 ft (b), 18.8 ft (d); 2555 gross tons

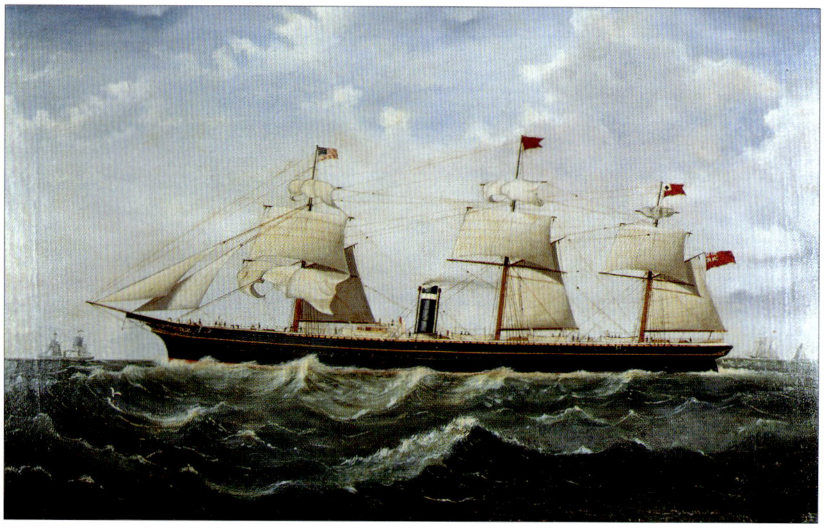

City of Paris is shown in port profile at sea under steam and auxiliary sail. She was rigged as a barque and she is making use of her aft sails and her topsails and topgallants and the crew are just raising the main course on her foremast. She is identifiable from the name on her bow. She flies the Stars and Stripes at the foremast, indicating her destination, a red swallow tail at the main mast, probably indicating that she is carrying the mail, the Inman house flag at the mizzen and the red ensign at the peak. On the horizon is other shipping including a brig rigged steamer, probably of the Lamport and Holt Line,[1] and a brigantine.

City of Paris was built by Tod and McGregor of Glasgow in 1865 for the Inman Line transatlantic service to New York. She was a fast ship and held the Blue Riband from 1867 to 1873. She was lengthened in 1870 and fitted with compound engines in 1879. She was withdrawn from service in 1883 and was sold to French owners in 1884. As *Tonquin* she sank in a collision off Malaga, Spain in 1885.[2]

Samuel Walters painted two version of the vessel - leaving the Mersey and also at sea, for which there is a carte de visite.[3] The museum has a builder's model of the vessel in the collection. (1932.91).

1 The funnel colours are correct but the bands of black and white above the blue are narrower than usual.
2 Bonsor North, p.242.
3 For the Mersey view see Maginnis, p.60, (Ill); for the carte de visite see Davidson, 1994, p. 202.

Isaac Joseph Witham (1832-1901)

Joseph Witham was born in Bognor, Sussex and spent a number of years at sea before coming ashore. He is first listed as a "marine artist" working in Liverpool in 1874.[1] He mainly painted steamers and boats in the local pilot service but occasionally producing larger and more imposing canvases, such as S S *Sarmatian*, see below (no. 259).

1 GDL, 1874. For details see Davidson, 1986, pp. 103-5.

254 *Follow the Leader*

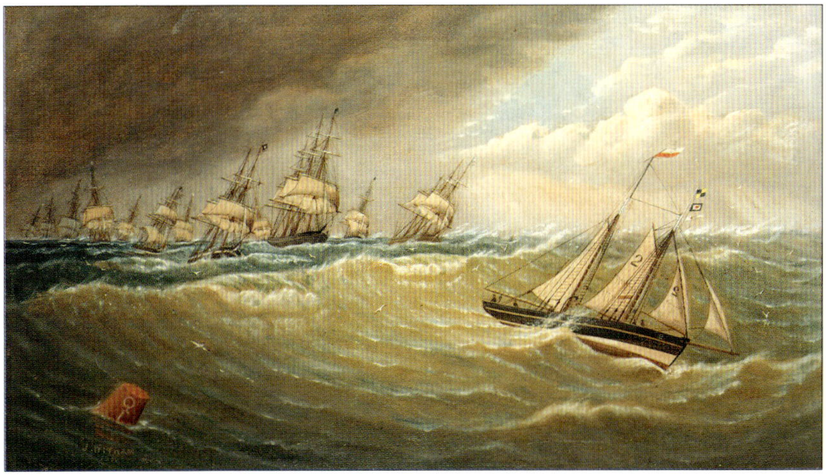

1982.328
Oil on canvas
44.5 cm x 80 cm
Signed and dated (bl) "J. WITHAM / 1896"
Prov: Mrs A Martin, presented by the Cape Horners Association in memory of Captain W Martin, 1982.

Vessel: *Leader* 76 ft (l), 18.9 ft (b), 9.2 ft (d); 61 gross tons

This painting records a famous local incident when the No.2 Pilot Boat *Leader* led a fleet of twelve ships over the Bar at the entrance to the Mersey during a gale on 8 February 1881.

An assorted group of vessels had arrived at the entrance to the river but there was insufficient depth of water to cross the Bar. The master pilot of *Leader*, which was on station, instructed them to heave-to and established an order of precedence according to their draughts. As the tide turned he ordered them to "Follow Me" as he led them over the Bar to the relative safety of the Mersey.

Witham shows the fleet as they are crossing the Bar. *Leader* is in the right foreground entering the Queen's Channel with the other vessels grouped across the far side of the canvas. She is rigged for the conditions with a special storm sail on the main and a storm jib. The entrance to the channel is marked on the starboard by the red buoy "Q1" in the foreground and its companion black cone in the right middle distance. The pilot vessel flies the pilot jack at her main mast and the flag hoist L W C the code for "Follow Me". The fleet comprised a variety of vessels including ships and brigs, all well-reefed.

The schooner rigged *Leader* was built by Thomas Harvey & Sons of Ipswich in 1854. She was withdrawn from service in 1896 and sold to the Preston Pilotage Service in April 1897.[1]

Witham produced a number of versions of this painting over a period of some years, including no. 255 and there are examples in the Irish Maritime Museum, the Vallejo Gallery, California,[2] and several in private collections.[3] An unsigned watercolour in the collections also closely follows these compositions.[4] There is a version of the incident by Parker Greenwood in the National Maritime Museum.[5]

There is a contemporary hull model of the pilot boat in the collections (accession No. 15.4.1862).

1 Rees, p.203.
2 Signed and dated 1897, see *Spirit of The Sea, The Vallejo Gallery Collection*, 1993, p.46 (ill).
3 DCF. The situation can be confusing; one version was offered for sale at auction three times in 1996.
4 Accession no. 1955.233.
5 Signed and dated 1899, Concise NMM, p.473 (ill).

255 *Follow the Leader*

1984.506
Oil on canvas
40.5 cm x 71 cm
Signed and dated "J. WITHAM / 1900"[1]
Prov: Mrs M Southworth, Liverpool, who bequeathed it, 1984

1 On reverse of frame, note in pencil reads "By Joseph Witham 127 (?) St Domingo Vale 1900"

This is the second and later version of this subject in the collection. The canvas is slightly smaller and there are very slight variations of detail but these are not significant. (See no. 254)

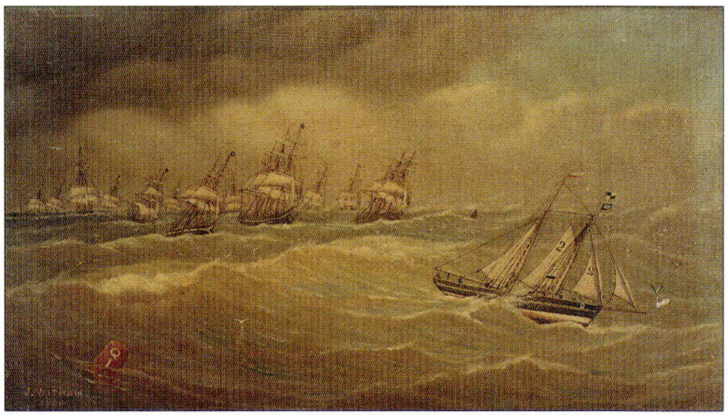

256 *S S Graceful*

1967.180.2
Oil on canvas
61 cm x 91.5 cm
Signed and dated (bl) 'J. WITHAM / 1894'
Prov: F H Powell & Co., Coast Lines, on permanent loan, 1967.
Exh: Liverpool 1986
Ref: Port Panorama, 1986, p.36 (ill)

Vessel: 244.2 ft (l), 33.3 ft (b), 23.6 ft (d); 1372 gross tons

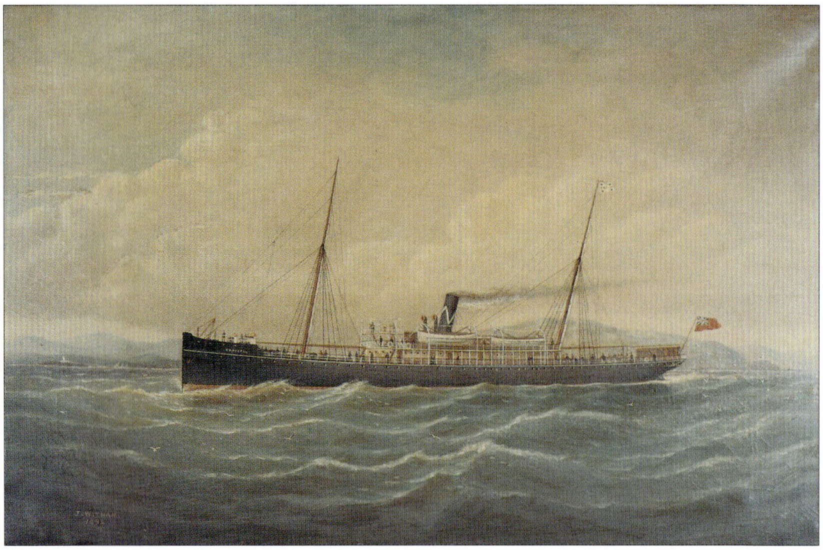

The coastal steamer *Graceful* is shown in port profile off Anglesey on her way into Liverpool. Her engines were placed amidships and she has a characteristic double storey open bridge. A number of passengers and crew can be seen on deck. The vessel is identifiable from her name on the bow and she flies the house flag of F H Powell of Liverpool. Her funnel is also painted in the Powell colours of a white zigzag against black. The Skerries lighthouse is visible in the far left distance and the South Stack lighthouse to the far right.

This vessel was originally built in 1886 as *African* by Sir Raylton Dixon of Middlesborough for service with the Union Steam Ship Co. in the South African coastal trade. She was fitted with triple expansion engines by Thomas Richardson of Hartlepool and had auxiliary powered derricks for cargo handling. She was acquired by F H Powell & Co. in 1893 for their coastal passenger service to Bristol and London[1] but was sold to Ostlandske Lloyd in 1902 and scrapped in 1931.[2]

1 Also frequently calling at Falmouth, Plymouth, Southampton and Dunkirk.
2 See LCR vol. 98, no. 79, 20 December 1893. From 1895 Powells was under the sole control of Alfred Read who brought together various other coasting firms to establish Coast Lines in 1913. Coast Lines adopted the Powell livery.

257 *S S Hopeful*

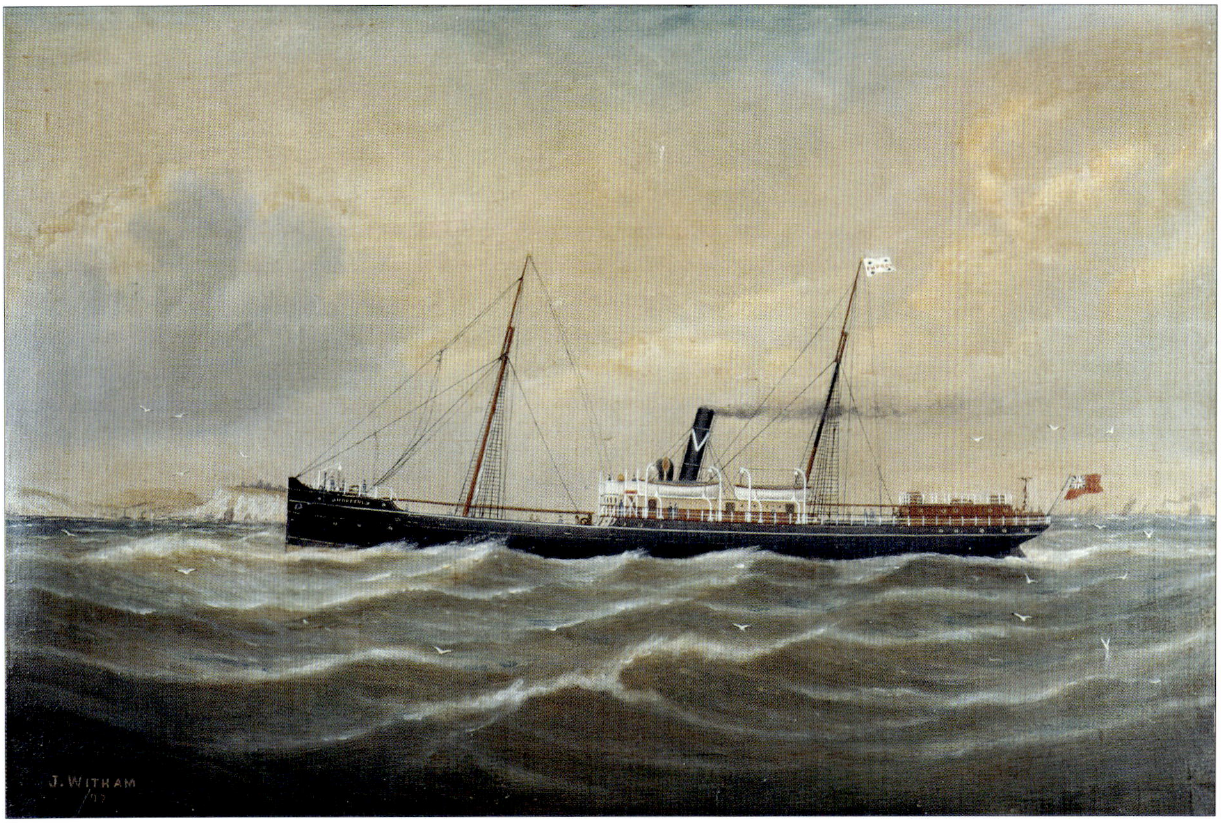

This port profile of the coastal steamer *Hopeful* is virtually a companion picture to no. 257 of *S S Graceful*, except that in this case she is shown off Dover. Again the vessel is identifiable from her name on the bow and the house flag and funnel in the colours of F H Powell of Liverpool. The red ensign flies at the stern. The white cliffs of the Kent coast can be seen in the distance behind the ship and to the left is a cluster of vessels in the entrance to Dover harbour. Further unidentified shipping is shown on the horizon behind her stern.

The steel-hulled screw steamer *Hopeful* was built as *Lady Alisa* by the Ailsa Shipbuilding Company of Troon in 1888 for J A Wyllie of London. She was fitted with triple compound engines by David Rowan of Glasgow. F H Powell & Co. acquired her in 1897 and she sank off the Longships in February 1903 after colliding with *S S Raloo*.[1]

1967.180.3
Oil on canvas
40 cm x 60 cm
Signed and dated (bl) 'J. WITHAM / 97'
Prov: F H Powell & Co., Coast Lines, on permanent loan, 1967.
Exh: Liverpool 1986
Ref: Port Panorama, 1986, p.36

Vessel: 231.2 ft (l), 33.2 ft (b), 16.9 ft (d); 1215 gross tons

1 LCR, vol. 95, no. 61, 29 September 1897.

258 *S S Potosi* (page 240)

The iron steamship *Potosi* is shown in port profile, possibly off Anglesey. The vessel was barque rigged and is portrayed under steam and square topsails. She flies the Chilean flag at the foremast, the house flag for the Pacific Steam Navigation Company at the main, a name pennant at the mizzen and the red ensign at the gaff.

1984.269.11
Oil on canvas
50 cm x 76 cm
Signed (bl) "J. WITHAM / (date indistinct)"
Prov: Pacific Steam Navigation Company, on permanent loan.

Vessel: 421.6 ft (l), 43.8 ft (b), 35.5 ft (d); 4218 gross tons

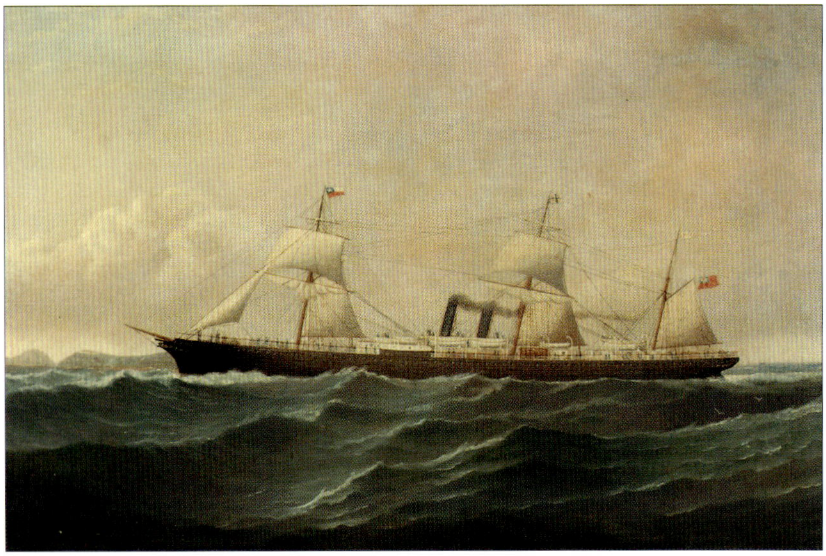

Potosi, named after the Bolivian town, was built by John Elder & Co. of Glasgow in 1873 for the Pacific Steam Navigation Company's service between Birkenhead and Valparaiso. In 1880 she was transferred to the Orient Line, which was a joint operation between PSNC and Anderson, Anderson of London providing services to Australia. She reverted to the Valparaiso service in 1887 and was broken up in Genoa in 1897.[1]

1 Haws PSNC, p. 48.

259 *S S Sarmatian leaving the Mersey, 14th November 1878, with the Marquess of Lorne and Princess Louise on board.*

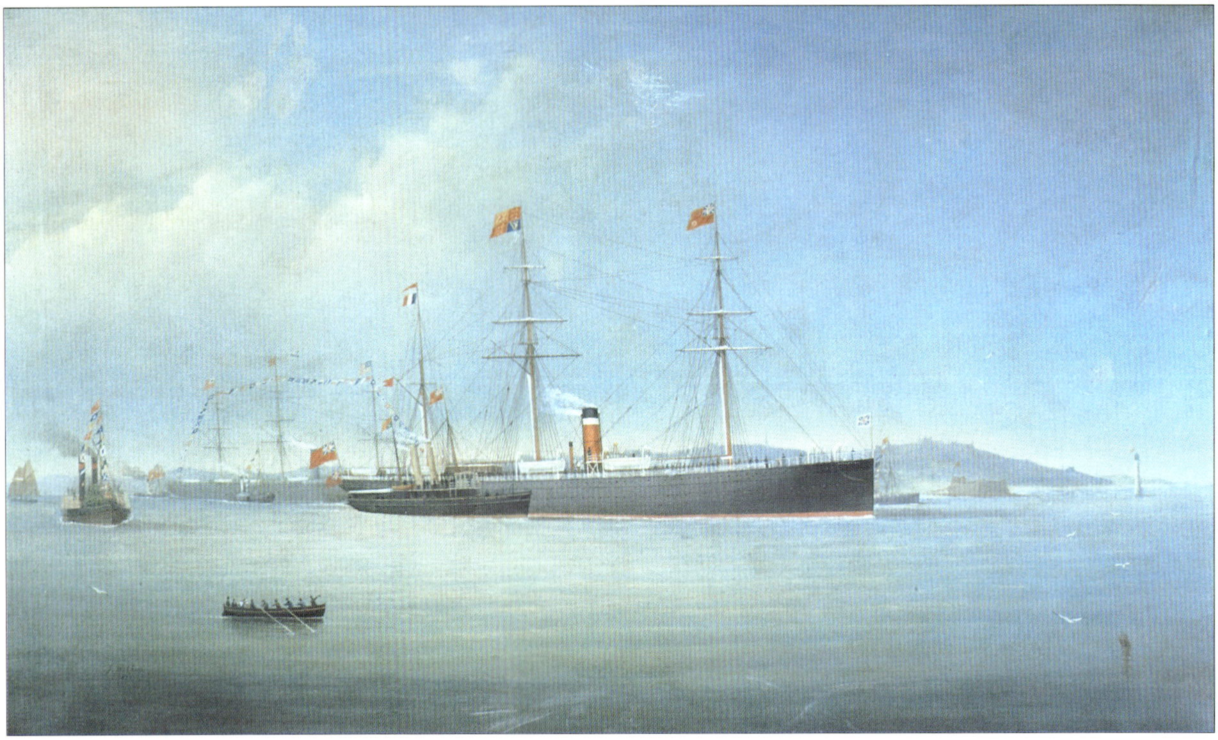

This view shows *S S Sarmatian* leaving the Mersey on 14 November 1878 carrying Queen Victoria's daughter Princess Louise and her husband the Marquess of Lorne on their way for him to take up his appointment as Governor-General of Canada.[1] *Sarmatian* is shown in starboard profile with the steam tender *Storm Cock*, responsible for conveying the royal couple, alongside. In the background, to

Sarmatian's stern, is the outward bound Inman liner *City of Berlin*[2] and there is a paddle tug of the United Steam Tug Company to the far left, a small rowing boat in the foreground and other tugs[3] and small craft in the vicinity.
In honour of her guests, *Sarmatian* flies a Royal Standard at her main mast and the red ensign with the insignia of the Governor-General at her fore mast; the Allan Line house flag below a red pennant[4] is on the mizzen, a red swallow-tail at the after peak, the red ensign at the stern and the pilot jack on the bow. *Storm Cock* also flies the Royal Standard and special red ensign. *City of Berlin* flies the stars and stripes at the fore, the red swallow-tail at the main, the Inman house flag at the mizzen and the red ensign at the stern.[5] There are passengers observing the proceedings all along the liner's deck and men are standing on the paddle boxes of the tug, one raising his hat in farewell. She is dressed overall in celebration of the occasion, as is the United Steam paddle tug.
The scene is set in the Mersey against the Wirral coast off New Brighton and the familiar landmarks of the Perch Rock Fort and Lighthouse are depicted in the right hand distance.
Sarmatian[6] was the largest vessel in the Allan Line fleet at the time. She was built in 1871 by Robert Steele & Company of Greenock with compound engines by MacNab, also of Greenock. She maintained regular voyages to Canada from Liverpool, except for a brief period in 1874 when she was used as a transport ship for the British Government's Ashanti Expedition. From 1889 she sailed in the cargo service from Glasgow or London and was scrapped at Rotterdam in 1908.[7]
Storm Cock was built in 1877 of iron and steel construction by Laird Brothers of Birkenhead and was owned by Liverpool Screw Towing and Lighterage Company. She was a pioneer in her day both in power and manoeuvrability. She was sold to the Admiralty in 1882 and subsequently survived until 1953.[8]
A lithograph after the painting was produced.[9] There is a wash drawing of *Storm Cock* by Gilbert Stevens in the collections. (1984.69.1).

1955.230
Oil on canvas
73.5 cm x 127.5 cm
Signed and dated (br) 'J Witham / 1878'
Prov: In collections, 1955
Exh: Liverpool 1986
Ref: Port Panorama 1986, p.37 (ill)

Vessels:
Sarmatian 370.9 ft (l), 42.2 ft (b); 3647 gross tons.
Storm Cock 155.5 ft (l), 25.1 ft (b), 12.1 ft (d); 328 gross tons.

1 Princess Louise (1848-1939), sixth daughter of Queen Victoria, married the Marquess of Lorne (1848-1914), eldest son of the 10th Duke of Argyll, in 1871. For the departure see Annals, 1878.
2 *City of Berlin* was bound for New York, as indicated by the stars and stripes, see LL 15 November 1878.
3 The single funnel tug is another Hill vessel and the two funnel tug, with white and black funnels, belongs to William Jolliffe's company.
4 The house flag was the same as the French tricolour but was always flown beneath a red pennant.
5 The red swallow-tail probably indicates that both liners are carrying the mail.
6 Sarmatia, an ancient name for parts of Russia and Poland.
7 Bonsor North, p.313.
8 The founder of the company, William Becket Hill, was also freight manager for the Allan Line. LCR, vol. 93, no. 29, 13 February 1878;
W B Hallam 'Cock Tugs of Liverpool' in *Sea Breezes*, vol. 36, December 1963, pp. 429-31.
9 Parker & Bowen, pp.264-5.

Woolston & Barratt (active late nineteenth century)

George Woolston (1862 -1937) was a photographer and Walter Barrett a painter who worked in partnership in Newcastle, New South Wales. Barrett used plans and photographs to produce a painting of a vessel; Woolston then offered photographic copies to the crew as well as his normal photographic services. Such arrangements were not uncommon in Australian ports at the turn of the century. Barratt also worked with other photographers.[1]

1 I am grateful to Diane Fletcher, Senior Curator, Australian National Maritime Museum, for this biographical information.

260 *Orellana* (page 242)

The steel barque *Orellana* is shown in starboard profile with all sails set approaching Dunedin, New Zealand. According to the donor it commemorates an occasion when the vessel entered the harbour at Dunedin under full sail, reputedly the only ship to have ever done so. Four copies of the event were painted by the artist. One is said to have been presented to the Mayor & Corporation of Dunedin and the three others were offered for sale. The present version was bought by Thomas Higson, an apprentice on the ship.[1] However, there is no record of the event or of a copy of the painting in Dunedin and on the one occasion when *Orellana* entered the harbour she was towed from the pilot station at Taiaroa Head.[2]
Although the features of the vessel are accurately painted much of the detail, such as the crew, are only sketchily indicated. The flag flying on the main mast is the house flag of Nicholson & McGill and the red ensign is at the after peak.

1960.116
Oil on board
46.5 cm x 61.5 cm
Signed (br) in red "WOOLSTON & BARRATT / NEWCASTLE N.S.W."
Prov: Purchased by Thomas B Higson; to his sister Miss F E Higson, Liverpool, who presented it, 1960

Vessel: 198.6 ft (l), 33.7 ft (b), 19.8 ft (d); 866 gross tons.

1 Information from donor, DCF. It may be that some or all of the others were photographic copies.
2 *Orellana* arrived in Dunedin from Liverpool on 15 August and was towed to Dunedin by the Harbour Board tugs *Koputal* and *Plucky*. She sailed for Newcastle, NSW on 31 August. *Otago Daily Times*, 16 August 1905. (Arrival and departure confirmed in LL 6 October, 12 October 1905). It is unlikely a vessel could make the eleven mile passage to Dunedin, which is full of twists and turns, under full sail. I am grateful to S Kirkpatrick Honorary Curator of the Maritime Hall, Otago Museum for checking local information in Dunedin.
3 Orellana was the former name of the Amazon, named after Francisco de Orellana (c.1500-49), the first European explorer of the river in 1541.
4 LR 1886; LCR no. 120, vol. 96, 12 November 1885.

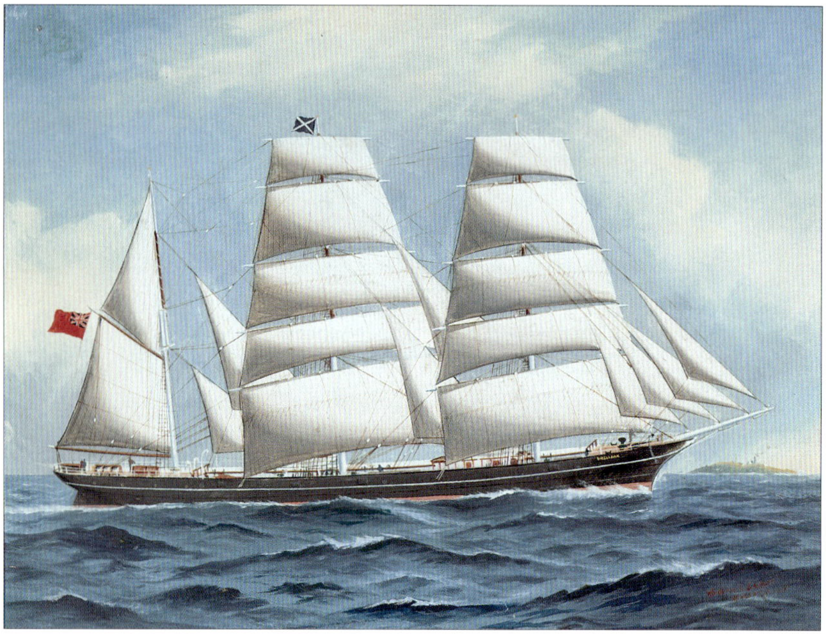

Orellana[3] was built by J Reid & Co of Port Glasgow in 1885 for the Liverpool firm of Nicholson and McGill. At this time they owned a fleet of about a dozen steel and iron barques of under 1000 tons involved in deep sea trade to Australia, New Zealand and the Pacific basin. The vessel was sold to J C A Johannesen of Moss, Norway and was lost after a collision off Barnegat, New Jersey, on a passage from Boulogne to New York in April 1914.[4]

Charles W Wyllie (1859 - 1923)

Charles William Wyllie was the younger brother of William Lionel Wyllie (1851 - 1931). Although less well-known and less prolific than his older brother he was an artist of considerable achievement, working in oils and watercolours to produce harbour, river and canal scenes. He is represented in the National Maritime Museum and the Tate Gallery, London.

261 *First boat race on the Mersey between cadets of HMS Conway and HMS Worcester, 11 June 1891*

A boat race between the cadets of the training ships *HMS Conway*, moored on the Mersey, and *HMS Worcester*, moored on the Thames, had been proposed in 1889 but refused by *Worcester*. The challenge was taken up the following year with a race on the Thames won by the *Worcester* cadets and it thereafter became an annual event. The race was first held on the Mersey in June 1891 when the home team from *Conway* won by twelve lengths.[1]

This painting shows the moments immediately after the end of the race with the winning boat from *Conway* in the centre of the canvas. The crew are celebrating their victory by standing and waving their arms in the air. Some way behind, the *Worcester* cadets are still struggling to complete the course.

To the left are a group of small boats with officials and well wishers, together with three steamers filled with spectators and including the largest of these vessels, a tender of the Mersey Docks and Harbour Board with its buff funnel.

Immediately to the right is *Conway* herself. Cadets are lining the decks and are in the rigging and on the yards cheering on their shipmates. Behind *Conway* are three further training ships, *Indefatigable*, *Akbar* and *Clarence*. The vessels were moored

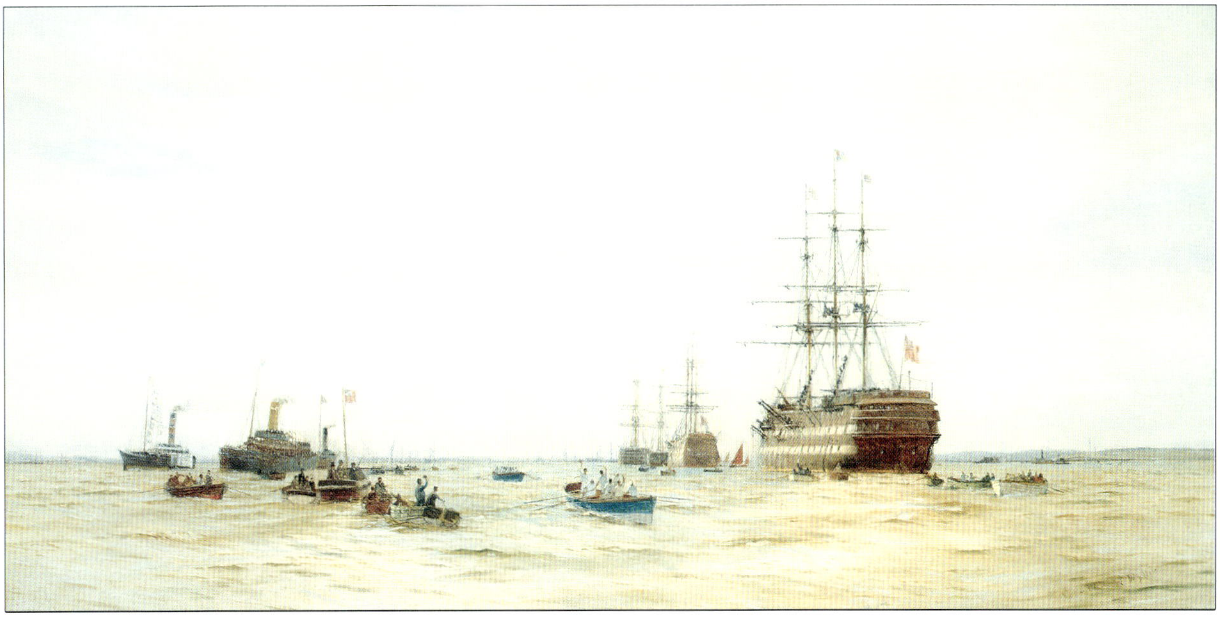

MMM.1998.44
Oil on canvas
50 cm x 102 cm
Signed (br) "Charlie W Wyllie"
Prov: *HMS Conway*; Seafarers Education Service (The Marine Society); sold Sotheby's London, 3 May 1995, lot 188 (mis-identified as "Hearts of Oak"); Royal Exchange Art Gallery, London, from who purchased 1988.

off the Wirral shore between New Ferry and Rock Ferry and the pier for the ferry boats at Rock Ferry can be seen in the far right hand distance.

HMS Conway was first moored in the Mersey in 1859 as a training ship for boys of good character who were destined for careers as officers in the merchant service. She was twice replaced by other former naval vessels, the last being *HMS Nile* in 1872 which is the vessel depicted here. She was moved to North Wales in 1940 and sank off Anglesey in 1953.[2]

Indefatigable was a training ship for the orphaned sons of seamen and other poor boys. Built as a 4th rate naval frigate in 1848 she served in her training capacity from 1864 to 1914.

Akbar was the training ship for Protestant boys and was run by the Liverpool Juvenile Reformatory Association. She was built in 1816 and replaced an earlier vessel in 1862. She was scrapped in 1907.

Clarence was the Roman Catholic reformatory training ship. Built in 1816 she took up her retirement role on the Mersey in 1884 and was burnt by the boys in 1899.

There is a companion painting by Wyllie of the first race on the Thames in 1890, now in the National Maritime Museum.[3]

The collections include a number of artefacts from these training ships including the anchor from *Conway* and the figurehead of *Indefatigable*. Archives from *HMS Conway* are also on deposit.

1 There is a contemporary description of the race in John Masefield *The Conway*, London, 1933, pp. 72-3.
2 For Conway see Masefield, op. cit., and other training ships see J Smart "Reformation afloat" in *Transactions of the Liverpool Nautical Research Society*, vol. 9 for 1955-61, Liverpool, 1963, pp. 90-95. All four training ships eventually became shore-based establishments.
3 OP1970-15, Concise NMM.

William Howard Yorke (1847 - 1921)

W H Yorke was born in New Brunswick, the son of William Gay Yorke (1817-1886) also a marine painter. The family moved to Liverpool about 1855 where W H Yorke lived for the rest of his life, though his father moved to New York about 1871. The work of father and son is often confused and variation of York or Yorke and other misspellings has further complicated matters. However, most of his work is clearly signed and readily recognisable on stylistic grounds. There are works in the National Maritime Museum; Peabody Essex Museum at Salem; New Brunswick Museum.[1]

1 See Davidson 1986, pp. 90-8.

262 *Anselma De Larrinaga*

1983.3335
Oil on canvas
56.5 cm x 90.5 cm
Signed (bl) (worn) " W [H] Yor[ke]"
Prov: Private Collection, on permanent loan.
Exh: Liverpool 1986
Ref: Port Panorama 1986, p. 37

Vessel: 364.5 ft (l), 46.9 ft (b), 26.6 ft (d); 4094 gross tons

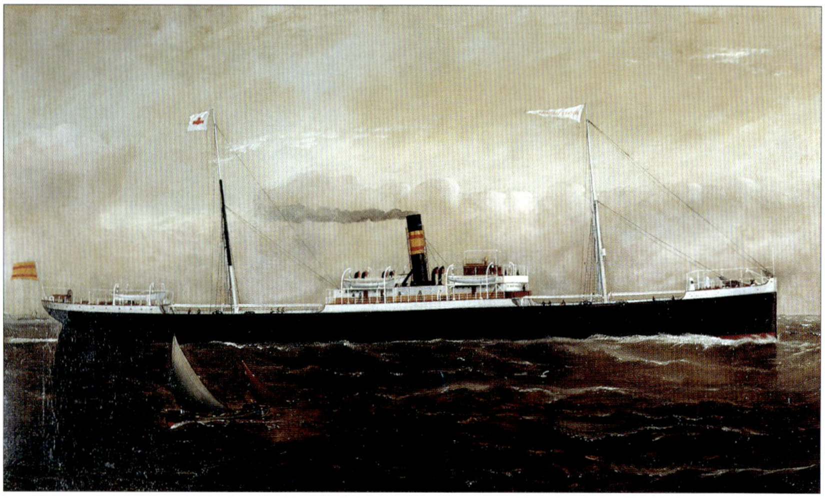

The steel steamship *Anselma De Larrinaga* is shown in starboard profile probably in Liverpool Bay. She fills virtually the full width of the canvas but there is a two funnel paddle steamer in the background astern and a small sailing gig boat with two men in oil skins on the bow. Her masts no longer carry spars and only support purpose-built derricks. She still has an open bridge and two of the crew are shown on duty there. The vessel is identifiable by a name pennant and the funnel colours and the house flag. As with other Larrinaga vessels, she flies the Spanish flag at her stern.

Anselma De Larrinaga[1] was built in 1898 by A Russell of Port Glasgow with triple expansion engines by Dunsmuir and Jackson also of Glasgow. At this stage, the company was involved in the deep sea tramp trade particularly to the Philippines, the Spanish Caribbean and the United States. She was sold to Italian owners in 1924.[2]

There are two notebooks in the Archives by Annie Stephens, wife of the vessel's captain, T. Stephens, which give details of a voyage she made on board the ship from Eastham to Buenos Aires in 1909.[3]

1 The vessel was named after Anselma, daughter of Ramon da Larrinaga, one of the founders of the line.
2 LCR vol. 99, no. 57, 21 May 1898.
3 DX 1128.

263 *The capture of S S Buen Aventura*

1983.3333
Oil on canvas
51 cm x 76 cm
Signed (br in red) indistinct "[ ] 01"
Prov: Private Collection, on long term loan, 1983
Exh: Liverpool 1986
Ref: Port Panorama, p. 37

Vessel: 278 ft (l), 34.4 ft (b), 23.9 ft (d); 1763 gross tons

Although on first appearance this painting seems to be composed as a fairly standard ship portrait, it does in fact depict the initial stages of the capture of the Spanish registered steamer *Buen Aventura* at the outbreak of the Spanish-American War of 1898. She was seized on April 22 by the US Warship *Nashville* on a passage from Pascagoula, Mississippi, to Rotterdam with a cargo of timber. In the painting the steamer is shown in port quarter profile with a line of American warships on the left horizon. *Nashville* has just fired a shot, which will go across *Buen Aventura*'s bow. She was forced to surrender and taken to Key West, Florida, where she was forfeited and sold.[1] She ended her days as a coal hulk in Chesapeake Bay, Virginia.

The vessel has her funnel painted in the Larrinaga house colours and flies the house flag from the mainmast and the Spanish national flag at her stern. Part of her deck cargo can be seen.

The iron screw brig *Buen Aventura* was built by T R Oswald of Sunderland in 1871 and was the first steamer to join the Larrinaga fleet. Although Larrinaga were originally a Spanish firm, they moved to Liverpool in 1862 but continued to register

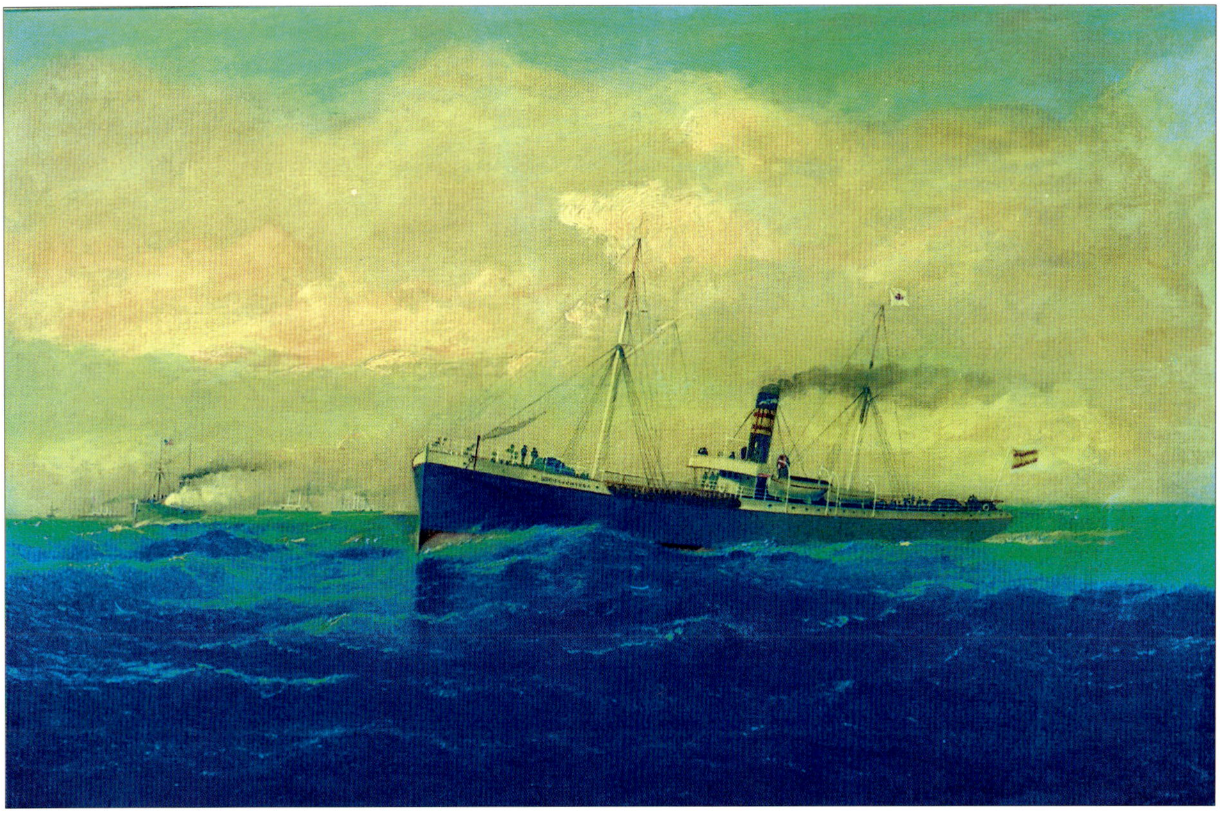

their ships in Spain. *Buen Aventura* had the distinction of being the first Spanish vessel to pass through the Suez Canal.[2]

Although the signature is now so badly degraded that it is illegible, the painting is clearly the work of the younger Yorke.

1 LL 23, 25 April, 13, 28 May 1898. The vessel ran aground at Key West and there was a suggestion that the crew tried to scuttle her.

2 LR 1872-3.

264 *Dora*

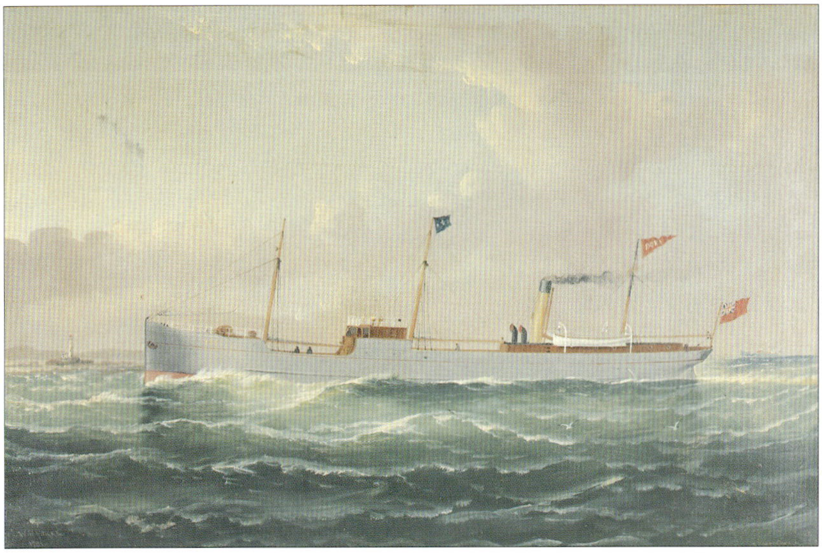

1976.282
Oil on canvas
51 cm x 76 cm
Signed and dated (bl) "W. H. YORKE / 1901"
Prov: Mr R L I Williams, Conwy, from whom purchased, 1976
Exh: Liverpool 1986
Ref: Port Panorama, 1986, p.38 (ill)

The steam coaster *Dora* is shown in port profile off the Skerries lighthouse, off Anglesey, en route for Liverpool. She is a typical functional coaster with her engines aft and the bridge relatively forward. She flies a red ensign, her name pennant and a house flag of blue ground with a fleur-de-lys between R and D. Another steamer is visible in the far distance and, with the same funnel colours as

Dora, is no doubt the company's other vessel, *Telephone*[1].

Dora was built by J Fullerton of Paisley for the Aberdovey and Barmouth Steamship Company in 1901. She spent her career between Liverpool, Aberdovey, Barmouth and Porthdinllaen, mainly carrying groceries and provisions for David Jones & Company of Liverpool. In fact, the vessel was named after the daughter of Owen Jones, a partner in the firm. She also carried deck cargoes of timber and provided a regular passenger service between the ports. *Dora* was requisitioned on the outbreak of war in 1914 and henceforth traded between Liverpool and Belfast. She was seized and sunk by a German submarine off the Mull of Galloway in May 1917. Her captain from 1909 until her loss was David Williams.[2]

1 For details of *Telephone* see R S Fenton *Cambrian Coasters*, Kendal, 1989, pp. 37-9.
2 ibid; and *Maritime Wales*, vol. 6, 1981, pp. 46-48.

265 *Reina Mercedes*

1983.3334
Oil on canvas[1]
66 cm x 105 cm
Signed and dated (bl) "W. H. YORKE. / L.pool 1879." Inscription (bc) "S. S. REINA MERCEDES" (partly faded)
Prov: Private Collection, on loan.

Vessel: 351 ft (l), 38.1 ft (b), 23.2 ft (d); 3060 gross tons

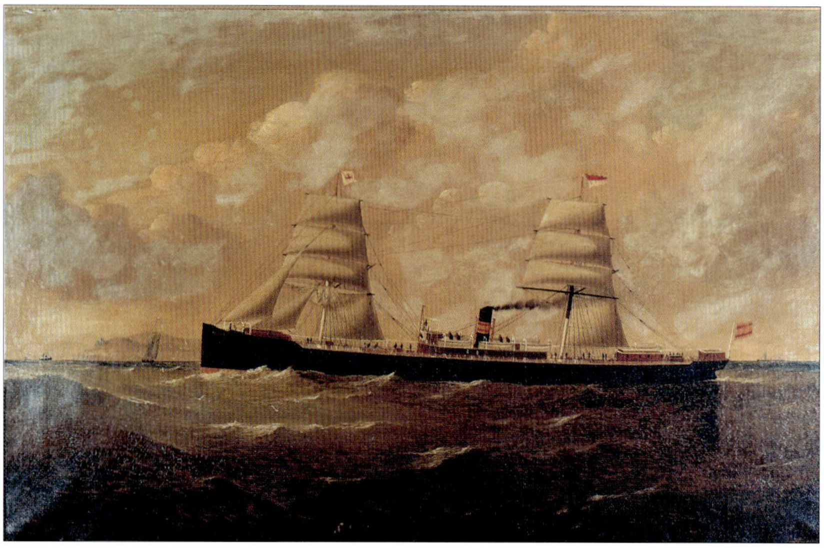

The steam ship *Reina Mercedes* is shown in port profile off Point Lynas, Anglesey. She is under full steam and is also using all her auxiliary sail except for the main courses. In fact, members of the crew can be seen on the foredeck in the process of hauling the main sail. The No. 10 Pilot schooner is approaching on the left but will not be required by *Reina Mercedes* as she flies the red over white flag from her main mast which indicates "Master holds pilot's certificate." She also flies the Larrinaga house flag at the foremast and the Spanish merchant ensign at her stern. Behind the pilot vessel is the Point Lynas lighthouse with Parys mountain in the background.

Reina Mercedes was built by A McMillan and Sons of Dumbarton in 1878 for the Larrinaga Line's service to the Philippines. She was sold to Marques de Campo of Madrid in 1881 and subsequently to the Compania Trasatlantica of Cadiz and Barcelona. She was broken up in 1898.[2]

The No.10 Pilot Schooner is *Criterion* built by Harvey of Ipswich in 1854 and withdrawn in 1898[3].

1 Printed label on rear stretcher for Boydell Galleries, Liverpool.
2 LR 1879-1898; Roger W Jordan 'Larrinaga's of Liverpool', *Sea Breezes*, n.s. 48, 1964, pp.82-85.
3 Rees, p.203.

266 *Reliance*

In this characteristic painting, Yorke shows the steel barque *Reliance* in port profile off Anglesey. All her sails are set and drawing and she is moving through the water at speed. She is almost festooned with flags, carrying from forward a pilot jack, a house flag for W T Dixon, the flag of the Merchant Marine Services Association, a name pennant and below the red ensign, her signal flags of J F N K. Another large

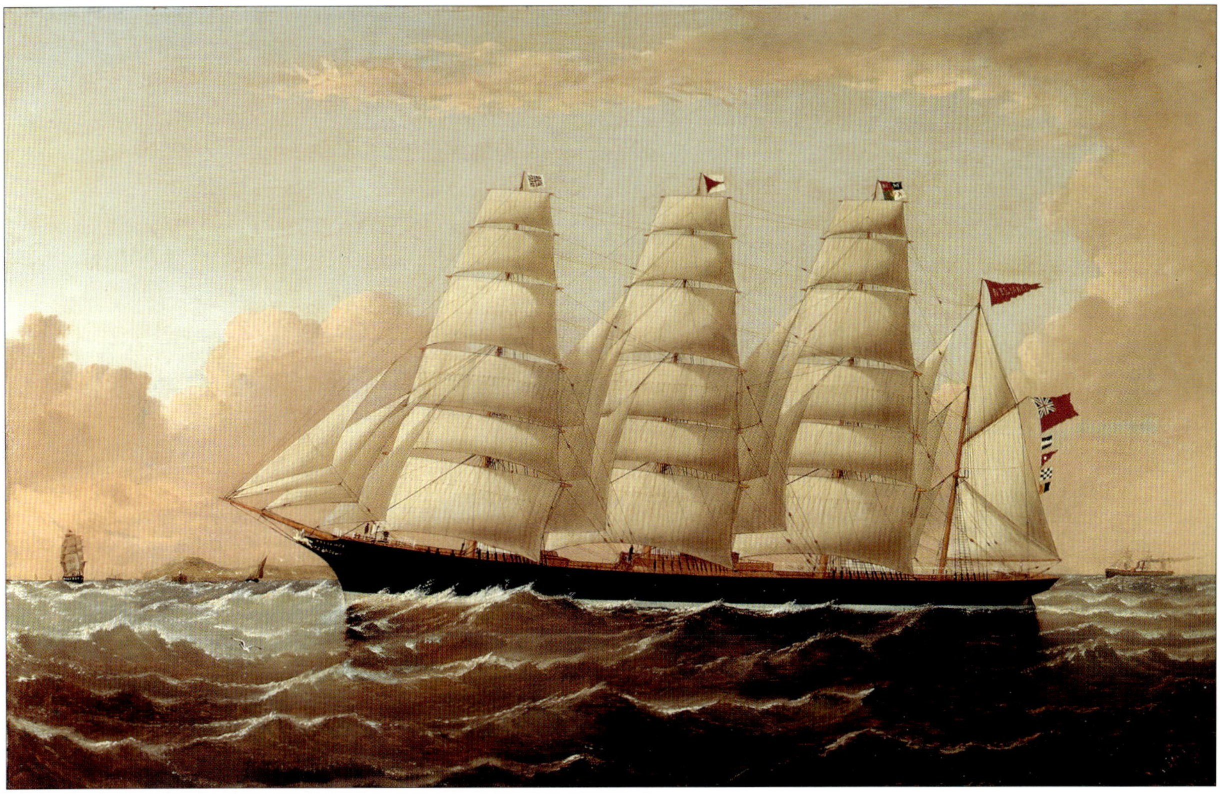

barque is approaching on the left of the canvas and in the distance astern is a 3 masted Cunard liner,[1] heading into Liverpool.

Reliance was built as a 4 masted ship rigged vessel in 1884 by W H Potter & Sons of Liverpool for W T Dixon & Sons in association with various others, including W H. Corsar, the well-known canvas maker.[2] The flying horse figurehead, prominently depicted here, appears on a number of vessels in which Corsars had shares. Her voyages were mainly up and down the Pacific coast of America and across to Australia, carrying coal, nitrate and timber. In 1893 Corsars took over direct management under the name of the Flying Horse Line. She was burnt out at Iquique in 1901 and her hull was bought by S Soler. She was rebuilt and re-registered in 1908 as *Ricart De Soler*, sold to Spanish owners in 1917 and finally broken up in 1924.[3] Her sister ship, *Pegasus*, is also represented in the collection, no. 63.

The vessel is shown in a standard location off Anglesey with the South Stack lighthouse in the far distance under the bowsprit. The first master of *Reliance* was Captain J English, presumably an ancestor of the donor.[4]

53.102
62.5 cm x 95 cm
Signed and dated "W. H. YORKE / L.pool. 1885"
Prov: by descent to Captain English, Parkgate, who presented it, 1953.
W H Yorke, Attributed

Vessel: 313.7 ft (l), 42.3 ft (b), 24.9 ft (d); 2631 gross tons

1 One of the following, most recent additions to the fleet, *Servia* (1881), *Aurania* (1883), *Umbria* (1884) or *Etruria* (1885), see Bonsor North, pp. 95-7.
2 W H Corsar (d.1886) was from Arbroath, Forfarshire.
3 Lubbock Windjammers, I, pp. 307-8, 483. Lubbock also includes a photograph of her on fire.
4 John English, born South Shields, 1825, LCpR 1869, CR no. 28, 27 February 1884.

267 *Saturnina* (page 248)

This portrait of the steamship *Saturnina* in starboard profile off a lighthouse and headland is probably related to the vessel's capture by the American navy at the beginning of the Spanish-American War of 1898. A group of three warships and a steam tender are shown to the right of the bow in the far distance. In fact, *Saturnina* was seized by the US cutter *Winona* in Biloxi harbour on 25 April. She was released by order of the Treasury Department in Washington on 28 April.[1]

The vessel is shown in the colours of her owners, the Larrinaga Line. The house flag of three clasped hands, said to indicate the three partners' agreement to build steamships in 1871, flies at the main and the Spanish ensign at the stern.

Saturnina[2] was built by Doxford & Sons of Sunderland in 1884 for the Larrinaga Line and remained in service until 1910. Although the vessel was registered in

1983.3337
Oil on canvas[3]
51 cm x 76.5 cm
Prov: Private Collection, on long term loan, 1983

Vessel: 340 ft (l), 37 ft (b), 25.9 ft (d); 2808 gross tons

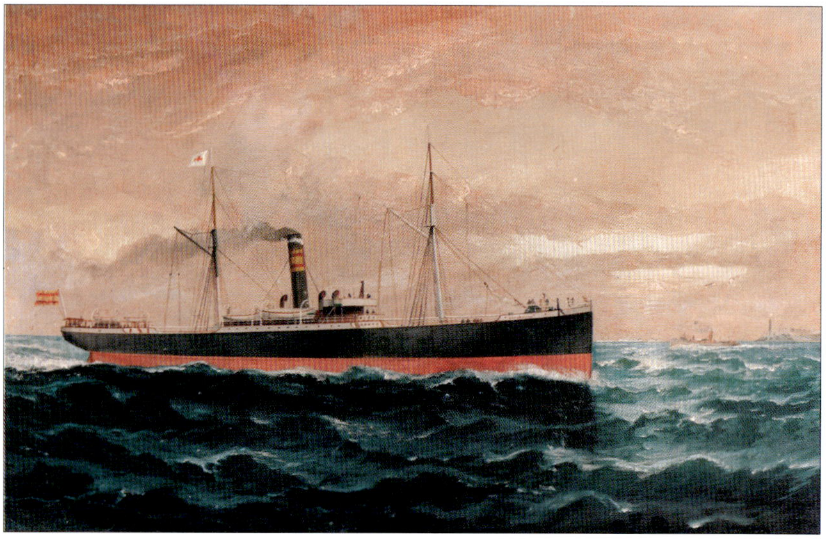

Bilbao, where the owners had been based since 1773, the company had moved its main offices to Liverpool in 1862. She traded mainly between Liverpool, Spain, the Caribbean and the southern American states.[4]
Although not signed, the style and composition are very reminiscent of W H Yorke, to whom the work is here attributed.

1 LL, 25 and 29 April 1898.
2 The vessel was named after Saturnina, sister of Ramon da Larrinaga, one of the founders of the line.
3 Canvas stamped "G. ROWNEY & CO. / LONDON, W. / QUALITY F"
4 For Larrinaga see R W Jordan 'Larrinaga's of Liverpool' in *Sea Breezes*, vol. 48, February 1974, pp. 81-94

J Young (active 1837)

268 *Shipping off Perch Rock Fort*

1985.162
Oil on board[1]
26.7 cm x 43 cm
Signed and dated (br) "J. YOUNG / 1837"
Prov: Mrs J A Patterson, Wallasey, who presented it 1985.

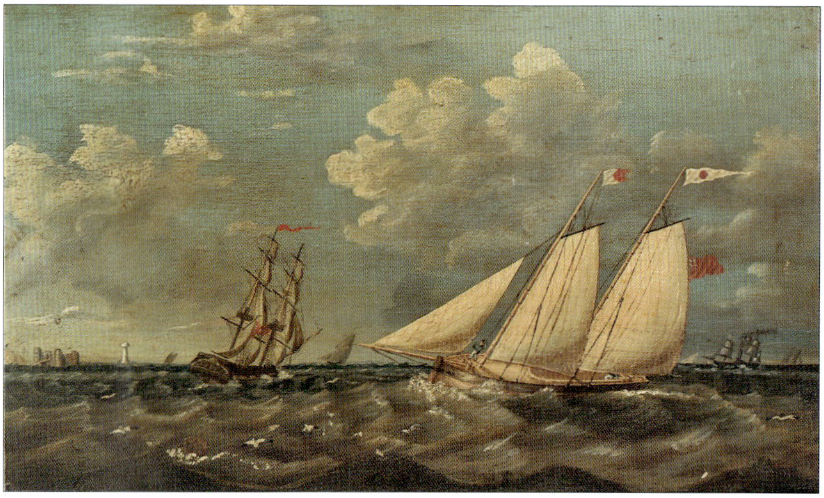

This lively scene shows a small schooner rigged pleasure vessel, with a brig and a paddle steamer off the Perch Rock Fort at the mouth of the Mersey.
To the right of centre the schooner is in port profile under full sail. There are two members of crew at the bow and two at the stern. She flies a white and red swallow-tail flag at the foremast and a white pennant with red circle at the main. This latter is the first distinguishing pennant in the Marryat code. However, it is not clear if these flags have any significance.
To the left of centre, in starboard quarter view is a brig heading out to sea. There is a hint of a name on the stern, possibly HAV and [LIVERP]OOL, and the red ensign and red pennant at the main but these do not allow identification. In the far right hand distance is a single funnel, brig rigged paddle steamer. The Perch Rock Fort and Lighthouse are placed to the left. Whilst these structures and the steamer are painted rather crudely, the detail of the other vessels is generally well-handled.

1 On rear of board inscribed in pen "No 2"

Index

(References are to pages. Vessel names are in italics)

D

E

F

G

M

N

O

P

Q

R

S